Following the publication of Al Venter's successful *Portugal's Guerrilla Wars in Africa* – shortlisted for the New York Military Affairs Symposium's 'Arthur Goodzeit Book Award for 2013' – his *Battle for Angola* delves still further into the troubled history of this former Portuguese African colony. This is a completely fresh work running to almost 600 pages including 32 pages of colour photos, with the main thrust on events before and after the civil war that followed Lisbon's over-hasty departure back to the metrópole. There are also several sections that detail the role of South African mercenaries in defeating the rebel leader Dr Jonas Savimbi (considered by some as the most accomplished guerrilla leader to emerge in Africa in the past century).

There are many chapters that deal with Pretoria's reaction to the deteriorating political and military situation in Angola, the role of the Soviets and mercenaries in the political transition, as well as the civil war that followed. With the assistance of several notable military authorities he elaborates in considerable detail on South Africa's 23-year Border War, from the first guerrilla incursions to the last. In this regard he received solid help from the former head of 4 Reconnaissance Regiment, Colonel Douw Steyn, who details several cross-border Recce strikes, including the sinking by frogmen of two Soviet ships and a Cuban freighter in an Angolan deepwater port.

Throughout, the author was helped by a variety of specialists, including the French historian Dr René Pélissier and the American academic and former naval aviator Dr John (Jack) Cann. With their assistance, he covers several ancillary uprisings and invasions, including the Herero revolt of the early 20th century; the equally-troubled Ovambo insurrection, as well as the invasion of Angola by the Imperial German Army in the First World War.

Former deputy head of the South African Army Major General Roland de Vries played a seminal role. It was he – dubbed 'South Africa's Rommel' by his fellow commanders – who successfully nurtured the concept of 'mobile warfare' where, in a succession of armoured onslaughts 'thin-skinned' Ratel Infantry Fighting Vehicles tackled Soviet main battle tanks and thrashed them. There is a major section on South African Airborne – the 'Parabats' –by Brigadier-General McGill Alexander, one of the architects of that kind of warfare under Third World conditions.

Finally, the role of Cuban Revolutionary Army receives the attention it deserves: officially there were almost 50,000 Cuban troops deployed in the Angolan war, though subsequent disclosures in Havana suggest that the final total was much higher.

British national Al Venter has written more than a dozen books on recent military history including *War Dog: Fighting Other People's Wars* on mercenaries as well as *Gunship Ace* (which covers the exploits of Neall Ellis, the world's most famous mercenary aviator). He spent much of his professional career reporting on wars for Jane's Information Group as well as for various news and photo agencies. These assignments ranged from visiting Beirut several times to cover the Lebanese civil war from the Christian side to a spate of African conflicts that included Biafra, South Africa's border wars, the Rhodesia insurgency, the Congo, Tanzania's invasion of Idi Amin's Uganda, Executive Outcomes mercenary operations in Angola and Sierra Leone and others. He was operational in El Salvador's guerrilla struggle and later, in the Balkans. At the behest of the CIA, he made a one-hour TV documentary on the Soviet offensive in Afghanistan in the mid-1980s. Venter has written three books on nuclear proliferation, including *Iran's Nuclear Option* and *How South Africa Built Six Atom Bombs*. He originally qualified as a Fellow of the Institute of Chartered Shipbrokers at the Baltic Exchange in London.

BATTLE FOR ANGOLA

The End of the Cold War in Africa *c* 1975-89

Books by the same author

Underwater Africa
Under the Indian Ocean
Report on Portugal's War in Guiné-Bissau
Africa at War
The Zambezi Salient
Underwater Seychelles
Coloured: A Profile of Two Million South Africans
Africa Today
South African Handbook for Divers
The Second South African Handbook for Divers
Challenge: South Africa in the African Revolutionary Context
Underwater Mauritius
The Ultimate Handbook on Diving in South Africa
Where to Dive: In Southern Africa and off the Indian Ocean Islands
War in Angola
The Iraqi War Debrief: Why Saddam Hussein was Toppled
Iran's Nuclear Option
War Dog: Fighting Other People's Wars
Allah's Bomb: The Islamic Quest for Nuclear Weapons
Cops: Cheating Death: How One Man Saved the Lives of 3,000 Americans
How South Africa Built Six Atom Bombs
Dive South Africa
African Stories by Al Venter and Friends
Barrel of a Gun: A War Correspondent's Misspent Moments in Combat
War Stories by Al J. Venter and Friends
Gunship Ace – The Wars of Neall Ellis, Helicopter Pilot and Mercenary
Shark Stories by Al J. Venter and Friends
Portugal's Guerrilla Wars (shortlisted for the New York Military Affairs Symposium's 'Arthur Goodzeit Book Award for 2013')
Shipwreck Stories by Al Venter and Friends
South Africa's Border War (Photographs, with Willem Steenkamp), Helion & Company
The Chopper Boys: Helicopter Warfare in Africa (New, revised and enlarged edition Helion & Company)
Biafra's War 1967-1970: A Tribal Conflict in Nigeria That Left a Million Dead

BATTLE FOR ANGOLA

The End of the Cold War in Africa *c* 1975-89

Al J. Venter

Helion & Company

Helion & Company Limited
Unit 8 Amherst Business Centre
Budbrooke Road
Warwick
CV34 5WE
England
Tel. 01926 499 619
Email: info@helion.co.uk
Website: www.helion.co.uk
Twitter: @helionbooks
blog.helion.co.uk/

Published by Helion & Company 2017. Reprinted in paperback 2021
Designed and typeset by Mach 3 Solutions Ltd (www.mach3solutions.co.uk)
Cover designed by Paul Hewitt, Battlefield Design (www.battlefield-design.co.uk)

Text © Al J. Venter 2016
Images © Al J. Venter or open source unless noted otherwise.

Every reasonable effort has been made to trace copyright holders and to obtain their permission for the use of copyright material. The author and publisher apologize for any errors or omissions in this work, and would be grateful if notified of any corrections that should be incorporated in future reprints or editions of this book.

Front cover photograph originally sourced to UNITA, cameraman unknown; rear cover: top left and bottom photographs courtesy of John P. (Jack) Cann; middle left Douw Steyn; all others taken by the author.

ISBN 978-1-914059-02-5

British Library Cataloguing-in-Publication Data.
A catalogue record for this book is available from the British Library.

All rights reserved. No part of this publication may be reproduced, stored in a retrieval system, or transmitted, in any form, or by any means, electronic, mechanical, photocopying, recording or otherwise, without the express written consent of Helion & Company Limited.

For details of other military history titles published by Helion & Company Limited, contact the above address, or visit our website: http://www.helion.co.uk

We always welcome receiving book proposals from prospective authors.

To my eldest son Johan who, like his dad, shares the unusual distinction of having been blown up by a Soviet anti-tank landmine in the same war. In fact, in the exact same Angolan theatre of operations, and within a year or so of each other: At the time Johan was operational with 61 Mechanised Battalion Group just south of Cuvelai . For my part, I was perched on top of the gun turret of a Ratel-90 infantry fighting vehicle during Operation Daisy when our right front wheel triggered the bomb.

… Like father, like son …

Contents

Glossary		ix
Acknowledgement		xvi
Introduction: Portugal's Wars in Africa		xviii

Part I: Overview — 43

1	Angola's War Against the Rebels – The Beginning of the End	45
2	The Cafunfo Campaign Gathers Momentum	54
3	Cafunfo Done and Dusted	64
4	Portugal's African Origins	76
5	Angola: More Recent Colonial Scenarios	89
6	Luanda – A Very Personal View	102
7	Portugal's Armed Forces Against its Guerrilla Adversaries	114
8	South Africa's Air Force Joins in the Fray	125
9	The South African Army Moves In	140

Part II: Aftermath — 153

10	A Two-Decade War on Angola's Southern Frontiers	155
11	Late 1975 – Luanda in the Final Stages of a Political Handover	174
12	Cuba's Revolutionary Role in Angola	188
13	Angola's New Political Dispensation and South Africa's Border War	204
14	Civil War: The Start	220
15	The Trial	234
16	Task Force Foxbat – The South African Army Moves into Central Angola	245
17	Fred Bridgland – Uncovering the Cover-Up	261
18	32 Battalion – A Crack Strike Force	271
19	Airborne: Countering the Angolan Threat	287
20	Into Angola with Charlie Company	304
21	Caught in an Angolan Minefield	321
22	Special Forces: The Recces – Best of the Best	338
23	The Recces Blow the Bridge at Cuito Cuanavale	354
24	The Commanding Influence of the Ratel Infantry Fighting Vehicle on Mobile Warfare in Southern Africa	369
25	Angola's Tank Battle on the Lomba: David Mannall Tells Us How South African Armoured Vehicles Knocked Out Soviet Tanks	384

Part III: Backblast: Civil War and Enter the Mercenaries   405

26 The African Adversaries   407
27 Consequences That Followed Lisbon Abandoning its African Possessions   423
28 The Soldier of Fortune Syndrome   442
29 Executive Outcomes – The Private Military Company that Altered the Balance of Power in Angola   451
30 The Battle for Angola's Soyo – African History in the Making   465
31 The Fighting Continues   476
32 How Executive Outcomes Ran It's Campaigns in Angola   486
33 Mercenary Air War in Angola   495
34 The Mercenary Air War Continues   505

Select Bibliography   518
Index   522

Glossary

A-76:	Military radio set
AAA:	Anti-aircraft artillery
ACIG:	Air Combat Information Group
AEB:	(South African) Atomic Energy Board
AK, AK-47:	*Avtomat Kalashnikova* 7.62mm assault rifle
ANC:	African National Congress: ruling South African political party, Socialist in orientation and in its day, closely allied to Portuguese opposition groups like Angola's MPLA and FRELIMO
aldeamento:	Portuguese protected camp
Alpha Bomb:	A circular shaped anti-personnel bomb weighing 6 kgs, normally dropped from level flight that gave a natural dispersion pattern. The bomb would strike the surface, activating the fusing mechanism, and then bounce into the air to explode about six meters above the ground
ALN:	*Armée de Libération Nationale* – the military wing of the FLN nationalist movement
ALO:	Air liaison officer
ANC:	African National Congress
APC:	Armoured personnel carrier
APILAS:	Armour-Piercing Infantry Light Arm System. French portable one-shot 122 mm recoilless anti-tank rocket
AR-10:	7.62mm battle rifle later developed into US Army's M16
ARMSCOR:	Armaments Corporation of South Africa
Assimilado:	Africans overseas who had 'assimilated' sufficiently to earn full Portuguese citizenship rights
AU:	African Union (See OAU)
Bergen:	Military-style multi-part backpack
BfSS:	(South African) Bureau for State Security, generally referred to in its day as 'BOSS'
BM-21:	Stalin Organ – Multiple Rocket Launcher
BMP-2:	*Boyevaya Mashina Pekhoty*, Soviet amphibious tracked infantry fighting vehicle
BND:	*Bundesnachrichtendienst*, West German/Federal Republic of Germany Federal Intelligence Agency
Boere:	A somewhat disparaging term used by both SWAPO and the Angolans to describe the RSA/SWATF security forces
BRDM:	*Boyevaya Razvedyvatelnaya Dozomaya Mashina*, 4x4 (converting to 8x8) amphibious 'Combat Reconnaissance Patrol Vehicle'

'Browns':	South African army personnel, or their uniforms (slang)
BSAP:	British South Africa Police, Rhodesian police force
BTR:	*Bronetransportyor*, 'armoured transporter', 8x8 armoured personnel carrier
C-4:	Common variety of the plastic explosive known as Composition C
CAS-sorties:	Close air support sorties
CCB or Civil Cooperation Bureau:	Secretive quasi-military organisation formed in latter stages of apartheid rule in South Africa
Chefe do Posto:	Local Portuguese administrator, roughly equivalent in British colonial Africa to district commissioner
CIA:	(United States) Central Intelligence Agency (also referred to by those 'in the know' as Langley)
CIO:	Rhodesian/ Zimbabwean Central Intelligence Organisation
COIN:	Counter-insurgency
Comintern:	Communist International, abbreviated to Comintern
COMOPS:	Combined Operations
Congo-Brazzaville:	The Republic of the Congo (*République du Congo*), also referred to as Congo-Brazzaville or simply Congo. Not to be confused with Democratic Republic of the Congo (Kinshasa)
CSI:	Chief of Staff Intelligence, South African military
CSIR:	(South African) Council for Scientific and Industrial Research
CT:	Communist Terrorist: term used for Chinese Malayan guerrillas by the British
DF:	Direction Finding
DGS:	(Portuguese) *Direcçao Geral de Segurança*, General Security Directorate
DHQ:	(South African) Defence Headquarters (in Pretoria)
DMI:	(South African) Directorate of Military Intelligence
DRC:	Democratic Republic of the Congo, formerly Zaire, formerly Belgian Congo, also called Congo-Kinshasa
DShK:	*Degtyaryova-Shpagina Krupnokaliberny*, Soviet 12.7mm heavy anti-aircraft machine gun
D Tels:	(South African) Directorate Telecommunications
ECCM:	Electronic Counter-Counter Measures
ECM:	Electronic Counter Measures
EO:	Executive Outcomes, mercenary group that ended civil wars in Angola and Sierra Leone
ESM:	Electronic Support Measures
EW:	Electronic warfare
FAA:	*Forças Armadas de Angolanas*, the Armed Forces of Angola
FAF:	Forward airfield
FAL:	The *Fusil Automatique Léger* (Light Automatic Rifle), a self-loading, selective fire battle rifle produced by the Belgian armaments manufacturer Fabrique Nationale de Herstal (FN)
FALA:	UNITA's military wing

FAP:	*Força Aerea Portuguesa*: Portuguese Air Force
FAPLA:	People's Armed Forces for the Liberation of Angola (*Forças Armadas Populares de Libertação de Angola*) – today *Forças Armadas de Angolanas*
FIA:	Field Intelligence Assistant
FLEC:	Cabinda Liberation Movement
FLING:	*Frente de Luta pela Independência Nacional de Guiné-Bissau/Front de Lutte de l'Indépendence Nationale de Guinée,* Struggle Front for the Liberation of Portuguese Guinea
FLN:	Algerian Liberation Group
FN:	See FAL
FNLA:	*Frente Nacional de Libertação de Angola*, National Front for the Liberation of Angola
FRELIMO:	*Frente de Libertação de Moçambique*, Liberation Front of Mozambique
FPLN:	*Frent Patriotica de Libertação National*: Guiné-Bissau liberation movement with headquarters in Algiers
G3:	7.62mm battle rifle developed in the 1950s by the German armament manufacturer Heckler & Koch GmbH (H&K) in collaboration with the Spanish. Adapted by the Portuguese Armed Forces
G-Car:	Transport Alouette helicopter
GOC:	JCFs General Officer Commanding Joint Combat Forces
GP:	*Garde Presidentielle*
GPMG:	General purpose machine-gun
GRAE:	Revolutionary Government of Angola in Exile (*Govêrno Revolucionário de Angola no Exílo*)
Grupos Especiais:	Portuguese Army Special Force units
Grupos Especiais Pára-Quedistas:	Paratrooper Special Groups (volunteer black soldiers that had paratrooper training)
Grupos Especiais de Pisteiros de Combate:	Special units trained in tracking
GRU:	*Glavnoye Razvedyvatel'noye Upravleniye* – foreign military intelligence main directorate of the Soviet Army
HAA:	Helicopter Administration Area
HAG:	Helicopter Administrative Group
HC: (*Honoris Crux*):	The highest decorations for military valour that could be awarded to members of the South African Defence Force. There are four classes namely: a) Bronze HC; c) Silver HCS; c) Gold HCG; d) Diamond HCD (never awarded)
HEU:	Highly enriched uranium
HF/DF:	High frequency direction finding (radio system)
HK21:	Heckler & Koch 7.62mm general purpose machine gun
HVAR:	High velocity aircraft rocket, also nicknamed during the Second World War as 'Holy Moses'
IAEA:	International Atomic Energy Agency
IDI:	Illegal Declaration of Independence (British rendering of Rhodesia's UDI)

IFP:	Inkatha Freedom Party (Zulu-based)
IFV:	Infantry fighting vehicle
INSS:	(United States) Institute for National Security Studies
ISIS:	(United States) Institute for Science and International Security
JARIC:	Joint Air Reconnaissance Intelligence Centre; JOC command centre
JMC (Joint Monitoring Commission):	This commission was brought into being by the recognised need by both the South African and Angolan antagonists to establish a forum wherein matters that could lead to a peaceful settlement were to be discussed
Joint-STAR:	United States Air Force E-8 Joint Surveillance Target Attack Radar System
K-Car 'Kill Car' (as in Rhodesian war):	Alouette helicopter gunship armed with machine guns
Katyusha:	Soviet 122mm multiple rocket launchers
KGB:	*Komitet gosudarstevennoy bezopasnosti*, (Soviet) Committee for State Security. See also GRU
KIA:	Killed in action
LAW:	M72 LAW (Light Anti-Tank Weapon), also referred to as the Light Anti-Armour missile
LZ:	Landing zone
Maanskyn:	The Afrikaans name (Moonshine) given to the successful night interdiction operations carried out by Impala jet ground-support aircraft from the early 1980s until the war ended. It involved a highly skilled form of flying that required intense concentration and came to dominate the battle area of Angola's Cunene province for a large period of the war.
MAG:	The FN MAG is a Belgian 7.62mm general-purpose machine gun
MANPAD:	Man-portable air defence system (like the Soviet Strela)
MASH:	(United States) Mobile Army Surgical Hospital
MBE:	Member of the Order of the British Empire
MBT:	Main battle tank
metrópole-províncias ultramarinas:	Portuguese overseas provinces
MG-42:	A general purpose machine gun, originally German and much favoured by Portuguese ground troops in all three African theatres of war
MG-51:	20mm cannon
Mi-8:	'Hip' transport/gunship helicopter
Mi-17:	Development of Mi-8 'Hip' transport/gunship helicopter
Mi-24:	'Hind' helicopter gunship/attack helicopter
MID:	South African Military Intelligence Division
MK:	*Umkhonto We Sizwe* (Spear of the Nation) – ANC military wing (South Africa)
MAOT (Mobile Air Operations Team/s):	These small teams were usually under the command of a Pilot with ranks at least at the level of major. It consisted of an operations officer, an intelligence officer and a radio operator. They were sometimes deployed by air, but were more likely to be mounted on board Buffel, Ratel and later Casspir vehicles

MPLA:	Popular Movement for the Liberation of Angola or *Movimento Popular de Libertàcao de Angola*
MPRI:	Private (mercenary) American military company
MRBM:	Medium range ballistic missile, such as the South African produced RSA-3
NATO:	North Atlantic Treaty Organisation
NCB:	Nuclear, chemical and biological (warfare)
OAS:	*Organisation de l'armée secrete*: a short-lived, French dissident paramilitary organization that was founded in French Algeria
OAU:	Organisation of African Unity, today African Union
OB:	*Ossewa Brandwag,* anti-British and pro-German Second World War organization in South Africa
OCC:	Operations Coordinating Committee
OP:	Observation post
OPO:	Ovambo People's Organisation
OZM-4:	Metallic bounding fragmentation mine
PAF:	Portuguese Air Force
PAIGC:	Guerrilla group in Portuguese Guinea – *Partido Africano da Independência da Guiné e Cabo Verde.* Took power by force after the Portuguese had hastily departed
Panhard AML:	*Automitrailleuse légère*, light 4x4 armoured car, developed by South Africa into the Eland
Panhard EBR:	*Engin Blindé de Reconnaissance*, French-built, light 8x8 armoured vehicle
PATU:	Police Anti-Terrorist Unit (Rhodesian War)
PCA:	Angolan Communist Party
PR:	Photographic Reconnaissance
PIDE:	Portuguese International Police for the Defence of the State or *Polícia Internacional e de Defesa do Estado* – Lisbon's equivalent of the secret police
PKM:	A Soviet 7.62 mm general-purpose machine gun much favoured by anti-government guerrillas
PLAN:	People's Liberation Army of Namibia – military wing of SWAPO
PLUA:	The Party of the United Struggle for Africans in Angola
PMC:	Private Military Company
PMD-6:	Anti-personnel mine
PNE:	Peaceful nuclear explosives
POM-Z:	Soviet anti-personnel stake-mounted fragmentation mine, much used in Africa
PPsH-41:	Soviet Second World War submachine gun
PSYOPs:	Psychological warfare operations
RAD ALT:	Radio-altimeter. System provides the pilot with accurate indication of the aircraft's height above the terrain, usually in the range of zero to 2500 feet AGL (above ground level)
RAF:	Royal Air Force
Recce/s:	A general term of common usage that could be used to describe a member or unit of the South African Reconnaissance Regiment

RhAF:	Rhodesian Air Force
RLI:	Rhodesian Light Infantry
RPD:	Soviet-made light machine gun, similar to the Degtyaryov, 7.62mm calibre
RPG:	Rocket propelled grenade – either RPG-2 (used by guerrillas in Portuguese African conflicts), or RPG-7 more recently, with additional variations
RPK:	Soviet-made light machine gun, 7.62mm calibre
RSA:	Republic of South Africa
RUF:	Rebel unit (Revolutionary United Front in Sierra Leone) destroyed by the South African mercenary group Executive Outcomes
SAAF:	South African Air Force
SABC:	South African Broadcasting Corporation
SACP:	South African Communist Party
SACS:	South African Corps of Signals
SADF:	South African Defence Force (in apartheid era)
SAEC:	SA Engineers Corps
SAFARI:	South African Fundamental Atomic Research Installation
SAFMARINE:	South African Marine Corporation
SAM:	Surface-to-air missile, SA-6, SAM-8 et al
SANDF:	South African National Defence Force (in post-apartheid era)
SAP:	South African Police, changed to South African Police Services in post-apartheid South Africa
SAR&H:	South African Railways and Harbours
SAS:	Special Air Service Regiment
SDU:	Self-defence unit
SF:	Special Forces
SG-43:	The SG-43 Goryunov – a Soviet medium machine gun (equivalent of the American M1919 Browning)
Shona/Shana:	An open area in the bush that floods during the rainy season: invariably dry during winter months
SIS:	Secret Intelligence Service or MI6
SNEB:	37mm Matra rockets
SO1 Ops:	Staff Officer 1, Operations
SS:	Nazi SS or *Schutzstaffel*: originally a protection squadron or defence corps; a major paramilitary organization under Hitler and the Nazi Party
SSO:	Senior Staff Officer
STASI:	*Staatssicherheit*, East German Ministry for State Security
Sten:	Second World War-era 9mm submachine gun
Stick:	(Rhodesian Army) – usually four troops on patrol
SWA:	South West Africa, now Namibia
SWAPO:	South West African People's Organisation
T-34 and T-55/T-54:	Soviet tanks supplied to Angola and Mozambique
TBVC States:	Transkei, Bophutatswana, Venda and Ciskei (apartheid-era regional entities within South Africa, ostensibly supposed to be independent of Pretoria)

TM-46 and TM-57:	Soviet anti-tank mines used by liberation groups
TNT:	*Trinitrotoluene* is a chemical compound best known as a useful explosive material with convenient handling properties
Tropas Especiais:	Special Troops, commonly known by the acronym TEs, which came into effect when one of the UPA/FNLA guerrillas defected to the Portuguese with 1200 of his men
TTL:	Tribal Trust Land
TYPHOON:	The name given by SWAPO to their elite group of most highly trained troops, whose specific task was the infiltration of SWA
UAV:	Unmanned Aerial Vehicle
UDI:	Unilateral Declaration of Independence
Uitmergel:	An Afrikaans word that literally translated means to exhaust or grind down
UNAVEM:	United Nations Verification Mission in Angola
Unimog:	A four-by-four medium-heavy transport, based on a Mercedes Benz chassis and engine, widely used in counter insurgency bush operations by the Portuguese Army and initially by the SADF until SWAPO mine-laying forced the introduction of wide variety of mine-protected vehicles
UNISA:	University of South Africa
UNITA:	*União Nacional Para a Independência Total de Angola*, National Union for the Total Liberation of Angola
UPA:	*União dos Populacèes de Angola*, Patriotic Union of Angola
USAF:	United States Air Force
VHF:	Very High Frequency
VOLCANO:	The name given by SWAPO to the training base roughly 14 kilometres north-east of Lubango where specialised training was conducted by Angolan troops.
WMD:	Weapons of Mass destruction
WO I:	Warrant Officer Class I
WO II:	Warrant Officer Class II
ZAF:	Zimbabwe Air Force
ZANLA:	Zimbabwe African National Liberation Army (guerrilla group)
ZANU:	Zimbabwe African National Union
ZAPU:	Zimbabwe African Political Union
ZIL:	Angolan *Zona de Intervencao Leste*
ZIPRA:	Zimbabwe People's Revolutionary Army (guerrilla group)

Acknowledgement

I have written quite a few Acknowledgments during the course of a career that spans five decades, but there have been none where I owed so much of what went into a particular title as *Battle for Angola* to others who contributed.

Length aside, it was a monumental task, originally scheduled as a single volume of about 500 pages. But it is impossible to ignore the realities of history and veracity demands that a second volume will follow.

My research took me into the homes of many of my colleagues as well as quite a few notable authorities with whom I had only glancing contact in the past. Almost without exception everybody came out tops and I am deeply grateful to them all because while I covered most spheres of hostilities, it would never have been possible to achieve what I did without their help. My gratitude is heartfelt.

One man, above all others, needs to be accorded the recognition he deserves and that is Duncan Rogers who owns and runs Helion, one of the biggest publishers of military titles in Europe. In originally giving me the go-ahead, I doubt whether he realised that it would become a project that encompassed continents and take twice as long as originally envisaged. In the process there were moments when we both threw up our hands in despair, but like me, Duncan is a fighter. I salute both him and his family for standing by my side throughout so much travail.

Among the 'players' in my corner were several individuals who were themselves involved in the wars featured here. First among equals is former officer commanding of 4 Reconnaissance Regiment Douw Steyn who has the unusual distinction of having been involved – with his strike teams – in destroying several Soviet and Cuban ships in Angolan ports.

I cover that story in detail, exactly as it appears in the book that he and his compadre Arné Söderland set down in *Iron Fist from the Sea*, coincidentally also published by Helion. They too gave me some relevant photos.

Former United States Navy aviator Captain John P (Jack) Cann – himself well-published on Portugal's wars in Africa – helped enormously with photos through his connections in Lisbon. I must mention that I rate Jack's book *Flight Plan Africa: Portuguese Airpower in Counterinsurgency 1961-1974* as the best volume on Portugal's air wars in Africa.

There is no question that with al-Qaeda making great strides in parts of this volatile continent that his work will be carefully studied by future strategists on both sides of the Atlantic. His pointers as to the way Lisbon handled their problems under sometimes atrocious Third World conditions are enormously instructive.

Other photos came from Manuel Ferreira, Stephen Dunkley, 'Kaas' van der Waals, Neall Ellis, Cloete Breytenbach, Cobus Claassens, David Mannall, Ariël Hugo, Ferdi de Vos as well as Dean Wingrin who provided a bunch of striking C-130 studies.

Former Recce commander Hennie Blaauw needs special mention because I spent time with him while covering Executive Outcomes' efforts during the Angolan civil war. He was generous with his photos, quite a few of which he will recognise between these covers. The same must be said of Pierre Victor from Pretoria, a skilled artist who produced some brilliant sketches of some of the weapons involved in these campaigns. *Dankie ou maat*!

There are a few others, I am sure, but if I have forgotten to include you, please regard it as the kind of oversight likely to be made by a 'Senior'...

For the rest, solid support came from someone with whom I rubbed shoulders when I was embedded – under his command – with 61 Mech during Operation Daisy: then-Commandant Roland de Vries and later, deputy chief of the South African Army.

Roland's book, *Eye of the Storm* is another work that future African strategists will carefully examine because this was the man who successfully devised 'African style' mobile warfare and went on to knock spots off the Soviets and their Cuban surrogates. It says a lot that these days Roland is linked to the Australian Command and Staff College in Canberra.

On the role of the Ratel infantry fighting vehicle in Africa – the mainstay of Roland de Vries's philosophy on mobile warfare in primitive regions – I must also thank that delightful fellow Tony Savides: he helped develop that remarkable machine and also William Marshall, who provided some excellent drawings, the best of which I used.

Chapter-wise, David Mannall allowed me use of a chapter from his book *Battle on the Lomba 1987: The Day a South African Armoured Battalion shattered Angola's Last Mechanized Offensive*. An outstandingly graphic account of actual combat, Roland de Vries rates it among the best of the works to emerge from the Border War.

I also used excerpts from Fred Bridgland's *The War for Africa*, which I originally published when I headed Ashanti Publishing; 'Kaas' van der Waals during Op Foxbat as well as that seasoned veteran of South Africa's own Airborne Forces McGill Alexander.

McGill went much further that he was originally tasked and gives the reader a lot of solid detail how the 'Bats' actually operated, comparing the way his Parachute Battalions went to war in relation to how the Rhodesians did it. It is the kind of insight that can only come from a professional and adds a good bit of lustre to this work. He includes a section on the Cassinga strike which is incisive.

Though my old friend Ares Klootwyk – originally trained in the SAAF and from there to the RAF, from where he hopped across to fly fighter aircraft and helicopters as a mercenary in the Congo – was not involved in either the Border War or Portugal's African campaigns, he sets the scene for what was taking place militarily in Angola's neighbour, formerly a Belgian colony. Quite a few of his pictures are used where appropriate, with grateful thanks to him and his delightful Sally.

Manie and Elize Troskie in Pretoria have always been a valuable and trusted adjunct to this work, Manie with easy access to information needed at short notice, and the extended Troskie family hosting us whenever we are in that part of South Africa, sometimes for fairly lengthy stays. As a section leader, Manie headed the squad with whom I went in when Charlie Company took Cuamato in south Angola on that fateful day so many decades ago.

Finally to the three people most closely involved with the production of this work, the first being Kim McSweeney who used her considerable skills and patience (if you consider my nagging throughout) to string it all together. It was a mammoth task Kim, and a simple thank you is not enough. I owe you big time.

Jerry Buirski in Cape Town proof-read the book and he too, needed to have patience because I fear I might have been extremely demanding. And last, there was Bruce Goneau who handles my photo library and is constantly on call. Bruce has the advantage of having fought in the Border War and is quick to spot any error of judgement, of which there have been a few. Thanks Matey!

Last, my lovely Caroline, to whom I am indebted more than anybody else because she had to suffer two long years of upheavals, frustrations, distractions and the rest. You stuck by me darling and I'd like to think we are both that much the better for it.

What else can I say but thank you?

Al J Venter, Surrey Hills,
November 2016

Introduction: Portugal's Wars in Africa

To understand the nature (and complexities) of this book, which deals not only with a historical background to Lisbon's five century-long occupation of Angola, but also some of the military struggles linked to maintain that presence – including the 13-year *Guerra do Ultramar* or what the guerrillas liked to call the War of Liberation or *Guerra de Libertação* – I need to start by dispelling a few myths and make clear my role as a military or foreign correspondent. In a search for answers, I visited all three of Lisbon's *metrópole províncias ultramarinas* many times during the course of more than a decade …

I

Following the publication in Britain of my book *Portugal's Guerrilla Wars in Africa* and subsequently translated in Lisbon, which was when *Portugal e as Guerrilhas de África* – to the surprise of many – became an immediate best-seller, I decided it was appropriate that I tackle Angola's historical and contemporary travails as a subject on its own.

For roughly 40 years after the last member of Portugal's armed forces flew out of Luanda, the nation tended to ignore the fact that for more than a decade a series of bitter wars were fought in Angola, Mozambique and Portuguese Guinea (today Guiné-Bissau). In the process, a lot of lives were lost.

These colonial insurrections exhausted the nation and nobody needed to be reminded that hostilities ended ignominiously. In the minds of most, Portugal was driven out of Africa; there was simply no other way of viewing the outcome other than as a defeat.

But then, quite suddenly in the second decade of the New Millennium, a lot of people started to ask questions about those conflicts in faraway Africa. A new generation of young (and not so young) Portuguese were eager to learn what their fathers, uncles, husbands, lovers, granddads and others had done while hostilities went on. Did those older folk actually get involved in jungle skirmishes, set ambushes, get blown up by landmines and possibly even killed people who were regarded as enemy? In turn, did they see some of their friends suffer similar fates?

Suddenly a variety of books started to appear in Portugal and they were snapped up. Mine was followed by other titles; unquestionably, there will be more.

A similar trend had already been set in motion in Southern Africa with regard to Pretoria's 23-year insurgency war along the southern fringes of Angola and, to a lesser extent along the frontiers of Zambia and Mozambique. In the past decade there must have been about a dozen books a year published on those conflicts and as a scribbler, I have been involved there too.

After *Portugal's Guerrilla Wars* appeared in print, I received a lot of requests from Portuguese media about Lisbon's troubles in Africa. I was asked numerous questions and answered as best I could, even though I sensed an underlying hostility among some of the hacks involved, in part because it is impossible to please everybody.

Also, there were radical elements who believed that everything about these wars was either tainted or evil and needed to be condemned. I didn't argue: my role was to tell it like it was and that was that.

But some of the interviews provided a certain measure of depth that none of us had plumbed before. Questions and answers not only made good sense but were intrusive and interesting, especially from an historical perspective. Like the individual who asked whether Portugal had actually *lost* her African wars, or whether she was driven out by radical political sentiment? That query suggested that the demon might have been communism, which, of course we now know is partly true. Or, on another tack, this time from an 'Old Africa Hand' who questioned whether there were ever any massacres of innocents like the Americans experienced at My Lai in Vietnam?

Somebody else persisted in asking whether the average Portuguese combatant was any good at this kind of conflict…and so on…

Most of the people I dealt with were seasoned, well-experienced Portuguese journalists and writers, with a book or two under some of their belts. Their number included Manuel Carlos Freire of the *Diario de Noticias*, a newspaperman who had spent 20 years on the Africa beat and who had seen and done just about everything. His review covered two full pages of copy and photographs, together with a map detailing where the wars were fought. It appeared in the issue published on 22nd November 2015.

That was preceded on the 27th October by a double-page spread that also included quite a few pictures, this time in Lisbon's *O Diabo*. Written by its editor Duarte Branquinho, a seasoned military correspondent, his piece was arguably the most intrusive because he has a strong following of military veterans and rarely pulls punches. Before that, the Portuguese national news agency ran several stories on the book, all of which, cumulatively, suggests an enormous resurgence of historical interest in that country's African military campaigns.

That said, a lot of people have since questioned me about these wars and the eventual outcome. The most persistent query that came up in the process was whether Portugal actually lost her wars in Africa.

The truth is that with the army mutiny of April 1974, hostilities were effectively brought to an end. And while it was certainly not a cataclysmic disaster like Nazi Germany suffered in 1945, conflict was abruptly halted and the men in uniform came home.

You could almost compare it with the French exit from Indo-China in 1958 or the inglorious departure of the Soviets from Afghanistan in 1989. All these 'superior' powers suddenly abandoned their stated military aims and the guerrillas/Freedom Fighters/adversaries on home ground went on to declare victory. They could hardly be faulted because there was no other way of looking at it.

The guerrillas in Angola, Mozambique and Portuguese Guinea were no less elated. They celebrated until those in Angola and Guinea started squabbling among themselves and that led to more wars and many more senseless killings.

In my personal view exactly the same sort of thing is going to happen to Putin's Russia in Syria in a few years' time…

The bottom line here is that anybody with a modicum understanding of history could, by the early 1970s, see the writing very clearly on the wall. The war had been going on for half a generation and frankly, things in Lisbon's African dominions could not go on like that forever. The country was being bled dry by a war that pitted one of Western Europe's smallest and poorest nations against the might of the Soviet Union.

One also has to take into account that just about everything that happened to Portugal at the time took place at the height of the Cold War, no small issue in the 1960s and 1970s.

Thus, with the Carnation Revolution, everything changed and literally, it was an overnight thing. As I said in my earlier book, when that happened, almost the entire Portuguese nation breathed a collective sigh of relief. In truth, it was a complicated process, largely because the single biggest problem for Portugal was strategic vision, or lack of it. With one notable exception: General Antonio de Spinola…

Certainly, as United States Naval aviator Captain Jack Cann pointed out, you go to war to achieve this vision when no other acceptable way is open; however, while there had to be a response to the March 1961 attacks, the big question was about where Salazar was going with it all?

As Cann declared, '…the military component did its job quite well, and it is a well-chronicled, fascinating, and laudable story. The problem lay in the politics. There was no flexibility in Salazar's position. His opponents were sidelined, and only his single-dimensional vision prevailed.[1]

> After Salazar's stroke, the future Prime Minister Marcelo Caetano was welcomed as a vehicle for change but he soon became an extension of the same unimaginative policy. His reaction to Spinola trying to negotiate with the PAIGC guerrilla leader Amilcar Cabral in 1972 and establish what was termed a 'Commonwealth' made infinite sense, but that proposal was soon quashed by Caetano.

As my American friend declared, there was literally no useful strategic vision at the top. With no ability to vote the government out of office, revolution was the only alternative. Of course, the revolutionaries had strategic myopia too, but then that is another topic worth discussion, but not between these covers.

Looking back, it was just as well that the wars ended when they did. I went to Lisbon often enough in the 1960s and 1970s and knew quite a few of the major players: people like the venerable Generals Spinola and Bettencourt Rodrigues (I have immense respect for them both). Also, there was no question that the nation was tired of conflict.

The Americans coined a phrase for it towards the end of the Second World War and they called it 'war weary'. The Portuguese nation – after 13 hard years of hostilities – was utterly exhausted.

You have to recognise that the difficulties faced by Lisbon were almost insuperable, finances being a major part of it: Portugal had very little cash to spare and it stayed that way for decades. Compared to today – with instant communications and jet travel – Angola might have been on the other side of the globe.

Troops didn't fly there like the Americans were doing in Vietnam: they went by ship and that took time and money.

Another question asked often enough was what kind of differences did I manage to discern between those three African wars?

Portugal's colonial conflicts adapted to circumstances in all three theatres of military activity. In miniscule Portuguese Guinea, where the insurgents were rarely more than a day's march away from any of that enclave's frontiers, things were tough for government forces because the guerrillas could bring so many more weapons to bear.

Angola, in contrast, became an expansive (and expensive) war with huge distances needed to be covered by both sides. But there, the mindless killings of 1961 remained constantly in the minds of the defenders and everybody accepted that if they did not take care, such brutal excesses could happen again.

---

1 Personal correspondence with Dr John Cann, 2016.

Mozambique was even more diverse, with hostilities restricted mainly to the jungle north and central regions. In Lourenco Marques (Maputo today) you might be forgiven for thinking that there was no war because the enemy never got far that far south. In fact, you never travelled in convoy on the roads south of Beira.

There were other differences. One needs to take into account that the Portuguese had almost no experience or training for an insurgency-backed war in *one* of their overseas provinces, never mind all three. Prior to those colonial struggles, the last time Portuguese troops had heard shots fired in anger was in the First World War, something that then had also happened in Africa (against the German Army in both Angola and Mozambique). I deal with that as well between these covers.

That the Portuguese Army was able to haul itself out of what was clearly a soporific haze and rally to a cause that had suddenly become an urgent 'do or die' affair is enormously commendable. In the eyes of most European observers, it was totally unexpected.

More salient, the country had no real armaments industry, but it didn't take long to get things going; first by acquiring from West Germany the rights for the local manufacture of the G3 rifle (and several other weapons), buying and then building the kind of heavy vehicles needed in a modern war (Unimog and Berliet) and, of course, the air components that went with it all. A lot of that stuff was in place, but much of it was part of Lisbon's commitment to NATO and the Americans, though helpful at first, soon began to restrict some of those assets from deployment to Africa.

US Navy Captain John Cann[2] (who we all know as Jack and who has written several books on these hostilities) phrased it well when he declared in his introduction to my earlier book that Portuguese troops were incredibly brave. As he phrased it '…those young men had the ability to fight under conditions that would have been intolerable to other European troops.'

He went on: 'They could go for days on a bag of dried beans, some chickpeas and possibly a piece of dried codfish – all to be soaked in any water that could be found…'

Captain Cann added that they were able to cover on foot and through elephant grass and thick jungle distances sometimes hundreds of kilometres over a three day patrol period. They quickly learned how to fight well, and did so successfully for more than a decade across three fronts in regions that were almost half the size of Western Europe and stretched much of the distance across the African continent. Remember, Angola fringes the Atlantic while Mozambique stretches for 2,600 kilometres all the way down the western littoral of the Indian Ocean…

More to the point, the Portuguese fought in Africa for twice as long as the American Army did in Vietnam…

On reflection, while it was an extremely difficult ongoing process that took lives, there are few countries that fared as well in any lengthy guerrilla conflict in the past two centuries. But in the end, it just became too much for the nation and the self-elected leaders decided to move on, not without good reason.

Another question which raised its ugly head several times was whether I witnessed any slaughters like those experienced at Wyriamu and My Lai while the Americans fought in Vietnam?

This is something often raised. And yes, at the start of hostilities in Angola in 1961 there was an incredible level of mindless violence on both sides.

That all followed the invasion of North Angola by UPA insurgents, a force composed of large bands of armed insurgents determined to overrun Luanda in as short a time as possible. They

---

2   John P. Cann: *Counterinsurgency in Africa: The Portuguese Way of War 1961–1974*, Hailer Publishing, Florida 2005; *Brown Waters of Africa; Portuguese Riverine Warfare 1961–1974*, Hailer, 2007; *Flight Plan Africa: Portuguese Airpower in Counterinsurgency, 1961–1974*; Helion, 2015.

actually came close to doing just that, penetrating southwards to within a couple of days' march of the capital.

So while some sources make out the invading force was largely composed of 'bandits' or 'rabble', that cannot be altogether true because they had their share of successes. They took control of the regional command centre at Nambuangongo from government forces with little resistance.

The rebel agenda was as clear as day: shock and intimidate the Portuguese nation into a state of terror and force them to leave Africa. And let's be blunt: thousands of people, both black and white Angolans died in the process because the attacks were so bloodily ferocious. Some kind of insurrection had been anticipated by Lisbon's intelligence agencies, but certainly not on that enormous scale.

UPA cadres killed everybody: men, women and children. Peoples' eyes were gouged out and pregnant woman had their bellies slashed open. In Leopoldville, capital of the Congo, UPA leaders boasted openly about their deeds: One of them told a French journalist *'avec un large sourire'* about Portuguese logging families in the north that he and his men had slaughtered.

His exact words were: 'we fed them lengthwise into the circular saws' (and this is on record with *Agence France Presse*).

That initial bunch of Portuguese soldiers thrust towards the frontline to face oncoming rebels in those first jungle forays was untrained and undisciplined and consequently created almost as much damage among the civilian population as the UPA. Afterwards, as the war came under control, a better relationship developed with the locals.

In retrospect, it was perhaps to be expected that Portuguese security forces retaliated with brutal vigour, as has happened in just about every violent revolution on every continent. They spared no effort, and in retaliation, many thousands of local people were killed, whether they were attached to invading groups or not. It is all there, documented in the archives in Lisbon. A hallmark of this period was the number of heads cut off and put onto stakes to rot in the sun (something both sides were guilty of).

Lisbon's forces having stabilized the situation in the *Dembos* north of Luanda, a measure of sanity did return. The army imposed severe strictures on any kind of brutality.

Obviously, there were still excesses when units came under fire or when troops were found mutilated, but the rule of law eventually did prevail. In fact, while covering the war I discovered several units where the United Nations Declaration of Human Rights was pinned up in the mess hall. I never saw that either in Lebanon or in the Rhodesian war, not once.

Were there any massacres like My Lai in Portugal's overseas wars? I would say yes, but only in the very early days of Angola's mayhem. That was a lunatic period of excessively violent exchanges on both sides and lasted less than a year.[3]

In Mozambique's war zones, in contrast, General Kaulza de Arriaga presided over some unfortunate events in various areas including Tete, Wiriyamu and Inhambane. But you will find very little of this in the archives because the Portuguese are extremely sensitive about those blots on their record.

Nothing like that happened in Guinea, though the massacre of 50 workers at Pijiguiti Docks in Bissau in August 1959 (during a non-violent demand for rights) might be categorised as such. It was certainly a senseless slaughter on the part of the authorities and led directly to Amilcar Cabral preparing the PAIGC for war.

---

3 http://www.concordmonitor.com/article/portugals-hidden-atrocities

The revolt by rural blacks in Angola early 1961 caused an enormous rush of emotions in the Metropolis. Salazar wasted little time in despatching all available military reserves to Luanda to quell the uprising which everybody thought would last months. Instead, it quickly developed into a major series of wars that ended 13 years later.

Portugal and its colonies became the focus of a new propaganda war.

Portuguese troops marching along Luanda's oceanfront Marginal. (Author's collection)

It did not take long for Lisbon to learn from other colonial insurrections: they implemented the *aldeomentos* system of containing the civilian groupings in protected villages, similar to that employed by the British during the Malayan Emergency. (Author's collection)

As conflict progressed to involve the Great Powers, Washington sided with UNITA and supplied Jonas Savimbi's people with Stinger missiles which were used to shoot down Soviet helicopters. (Author's collection)

Tanzanian President *Mwalimu* Julius Nyerere is regarded as the architect of many of the anti-colonial/anti-white insurrections that beset vast swathes of Southern Africa from the early 1960s on. (Author's photo)

A captured insurgent wounded in a contact with government forces in a Luanda prison during the author's visit. (Photo: Cloete Breytenbach)

> The blacks, those magnificent examples of the African race who have maintained their racial purity thanks to their lack of an affinity with bathing, have seen their territory invaded by a new kind of slave: the Portuguese.
>
> — *Che Guevara* —
>
> AZ QUOTES

Che Guevara was an early visitor to the region where the war was being fought.

Early photo of counter-insurgency hostilities in bush country east of Luanda. (*Revista Militar*)

Portuguese *Fuzileiros* (Marines) on ops. (Photo: *Revista Militar*, courtesy of US Navy Captain Jack Cann)

As hostilities progressed and South Africa became more involved in the war, the South African Air Force started to play a significant role, including deploying its C-130 transporters in operational roles in South Angola. (Photo: Dean Wingrin)

Portuguese Air Force crews attached to American-built F-84 fighter jets at Luanda Airport. (Photo: *Forca Aerea Portuguesa*)

MPLA Adolfo-Maria base at Kalunga, 1973.

Portuguese Air Force Alouette gunship with 20mm cannon mounted and operational in Angola.
(Photo: *Forca Aerea Portuguesa*)

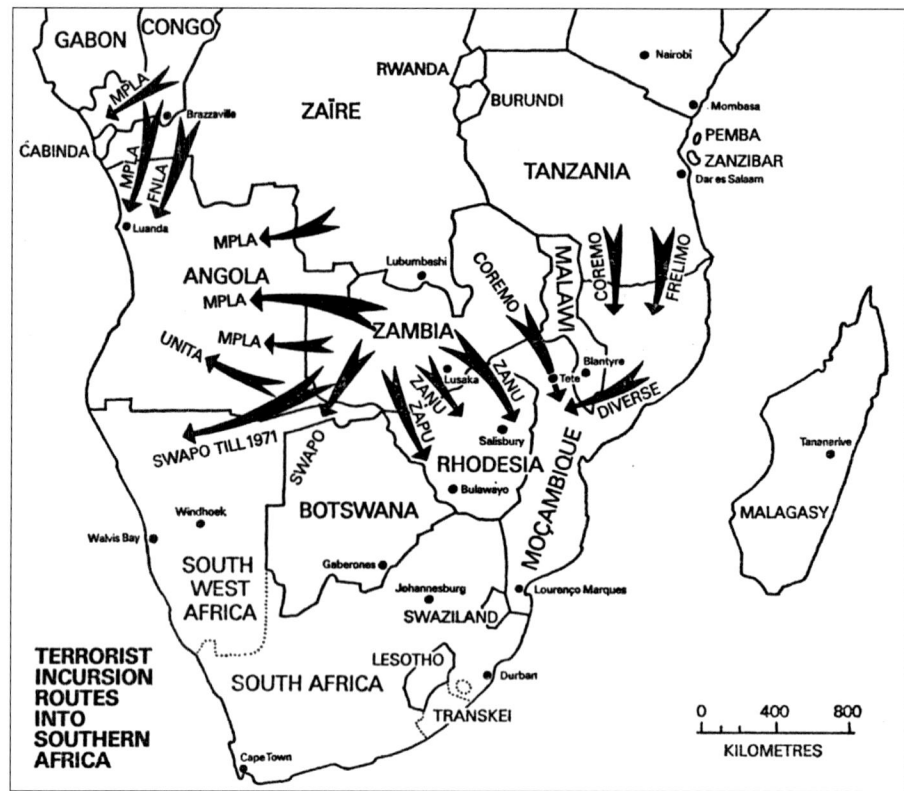

Map showing the extent of the insurgent onslaught throughout southern Africa, taken from the author's book *The Zambezi Salient*.

The bush war was to take on a radically new dimension once Pretoria started to involve some of its more modern weapons, including Ratels, such as the one shown here during Operation Askari.

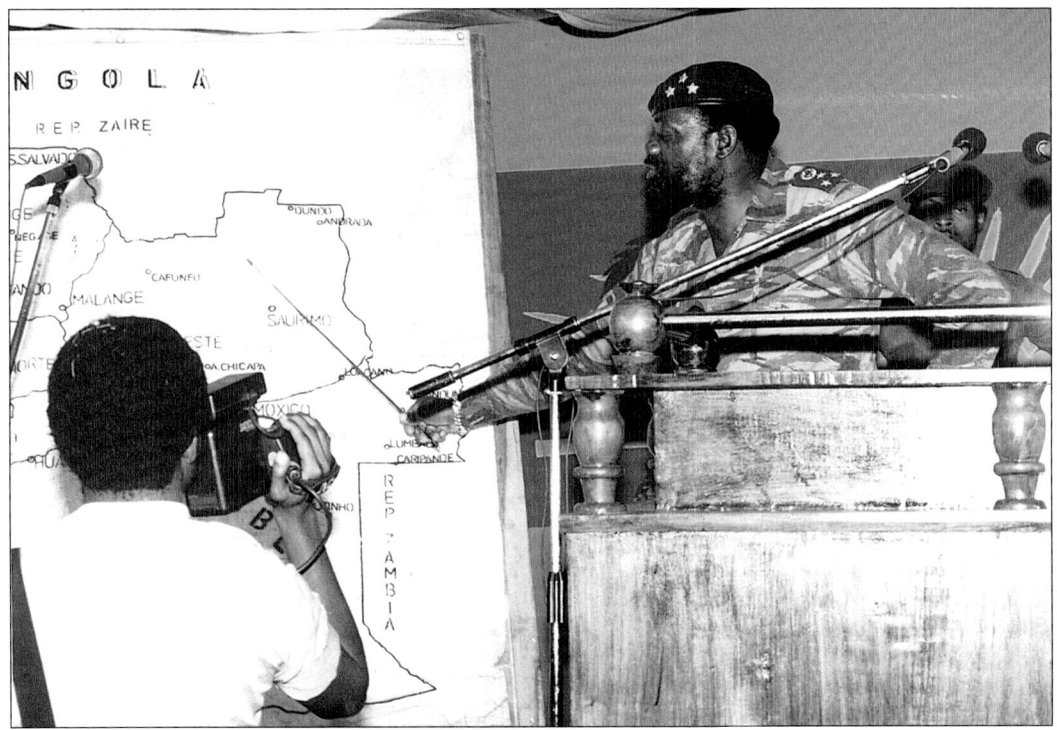

UNITA'S leader, Dr Jonas Savimbi caused the civil war to go on for another decade, until he was eventually tracked down by Luanda's security forces and killed. (Author's collection)

The author on a Rhino mine-protected vehicle at Ondangua in 1985. (Photo: Alwyn Kumst)

In the final stages of the bush war, South African refurbished Olifant tanks played a predominant role in some of the battles that preceded a cease-fire. (Author's collection)

Many advanced Soviet weapons were captured by South African forces during the course of hostilities, including these hand-held ground-to-air MANPADS. (Author's collection)

Overall though, Lisbon fought the rest of its colonial conflicts 'by the book'. This, obviously, did not please everybody and did not restrain PIDE and other government security agencies from regularly and often brutally overstepping the mark.

II

Another query pertained to my impartiality as a writer and journalist, and whether I followed the wars *only* with the Portuguese Armed Forces or also with some of the guerrilla groups.

Fundamentally, I – and many Western journalists – could not risk going into combat with the guerrillas. That would have been like spending time with the Israeli Army and then asking to be attached to a radical Arab Jihadi unit that had sworn destruction on the Jewish State: it just does not happen. Unlike Basil Davidson, or that radical nonconformist Portuguese Admiral Rosa Coutinho, my ties with Moscow were, if anything, guarded.

Also, were my articles censored by the Portuguese authorities?

There I can be specific: The authorities in Lisbon (or any of the overseas colonies) never once asked to vet my material. In those days it was not done.

I suppose they could have censored my writings because I could be critical – and sometimes was – especially with regard to the way the war was being fought in Mozambique. The truth is, they did not. Nor did they ask to view the photos I took, though obviously there were some classified issues (like the deployment of helicopter gunships and F-84 bombing missions) from which I was discreetly steered clear of.

Once in the field, I was usually on my own (without an escort officer). Obviously, there would be liaison officers appointed to coordinate my trip, but they almost never ventured into the field with me. We called them 'Jam Stealers' because so few of them ever saw any real action.

Notably, my contact in Bissau was Captain Otello Saraiva de Carvalho, then serving on General de Spinola's staff. There is actually a photo of him in *Portugal's Guerrilla War,* taken in Portuguese Guinea.

An important issue raised by Manuel Freire of *Diario de Noticias* revolved around Portugal being the first European Nation to arrive in Africa and the last to leave. He queried whether the Portuguese presence in Africa was any different from that of other European nations?

In point of fact, it was. During the many decades that I covered Africa for newspapers and magazines, as well as news and photo agencies, I was able to visit all the African states. I also made dozens of TV documentaries. This 'total immersion' process gave me a very good insight as to how things were in the various African states and how their respective governments worked and there is no question, there were enormous differences.

Liberia for instance, though totally free, was actually more of an American colony than neighbouring British-run Sierra Leone or Francophonic Cote d'Ivoire. For almost a century Liberia's currency was the American dollar and it was only after President Tubman died (in his sleep, in contrast to those who followed) and ethnic violence emerged, that Monrovia had to establish its own currency.

Also, ties with Washington were so strong that Liberians could come and go to and from the United States as they pleased. Freed slaves had originally been the basis of it all, but then Firestone got a grip with the rubber industry which became of strategic importance during the Second World War. In the end, Firestone almost ran the country.

Elsewhere on the continent, the two colonial powers that stood out rather starkly were Britain and France, both quite benevolent in their approach to imperial rule. Paris's mission was always to draw its colonies closer to what it termed the 'motherland'. In turn, Africa provided France with much of the raw materials it needed as a commercial and industrial power (and still does). For all that, very few important matters were *not* referred to Paris.

It did not take long after the end of the Second World War for the Elysees Palace to accept that all her African colonies would not remain subservient forever. The rebellion in Indo-China had already started and the knock-on effect extended half way across the globe. It resulted in a form of self-rule being implemented in places like Dakar, Yaoundé, Abidjan, Libreville, Bangui and elsewhere. The naysayers in Paris were aghast of course, but the new system worked quite well because the French rule of law prevailed and with a good sense of fair play, ordinary people were protected.

The British went a step further. Though they had their 'all powerful' governors in capitals like Nairobi, Lagos, Freetown, Dar es Salaam and the rest, Whitehall did not meddle in matters linked to tribal affairs. Lord Lugard had originally established what was referred to in Nigeria as 'Indirect Rule' for the Moslem people in the north: that meant that day-to-day government and administration was left in the hands of traditional rulers (coupled to a relatively moderate form of Sharia Law that did *not* include the cutting off of hands for minor transgressions).

It is worth mentioning that when I met General de Spinola at his Bissau headquarters, I had already observed his approach to local tribal leaders in Portuguese Guinea (some of my photos in *Portugal's Guerrilla Wars* cover this aspect) and the 'Lugard' issue was raised. I got the impression that Spinola had already considered that this might be the way forward, though I also sensed that I might be stirring muddy waters and he soon changed the subject.

My opinion is that if General Spinola had time and the resources – he had neither – he could have made it work: the village 'self defence' concept was quite widespread in Portuguese Guinea and once in place, it worked reasonably well.

With regard to black Africa generally, one must accept that Britain and France – as well as Spain, Italy and Belgium (and Germany, before it lost all its African possessions after the First World War) – were relatively newcomers to actually *colonising* Africa.

Though the French and the English had traded with the continent for a couple of hundred years, the British only annexed Lagos in August 1861 under the threat of force by Commander Beddingfield of HMS *Prometheus*. Ceremoniously, he was accompanied by the Acting British Consul, William McCoskry.

Nairobi, in East Africa, was only established in 1899. Portugal, in contrast, put roots down on the African continent more than four centuries before that.

Which raises another issue: Does that explain how Portugal could maintain a war in three African fronts for more than a decade?

The answer is no. In trying to explain why Portugal fought so hard for 13 years to prevent its provinces in the *ultramar* from being lost, one has to consider the fact that Lisbon knew and understood Africa a lot better than any other European power. Also, she tolerated nobody – black or white – from interfering with those interests.

Further, the rebellion in Angola's north in 1961 was nothing new. There had been many uprisings, rebellions and revolutions in the past, some minor and quite a few that needed a good deal of effort, time and manpower to quash.

When explaining reasons why Lisbon had reacted so strongly to the Angolan attacks in the early 1960s, Prime Minister Salazar said on numerous occasions that the provinces were, as he phrased it, 'an extension of Portugal itself.'

'All three territories are part of the greater Portugal' he stated on many occasions, adding that he was not going to allow centuries of historic civilizing tradition give way to radicals with guns. The consensus in Lisbon at the time was that this sort of thing had happened before and everything would eventually settle down.

Those who were 'in the know' would remind the populace that some of the early rebellions in both Angola and Mozambique had been extensive and more often than not, quite bloody. All had been put down, some quite brutally, particularly in regions adjacent to German South West Africa (before Kaiser Wilhelm's war). It is interesting that there are many recorded instances of South African Boers having been hired to fight in some of the earlier conflicts; according to French historian René Pélissier, several dozen times during the course of the century before.

What is astonishing is that Portugal was able to rally the way it did when, for a time, all seemed to be lost in Northern Angola in 1961. Portugal then, was a nation of nine million people and, after Albania, the second poorest country in Europe.

One needs to accept too that while the Portuguese were not battling the most sophisticated enemy on the planet, the rebels quickly evolved into a fairly effective fighting force and were kept well supplied by the Soviets with the same weapons then being deployed against the Americans in Vietnam. Also, guerrilla cadres from all three territories were being trained in their thousands in military establishments behind the Iron Curtain, China and Cuba, as well as in a dozen African states that enjoyed Moscow's support.

It is also true that the guerrillas trained by Eastern Bloc states were streets ahead of those funded by the West, with the single exception of UNITA which at one stage, went on to control roughly 90 percent of Angola's rural regions. The initials, in Portuguese, stand for *União Nacional para a Independência Total de Angola:* National Union for the Total Independence of Angola.

The Washington-supported FNLA (Front for the Liberation of Angola) in contrast, was little more than a token force, its morale and fighting capability destroyed in a single major defeat immediately after independence at the Battle of Quifangondo (which became known among those who survived it as the 'Road of death'). I deal with this at some length in Chapter 12.

It is axiomatic too, that from the many guerrillas sent abroad for training, a significant number of brilliant, totally committed and determined fighters would emerge.

Guinea's João Bernardo Vieira (His *nom de guerre* was Nino) was one of them. Very much a 'hands-on' fighter, 'Nino' demonstrated an utterly ruthless skill and daring while active militarily against Lisbon's forces, to the extent that his forces ended up controlling several 'no-go' areas off the coast from which he was never properly excluded by the Portuguese Army.

I met the man – by then President of his beloved Guiné-Bissau – during a visit to Bissau long after the war had ended while making a television documentary there, and I found him a remarkably reticent, quiet-spoken individual. That, I subsequently heard, belied his ruthlessness and when it came to settling scores, his enemies murdered him, cut his body into small pieces and spread them about the city.

Jonas Savimbi was an altogether different kind of individual who went on to become a favourite with the Washington Central Intelligence Agency: they eventually supplied him with Stinger ground-to-air missiles (together with a group of American specialists who took up permanent residence at his bush camp at Jamba in the extreme south-east of the country, an event that was to cause serious damage to the Angolan Air Force.

It should be noted too, that in the post-independent phase, many of Savimbi's frontline troops were trained by South African military Special Forces operators, and with it all, UNITA became a fearsome insurgent force.

It is ironic that those same South Africans were eventually recruited as mercenaries and hired by Luanda – their former arch-enemy – to destroy UNITA, which they did in a series of short, sharp campaigns, something I deal with in detail in the first three chapters of this book.

In truth, Savimbi was every bit as ruthless as Guiné's Nino, probably even more so. In a subsequent exchange of messages with British journalist Fred Bridgland, who wrote one of the best books to emerge from the war, Savimbi murdered just about everybody whom he even thought might oppose him.[4]

As with so many African leaders, his measure of power became absolute and, in turn, absolutely bloody. Bridgland is currently updating his earlier work on the UNITA leader.

Diario de Noticias also questioned whether Lisbon's African wars could be compared to the US intervention in Vietnam?

My answer was this: The Vietnam syndrome in relation to what was going on militarily in Africa at the time had been a subject of much debate, and here one has to recall that the first of the 'Liberation Wars' in East Africa was launched against the Mau Mau in Kenya and effectively put down by the British military using largely conventional means. All that took time and it gave London the necessary breathing space to formulate fresh and more innovative sets of tactics.

It soon became clear to insurgent groups that Mau Mau tactics – and the way they were implemented, usually piece-meal against the British – did not work. So a more conventional approach was adapted by the guerrillas once the Angolan war got into its stride, followed quickly by similar struggles in Rhodesia and Mozambique.

What subsequently did emerge was that many of the instructors who put Angolan, Guinean and Mozambique insurgents through their paces, had good experience of insurgent warfare in Vietnam, as did Luanda's Cuban allies. Also, identical weapons were deployed, both in Asia and in Africa: the AK, RPG-2s, the RPD light machine-gun and the TM-46 anti-tank mine as well as a range of anti-personnel bombs like the POM-Z. With time, these weapons progressed to more advanced versions (RPG-7 and TM-57 among others).

Obviously, guerrillas being trained in Soviet countries were inducted into many of the systems employed by Vietcong veterans who had seen a considerable amount of action: being 'Third World' and both regions largely undeveloped, it made good sense. Trainees were shown news clips and propaganda films and seasoned battlefield commanders would come through and, with the help of interpreters, would explain how they fought.

Also raised were reasons that I believed led Portugal's military forces to defeat, which has no immediate answers.

In the modern period – post Second World War – there have been few wars that have been 'won' outright: that is, one side going in and crushing another, the Malayan 'Emergency' being the exception. Most recent wars have ended up at the negotiating table and fairly clear victories have ended up with the 'winner' having to yield, often quite substantially: the Korean War (still undecided); Israel after the Six Day War (the Jewish state having to hand back all of the Sinai Peninsula), American efforts in Vietnam, the Iraq-Iran War (one of the bloodiest) and South Africa's so-called Border War which, to those involved, seemed to go on forever. In most cases both sides claimed victory…

The same could be said to apply to Lisbon and its African 'provinces'. The Portuguese were not, in the classic sense 'defeated' in Angola, Mozambique and Portuguese Guinea, but then she did not win either. Like other conflicts, guerrilla or otherwise, everything eventually centred on politics, in this case driven by a disaffected military establishment. The reality is that the African people who challenged Lisbon's hegemony for their freedom in these overseas territories eventually got it.

It is interesting that exactly the same sort of thing happened in the Rhodesian War, though obviously on a much smaller scale. I knew former Prime Minister Ian Smith quite well and after

---

4 Fred Bridgland, War *for Africa: Twelve Months that Transformed a Continent*, Ashanti Publishing, 1992.

the hostilities had ended, he confided that he became aware of his own military shortcomings when it was reported that he was losing a company of men *every month,* not to any kind of enemy action, but rather, to emigration.[5]

These were the same people who had been doing the fighting and they moved on, because like many young Portuguese who fled abroad, they felt they had to make new lives for themselves in a more secure environment.

In both countries (as well as with South Africa towards the end of the Border War in the late 1980s) the consensus was that there was essentially nothing to be gained by unnecessarily losing more lives in a succession of African wars.

Critically, of all the wars in the post-Second World War epoch, Portugal was arguably the most 'unready' nation to embark on a major conflict, never mind one that lasted more than a decade.

That the Portuguese Army was able to haul itself out of what was clearly a soporific haze and rally to a cause that had suddenly become desperate is commendable. In the eyes of most European observers, it was totally unexpected, especially since the French had recently been driven out of Algeria. If the powerful and seasoned French Army couldn't do it, ran the argument, how the hell could poor little Lisbon's cohorts?

But then, to the surprise of all, it wasn't long before young Portuguese troops were giving as good as they got. In record time they managed to recapture many of the gains made by the revolutionaries in north Angola – including the new-found rebel regional capital Nambuangongo in the heart of the *Dembos*. It took a while, but with application and an astonishing determination, they got themselves back onto the offensive.

I deal with these events in some detail in Chapter Four of *Portugal's Guerrilla Wars in Africa*.[6]

III

It was Portugal's youthful soldiers – the majority of them conscripts – who finally had the last say, commented one observer who had spent time at the front. He was right, because if you had to suggest today that there is any nation, big or small, that would send its boys into a war for more than a dozen years, you'd be laughed out of the room.

The sentiment then and now is that this is a virtually impossible concept, not only in terms of money but in manpower, logistical limitations and, of course, the ultimate test: attitude.

In reality, the youth of yesterday was very different to today's youngsters. That applies as much to Portugal as it does to the average American, Israeli or Brit. Four or five decades ago young people accepted challenges as part of life because, simply put, the majority of them had to.

One example puts this into perspective. When the Israeli Army invaded Hezbollah strongholds in 2006, conscripts were ordered to leave all personal electronic gear behind. Many did not, with the result that when they called their families and their girlfriends from their bunkers inside Lebanon, Hezbollah communications specialists were able to triangulate those positions and rain mortars down onto their heads.

Can you imagine your son or your neighbour's son being sent to Africa for two years' military service without once being allowed to come home? And without their omnipresent cell phones, iPads and computer games? Forget it…

---

5   Talks with the former Prime Minister at his Harare home prior to his retiring to Cape Town.
6   Al J. Venter; *Portugal's Guerrilla Wars in Africa*, Helion, UK, 2012.

While war raged in Africa, those who were called up tended to accept their lot. It was only at later stages that many of the young men waiting to be called up slipped across the border and sought succour in other countries. For the majority, that 'faraway' continent of Africa was as alien to the average kid who has just left school in Vila Real, Lisbon or Castelo Branco as landing on the moon.

Yet, for those who did not take the gap, almost all accepted their lot because it was considered in the national interest. Just as youthful American, British, Australian and Canadians rose to the occasion when the world was threatened by the Japanese and the Nazis in the Second World War and scores of conflicts before that.

The command factor obviously played a role. While there were innumerable laggards – as there would be in any large-scale gathering of individuals – there were many excellent officers fighting Portugal's wars in Africa. Some were quite brilliant. I rate General Antonio de Spinola as one of the best. In one of my recent books, I put him way up there with the likes of Orde Wingate of Chindit fame, France's Roger Trinquier and Vietnam's General Vo Nguyen Giap.

So too, with General Bethencourt Rodrigues, with his classically aggressive and intrusive approach that clearly reflected an excellent historical understanding of guerrilla warfare, and who went on to turn the war in Angola on its head. By then, the people of Angola believed he had won the war and that it was time to move on, but a group of dissident officers in Lisbon thought otherwise.

To return to the older veteran, I found General de Spinola to be an unusual man, friendly and direct, sometimes almost embarrassingly so. He was also tough, a stickler for discipline and often uncompromising. He never tolerated slackers within his upper command, some of whom would be removed from positions of trust and put on the next plane home.

His most significant attribute was that he was modest enough to sit down with people and listen to what they had to say, not only his own officers and men but most noteworthy, the people whom he governed in Portuguese Guinea. Following his arrival in this West African enclave, he'd decided early on that in order to achieve results, he had to get the local people involved and he did so in a positive, pro-active manner.

Seminally, the man had a solid military background. It is not generally known that during the Second World War, he spent time as an observer of *Wehrmacht* efforts on Hitler's eastern front during the encirclement of Leningrad. Groups of Portuguese volunteers were then fighting for the Nazis, having been incorporated into what was known as the 'Blue Division' and they apparently gave a pretty good account of themselves.

What is also not known is that Spinola met clandestinely at least once with Leopold Senghor, the much-esteemed President of Senegal. The two men shared a common interest in what the Leninist lunatic Sekou Toure would do next.

Nor was General Antonio de Spinola afraid to take chances. When he was offered the opportunity to rescue a bunch of Portuguese soldiers who were being held in a high security prison in Conakry, he sent his commandos into the enemy port to haul them out. It was an extremely risky venture listed in the record books in Lisbon as 'Operation Green Sea'.

It is worth mentioning that he was occasionally happy to bend the rules. Scribes such as myself were well down the list of priorities in Portugal's African wars, but when my plane almost came down in the Atlantic because of engine failure and had to limp back to Bissau, I appealed to him (through my liaison officer, Captain Otelo Saraiva de Carvalho) to help me out.

I told him that I had an interview scheduled with the Ghanaian foreign minister in Accra a few days hence and unless he put me on the regular TAP jet flight back to Lisbon the next day, it would be forfeited.

I flew out the following morning.

Another issue raised, was a question about enemy forces: how did they rate in a comparatively modern war? This was something that surfaced quite often when I spoke to some of today's journalists in Lisbon.

The ability of the guerrilla armies, I suggested, varied between the three overseas provinces at war, as they did in Rhodesia and with the South Africans along the southern frontier of Angola.

In fact, as all these wars progressed, the guerrillas improved markedly. South African troops who fought their own 'Border War', often talked disparagingly about the SWAPO enemy, but one must accept that it takes a specially committed type of combatant who is willing to go to war for 23 years (which is how long that war lasted). Make no mistake, SWAPO cadres were good fighters and they ended up teaching Angola's MPLA a thing or two when it came to fighting a bush war.

From personal observation, I would rate Amilcar Cabral's PAIGC at the top of the pile, with a few MPLA units a close second. Obviously, a lot depended on training and, as hostilities dragged on, the ability to be able to handle complicated weapons systems efficiently made the difference.

Quite a few insurgents were killed laying heavy anti-vehicle landmines that had been hauled hundreds of kilometres across country because they did not observe the basics. Some ignored the simple task of keeping the detonator clean, so that when it is screwed into place it does not jam. You don't use your fist to slam a TM-57 detonator home if something is lodged in the thread causing it not to fit properly…

At the same time, the majority of guerrillas were a remarkably resilient force. They could march for weeks across the most inhospitable parts of Africa and survive quite comfortably off the land. Few European troops – apart from Special Forces units, of course – could do the same. Those black fighters came from the land and they managed to live off it.

Also, the guerrillas like to keep almost all their needs on them, close by, which helps when you are mobile. Modern armies need enormous logistic back-up. And when wounded, I have seen black troops (both guerrilla as well as those serving in the Portuguese Army) with horrendous wounds that would have killed most white youngsters.

It was the same in Biafra where there were no drugs and most times, no anaesthetics. I spent time with the French doctors attached to a small group who became the forerunners of *Medecines sans frontiers,* cutting off limbs without chloroform. It must have been hell, but these victims accepted their pain and very few cried out.[7]

And then, the ultimate question: what was my interest in these wars? Several times questions were raised about my bona fides: what it was that gave me the right to pass judgement on conflicts in distant lands, almost always involving people I hardly knew? It was a valid criticism that I answered as best I could.

My reply became standard because I had seen a lot of wars and, in the process, was wounded twice, once because of my own stupidity. I had been covering conflicts for most of my professional life, more often than not for Britain's Jane's Information Group and for London's *Daily Express,* as well as a host of publications on four continents. Also, I was circulating my photos to *Gamma Presse Images* and *Sipa*, both originally in Paris.

I made something like 100 TV documentaries over a dozen years, few of them of a military nature but some quite specifically so. That included producing and directing a TV film on the war in El Salvador as well as a one-hour TV documentary on the Soviet invasion of Afghanistan (1985). My film on the civil war in Uganda was screened coast-to-coast in the United States by American Public Television (PBS).

---

7   Al J. Venter: *Biafra's War: 1967–70 – A Tribal War in Nigeria That Left a Million Dead;* Helion, 2015.

Apart from my work in Africa, I was in and out of the Lebanese civil war for a decade, covering largely from the Christian Arab side. During this period I accompanied units of the Israeli Army into Lebanon when they invaded Beirut in 1982 and thereafter with the Israeli Navy patrolling the Eastern Mediterranean on *Dabur* gunboats.[8]

During the Balkan War I was mainly with the United States Air Force operating out of Frankfurt and afterwards, briefly involved with landmine removal in Croatia.

Before that I covered numerous conflicts ranging from Biafra (the subject of *Biafra's War*, my most recent book published by Helion), travelled through some of the more accessible parts of the Congo (where I was arrested on an espionage charge), Somalia (many times), the Rhodesian War (about a score of operational visits) and off and on for 20 years with the South African army and air force along the Angolan frontier.

Then came the Sudan (arrested once more and marched through the streets of Khartoum at gunpoint), the civil war in El Salvador as well as going operational with mercenaries in Angola (twice against Savimbi's forces), and in Sierra Leone with the same South African mercenary group, Executive Outcomes and thereafter, flying combat in a Mi-24 helicopter gunship with Neall Ellis. The former Portuguese overseas territories were consequently very much a part of it

I never covered Vietnam because I was too busy elsewhere, but in the process I was able to write dozens of books which can be viewed under my name on amazon.com.

In preparing this book, I have to mention that it was impossible for me not to look back in some detail at what I'd had published in the past on Portugal's African campaigns and in so doing, I could easily have skirted everything I'd included in *Portugal e as Guerrilhas de Africa*. But that would have meant ignoring the single most important factor that affected this nation's history over the centuries: how Lisbon was ultimately ousted from Africa.

So, if some readers do spot familiar tracts from my earlier works, I ask you to bear with me because cumulatively, that material is a vital component to exactly what went on in the *ultramar*. Additionally, we have the benefit of it all being suitably updated. I am constantly getting comments from some of those who were there about events I'd dealt with. Invariably some of these arrive with additional data, which adds lustre to it all.

That, I believe, is how history should be handled: a sometimes disjointed hodge-podge of detail, investigative fact and speculation strung logically together to make good common sense but also to add another tiny piece of the national puzzle in its proper context.

This book closely examines what happened to Angola both before and after the so-called 'Colonial Wars' had ended. In fact, having dealt with Portugal's efforts in Angola, Mozambique and Portuguese Guinea, a lot of the material in this work covers Angola in its post-*coup d'état* phases.

Indeed, there were several, including the hectic (and often bloody) transitional period, since the civil war lasted for a couple of decades, as well as the use of South African mercenaries to force UNITA to the negotiating table and eventually to give up the struggle. For Dr Jonas Savimbi it had become a hopeless struggle for survival and he could never match the kind of money then flowing into Luanda's coffers from its oil industry.

What does emerge in this work are the exceptionally heavy odds that were ranged against South Africa in its Border War, most of which was contested along the southern borders of Angola.

In countering Moscow and its surrogates, Pretoria was pitted against a far more powerful enemy that it initially realised. Though not a poor nation, the South Africans struggled to match what the

---

8   Al J. Venter: *Barrel of a Gun: A War Correspondent's Misspent Moments in Combat*; Casemate Publishers, USA 2010.

Soviets, Cubans, East Germans and other Comintern nations were committing to a struggle that at one stage almost ended up with both sides using weapons of mass destruction (WMD).

In the closing stages of the war, the Angolans did use chemical weapons against South African troops, but whether by accident or design, these did not work properly. Pretoria had consistently warned that any use of WMD by their adversaries would result in an 'appropriate reply'.

South Africa had already built six atom bombs and there is no question that pre-emptive planning involved the actual use of them, with Luanda a prime target. It was then that Washington and Moscow decided that enough was enough and that with a chemical or nuclear outcome imminent, nobody needed a further degradation of hostilities. But more of that later…

For now, it is apposite to look at the money involved, specifically in relation to the sophisticated material the Soviets and their allies pumped into the Angola war.

With Portugal out of the way, there is no question that the next step for Moscow was the big push: to remove South African forces from the military equation, aimed specifically at Cape Town as the ultimate target. With a battered South African government acquiescing to superior (and as far as Moscow was concerned) more pliable forces, the sea route around the Cape, strategically, would be theirs.

This is something that has been consistently pooh-poohed by some strategists, but you need to look at the numbers in Chapter Seven, if only because it makes good sense.

A typical Ovambo town in South West Africa's northern reaches as observed from an Alouette helicopter gunship. Though SWAPO guerrillas moved in and out of these villages and had the support of locals against government forces, they were never able to maintain a strong enough grip to dominate and hold a region. Almost always the insurgents would arrive after dark and conditions allowing, disappear back into the bush before first light. (Author's collection)

Official emblem of the once-proud SADF

PART I

OVERVIEW

Portuguese warfare in Africa revealed the limitations of the European state and its technological approach to warfare. Unlike Europe, Africa had almost limitless land and few easily identifiable strategic targets for the control of its wealth. Military objectives – as European strategists understood them – were hard to identify. Consequently, the rewards of campaigning for European troops were slight and the logistical problems often insuperable. The Afro-Portuguese therefore, not only learned to fight their wars in the only manner possible in Africa, but these wars came to have objectives which were only understandable and therefore achievable in an African context.

With apologies, source unknown

In contrast, Portugal did pretty damn well dominating its African dominions for five centuries. The last time anything like that was achieved was by Rome. Britain's expansive fiefdoms across the globe lasted only a couple of centuries…

The author

I began my history at the very outbreak of the war, in the belief that it was going to be a great war …

Thucydides

1

Angola's War Against the Rebels – The Beginning of the End

Private armies are a far cry from the Sixties dogs of war.
John Keegan, Former Defence Correspondent, *Daily Telegraph*, **London.**

Very few military histories start halfway through the campaigns on which they are focussed. This book does exactly that, and for good reason. By capturing Jonas Savimbi's diamond fields at Cafunfo (near the border with the Congo), a small group of South African mercenaries involved in Angola's insurgent war effectively severed rebel access to the world outside. Once they had removed diamonds from the battlefield equation almost all UNITA's external bank balances were effectively 'frozen'. No sales of precious stones were being generated and that meant no money for weapons…

The great battle of Cafunfo lasted several weeks, though if you include the planning stages and movement of assets needed for such a military adventure, it took months.

The process involved a mechanized strike force that covered hundreds of kilometres in a distant corner of Africa that few of us had heard about, never mind visited. Throughout, the attackers consistently came under fire from an extremely determined adversary, many of whom were not afraid to die for a real or imagined ideal.

These battles – short, sharp and brutal – were fundamental to the kind of conventional onslaughts launched by both sides, the likes of which are rarely taught in such august establishments as West Point, Sandhurst or France's elite *École Spéciale Militaire de Saint-Cyr*.

At the end of it, the consequences of government forces – sternly backed by a modest group of freelance fighters – taking the diamond fields after the Cafunfo battle were long term. In turn, the rebels had blown it.

Though hostilities would continue for a good while longer, UNITA – a political and guerrilla movement founded, nurtured and commanded by maverick insurgent leader Dr Jonas Savimbi – appeared to lose both the initiative and the momentum linked to the struggle, which had always been a hallmark of this rebel force.

Without the $200 million delivered annually by Cafunfo's and Catoca's alluvial diamond diggings, the rebels were deprived of a hefty proportion of the wherewithal they needed to fight their war. In contrast, the Luanda government was coining billions from oil, supplemented by the comparative 'small change' it got from diamonds.

In reality, the mechanized assault in Angola's remote Lunda Norte Province in July 1994 should never have happened. The target lay at the far end of a virtually non-existent road in the middle of nowhere. Throughout, while moving towards its objective, the strike force was exposed in a region that had little cover and almost no prospect for back-up should things go wrong.

Air cover from several Mi-17s operating out of Saurimo – the city lies 300 kilometres to the east of Cafunfo (or roughly three hours flying time there and back) – and almost the entire area in-between was hostile. Should one of the helicopters be forced down, it would have been difficult for help to arrive in time. That did happen, several times in fact, but the saving grace was that South African mercenary aviators always insisted on two-ship operations. If one helicopter went down, the other would land and rescue passengers and crew.

In one such incident, where a Mi-17 Hip was forced down by ground fire, the second helicopter landed and loaded everybody onboard. It was a remarkable achievement: the handbook of the older version of that former Soviet helicopter suggests a maximum load of about 20 troops. By the time everybody had clambered onboard and was ready to head towards Saurimo this time round, the total had upped to 40.[1]

For all that, South African mercenary pilots operating under Angolan Government auspices did what was expected of them and were able to provide several hours of top cover when weather allowed, and sometimes when it did not. It did not help that UNITA had acquired SAMs, and these were used several times against the Hips: mostly Stinger missiles provided some years earlier by the CIA for use against pro-Soviet government forces.[2]

Having given this sophisticated equipment to Savimbi to fight his war against the Marxist Luanda government – quite a few Angolan Air Force jets and helicopters were downed with them – there was no way that Washington could take them back after Soviet influence in Africa had waned.

Still, the missile threat did not deter the South African-backed mercenary force from moving onto Cafunfo and throughout, the Angolan Hips were an invaluable asset. But Angola's main operational base at Saurimo in the diamond-rich north-east of the country was a long way from the diggings. That meant that quite a few improvisations needed to be implemented, fuel being the main concern.

Since the average Mi-17 has a flying time of about 150 minutes, getting adequate supplies of avgas to intermediate points along the way was a priority, though the mobile column heading towards Cafunfo did provide some fuel, carried onboard trucks in the two-kilometre-long convoy. Additionally, a refuelling point was established at a small town that had been militarily secured on the main east-west road that snaked through the heavily foliaged region some distance south of Cafunfo.

There were many ancillary problems linked to the onslaught. To avoid landmines and ambushes (which took place anyway, two, three and sometimes four times a day) the column had to cut or plough its own route across some of the most difficult bush and jungle terrain on the African continent.

There were several rivers that needed to be crossed, Savimbi having blown the bridges over most of them as soon as he realised in which direction the column was heading. This the South African commanders did with great difficulty even though their column included several Soviet armoured vehicle-launched bridges (AVLBs). Like much else in this improvised strike force, just about everything in the column moving towards the ultimate objective was 'make-do'.

---

1 The complete story can be found in Al Venter's first book on mercenary involvement in the Angolan war, *War Dog: Fighting Other People's Wars* (Casemate). See Chapter 17 'The Mercenary Air War in Angola'.
2 There were also some SAM-7 Soviet-built 'Strela' ground-to-air missiles deployed by the rebels, most of them given to Savimbi after these weapons had been captured from the Angolan Army during several campaigns that took place each year prior to the rains to the immediate north of the South West African border.

In the end, having fought the rebels off more times than anybody could recall, the mercenary-led attack group – headed by former Reconnaissance Regiment commander Colonel Hennie Blaauw – managed to reach the diggings, though it took twice as long as they initially expected. Once in Cafunfo and the enemy forced back into the jungle, more Angolan Army troops were airlifted into the area and the combined force set about driving the guerrillas further into the interior.

A difficult process of holding onto their gains followed, which, even with helicopter gunship support, was always tenuous; nobody ever knew if Savimbi had sent for reinforcements and whether another 10,000 guerrillas would suddenly descend on the occupiers. Also, the region was remote from any large or small government post and re-supply was always a problem.

Though the attack force was eventually joined by a second large force of government troops who were brought in overland and who set about consolidating the defences of the *Forças Armadas Angolanas* (FAA, the successors to FAPLA), the process remained touch-and-go. Ambushes, landmines and booby traps were a constant threat, in large part because the rebel force had originally been trained by the South African Army.

The battle for Cafunfo was to become one of Africa's classic examples of contemporary insurgency bush warfare.

With Angola's armour, ground and air assets preparing for battle, Cafunfo almost overnight became the magic word. Nobody had any doubt that the rebels would eventually be dislodged: especially since a new bunch of toughies on the block was involved and Luanda was confident that, as with Soyo, the newly-recruited bunch of mercenaries would do the trick.

Colonel Blaauw knew from the start that the task was daunting. There were innumerable delays, false starts and cancellations, coupled to some Angolan commanders playing mind games in their bids to either enhance their influence or start their own not-so-little diamond-buying cartels. Much of this obfuscation could be sourced to Luanda's mind-blowing bureaucracy.

At one stage a group of MPLA political commissars[3] arrived at Saurimo. Like a gaggle of Auschwitz *oberleutnants*, they jackbooted about the base and demanded to know about things that were not only of no concern to them, but had nothing at all to do with the campaign ahead. A quick radio call to Luanda got them all back on their plane.

In Saurimo, during the preparatory stages, there were endless messages, contradictions, debates, not a few heated arguments about who was in charge of what, as well as questions that sometimes made little sense. Forms had to be completed (sometimes in quintuplicate), much of it linked to order groups or staff meetings, though Blaauw and his associates believed that very little of what they wrote or reported in these missives to Luanda were ever read or passed down the line. Additionally, strings of military brass would flip in and out of Luanda and head east towards the diamond fields.

Kafka would have loved the place, especially since most of the senior Angolan commanders had been put through their paces in the Soviet Union. Almost to a man, they tended to do things by the book. The South Africans did not, which was the prime reason these former Special Forces operators were hired to fight Angola's civil war in the first place: they were totally unconventional in their approach.

That, in essence, was the start of it. Issues were further compounded by delays in the supply of men, equipment and machines, none of which was helped by the fact that Luanda lay on the far

---

3 Angola has been run along the lines of a Soviet-style Comintern state almost from the time that the Portuguese left Africa in the mid-1970s. Much of it came into play during the incumbency of the last Portuguese military governor Admiral Rosa (Red) Coutinho, a notorious communist. And what a legacy he bequeathed this sad state. As one Angolan politician was heard to comment when his duplicity was finally exposed: 'a pox on his house and all his children!'

Recruited by the mercenary organisation Executive Outcomes, former Reconnaissance Regiment Colonels Duncan Rykaart (left) and Hennie Blaauw handled most of the company's operational duties while serving in Angola. They are seen here on Luanda's Marginal. (Author's Photo)

Alluvial diamond diggings in Angola: source of much of the wherewithal which funded Savimbi's guerrilla war against the Luanda government.

At Saurimo, in Angola's diamond-rich northeast the mercenaries found many Soviet missiles lying around the air base, obviously abandoned. To the chagrin of the Luanda government, some of these were 'spirited away' to South Africa. (Author's photo)

Black marble memorial to those Executive Outcomes combatants who died in action in Angola and Sierra Leone. It originally stood in EO's home base in Pretoria. (Author's photo)

The EO logo which became very well known while the company remained active.

'Demo Day' at EO's main training base at Cabo Ledo, a scary 90 minute drive south of Luanda. The parade was attended by a number of senior Angolan Army officers and EO mercenary commanders, including Nick van den Bergh and his wife (nearest camera). An array of weapons is laid out on the table before them. (Author's photo)

Former Recce Captain Wynand du Toit, captured by Cuban commandos during an abortive raid in Cabinda and held in isolation for years in an Angolan prison, ended up running the EO training centre at Angola's Rio Longa. He is seen here with some of his charges. (Author's photo)

Map showing main operational areas in Angola's north-east where UNITA was most active because of diamonds.

Saurimo, the hub of Angola's diamond industry in the north-east: a dirty, dusty conurbation, the town was completely surrounded by minefields because of persistent UNITA raids. (Author's photo)

side of the country. The distance between the capital and Saurimo – heart of Angola's diamond industry in the east – is about 1,000 kilometres by road.

To cap it, the mercenaries hired by Executive Outcomes – or EO in private military company (PMC) jargon – had to contend with staff officers who were sometimes political appointees with no real experience of warfare. There were quite a few instances where petty jealousies became squabbles, equipment arrived from abroad that didn't work, and spare parts that would disappear within an hour of arrival or simply didn't fit because they weren't the ones that had been ordered. Not to mention an army that seemed permanently smashed or, more often than not, was smoking something noxious.

Also, there was little love lost between the mercenaries at their Saurimo base and the Angolan security people, in particular the black-uniformed, so-called 'Ninjas', a foreign-trained group of quasi-secret police who would not hesitate to shoot a man if they believed he was anti-government. There were several impromptu fire-fights between EO mercs and the 'Ninjas' at the airport, almost none of which resulted in casualties. I was arrested by them for taking photos of some of the planes, inoperable as it transpired and an event I deal with later.

Even Angolan pilots who – with their South African counterparts – were intended to be part of the show, weren't immune to these inanities.

Immediately prior to the column setting off, there were a number of aircraft involved in accidents, with those at the controls later found to be drunk. One of these African aviators took a Mi-17 out and after cutting enough of a crooked line across the skies above Saurimo, he had everybody on the ground gaping. More by luck than design, he eventually brought his helicopter down with a thud and in the process buckled the chopper's undercarriage and snapped several rotors on impact.

Unlike civilian air crews, this crowd was *not* regarded as expendable and such transgressions were ignored, most times, anyway.

Add to all these quandaries the weather, which, in that part of tropical Africa seemed to have a priority all its own. Though it was technically winter in the Southern Hemisphere, the occasional storm – black, billowing tropical cu-nimbus clouds stretching from one horizon to the other – would roll in and make things as difficult for those on the ground as in the air. There would be downpours that could make quagmires of areas sometimes half the size of Ireland.

Finally, there was Savimbi, a tough adversary whose entire career revolved around taking absurd chances. Indeed, as the South Africans were aware, he – and the forces under him – had never been a pushover because so many had been trained by them. Together, all these factors seemed to contrive to end everything before it began.

Yet, whenever things looked hopeless, somebody would recall that Executive Outcomes had done it all before. Never mind that circumstances at Soyo, where the South Africans first made their mark in this ongoing military struggle (See Chapter 30) were different, Soyo had conclusively demonstrated – with the loss of several EO lives – that the UNITA nut could be cracked.

Throughout, even when there were sharp differences between Blaauw and the FAA high command – which was often, because the approach to most things military by so many of these black brigadiers was cumbersome – it was taken for granted that this tough, mostly bearded bunch of mercenaries could and *would* repeat the process. In reality then, Cafunfo was a critical test of the firm's ability to counter UNITA insurgency across a huge swathe of Africa's seemingly impenetrable interior.

Every one of those involved knew that without diamonds, Savimbi would falter. Thus, should the boys fail in their efforts, the implications weren't lost on any of those linked to Executive Outcomes. Future PMC contracts would stand or fall by the outcome of this extended jungle campaign.

Hennie Blaauw explained some of it shortly after I arrived in the diamond capital. He pulled out a set of Angolan government maps of the north-east of the country (near a part of the Congolese border that had recently been ravaged by Ebola). Marked in bold capital letters across the top was the word, in Portuguese: *SECRETO*.

The Cuango, the river which lay adjacent to Cafunfo, he explained, emptied into the great watershed of the Congo. It also drained much of the huge Malanje basin.

Pencilled in across the chart were tiny shields of crossed picks and shovels – geological markings that identified deposits: gold, diamonds, aluminium and the rest. Many highlighted diamondiferous pipes, which, though largely alluvial, stretched all the way to the Congo's frontier and beyond. A source at De Beers confirmed afterwards that the entire riverine region was potentially Kimberlitic and regarded by some geologists as being blessed with some the richest diamond deposits in the world.

With a stubby, nicotine-stained finger, Blaauw poked at a few places until he finally found what he was looking for. He chortled gruffly in Afrikaans: '*Ja. Hier's dit!*' ('Yes, here it is!').

That place was Firiquichi, he declared, pulling himself up full stretch. A hefty Red Heart rum laced with coke in one hand, a pencil in the other and the map laid out before us, he added that I probably wouldn't find it on any conventional chart.

He and many of the others who went in with him weren't to know until afterwards, but just about everything that eventually took place in a succession of battles that lasted a month, hinged on that tiny anonymous cluster of mud and grass huts perched on the banks called Firiquichi. Until then, nobody had ever heard of the place before.

2

The Cafunfo Campaign Gathers Momentum

> 'Without doubt, the Afrikaner people [most of the whites in EO were Afrikaners] understand Africa better than any other whites have ever done, for the simple reason that for much of their tortuous history they have lived like Africans, close to the land, risking all its hazards, its harshness and its caprice.'
>
> Peter Younghusband, decades-long correspondent in Africa for the London *Daily Mail* and *Newsweek*

When the armoured column eventually did transmogrify itself into a potent fighting force – part of it having moved overland across Angola from Luanda, the rest coming out of Saurimo in the east – it was comprised of about a hundred vehicles. Apart from the 28 BMP-2s, all brand new, there were an additional 60 logistic and fire-support vehicles, among them Russian bridge-building TMMs.

In terms of manpower, there were about 500 Angolan troops, many of them trained at Wynand du Toit's Rio Longa base.[1] They, in turn, were supported by perhaps a hundred or so Executive Outcomes mercenaries, the majority black.

Also in this array was a group of a hundred Katangese regulars; tough, aggressive combatants who years before had fled Zaire and taken refuge in Angola. Though older than the rest, everybody knew they could dish it out when needed. Blaauw regarded them as a rather odd, irascible French-speaking bunch, but as everybody knew, they kept themselves in a constant state of readiness for the day they could 'return in triumph' to the old country.

On the road to Cafunfo these Katangese were to prove their worth many times over, even though Colonel André, their leader, was sometimes unnecessarily castigated by his Angolan counterparts. For Blaauw that was uncalled for; it was sometimes meted out in the presence of junior officers and as far as this veteran was concerned, that was just not on. But then, as even he would

---

1 Captain Wynand du Toit, formerly a member of South Africa's crack 1 Reconnaissance Regiment was taken into Angolan waters off Cabinda with a small strike force by submarine and put ashore on a clandestine mission to destroy oil installations. But the operation had already been betrayed and a Cuban Special Forces team was waiting for them. Two South Africans were killed and a wounded du Toit taken prisoner. He spent seven years in solitary in Luanda. After his release he joined EO but because of what had happened, was not allowed to take part in actual operations. Instead, he was first employed in training at the mercenary base at Cabo Ledo base on the coast, south of the capital and later at the Special Forces camp on the Rio Longa, further south.

admit, the Angolan military code of ethics had a very different texture from his own. This former Recce commander was old school and he liked to play by the rules.

There was little doubt, the colonel recalled afterwards, that the Katangese had seen a lot of fighting. With Angolan support during the course of the previous 20 years, they had launched three invasions of Zaire against the hated Mobutu regime. The last time they tried to take the copper mining town of Kolwezi in Katanga and were twice beaten off, but only after the Congolese tyrant had appealed to Europe for help.

Both times a combined force of French parachutists and Legionnaires were sent to Africa to sort things out[2].

The armoured thrust on Cafunfo would eventually cover hundreds of kilometres and was extremely tough going. Blaauw commented that he knew it would be more difficult than anything he had experienced before; 'worse than Soyo, because there we were static – here we were constantly on the move.'[3]

He added that there was no way of predicting events, 'We could only guess what UNITA might pull out of the hat to counter our efforts.'

In the end, the operation – in its various disjointed phases – lasted three months, though the final stage out between Cacolo – just off the main road that linked Saurimo with Luanda – to the Cafunfo diamond fields, took only 25 days, when the attacking force had to build its own stretches of road through terrain that was almost primeval.

Throughout, the column was harassed by a succession of attacks, ambushes and mortar stand-offs. At one stage, Blaauw recalled, 'they were hurling 60mm mortars at the column as if they were firecrackers.' There were also landmines laid by Savimbi's people, but because the attackers covered virgin ground almost from the start, there was no way that UNITA commanders could predict which route the mobile force was likely to follow.

A glance at the *dagboek* (diary) kept by Colonel Blaauw for the duration, provides a graphic insight. This extract is from the final stages of the march on July 25, 1994, the day before Cafunfo was overrun. Measurements are in metric while non-italic notes (in brackets) are for the readers' benefit:

0829 *Mortar fire from 100 meters ahead. Line of UNITA infantry behind. BMP throws a track. Scramble MiGs* (MiG-23s)

0940 *MiGs in air taking heavy 23mm fire from positions around us. More UNITA troops in trenches near thick bush. BMPs overrun them. 250 kg aerial bomb falls 100 meters behind us. Close! Mortars incoming!*
   Move column forward. Prepare mortars and artillery for reaction. UNITA on left flank and hitting us. Nick wounded in lung (Presumably Nick Hayes who later died in a South African hospital). *About 60 enemy dead*
   Move into town. More mortar and small arms. Heavy going!

---

2 They were despatched from France and air-dropped at the behest of a much-beleaguered Mobutu Sese Seko.
3 The 'Battle for Soyo' was the touchstone on which the entire mercenary-led operation in Angola was based and is dealt with in great detail in Chapter 30. In fact, Soyo set the scene for the subsequent use of private military companies (PMCs) in other regions of turmoil, notably Iraq, Afghanistan, Colombia and elsewhere. At one stage there were more than 10,000 South African private military contractors working in Iraq.

One of several Soviet-built BMP-2 amphibious infantry fighting vehicles that guarded the approaches to Saurimo while Executive Outcomes was still around. (Author's photo)

All Mi-24 helicopter gunships flown by Executive Outcomes pilots in Angola and Sierra Leone were fitted with air-to-ground rockets. (Author's photo)

EO side-gunner on board one of the Mi-17 helicopters operated by EO. (Author's photo)

A nondescript town in Angola's interior: a UNITA military presence was invariably around, which meant that SAM-7 or American Stinger MANPAD missiles were always a threat. (Author's photo)

Colonel Hennie Blaauw conducts his early-morning briefing to section leaders with his operational map affixed to the hull of one of the BMPs involved in the Cafunfo strike.
(Photo courtesy of Hennie Blaauw)

Some of the former Special Forces operators – most had served in South Africa's Reconnaissance Regiment – who were involved in the Battle for Cafunfo. This photo was taken soon afterwards in Sierra Leone where EO played a significant role in defeating the rebels. (Photo: Cobus Claassens)

An EO operator with two of the newly arrived Soviet T54/55 main battle tanks that should have been used in anti-UNITA counter-insurgency operations but were not because they were unsuited to the largely jungle terrain of north Angola. (Photo courtesy of Hennie Blaauw)

Cafunfo's diamond diggings stretched for several hundred kilometres along a series of rivers in the north-east of the country and were inordinately productive, one of the reasons why Jonas Savimbi could fight his guerrilla war as long as he did. (Photo by Jose-Paulo in 2009)

Another contact. FAA soldiers fired rifle grenades at enemy from behind us and almost hit our BMPs! Gadaffi wounded (referring to a black EO operator who was seriously wounded in Sierra Leone 15 months later)

Stopped for eats. Instructed drivers to go on both sides of the track rather than on it because of mines. Two sections in front, one in depth. Caught UNITA patrol on open ground. All killed…

Mortar and small arms incoming

Reach Alberto Fernandez. Go round town. Heavy incoming. Hatches down. Just go! Mines!

Into TB (temporary base). *Overnight.*

Colonel Blaauw made two further observations…

The first concerned night flying activity by the Pilatus Porter PC-7, where former SAAF veteran Louwrens Bosch – using his 68mm rocket pods – hit two UNITA trucks moving through thick bush, having targeted their lights. *'Huge explosions'* was scribbled in the margin.

The other mentioned the enemy using their ZSU-23s in ground support roles in conjunction with mortar fire. That took place a few hours later. As usual, *die waens* (the wagons), as he phrased it, had been pulled round into a traditional Boer laager position.

Earlier, Blaauw had ordered his men to dig slit trenches at least two feet deep, though most of his combatants – because of the intensity of incoming fire – went down half as much again.

It was a complicated process getting all the components together for what was to become the biggest single FAA operation of the war. The airlift of BMP-2s to the east began in February 1994 – all 28 were taken in by Russian cargo planes – and even that took longer than anticipated because there was always something else that needed shifting.

Originally EO Management had put forward the proposal that for logistical, maintenance and other reasons, the entire force be marshalled at Saurimo. But this proved impractical and the onslaught became two-pronged. Thus, once FAA's heavy-duty Russian-built Ural logistics vehicles arrived, Combat Group Bravo with Brigadier Pepe de Castro in command – together with Roelf van Heerden and the rest of the mercenary force in tow – departed Saurimo on April 21. The PC-7 ground support aircraft had arrived the previous month.

An immediate problem facing Luanda was that most of the bridges linking Saurimo with the west had been destroyed. Also, all approach roads were mined, which was why the column struck out first towards the east, then south and finally north-west towards the junction town of Cacolo, where the intention was for them to link up with Combat Force Alpha.

Mines were more of a problem than first anticipated and within a week several BMP-2s had been destroyed. Every single road that UNITA believed might be used by the attacking force was peppered with these bombs, many of them electronically command-activated from higher ground, which suggested fairly technical foreign input, probably Israeli.[4]

UN specialist teams said afterwards that it would take years to clear the main roads, never mind secondaries.[5]

Also, fuel for the air support element became so much of an issue that the MiG-23s (which only became operational in that north-eastern sector in mid-May) were grounded halfway through. Eventually the problem was partly solved by aircrews tapping fuel directly into their fighters from the tanks of the cargo planes that regularly flew into Saurimo.

---

4 Savimbi wasn't shy to use foreign military specialists to bolster his forces: in fact, commented Duncan Rykaart, 'why shouldn't he? We South Africans were 'foreign' and our boys had originally trained a large segment of his military, including all his Special Forces, which was why UNITA gave us such as hard time at Soyo.'

5 'Angola: New Mines, What Ban?' *Bulletin of the Atomic Scientists*, Al J. Venter, Volume 55 #03, May/June 1999, pp 13/15.

Totally unexpected, Roelf van Heerden was called back to South Africa. The always-affable Blaauw was pleased, in part because until then he'd been kicking rocks back in Cabo Ledo and, as he told me, he wouldn't have missed what was to turn into some of the best action of his life. Always keen for a scrap, Blaauw probably would have *paid* the Angolans to let him get involved.

Flown to Saurimo on June 1 and having been familiarized with what was going on in the field at EO's command centre, he was taken in one of the Mi-17s to join the column at Tchicuza the next day. As it happened, Blaauw was to become Brigadier de Castro's most valued counsellor: in fact, it wasn't long before the South African led most of the day-to-day planning sessions in the field.

Advisor or not, Blaauw countered some of de Castro's more debatable decisions: irrational man that he was, the Angolan brigadier quite often let his emotions rule. In other Angolan quarters, de Castro had already acquired a reputation of being something of a loose cannon whenever he came under pressure.

The first phase of the operation – after several punch-ups with UNITA at Dala, Alto Chicapa and Cucumbi – was the capture of the crossroads town of Cacolo from where all routes, such as they were, led to Cafunfo. But first the Alto Quilo River had to be bridged by a TMM team. Only two of these mechanical systems were allocated to the force and they were carefully husbanded by the South Africans. Without them, the column would have been halted dozens of times and, in the end, would probably have got nowhere near the target.

Also included in the column was what Blaauw regarded as his most valuable asset: a Caterpillar front-end loader. At one stage it was almost discarded in a sloppy recovery operation that had been completely misdirected by de Castro. On a whim, the Angolan officer decided that because the machine didn't work quite like he thought it should, it would have to go. He'd already given instructions for it to be blown up and it took a hefty argument from Blaauw to persuade an Angolan staff officer to desist.

As it subsequently turned out, it was just as well that de Castro's orders were not obeyed. Several times the column ground to a halt, its vehicles paralyzed because of obstacles. This usually happened at river approaches where vehicles might have tumbled into the water. Most times it was because bridges weren't level or they hadn't been built strong enough to take armour. Then this extremely versatile and reliable old machine would be hauled forward to remove whatever was causing dislocation.

The question of adequately supplying the column was always a serious issue. Very literally, everything had to be flown to a mobile force that could never predict in advance where it would be at any specific time. For this reason, EO personnel spent long hours prior to the operation planning air drops with former Soviet pilots who were at the controls of a small fleet of Ilyushin-76s, all hired on contract for this military operation.

'We couldn't afford mistakes while we were out there. So we would improvise as we went, usually working with our own support pilots when looking for safe drop zones. They'd do an aerial recce for us and come back with suggestions about likely places where a drop could take place.

'At the same time, the guys bringing the stuff to us had to be scrupulously familiar with our routines, in large part because we had to remain flexible. Everything that might be needed was listed…we'd prepared pages of detailed instructions, where everything was stored or from whom it could be ordered. Then followed complicated delivery arrangements, which also had to be coordinated and which could sometimes become a nightmare in a city like Luanda.

'With all these factors in mind, we established some good parameters for the drops and our new Russian friends were more than up to the task.'

Blaauw detailed what was involved at the delivery end:

'Supply drops were made from about 20,000 feet with between 16 and 20 drogue-stabilized pallets per flight. Each time about 20 tons of fuel, food, spare parts and medical needs would freefall to about a thousand feet where KAP-3 systems would automatically open the chutes.' Obviously, explained Blaauw, altitude had to be strictly maintained because of the threat of SAMs.

'At the end of it, things were very professionally handled. The Russkies dropped their cargoes spot-on and actually, for all the doubts some of the guys had about these people, they never missed a drop zone. They were a real pleasure to work with, very professional,' said the former Recce colonel, speaking of his former enemies.

UNITA threw everything they could into the campaign which, as some of the men commented afterwards, might have become a rout had the rebels been anything of a lesser adversary. Though UNITA hardware was every bit as good as that used by FAA, Savimbi's combatants – many of them crack specialists with years of bush war – were in an altogether different class.

At the same time, there was evidence of extreme hardship endured by many rebel units. As the people attached to the column could see from casualties after a battle, nearly every UNITA soldier was malnourished. Also, their uniforms were threadbare. 'They would use rucksacks made of sacking and sometimes the fighters did not even have slings for their AKs,' said Blaauw. So they made their own of a rough bark that had been treated in an improvised kind of bush tanning process and made malleable.

UNITA would attack wherever and whenever the opportunity presented itself, which underscored a determination that was not only fierce but dedicated. According to Blaauw, while these rebels did cause damage, their efforts had very little effect on the BMPs which, built for Third World conditions by the former Soviets, could take an inordinate amount of punishment.

'We would shut our hatches and plough right through their lines, sometimes right over the top of their bunkers and trenches…they suffered terrible losses,' he declared.

'We'd be travelling along in the bush in line-ahead and as soon as we heard that distinctive mortars 'plop…plop…plop', we'd close down everything and just go. Sometimes their aim was well off but even when they homed in on us, their 60mm shells had little effect. The BMPs were built to take that kind of hit and when it happened, the guys inside would be deaf for a week, their eardrums blown. But they were very much alive and still fighting.'

Were 81mm mortars used instead, he reckoned it would have been much more devastating…'

The route to Cafunfo chosen by Blaauw and Brigadier de Castro was a series of remote bush tracks that headed roughly in a northerly direction towards the Congo border.

A second, smaller column made a perfunctory feint westwards from Cacolo in a bid to keep the enemy guessing. In fact, said Blaauw, either of the forces could have ended up in the diamond fields, so it was a solid, practical approach to anything that Savimbi might have planned in the way of interdiction.

'They'd actually expected us to hog the road, which suggested that Savimbi planned accordingly. He ordered that huge supplies of mines and booby traps be lugged south from the Cafunfo area in preparation for the confrontation.

'More significant, they never believed that we'd go in a straight line all the way across that part of tropical Africa, in part because it had never been done before in the conflict, even though we South Africans had used that tactic often enough in decades past during the Border War, usually in our cross-border raids against the Angolans and Cubans.'

One of the immediate effects of these developments, observed Duncan Rykaart, Blaauw's deputy and another senior Recce commander, was that UNITA's crew-served weapons – artillery and some of their heavier stuff – was invariably out of position. It would sometimes end up a day or two from where the real action was.

'Also, they couldn't move it about that easily because just about anything mobile on the roads was blasted by our pilots,' Rykaart added

THE CAFUNFO CAMPAIGN GATHERS MOMENTUM 63

'Of course, those guys helped enormously.' The MiGs and Pilatus Porters flown by Bosch and Pine Pienaar and the others would plaster a UNITA town or troop concentration long before we got there. Then they'd zap them again as we approached.'

The ploy underscored one of the fundamental principles of a modern insurgency, especially in a primitive environment: field commanders that control the skies, dominate just about everything.

This was something that would be put to very good effect when Executive Outcomes moved into Sierra Leone not long afterwards.

Savimbi's ragged band of defenders did their best to try to stop Hennie Blaauw's attacking force, even laying anti-tank mines, but to no avail.

3

Cafunfo Done and Dusted

Despite vigorous disrupting efforts on UNITA's part, the column made remarkable progress. A good deal of it Colonel Blaauw attributed to what he regarded as one of the most efficient infantry fighting machines of the modern period, the Soviet-era-designed amphibious BMP-2.

A product of the Cold War, this 14-ton infantry fighting vehicle (IFV) first appeared in public in Moscow during the 1982 May Day parade. Since then it found its way into many Third World conflicts.

Although originally designed for the both the battlefields of Europe and some of the primitive regions in which Moscow believed it would eventually be involved (Angola, Central America, East Asia), this classic tracked troop carrier with its distinctive pointed nose and almost horizontal ribbed glacis plate has always performed well in Africa.

Usually carrying ten men, which include a three-man crew, the Angolan versions came with 30mm cannon mounted, together with a coaxial 7.62mm machine gun. Indeed, it was a remarkably lethal fighting machine.

In all, said Duncan Rykaart, 'it's a pretty formidable weapon and only a direct hit with an armour-piercing RPG grenade or a heavy mortar can cause serious damage.' It was his view that the BMP was the best light-skinned piece of armour for the job.

Also, for that of Angolan terrain, being primitive and in places impassable for normal vehicles, its tracks were an advantage over wheels whose tires were vulnerable to bullets and mortar shell fragments. Its secret, said Blaauw, was that it needs almost no regular maintenance. 'As long as it is regularly greased and its water and oil kept topped up, the BMP-2 will accomplish everything that is expected of it, including lengthy safaris across the face of Africa.'

Like many other Western force commanders who only got the feel of Soviet hardware in later years, Blaauw always talked well of this IFV, as did a group of South African mercenaries who used it to good advantage in Sierra Leone not long afterwards.

Trouble was, only days out of base on this campaign, the engines of at least three BMP-2s seized because their FAA operators didn't bother with routine maintenance, as they had been tasked to do before they pulled over the covers at night. They'd allowed their machines to run dry, with the result that they had to abandon them where they ground to a halt in the bush. After that, Blaauw put the word out: 'if your machine fails because you didn't maintain it, you stay behind with your crippled vehicle.' The prospect of being picked off or taken captive by the rebels had the requisite effect.

As might have been expected, the last 30 or so kilometres northwards towards Cafunfo ended in a series of land battles that were both intense and, by African standards, classic.

What had become clear to the attackers was that Savimbi was desperate. He threw at Combat Group Bravo all that remained of his reserves. As one of the EO officers recalled, 'those bush fighters would sometimes come at us in waves, and quite often with an almost total disregard for their fate…they were as brave as hell.'

He reckoned that some UNITA attacks were nothing short of suicidal because, as he declared, 'let's face it, guerrilla or not, men on the ground or in soft-skinned vehicles are no match for armour…it was the same for us heading towards the diamond fields.'

By the time the Cafunfo operation happened, both UNITA's senior commanders, General Bok (Chief of Staff, Logistics) and General Ben Ben (Head of Operations and Savimbi's deputy), were driving the war from a set of bunkers in Cafunfo. In the northern sector was General Luzamba, a fine tactician with much experience of battle. Like General Ben Ben, some of the South African veterans who had worked with him the in the past had a high regard for the ability of these men. As one of them suggested, 'these guys think out of the box…and you never know what they'll do next.'

Significantly, the apartheid-era South African Directorate of Special Tasks personnel had trained them all.

The last resistance offered by UNITA was at the village of Firiquichi, where a very substantial rebel force had gathered together for a 'Hail Mary' ambush. This was the same place that the former Recce commander had pointed out on the map to me when he detailed the campaign while we were still in Saurimo. As Blaauw recalled, they took some heavy fire and there were a handful of FAA troops wounded, but in the end, it was no different from what had taken place before.

As soon as the UNITA whistles sounded – another trick taught by the boys from Pretoria – the Angolan BMPs made straight for UNITA lines and overran all resistance. With that, the attackers scattered. Almost a hundred bodies were counted after the first Firiquichi attack, including one of Savimbi's most resourceful field commanders, Colonel Antonio Neves. An acknowledged expert in unconventional warfare, even by FAA's senior commanders, it was a huge loss for the rebel command.

Just after that line had been broached, the column had a remarkable run of luck. They were approaching Muvuca when Louwrens Bosch – overhead in his favourite PC-7 and flying one of his last sorties before he was killed – suddenly took Triple-A fire from an area of thick bush about 15 clicks to the north. This was unusual, Bosch reported afterwards because UNITA never wasted ammo.

The South African pilot immediately felt that there had to be something there, and being curious, he went down to have a look. Though there was nothing immediately obvious, except a partially camouflaged blue truck, he did spot a lot of tracks. Specifics were passed on to Blaauw.

The next day the South African commander decided to investigate. Having been given coordinates, he detached two BMPs and with Jos Grobelaar, a former Koevoet regular, led a sortie into the bush. For once there was no resistance. Shortly afterwards they came upon the same vehicle tracks that Bosch had noticed. Having reported back to de Santos, Blaauw pushed deeper into a remote, largely unpopulated and undeveloped region.

Then things began to happen. Sending his own BMP into a craggy outgrowth, Blaauw's people stumbled on to what must have been the biggest supply dump of the war. It was immense.

As Blaauw recalled, it easily covered an area as big as several football fields, with as much stored below ground as above it. The material that had been accumulated must have taken Savimbi years to gather together. Every single item had been either flown in or hauled overland through the Congo, itself an often impossible task considering the state of that country's roads. In terms of raw diamonds mined at Cafunfo, the cache must have cost UNITA tens of millions of dollars.

'There was everything there that an army might pray for,' Blaauw said. Carefully hidden from curious eyes were hundreds of fuel drums – at least six months' supply for the column.

Apart from more TM-57 mines that anyone had ever seen stacked together, there was hardware for scores of 106mm recoilless rifles, crate upon crate of ammunition for B-10s and B-12s, mortar bombs by the thousands together with millions of AK rounds. 'You could have started another war with all that stuff,' the South African reckoned.

Topping it all off was a hundred tons of food: canned meats, hams, fish, vegetables and the rest, all of it good quality, like you might have found in any European supermarket. It was gone in a stroke because a lone rebel soldier who was probably bored and had fired a single burst at an aircraft passing overhead.

The reality of this catastrophe really came home when it was reported later that with those supplies alone, Savimbi might have kept the war going for several more years. All was lost, in part, because the guerrilla leader never envisioned that the attacking force would move overland through some of the most difficult terrain imaginable. Nor that their route would take them within a rifle shot of his most valuable strategic reserve.

Though Savimbi remained steadfast, not so his commanders. Thereafter, some of them simply lost the will to continue, said one of his senior officers after it was all over.

It was during the final approach to Cafunfo that Hennie Blaauw had what was possibly the narrowest escape of his career as a fighting man. I quote:

> I'd called the column to a halt fairly early one afternoon a couple of days out of Cafunfo. Because there had been harassment from UNITA after dark, some of it pretty concerted and involving mortars and encirclements, we were in the habit of bringing our vehicles round into a defensive ring and positioning them all into what us Boers would call a laager. We'd arrange the BMPs so that their guns pointed outwards: if we had to retaliate, it would be pretty easy to do so.
>
> The forest around us was thick, typically jungle and almost impenetrable in places. The bush encroached right up to where we'd parked. It was also the season for mist, which would roll in across the valleys within an hour or two of sunset and then only lift again the next day about mid-morning. Although UNITA tended to mortar us whenever we stopped, we weren't overly bothered because we'd all dug slit trenches. Or for those who preferred, they could sleep inside or under their IFVs.
>
> It wasn't quite light when I got up the next morning and did the usual rounds. If a man was asleep at his post, it was better that I should find him than his bosses. Angolan officers and NCOs would have no compunction about shooting a sleeping man where he lay. We only docked their pay.

The colonel asked his signaller-driver Paul Ditrich[1] for a roll of toilet paper. He then did what he'd spent a lifetime in Special Forces telling others not to: he set off into the bush for a dump *alone*.

> I ambled off towards a clump of bushes. By then Ditrich was headed back towards the perimeter of our defences. Moments later, facing outwards from the column and having just undone my belt, I was watching something on my flank and not paying too much attention to what

---

1 Ditrich was to die in a bizarre accident near Saurimo two months later. While at the wheel of a BMP-2 and crossing the Lauchimo River to the immediate east of the city, the machine veered off a bridge and ended upside-down in the water. Though his colleagues did what they could, Paul was dead before the BMP-2 could be righted. His passing is commemorated with the dozen or so others who were killed in company service on the granite plinth that stood in the grounds of the house in Raslouw Street in a Pretoria suburb.

was immediately in front of me when suddenly, a rebel popped out of the bush, right there, only metres away.

He was as surprised to see me as I was him: we had eye contact for about a second.' Armed only with a toilet roll, Blaauw threw himself sideways and sprinted for the nearest BMP.

I had perhaps 20 metres to cover when the ground erupted all around me: the bastard targeted me on full auto. A second later the entire column came under attack as a huge rebel force that had crept up close during the dark hours opened up. I got back OK, but I reckon I must have been as lucky as hell to have done so.

Blaauw was to establish later in the day that it was an attack in battalion strength: about 250 of the enemy were involved. His own people were able to retaliate immediately, something they'd learned to do many times over. Looking back, he reckons it was probably their quick reaction time that saved them.

'Meanwhile, Ditrich, who hadn't seen me cut and run, assumed that I'd been killed. When he heard the first volley, he turned towards where he'd left me and all he could see was a UNITA soldier, AK in hand and letting rip. He promptly also threw himself down on the ground shouting 'the colonel's been shot! The colonel's dead'!'

Indeed, Blaauw didn't come out of it unscathed: he took a flesh wound in his arm, probably from an AK. He's convinced too, that the attack had been pre-empted.

'I'm as sure as hell that the entire group was not yet in its final position. In fact we heard as much afterwards from one of the rebels we took captive. There were apparently some UNITA troops that were held up for some reason in a shallow defile to the north of our position; had they been there as well, things might have been a lot different because they were almost on top of us when the shooting began…some of the enemy were lying three or four metres from us.

'Yep! I was lucky,' was his comment, adding that 'it's the first time that the outcome of a battle was decided by someone needing a shit.'

Only after UNITA had withdrawn was he able to evaluate his good fortune. The BMP behind which he had taken cover seemed to have taken the brunt of the onslaught. It was hit by thousands of rounds. 'In fact, examining it afterwards, I could see that the firing was so intense it wasn't possible to put two fingers together over any patch of armour without touching a dent where the paint had been sheared,' he explained.

'Also, all the trees around our positions were cut down by the salvoes that followed. Most were completely stripped of their leaves. But then it ended as suddenly as it began because a few minutes later, when more of our IFVs got into the act, the attackers dropped everything and ran.'

Blaauw was pulled out later by one of the helicopters, had his arm dressed at Saurimo and was back with his unit before nightfall.

Another equally unlikely survival story to come out of the war involved 'Juba' Joubert, who was later to fly combat in Sierra Leone with Neall Ellis, the mercenary aviator who, with his trusted and barely airworthy Mi-24 helicopter gunship helped turn the rebels away from the gates of Freetown.[2]

Juba Joubert, with John Viera as his co-pilot, had their Mi-17 take a hit from a ground-to-air missile – probably a Strela MANPAD – a few days after the column had occupied Cafunfo.

Though the air crews were assured that the area around the diamond town was clear of threat, including missiles, these veterans of several wars tended to remain a little circumspect and it was

---

2 Al J. Venter; *Gunship Ace: The Wars of Neall Ellis, Helicopter Pilot and Mercenary:* Casemate Publishers, US and Britain, 2011

Black troops fighting for EO included many veterans of the Border War, trusted colleagues who had experienced many operations with their white counterparts. More than half of EO's operators in Angola and Sierra Leone were African. (Author's photo)

Duncan Rykaart with his back to the camera consults with the senior Angolan Army commander at Saurimo about defences around a narrow bridge to the north of the town. (Author's photo)

Former South African Air Force helicopter gunship pilot Juba Joubert slotted in well at the controls of one of EO's Mi-17s at Cafunfo. He was to take a SAM-7 hit while flying out of the diggings (UNITA was encamped on the outskirts) but was able to crash-land without injury. (Photo: Juba Joubert)

Chopper pilot's view of the Cafunfo alluvial diamond diggings.

The threat of hand-held ground-to-air missiles (MANPADS) was constant. Many Angolan Air Force and quite a few civilian aircraft were downed by these weapons, including this one, probably hit by an American-supplied Stinger in the south-east of the country. (Photo: UNITA)

Arthur Walker, one of the most experienced helicopter gunship pilots on the African continent, had several tours of duty with EO. He later fought against Boko Haram in Nigeria, where he was wounded after his chopper was hit by an RPG-7.

The author covered Executive Outcomes operations several times, both in Angola and Sierra Leone. He was initially 'blooded' in the early days of the Border War, seen here in a white T-shirt, his hand on the shoulder of veteran Associated Press Vietnam correspondent Bob Poos.

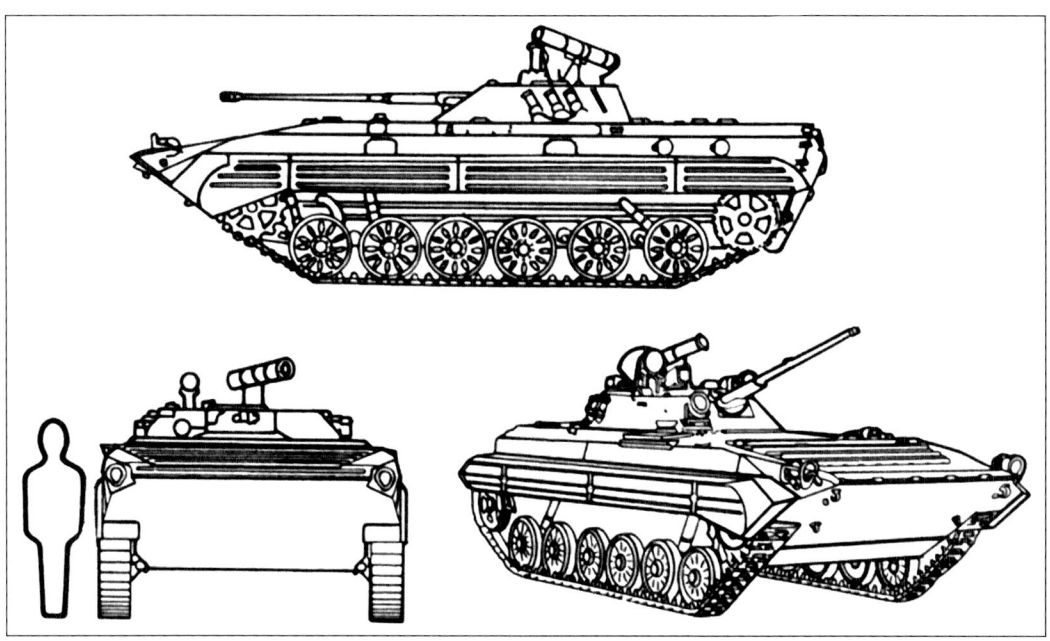

Diagrammatical drawings of the Soviet BMP-2 which became the mainstay of many of the attacks launched in both Sierra Leone and Angola by Executive Outcomes.

just as well they did. When they were required to head for the sharp end, they flew high and came down fast – invariably in a spiral and as steep as their rotors would allow. It was the same on the way out again: straight up and then a swing away when the required altitude had been achieved.

Cafunfo presented the same problems as anywhere else in this ongoing war. The pilots noticed that as soon as they got anywhere near Cafunfo, UNITA guns and mortars from across the river would open up. Rebel gunners would shell the landing strip and they would keep hammering away as long as there was a helicopter on the ground.

On that day, 'Juba's old Border War colleague, the late Arthur Walker – sensing that this activity was become more intense – decided that they should put down at an old disused airstrip on the south-western side of town.

Flying in support of Walker and Alberts, Joubert's Hip had just delivered its two-and-a-half ton load and taken onboard about a dozen casualties when he prepared for departure to Saurimo. With that, the two Hips took off again and, as Walker always said, 'there's no hanging about when you've got people throwing things at you.'

The two machines were about 600 feet in the air when several people on the ground saw the brilliant white flash of a missile being launched from the opposite bank.

'SAM!' somebody shouted, pointing at the missile's contrail heading straight for the circling choppers.

Walker saw it first but it happened so fast that there was no time for any kind of evasive action. At Mach-2, the missile shot right past his nose and headed for Joubert, hitting his chopper's exhaust just above the starboard engine. The South African pilot recalls an enormous blast above his head.

Talking about the incident afterwards, both pilots extolled the ruggedness of this Soviet-type helicopter for not being immediately knocked out of the sky. Walker was always of the opinion that no Western helicopter would take that kind of punishment and come out of it still airworthy.

Having got down onto the deck again, shaken but safe, the crews were able to examine the damage. Altogether five pockets on one of the rotor blades had been blown away and the blast missed the main spar by a centimetre. Had any one of the Mi-17's five blades been sheared, it would have resulted in the gearbox being torn out and they would have crashed. Exactly that had already happened to 15 other Angolan Air Force Mi-17s in the war by the time that incident took place. Worse, there wasn't a survivor among any of them.

Nor did Hip crews get out alive when three more SAMs destroyed Angolan Air Force choppers in the following six months.

It's interesting that during the period the South Africans manned Mi-17s in Northern Angola, each of the three helicopter teams was picked up at least once by other crews after having been brought down by ground fire: which was why they always insisted on two-ship sorties. The same policy held afterwards for Sierra Leone.

The SA-7a was codenamed Grail by NATO, and probably reverse-engineered from the US Army 'Redeye', with a high explosive warhead and passive infrared homing guidance.

Earlier versions of this man-portable, shoulder-fired, low-altitude, surface-to-air missile system (MANPAD) was no lightweight. Once fired, it quickly picked up speed and zeroed in at almost one-and-a-half times the speed of sound (Mach 1.4) with a slant range of 3.6 km and a 'kill-zone' almost from ground zero to 1,500 metres in altitude.

Later versions were known as the SA-7b and were both deadlier (larger warhead) and more accurate with proximity fuses. It is almost certain that it was 7a's that were used in most of the southern and central African conflicts. Introduced for service in 1968 and classed as 'fire and forget' types, the missiles were easily overcome by solar heat and, when employed in hilly terrain, by temperature upsurges from the ground.

SAM-7 Missile Experiences

Famed freelance chopper gunship pilot Neall Ellis recalls the first time he experienced a SAM-7 launch. That was in 1980 while on a SAAF cross-border operation in the Cuamato area, Southern Angola.

As he remembers the event, he had been deployed to a 32 Company temporary base to be on standby for a patrol that expected to make contact with SWAPO elements who had entered the country from Angola and who were active in the area. On such operations, he recounted, they normally deployed in a formation of a pair of Alouette III gunships, armed with a side-firing 20mm cannon.

The helicopters were equipped with metal covers which shrouded the engine: exhaust fumes were directed into its rotor wash in order to reduce any heat signatures. The entire helicopter, except for the undercarriage and Perspex canopy, was painted with a special paint which reduced temperatures in the heat frequency spectrum emitted by the aircraft. It was this that attracted the 'seeker head' of the missile.

Neall Ellis takes up the story:

> The modification was developed by the South African CSIR (Council for Scientific and Industrial Research) and according to the 'boffins', we would be safe from any first-generation heat-seeking missile.
>
> The only heat source that could attract the missile was the exposed silver metal of the extended oleos on the undercarriage, or possibly, sun reflections off the Perspex canopy. But, according to the engineers, the helicopter is an unstable platform, so the infrared source would be intermittent and therefore incoming missiles would not have a constant heat source for a proper 'lock-on'.
>
> As this theory had not yet been battle proven, it was with great trepidation that we flew out across the border into Angolan skies.
>
> To date, there had been no reported use of MANPADS against low flying helicopters in South African or South West African air space, though a Portuguese Air Force Dakota – with a full complement of foreign diplomats on board – had taken a hit from a Strela in northern Mozambique towards the end of that war.
>
> In southern Angola that day, around midday, we were scrambled following a call-out from one of the ground patrols who reported having stumbled onto a SWAPO position and were taking fire. The position was not too far from our headquarters position, and after ten minutes of flying we were overhead. Immediately we came under attack.
>
> Initially it was not easy to determine from where the enemy were shooting from, but after taking a couple of hits from a 14.5mm Triple-A gun, I saw the firing site position and banked sharply to engage.
>
> The first couple of rounds from our 20mm cannon helped subdue things a bit, which enabled me to observe the layout of the enemy camp and its size. It was a fairly regular unit, not the small enemy camp reported by the patrol.
>
> I decided to widen our orbit and increase my height to around 1,500 feet AGL in order to first silence the anti-aircraft positions before engaging enemy troops on the ground. While initiating my second pass towards the camp, I noticed from my 9 o'clock position through the

open side door, a cloud of dust suddenly emerging from a thicket around a click-and-a-half away.

A second or two later, a very fast moving bright yellowish light with a corkscrewing trail of thick grey smoke was headed our way. Lange, my flight engineer, shouted a warning.

I immediately realized from intelligence briefings at base that the object coming towards us and moving at great speed was most likely a SAM-7 and frankly, there was not much I could do to avoid the missile by banking, climbing or even attempting to dive. The missile was locked on and flying a helicopter at 80 knots an hour, there was no flight energy or time to attempt any kind of evasive manoeuvre.

I steadied my fears and decided to do nothing because the missile was almost onto us. Instead, I'd fly as smoothly and not reduce speed because we were still under fire from the ground. I knew that if I flew any slower, I'd give enemy gunners an easier tracking solution.

I recall thinking that I hoped that the CSIR people were correct in their theory that we would be safe from SAM-7 missiles and that the statement was not another piece of bullshit to make us feel happy about flying into battle. But those thoughts didn't last long: the missile was now only metres away.

A moment later the missile disappeared behind me and there was a loud bang: I thought we'd been hit in the tail boom area because the chopper shuddered. From where we were flying, the ground was a very long way down in what would obviously be a helicopter out of control. But to my surprise, nothing happened. Instead, we carried on flying and after a quick glance at the instruments, I realised that a sonic boom had been generated by the missile as it passed.

The result was that the SWAPO cadres had not only revealed that they now had SAM-7 missiles – which, until then, was just another rumour – but with the firing of the Strela and the dust cloud it generated, the launch site was easily determined. From where we hovered, there was a great grey smoke trail leading all the way down to its original position. We positioned overhead and killed the missile crews with our 20mm cannon.

We had survived the first known missile launch against a helicopter in the southern Angolan Border War and also proved that South African technology was up there with the best. From then on, I determined that I could taunt our foes into revealing their position by flying high enough to entice a SAM-7 launch and follow up by knocking them out.

That tactic I used several times afterwards and because of protection measures installed on the helicopter, the SAM-7 never became a threat to our operations as it had with the Portuguese Air Force in Guinea.

In a subsequent contact I had three missile launches against our chopper, with none coming close enough to cause damage. That said, sonic booms always tested us, because the blasts were so bloody unnerving.

I reckon that during the period I operationally flew Alouette gunships in the SAAF, approximately ten SAM-7 missiles were launched against my helicopter: each time CSIR protection measures prevailed.

However, into the 21st Century, newer generation missiles are much more efficient and the protective measures we used would not suffice, if only because SAMs are now fitted with proximity fuses.

This was not Ellis's first brush with SAMs. Indeed, there cannot be many people alive who saw so much combat in these tiny French combat-support helicopters.

Nellis to his friends, the pilot once rated as the world's best known mercenary aviator has been involved in conflict since leaving university in his early twenties. In the book I wrote about the man, I quoted the words of General David Richards, former Chief of the Defence Staff in Britain who commanded the British contingent that finally brought the war in Sierra Leone to an end. He declared in a personal note that 'Neall Ellis is a very brave man.'2

It's no surprise that Ellis, like his old pal Arthur Walker, is extraordinarily good at what he does and possibly, why he has survived for so long.

One attack with SAMs took place in a remote, isolated corner of south Angola, not far from the Namibian border. The area is a barren, eroded and generally vacated region that the Portuguese originally called *Terras do Fim do Mundo:* Land at the End of the Earth. Ellis was at the controls of one of a pair of Alouette gunships that were providing close air support to a combat detail on the ground, all members of a 32 Battalion combat unit.

The moment Nellis and Tony Maranta, his wingman, got over the battlefield, the guerrillas retaliated.

'The entire insurgent force was shooting at us simultaneously. Our choppers were the only things in their sights!' he related some years later. Ellis goes on:

> The first rounds from our choppers stopped the run and the insurgents dived for cover, such as it was. Then all hell broke loose. I heard a loud blast towards our rear as an RPG-7 exploded near the tail. Maranta shouted over the radio, 'SAM launch: six o'clock'.
>
> Again, I could see the distinctive thick, white-gray smoke trail of a Strela twirling up towards us. Immediately I put on more bank to find the firing position. As I turned through 180 degrees a second missile was launched in our direction, this time directed at Tony. I called sharply: 'SAM launch: nine o'clock.'
>
> We were now so low that by the time I'd used my radio, the missile was already travelling at almost bore, which was half again the speed of sound. As Ellis recalled a long time afterwards, it passed harmlessly just in front of his nose.
>
> But by now we were coming under heavy automatic fire, which included machine-guns, RPGs and a lot more – all of it accompanied by curtains of green tracers. The noise was deafening, even with our headsets on…
>
> Another Strela shot past our nose. Once the firing position had been established, Coetzee (the gunner) killed the missile team. With the Puma transport helicopters arriving – they were quite close to an LZ that I had identified earlier – I shifted my position to mark the spot with a smoke grenade and went into top cover mode.

Altogether almost 200 SWAPO guerrillas died that morning. It was the guerrilla group's largest single loss to a small field force in any battle during more than two decades of border conflict, more details of which are to be found in Chapter 18.

Many of the Angolan enemy who were subsequently captured by the South Africans were eventually 'turned' to fight their old comrades. Quite a few ended up as mercenaries elsewhere in Africa a decade later, some in Angola and Sierra Leone with EO.

4

Portugal's African Origins

Five centuries firmly ensconced as a European power on the African continent made Lisbon's presence in her overseas colonies – Angola, Mozambique and Portuguese Guinea – the most enduring. In the early 1500s, Prince Henry the Navigator (also referred to as the Infante Dom Henrique de Avis and the Duke of Viseu) was only 21 when he and his brothers – led by their father King Joao – captured the Moorish port of Ceuta in present-day Morocco. With nearby Melilla, these are the only remnants of a vast European colonial empire that remain on the African continent, the only difference that both enclaves are Spanish.

One of the questions most often asked these days when we read about Portugal's wars in Africa, was what in the name of heaven were those Europeans doing on such an unstable continent anyway?

More salient, Lisbon held out in Africa with its *metrópole províncias ultramarinas* for something like 500 years, which eclipsed France, Britain, Italy, Germany and Belgium, together with one or two other colonising powers. Britain's colonial role in India lasted 350 years while Nigeria, on the west coast of Africa, boasted a colonial tradition that lasted only 60 years, from 1900 to 1960.

To be fair to London, as Daniel Hannan tells us in a *Spectator* book review, plenty of conquered territories – the diamond and gold fields of South Africa apart – were immediately handed *back* to their original owners, and requests from the inhabitants of Ethiopia, Mexico, Uruguay, Sarawak, Katanga and Morocco to join the empire were firmly turned down.[1]

Several factors motivated the early navigators to explore beyond Europe's frontiers. The first was the knowledge that, somewhere beyond the horizon, there were other civilizations and cultures that were not only enormously enticing, but had much to offer. Make contact with those far flung societies and there are fortunes to be made, was the dictum.

Until this new bunch of intrepid seafarers arrived, all trade with the East had been by land. A range of Eastern goods had been reaching Europe from the East for centuries, including silks, spices, medications, gemstones and a huge variety of trade goods that wealthy Europeans sought. The one impediment was that all movement was overland, much of it directed across that huge stretch of semi-desert that historians refer to as Asia Minor and its legendary Silk Road. It would certainly have included present-day Iran, Syria and Iraq.

Still more of it filtered through Egypt, or across Turkey's porous borders, or what was later to be called the Ottoman Empire.

It worked like this: limited quantities of goods would, for instance, leave India and, for the most part be transported on mules or packhorses. Once arid regions were reached, cargoes would be

---

1 Daniel Hannan, review of *The English and their History* by Robert Tombs, *The Spectator*, London 13,20/27 December 2014, page 87.

shifted onto the backs of camels. Back on hard ground again, it would all be shifted onto horses or perhaps primitive wagons with solid wooden wheels. Usually covered in sackcloth – which, to some extent, took care of wear and tear (but not rain) – this stuff was transported to the nearest Mediterranean port and from there moved westwards by ship.

Overall, it was a journey of several thousand kilometres, depending on destination. With the additional sea-leg, it could sometimes take a year.

Clearly, there was a huge amount of effort and labour involved, never mind risk. Small wonder then that everything that eventually reached Europe was inordinately expensive and the only people who could afford such things were the ruling classes. Pepper and cloves, for instance, were so scarce that ounce for ounce, these condiments were worth their weight in gold.

While many of us are aware of the role played by Bartolomeu Diaz in discovering that elusive sea route to India – even though he only made it to Southern Africa on his first exploratory voyage, it is not generally known that he actually accompanied his younger compatriot Vasco da Gama on that expeditionary voyage to the Indian subcontinent. Indeed, of all the early Portuguese exploratory journeys, Da Gama's mission to India was to be the most rewarding, not only for Lisbon, but ultimately, for all the nations of Europe.

In that early period, it was Lisbon that was the first to take the initiative. Prince Henry's navigators forged alliances and trading pacts with the Indians, the Ceylonese, Javanese and others. In time, others followed. It wasn't long before these links were extended all the way across to the fringes of the Pacific Ocean, which was when China and Japan came firmly into the picture.

But to do that, the Portuguese – intrepid and forward-looking in the earlier period – needed stopping points along the way. Their ships had to be assured of safe anchorage where they could be resupplied (and sometimes repaired), crews rested and the sick left in comparative safety to await craft heading home.

One of these first so-called 'Halfway Houses' was the port of Luanda on the west coast of Africa. In those days it was known as *São Paulo da Assumpção de Loanda,* and the general consensus in Lisbon at the time was that since Africa had been the source of much gold in the past, there had to be precious metals somewhere in the interior of this vast tropical region. When that didn't work out, the new arrivals turned to slaves.

Meantime, the first group of colonists attracted to Africa by promises of riches – all 400 of them – arrived in Luanda in 1587 backed by a fairly large military detachment. They were soon followed by more hopefuls who settled at Benguela, further down the coast.

Once settled and protected in these two far-flung outposts fringing the Atlantic, the Portuguese, always adventurous, expanded from there, eventually consolidating the vast, uncharted and unexplored hinterland into a single colony.

At the same time, it was an extremely diverse society which subsequent research has revealed was – and still is – composed of almost a dozen ethnic groups, headed initially by the preponderant pre-colonial Kongo Kingdom. Today that same homeland – Kikongo, as we know it and about 10 million strong – stretches from the jungle regions immediately north of Luanda and reaches deep into present-day Congo.

An interesting feature of these adventures was the ships that took Europe's navigators to these distant lands. They were an assorted lot and ranged from as little as 80 or 100 tons (and possibly 20 or 25 metres long) to the leviathans of their age, cumbersome wooden East Indiamen well in excess of 1,000 tons that the Dutch introduced later. That kind of tonnage would have placed them in almost the same bracket of some of the naval corvettes deployed by Britain during the Second World War.

The Portuguese employed for their voyages of discovery the caravel, a vessel that would certainly never have been granted a seaworthy certificate today. Originally derived from small offshore fishing boats – diminutive examples of which are still sometimes to be seen off the coast of the Azores island group and along the Portuguese coast – all had straight stern rudder posts and were three-masted, lateen-rigged square riggers of about 20 metres, depending on where and by whom they were built.

Their manpower was modest, if only because they were easily handled by a 24-man crew. By the time that Diaz set out for Africa, early Portuguese navigators had already used them for generations to traipse the length and breadth of the Mediterranean.

Ideally suited for making downwind runs, such was their versatility that Lisbon's shipping community would boast that while just about anybody could make the long haul to the Guinea Coast, only their *caravela redondas* were able to get back home again. The difficult part was that these early merchantmen sometimes needed tacking against prevailing West African westerlies, always something of a risky grind in uncertain weather, of which there is a lot the closer you get to Europe.

Once the Dutch, and then the British entered the trading scenario to the East, both the shape and the size of ships involved in this trade changed.

There were numerous stratagems involved in maintaining the kind of secrecy that surrounded these trading routes, a subject that could be worth a book on its own because Lisbon disclosed absolutely nothing that might help her competitors achieve the same. As we have since learnt, European nations were extremely reticent when it came to revealing anything that might be of help to their competitors: indeed, it took the Dutch decades to uncover some of Lisbon's secrets and the English even longer.

This was an era of great intrigue, with each of the European maritime nations eager to expand their interests, much as Spain had done in the New World and the Portuguese in the East. While others carefully observed the activities of these two seafaring countries, small wonder they were desperate to make a few navigational breakthroughs of their own.

For a century the sailors that Prince Henry sent out into the 'unknown' were pretty much in control of their own destinies and, by all accounts, were both bold and astonishingly successful. News of their overloaded carracks returning to Lisbon filled with precious – and useful – trade goods spurred others. Meantime, King Joao II, Henry's successor, forbade any foreigner access to his country's precious charts and any person suspected of passing on these vital keys to trade and treasure was summarily dealt with.

Then, in 1502 came a breakthrough. An Italian secret agent, Alberto Cantino, paid 12 gold ducats – an immense amount of money at the time – to be allowed access to a copy of the *Padron*, the ultimate explorer's guide. This was the reasonably accurate world map on which all Portuguese activities were recorded, a copy of which was supplied to the master of every ship that set out from Lisbon.

It was essentially a picture of all the areas of the world that had so far been discovered and extended from the Americas in the west all the way across three oceans to China. The African coastline was astonishingly well detailed, though the interior was filled with illustrations of wild animals, fuzzy-wuzzies and dragons. The source of the Nile was shown somewhere around present-day Zimbabwe.

These charts were so valuable that every ship's captain had a weighted box in his cabin with express instructions that should the ship be about to be overrun by the enemy, that box had to be the first to be dumped overboard.

Then the Dutch got a windfall of their own with the return home of Jan Huygen van Linschoten after he had spent 13 years in service with the Portuguese, including five years in Goa.

In three volumes, he recorded his experiences in Lisbon's possessions in India, one of which was titled *Reysgheschrift* (roughly translated as 'Traveller's Journal'). That was rushed through for publication in time for use by the Dutch navigator Cornelius de Houtman who led Holland's first four-ship expedition to the East Indies in March 1595. That expedition became an unmitigated disaster, in large part because Holland's emissaries treated the local people they encountered in the east so badly.

To the Dutch, Huygen's reports were worth a good deal more than money. He gave his fellow countrymen details of everything he had learnt while employed by his old masters in Lisbon: specific details of routes as well as advantages and dangers in all the regions where he had worked. His descriptions of dozens of harbours – in Africa especially – inlets, islands, reefs, navigational hazards, together with a thorough assessment of all the countries he visited – Portuguese as well as Spanish – made his three volumes the equivalent of the Dutch seaman's manual of the day.

Just in time too, because the Dutch arrived at their first East Indies base at Bantam (Banten today, on the western shores of the island of Java) in 1596. That was only six years before the first flotilla of English East Indiamen got there and were forcibly urged to move on by Dutch East India Company officials, otherwise known as the *Vereenigde Oost-Indische Compagnie* or VOC.

This was a pattern to be repeated many times over during the course of the next century, not only with the British but with other European nations trading in the East as well.

In those parts of Africa where something of a footfall had been achieved – notably Angola and Mozambique – things were really tough in the early days, and they continued to be hard for the majority of Europeans who sought unspecified promise on what soon became known as the 'Dark Continent'.

Even in the 1960s, when I spent time working in Nigeria, we had constant problems with tropical diseases, the most common being malaria. I ended up with hepatitis because my steward, while dutifully boiling all my drinking water, used the tap when he made ice, a common mistake in the tropics.

There were also outbreaks of cholera and you had to be careful what you imbibed because typhoid and typhus – and sometimes encephalitis – were regular visitors. You still hear of people, children especially, dying of yellow fever and in more recent times, these regions have been wracked by Ebola and further towards the west, Lassa Fever, both acute viral haemorrhagic illnesses, neither of which needs elaboration because newspapers have been full of those reports.

Yet, over the centuries, a lot changed. You just have to look at antiquarian maps of the West Coast of Africa produced more than a century ago: many showed precious little detail of Africa's interior. It was only the first major war with Germany that forced the pace of progress in Africa, both for Britain and France and, to a lesser degree, Belgium, Spain and Portugal.

In his book, *Sierra Leone*, published in London in 1954, Roy Lewis – then on the staff of Britain's *Economist* – took serious issue with the colonial government for so effectively 'shielding the tribes from hasty interference in their settled customs.'

It was not until 1927, he declared, that the world discovered that London 'still firmly upheld the principle of domestic slavery' in the hinterland. As recently as the mid-1950s, the folk around Kailahun in the east of the country (and for a long while, a rebel stronghold during the recent civil war) were still using for currency the famous Kissi pennies. These were iron bars about 18 inches long and used for trade.

A lot of the history of these African countries can be found by just wandering about some of the colonial graveyards. I did so in Freetown while I covered the war against the rebels, though I had to be careful of snakes; they were everywhere, especially on the edge of town.

One of the early sailing ships that took Prince Henry's navigators around the Cape of Good Hope to India.

Queen Nzinga was regent of the largest tribe in the Lower Congo region in the mid-1500s. Lisbon's emissaries paid tribute to her.

As the Portuguese progressed towards the East, they left behind many stone crosses or what was known as a *Padrão*, similar to this contemporary version which was raised at Cape Cross in Namibia by Diego Cao in 1485. (Author's photo)

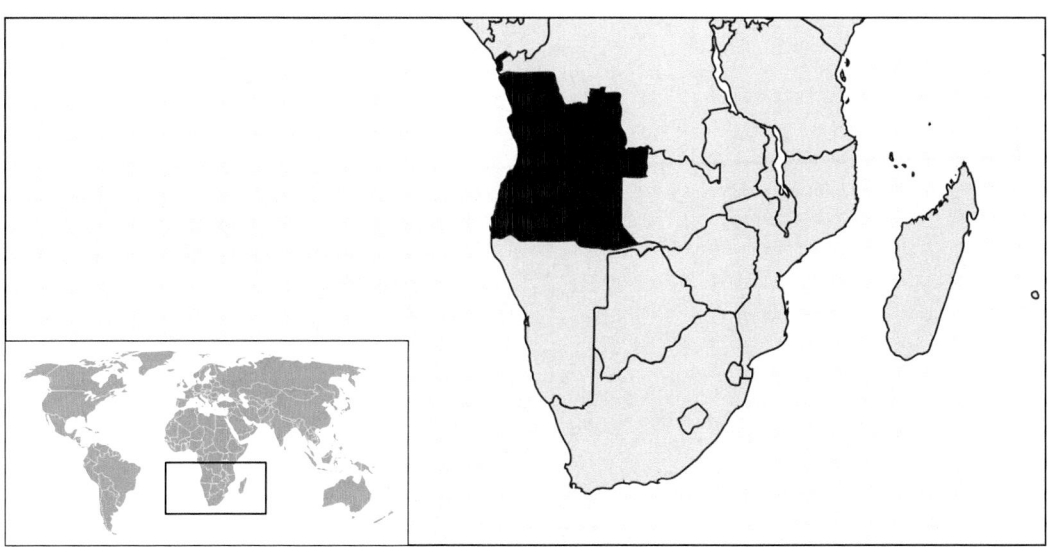

Sketch map showing the African coastline rounded by Diego Cao, Bartolomeu Diaz and those who followed on their trips to India.

Early Portuguese coinage used in the African territories. The coin was known as the *Macuta*.

Monument to Portugal's early navigators overlooking the Tagus River in Lisbon. (Author's photo)

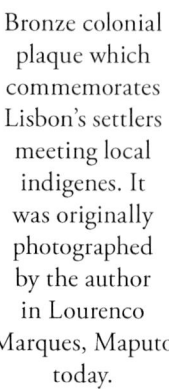

Bronze colonial plaque which commemorates Lisbon's settlers meeting local indigenes. It was originally photographed by the author in Lourenco Marques, Maputo today.

Following the invasion of south Angola by the Kaiser's army, Portuguese troops were rapidly despatched from Lisbon to counter that threat.

One of the earliest photographs taken by an explorer who ventured into the remote interior, of a group of natives linked to the present-day Ovimbundu tribe of south-east Angola.

Portuguese administrators dealt brutally with African communities that rebelled against the colonial presence. Lisbon all but wiped out Angola's Hereros and caused most Ovambos who resisted to flee southwards into what was then still German South West Africa, Namibia today. This is a starving group of Ovambos.

Following the invasion of north Angola by an army of revolutionaries who killed anyone who opposed them – as well as many innocents who did not – the authorities retaliated with vigour: the heads of some of the rebels are shoved on stakes in the forest.

In one of the old burial plots adjacent to Tower Hill, I found the grave of a woman, Elizabeth Murial Duncan, a mother from a small town in Essex who, at the age of 22, was 'taken' unexpectedly. The 1822 inscription on her grave noted that she had become ill in the morning 'and died of high fever' before the sun went down.

It must have been bad, because almost all of West Africa – and the Portuguese colonies included – soon acquired sinister reputations. Roy Lewis tells us that the colony exacted a dreadful toll. He wrote that between 1814 and 1885, 'five British governors and seven acting governors died at their posts or on the ship home.'

Harrison Rankin, in his book, appropriately titled *White Man's Grave* – which was published in 1847 – records a discussion that went something like this: 'One kind friend, more facetious than the rest observed that, inasmuch as I was bound for such a deadly place, it would be judicious to include a coffin in my equipment since it might come in handy at an early date.'

Another visitor to West Africa said at the time, that in the first years after its settlement, it was quite customary of a morning to ask: 'How many died last night then?'

Africa's early European settlers soon became remarkably adept at separating the pathetically trusting locals from just about all they possessed, or, more appropriately, from what they believed belonged to them.

Take one example: the Portuguese in Angola shipped in cargoes of cone shells from their possessions in the Indian Ocean and told the natives that these large and peculiarly-shaped molluscs – a genus of predatory sea snails – had magic qualities. They traded them with the locals – one cone shell for a single head of cattle – and it was not all that surprising that they could get away with it because the Portuguese told these simple tribal folk – who knew absolutely nothing of European trading scams – that they were a God-fearing trustworthy people.

Even today, you will find some of the more primitive clans in the south of the country – and even the Himba people of Northern Namibia – still wearing cone shells around their necks. Examine these obscure forms of adornment more closely – as I did when I visited Namibia in 2015 – and it soon becomes clear that somebody, somewhere, has been wearing these adornments for a century or more.

It's exactly the same with cowrie shells which are not at all native to Africa's Atlantic coast. Shiploads of cowries were dumped all along the West African coast, in Nigeria and the Gold Coast especially and there is no question that the Europeans made a killing. They were so successful that many of the antiquarian artefacts found along the coast – especially those of Nigerian origin – and to be seen in European or American museums these days, are decorated with cowries.

The history of all these black states reflects a level of exploitation that, were it to take place today, would in all probability involve Interpol. It is also true that most West African cities, Luanda included, are the sites of some of the first efforts by the West to redeem four or five centuries of plunder, slavery and piracy. As always, the original intent – backed by the ubiquitous church – was honourable, but then, we all know about the road to Hell…

Many of the actions that followed the arrival of the first European settlers became mendacious, especially that of acquiring real estate. Moreover, we need to be reminded that this was something that more often than not took place on both sides of the Atlantic and way south, in the Antipodes.

Take one example: the first strip of land granted to the British Government by King Tombo, the Temne chief of the coastal mountain peninsula of Sierra Leone further up the west coast of Africa. He gave the British a large site overlooking the sea in exchange for a load of trumpery that included some rum, a few muskets and an embroidered waistcoat. If it sounds like *déjà vu*, you've got it!

And so it went, with everybody making money except those to whom the country belonged. It was also a period that has since been labelled the 'Scramble for Africa', much of which is encapsulated in a marvellous book by that name and which lays bare some of these nefariously activities.[2]

From the earliest period of settlement of the Portuguese, there were sporadic rebellions on the part of some of the northern African tribes who had their headquarters in or adjacent to what is the present-day Congo. This came about in large part because of the high-handed manner in which Lisbon's administrators conducted their affairs: they often took that which was not theirs without asking, land especially, something I deal with in a later chapter.

From late 1500 onwards, Nzinga Mbandi the paramount queen of Ndongo – today modern-day Angola – fought a series of bitter wars against the Portuguese. Unfortunately it was spears against muskets, coupled to an unsavoury chapter of a century-long campaign of resistance waged against the slave trade.

Of all the people with whom I have communicated over many years with regard to Portugal's wars in Africa, the French academic and historian René Pélissier has always been at the forefront when it came to facts, statistics and the little asides that sometimes are quite remarkable stories in themselves.[3] We corresponded many times over the years, and it was René that added the final touch to my Bibliography in *Portugal's Guerrilla Wars in Africa*, published in Britain in 2013.[4]

One of the most interesting details that subsequently emerged and that he shares with us was that Lisbon conducted something like 180 military campaigns in her African possessions between the years 1848 and 1926. That kind of statistic makes South African interracial issues that involved violence in one form or another within that same timeframe quite trivial by comparison.

It was René too, who first told me about 'The Grey Wars', or, in its original French, *Les guerres grises: Les campaigns colonials du Portugal*, published in France in 1978. Part of this document is included in Appendix D.

In a subsection titled 'The Great Cemetery', he refers to the tragic consequences of the southern Angolan military campaigns after 1906.

There were a lot of them, his sources being Catholic and Protestant missionaries who had been active in the region, interpreters, medical aides, intermediaries linked to these struggles as well as people who lived near the various battlefields. Lisbon was clearly unhappy with his research, even though it was hardly hostile, which was why, for many years, René was denied access to most Portuguese library, archival and research establishments both in Europe and in Africa. He was even refused visas to visit some of the *ultramar* historical depositories.

In a review of Pélissier's book, Douglas Wheeler provides a brief study of a little known resistance episode of 1940–1941 which gives a rare glimpse of a terrifying 'pacification' campaign in south Angola, a tribal Armageddon for the Herero of the south Angola borderlands.[5] I quote:

> In the dark recesses of the Lisbon Society of Geography, Pélissier came upon the kind of revealing document historians sometimes only have dreams about: the operations report by the Portuguese General Abel de Abreu Sotto-Maior of 1940 – 1941. This tragic case is surely

---

2   Thomas Packenham: *The Scramble for Africa: White Man's Conquest of the Dark Continent from 1876 to 1912;* Avon Books, 1992.
3   René Pélissier; *Les Campagnes Coloniales Du Portugal; 1844–1941.* Editions Flammarion, departement Pygmalion, 2004.
4   Al J. Venter; *Portugal's Guerrilla Wars in Africa: Lisbon's Wars in Angola, Mozambique and Portuguese Guinea 1961–74;* Helion Books, UK 2013.
5   Professor Douglas Wheeler adds his own interpretation in an insightful article titled 'Independent Scholar Conquers a Military History Battlefield – But who Will Follow?' in *Portuguese Studies Review* published by Trent University, Peterborough, Ontario, Canada, in the 2004/2005 Summer/Fall edition. It is subtitled 'A Review Essay in Honour of Dr René Pélissier'.

the Angolan Hereros' 'Wounded Knee' in history, the virtual extirpation of a people (some 4,000-5,000 in number) virtually unknown and isolated.

Even the facts revealed by Pélissier jar the imagination: a five-month campaign, the capture of nearly 4,000 Herero as 'prisoners of war', the confiscation of 20,000 cattle, the dispersal of these people by execution and the transporting of the survivors as forced labourers (or salaried labourers with very low wages) to various parts of Angola or the *roças* (plantations) of São Tome island.

From the evidence Pélissier presents about Portuguese methods in this disgraceful campaign (including the use of airplanes with bombs against a people who did not have even firearms with which to defend themselves), one wonders if the South African Government's suppression of the Bondelswarts communities in 1922 in Namibia formed a precedent.[6]

He also notes the three colonial wars that subsequently took place in Angola, Mozambique and Portuguese Guinea from 1961 onwards and which eventually claimed almost 10,000 lives. These campaigns were huge, involved hundreds of thousands of men and women and some consisted of several operational areas hundreds of kilometres apart. Things stayed that way for 13 years, until Portugal's young officers revolted in 1974. Up to that point, these three military struggles were the longest such armed conflicts in Africa's history of colonial affairs. Only South Africa's so-called 'Border War' lasted longer: 23 years.[7]

It is also curious that René Pélissier once referred to Angola in one of his books as 'a Brazil with all the sorrows.'

In the earlier period of endemic warfare with the tribes, – during the 19th Century and into the early years of the 20th – Lisbon retaliated with a fury. There was very little remorse shown and sometimes entire communities were eradicated. Because Angola was several months' distant sailing from Europe, there was no question of the European government intervening, had it even wanted to. As long as recalcitrant tribal people were put down, natural resources and taxes recovered, everybody was happy.

What is pertinent is that all these uprisings necessitated a series of systematic military campaigns of conquest and, with time, local kingdoms were overwhelmed and in some cases so-called 'seats' of power – which meant the chief together with his entire entourage – would be abolished and the principals sent into exile.

It was never easy because many African tribes believed their territory had been usurped by their colonial overlords. So too they had, but as the aphorism states, to the victor goes the spoils, for the simple reason that African people living in the bush were never (until 1961) able to muster enough firepower to counter what was obviously a superior European military force.

Consequently, by the end of the Great War in 1919, almost the whole of Angola was under government control.

---

6 In 1917, the South African mandatory administration in South West Africa – appointed by the League of Nations to take the country over from the defeated Germans – had created a tax on dogs and increased it in 1921. This tax was rejected by the Bondelswarts, a group of Khoikhoi who were opposed to various policies of the new Pretoria administration. They were also protecting five men for whom arrest warrants had been issued. The de facto authority in Windhoek brought in 400 armed men and sent in the air force to bomb these recalcitrants. Casualties included 100 Bondelswarts deaths, including a few women and children. Almost 500 more were either wounded or taken prisoner.
7 Willem Steenkamp and Al J.Venter (photos); *South Africa's Border War*; Helion Books, UK 2014.

Granted, slavery had been abolished, but powerful commercial interests in the metropolis moved in and took over most of the country's trading rights as well as its plantations which were worked on a mandatory system of forced African labour.

Obviously there were many Africans who resisted and with time, similar insurrections began to take place in the south of the country, with the proud Ovambo Nation – split in half between northern German South West Africa (Namibia today) and Angola following the 1884 Congress of Berlin.

In these excesses, the Portuguese were hardly alone. Joseph Conrad graphically detailed what the Belgians were doing in the Congo in his brilliantly evocative book *Heart of Darkness*. In neighbouring *Deutsch-Südwestafrika* Kaiser Wilhelm's Imperial German Army murdered 65,000 ethnic Hereros in a tribal uprising between 1904 and 1908 that lasted five years, events that are still vividly recalled today by the descendants of the victims.

It is worth mentioning that one of the war memorials to German troops killed in that internecine struggle still stands untouched a century later in a very prominent public site in Swakopmund, Namibia's third largest city.

In 2015 the German Foreign Ministry labelled these excesses as genocide and said that reparations would be made, though it is doubtful to whom, since early records in African societies were never properly kept. Still, it had the necessary media effect and as one commentator said, 'it looked good…it was the thing to do…'

For its part, Brussels has nothing to say about atrocities committed in the Congo by its civil service and military which were much worse, and, if that were possible, even more brutal. Some of the punishments handed out by government functionaries involved the cutting off of hands of tribal people who did not (or who were unable to) pay their taxes. Others were shot outright for protesting, but these measures – violent, often mindless and unspeakably horrific – were rarely questioned.

The truth is that the Belgians were directly instrumental in several million people subsequently dying in the Congo after Brussels abruptly vacated its African colony in 1960. They left no proper infrastructure in place to effectively run the country and in this, they are particularly culpable. Brussels never took any positive steps to ease the transition, such as establishing basics needed to run a country after their civil servants had hastily departed. As a consequence, the country, run by a succession of despots, continues to be ripped apart by civil war.

As far as the early Angolan settlers were concerned, civil unrest in the interior was hardly likely to appeal to potential new arrivals from Europe in the 19th Century. Early in the 1800s, the government headed by Marquis Sá da Bandeira attempted to encourage Portuguese farmers to move to Angola, in much the same way as Europeans were then flocking to the Americas.

Yet, something must have happened to attract more settlers because by the time of the 1961 rebellion, Angola's Portuguese community numbered several hundred thousand souls.

Once the Portuguese Army had thrown in the towel, everybody just grabbed what they could and returned to Europe, a 'Homeland' that some of the families had had little real contact with for almost 500 years…

5

Angola: More Recent Colonial Scenarios

Angola was never receptive to outside influences when Portugal ruled, certainly not those that did not originate in the Metropolis. Obviously, a steady flow of visitors arrived over the centuries, most intent on finding a foothold in the reasonably developed coastal regions, doing business or possibly appointing a local agent before heading home. But there was no stopping the missionary influence, and though Lisbon restricted many who were not of Roman Catholic persuasion, less orthodox proseletysers started to make their mark at about the time that David Livingstone briefly ended up in Luanda in 1854.

In the more modern period, most tourists intent on a casual holiday visit to Angola – except those wanting to hunt big game which was always a big money issue – invariably had a hard time explaining why they would want to go to what Stuart Cloete once called 'one of the remotest parts of Africa' and spend time there.[1]

Journalists came under particular scrutiny because justifiably, few members of the Fourth Estate were kindly disposed towards what was still clearly a Fascist state. It had been that way for decades.

The government was ruled as a virtual dictatorship for more than 30 years: its prime minister, a career economist by the name of Dr António de Oliveira Salazar having taken over the government in 1926, after a lengthy period of chaotic misrule that included a revolution and the monarchy being deposed, as well as army revolts.

Using authoritarian control that included censorship, several layers of security (and a ruthless and efficient secret police) as well as arbitrary imprisonment, he declared that his *Estado Novo*, or 'New State' would pave the way for the country's future. Or so, he and those who accepted his edicts, believed.

For all that, the *ultramar* – Lisbon's overseas possessions – thrived. Basically one of Europe's poorest nations, there never was much ready cash about in the streets of Lisbon or Oporto, but

---

1 Stuart Cloete, with whom I communicated for some years before he died, wrote a remarkably prescient book in 1956 called *African Giant* which was published by Collins to worldwide acclaim. With his American wife Tiny, he travelled the continent in the 'twilight years of colonialism' and detailed much of what had happened after the Second World War. 'The giant was awakening' he declared, adding that a bunch of new and powerful social and political figures had emerged. It was Cloete's writings that played a seminal role in inspiring this writer to explore the 'emerging' continent for himself. Even today *African Giant* is a fascinating read because it brings into context much what subsequently took place in Europe's colonies on a continent that was still quite often referred to as 'dark'.

in Mozambique – and Angola especially, with its huge natural resources – there was money to be made if you bent your back. More to the point, nobody starved. Everybody, black and white, seemed to manage, as long as they 'knew their place'.

Indeed, looking back – I went into all three African territories many times before the 1974 army mutiny in Lisbon and broadly speaking, things were a lot better then for ordinary folk than they are today. For a start, just about every town had a clinic, nothing fancy, but if you were hurt, you got help, if not from a qualified doctor then from a medic who had studied for that role.

Also, there were schools just about everywhere that were basic, functional and if not as efficient as they might be in the Western World, they managed to impart the elements of the 'Three Rs'. To achieve that much, there were teachers on call. Instruction, as in Brazil, another of Lisbon's former colonies, was in the Portuguese language.

It must have been reasonably successful because that tradition continues today in all of Lisbon's former African possessions: 40 or more years after independence, Portuguese remains the *lingua franca*, though most Africans also speak one or two tribal dialects.

That said, life was cheap. Real politics, such as it was – because there were no free elections – was for ethnic Portuguese only, almost all of whom were white. Once the war started, things began to change and more black and *mestiço* people found themselves in uniform in the perpetual 'battle against *comunismo*.'

The name of the game – as in Rhodesia and afterwards, South Africa – was the fight against what was referred to as terrorism and in the minds of those in charge, the threat was global.

Not all military types subscribed to that dictum because by the early 1960s Marxism had made discreet but significant inroads into Lisbon's military establishments. Slowly, inexorably, these sentiments eventually came to play a role in the anti-colonial struggles that followed. Indeed, it was elements from the 'Radical Left' that devised and implemented the 1974 young officers' revolt.

But that was still some way ahead, and until the government was overthrown, conscription was as much a part of life for young men just out of school or university as *bacalhau* might have been on the menu at least once a week.

What did become apparent was that from fairly early on, there were never enough soldiers around to do what was necessary. So Lisbon had to acknowledge that the strategic role of 'people of colour' might be part of the answer. By doing so, those back home in charge of recruitment started to make a number of concessions, including the ability of suitably qualified blacks to achieve officer status.

But, as critics of the system subsequently conceded (even though there were now black officers in the Portuguese Army) it was, as the well-worn aphorism goes, much too little and far too late...

Going back more than a century, the British missionary David Livingstone was to become a notable and long-standing link to the period when he arrived in Luanda in May 1854, after travelling the full width of the continent from East Africa by foot. His diaries, published posthumously, tell us that in the final stages of the journey – some hundreds of miles – he got a lot of help from Portuguese settlers in the region who were friendly and helped him on his way.

Paraphrasing his notes and I quote, he told us that he started his descent towards the coast and ten days later 'was hospitably welcomed by Mr Gabriel, the English commissioner for the suppression of the slave-trade and consul for Angola.' He was also hosted by the Bishop of Angola, at the time acting-governor-general and by the leading Portuguese of this faraway settlement that had been founded centuries before.

Livingstone: 'The captains of Her Majesty's ships HMS *Pluto, Philomel and Polyphemus* came shortly after into port and offered to take me either to St. Helena or home. But I would not leave my Makololo followers to return without my assistance now that I was aware of the difficulties of the journey and the hostilities of the tribes on the Portuguese frontier.'

Like many other expatriates who chose to live in the tropics in those early years, the good doctor suffered much from dysentery and it was not until four months later that he started on the return leg, well supplied with stores and the good wishes of Lisbon's officials.

What is also clear is that while David Livingstone was respected, well received and treated by his hosts, his presence was unquestionably an embarrassment to the authorities. He had always been one of the most vociferous opponents of slavery, and while the infamous Atlantic slave trade had been outlawed by the majority of European countries decades before he reached Angola, he encountered several parties of Portuguese slavers driving their wretched booty to market in Luanda. It was nothing new and he was appalled, in large part because he had seen much the same while travelling about East Africa and there too, Portuguese traders operating out of Mozambique were sometimes involved.

As with many other African countries on both the Atlantic and Indian Ocean littorals, the slavery issue had become pervasive centuries before. In Angola, from 1617 to 1621 – during the governorship of Luís Mendes de Vasconcellos – up to 50,000 Angolans were enslaved and shipped to the Americas.

The Portuguese never worked alone. They were enthusiastically helped by several tribes who were willing participants in bids to capture their fellow countrymen and market them to European slave merchants. This influence was widespread, as it already was in East Africa with Arab slavers among the most active on the African Continent.

In Angola in the 17th century, the Imbangala tribe in the north of the country became the main rivals of the Mbundu in supplying slaves to the European colonials and a century later the Portuguese sold 5,000 to 10,000 slaves annually, devastating the Mbundu economy and population. To achieve such dividends, Portuguese and Imbangala soldiers attacked and conquered the Kingdom of Ndongo from 1618 to 1619, laying siege to the Ndongo capital of Kabasa.

The Portuguese and their black allies captured and sold thousands of Kabasa residents with 36 ships leaving the port of Luanda in 1619 and setting a new record of slave exports destined for European plantations abroad.

The system employed was basic. The Portuguese traded guns with Imbangala soldiers in return for slaves. Thus, armed with superior weapons, soldiers from this primitive tribe captured and sold their black brothers to the colonials on a far larger scale: every new slave translated into a better-armed force of aggressors.

Officially, Lisbon subscribed to the anti-slavery dictum as expounded in several treaties, the first dating from 1803 and finally enacted into law in Portugal 30 years later. But this had little effect on halting this nefarious traffic to Brazil, where the demand for slaves persisted. Indeed, David Livingstone was not shy to castigate Luanda's colonial representatives for what was clearly a breach of trust and there is no doubt that authorities in Luanda were delighted to see his back once he started on the long haul back to East Africa, again on foot.

Livingstone does not make much mention of African efforts to curtail these crimes while in Luanda, though the French historian and pre-eminent authority on Africa, Professor René Pélissier has devoted almost his entire professional career to recording these and related events.[2]

---

2 Pélissier, René: *Les Guerres Grises: Resistance et Revoltes en Angola (1845-1941),* Editions Pélissier, Orgeval, 1977; And also *La Colonie du Minotaure, Nationalismes et révoltes en Angola (1926-1961)*, Editions Pélissier, Orgeval, 1978.

What does emerge from his research (which at one stage got him banned from actually doing personal research in Lisbon's historical archives) is that from the earliest days of settlement along the Angolan coast, local tribes often revolted against Portuguese control subjugation and the consequences could be brutal.

Lisbon's colonial wars in Africa rarely lasted more than a year or two, though in the period from the turn of the century to around the First World War, conflict seemed to have been unending and involved numerous dissident tribal groups.

In the 19th Century – at one time or another – conflict stretched across almost the entire country and incuded confrontations with the Ovimbundus of the south-east (Jonas Savimbi's homeland), the Ambo, Humbo, Kuvale and others, all the way through to the war against the Cuanhama/Ovambo people of the south in 1914/1915 – which I deal with below – and the subsequent Seles Revolt (*Guerra dos Seles*) of 1917/1918.

That uprising as well as the Binga Revolt involved large numbers of fugitives who had fled forced labour edicts and sought succour in a region in Benguela Province in the south. Documents dating from that period roughly described the area as a no-man's land – a *Terra de ninguém* – because Luanda lacked the resources to properly administer it. René Pélissier deals with this in considerable detail in his book *Les campagnes coloniales du Portugal*, published in Paris by Flammarion.

He also covers events involving the Kuvelai Tribe, a community that existed on the fringe of the southern desert near the port of Moçãmedes (Namibe today). This was a large African community not easily intimidated, especially by the *de jure* system of forced labour which was finally abolished in 1913. But not before it provided the basis for development of a plantation economy and, by the mid-20th century, a major mining sector.

In the process, forced labour combined with British financing to construct three railways from the coast into the interior

An interesting observation made by Professor Pelissiér is that during the course of quelling African rebellions, the Portuguese were not averse to emptying their prisons in search of men who were fit and capable of handling firearms to fight recalcitrant indigenés. In the Cuamoto campaign of 1915 for instance, he states that the force included 56 officers, 1208 white soldiers, 138 African soldiers, 5 auxiliaries and 30 convicts.

Luanda also made regular use of South African mercenaries, mainly Afrikaans-speaking Boers who easily slotted into the ranks with regular Portuguese troops because they were renowned for being able to shoot extremely well, something the British discovered during the two Boer Wars (the first in 1881 and the major campaign from 1899 that eventually involved several hundred thousand British and Commonwealth forces fighting a brutal guerrilla war that lasted almost three years).

In truth, while Lisbon had planted the Portuguese flag over an enormous part of west and central Africa, full administrative control of the interior did not occur until the beginning of the 20th century, and then only when resistance from a number of population groups was overcome. Chief among these was the uprising of the Kwanyama, led by their leader Mandume Ya Ndemufayo. There were numerous battles involving these people: In September 1904 a Portuguese column lost over 300 men, including 114 Europeans, in an encounter with the Kwanyamas in the vicinity of the Kunene River, not far from the German frontier.

In the earlier period it was the northern Mbundo and Bakongo-linked tribes (adjacent to what is today the Congo) that were the most difficult to deal with, but eventually these insurrections spread south.

ANGOLA: MORE RECENT COLONIAL SCENARIOS 93

Colonial Luanda at about the time of Livingston's visit.

Livingtone constantly encountered slavers during his travels through Africa.

Primitive but tough Luba Angolan tribesmen were targeted by slavers.

Effective means were found to keep slaves shackled.

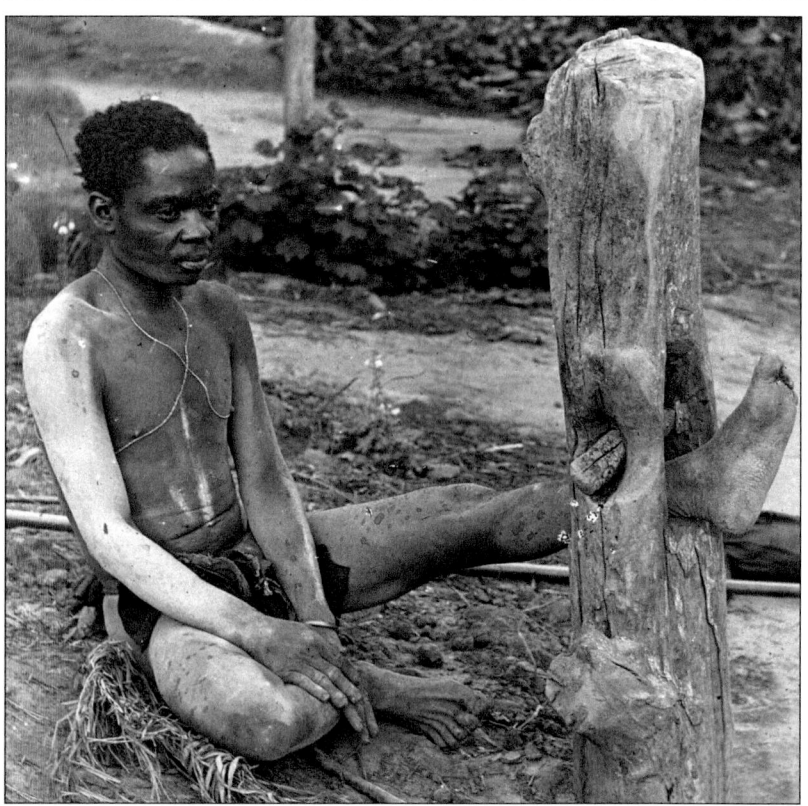

Turn of the century postcard from the colonial town of Dondo in Angola's interior.

Portuguese troops embarking for Angola during the First World War.

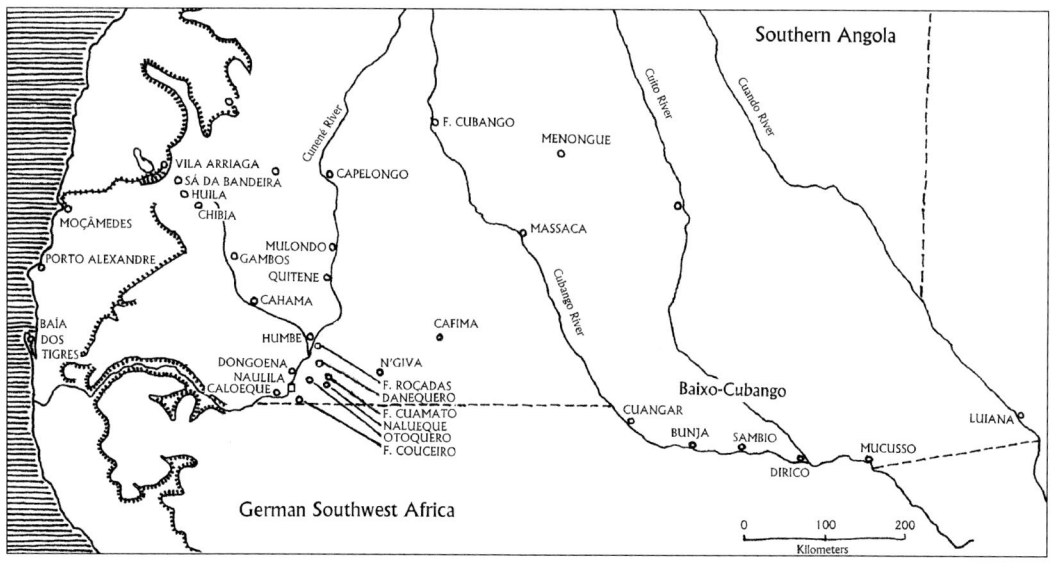
Map of south Angola showing where hostilities with the Germans took place.
(Courtesy John P Cann)

South African troops embarking in Cape Town in 1915 for war in German South West Africa.

Armoured car used against German forces in Africa in the First World War.

This portrait of Dr David Livingstone appeared in an edition of the *London Illustrated News*, as did an encounter with an extremely angry hippo that he and his boatmen encountered while on the Zambezi and which cost the life of one of his men.

Communications – or lack of – was obviously implicit in the days before the telegraph. In most cases, if Luanda did not have the resources to quell a rebellion, the governor would summon help from Lisbon. But that invariably meant sending sometimes desperate appeals to Europe by ship – and occcasionally a delegation or two – and then waiting for reinforcements to arrive, also by sea. The process took months.

Over almost five centuries of Portuguese dominance there were many hundreds of uprisings, some of which petered out after relatively peaceful protests while others required military force and the loss of hundreds, sometimes thousands of lives to put down.

Pélissier's works encompasses thousands of pages of research and would be impossible to accurately enumerate within these covers. But it is worth looking at his comments about some of the uprisings that took place little more than a century ago, especially those affecting the Herero and Ovambo communities that had been living on Angolan soil for centuries.

At the end of it, the Hereros all but ceased to exist in their own homeland in the south of that vast country, while the hardier Ovambos, after fighting a series of fairly protracted campaigns, eventually upped sticks and moved south for protection – such as it was – into German territory.

Namibia, prior to being conquered in the First World War by South African forces headed by a former Boer leader General Louis Botha and being renamed South West Africa, was originally listed on early maps as *Deutsch Südwesafrika*.

One of the most interesting campaigns that lasted more than a year, involved the Portuguese General Antonio Júlio da Costa Pereira de Eça, whose job it was to reconquer some pretty extensive swathes of territory in South Angola from which the colonials had been driven out of by an invading German military force.

This was not something that happened by chance. As John P (Jack) Cann, United States Navy captain and military historian explains, Germany had always held a covetous eye for the southern portion of the Portuguese colony of Angola, and the First World War provided the long-sought opportunity for it to take what it wished. He goes on:

> Neutral Portugal was initially intimidated into concessions in Angola and then invaded there by a small German force that wreaked havoc well beyond the interesting one-day battle. The German action turned out to be an isolated tactical engagement that bore little relation to its long-stated strategic objective of making southern Angola part of German South West Africa.
>
> The Portuguese recovered from the chaos that the Germans had created and by September 1915 had established a peace that lasted 46 years until the uprisings in 1961.
>
> The root of the First World War German offensive into southern Angola lay in the severe difficulty that Portugal experienced in bringing order to this colony and thus its perceived vulnerability to a covetous neighbour. In the less than 80 years between 1848 and 1926 Portugal conducted more than 180 campaigns and military operations there to subdue the resistance of its population. No other European power met with such resistance or faced so many uprisings in its colonisation of tropical Africa.
>
> Southern Angola, the scene of the German incursion, is particularly noteworthy because of the number, fierceness, and scale of military operations. The area symbolised war and was the acid test of the Portuguese colonising ability. Indeed, it was only in the south that the Portuguese waged a European-style war with large troop deployments from the *metrópole* and the use of heavy weapons.

Even before a German force of 2,000 men under the command of Major Victor Franke attacked Lisbon's army ensconced at the small town of Naulila, just north of what is today the Caleque

Dam on the Kunene River on the 18th December, 1914, there had been hostilities between the two forces going back months. The Portuguese Army resisted but was forced to withdraw towards the Humbe region (the site of the riverside town of Vila Roçadas, Xangongo today). Their losses were 69 dead, 76 wounded and 76 men taken prisoner.

The Germans stayed on in Angola for another seven months before they withdrew in the face of the South African Army advancing from the south. Two days later, on the 9th July 1915, Kaiser Wilhelm's forces in South West Africa surrendered, ending the campaign.[3]

The problem then, was that all the tribes in the south were in rebellion against continued Portuguese rule, their emotions fuelled by large quantities of weapons that the Germans had passed on to African dissidents. Essentially, Lisbon had a major war on its hands, and not only with the powerful Cuanhama people who were at the vanguard of the rebellion.

Lisbon despatched two expeditionary forces to the southern port of Moçãmedes totalling more than 7,000 men as well as 60 cannon and machine-guns.

Because the country had been laid waste, the Portuguese had to bring with them everything they were going to need to fight a lengthy campaign. That included 80 motor lorries (the first to be used in an expedition in Angola), three locomotives as well as sets of what were termed 'temporary barracks'. Much of this material came from South Africa and some from Mozambique.

General Pereira de Eça also needed the wherewithal to construct 800 kilometres of roads and to install equal lengths of telegraph and telephone lines. Water in this remote region was obviously a major problem for both sides. If it did not rain, some people died of thirst in a semi-arid region that was among the harshest imaginable anywhere and where temperatures in summer were often in excess of 40° Celcius.

He augmented his strength with another 7,000 men from Europe, almost a thousand African troops, 300 European auxilliaries which, one surmises, included South African Boers who had settled in Angola and who who had fought many times in the pay of the colonials, as well as a further 3,700 African auxilliaries. They came with another 26 pieces of artillery, 28 machine-guns, thousands of rifles, more than 400 horse vehicles as well as 40 'Boer carts' (Pélissiér suggests that these were horse-drawn armoured vehicles).

The enemy, mostly Ovambo, were reckoned to number about 40,000 warriors.

Losses of the Portuguese Army in 1914–1915 (South)

	Deaths from wounds in combat	Deaths from sickness or accident	Deaths from wounds or sickness	Total
Officers	10	18		28
European soldiers	99	618		717
African soldiers			68	68
White auxiliaries			6	6
Total	109	636	74	819

Source: After Jose Ribeiro da Costa Junior: Servicos administrativos na campanha do Sul de Angola em 1914 – 1915 2nd edicao, Lisbonne 1921, page 208.

---

3 The country was taken over as a League of Nations Mandated territory, administered by South Africa from Pretoria and renamed South West Africa

Jack Cann's comments on the overall German invasion plan of south Angola are illuminating. I quote:

> The key German aim in Africa in the First World War centred on the concept of a 'German Central Africa' in which a zone of economic opportunity would be acquired principally from the French, Belgian and Portuguese possessions and carved from the French West Coast, the Congo Free State, Angola, and Mozambique. The reason for demanding Angola was to connect the mining area of Katanga to the west coast ports of Moçâmedes, Benguela, and Luanda. British colonies were avoided in this plan, as Germany did not believe that Britain could be defeated as could France and Belgium.
>
> The German strategy with Portugal, a neutral, was to compel it to abandon its position of neutrality through a contrived border dispute and associated incident. This action would serve as a pretext to provoke a break with Portugal, so that it could be among the defeated German adversaries and be forced to part with its colonies when a victorious Germany dictated the peace terms.
>
> German designs under the *pénétration pacifique* became less subtle in November 1913 with an agreement to open Angolan ports to its commerce and establish a consul general in Luanda. While these moves might seem innocuous, the Portuguese government was intimidated by Germany and agreed further to the establishment of a joint German-Portuguese mission for scientific studies in the south of Angola. When the mission arrived in Luanda, Governor-General Norton de Matos was taken by complete surprise, not having been consulted or informed by Lisbon.
>
> The vastness of Angola, the long uncontrolled southern border, and the relatively primitive communications made it particularly vulnerable to any German offensive. Norton de Matos had few troops with which to police the frontier, much less to defend the colony. With the German mission travelling through the area gathering intelligence on every aspect of the colonial defences and able to engage in other activities – and the consul general vigorously pursuing German interests – it was not difficult to foresee trouble.
>
> As the implementation of German war aims in Africa became more obvious, it produced considerable anxiety in Lisbon and Luanda. Even though the borders between Angola and South West Africa had been fixed by treaty dated 30 December 1886, the Germans sought certain convenient interpretations.

As with Tanganyika in East Africa, also a German possession and one that bordered on Kenya, a British colony, there was much subterfuge prior to the Great War as to how Berlin would deal with this territory once hostilities had started. The Kaiser was hesitant about creating another battlefield as distant as Kenya because he was aware that Britain would rush to help, as it certainly did once German objectives became clear.

Angola, as we have seen was a totally different matter and here, too, Cann paints a vivid picture, specifically with regard to intent:

> In South West Africa an *Angola Bund* was formed and actively prepared to absorb the colony. Its formation was part of an official German effort to co-ordinate the activities of interested groups and institutions in its drive for colonial expansion.
>
> Increasingly, the state and the financial and industrial sectors were combining their activities through such organisations and joining in co-ordinated public expressions of each's wishes and demands.
>
> At its inauguration in 1912, its founder declared, 'We must possess the south of Angola! Only then, through strong effort and serious work can South West Africa be for us a country, a nation.' Such rhetoric put Angolans on edge.

As the German-Portuguese scientific mission of 1914 travelled through southern Angola, the German vice-consul at Moçâmedes, a gentleman named Schoss, used the opportunity to preposition provisions for the German Army under the pretext of resupplying the mission. All of these activities were perhaps suspected in Lisbon, but Portugal was so intimidated by Germany that no protest was made. As war developed in Europe in early August 1914, so the Germans began to conclude their various civil operations in southern Angola.

The steady exodus of Germans from the country was a clear indication that open hostilities were just around the corner.

What is also pertinent, said Cann, is that Angola had become Portugal's nightmare colony with conflict taking place practically all of the time in the north, south and east. As a result, on the eve of the First World War at least 20 percent of the colony remained independent of Portuguese rule. In the south, Xetaquela had become the chief of the Ovambo-linked Cuamato in 1907 and had succeeded chief Igura, who had been responsible for the 1904 massacre of an ineptly-led Portuguese force.

> The Portuguese returned in a determined effort during the summer of 1907 and concentrated a large force at Fort Roçadas. The colonials marched on the Cuamato, defeating them decisively in the fall of the same year, and Xetaquela consequently fled south across the border to the German sanctuary of South West Africa.
>
> [Once the Germans had left] the Cuamato, who had been practically disarmed in the re-conquest of 1907, took up the abandoned weapons originally left by the Portuguese and sought their revenge. Naulila had become a signal for a vast uprising in southern Angola.
>
> The line of forts established in 1907 beyond Humbe were evacuated by Roçadas in great disorder: Nalueque, Otoquero, Damequero, and Fort Cuamato were all attacked by the Cuamato. The garrison of this last fort lost a third of its 104 local troops.
>
> Many believed that the Germans were still around creating mayhem. Eventually Humbe, which had been maintained at great sacrifice for half a century, was abandoned. The disaster continued with the loss of Quitene and Mulondo and stopped only at Capelongo. Further east troops abandoned Cafima for Massaca.
>
> By the end of December 1914, there was no Portuguese presence east of the Cuneré in southern Angola. The Cuamato had taken their cue from the retreating Portuguese and had destroyed the abandoned forts.
>
> The territory had become independent again for all practical purposes, and the area beyond the outposts of the plateau was now chaotic and developing into a tragedy in the absence of any rule of law. In the vacuum of the Portuguese withdrawal, an orgy of pillage ensued. As a result of this chaos, in 1915 there was a vast famine that left the population helpless and in which it is estimated that 80,000 perished. This catastrophe was to facilitate the return of Portuguese rule.

In the final analysis the Germans won the day through superior training, discipline, and leadership. Its troops, says Cann, were tough, hardened colonial regulars augmented by reservists who had settled in Berlin's southern colony. The all-European German force contrasted with the Portuguese, a mixture of Europeans and local troops, poorly trained and indifferently motivated. The *straf expedition* had not lost its utility or effectiveness over time.

Cann: One only has to view the South African 'externals' in use during the late 1970s and early 1980s to draw a parallel. Those mobile forces of European troops struck across the Angolan border from what is now Namibia to devastate equally well-armed but less well-trained mixed troops of white Cubans and black Angolans during South Africa's Border War...

6

Luanda – A Very Personal View

In Africa's so-called 'Colonial Era', Luanda and Mozambique's Lourenço Marques – Maputo today – were regarded by many who travelled extensively to be among the most progressive cities on the African continent. The most striking of all was Luanda, sometimes referred to as 'Paris in Africa'. By any standards, the Angolan capital was once a beautiful, expansive and innovative city.

The first time I sailed into Luanda harbour was on a bright tropical day in 1959. I was a lowly 20 year-old crew member onboard a navy frigate, then in the process of 'showing the flag' in the Portuguese overseas 'province' as Lisbon liked to call it. Thereafter, we would visit Matadi, the Congo's largest port, still under Belgian colonial administration and about to become independent.

The visit to a West African destination was a revelation for those of us who had never been further north than Rhodesia's Salisbury or Lourenço Marques.

In Luanda, we were to discover a bustling, prosperous and cosmopolitan city with all the trappings of a European capital, including modern buildings, restaurants that were far beyond our meagre earnings and suburbs that vied with anything that Cape Town or Johannesburg had to offer. That and the craziest traffic south of Marseilles where, to our astonishment, the locals drove on the wrong side of the road…

The entire city fringed a lagoon that stretched some distance down the coast and was overlooked by the impeccably-kept Fortress of São Miguel that was built almost a century before the Dutch settled the Cape of Good Hope. This massive structure, with its unusual polygonal shape and numerous bastions, overlooked the favourite hangout of the crew during our brief visit, the *ilha*, or island, connected to the mainland by a bridge and with more restaurants, clubs, jazz joints and whorehouses than any other city on the continent.

The intention was for the ship to stay a week. But after a first night of cheap booze and licentious broads in town, coupled to the kind of sometimes violent dislocation that ended up making the newspapers back home, our rather ostentatious state visit was abruptly cut short.

Much of the drama was centred on the 'plunder' of a number of thousand-litre wooden wine barrels that were standing on the quay alongside our frigate. There were no barriers around them, or, for that matter any guards. As the Luanda police said afterwards, who in his right mind would take the trouble to steal something as mundane as wine, anyway? There was so much it was all over the place and not even the locals bothered to take it without paying.

My shipmates did not share that view. Those crew members who were required to remain onboard used hammers to broach several of the wooden vats to help themselves, and that soon turned into a disaster that eventually involved the police. As we were to discover the next day, the alcoholic-inspired melee resulted in the arrest of several South African sailors, with the rest of us remanded to remain onboard, or as they say, even in the navy, 'confined to barracks'.

The bottom line was that our ship – to the exasperation of Captain Terry-Lloyd, our captain and a man who was always a stickler for discipline (as well as an utterly perplexed South African consul ashore) – had been disgraced. It did not take the skipper very long to call it a day and the order that followed from the bridge was to let go fore and aft. We continued our journey up the coast towards the Congo and the final west coast port of call.

In Matadi none of the ship's company was allowed ashore, even though we were there for several days: the reason given was that they feared the crew would turn that harbour upside down as well.

I returned to Luanda not many years later. I'd left the navy, qualified professionally in London, returned to South Africa and decided to head back to Britain in 1965. That expedition involved a four-month overland journey that took me up the west coast of Africa, through Lambarene and Albert Schweitzer's famous jungle hospital, and along the coast all the way to Senegal. I deal with it all quite expansively in one of my books, *African Stories by Al Venter and Friends* which I regard as one of my best titles ever.[1]

You'd have to be a little loco to try that today, but in the 1960s it was feasible and actually quite safe, that is if you survived Africa's crazy traffic.

In the process I entered Nigeria by dug-out canoe from Victoria in West Cameroons, spent time in Ghana, from where I had to make a run for it because somebody in Accra spotted my South African origins, travelled the length of the Cote d'Ivoire by bush taxi and continued overland through Sierra Leone, Gambia and eventually made Dakar, another beautiful African capital in those early halcyon, pre-Uhuru days.

It was a tough, arduous journey that included my going down with malaria in Lagos, a lonely trudge through Liberia and a nightmarish visit to Guinea, then in the throes of its own Marxist revolution under the dictator Sekou Toure. A ruthless tyrant who, word had it, appeared to get off murdering his political opponents, Toure (and his modern harbour at Conakry, a large city on the Atlantic Ocean that until then had been a virtual NATO preserve) was embraced by the Soviets after the dictator had seriously fallen out with France's President Charles de Gaulle.

Moscow flooded Guinea with all sorts of gifts that included a shipload of snowplows and another of cement. The first ended up rusting on a quay in the harbour – because nobody in tropical Guinea knew what the machines were for – while the cement was delivered in the rainy season in paper bags. That meant that Conakry still has the largest rock-hard mountain of concrete of any port in Africa. Clearly, there was somebody in the old Soviet Union who wasn't paying much attention to African geography, or its climatic conditions while still at university.

I reached Luanda the second time round on a fairly long haul north from Angola's port city of Lobito, where I'd been arrested by the local military because foreigners travelling overland were not only a rarity, but suspect as well.

The guerrilla war which the Portuguese Army was trying to contain in the north of the country was on the upswing and somebody concluded that because I was hitch-hiking, I could only have been a foreign spy. Though I spent a night in the cells devoured by mosquitoes, my South African passport and valid visa got me released the following morning.

I reached the outskirts of Luanda late the following day. It was rush hour and the truck driver who had given me a lift was in a hurry and sped through the outskirts into the centre of town, dropping me off adjacent to the city's famous lagoon-side Marginal.

From the moment I arrived, I was awed at the astonishing pace of a great city in the process of closing shop for the night. This time, I had no ship to report back to and, in any event, not enough

---

[1] *African Stories by Al J. Venter and Friends*, Protea Books, Pretoria, 2013.

money to think about making a habit of getting drunk. At something like a dollar or two for a good bottle Douro *vinho tinto*, I was easily tempted.

The Luanda of the mid-1960s was a somewhat different place from what I'd experienced five or six years before, while still in the navy.

For a start, with an ongoing war in the *Dembos* – the jungles to the north of the port city – there were people in uniform just about everywhere. These included soldiers, sailors and airmen. In the bars and restaurants that I frequented, I observed that the military component appeared to mix easily with the civilian population, both black and white. In fact, the informality of interracial association astonished this newcomer from a South African society just then in the process of shoring up its racial barriers.

Part of the reason was that Lisbon, a decade or two before, had changed its citizenship laws in a bid to encourage those Africans and people of mixed blood in the colonies – the mulattos – by granting them what could best be deemed 'honorary' Portuguese' status. They were officially referred to as *assimilados*, or people that had been assimilated by the mother country, and though it was a shrewd but cynical political move to get more support from the locals, it actually worked.[2]

More to the point, as mentioned by somebody who had been born and brought up in colonial Angola, an *assimilado* was someone who had, as the word was supposed to imply, assimilated the Portuguese language and customs, had a formal education, would adopt European names and, of course, eat with a knife and fork…

Looking in from the outside, it was obvious that this form of inverse racial classification in Portugal's African possessions was both demeaning and insulting, but it was certainly an enormous step and streets ahead of anything going on in an apartheid-obsessed South Africa at the time.

Obviously there were many people in Angola, Mozambique and Portuguese Guinea who seized the opportunity to improve their station and, with time, *assimilados* became a significant bridge between the cultures of Africa and the *metrópole*. These 'chosen few' – in theory – were able to be elected to public office (and indeed, some were), work in jobs of their choice, travel without permits and observe their children enjoying higher education.

More salient, with the war gathering strength, they could aspire to commissioned rank in the military.

One of Lisbon's most famous 'sons' was a young officer then fighting in Portuguese Guinea. Declared an *assimilado* some years before, Captain João Bacar became one of the most celebrated and decorated men in the Portuguese Armed Forces. Shortly before I spent time with him at his base in Tite (not to be confused with Tete, in Mozambique) he had been awarded the coveted Gold Order of the Tower and the Sword, Lisbon's rough equivalent of the Victoria Cross.

A week after I'd returned from a patrol with Captain Bacar and his seasoned squad of *Comandos Africanos* in a swampy area to the south of the capital he was killed in an ambush. The entire Portuguese nation mourned his death.

Very much the same situation held for Angola, where I was to meet still more African war heroes and even travelled to Cabinda with a distinguished young combatant who had taken on a group

---

2   Over 95 percent of Angolans received the classification *indígena*, equivalent to the legal designation n*ative* in British colonies in Africa. According to a 1913 report: '*Indígena* is the individual of colour (black or mulatto) that satisfies all of the following criteria: a) was born in the province; b) does not speak correct Portuguese; c) has the habits and customs of a native.' Legally *indígenas* had none of the legal rights of a citizen. For a terrific study of legal classifications in Portuguese colonialism, see: M. Moutinho, *O Indígena no Pensamento Colonial Português* (Lisboa, Edições Universitários Lusófonas, 2000). Source: Jeremy Ball: *Colonial Labour in Twentieth-Century Angola*: Dickinson College, Carlisle PA 2005.

of guerrillas on his own and saved the day for his company. Yet, in other respects, Angola was very different from Mozambique and Portuguese Guinea.

In the East African Lusitanian colony that fringed the Indian Ocean for its entire 2,600 kilometres, those with money tended to congregate towards Beira, Lourenço Marques and the south; they left the rest of what our elders often referred to as Portuguese East Africa to a rugged bunch of more adventurous farmers, settlers and entrepreneurs. It was also a reality that, unlike Angola where farming had always been intense and foreigners were encouraged to buy land in the interior, four-fifths or more of Mozambique had never been developed or exploited, which meant it was Portuguese in name only.

Also, the average white Mozambican in Lourenço Marques had little time for those members of the military who had arrived from Europe to fight guerrilla insurrection from Tanzania and the north. They made few attempts to support them, and unlike Angola – where the army was embraced by the settlers – it was uncommon for the average white resident of Lourenço Marques to invite military personnel into their homes for a meal or a chat.

In fact, this kind of hospitality was something of a two-edged sword because there were several incidents in which Portuguese soldiers 'misbehaved' in the homes to which they were invited, making passes at the wives of their hosts and things of that sort, in part because the majority of young conscripts in the Portuguese Army were rural, or of the *fadista* type from Lisbon.

In Portuguese Guinea conditions were even more severe. An unhealthy, low-lying country with mangrove swamps stretching deep into the interior, the tropical climate was too severe to foster any kind of permanent residence by the majority of Europeans who were sent there on government business or to trade. Consequently, the military deployed in that country were very much on their own.

For their part, the Angolans took the initiative in most things that affected their ultimate destiny and, for good reason. The first Portuguese had originally landed near the mouth of the Congo River in 1482, which meant that by the time I got there, the country had been either sporadically settled or colonised by Lisbon for more than five centuries. More to the point, there were Portuguese families in Angola of all races who had been there for centuries and they were proud of their Angolan heritage. They were also willing to fight for it.

Indeed, Angolan whites, and those locals who supported them, believed that they had become an inviolable part of Africa. There was even surreptitious talk at one stage to launch the same kind of unilateral declaration of independence or UDI, as Rhodesia had done a short while before. In the end, nothing came of it, which was probably just as well because the Angolans would truly have been on their own in the face of an encroaching insurgency that claimed more lives each year.

Instead, these white, *mestiço* and black nationalistic elements, with strong government support, would loudly proclaim that the country was theirs, to the point where radio stations throughout Angola would routinely broadcast the slogan *Angola é Nossa* – 'Angola is Ours' – and they did so dozens of times each day. They really believed it!

Though the *assimilado* concept had its uses, partially by marshalling the aspirations of some of the more politically astute African citizens towards the interests of the Prime Minister Salazar's *Estado Novo* regime, it also resulted in the alienation of some of the more politically-seasoned dissidents; those people who refused to be categorized as 'second class citizens' as one youthful firebrand at a Luanda University viewed it.

I only remember him by his first name, which was Saraiva, but this was clearly a very bright young man who had had a tough time of it because he totally disagreed with his white classmates about the future of what he referred to as *my* country, and, by inference, not theirs….

A true mixed-blood patriot – his father was a white trader and his mother was black. But he deeply resented the prospect of having to serve as a conscript in the Portuguese Army in a conflict

View of Luanda from the fort at the time of the visit by the author's ship, the South African Navy frigate *SAS Vrystaat*.

The Roman Catholic Church played a dominant role in the country's social norms: every town had its church and Luanda had this cathedral.

An early 18th Century sketch of an area adjacent to Luanda's present-day Marginal.

Distinctive Portuguese blue tiles were as much a feature of Luanda's architecture as it might have been in the Metropolis.

Government Palace in Lobito.

An aerial view of Luanda in 1960: the often nearby insurgency very rarely affected life in the cities.

Luanda's famous Palace of Iron, originally built by the same man who constructed the Eiffel Tower.

Luanda Bay 1960. – a marvellous laid-back backwater where life was good and you could exist on a few dollars a day.

View of Luanda's beach area from the fort.

that he unswervingly believed was totally unjustified. He'd been called up and was due to go into the army within months.

The Portuguese must all go back to Portugal from where they originally came, he would tell me, and then he'd wait for a reaction. But on his patch I was not prepared to argue politics. It did surprise me that he would pour out his soul to me, an *estrangeiro* (his word, not mine) in a way that he would never have done with one of his own white countrymen. Frankly, his views were sobering for somebody who had never experienced 'somebody of colour' with such strong views.

'Africa is for the African', Saraiva would state with undisguised contempt, and the more Cuca beers he drank, the more outspoken he would become.

He had clearly had a tough time at school, not necessarily because of the colour of his skin, but because he would tell everybody who was prepared to listen that there were other forces active that would eventually change the status quo in Angola. These, he intimated, were to be found in Angola and abroad, and offered him something better than the role as a minor functionary in the local administration when he eventually got out of uniform.

His hero, he made clear, was Agostinho Neto, somebody whom I'd never heard of before. But I would come to recognise that name often enough in the future, after I'd started covering those African guerrilla struggles for the various publications for which I wrote.

Like Saraiva, Neto came from an *assimilado* background. His father was a Methodist pastor in Luanda and, having finished school, the younger Neto left Angola for Portugal and studied medicine at the universities of Coimbra and Lisbon. He combined his academic life with covert political activity of a revolutionary sort, was arrested by PIDE – the Portuguese secret police – for his separatist activism in 1951 and spent seven years in prison. On release, he finished his studies and, on the same day he graduated, Neto married a 23-years-old Portuguese woman, like him, a *mestiço*.

Two years later this youthful revolutionary was back in Angola where he helped put the MPLA firmly on the map, the same political party that has ruled Angola since the mid-1970s and is better known internationally as the MPLA.

I stayed in Luanda on that visit for almost two weeks and it was a charm.

It was not long before I'd joined a small group of student friends and after hours, we'd move about the city from one night spot or restaurant to another. In the process I discovered a vital, dynamic and charming conurbation, the likes of which I had never dreamed possible on the continent of my birth.

The city was well ordered and while the majority of blacks were poor, they seemed to keep their spirits alive by decorating or cleaning their front and back yards and sometimes even mended potholes in their streets.

Compared to other major African cities like Lagos, Leopoldville in the Congo or Liberia's Monrovia, there were relatively few of the enormous hardscrabble shanty-towns – locals refer to them as *musseques* – and that these days encroach every available (and sometimes unavailable scrap of space) just about all the way across the city.

These days, these enormous slums – together with the hill-tops of filthy garbage they invariably accumulate – are a brutal feature of everyday Luanda life and not at all unlike Rio's notorious *favela*s.

Very much like South Africa, the European settler community in Angola was forthright and uncompromising in its views, whether about food, entertainment, politics or sport. This was also a much healthier outdoor community than that of their relatives in the Metropolis.

Army instructors in Lisbon would complain that new conscripts – when they arrived for their basic military training – were often below par physically, but that was a rare event in Angola. In this African colony people were accustomed to lengthy sporting sessions while at school or perhaps heading out into the bush with their families or fishing down the coast, for no other reason than that they liked doing so. Also, just about everybody and his uncle was a hunter of sorts and in this regard, Angola's resources were endless.

In Luanda, Lobito and Nova Lisboa – which, after independence was to change its name to Huambo – the emphasis among the youth was on education, sport and culture: just about every youngster whose parents could afford it aspired to a university degree. In Luanda there were academic clubs that catered for these needs with mathematics and science clubs and even a privately owned observatory in one of the suburbs.

Traditional and classical concerts were regular, with chamber groups and even a small national orchestra. Overseas artists performed routinely in all major centres and the lovely Amália Rodrigues, with her distinctive *Fado* following, was almost regarded by locals as a regular. While musical fare was largely European or American, one of Luanda's most elite clubs, Xavarotti, sometimes engaged prominent artists from Brazil.

For the majority who had almost nothing, their music was traditional, African and enjoyable, with the *kissange*, a primitive thumb piano typically constructed with metal strips on a wooden base, predominating. It is called the *mbira* in Rhodesia.

Things were cheap in Angola in those days, in part because prices had not been bumped up by expatriates. There were hardly any. Portugal was coping with its conflicts and anybody who wished to visit the country had to have a very good reason for doing so before they could gain entry. That category obviously excluded the American and European hunting fraternities, because Angola boasted some the best safaris on the continent. But that, as the saying goes, was strictly 'big bucks'.

Ensconced as I soon was, in Luanda, I had a clean room in one of the local hotels for about $10 a night, and I could eat an excellent seafood dinner for about half that. After I emerged in the mornings, I would saunter down to a huge open coffee house near the harbour with windows as big as doors and get myself a jug of *café com leite* with enough bread to carry me through to lunch. The place was the haunt of many of the white Portuguese dock workers, taxi drivers or trades folk who would noisily start their day, very much as I did.

There was an excellent public transport system in Luanda in those days and it was possible to move about the city for a pittance. Like today, the city was divided into two parts, the Baixa de Luanda (lower Luanda, the old city) and the Cidade Alta (upper city or the new part).

The Baixa with its narrow streets and old colonial buildings was situated next to the port, and it was there that my friends and I would spend most of our evenings. And, if the mood took me, I could get a day job on one of the boats that plied the coast and accept my wages in fish once we got back to port, which would provide me and my student friends with dinner: Angola was that kind of place in the old days.

It was an idyllic life, and I would have liked to stay. But the rest of Africa, and, at the end of it, London called.

Interestingly, I had a contact in Luanda that I was urged to visit by a friend back home and his name was Jannie Geldenhuys, who a short while before had been appointed vice-consul at the South African diplomatic establishment in the city.

'Unofficially', as this future head of the defence force told me over dinner on my second night there, he was a major in the South African Army. But Angola, being a province of Portugal, did not have full diplomatic status and military attachés were restricted to Lisbon. Since the war had become a reality and Angola fringed on South West Africa's northern border, somebody in Pretoria thought it a good idea to have somebody there who could keep tabs on the war.

From what I could see, Vice Consul Geldenhuys had a good life in Luanda. He and his wife enjoyed the company of a growing circle of friends, diplomatic and otherwise and a delightful home in the main part of the city. He was to stay at his post for four more years, and another South African military man, Major 'Kaas' van der Waals – today Brigadier General van der Waals (Retired) – was appointed in his place.

'Kaas' went on to write the definitive book on the guerrilla struggle, then steadily edging closer to Luanda; *Portugal's War in Angola: 1961–1974*.[3]

Indeed, when I returned three years after my first meeting with the future General Jannie Geldenhuys – specifically to cover that war and write a book about it – I was taken on a Portuguese Air Force supply mission to one of the beleaguered military bases immediately north of Luanda.

We took off from Luanda International Airport – which doubled as the country's largest air force base – in a creaking old French-built Noratlas transport plane and my first impressions were instructive.

I was surprised that the actual supply drop – about a dozen crates and bags attached to parachutes – were physically hurled out of an open hatch by the loadmaster as we circled several rows of granite hills that were completely surrounded by jungle. All that took place barely 30 minutes flying time out of Luanda's international airport, which meant that hostilities were not that far from the Angolan capital.

Things were obviously getting tough for the Portuguese Army…

Even with the war, life in much of Angola continued much as before. Conflict was restricted very much to the jungle regions adjoining the Congo and to the east, out of the Congo's Katanga and Zambia. None of these regions were economically viable, though the north had been the source of much of Lisbon's hardwood as well as some of its tropical produce. The coffee industry, diamonds, gold, the oil and much else besides were totally unaffected by ongoing hostilities.

During my initial visit, you could not miss the cut and thrust of many of the trading companies active in the interior that made millions for their owners back in Portugal.

The name of the game was exports – commodities like palm oils, cotton, cocoa, timber, tobacco and some of the best coffee to be found anywhere. The Angolan bourgeoisie was born trading in rubber and ivory, in much the way that earlier generations had made their fortunes in the slave trade.

I spent quite a bit of time in a huge metal structure in the city that is still known by its original name, the Palácio de Ferro, or, in English, the Iron Palace. It was originally built by the French engineer Gustave Eiffel, who gave his name to the most famous tower in Paris. In Luanda, this edifice became a kind of home from home to many of the city's artists.

The origins of the place remain shrouded, because it was originally intended for Madagascar, but the ship taking it there sank off Angola's southern desert Coast, from where its modular sections were salvaged and hauled to Luanda.

Much else has changed in Luanda since the Portuguese scarpered back to Europe decades ago. Since then, many Portuguese nationals have returned and the city's population has burgeoned, in large measure because of the 27-year civil war. Luanda is now the third biggest Portuguese speaking city in the world, after Santos and Rio de Janeiro in Brazil and about twice the size of Lisbon.

Just about everything in the country today centres on the oil industry, with Angola having become the second largest producer of crude in Sub-Saharan Africa after Nigeria. As a consequence,

---

3 WS Van der Waals; *Portugal's War in Angola, 1961–1974*, Protea Books, Pretoria, 2011

the country's agricultural sector collapsed, with just about everything given over to burgeoning oil revenues. The year 2016 – with the collapse of the oil price – saw a reversal of those policies...

Another downside is that in 2015, Luanda was declared the most expensive capital in the world, having donned that dubious mantle after it was claimed from Tokyo, which had held it for decades. There are no more hotel rooms for $10 a throw like I enjoyed during my visit in 1965.

These days prices range from $400 upwards, with the run in from the airport likely to cost you $50 or more.

A simple hamburger at one of the fast food joints in Luanda – of which there are many and all thriving – will put you back $15 or more while 100 grams of spaghetti costs $8.

As in the old days, tourism is not encouraged and, again, anyone intending to visit the country will need a jolly good reason for doing so.

The wheel has almost completed its cycle…

Luanda today.

7

Portugal's Armed Forces Against its Guerrilla Adversaries

It was Africa's 'Liberation Wars' of the early 1960s that thrust Portugal firmly into the contemporary era of modern insurgency warfare. By the time the first rebels had crossed into Northern Angola from the Congo, the Vietnam debacle had been on the go for decades, first with Viet-Minh driving out the French, followed by the United States who faced a resolute and determined Viet-Cong.

The argument in revolutionary circles at the time went something along the lines that if the Americans were battling to cope in South East Asia, an impoverished, ill-prepared Portugal would be almost certainly be a walkover in any African insurgency.

The theory was right, but being Africa, its application was a disaster. Lisbon, one of the poorest nations in Europe, held out for twice as long as the American Army in Vietnam, even though *proportionately*, Portugal with its nine million inhabitants, took as many casualties during the course of its African military campaigns as did the Americans in South East Asia.

This series of military campaigns waged halfway across the continent of Africa had numerous facades. The Portuguese colonial war (in Portuguese, the *Guerra Colonial Portuguesa*), was also referred to as the Overseas War (*Guerra do Ultramar*) or in the former colonies as the War of Liberation (*Guerra de Libertação*). In effect, three separate campaigns were fought between Portugal's military and the emerging nationalist movements between 1961 and 1974.

Real conflict took a time to get underway. On January 3 1961, Angolan peasants in the region of Baixa de Cassanje, Malanje, boycotted the Cotonang Company's cotton fields where they worked, demanding better working conditions and higher wages. Cotonang, a company owned by Portuguese, British and German investors used native Africans to produce an annual cotton crop for export abroad. In effect, it was a labour dispute.

The uprising, later to become known as the Baixa de Cassanje revolt, was led by two previously unknown Angolans, António Mariano and Kulu-Xingu. During the protests, African workers burned their identification cards and attacked Portuguese traders.

The Portuguese Air Force responded to the rebellion by bombing 20 villages in the area, allegedly using napalm in attacks that resulted in some 400 indigenous Angolan deaths.

In Angola, the call for revolution was taken up by two insurgent groups, the People's Movement for the Liberation of Angola (MPLA), and the *União das Populações de Angola* (UPA), which soon became the National Liberation Front of Angola (FNLA) in 1962, of which GRAE (*Govêrno revolucionário de Angola no exílio*) was its 'Government in Exile'.

Then both GRAE and MPLA commenced activities in a part of Angola known as the *Zona Sublevada do Norte* (ZSN or the Rebel Zone of the North), consisting of the provinces of Zaire, Uíge and Cuanza Norte.

Throughout the war period Portugal faced increasing dissent, arms embargoes and other punitive sanctions imposed by most of the international community. By 1973, hostilities had become increasingly unpopular due to its length and financial costs, the worsening of diplomatic relations with other United Nations members and the role it had always played as a factor of perpetuation of the entrenched *Estado Novo* (new State) regime as well as the non-democratic status quo.

While the Portuguese pulled their forces out of Africa at the end, these three African military struggles – which started in Angola, followed soon after by Portuguese Guinea and Mozambique – were remarkable, if only because Lisbon managed to hold on for as long as it did.

As we have already seen – and it needs to be stressed to put matters in perspective – the country was fighting uprisings in three different theatres, each thousands of kilometres from home and separated from one other by half the width of the continent. Clearly, the odds were powerfully stacked against Lisbon managing to control things for even a year…

Much of the credit for what follows comes from my colleague John Pike, who originally founded and runs GlobalSecurity.org in Georgetown in the United States. He has clearly devoted a lot of time and effort to compiling his assessments on Lisbon's African campaigns.

I can do no better that use these arguments as the basis for much that took place, because briefly and concisely, Pike shapes developments that would otherwise take volumes to properly elucidate. The American essays a fair and thorough assessment of events.

As GlobalSecurity.com declares on its website, Lisbon based its commitment on its several centuries-long presence in the African territories, regarding them essentially as integral parts of Portugal and totally subject to the Portuguese constitution and supreme authority in the Homeland. Indeed, Portugal believed it had built a multiracial society which was quite different from that of the former colonial powers [in the French, Belgian and British African dominions] and from the white minority governments of the Republic of South Africa, South West Africa and Rhodesia.

The Portuguese were emphatic that their overseas territories were a national heritage which could not be honourably relinquished. Its leaders also believed that they needed these colonies (though in Lisbon colonial implications were rarely allowed to come into play) and their potential wealth and strategic location to maintain the country's international status and its economy.

Except for Portuguese Guinea, the African provinces did offer significant immediate and long term economic returns to certain economic groups in Portugal. Large corporations in the *metrópole* – owned by a few powerful families – controlled virtually all aspects of the territories' modern economic sectors, including local industry, commerce, banking, and plantation agriculture. Indirectly, these entities also had control of a huge source of labour, almost totally dependent on earning a living from one or other of these sectors. There were no labour laws and any form of trade unionism was forbidden by law. Labour unrest, as a consequence, was rare.

The Metropolis received preferential trade treatment, and it controlled the territories' sizeable foreign exchange receipts. But the overall returns were not sufficient to offset the expense of economic development and of fighting the insurgents. Only Angola came close to paying its own way and by 1974 may have been contributing as much as 60 percent to its development and war costs. In the context of the authoritarian system that prevailed for so long, stirrings of dissent were regarded by many observers as unusual.

Since Salazar's time, a group of perhaps 40 families who controlled most of the country's wealth played a decisive role in the exercise of political power. Their position derived from their control of the economy, the actual ownership of news media, representation in the legislative bodies and also their close connection with top government officials. Consequently, government policy reflected the strong conservative political, economic, and social views of this group.

It was a given that their business interests in Portuguese Africa were profitable, immensely so. The 'moneyed-few' long opposed any loosening of Portugal's overseas ties, even though this meant the continuation of a large and expensive military force to counter a series of home-grown revolutions.

At the same time, Portuguese oligarchs – like their Russian counterparts today – were clearly an astute group of businessmen, and with time, would probably have adjusted to a new kind of government relationship with the African provinces. Indeed, many favoured more rapid economic growth and closer association with Europe, and most had already diversified their investments so that their wealth was not dependent solely on what came from Africa.

Portugal's economic ties with Western Europe, which in the period under review had developed more rapidly than its economic links with the African territories, provided an alternative to the African association. This factor would make it easier than before for Portuguese commercial interests to consider alternatives other than in Africa, should the financial burden of hostilities become too burdensome.

To do justice to the Portuguese war effort, one must also examine the role of the communist leaders in Moscow in keeping their African adversaries supplied with most of their military (and other related) needs, in much the same way that the Soviets were the principal suppliers of military hardware to North Vietnam. The figures are staggering and come from a Unites States Marines Corps *Country Study: Angola.*[1]

The report is explicit, declaring that from 1982 to 1986, the Soviet Union delivered military equipment valued at US34.9 billion, 'which represented more than 90 percent of Angola's arms imports and one-fourth of all Soviet arms deliveries to Africa.'

Additionally, 'Poland and Czechoslovakia transferred arms valued at US$10 million and US$5 million, respectively, over the same five-year period.'

During 1987 and 1988, Moscow more than compensated for FAPLA losses [to the South Africans] with accelerated shipments of heavy armaments. In addition to armour, dozens of aircraft, heavy weapons, and air defense systems were delivered.

The report goes on: 'Beyond material deliveries, Moscow and its allies continued to provide extensive technical aid. Soviet military, security, as well as intelligence personnel and advisors who helped establish the defense and security forces and served as advisors at all levels, from ministries in Luanda to major field commands.'

The report provides a good deal of information about the structure of this wherewithal: 'The Soviet Union provided most of the air force pilot and technician training as well as technical assistance in the operation and maintenance of the most advanced equipment: aircraft and warships, major weapons such as missiles, artillery, rockets, and sophisticated radar and communications equipment.'

Also, declares the report, the number of Soviet service members and advisors varied. 'In 1988 it was estimated by most sources to range between 1,000 and 1,500 personnel, including some fighter pilots. UNITA claimed that the Soviet military presence increased during 1988 to 2,500 or 3,000 and that seven officers were assigned to each FAPLA brigade.

---

1 Website – United States Marine Corps, Quantico, Maryland: http://www.marines.mil/News/Publications/ELECTRONICLIBRARY/ElectronicLibraryDisplay/tabid/13082/Article/125400/country-study-angola-click-here-fpts.aspx

A guerrilla group fighting the Portuguese Army is addressed by one of its leaders.
(Photo: Basil Davidson)

The church in the embattled town of Nambuangongo in Angola's *Dembos* (Jungle) region – it was captured by the rebels and briefly served as their headquarters – shortly after it was retaken by government forces. (Photo: Manuel Graça)

Artillery featured strongly in this war very early on, especially attacks on known rebel positions or towns. (Author's collection)

White civilians caught by the rebels were brutally tortured and executed. Rebel leaders were reported by *Agence France Presse* as being overheard that they had fed saw mill managers and their families lengthwise into the blades.

Leopoldville – soon to be renamed Kinshasa – became the focal point of rebel activity in the early days. (Photo: Ares Klootwyk)

It did not take Lisbon long to re-orientate its strategy in countering the rebels. Priority was soon given to training airborne troops. (Photo courtesy of John P Cann)

Radio communications in the early days of hostilities were basic: many units were equipped with equipment that dated from the Second World War. (Author's collection)

The former rebel capital of Nambuangongo from the air after it was recaptured. An enormous number of vehicles were thrown into the fray by Luanda but very little armour: there was almost none available in the early days. (Author's collection)

With hostilities on the increase, the army took increasing numbers of battle casualties. It was only after Alouette III helicopters were acquired from France that more adequate support was provided. (Author's photo)

In neighbouring Congo meanwhile, a full scale uprising necessitated the black leaders hiring white mercenaries to counter the rebels. Constantia's Ares Klootwyk flew fighters for three years and took this photo of refuelling his plane at a jungle airstrip.

One of the touchstones of the 'Liberation Wars' during this early period was the murder of Patrice Lumumba, instigated by the CIA. The Soviets used his death as a rallying point for many years and founded a university named after this political martyr in Moscow. (Author's collection)

'Cuba was the main provider of combat troops, pilots, advisors, engineers, and technicians. As the insurgency war expanded, so did Cuba's military presence.

'By 1982 there were 35,000 Cubans in Angola, of which about 27,000 were combat troops and the remainder advisors, instructors, and technicians. In 1985 their strength increased to 40,000, in 1986 to 45,000, and in 1988 [before a cease-fire was signed with South Africa] to nearly 50,000.

All told, it tells us, more than 300,000 Cuban soldiers had served in Angola since 1975. Angola paid for the services of the Cubans at an estimated rate of US$300 million to US$600 million annually.

One has to look back to the start of the conflict and work through the various phases to place these numbers in some kind of objective viewpoint.

From the earliest days of hostilities, military operations for the Portuguese – in contrast to the insurgents, who had almost no financial problems – were costly both in terms of manpower and in money. When the rebellion began in 1961, Portugal's armed forces numbered 84,000 men, of which less than 30,000 were stationed in Africa.

As the insurgencies spread, figures rose exponentially and ultimately levelled off at around 216,000 in 1973, with more than 150,000 of them serving in Africa.

Although about 60 percent of these forces were from the African territories, the majority black, military service caused a manpower shortage back in the metropolis, aggravated by the emigration of young workers from Portugal to Western Europe. But the situation appeared to have been bearable because the number of soldiers killed in action was relatively low, amounting to about 400 in 1973.

There is no question that Lisbon's military effort in Africa soon became crippling. In 1960 Portuguese defence spending totalled only $105 million [in then-year dollars]. By 1973, the figure had increased almost five-fold, amounting to more than $521 million. As a percentage of the Portuguese national budget, defence expenditures represented 27 percent in 1960, 45 percent in 1966–1968, and 30 percent in 1973.

As a percentage of GNP, defence costs increased from 4.2 percent in 1960 to a high of 7.4 percent in 1968, levelling off at around 6 percent after 1970. This was almost twice the figure for the principal NATO countries, Britain, France and Germany included.

The truth is that the cost factor was high enough to raise serious doubts about Lisbon's long-term chances of retaining its *ultramar* provinces. An upsurge of attacks by black insurgents in Mozambique in January and February 1974 caused serious worries in Lisbon that the internal security problem there might get out of hand. However, the real concern was over the stalemate in Portuguese Guinea where the colonial war was at its worst. There the Portuguese controlled the towns and principal roads, but the guerrillas dominated much of the rest, including the hinterland and some of the offshore islands with neither side able to oust the other.

The situation was discouraging enough to have led some military leaders, such as General António de Spínola [governor and military commander, of Portuguese Guinea from 1968 to 1973], to declare that a military victory was impossible and to urge a political solution, such, as a plan for federation. But such alternatives appealed neither to the far right, nor to the insurgents, who naturally wanted immediate freedom.

On February 22, 1974 General Spinola – then vice chief of staff of the armed forces – published his book *Portugal and the Future*. Its original title was *Portugal e o Futuro*.

Spinola, always outspoken, called for a new Portuguese constitution to provide civil liberties and democratic institutions in all areas administered by the Motherland, and also to create a federation of sovereign states between Portugal and its overseas possessions. Plebiscites to determine whether the Africans wished to remain within the Portuguese ambit would be allowed.

Spinola acknowledged that this policy could risk the eventual severance of all ties between Portugal and its overseas territories, but he did accept this risk in the belief that continuation of past policies would virtually guarantee such an outcome anyway.

As the first major and public challenge to the regime by a high-ranking figure from within the system, Spínola's experience in the African campaigns gave his opinions added weight. The book was widely regarded – a correct assessment as it turned out – as the opening salvo in the general's ambitious campaign to become president.

Rightists were outraged by the public airing of such views and demanded the general's immediate removal along with that of his chief, General Costa Gomes, who supported him. Prime Minister Caetano, who initially resisted this pressure, finally succumbed and removed the two generals. The very conservative General Luz Cunha was appointed to Costa Gomes' post and some officers sympathetic to Spinola were reassigned.

In response, some petitions were circulated in favour of Spinola, and on March 16, 1974 an army unit near Lisbon – led by a group of young officers sympathetic to Spinola and Costa Gomes – attempted to march on Lisbon. They were intercepted and arrested by troops loyal to the government.

By now, the military was deeply divided. Most of the senior officers, led by the new chief of staff of the armed forces, General Luz Cunha, were opposed to General Spinola's ideas which, in their opinion, would lead to the loss of Lisbon's African provinces. These officers participated in a public oath of loyalty to the government, and the refusal of Costa Gomes and Spinola to participate on the grounds that the military were not supposed to be involved in politics was the ostensible reason for their being sacked.

At the same time, there were some high ranking officers who supported Spinola, especially his thesis that a military victory had become impossible. What they did not want was the military becoming a scapegoat for giving up in Africa and they thus viewed his proposals as an honourable way out.

However, it did not appear that these moderates were interested in going so far as to overthrow the government on contentious issues surrounding African policy. Indeed it was not at all clear whether Generals Spinola and Costa Gomes wanted that either. Neither had any known contact with the military regiment that marched on Lisbon and Spinola declared publicly that he was awaiting another military assignment.

A number of junior and middle grade officers also supported Spinola's sentiments. Some were angered enough over his firing and the arrests and reassignments of his supporters to circulate protest petitions. Several even participated in another small-scale march on Lisbon. There were also reports in March and April 1974 of dissent among the military in the African provinces, that apparently aroused the concern of the Directorate of Security. Finally, as we now know, a group of younger officers became attached to an underground organisation, the Armed Forces Movement, staged a putsch and ousted Caetano and company....

General Antonio de Spínola emerged as the titular head of the new government, but not for long because in the minds of some of the young revolutionaries, pumped up with Guevara-like ideals that later proved excessive, Spinola was not radical enough.

But where the coup did succeed, brilliantly it transpired, was that everything happened within a few hours and virtually no bloodshed resulted.

Clearly the nation wished to be rid of the wars being fought in Africa. The Prime Minister and other high-ranking officials of the old regime were arrested and exiled, many to Brazil. The military seized control of all important installations, first in Lisbon and shortly after, in all other cities in the country.

Spínola regarded the military's action as a simple military *coup d'état* aimed at reorganizing the political structure, with himself as the head. It was a *renovação* (renovation) in his words. Within days it became clear that the mutiny had released long pent-up frustrations when thousands – and then tens of thousands of Portuguese – poured into the streets celebrating the downfall of the regime and demanding further change.

The coercive apparatus of the dictatorship – secret police, Republican Guard, official party, censorship – was overwhelmed and abolished. Workers began taking over shops from owners, peasants seized private lands, low-level employees took over hospitals from doctors and administrators, and government offices were occupied by workers who sacked the old management and demanded a thorough housecleaning.

Spínola's position was weakened when he was obliged to consent to the independence of Portugal's African colonies, rather than a bid to achieve the federal solution he had outlined in his book.

Guinea-Bissau gained independence in early September 1974, and talks were underway on the political freedom of the other colonies. Spínola attempted to seize full power in late September but was blocked, and then resigned from office. His replacement was the more moderate General Francisco de Costa Gomes.

The People's Republic of Mozambique became independent in September 1975. A few months after the 'Young Officers' revolutionary government came to power in Lisbon in 1974, it initiated negotiations with several Angolan political factions.

Full independence for what had been Portugal's largest colonial possession was granted on November 11, 1975, setting in train two decades of civil war that followed.

8

South Africa's Air Force Joins in the Fray

Southern African military personnel were involved in Angola and Mozambique while the Portuguese were fighting rear-guard actions to save their African possessions. Rhodesian Special Forces were active in both countries. That followed the deployment of South African helicopter gunships to assist Portuguese troops in Angola. Former South African Air Force Brigadier the late, great Peter 'Monster' Wilkens was among the first to be tasked in this role. His recollection of events follows:

After Operation Blouwildebees in Ovamboland, – adjacent to Southern Angola, where the South African Police assault on Ongulumbashe took place in 1966[1] – South African Air Force elements soon became involved in a low-key security role in south Angola. Essentially, they went in to provide back-up to the Portuguese Air Force: this largely clandestine arrangement survived until 1973, roughly a year before Lisbon pulled out of Africa.

Initially, the main areas of operation involving gunships included northern Namibia, southern Angola and what was then Rhodesia, where SAAF pilots fought alongside their Rhodesian counterparts. The primary instrument for what had earlier been dubbed 'The Chopper Boys' was the venerable Alouette III, a remarkably resilient machine, which, despite being able to take innumerable hits, usually managed to haul their crews and passengers back to base. If a round pierced the helicopter's hydraulics or perhaps removed a rotor blade – and that did occasionally happen – it was another story.

Among these survivors was Dave Atkinson (known as to his buddies as 'Double Dave' or 'Size Twelves', due to his boot size) who once emerged from a significant contact with enemy guerrillas after his chopper had taken more than three dozen AK hits in and around the fuselage and a rotor almost separated from its spar.

---

1   Paul Els: *Ongulumbashe* – Start of the Bush War, Pretoria, 2011.

Brigadier Wilkens continues:

Before the acquisition of Pumas by the SAAF, all military trooping was handled by light utility Alouette III helicopters that Pretoria acquired from the Aerospatiale group in France. A versatile machine, it was small by modern military standards, lacking both space and range. At best, they could handle five plus a crew of two, depending on the amount of kit, weapons and ammunition carried.

America's ubiquitous Bell UH-1 Iroquois – universally known as the Huey and which saw wide service in Vietnam – had a lifting capacity of almost two tonnes, which meant something like 14 troops or six stretchers. It was also the first turbine-powered helicopter to enter production for the US Military with more than 16,000 Hueys built during the course of an unusually lengthy career that began with development in 1952 and production eight years later.

Initially, operational SAAF helicopters were based at the air force base at Ondangua. They were later deployed to positions further afield, including Rundu (on the southern bank of the Okavango River which bordered on Zambia) as well as Katima Mulilo, further towards the east. Operations included stealthy day-time flights into Angola in support of Portuguese ground forces.

Lisbon had its own Alouette IIIs in these areas, but, having to cope with three major wars, their numbers were limited, often severely. As a consequence, the Portuguese Air Force was hard-pressed to meet its military needs. It was axiomatic that the SAAF would be tasked to lend a hand.

The fact was, guerrilla armies then active in South Angola were also South Africa's enemy, and at the time they were giving good support to SWAPO cadres intent on infiltrating southwards into the country that was eventually to become Namibia. It was more or less taken for granted that Lisbon's request for help would elicit a positive response from helicopter wings with combat experience.

There was a catch to the deal (isn't there always?): SAAF operations inside Angola were to remain classified and the media was never to be privy to these developments, though obviously, with some of the hacks moving about those war zones, the machines were sometimes spotted when operational. The usual excuse given when enquiries were made about these 'helicopter gunships' was that there were none and that the 'Alos' were for casualty evacuation.

Also, the heavy machine guns mounted to port were for 'protection', which, of course, those who saw them knew was simply not true.

By the time the SAAF was 'unofficially' deployed into South Angola, the most active anti-Portuguese insurgent movement in that region was Dr Jonas Savimbi's UNITA.

Those who met this guerrilla leader in the flesh coined a range of epithets for someone who was said to know no fear. 'Mercurial' was one, 'dogged' another, while there were those in his own camp who feared him greatly. According to Fred Bridgland, a British journalist who spent time with him at his bush headquarters at Jamba, he was regarded by many of his own people as sometimes extraordinarily irrational.[2]

Based largely in the south-eastern Cuando Cubango province – which lay north of Caprivi – it made good sense to help the Portuguese. That was where we came in…

Because the first Pumas had not yet arrived from France, we were equipped only with our modest little troopers, almost all of them unarmed Alouettes and it remained that way from 1966 to 1969. The Portuguese, in contrast, fielded full-blown gunships – the same Alouette helicopters

---

2 Fred Bridgland: *The War for Africa*, Ashanti Publishers, Johannesburg, 1993.

– but with 20mm cannon facing out the left rear door. We were only to receive our first gunship in the Caprivi in the third quarter of 1969.

I was operating out of Rundu at the time and I clearly remember the strict set of rules with which we were issued on arrival at the base. The thrust was that restrictions imposed by Pretoria severely limited the versatility of the machines we operated under wartime conditions. But, as in most conflicts, the chopper crews had their own way of doing things and we soon figured out ways to get the most out of our whirly-birds.

Bluntly put, South African air crews were not allowed 'to take the war to the guerrillas'. Instead, we were expected to account for every single round of HE (high explosive) fired by us.

The word from Pretoria was that we were only to 'protect our own' and SAAF helicopters were not allowed to engage in any kind of 'seek and destroy' engagement. In short, we were *never* to be the aggressors, which, in wartime, was hogwash. It also demonstrated a complete lack of operational procedures by those making these decisions back home.

We actually doubted if any of those big-wigs – with the single exception of General Dennis Earp, who, with great distinction, had flown Mustang fighters combat in Korea – had ever heard a shot actually fired in retaliation.

Of course, there were ways of circumventing this nonsense. The business ends of our HE rounds were painted green. Portuguese ones, in contrast, were orange and yellow, which made them easily distinguishable from each other.

But we soon became aware that Portuguese aircrews had a singular weakness, which was the need for good South African wines, of which we had a lot. It wasn't long before we established a primitive barter system that involved trading a good bottle of wine for so many rounds of Portuguese HE: thank you very much…

That done, our gunners would insert scrounged Portuguese high explosive rounds into their ammo belts and leave a distinctive gap before inserting our own rounds, which ensured that the weapon stopped firing before our own rounds came into play. In a really hot contact, a quick pull by the gunners to re-load their heavy machine-gun was a formality and the fire-fight would continue. We ended up using a lot less of our own ammunition to achieve the same result.

At the same time, ball or solid 20mm rounds were also studiously hoarded. Because we were officially allowed to use them for target practice, they were more freely available than HE rounds, so we guarded our supplies of ball ammunition as well, and for very good reason.

We had long been made aware of the fact that in the kind of heavily wooded country we encountered in areas where the Portuguese forces were active, HE would explode on contact with tree branches, often well short of the intended target sheltering below. Obviously, that achieved few results. But by inserting ball rounds into the ammo belts, we had excellent penetration. Though not spectacular, ball ammo was very effective against an enemy using clumps of trees and forest cover to hide.

Interestingly, this was a lesson we used in later years, when 20mm ball ammunition would easily penetrate the hulls of armoured vehicles like Soviet BRDMs and BTRs whenever they were deployed by the Soviets against South African forces.

Our choppers were also used to torch guerrilla camps by using our Very Pistols. Every Alouette had at least one of these signal guns, ostensibly supposed to be used for rescue purposes.

My first border trip was scheduled for a combined strike – ground forces and air – that was launched in September 1966, but I had a problem with my ears and was grounded for the duration. The result was that I only experienced my first operational 'bush tour' after I'd returned to Ondangua in May 1967. It lasted more than two months, the first of many.

Over a three year period, I completed more than two dozen postings to the Operational Area, some as long as three months and others, mostly on Pumas, for perhaps a week. More than a thousand of my operational hours were on Alouettes, with about 300 on Pumas. The first really 'hot' operations to which I was subjected came in 1968, when we were supposed to act solely in a supportive role for the Portuguese.

While our troopers were initially not armed, they were later fitted with light machine-guns for self-protection. Additionally, our flight engineer carried an automatic rifle, whereas the pilots would take a 9mm pistol as well as a hand machine carbine (HMC), or perhaps an Israeli Uzi on board.

We would load up a couple of eager-for-combat Angolan soldiers – usually commandos or Airborne Forces, termed *Grupos Especiais Pára-Quedistas* in local lingo – and they would lead us in the general direction of what they would claim were 'known' insurgent camps. It was all very much a hit-or-miss affair. Once arrived, in theory, we were required to circle overhead while the Portuguese gunships would go straight in. Frankly, this wasn't our idea of fighting a war and the SAAF crews wouldn't waste much time before also getting involved.

The upshot was that there was a good deal of illegal firing from our choppers, which often included the pilots who would sometimes join in the fray. Most of the 'Fly Boys' quickly mastered the art of keeping the cyclic stick between their knees steady and firing at the enemy from their little side windows with their hand machine carbines.

But these were still early days in the bush war and the guerrillas rarely looked overly-threatening, which meant, that we usually had things our own way because this was no Vietnam. When the enemy did fire back, it was invariably inaccurate and usually 'blind': firing their guns over their shoulder while on the run.

Their first mistake was actually to display their weapons, so we knew exactly which individuals running about below us needed to be picked off…

On these cross-border operations into South Angola, we usually set out of Rundu with a squadron of six Alouettes.

Five of the troopers would form into a 'V' or 'Vic' formation, though this was customarily quite loose, individual choppers being a kilometre or more apart throughout the flight. The lone gunship would slot in behind this formation, riding shotgun and keeping all the troopers in view. Because of weapons and the amount of ammunition on board, this helicopter was much heavier than the others and also the slowest. It was left to its pilot to call a power setting for the leader to use.

Progress once across the Okavango River and northwards into the vast and almost featureless Angolan landscape was sometimes very slow, especially when our machines were still heavy with fuel. Returning to base half-empty in contrast, was a breeze. In-between, we billeted at established Portuguese bases in the interior.

The weight problem was a consistent problem, as the ops were usually three weeks long and we needed to take along with us just about everything we might need. Another problem was the shortage – in some areas, the non-existence – of drinking water and most times we had to take our own. For weight reasons, this was usually limited to a five-gallon canister per crew member.

With the crew, their clothes and water for three weeks, as well as the 20mm cannon and up to 480 rounds of ammunition, weight was a perennial problem. Maximum fuel to keep the gunship within limits was usually 600 pounds (60 percent) for ops. But due to the shortage of infrastructure in Angola, one needed at least that much for the heavy ferry flights too, so flying out of Rundu we were always overweight.

The legs between refuelling points were each about an hour-and-a-half's flying time.

Map of colonial Angola in 1961, and below, during their almost-500 years in Africa the Portuguese constructed many forts and castles in their colonies, the very first at Cacheu in Portuguese Guinea (right) and later on Ibo Island, Mozambique. (Author's photos)

Top left: The Congo soon became a focal point for early explorers after sovereignty treaties were signed with tribal kings. (Author's photo) **Top Right:** One of the beautiful ivory statues pulled off a shipwreck by Cape diver Charlie Shapiro. **Middle Right:** The Caravels that took Portuguese navigators around Africa were tiny by today's standards and manned by possibly 35 men. **Below:** Salvage diver Peter Sachs with a cannon taken off the Portuguese East Indiaman *Senhora da Atalaia do Pinheiro* in the Eastern Cape.

Above: Munster's map of Africa dating from 1554 is one of the earliest and shows just how little was known of the continent. *Fortaleza de São Miguel* fortress. **Below**, was built by the Portuguese overlooking Luanda Bay in 1634. (Author's photo)

Top left and immediately below: The first *Padrao* (stone cross) was erected in 1485 as a landmark by Portuguese navigators at Cape Cross in present-day Namibia. (Author's photos) **Top right and middle**: By the time the war started in Angola, neighbouring Congo was grappling with rebellion which necessitated bringing in South African mercenaries. (Photos Ares Klootwyk) **Below:** Portuguese troops on convoy duty. (Author's photo)

PORTUGAL É SENSACIONAL

Top left: Mercenaries flew CIA supplied WW2-era bombers to counter rebel advances in the Congo in the 1960s. **Below:** a Portuguese soldier uncovers a Soviet mine. **Top Right:** Postcard from 1960s Luanda and below that, Cape Point, South Africa, the ultimate Soviet target never realised. **Middle:** Much of Luanda's architecture reflected structures in Lisbon or Oporto. **Bottom:** An Angolan Escudo banknote from the colonial epoch.

Two photos from Angola's air war against the insurgents from military historian John P Cann. **Top**: Portuguese Air Force Harvard returns to base after strikes in the interior and **Below**, French-built Puma helicopters only entered service in Africa fairly late in the conflict.

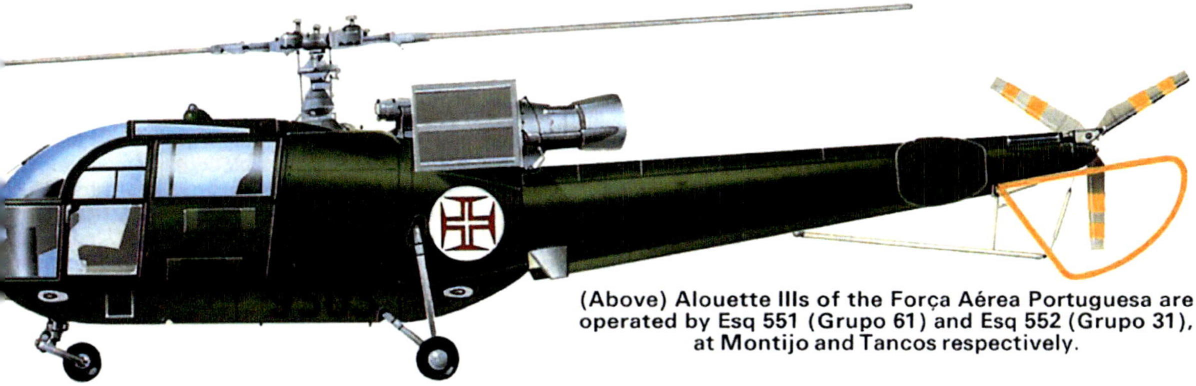

Top: Mainstay almost from the start of the colonial war in Angola was the small but versatile Alouette III, deployed as a gunship and troop-uplifter. (Photo source unknown) **Middle Left:** Improvised tank deployed by mercenary forces in the Congo. **Middle Right:** Gunner's view of the *Dembos* (jungle) north of Luanda. **Bottom:** Two Mercenary commanders from 4 Commando *Force Katangaise* in the Congo with Colonel Bob Denard on the left.

Above: Landmines exacted a terrible toll among Portuguese forces during the course of the guerrilla struggle. Lisbon never really got to grips with the problem as did the South Africans and, to a lesser extent, the Rhodesians. A Soviet TM-46, precursor of the far more deadly TM-57 did the damage here. **Below:** As the war progressed, more African troops joined colonial forces to counter the insurgent threat. (Author's photos)

Above: As hostilities in Angola progressed, tactics – as well as weapons – became more sophisticated and eventually involved artillery strikes in regions north of Luanda where the fighting could sometimes be quite intense. **Below:** A military parade in Luanda took place on the morning the author arrived in Angola to cover the war. National holidays were celebrated with much pomp and ceremony.

Bombing up, Luanda airport **Top left** and **Right**, the ubiquitous French-built Panhard Reconnaissance Armoured Vehicle deployed with road convoys in the Angolan interior. **Middle Left:** Captain Ricardo Alcada, the author's escort officer while in the north of the country. **Middle Right:** Colonial troops on parade in the interior. **Immediately below:** Bush ops with an Alouette gunship. **Bottom:** Ragged band of insurgents undergoing training in the Congo.

Top left: As the Angolan war progressed, the South Africans started gearing up for their own conflict along their frontiers. SWA (Spes) forces were among the first to include black soldiers within their ranks. (Author's photo)
Top Right: In Angola's north the terrain was tropical, often waterlogged and sometimes extremely harsh: hardly ideal for fighting a guerrilla war. (Photo Peter Wilkins)
Below: South African military base in Sector 10. **Middle Left:** Eland armoured cars patrol Caprivi's roads early on. **Right:** Troops destroy a cache of food uncovered in a cross-border follow-up raid. **Bottom:** The partially destroyed border post at Oshikango. (Author's photos)

Top Left: Portuguese Air Force Noratlas transport aircraft used throughout the war. **Below:** SAM-7 hand-held MANPADS issued to the guerrillas by the Soviets. **Top Right:** Satellite view of Lobito harbour. **Immediately Below:** Bush ops with gunships in support. **Middle Left:** Harvard T-6s on operations in Angola (with Luanda in background). **Bottom:** Remote bush airstrip in Eastern Angola with a Noratlas taking off (Photos: *Forca Aerea Portuguesa*)

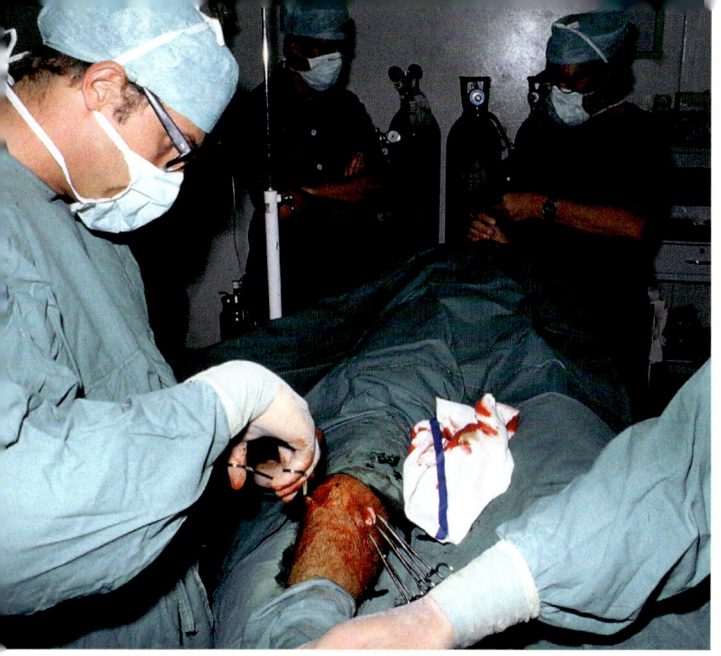 

Top Left: South African surgeons remove shrapnel from the leg of a wounded soldier at Oshakati Military Hospital in Sector 10. **Right:** Memorial to the founder of the MPLA Agostinho Neto. **Middle:** American-built jet fighters at Luanda Airport. (Photo: *Forca Aerea Portuguesa*) **Bottom Left:** The Angolan flag – with distinct Marxist hammer and sickle motif - hoisted after the Portuguese had been expelled. **Bottom Right:** Portuguese troops on a Unimog truck ready to move into the interior. (Author's collection)

Left: Special forces operations in north Angola involving French-built Puma helicopters. (Photo: Forca Aerea Portuguesa)
Middle Left: Landmines were a perpetual problem for the defenders. (Author's photo)
Right: Burnt-out Cuban-manned APC caught in an ambush during Op Savannah.
Bottom: Massive UNITA parade in south-east Angola towards the end of the Border War.

Top left: Bush ops in Eastern Angola. **Middle:** General Antonio de Spinola did offer an option to end the war but was eventually thwarted by some of his followers. **Top Right:** A Savimbi poster spread about the country by UNITA that offered supporters hope. **Middle Right:** Bush operations were tenuous when the army did not react promptly. Any delay meant the enemy had fled by the time security forces arrived. **Below:** A Portuguese Air Force pilot in the cockpit of a US-supplied F-86 jet at Luanda Airport just back from a strike on a guerrilla base. These fighters played a useful ground support role, especially in the earlier phase of hostilities. **Bottom Left:** 'Carnation Revolution' Lisbon's 'Young officer' billboard. **Bottom right:** Marines on operations in the interior. (Photo: *Revista Militar*)

Top: One of Angola's national banks trashed in the southern town of Ongiva prior to the South African Army arriving. (Author's photo) **Bottom**: Senior military officers gather in Lisbon shortly after the army mutiny which ousted the government had taken place. General de Spinola is seated in the middle with Admiral Costa Gomes, president of the revolutionary junta to his left. Behind the admiral stands Captain Vitor Alves, one of the original planners of the military putsch.

Portuguese F-86s gave good accounts in ground-support roles in Angola. In Portuguese Guinea, Lisbon was forced by Washington not to use these jets in the war. (Photo: *Forca Aerea Portuguesa*)

Portuguese commandos going into action from an Alouette in dense bush country.
(Photo: *Forca Aerea Portuguesa*)

Personal photo of one of the pilots.

Portuguese air crew on the wing of one of the T-6 Harvards.

In Angola's south, the terrain often levels out into savannah grasslands. (Author's photo)

The *Forca Aerea Angola* emblem.

Carlos Santos took this photo of an Alouette at one of the air bases in the interior.

Airlifting the wounded back to civilisation. (Photo: *Forca Aerea Portuguesa*)

SOUTH AFRICA'S AIR FORCE JOINS IN THE FRAY 133

From Pierre Gillard's photo collection: operational Alouettes in Angola.

PAF Dornier. (Courtesy of John P Cann)

Most of our ops in Angola were pre-planned between the Portuguese army officers at the camps from which we operated and our SAAF Air Liaison Officer or ALO, usually a major who was based in Angola with the Portuguese at Cuito Cuanavale.

The usual scenario was to fly troops into specific areas, close, but not too close, to known guerrilla camps. If the choppers ventured near to an enemy group and were heard approaching by our adversaries the operation could be compromised, in which case the guerrilla camp would be found deserted. Or, the troops could disembark into an ambush, which sometimes also happened. Most of our initial trooping consequently was not into heavily contested combat zones: that came with later Rhodesian ops and when the Angolan war escalated after Lisbon had decided to call it a day on the African continent.

Nonetheless, in those early forays 'into the interior', occasional shots were fired at us and the odd bullet-hole punched into an Alouette.

I was only hit once and didn't know about it until after we'd touched down back at base; a bullet-hole was discovered in the panel behind the fuel tank. Fortunately nothing vital was struck. In fact, we hadn't even been aware that there were guerrillas in the area during that sortie! One of our pilots, Geoff Clark, was shot in the thumb, but none of our Alouettes were downed by enemy fire in the early days.

However, we were required to operate in an environment of 'ever-present danger', with the gunship pulling ahead prior to the landing, to seek out a safe-looking landing zone or LZ. If an enemy presence was detected, it would be its job to flush them out.

Because weight was the critical factor, wind direction was important, which meant that when the troopers were on a long approach, the gunship would drop a smoke grenade into the intended area, give the lead trooper his LZ, wind direction and speed and allow him to make the necessary adjustments.

Drops were usually done beyond the tree line, as the choppers were usually too heavy for hover landings. Open ground between the trees and the many rivers in south-east Angola was usually suitable for getting five troopers into a landing. That meant they were in reasonably close proximity to one another, essentially to make sure ground forces were not too spread out once down.

The technique for landing, especially when heavy and while dropping troops, was to use whatever help was available. For instance, smoke grenades were an accurate indication of the wind, but the actual landings needed to be well timed: each chopper took advantage of the previous helicopter's down-wash, essentially to conserve fuel. As one machine landed, its down-wash would sometimes become a bit of an up-wash and add impetus to the wind factor; if the chopper behind had its timing right, wind factor would be increased and that would allow for an easier landing and use less fuel.

The guys with whom we were in operation were solid professionals: pilots like Hobart Houghton, Johan Ströh, Glen Williams, Gary Barron and Fritz Pieksma. They would get their timing spot-on and an entire drop would go off so smoothly and quickly that the gunship needed a single circuit before there were 20 soldiers deposited safely onto firm ground – literally within 30 seconds or so.

There were some difficult moments. Occasionally, on arrival over the LZ, one or two choppers would find there were obstructions on the ground, like tree stumps or possibly an anthill. For the troops this would necessitate deplaning while in the hover. Because speed was of the essence and there was often a chopper right behind you – also wanting to get airborne immediately the job was done – we practised for this eventuality.

Our flight engineers – who doubled as our gunners – taught the troops to slide open the side doors on final approach. This was done by way of hand signals, essentially showing both thumbs in a repeated reverse movement. The next signal was similar, but with thumbs pointed outwards – in other words, 'get the hell out'.

The regular Portuguese soldier, a youthful conscript, and many of them still in their teens, were really all that stood between Lisbon winning or losing everything in Africa.

Prior to being sent out to serve their two-year terms of military service, which, in the remote African context could be pretty demanding and rigorous, the majority had hardly been aware that the 'Dark Continent' even existed. Never mind that their country dominated several very substantial chunks of it that, cumulatively, were dozens of times the size of their home country.

Unlike Angola – and Mozambique with a coastline that stretched more than a couple of thousand kilometres along the East African coast – Portuguese Guinea (Guiné-Bissau today) should have been small fry.

But conditions there, in a terrain composed mainly of low-lying mangrove swamps and semi-habitable jungle were among the harshest of all the African postings. Also, Amilcar Cabral's PAIGC was way ahead the most determined and enterprising of all of Lisbon's enemies, in large part because the country was tiny and Moscow kept his insurgents very well supplied with the most modern weapons – including SAM missiles.

In Angola, for us, it was clear that apart from the odd exception, these youngsters weren't really interested in what was clearly a colonial conflict, with Lisbon seeking to dominate huge swathes of the African continent.

Few of these young fellows were looking for a fight and some were so inexperienced in bush craft that they could quite easily misread the map and trek away from the targeted insurgent camp instead of towards it after being put down by our choppers. That naturally meant that pick-ups after the supposed 'fire-fight' required dollops of patience and, often enough, extra fuel, so that a search could sometimes be conducted to find the troops who were nowhere near the designated LZ.

Those were all boys from the *metrópole*, as it was customarily phrased, and meant, of course, the Metropolis, or Europe.

Troops who hailed from Angola itself – those soldiers who were born in Africa – in contrast, were very different. Black and white, they had a stake in the country for which they were battling. Also, they knew their Africa and were aware that if they didn't counter subversion, they'd be out of it, very much like South African troops who followed in their wake not long afterwards in South West Africa.

'Home grown' Angolan troops were usually either Commandos – sometimes *Comandos Africanos* – or Airborne: they were proud of what they did and invariably meant business. We could immediately see that they were a pretty handy bunch of fighters who enjoyed getting into a scrap. As with Portuguese chopper pilots with whom we operated, they simply relished their bits of combat, especially since they always had a gunship or two hovering nearby to add something to the outcome.

Also, their basic intelligence was invariably more reliable than the kind of information provided by regular Portuguese army officers with whom we came into contact. Like the conscripts under them, their only interest was in staying alive: if they could avoid confrontation, they would take the gap.

Many of the contacts that resulted with elite Portuguese units were sporadic. Some would last minutes, others perhaps half an hour. No matter how long, there were usually a number of dead or wounded enemy troops left on the ground after their compadres had fled. So, with the pick-up effected, we'd head back to base with our satisfied 'customers', together with a variety of booty acquired by them, usually firearms and the inevitable AK bayonet.

This practice was almost always frowned upon by the Portuguese army officers back at base because it wasn't part of their 'plan'. But the ebullient Portuguese chopper pilots would be quite adept at calming things down and eventually singing everyone's praises for what happened during this 'sudden and unexpected' occurrence of 'discovering' a guerrilla camp 'somewhere out there in the bush.'

Our main base of operations in the Cuando Cubango region of Angola was the town of Cuito Cuanavale, not long afterwards to become a major staging post for FAPLA, the military wing of the Marxist MPLA. That came after the country had been handed over as a one-party state to the newly-formed Luanda government – without elections or a referendum – by the departing Portuguese, thanks in large part to the card-carrying member of the Communist Party Admiral Rosa Coutinho, the appropriately-named 'Red Admiral'.

In all the campaigns in which we South Africans were involved in Angola, the Portuguese Air Force fielded some great pilots and also quite a few characters unblinkingly brave and totally dedicated to their cause. One example was a fellow by the name of Vidal, who seemed to have the inordinate ability to find enemy camps in the kind of bush country that seemed to go on uninterrupted from one horizon to the next.

We were operating from Cangamba when one morning he got up from the breakfast table and moments later all but fell over. We knew he'd had a touch of malaria but weren't aware that it was quite so serious. The man could barely stand unaided. Still, this didn't deter him from heading out to the airstrip, getting into his Alouette and heading out into the bush. The operation that day was a marked success, in large part due to Vidal's efforts at egging on his own pilots: there were dozens of enemy killed and lots of captures.

Vidal was a remarkable character, always ready for a scrap. Our Cessna had flown me in to Cangombe before an operation to assist in the planning, which was when I met him for the first time. Some operations would last a week or two and then the Portuguese squadron from Luso, the *Saltimbancos*, would take over from us for another few weeks, or vice versa.

On one occasion, when a group of Portuguese officers were busy with an operation I popped in, but everything seemed to be pretty quiet. As it happened, the day had turned into a proverbial 'Lemon'.

Meantime, Vidal and another pilot by the name of 'Jailbird' – so-called by his colleagues because, with his head shaved clean, his mates thought he resembled an Alcatraz inmate – were convinced that the planners – all of them 'full-time Jam Stealers' from Portugal – were not really interested in 'mixing' it with the enemy. It was actually not difficult to sense the reticence of these backroom boys: they were very much more were interested in getting back to the mess at the end of their shifts and the grog that would be waiting.

Undettered, Vidal offered to take me up in his Alouette gunship, for what he termed would be 'an armed recce'!

In a discreet briefing after the planning session, he said that he had a bit of surprise for me, because he'd had info about a large insurgent camp not very far into the interior and he was eager that he and Jailbird hit it with their two gunships before dark. The troopers would come in afterwards, he confided.

Initially, he said, there would be just the two of us, plus Jailbird and his gunner. Those flying the trooping choppers believed that they were heading out on a routine reconnaissance mission. As the Portuguese gunships always ranged far ahead of the troopers, Vidal felt confident that nothing would seem amiss.

Once in the air, Vidal suggested that I fly his gunship, while he took up a position behind the gun. At least, that is what he told his colonel. So we got airborne and were on our way to the LZ for the 'dead' drop, when Vidal steered me off to the left, away from the troopers. About 20 minutes later we arrived over the camp.

This was no ordinary insurgent base, I soon discovered. From what I could see from where we were perched, it was actually a very large and well laid army base nestling in what seemed to a fairly secure position under the trees. There were even some rather untypical benches – probably for 'lectures' which was a feature of all guerrilla bases in Angola, only this facility suggested that there were an awful lot of 'students'.

Once the target had been confirmed, the turkey shoot began.

We were much lower than the usual 800 feet (on Vidal's insistence) and yes, as he'd enthusiastically declared earlier, it was a lot easier to pick up and knock off targets from lower down.

But that wasn't the problem: finding targets for us to shoot at was, as very few, if any of the guerrillas, fired back. In fact, we couldn't clearly make out much of value on the ground from where we hovered. Still, it was a job that had to be done.

One of the guerrillas, obviously a good deal braver than the rest, actually did shoot at us, but from the cover provided by one of the larger forest trees. So Vidal called in Jailbird, who took the recalcitrant out from the other side. Otherwise Jailbird did his own thing – there was more than enough room to do so – while Vidal and I went after a few other options including stragglers heading for thick bush.

The idea was that at some stage I would take my turn behind the gun, but by now Vidal seemed that he'd forgotten what we'd planned. Then I took the helicopter into a clearing and landed and he quickly got the message. But by then it was almost over: we were out of ammunition and the troopers had been called in to land the troops whose job it was to 'clean up'. A stack of documents and weapons were uncovered and loaded on board. They also took back several prisoners.

The operation that day was certainly far more successful than any of the other 'official' operations I witnessed while I spent time with the Portuguese. But, of course, I was not 'officially' involved and I'm certain that Vidal and Jailbird got a massive rocket for their enterprise from their commander.

Looking back, it was obvious that the entire effort was makeshift and planning was consequently pretty damn poor. For the rest of the 10 days our six Alouettes worked with the Portuguese, we plucked only lemons.

Clearly, at the behest of Vidal and 'Jailbird', they'd got the message and moved further into the bush.

One of the fixed-winged aircraft fielded by the Portuguese Air Force in Angola and its other African military theatres was the Lockheed PV – referred to in Angolan pilot-talk as the 'Pee-Vee'. It had a reputation of good power in reserve and versatility, which one might expect from the Americans, who had given the planes to Lisbon in the first place.

But, said one of the Portuguese aviators: 'beware the high wing loading if you have an engine cut.'

We were at Cuito once, when a PV was doing engine run-ups prior to going on a bombing raid. Initially, whenever the throttle was opened up, the starboard engine kept backfiring. Then the technicians would shut it down, work on it some more and fire it up again.

This rigmarole was repeated several times and went on until the pilot arrived, resplendent in a magnificent blood-red silk scarf and flying overalls that were so well pressed that he might have been heading out for a night on the town.

A few more adjustment followed, this time with him at the controls. Then the other PV started up as well. That meant that we all congregated at the edge of the runway for what was certain to be an 'Occasion'. We watched with great interest as the bomb-laden PVs rolled away for an uphill – into the wind – take-off.

The 'good' plane dutifully waited for the 'ailing' aircraft to go first, which it did, after a perfunctory final engine run-up before rolling. Then, to nobody's surprise, the first backfire sounded, just as the tail came up. There was a little wiggle at the far end of the runway, the plane went tail down again and finally its engines opened up with a roar.

After three more backfires the pilot got himself and his plane airborne, followed soon afterwards by his wingman. In echelon, they turned into the sun and headed out on their raid, obviously well-aware that we were all watching.

Everything must have gone off as expected, because the two Harpoons were back at the base within an hour, gun-ports whistling and pilots smiling proudly. Their mission had obviously been successful

The PVs carried an impressive array of weapons, not all of them standard. There might be a mixture of anything from .303 and .50 Browning to 7.62mm NATO and 12.7mm guns – all stuck away in the nose of the plane. Several times I did a count once and found that there could be anything from six to a dozen guns per PV, depending on availability. These were also taped before departure, but once used, would whistle gaily to herald the standard beat-up after a raid.

When the pilot of one of these large, noisy airframes swaggered up to his audience afterwards, we asked him whether the thought or the possibility of an engine cut on take-off – uphill, with a sick, backfiring motor – didn't worry him.

'Oh no!' he said in fractured English. 'Long runway and if I 'ave an 'undred knots, it is no problem!'

Cost Analysis of 'Operation Bombay' in Respect of Support to the Portuguese Armed Forces (Period Covered from June 1968 to December 1969)

The South African Air Force has been supporting the Portuguese in east and south-east Angola in a direct and indirect capacity since June 1968.

1. **Direct Capacity:** By direct support is implied, flights done against the enemy or flights done in a direct supporting role: e.g. flying in POL and supplies to security forces.
2. **Indirect Support:** By indirect support is meant flights done to support No.1 Air Component in its task of supporting the Portuguese.
3. **Basis of Calculations:**
    a) **Flying Costs:** Flying costs have been calculated on the cost per basic flying hour as at 1967 + 7% allowance for escalation costs, a conversion factor for the aircraft type: e.g. Basic flying hour in 1967 was R198.38. Thus R198.38 × 7% = R212.26 the conversion factor for the Alouette III is 1.4. Therefore one Alouette flying hour costs R212.26 × 1.4 = R297
    b) **Accident Costs:** Accident costs are based on the price paid for the aircraft less depreciation for hours flown.
4. **Flying Hour Costs:** The following table shows the flying hours done by type of aircraft in direct and indirect support of the Portuguese in Angola and the costs involved:

Aircraft Type	Conversion factor applied to R212.26	Hours flown on Direct support	Hours flown on Indirect support	Costs in Rands
Alouette III	1.4	4350.05		1,291,950
Cessna	0.5	2015.15		213,590
Super-Frelon	5.5	76.05		91,026
Harvard	0.7	124.15		18,352
Canberra	5.4	183.55		210,854
Dakota	2.2	262.30		122,821
Dakota (Ind)	2.2		534.05	249,378
C130	8.0		34.15	57,732
Totals		7013.25	568.20	2,255,713

TOP SECRET

It was not long before South African Air Force C-130 transport aircraft were making regular runs between Waterkloof air base in Pretoria and the Operational Area, ferrying men and equipment to areas where the effects of an upcoming insurgency had begun to be felt (Photo: Dean Wingrin)

9

The South African Army Moves In

While all these political shenanigans were going on in and around Luanda – as well as in the interior where the different factions were jockeying for power – South Africa briefly stood on the sidelines, uncertain how to react. Already fighting what was then still a low-key insurgency of its own against **SWAPO**, a home-grown liberation group, Pretoria was fearful that the **MPLA** – the major Soviet surrogate force in the region – might achieve dominance. If that were to happen, it was argued, then **SWAPO** would become a much more serious threat.

Within the upper echelons of the South African Defence Force, there were a series of debates for doing something – *anything* – to counter the MPLA's encroaching influence in Angola.

You needed only a fundamental understanding of the politics of the country to see that this Marxist/Leninist organisation (jump-started into a position of prominence by the radical Portuguese Admiral Rosa Coutinho) was on the verge of taking over the country. That would happen when independence was formally ceded on December 11, 1975.

Obviously, the South African cabinet was drawn into the melee, with those in favour of some kind of military action in the majority: this was very much when South African politicians constantly warned about discovering 'a communist under every bed'.

What these sentiments clearly suggested was that some kind of military action to prevent this happening was essential: it would involve sending the army into Angola to counter Aghostino Neto's aspirations of creating a communist state.

But, as some of the wiser counsels pointed out, it was not quite so simple: South Africa was not on a war footing, nor had it been for decades. The last time the SADF had seen any real conventional military action was during the Second World War and going into Angola in force would clearly involve at least some kind of armoured support, which it didn't have.

South African intelligence operatives – including quite a few former Portuguese security operatives like Oscar Cardoso who had worked for PIDE – had been keeping tabs on recent developments in Angola, including the unexpected arrival of several thousand Cubans, almost all of them military.

While the majority of Havana's forces were inexperienced, a number had seen action in Vietnam and still more with Arab forces against Israel in the Yom Kippur War. Of the 500 Cubans sent to fight in Syria as 'tank commanders' (obviously at the behest of the Soviets), a disproportionate number were killed in action against the IDF. Thereafter, Cuban contingents were involved with the Polisario Front in the Western Sahara.

Details of Cuban involvement in the Vietnam War against the Americans were published in an edition of *Juventud Rebelde*, a newspaper put out by the Union of Young Communists of Cuba. It carried an interview with Roberto León González, a retired colonel of Cuba's Revolutionary

Armed Forces (FAR) about his participation in a secret Cuban 'Internationalist Mission' with the North Koreans between 1973 and 1975. This was under the supervision of Commander Raúl Díaz Argüelles of the FAR's '10th Directorate'.[1]

According to American writer John Hoyt Williams, writing in the *Atlantic Monthly*, by 1973 Cuban military advisors and instructors could be found in the Middle East, probably earlier, often in combat roles. Hundreds of Cubans served in unstable Marxist South Yemen, not only instructing the Yemeni armed forces but also training Dhofari guerrillas, who were busily destabilizing Oman. The guerrillas were finally overcome by elite British units after years of low-intensity but bitter fighting.[2]

One of the first choices for possibly doing anything operational fell to Brigadier-General Willem (Kaas) van der Waals who was airborne-trained but then still a lieutenant-colonel in the South African Army. He had been directly involved in Angola during the colonial period while seconded to the Department of Foreign affairs as a Vice Consul at the South African Consulate General in Luanda. It was to be accepted that he would be regarded as a likely conduit for some kind of action.

There were several reasons, the first being that that officer had intimate knowledge coupled to several years experience of Angola. Also, the man was familiar with many of the players who had remained after the bulk of the Portuguese Army returned to Europe (a small force remained in the country until the actual handover took place). To cap it, he was fluent in Portuguese.

On his return to South Africa and shortly after the Lisbon military putsch, he was ordered by Major General Constand Viljoen, then Director General Operations of the SADF's General Staff, to go back to Angola, this time on a totally different mission.

As this brigadier-general told me, what was not yet known to him was that his government – including the South African Defence Force – was intensely involved in international discussions with regard to the future of the former Portuguese colony. That included contact with the CIA (whose directorate was just as alarmed as Pretoria at the way the Marxist MPLA was handling things) as well as the future role of the Congolese President Mobuto Sese Seko in what was obviously going to be a civil war.[3]

Others in that category were Angola's rebel leaders Holden Roberto, who headed the FNLA, as well as UNITA's Dr Jonas Savimbi.

By this stage Savimbi was no longer regarded by the South Africans as an adversary. Vigorously opposed to the MPLA (and by now receiving American military help) UNITA had become a potentially useful ally in whatever military action lay ahead. As the saying goes, the enemy of my enemy is my friend and in Africa that has currency.

Also, whatever happened, Savimbi's future – and that of his guerrilla movement – lay on the line, rather precariously as it was to emerge. Essentially, the idea was to mobilise support for pro-Western Angolan liberation movements in a bid to counter Cuban and Soviet gains in a country that had swung hard left.

As Van der Waals wrote in his subsequently published report, the overall plan – as stated by General Constand Viljoen – was to prevent a Portuguese handover of power to Angola's Pro-Soviet MPLA.

The brigadier-general takes up the story:

---

1   *The Militant*, Havana, Cuba, Vol 69/No 20: May 23, 2005.
2   John Hoyt Williams, 'Cuba, Havana's Military Machine', *The Atlantic Monthly*, August 1988.
3   Personal interview and unpublished manuscript on his role in Task Force Zulu.

The first time we discussed my new role, General Viljoen characteristically played straight cards. He asked me whether I'd personally like to become involved in recovering and maintaining the traditional areas of influence of the two western-oriented movements and if so, where?

My options were basic, he stated: I would either be linked to Holden Roberto's FNLA in the north, where they received most of their support from the Americans through the Congo or alternatively, in Angola's central regions where UNITA was most active. The choice was mine.

As a matter of principle I was almost totally opposed to involvement with the FNLA given their murderous actions from March to May 1961. All that, coupled to a dismal insurgency record, weak leadership, and their present status – being mainly the trumped-up consequences of the CIA-backed American propaganda machine – didn't make for a persuasive option.

A week later I would become directly involved in the South African Defence Force's largest military operation for 30 years.

By now too, preparations were in hand for what was to become known as Operation Savannah, a full-scale invasion of South Angola by the South African Defence Force.

This was not as unusual a development as some would have thought: the South African Air Force had already been involved in counter-insurgency operations in the south of the country for some time (as detailed earlier by Brigadier-General 'Monster' Wilkins) and Pretoria had a fairly good understanding of what things were like there.

Operation Savannah was to be the first full-scale cross-border operation of the bush war, at the time a very substantial undertaking. Strictly covert, it would involve four South African Army battle groups: Foxbat, Zulu, Alfa and Bravo, together with as much air support as could be mustered at short notice.

Their role, it was clearly laid out by Pretoria, would be to support the pro-Western Freedom movements then active against Luanda's Marxist-orientated MPLA in the immediate period prior to independence. A secondary role would be to clear SWAPO, together with its military wing PLAN (Peoples Liberation Army of Namibia), out of southern Angola.

Operation Savannah was launched from South West African soil on the 14th October 1975, which allowed precious little time to ensure a military and political victory for the pro-Western forces of FNLA and UNITA before independence just 28 days later. It says a lot that in this short space of time Task Force Zulu advanced more than 3,000 kilometres, fought 21 battles and skirmishes in addition to 16 hasty as well as 14 deliberate attacks.

Interestingly, the South Africans did astonishingly well. By the 6th November, a bit more than three weeks after the campaign had taken off through Angola's southern Cuando-Cubango region, Task Force Zulu – heading directly west and spearheaded by Lieutenant-Colonels Jan Breytenbach and Delville Linford (who was in command of the legendary Bushman Battalion) – captured the harbour city of Benguela. This was the western terminal of the railroad that linked Angola to the Congo's Katanga.

A day later they took Lobito, Angola's second city. All conurbations captured by the SADF were handed over to UNITA.

In central Angola, at the same time, combat unit Foxbat had moved 800 kilometres north toward Luanda. But by then the South Africans realised the Angolan capital could not be captured by Independence Day and seriously considered ending the advance and retreating. They did exactly that a short while later.

The CIA covertly assisted the South Africans, but only marginally, because of a powerful anti-South African lobby in the US Congress (a consequence of that country's apartheid policies). Any help proffered had to be clandestine.

Then, almost overnight, the Americans withdrew support with the so-called Clark Amendment Bill, in large part because the US was also dealing with its defeat in Vietnam. The matter was further compounded because American politicians were ill-informed about the real situation in Angola. The story might be apocryphal, but some members of Congress were so totally ill-informed about what was happening in Africa at the time that one politican actually believed that Angola might be a new brand of chewing gum.

This left the relatively small SADF Task force – never more than 3,000 men – without any Western support, fighting an enemy openly and liberally supported by the Communist Bloc. At the end of it, Pretoria decided to withdraw and Angola spiralled into civil war.

John Stockwell, a former CIA Station Chief in Leopoldville, captures much of these events in one of the best books to emerge on that period, *In Search of Enemies*. During this period he liaised closely with the South Africans and made the point several times that they were an extremely efficient and reliable military element during Operation Savannah.

As he stated, 'if they said they were going to do something or be somewhere at a specific time, they always delivered…'

After 13 years and seven tours of duty with Langley, he resigned from the CIA in disgust and became one of the most outspoken critics of US clandestine operations in Third World countries. The book is a most informative read.[4]

What does rather forcefully come across is that Stockwell was the ultimate intelligence maverick, ideally suited for his role as an intelligence chief in the Congo and adjacent countries. As a youngster, prior to returning to the United States with his family when he joined the US Marines, he grew up in the heart of the Belgian Congo. There he learned French and Tshiluba, one of the many native languages of the country.

Effectively, the man made good sense to some of the African people involved in these struggles because he could communicate, and in their own language.

Angola was a remarkable experience for almost all the young men who went into that country as part of Operation Savannah's aggressive mobile force.

Some of the youngsters were still in their teens and there were quite a few who had never been further from home than Durban during their July school holidays. Angola, as one of them wrote to his mother, was 'pretty damn dodgy'. It was dangerous too, he confided afterwards to a pal who still had to do his National Service.

'Nothing…*absolutely nothing* …prepared us for this…we had a vision of hell,' he wrote in his diary that he showed me years later.

It was beautiful in places, he conceded once his column got into the mountains leading towards the coast. But as another soldier commented on his return home: 'there were a lot of people out there just waiting to strike and what worried us most was that they had stuff that was way ahead of anything we were able to field…stacks of it.'

This was the first time elements of the South African Army had come up against weapons like BM-21 'Grad' multiple 122mm truck-mounted rocket launchers and Soviet BRDM amphibious armoured patrol cars that had been landed in Angola in considerable numbers by those who pulled

---

4   John R Stockwell: *In Search of Enemies: A CIA Story*: WW Norton USA 1984.

By now the South Africans were fully active along the northern border of South West Africa, largely countering SWAPO guerrilla incursions but also carefully observing developments in the neighbouring state. (Author's photo)

Puma helicopters bought from France started operating in northern South West Africa from 1972 onwards, mostly used as troopers following contacts with the enemy. (Author's photo)

The only real 'muscle' the SADF was able to deploy in the early days was the Eland armoured car – based on the French Panhard AML – like this Eland Mark 7, fitted with a 90mm cannon. Still more had heavy machine-guns mounted.

Youthful South African Army conscripts adapted quickly to border military regimes, in large part because they were very well trained. While there were many dissenters, a lot of the troops regarded their role as one of 'protecting the nation from the communist bogey.' (Author's photo)

In Lisbon's African territories there was much dislocation in the larger cities, with many Portuguese nationals opposing any kind of handover to what they regarded as 'terrorists'. In Lourenco Marques there was initially much violence. (Author's collection)

South West Africa's frontier with south Angola stretched from the Atlantic to the merging of borders of Botswana, Zimbabwe and Zambia in the middle of the Zambezi at Kazangula – a distance of almost 900 miles. Large stretches of this primitive terrain needed a military presence to prevent guerrilla incursions.

Many Portuguese who had served in Angola now drifted southwards and were eagerly recruited by the SADF. Portuguese war hero, Mozambique-born Danny Roxo ended up crossing into South Africa and joining the famed Reconnaissance Regiment. He was eventually killed in action. (Photo: Manuel Ferreira)

Almost overnight the SADF had to look at recruiting more Africans into its ranks, especially those familiar with conditions in South West Africa. (Author's photo)

the strings of the MPLA. Additionally, there was Cuban-fielded heavy artillery, rocket propelled grenades and much more.

By today's standards, South African casualties were hardly dramatic, due largely to poor training and the inability to handle sophisticated weapons on the part of their adversaries. That said, a number of South African troops took hits and quite a few more than were anticipated were sent home in body bags.

Essentially, Operation Savannah was not only badly planned, it was over-hastily conceived with no proper operational back-up in place should anything go wrong. In the words of Lieutenant-Colonel Delville Linford who led Combat Group Alpha and led the way from the start, 'the invasion was under-manned, under-supplied and under-armed.'

Alongside him was Jan Breytenbach's Combat Group Bravo, composed of large numbers of former Angolan soldiers and the legendary Portuguese Army 'Flechas', most of whom had fled into the arms of the South African military.

Nobody in Pretoria dreamed that this hodge-podge, hastily-put-together fighting group would make anything like the ground they did when they first set out. Also, the politicians back home had not actually considered the implications of an all-out onslaught that might feasibly prompt a Soviet reaction.

It was also a military campaign about which nothing was made public at the time. In 'domestic' South Africa, it was the 'non-event' of the decade and only years later did most of the details emerge, and then sporadically. But there are still quite a few gaps and even more questions that need to be answered. As a consequence, just about everybody paid a price.

It should never have been like this. Any foreign war needs a period of conditioning. You are taught local traits and customs, even some of the traditions likely to be encountered along the way. But with Op Savannah there simply was no time. Not one in a hundred of the men – apart from those Angolans who had thrown in their lot with the South Africans – could muster two consecutive sentences in Portuguese.

Also, Angola was a nation at war with itself. There were half a dozen factions consistently trying to score points against each other; an overnight killing here, an assassination there…and, in the field, sometimes an ambush.

Away from your buddies, one of the young South African conscript soldiers recalled, 'you could never be sure who exactly were your friends among so many of the people you encountered along the way north…they would smile at us, and sometimes wave when we passed. But once we were over the hill, we found out afterwards, they would retrieve their AKs and wait for the next bunch of Troopies to pass. In a sense, it was a precursor of what we see today East of Suez.

As Colonel Linford, then a commandant or half-colonel, recalled:

> Hand-over-fist, we took on everything thrown at us by Angola's field commanders. We all came to know the newly created military wing of the future Marxist government and its FAPLA army, an acronym for the People's Armed Forces for the Liberation of Angola, or, more correctly, *Forças Armadas Populares de Libertação de Angola*.
>
> Within my combat group I had a few hundred men that included a *Flecha* battalion which could be rated by today's standards as Special Forces, as well as two Bushman companies. They, in turn, were backed by two Eland armoured cars with mounted 90mm guns. These airportable, light fighting vehicles based on the French-built Panhard AML were supplemented by a single 81mm mortar platoon and a 140mm artillery platoon.

Breytenbach didn't do much better, though he did have an additional Eland and some howitzers. Taken together, this was not exactly an exemplary force with which to invade a neighbouring state, never mind try to overrun an entire country. Yet, in the end, we almost succeeded.

Both combat groups moved fast, quickly pushing back the Angolan military from their earlier gains, in large part because the South Africans relied on using surprise as a weapon.

Having first taken the southern town of Ongiva, the two fighting groups went on to capture the old Portuguese regional capital of Vila Rocades (Xangongo today). That was achieved by the 20th October or six days after the force had set out and roughly three weeks short of when the entire operation was due to be terminated.

Sa da Bandeira (Lubango) was taken with minimal losses by the 24th October and four days later the southern port of Mocamedes was in South African hands, again with little opposition. After this, FAPLA, under Cuban Army direction regrouped and things got tougher, Linford recalled:

> Less than a week later – having fought our way halfway across one of the biggest countries in Africa and covered almost a thousand kilometres in the process – we found ourselves in Benguela, a fine old coastal city that would hardly be out of place along Portugal's Algarve coast.
>
> There were very few Portuguese nationals who remained behind to greet us: because of earlier hostilities, most of the settler community had fled, the majority heading to Europe taking with them only what they could carry. By the time the two combat groups arrived the city was almost empty.
>
> What was sad was that all these events took place at the end of Lisbon's five-century rule in Africa. The continent's history was being rewritten by a small group of fighting men who stood up to be counted…
>
> We discovered, in occupying Benguela, a delightful coastal town. Both Jan Breytenbach and I were expecting the place to be heavily defended but there was almost no resistance.
>
> I deployed the troops and tried to make contact with our headquarters way back from where we had originally set out almost two weeks before, but without success.
>
> On the outskirts of Benguela was a tall, isolated hill that on its peak some religious functionary from long ago built a structure that resembled a chapel. We drove up there as far as we could, with the magnificent bay on which the city stands, to our left. I left my driver – he was also the radio man – to try to try to establish comms with our generals, most of whom did not yet know that we had reached the Atlantic Ocean.[5]

After a brief skirmish with a FAPLA unit they encountered trying to enter the city, Linford took his unit in tow and headed out to the city airport. A two-day battle ensued before they moved north and discovered that most of the bridges across rivers along the way had been destroyed by the retreating Cubans.

One of the immediate problems facing the South Africans, especially when it became clear that large numbers of Cuban soldiers were arriving in Angola in one of the biggest Soviet-sponsored air

---

5   Much more detail of this Angolan invasion can be found in one of Al Venter's recent books, a co-written biography of Colonel Delville Linford titled *As the Crow Flies*. It was published in South Africa in 2015 by Protea Books.

lifts yet seen in Africa, was communications. It did not take long before numerous Angolan radio intercepts monitored by Pretoria were in Spanish, reinforcing the view that Cuban involvement in this African state was long term.

Walter Volker, a Border War veteran and communications specialist and today an internationally-recognised banker, details this vital aspect in his book *Signal Units of The South African Corps of Signals and Related Signal Services*.

He tells us that one of the first tasks tackled by the South Africans as the Border War gathered pace was to establish an electronic warfare monitoring unit, or rather a series of them. There were already substantive Signals Intelligence (Sigint) as well as Electronic Warfare (EW) capabilities leading up to and during Operation Savannah, and once the Cubans appeared this would demand facilities to monitor Spanish-language signals as well.

The first intercept stations had already been deployed along the northern borders of South West Africa at Katima Mulilo and Rundu in Caprivi as far back as 1968. This was all part of Operation Brush, with the main focus at the time to intercept SWAPO/PLAN radio traffic in southern Angola and south-western Zambia. Obviously, this radio traffic was all in English – either voice, or more likely, Morse code.

In 1972 the SADF also deployed two monitoring stations at Binga and Chirundu in Rhodesia as part of Operation Falcon. This was to assist Rhodesian security forces with signals intelligence of ZIPRA and ZANLA forces operating out of Zambia and, to a lesser extent, the northern outreaches of Mozambique. These intercepts were also English-language based. It was left to the Portuguese to conduct similar efforts targeted against the rebel forces operating in Angola and against FRELIMO in Mozambique.

Following the army mutiny in Portugal in 1974, it was soon accepted that an independent covert intelligence collection capacity would have to be developed. It was essential that EW/Sigint efforts be expanded to include a Portuguese language and translation capability, with an expanded focus on monitoring guerrilla forces operating in the Lusophone colonies.

From the side of military intelligence, two officers from the Directorate Covert Collection (DCC) were deployed to northern South West Africa by mid-1975. Their orders were to start establishing an agent network and develop a more direct source of accurate intelligence.

Commandant Philip du Preez was sent to Rundu while Major Dries van Coller was based at Oshakati, headquarters of Sector 10. Many of their agents were former PIDE intelligence personnel or even Portuguese hunters still moving about in some of the remoter Angola regions in the east.

The initial response to the BRUSH stations included sending recordings of Portuguese radio traffic to translators at military intelligence in Pretoria. The main monitoring stations were expanded to include Mpacha, while the Rhodesian stations at Binga and Chirundu were also able to provide support as this was mostly monitoring of HF – that is, High Frequency radio waves which could travel vast distances (as opposed to Very High Frequency or VHF which have limited range).

With the arrival of the Cubans in Luanda, South African EW stations now faced a new challenge. The Cubans spoke a dialect of Spanish, and while Portuguese speakers were able to understand most of it, their interpretations were not always accurate.

Fortunately, policy demanded that all intercepts be recorded, and this material was then sent for translation to expert personnel working for military intelligence. Soon the need for Russian and German speakers arose as Soviets and East German military and security personnel arrived in Angola in numbers.

During the course of Operation Savannah (October 1975 to January 1976), the South African Army's 2 Signal Regiment was involved in Angola for the first time when a mobile EW station was deployed at Cela, deep inside Angola. This was a small town on the road to Luanda and at the time, headquarters of Task Force Zulu and 2 Military Area.

The value of the EW weapon to obtain valuable intelligence about the enemy had, by this time, been accepted by the South African command structure. It was also acknowledged that technological development in this area was urgent, something that had not bothered anybody in Pretoria since 1939.

Projects to modernise and expand the EW capability were launched. By then Project Molasses had already started, to establish a mobile High Frequency ECM capability.

Other projects initiated included Project Expanse for the development of a mobile HF and VHF ESM and ECM capability.

One of the British-built Buccaneer bombers of 24 Squadron SAAF that took part in the Cassinga raid, now retired to the War Museum. Its identity is unmistakable.

Forward SA Army obsevation position within metres of the Angolan frontier. (Author's photo)

The Border War started slowly in the early days. Troops were deployed, some Eland armoured cars brought in but for some of the time hostilities were restricted to Caprivi, because that sliver of land reached out eastwards towards Zambia from where the guerrillas infiltrated. (Author's photo)

PART II

AFTERMATH

The trouble with recording military history is that there are always so many different versions of the same event. As a British Army Captain named Siborne discovered in the 1830s when he set out to build his great model of the Battle of Waterloo and found out that 'if you ask 50 officers what time something happened at Waterloo, you get 50 different conflicting and partisan answers...'

On 4 July, 1975 SADF Director of Operations Constand Viljoen and BOSS Head of Foreign Operations Gert Rothman went to Kinshasa to consult Savimbi and Roberto as to their military needs. Viljoen recalled: Savimbi was there. Holden Roberto was there. They explained to me the situation. They said 'Can you give us any support that will be able to assist us in holding our positions?' I then made certain recommendations to the government that the two forces of Roberto and Savimbi cannot hold themselves against the MPLA forces supported by Cuba and the USSR and they had to find another way of fighting, which was the more conventional way.

'Into the Quagmire: Reassessing South Africa's Intervention in the Angolan Civil War, 1975' – Jamie Miller, University of Cambridge.

Foreign Policy, the Washington magazine that was founded more than 40 years ago, as it succinctly states, 'to question commonplace views and groupthink and to give a voice to alternative views about noteworthy political issues', recently published an article about 'the South African border war of 1966–1989.'[1] Written by Robert Goldich, it featured under a series titled *Annals of Wars we Don't Know About*. The piece, having come from the American capital, I was sceptical about it. But then Goldich makes the following comment, and I quote:

> **Reading South African accounts of the 23-year-long Border War between the South Africans and the Angolan liberation movement UNITA on one hand, and the Angolan government and army, supported by large Cuban forces, on the other, is almost hypnotically compelling. This is not only because for most of us north of the Equator it is so distant. The names of both natural features and people involved and the range of cultures they represent sound exotic to our ears and hold one's attention.**
>
> **The tactical and operational lessons from the Border War are mostly variations on usual military themes – solid and relevant training, doctrine and attitudes – but the most significant lessons for the United States are far broader, and sobering, in nature.**

The writer mentions the role of the ANC and its military wing *Umkhonto we Sizwe* (MK) in its freedom struggle and makes the point that they were 'mere pinpricks at best.'

Goldich goes on:

> **Far more formidable was a guerrilla movement against South African rule in South West Africa (SWA), later independent Namibia, beginning in the late-1960s by the South West African People's Organisation (SWAPO). The latter would have remained insignificant had not Portuguese colonial rule collapsed in Angola, directly north of SWA in 1974–1975. This left a military vacuum where SWAPO could train, equip and debouch into northern SWA without any hindrance…**
>
> **To make things far worse for South Africa, and potentially for the West in general, the Soviet Union committed huge amounts of military hardware and military advisors/trainers for FAPLA (the acronym for the Angolan army). Cuba made an even more massive investment. It ultimately dispatched an expeditionary force to Angola which reached a maximum strength of about 55,000, with a total of almost 380,000 Cuban military personnel serving in the country from 1975 through 1991…**

---

1 *Foreign Affairs*: 'Annals of Wars we Don't Know About – The South African Border War of 1966–1989'; Robert Goldich, Washington, March 12, 2015.

10

A Two-Decade War on Angola's Southern Frontiers

Southern Africa's longest war effectively ended on 1 November 1988, when South Africa and the South West African People's Organisation (SWAPO) finally called it quits. That was more than 20 years after the first shot had been fired. It had gone on for so long that for several generations of people of all races it was hard to believe that peace had come. During the course of hostilities a father and a son on the South African side could be wearing the same campaign medal for fighting on the same front, but a full generation apart. In the latter stages the brunt of the war was borne on both sides by young men who had not even been conceived when it started. Willem Steenkamp elucidates…

To understand what South Africans mean by the Border War, it is necessary to know something about the territory along whose northern reaches – that part of the country that adjoins Angola – where most things happened.

For decades, present-day Namibia was a German colony in Africa, but this proud European nation unfortunately left behind a legacy of brutality in its subjugation of the local people. Then came the First World War, and 'German South West Africa' was conquered by the South African Army and its fledgling air force, after which – like the other former German African colonies of the Cameroons, Tanganyika and Togo – it became a League of Nations Trusteeship.

This huge land, half the size of Alaska, was handed to Pretoria to administer, which the South Africans did for half a century, though not to everybody's acclaim. In this century-long process it was called, in turn, *Deutsch-Südwestafrika*, South West Africa, *Suidwes-Afrika* (Afrikaans) South West Africa/Namibia and today, simply Namibia.

Bounded in the west by the Atlantic Ocean, in the east by Botswana, South Africa in the south and south-east and in the north by Angola and Zambia, Namibia incorporates one of the longest desert coastlines in the Southern Hemisphere, the Namib, which includes the bleak and terrible Skeleton Coast and some of the richest diamond diggings on the globe.

There are also swamplands, the desolate Zebra Mountains in the north, one of the biggest game reserves in Africa at Etosha, vast open savannah plains and a winding riverine topography where the country nudges the great Cunene River in the north and the even larger Zambezi River in its tropical north-east. Most of the country is as flat as the surface of the moon, which, in places, it also resembles, though there is an elevated plateau between 900 and 1,200 metres above sea-level in the centre somewhere.

Namibia, to use a rather worn-out phrase, is a land of contrasts. It offers an almost infinite variety of terrain and quite often the landscape varies so abruptly and dramatically that travellers can scarcely believe they are still inside the same set of borders.

For 30 years Berlin's imperial flag waved over German South West and this brought progress, railway lines and a couple of harbours because its uninvited rulers were energetic developers. The Germans also built its first roads, health services and bridges, and created an efficient structure of civil government. At the same time they ruled sternly and, as with all colonial powers, frequently without concern for their subjects' property and other rights. As a result they were involved in a series of fierce and sometimes brutal tribal insurrections.

Then in 1915, to the surprise of many people, the majority of the South African electorate effectively threw in their lot with the Allies and invaded German South West at Whitehall's request.

Just 13 years earlier the two independent Boer republics had been savagely crushed in a horrific 'scorched earth' campaign by General Sir Herbert Kitchener in which thousands of farms were destroyed and upwards of 27 000 Boer civilians – mainly old people, women and children – and at least the same number of black farm workers – died of starvation and disease in badly administered and poorly-supplied British concentration camps.[1]

But in fact the South African government had no real choice: South Africa was not independent but a 'dominion', a type of super-colony, and was therefore automatically at war when Whitehall opened hostilities with Germany.

After the First World War the League of Nations entrusted South West Africa to South Africa as what was termed a 'Class C mandate' – a territory which through lack of population and resources was deemed incapable of ruling itself or eventually becoming independent. The new South West Africa, as it was now referred to in all official documents, was to be governed, in trust, as a virtual extra province for the betterment of its inhabitants. The mandate laid down certain requirements and required the South African government to report annually to the League of Nations.

When the League of Nations became moribund at the end of the Second World War, South Africa undertook to continue administering the territory, more or less in the spirit of the old mandate, but denied that the ultimate responsibility had automatically passed from the League of Nations to the United Nations. The UN, however, maintained – unsuccessfully – that South West Africa should be placed under its trusteeship.

South Africa stood firm and refused to give way, even though the issue was twice tested at the International Court of Justice at The Hague in Holland.

Not long afterwards, the seeds of the eventual South West African insurgency were sown. Curiously, that happened 1,400 kilometres south of the country when a 33-year-old former railway policeman and the Second World War veteran called Herman Toivo ja Toivo, who was living in Cape Town at the time, founded a political movement which he called the Ovambo People's Organisation (later the Ovambo People's Congress') and which was strongly supported by the South African Communist Party.

Ja Toivo, naturally, was himself an Ovambo tribesman, and as the South Africans were subsequently to discover (as did the Portuguese shortly before and at the turn of the previous century, because a fairly large proportion of the tribe also lived in Angola) this was an aggressive, purposeful society that tended to tackle challenges head-on.

During the 19th and most of the early 20th centuries the Portuguese had numerous brushes with the Ovambo people, but then – according to the French historian René Pélissier – their King

---

1   Gerald L'Ange: *Urgent Imperial Service – South African Forces in German South West Africa 1914–1915*, Ashanti Publishing, 1991. Personal communications 2013/15.

Mandume rebelled when resisting colonising attempts by local *Chefe do Posto.* He lost 5,000 of his people in military actions launched by the Portuguese Army and was forced to flee, many of his subjects to seek sanctuary on German colonial soil further south.

Clearly, the Ovambos have always been a mainly peaceable society but could be difficult and sometimes a belligerent people who did not take kindly to being wronged. This was what happened in the 1960s when Toivo ja Toivo's organisation began to offer resistance to SWA's unpopular contract migrant labour system. Almost inevitably the discontent and attempts to control it morphed from a mainly political movement into an 'armed struggle', egged on by the Soviet Union (the Cold War was at its height, and the ultimate prize was control of the highly strategic Indian Ocean area).

Before embarking on the story of the Border War, however, we should include a few words about the population that inhabits present-day Namibia.

The territory lacks many things, but most of all, it lacks people. In the entire vast extent of a region twice as big as Germany, there are a little over two million people living there today, though 40 years ago when the war started, it was less than half that.

In November 1986 the-then General Officer Commanding South West Africa, Major-General Georg Meiring, phrased it even more aptly when he described South West Africa/Namibia as being four-fifths the size of South Africa but with roughly the same population as the South African city of Benoni, which had more or less the same number of inhabitants as the British holiday resort of Blackpool.

In the interim, there has been a considerable amount of urbanisation, but in the tradition of Africa, most of these groups are still closely linked to their original tribal stamping-grounds.

The Kaokolanders, Ovambos, Kavangos and Caprivians have traditional homelands in the far north, immediately south of the official border with Angola and Zambia. The whites, Hereros and coloureds mainly inhabit the central part of the country and the Namas the dry south. This demographic distribution largely determined the battle zones of the Border War and it is no accident that most of the infiltration and fighting took place in central Ovamboland – Ja Toivo's ethnic heartland – where about a quarter of all Namibians lived at the time, including the major Kwanyama and Ondonga tribes of Ovamboland.

Because of this and other factors it would be futile to compare the subsequent insurrection – and its ultimate result – with any other of the regional southern African wars.

It is perhaps an indication of the generally low intensity of the Border War that during the course of hostilities, the population of the country actually increased and no part of the territory was laid waste. It was also remarkable how little the struggle impinged on the daily life of the average Joe.

South of the black tribal areas, especially central Ovamboland, there was little evidence of strife. The actual war was barely noticeable except for the occasional urban bomb blast and a few daring but small-scale SWAPO raids on white-owned farms in the midlands.

In places such as Ovamboland, the northern regional economies actually benefited from the conflict, thanks to local military expenditure; ironically, probably the greatest consequence of the war was the accelerated abolition of almost all racial laws and the inclusion of blacks in the previously all-white administration. By 1988, when the war ended, the territory's internal government was preponderantly non-white and included representatives of all SWA's political parties except Toivo ja Toivo's South West African Peoples Organisation, the new name his OPO had long ago adopted in a bid to broaden its popular appeal.

It is not known to what extent this ploy succeeded (given the absence of any impartial survey of its popular support) but it does not appear to have turned the new political movement into a truly representative organisation, possibly a reflection of the territory's history of internal conflict and ethnic divisions.

Although its political wing recruited some sympathisers from members of most other ethno-cultural groups, it still remained strongly Ovambo-orientated in the years to come, particularly as regards its military wing, which did most of the fighting. This can be seen from the fact that about 95 per cent of all SWAPO insurgents killed or captured in the decades-long Border War which was soon to break out were from the Ovambo tribal group.

One of the biggest steps forward was when a provisional SWAPO headquarters was set up in Dar es Salaam, Tanzania, in March 1961. A more exact dating, however, is to be found in the fact that in 1962 – soon after SWAPO had set up its headquarters in Lusaka – it founded a military wing called 'Peoples Liberation Army of Namibia' (PLAN). Given the South African government's complete disinclination, then or later, to yield to SWAPO or any other 'liberation organisation' other than through peaceful negotiation, this effectively set the stage for a shooting war.

Meantime, SWAPO had used South Africa's recalcitrance – and the resultant impasse – to recruit fighters for its embryonic military wing, many of whom slipped in and out of the country through Portuguese-controlled Angola. Progress was slow at first, but eventually some 900 recruits were gathered by a variety of means, ranging from signing up genuine volunteers to offering South West African black youths bogus scholarships for overseas study and then diverting them to PLAN for military training.

The recruits were given basic training in Tanzania, and those selected for advanced and/or specialised courses were then sent to countries such as Algeria, Cuba, Egypt, China, the Soviet Union, North Korea and Red China.

At the same time SWAPO forged links with the anti-Portuguese UNITA insurgents, then in the process of launching guerrilla operations in southern Angola. This was an advantageous relationship because the southern Angolan Ovimbundus and the Ovambos are part of the same broad ethnic group and such a friendship would give PLAN easier access to its main objective, South African-controlled Ovamboland.

The links were so close, in fact, that when the UNITA leader Dr Jonas Savimbi slipped back into Angola late 1966, he was carrying a Soviet Tokarev pistol given him by Sam Nujoma, SWAPO's new leader.

By September 1965, PLAN was ready to launch its first infiltration, and that month six trained insurgents slipped across the border from southern Angola into Ovamboland, an easy process, because the international frontier boundary lines existed more in name than in fact, with no-one to guard them except a handful of South West Africa's modest 600-man police force.

The insurgents busied themselves with basic political activation and also gave about 30 young Ovambos some elementary military training before sending them home to await a call to arms. By this time suspicious tribal elders had passed word of their activities to the police, but except for cursory surveillance, no immediate action was taken.

In February 1966 a second small group travelled through Angolan territory to infiltrate southwards, only to become the authors of a total fiasco when they murdered two Angolan shopkeepers and an itinerant Ovambo in the apparent – and mistaken – belief by its members that they had crossed the border. The group then dispersed, only to have three of its members arrested by police in the neighbouring tribal territory of Kavango, where local inhabitants had wasted no time in informing the authorities about the presence of foreign tribesmen.

In July 1966 a third group of insurgents came through from abroad. They were an unimpressive group, trained in half a dozen countries and armed in some cases with assegais and bows and arrows, a far cry from the uniformed, well-equipped and trained insurgents of later years. In spite of this they launched the 'armed struggle' by attacking a number of Ovambo tribal chiefs, firing at a white farmer's house in the Grootfontein district just south of Ovamboland, and shooting up the South West African border post at Oshikango.

This opening phase of the struggle was short-lived, however: the following month helicopter-borne policemen attacked their camp at Ongulumbashe, killing two insurgents and capturing nine others. The author Paul Els gives an account of this early phase of hostilities in his book *Ongulumbashe – Where the Bush War Began*.[2]

Later, acting on information passed on by the local inhabitants, they arrested many more, bringing the total number of captures to 45. This effectively strangled the infiltration and, incidentally, knocked out the only permanent base PLAN ever managed to establish anywhere in the operational area during the entire 23-year course of the war.

Following the crushing of this latest infiltration by police security elements – the army had not yet been called to handle what was still a relatively minor series of insurgent incursions – Ovamboland and the neighbouring Caprivi homeland were now so quiet that the police withdrew their counter-insurgency unit, but the Border War was far from over.

In October 1968 two large groups of insurgents slipped in from Angola and restarted the Caprivian end of what had become a moribund insurgency. Police retaliation was swift. Within a week no fewer than 56 insurgents had been arrested. At year's end a total of 178 PLAN members had either been killed or captured, and the infiltration ended with the remaining operatives withdrawing into Zambia.

The local population still declined to rebel *en masse*, and the insurgents concentrated on harrying the security forces. In April a Russian-made mine blew up a police vehicle near Katima Mulilo, heralding a new dimension to hostilities, and during 1971 and 1972 five policemen were killed and 35 wounded by landmine explosions.

What is surprising is that it took SWAPO so long to include landmines in their armoury, especially since the Portuguese had been trying to counter that menace for years. Indeed, of all actual casualties in these colonial wars other than in SWA (as opposed to troops who went down with tropical illnesses) mines took a terrible toll in both men and machines.

The difference between Pretoria and Lisbon was that one of the first priorities launched by the South Africans at the start of their military operations in the north of the former League of Nations mandated territory was to develop a comprehensive range of mine-protected vehicles, some of which performed so well that their descendants are still in use today by various peace-keeping and counter-insurgency forces the world over, including South Lebanon, Somalia, Iraq and the Congo. In fact, as early as the 1980s, while the SWA border conflict was still raging, discreetly purchased South African mine-protected Buffel troop carriers were spotted in just about every news clip that came out of Sri Lanka when the civil war there was at its height, and it says a lot that when the Border War ended, India bought a hundred of the more advanced multi-purpose Casspir infantry fighting vehicles from South Africa.

For the next few years the landmine was to become a prime insurgent weapon (as it was against the Portuguese in Angola and Mozambique), but in due course, thanks to new developments, its threat lessened and eventually became a minor one as the South Africans learnt from their experiences.

By the end of 1973 it was becoming fairly obvious to the Pretoria government – although not to the South African general public, which was still looking towards Rhodesia, where a police contingent had been campaigning for several years in support of the Ian Smith government – that

---

2 Paul Els, *Ongulumbashe – Where the Bush War Began*, 2008. Website http://paul.who-els.co.za.

What began in South Africa as a hesitant reaction to Angola's political transition soon became a way of life for many young men conscripted into the SADF, the majority straight out of school. Troops were airlifted on a daily basis to the far-flung border regions in air force C-130s and French-built C-160s. (Author's photo)

Among the first priorities facing the government was to find an answer to the landmine threat and various 'mine-protected' vehicles started to arrive in the operational area, including this appropriately-named 'Hippo'. (Author's photo)

Specialist units – tracking, motorcycle, mounted elements and others – soon arrived to counter the threat. (Author's photo)

Having observed Portugal's wars in Angola and Mozambique from up close, no money was spared to buy a variety of aircraft and helicopters abroad, and to start assembling some versions locally, including the all-purpose French Aerospatiale Puma 330. (From the author's original edition of *The Chopper Boys*)

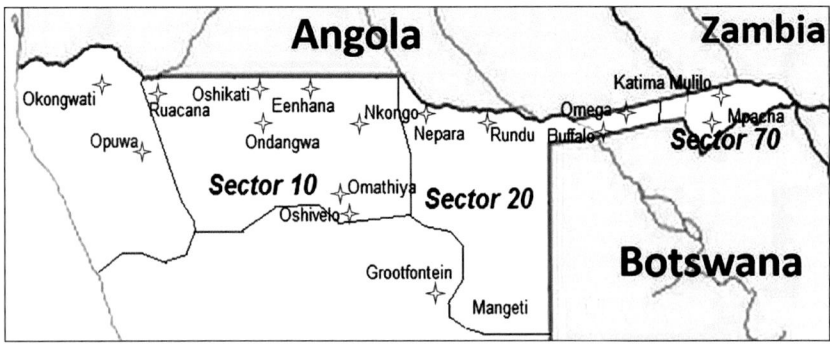

Top: Operational area adjacent to south Angola and Below: In spite of vigorous efforts to counter the threat of landmines, these weapons were still having an effect. This Hippo was badly damaged by an anti-tank mine but no casualties resulted. (Author's photo)

Mounted unit with which the author went operational in an area adjacent to the Angolan border. It was commanded by Lieutenant Johan Louw – here leading his troop. (Author's photo)

SADF Intelligence resources were expanded exponentially, with the result that the army had its share of successes: an enemy weapons cache uncovered and ammunition is airlifted back to headquarters in Pumas. (Author's photo)

Alouette helicopter gunships had already been active for several years, aiding the Portuguese in their efforts to counter subversion in south Angola. This front now shifted southwards. (Author's photo)

Senior officers arrive at a SWAPO position taken after a brief fire-fight. (Author's photo)

Army strongpoint along the Zambezi in east Caprivi. (Author's photo)

Once cross-border raids became the norm in the 1980s, infantry fighting vehicles like Ratels – as well as Sabres – adapted four-wheel-drive vehicles, seen here in south Angola, became a fairly regular event. (Author's collection)

A new development arrived in the Border War with a motorcycle unit, trained for operational duties along the frontier. Though fast and mobile, they were too noisy for effective deployment. (Author's photo)

During cross-border raids that struck at enemy positions often well inside Angola, the South Africans took with them their own mobile communications systems. (Author's photo)

Unlike the Portuguese, who always seemed to be struggling with radio communications, Pretoria wasted little time in designing and producing advanced compact radio systems that had good range. (Author's photo)

Vehicles and aircraft apart, much of the dog-work was still left to men on patrol in an often hostile environment. (Author's photo)

As the war progressed, more sophisticated weapons were brought into play, including a mobile 155mm howitzer dubbed the G-6. With base-bleed ammunition it had a range of 42 kilometres. (Author's collection)

the South African Police simply did not have the manpower or other resources simultaneously to keep the peace in South Africa itself, secure the South West African borders, and also to provide a contingent to help in the Rhodesian War.

The SAP had never been a large force, but it had always managed to carry out its tasks with reasonable efficiency; the additional burden of the growing low-key insurgency just south of the Angolan frontier was more than it could handle.

It was then decided that elements of the South African Defence Force would be deployed 'in support of the civil power', as the international usage has it, by taking over responsibility for all security operations in the as yet remote northern operational area, leaving the police to concentrate on their normal duties, while still maintaining their small anti-terrorist unit. The date for the South African Defence Force's assumption of responsibility was set at 1 April 1974, and in the second half of 1973 increasing numbers of military personnel and quantities of equipment started to arrive in the operational area.

Late in June of 1974 Admiral Hugo Biermann, Chief of the SADF, announced the death of the first known military casualty – Lieutenant Freddie Zeelie, 22 – who had died the previous week 'in a skirmish with a group of terrorists which attempted to cross the South African border … a unit of the Permanent Force killed and wounded a number of terrorists.'

The circumstances of his death were shrouded in secrecy – not even his parents were told exactly when, how and where he died. At the time it was not even known what unit he belonged to, although a green Infantry Corps beret lay with his sword on his coffin when he was buried with full military honours at his home town of Alberton, near Johannesburg. Much later it transpired that he had been a member of the very low-profile Reconnaissance Commando, the forerunner of today's Reconnaissance Regiments. About six months later his parents received his posthumous Louw Wepener Decoration for gallantry.

Although most South Africans did not realise it at the time, a new phase of the war was about to start, one which would have a radical effect on the country's still-porous frontiers and would force Admiral Biermann to regret his public assurances that there would be no South African intervention across the country's borders.

Then in the first quarter of 1974 the entire strategic picture changed when the regime of Portuguese leader Dr Marcelo Caetano was overthrown by a junta of far-leftist military officers. Up to that time the Caetano government's support had been of great value to Pretoria in its counter-insurgency campaign in South West Africa, principally because it had meant that PLAN could not freely use southern Angola as a sanctuary, training-ground and jumping-off place for infiltrations into Ovamboland.

But by 1974, more than a decade of fighting ongoing insurgencies in all three of its African provinces had brought Portugal to the brink of financial and spiritual collapse. The poorest country in Europe, it had long been carrying an insupportable burden: it was short of money, short of external support, short of manpower, short of the resources needed to produce effective mine-protected vehicles, of which very few existed then in any case. In the meantime its opponents – particularly Angola's MPLA (the 'Popular Movement for the Liberation of Angola' – were receiving lavish aid of various kinds from the Soviet Union, the rest of the Soviet Bloc and other sympathetic countries.

In late 1974 alone, for instance, an estimated 6 million US dollars' worth of heavy Russian weaponry – including 122mm BM-21 multiple rocket-launchers, obsolescent weapons but highly effective against unsophisticated African troops – was shipped to remote rural MPLA depots from Dar es Salaam and later Congo-Brazzaville, and large numbers of MPLA officers were flown to Russia for training (although in fairness, this happened only after Red China had sent some instructors and 450 tons of light arms through Zaire in June of that year to another Angolan insurgent body, the FNLA ('National Front for the Liberation of Angola'), followed by another shipment from Romania in August.

In addition, more and more Cuban military advisors and instructors were quietly slipping into Angola, many of them taken into distant airports well away from Luanda while still more, according to CIA sources, were flown to Brazzaville in the Congo Republic in Bristol Britannia aircraft for some months before independence, from where they were ferried into what was still a Portuguese possession.

Also used was Cabo Ledo, several hours' drive south of the capital. It had a lengthy paved runway (built by the Cubans) and good security. This was the same base that many years later was to become the headquarters of the South African mercenary group Executive Outcomes – an episode described at some length in Al J. Venter's book *War Dog, Fighting Other People's Wars*.[3]

The EO Boeing would come in two or three times a week with goods and provisions and would also be used for rotating manpower to and from the Republic. It was notable that EO was able to buy two of these Boeing 727s because their engines exceeded newly-promulgated American aircraft noise limitations in the US: they cost $500,000 each and were bargains because they were still almost new.

For years SWAPO and MPLA sympathisers inside and outside South Africa have claimed that Cubans started arriving in Angola only in late 1975, ostensibly to combat South African aggression. In fact, there was already a solid relationship between Neto and President Fidel Castro in place dating back a number of years: Cuba had been providing his socialist movement with instructors and a personal bodyguard since 1966.

With dismaying rapidity Angola began to slide into full-scale chaos as the three contenders went at each other, for survival in the case of Savimbi and for supremacy in the case of Neto and Roberto. As early as July 1975, the MPLA and the MPLA won the first round by throwing both the FNLA and the small UNITA presence out of Luanda and establishing itself in almost every sizeable population centre between the capital and the South West African border, though for the next year or so, the pendulum swung in both directions with the Marxists eventually coming out on top in the urban areas.

To the South Africans it was obvious that an extremely serious situation was developing. Refugees, who were now streaming in from Angola in their thousands, had started bringing word of the close Cuban involvement with the MPLA. Independent proof of this involvement – and possible future plans – was obtained when one of the numerous small hot-pursuits launched by the South Africans over the ever-more irrelevant border turned up Cuban-origin ammunition and arms dumps which, as one official spokesman later said, 'placed the security situation of southern Angola in a completely hazardous light.'

The Americans' grasp of the issues involved does not seem to have been very strong, if one is to believe John Stockwell, then a Central Intelligence Agency officer who came almost straight from the disaster in Saigon to be made head of the operation the CIA hastily set up in Angola in 1975. In a 1984 television documentary, Stockwell – who by then had severed his ties with the organisation and had become one of its strongest critics – described the first briefing on Angola to be delivered by the CIA director to the National Security Council, US President Gerald Ford's inner cabinet. According to Stockwell, who was at that briefing, the proceedings began as follows:

> The CIA director (said): 'Gentlemen, this is a map of Africa, and here is Angola. In Angola there are three liberation movements. There is the FNLA, headed by Holden Roberto, they're

---

3   Al J. Venter: *War Dog: Fighting Other People's Wars*, Casemate, US and UK 2006, Chapter 15 *et al.*

the good guys. There is the MPLA, headed by Agostinho Neto, who's a drunken psychotic poet with a Marxist background. They're the bad guys' – and they used exactly that terminology, 'good guys' and 'bad guys', so that those people on the National Security Council could get straight what the game was.

The reason why Savimbi did not get a mention (or recognition) at this stage was undoubtedly the fact that (as Stockwell noted), 'nobody knew much about Savimbi ... he didn't hit the international cocktail circuit the way FNLA and MPLA activists and leaders did. Instead, Savimbi stayed in Angola, tending to his business.'

The fact is that throughout the crucial first six months of 1975 the US government was virtually inert as far as Angola was concerned. No doubt the Americans' deeply ingrained parochialism was partly to blame. In addition the US was not only still too deeply mired in its post-Vietnam nervous breakdown to take positive action but was also entering its traditional pre-presidential election foreign policy paralysis phase.

And so South Africa was sucked into the burgeoning war, a conflict that went on for another 15 years.

Over the years, Pretoria's involvement in Angola has been put down to everything from blatant racism to out-and-out neo-imperialist expansion. Stockwell's theory is that the South Africans' main reason for giving in to the American urgings was because they scented a lever which they could use to force the US to support their (apartheid) policies – if true, a bad mistake.

The Border War was still of fairly low intensity, but an intermittent dribble of contacts, mine explosions and shoot-and-scoot rocket and mortar bombardments inexorably pushed up the casualty rate. For the PLAN insurgents, operating on their home turf against (at first) relatively inexperienced enemies, the environment was still comparatively favourable; the SADF's immediate reaction was to mount intensive counter-insurgency operations, and it learnt quickly from its mistakes.

For all that, South West Africa's northern conflict showed no signs of abating. Insurgents often operated in large groups and did not hesitate to fight if contact was made. In certain sectors of the South African public, the erroneous conclusion was reached that PLAN members always ran if attacked. In fact, this tactic was usually the only one that made sense.

A typical contact consisted of a short, fierce fire-fight, after which the insurgent group usually gave way and headed for the Angolan cut-line. Or these combatants would disperse into Ovamboland's endless stretches of bush country; to do otherwise would be to provide targets for the SADFs extremely efficient helicopter gunships and reaction-force units.

The Border War lasted for 22 years (or 23, if the final post-ceasefire outburst of violence is included). If the material losses of all the participants are counted, it cost billions in any reputable currency and destroyed the lives of thousands, especially in southern Angola.

Its total casualties will probably never be established; South African sources give known deaths by November 1988 as 715 security-force soldiers, 1,087 SWA/Namibian civilians and 11,291 insurgents and Angolan soldiers. It is quite possible that many more PLAN fighters died, given the fact that they did not have recourse to the sophisticated medical backup enjoyed by the security forces.

These figures do not include the thousands of deaths suffered by UNITA, the Cubans or the Angolan soldiers and civilians who died in a civil war intimately connected with all the fighting in that region.

The number of dead and permanently disabled is not, perhaps, very impressive when measured against the ghastly losses suffered in greater wars, Vietnam and the Middle East especially. By the standards of Southern Africa, however, where countries are vast but populations small, it is a heavy toll, and particularly Angola has been a long time recovering from the loss of blood and resources.

An interesting avenue of speculation is this: was it necessary for SWAPO to embark on its 'Armed Struggle' in 1962? Might it not have been better advised to fight for an independent Namibia on the national and international political battlefield rather than take up arms in its own backyard?

The answer, possibly, is 'no' to the first part and 'yes' to the second. But the question should be seen in the context of its times. The 1960s was the era of the 'Freedom Fighter', ubiquitous in many Third World countries suffering from 'growing pains'. And in any case, the South African government of the time was little disposed towards negotiations with an openly revolutionary organisation which had an open line with Moscow.

An intriguing idea some observers play around with in their idle moments is the theory that perhaps the war did not hasten South West Africa's progress towards independence, but actually delayed it. It is difficult to say, for there is no clear answer.

An interesting question is this: Should the South Africans have fought the insurgents?

The answer is probably that, apart from personal inclinations, they had no alternative, especially once it had become clear that the insurgency was not a nine days' wonder but an integral part of the Cold War struggle for control of the Indian Ocean and its vitally important east-west maritime route, the only all-weather link between Orient and Occident.

In addition, they were quite willing to confer independence on South West Africa, which annually swallowed tens of millions of South African taxpayers' rands for administrative and developmental expenses – but they were not willing simply to abandon the territory to its fate, and insisted that South-Westers of all ethnic and tribal groups get together and work out their own constitutional dispensation.

All the internal political parties agreed to participate except SWAPO, whose policy then was simply to conquer SWA by force of arms. From first to last the South Africans' main priority remained the same: to keep SWAPO in check so that the other internal parties would have the opportunity to develop their home-grown constitution.

The immediate after-effects of Operation Savannah sealed the matter. After 1976, when the insurgency became really viable for the first time because Angola's new masters threw solid support behind SWAPO, there was no turning back. The irony of it was that the seeds of the SWAPO movement were sown in the 1940s and 1950s, but did not come to fruition till late in the 1960s. By then, attitudes had changed a good deal and gave promise of changing even more: after all, because by then both the Rhodesian and Portuguese wars were history.

History teaches us a great deal. Angola's disastrous slide into chaos was largely due to the Soviet Union's undermining of Portugal's post-Caetano era. It might well be that the Russians were not working according to a pre-determined plan, but were merely seizing a handy opportunity. That hardly alters Moscow's culpability (and the 'opportunity' theory is suspect in any case, when one considers that Moscow, Cuba and the likes of Portuguese Admiral Rosa Coutinho had already started working in 1974 to manoeuvre the MPLA into power – details of which can be found in Chapter 12).

Then there is the matter of Angola, which is generally cast as the war's (and South Africa's) greatest victim. Yet to a large extent the Angolan government could be said to have brought its troubles on itself.

There have been many statements that thousands of young white South Africans left the country to avoid service in SWA/Namibia, but this has not been backed up by any conclusive research, and it seems likely that many of those who left did so because they considered that two years of full-time conscription – followed by 720 days of part-time service – were too onerous a burden on their careers and personal lives. But that is a different matter altogether.

Still, it was only half of what the majority of Portuguese conscripts ended up doing at the end of their colonial conflicts.

The ongoing conflict that stretched into South Angola was certainly not South Africa's Vietnam in the sense that the SADF was bogged down there, unable to bring an expensive war to a satisfactory end. Till far into the 1980s, the South Africans did pretty much as they pleased in southern Angola and scored many victories at little cost to themselves, and in any case by the late 1980s the main burden of the counter-insurgency campaign was being shouldered by the locally recruited SWA Territory Force. If Angola was anybody's Vietnam, it was the Cubans'.

Losses among Cuban conscripts who were sent there by Fidel Castro have never been made public, but it is accepted that the dead and wounded amounted to thousands – almost all victims of UNITA. Included in this tally were dozens of Cuban aviators whose jet fighters and helicopters were brought down by ground fire and American Stinger FIM-92 shoulder-fired SAM missiles that the USA supplied to UNITA.

Another popular misconception was that what went on in South Angola ended up destroying the 'myth of South African military superiority'. This was a handy phrase that rolled readily off the typewriter, but the contrary was true. South African military superiority was anything but mythical, then or later.

Unlike almost every other southern African army, the SADF was a long-established body, forged by six decades of independent development and two bloody world wars into the best-organised, best-trained force in Africa. It says a lot that a young South African farm boy from Grahamstown, M St J Pattle, was the highest-scoring British and Commonwealth fighter ace in the Second World War.[4]

Third in the number of *Luftwaffe* aircraft shot down, after the legendary Johnny Johnson, was another South African, A G 'Sailor' Malan who commanded the RAF's 72 Squadron at Biggin Hill, south of London.

What Savannah *did* prove was that the SADF was not in good shape after more than 30 years of peace. Its equipment was outdated and there was a good deal of deadwood – both in personnel and in doctrine – that needed to be lopped off.

To the South Africans' credit they took this lesson to heart, with the Border War supplying a handy training-ground. As a result they emerged with a standard of operational expertise which surpassed that of some of the most famous armed forces in the world, and the self-confidence that went with it.

Were the South African and SWA/Namibian soldiers better than the SWAPO insurgents? The answer is an unqualified 'yes', but one must understand why this was so.

It was not about courage or cowardice, but about better organisation, better planning, better utilisation of resources and, above all, superb basic training, all the way through to the most advanced military-related disciplines that involved fieldwork, retaliation, transport, armour, close-air support, the always-urgent evacuation of casualties and the kind of clandestine work that involved South Africa's Special Forces.

Most important of all, they understood something that generally seems to elude Western military thinkers: time is not automatically on the insurgent's side – it can be on the insurgent's if he

---

4   ERC Baker: *Ace of Aces, M. St. J. Pattle:* Top scoring allied fighter pilot of the Second World War, Crecy Publishing, UK, 1992.

accepts that he is in for the long haul, and tailors his tactics accordingly. The South Africans did so, and eventually the war ended in successful negotiations for a future democratic Namibia.

If the war proved anything, it was that although most insurgencies end in political solutions, he who has lost the penultimate military phase has no right to say anything when the armed struggle concluded, not with a bang, but with the rustle of papers being shuffled around at a conference-table.

To those who did not know better – and to some who did, but found it more convenient to avoid facing the facts – the Border War was a simple confrontation between racist whites and oppressed blacks.

The men and women who fought in it knew better, probably no other southern African war has ever featured such a motley, many-tongued array of combatants driven by such a variety of motives: patriotism, political belief, a hunger for vengeance, a desire for money, obedience to the authorities, and so on.

For some it satisfied a thirst for adventure. In a sense this 'Border War' was a fighting man's conflict; in that most of the action in it was Mark One, face-to-face soldiering at whites-of-the-eyes range rather than the impersonal killing of enemies at long distance.

It has also been called a 'colonial' war, but in at least one important aspect it was not. Where it differed from most such wars was that almost none of the fighters were foreigners, in the sense of coming to the battle-zone from distant lands, like the Americans in Vietnam and the British in Malaya. Most of those involved were southern Africans of one race or another and did not experience real difficulty in coming to terms with their environment.[5]

In some cases, in fact, the difference between the protagonists was tragically small: for the insurgents on the one hand and the Ovambo soldiers and policemen of 101 Battalion and the South West Africa Police it was nothing more or less than a civil war.

In the eyes of some observers, the so-called 'Border War' actually ended in a triple victory. The South Africans fought PLAN to an effective standstill, which was almost inevitable because of a variety of circumstances, and thereby prevented the establishment of a Soviet foothold in SWA; SWAPO achieved its ultimate aim, winning the pre-independence election by a narrow but decisive margin, thanks at least partly to the fact that the Ovambos were the largest ethnic group; and the peoples of Southern Africa avoided having the sub-continent turned into an endless maelstrom of intermittent warfare.

The only real losers were the Soviet Union, which made a huge investment in cash and kind but achieved nothing except more damage to its tottering economy; and the Cubans, who had expected a quick 'internationalist' victory but instead became mired in a protracted struggle which brought them nothing but death, wounds and financial disaster.

---

5 There was an army unit formed later in the war that recruited foreign volunteers: 44 Parachute Brigade. It was founded and commanded by the legendary Colonel Jan Breytenbach (the same man involved with Colonel Delville Linford in Operation Savannah in 1975). Into the ranks of its Pathfinder Company came veterans from Britain, the United States, Australasia, Rhodesia and elsewhere, many having spent time with the SAS, Selous Scouts, the Rhodesian Light Infantry and other crack combat units.

11

Late 1975 – Luanda in the Final Stages of a Political Handover

November 1975, only days before Lisbon finally gave power to a newly-formed Marxist government in Luanda, things were tight. I was in Luanda at the time, totally unaware that the South African Army had invaded in the south of the country and that Commandants, or in today's language, Lieutenant-Colonels Linford and Breytenbach were targeting the Angolan capital. Their forces were already well north of Lobito and they were beginning to accept that indeed, there were Cubans all over the place, many more than their intelligence services said there were…

As a foreign correspondent that had spent a good deal of his life covering the Africa 'beat', I had done a few things. Among the most unusual was observing Angola's transition from fairly close-up. Though operating out of Johannesburg – and from a country hostile to the Marxist MPLA whose commissars were calling the shots – I could do so because things had not yet got out of hand. And anyway, everybody in Luanda had already started to celebrate because independence was imminent.

Those journalists with whom I associated were a diverse bunch and included some very well known names from London, New York, Moscow, France, Portugal and elsewhere. Some were good at what they did, a number were mediocre and quite a few were really evil 'uns. Of the names, there were those who might be forgotten today, but the majority left their mark – often indelibly so.

Members of the Fourth Estate in Luanda just then included people like the incorrigible Peter Younghusband of *Newsweek* and London *Daily Mail* fame as well as the always delightful Chris Munnion who reported for the *Daily Telegraph* for most of his career. Graham Linscott who today writes the *Idler* column for Durban's *Mercury* had been there a short while before, so had John Edlin of the Associated Press, who tended to drink a lot more than was good for him, together with a host of others.

Other notables who covered Lisbon's travails over the years, included *Washington Post's* 'uppity' Jim Hoagland (who I first met while covering the war in Portuguese Guinea) CBS's Canadian-born Allen Pizzey with whom I shared an adventure or two in Angola and last heard, was living in Rome, as well as the always-alluring Robin Wright then with the *Los Angeles Times*.

I should mention Fred Bridgland, who was working for *The Scotsman* because our paths crossed many times over the years, including my having published his book on the Angolan struggle, *The War for Africa*, when I still owned and ran Ashanti Publishers. He and Mike Nicholson – ITN's first bureau chief in South Africa – eventually went on to break the news that the South African

Army had invaded Angola's south, an event that had a direct bearing on my stay in Luanda at the time. But more of that later...

Nor should we not forget German nationals Peter-Hannes Lehmann of *Der Spiegel* and *Stern's* Gerd Heidermann, one of whom was later prosecuted for trying to peddle bogus Hitler Diaries.

Ryszard Kapuściński, the Polish foreign correspondent, was also one of the journalists there, but he was in a class of his own. Apart from fabricating many of his stories, there was a good bit of evidence that he worked closely with at least one Eastern Bloc intelligence agency and we viewed him warily. With Ryszard, in a potentially hostile environment like Luanda, you never knew where you stood. In fact, in a book published in his own country after he died, London's *Guardian* tells us, he was accused of 'repeatedly crossing the boundary between reportage and fiction writing', or more directly, made stuff up.[1]

Even worse, and this is a personal gripe, he used one of my photos on the cover of his book on the Angolan war without payment or acknowledgment. It was a memorable illustration, taken near one of the South African Army camps adjacent to Angola at sunset, framed by a Buffel troop carrier on one side and a Makalani palm on the other. Some old-timers will remember it.

Indeed, while each of us did have our quirks, there was no question that the majority of journalists in Luanda in October 1975 were as professional as they come. Simply put, they had to be or they would never have kept their jobs: that of reporting on developments on the African continent. So it happened that I found myself in Luanda roughly 18 months after the Portuguese Army had beaten an inordinately hasty retreat back to the Metropolis.

The city then was firmly in the hands of the MPLA and there was no question: those calling the shots were utterly ruthless in their opposition to any of the other guerrilla groups, the FNLA and UNITA especially. Both had been run out of the city in a series of urban battles that had left many people dead. Consequently we hacks were treated to the emergence of an extremely radical group that had all but deified Lenin and Karl Marx. In fact, the party not only declared its communist affiliations, but included its own version of the hammer and sickle on what eventually became the country's national flag.

I was doing work at the time for a variety of publications including the Johannesburg *Sunday Express*, Geneva's *Interavia* as well as *Scope*, a news magazine that sometimes liked to emulate *Playboy* with lots of scantily-clad bimbos. And while the independence of an African state didn't appeal to everybody, the country and the violence that followed Lisbon's departure tended to make news.

So, quite happily, I joined this fairly large bunch of scribblers who had arrived to report the goings-on in Luanda; that is when we weren't quaffing *Cuba Libres* by the tumbler-full. But what should have been a rather august event – a young and aspiring country joining almost 50 other African states that had earlier achieved their sovereign independence from Britain, France, Belgium and others – it was anything but.

Security had already become a problem in the country and some parts of Angola were plunged into what can best be described as 'mindless violence'. Even Luanda was not secure. Allen Pizzey and I were strolling along the city's lagoonside Marginal one afternoon and we had to take cover because a machine-gun opened up somewhere on the heights that overlooked the city, either on us or somebody uncomfortably close to where we were.

Because so many of the original Portuguese inhabitants of Luanda had already decamped, accommodation had become a problem, so most of us stayed at the few local hotels still open.

---

1 Luke Harding: Poland's ace reporter Ryszard Kapuściński accused of fiction-writing, *The Guardian*, London, March 2, 2010.

Also, on accounts of national currency issues, linked to the Portuguese escudo – and a lot else besides that had not yet been sorted out – we were required to pay in greenbacks. That we did not mind, because our offices back home were picking up the tabs, except that it made a bottle of Scotch hellish expensive.

But even those conditions soon became uncertain. Almost overnight there were scores more 'journalists' joining our throng, only these came from Cuba as well as a good sprinkling of Soviets, Poles, Bulgarians and even a North Vietnamese or two. Africa was represented by some really ominous people from Cairo, Dar es Salaam, Algiers and Ghana and there was no question that many were what we usually referred to as spooks.

Obviously it was impossible for me to retreat into any kind of shell because, British passport or not, everybody with whom I came into contact knew that I worked from South Africa. That had gone over well enough when Lisbon still ruled, but with Portugal almost out of the local political spectrum, I suddenly had to answer a lot of questions about apartheid.

Because I had been covering the African beat since the mid-1960s, I could handle that – including the fact that I had written a book two years previously that viciously castigated apartheid – which was fine, except that things took a more serious turn when I was approached one evening by a couple of enthusiastic young journalists of doubtful origin. They asked whether I was aware that the South African army had invaded Angola.

This was all totally new to me and I told them that it really did not make sense. My reply was direct: why would Pretoria be so stupid as to actually *invade* a neighbouring country?

I knew nothing about it, I said, but there was no question their eyes told me they believed I was lying.

Later that evening I was befriended by a Cuban who didn't identify himself except to say that his name was Óscar and that he lived in a small town close to Havana, the Cuban capital. His approached was friendly but soon became ingratiating, which worried me. You said nothing untoward in Luanda during the difficult period, but he was clearly intent on getting under my skin.

We talked about everything: where I was born, my parents and where I was educated. He was surprised to learn that this South African-born journalist had finished his professional studies in London and carried a British passport. It wasn't long before he asked me, nudge-nudge, wink-wink how I'd managed that? That irked. So did the obsequious way he would occasionally preface his questions with the expression '*hablando se entiende la gente*' (By talking, people understand each other) which might have worked under interrogation in a Cuban jail but not in a Luanda nightclub where everybody was enjoying themselves. I slipped out shortly afterwards.

The following night I was again approached, this time by half a dozen of my putative colleagues. Again I was questioned about the 'invasion'. One of them mentioned that the 'Boers' had taken Pereira d'Eca, a provincial administrative centre in the far south I knew quite well from visiting it several times in previous years. Somebody else used the word 'Savannah', and then qualified it asking if I knew the meaning of 'Operation Savannah'. I did not, I replied truthfully.

Things were really bad when one of my inquisitors said that I was a known supporter of the South African Government. 'Yes', I replied, 'as the rope does the hanging man.' I reminded him of my track record and having even written a book about the iniquities of the apartheid system.[2]

In my mind, at that moment, several alarm bells rang. Obviously there was something going on in South Angola that I knew nothing about and because everybody with whom I mixed knew that I worked in racist South Africa, things started becoming uncomfortable, especially after someone on the fringes of our social group had been found shot a few days previously. It was suicide, we were told…

---

2   *Coloured: A Profile of Two Million South Africans:* Human and Rousseau, Cape Town, 1974.

Worse, there had been several battles in the streets of Luanda during the week. It was nothing serious because there were guns being fired every night in the streets of this great city, but successive volleys of automatic fire adjacent to your hotel does tend to focus the mind. And were it not for the fact that some of my colleagues with whom I and the others had been socialising moved away when I approached in the clubs and restaurants we all frequented, I might have stayed longer. In short, I was being given a bums rush by my erstwhile mates.

The thought had already crossed my mind — several times, in fact — that I was possibly being regarded by some of them as a South African spy. That was when I began to consider my options, or what was left of them.

I had not yet got my story, so I was obviously hardly ready to return home. Also, every one of these scribes with whom I associated was aware that there was a fairly hefty war going on in the interior, with one group of fighters opposed to the future government — the Front for the Liberation of Angola or FNLA — having taken Nova Lisboa, the country's second largest city in the Central Highlands. The real war between the various factions was still to come.

Meanwhile, scheduled flights between most urban centres in the country — sporadic for the most part — did continue and this seemed hopeful. So I made a few discreet inquiries and discovered that there was a plane leaving Luanda for Nova Lisboa every night at about nine. Whether or not there would be a seat available was another matter.

Two nights later, telling nobody of my intentions, I paid my hotel bill, slipped out through one of the rear entrances and got a friend to drive me to Luanda Airport. There I joined a queue about a mile long, with just about everybody trying desperately to get to Nova Lisboa. It did not help that the Angolan Airline offering this service was equipped with high-wing Fokker F-27 Friendships, which at max, could take something like 40 passengers.

So there was I at the airport, very much aware that just about everybody around me was desperate to get on that plane. Angolan independence was officially scheduled for November 11th, a week or so away, and since fighting in the adjacent hinterland had intensified, the majority believed that the city was about to become a battlefield. That never happened, but with a civil war threatening, who could really be sure?

Bag in hand, and standing behind a line of hopefuls that seemed to go on forever, I had to do something, only too aware that even being there was a risk. One of my American colleagues had mentioned the day before that MPLA political commissars — backed by still-discreet squads of Soviet agents who were already in the country — were monitoring all movement at the airport, both in and out. And at six foot two and not being the most inconspicuous fellow on the block, my presence there that evening would almost certainly have been noted. There was no question: I had to make that flight, which is when I made my move…

With the kind of determined, poker-faced purpose that suggested I had a firm booking in hand, I strode directly towards the check-in counter and in the best Portuguese I could muster, I demanded to know who was in charge.

'I am,' said an officious white youngster with gold braid on his shoulder, obviously displeased at my approach. Under any other circumstance he probably wouldn't have given me the time of day.

'Well,' I said, 'my name is Venter and I am pleased to meet you.' With that, I thrust out my hand. He could hardly ignore my outstretched paw, so reluctantly he took it. I knew immediately that he'd felt that rustle of a banknote in my palm.

It was the oldest trick in the book and he knew very well how to discreetly accept a tightly-folded $100 bill. And he did so without anybody being aware that a transaction had taken place. But before he took my passport he went out back for a moment or two, probably to check the amount.

That night I slept in Nova Lisboa.

Prior to independence, there was bitter (and most times violent) rivalry between the various political factions. Both the FNLA and UNITA (see here) would seek out MPLA cadres and the battles that followed were always bloody. (Author's collection)

Among the last of Lisbon's forces to leave Angola were its commandos, considered to be the most reliable to maintain some semblance of order.

Daniel Chipenda, a former MPLA regional commander who had switched sides to the FNLA, was among the more prominent Angolan political figures opposed to Marxist rule in Angola. (Author's photo)

Whatever else took place in Angola during this difficult period, Neto's MPLA had to display a measure of control and in this the national bank in Luanda was pivotal. (Author's photo)

Efforts were made by both Lisbon and the Americans to bring opposing leaders together: as happened when Neto and Savimbi held discussions, seen here together on the flight to Luanda. (Author's collection)

Some of the posters which decorated the walls of most buildings throughout the country.

The author flew from Luanda to Nova Lisboa in a Fokker F-27: one of the last flights to maintain links between the two cities. (Author's photo)

Within the ranks of the MPLA, female combatants played a major role. (Author's photo)

FNLA troops prepare for battle. (Author's photo)

As Executive Outcomes was to discover, many MPLA soldiers had been shanghaied into the ranks, some not yet into their teens.

Black fighters attached to one or other of the political contenders.

MPLA march past at a remote bush camp. (Author's collection)

The flight itself was not entirely uneventful. Because there were so many military factions involved in the transitional 'freedom' process – there were more people with guns in Luanda than there had ever been, even during the Portuguese colonial period – and I was pleased to be out of it.

And since there was always somebody emptying his AK magazine at some real or imagined target – and that included low-flying aircraft – it also meant that after the pilot had lifted the Friendship's wheels off the ground, he had to make a long, lazy circle over the airport to gain enough height, just in case anybody did end up firing at us.

Once on board, I found myself sitting next a pleasant young fellow who said he was off to visit his mother in Nova Lisboa. He, too, lived in Johannesburg, he told me, and was intrigued to hear that I had just spent a couple of weeks in the Angolan capital.

Because he expressed fears about the upcoming handover, he quizzed me keenly as to what conditions were like in the big city – the East European presence especially, which, I thought, was a bit odd. But since I was out of that dreadful place, I confided that I was not only pleased to have moved on, but *damn pleased*.

I was really pretty candid indeed about fears for my personal safety had I stayed on there.

The 500-odd kilometre flight went quickly, with the two of us sharing half a bottle of Johnny Walker because we'd all heard that Nova Lisboa was not only cut off from any of the coastal cities but almost under siege.

On arrival at our destination about midnight, the pilot addressed the passengers through the intercom. He told us to remain in our seats because a certain unnamed VIP had to disembark first.

The Fokker came to a stop alongside the terminal, and from what I could see through the aircraft window, there was a fairly smart military escort group formed up on the apron as the steps were brought alongside. At this point my new-found pal quietly excused himself, got out of his seat and made his way towards the back of plane. As he appeared at the door, the troops outside were ordered to attention and their officers saluted.

Only afterwards was I to discover that my companion was actually one of the senior military commanders of the FNLA force then holding Nova Lisboa. He'd successfully slipped past the goons at Luanda Airport and I am pretty certain that once they had learned who it was that had boarded the F-27, they would have seriously upgraded security for all future flights. Flight services between Luanda and Nova Lisboa ended shortly afterwards.

One of his last gestures before we parted was to suggest that I give him a shout once I'd settled in. I would find him at the local headquarters were his final words. So I did, a day or two later, only we met for lunch at my hotel, one of the few restaurants still functioning in a large city in the process of preparing for war.

One of the first comments he made was to apologise for telling me that he was visiting his mother. His family were all in Portugal, he said, but he did live in Johannesburg and without going into detail, confided that getting back to Nova Lisboa was vital because hostilities had already started.

What was interesting was that while he was aware that I intended to write about my experiences, he was candid about what was going on. There were daily clashes in the hills to the west of the city, where some MPLA elements had tried to make inroads, and though these were still moderate threat-wise, things would soon escalate, he intimated. As it was, he had some of his forces deployed in depth on all roads leading towards the coast and contacts with the enemy were now happening daily.

When he explained that many of his troops were irregulars and included a sizeable body of soldiers who had formerly served in the Portuguese Army – as well as a few foreigners who 'believe in our cause' – I chose that moment to ask whether I could join.

'*Join*? What do you mean?' he asked incredulously. After all, he added, I was supposed to be a journalist…

'Join your crowd, for the upcoming showdown', I replied.

At which point he hesitated, before looking at me straight in the eye and adding that his people had no money and that everybody in his ranks were there because of their political convictions.'

'Well, I said, 'I'm not in favour of a Soviet take-over of Angola either, so count me in.' He obviously could not help smiling and suggested that I report to his barracks the following morning to pick up a uniform and some hardware.

I had already explained that I was thoroughly familiar with firearms, having spent three years in the navy and was also a member of a gun club in Midrand between Johannesburg and Pretoria, where I regularly competed at competition level at the Guthrie shooting range with my .45ACP pistol. It had originally belonged to *Soldier of Fortune's* owner Colonel Robert K. Brown, with whom I had covered the war in Rhodesia several times.

So it was, a day later, I was issued with a camouflage uniform and what I thought was a brand new *Fabrique Nationale* FAL in 7.62mm NATO calibre. Had I taken the trouble to examine my piece more closely, I would have seen that it was not Belgian-made at all, but a standard-issue R1 rifle, then in everyday use by the South African Army. The weapon was manufactured by Lyttelton Engineering outside Pretoria.

I was also not yet aware that an entire South African battle group was in the process of leap-frogging halfway across the length of Angola as part of what was to become known as Operation Savannah.

My fellow combatants in Nova Lisboa could hardly be described as 'Great Guns'. The majority were Angolan nationals, split between the country's three racial groups; mostly black, some white and quite a few more of mixed blood or *Mestiços*. Almost all, if asked, would tell you that they regarded themselves as the country's new breed of *Angolanas*; proudly so.

The few officers with whom I came into contact – at least those who showed their faces – were mostly of European extraction and had served in the Portuguese Army.

Though the unit was strictly military, many of the Angolans in our ranks had grown up in the highlands and had spent most of their lives outdoors. Being African, they had their own hunting rifles which, when needed, would be used in preference to either AKs or the newly-arrived R1s.

The reason was simple, one of them told me. 'When we go out, we never bunch up while on the move. Some of us head out to high ground…and there we wait for those bastards to show themselves. All we need to see is a head,' he declared, fondly patting his Holland and Holland .375 Magnum rifle fitted with a decent power scope.

He reckoned he'd killed quite a few of the enemy at ranges in excess of 500 metres. Nor was he shy to use soft-nosed bullets – referred to as Dum-Dums in the lingo – which, under the Geneva Convention, is illegal.

The African military component in Nova Lisboa's new-found military unit, to my mind was certainly the most interesting of the group of combatants I'd joined.

This shadowy bunch of guerrillas had seen a lot of action in the past, commanded as they were by a disillusioned former communist by the name of Daniel Chipenda.

Numbering several hundred, the squadron had started out fighting the Portuguese by loudly proclaiming fealty to the MPLA. They then switched to the CIA-financed FNLA and it was the money that did it, maintain Chipenda's detractors. You were left in little doubt that the moving force behind this unit was Chipenda himself, whose background was almost as complex as that of the war in which he was involved, but nobody was ever certain where he was, or even whether he lived in Nova Lisboa.

A testy but competent military man, he had fallen foul of the elders of the founding party while serving as the MPLA representative in Dar-es-Salaam. His job, early on, was to coordinate training and supply programmes with other liberation groups in Southern Africa, which was a significant posting because a large proportion of the military hardware used by the MPLA – as well as Mozambican and Rhodesian liberation groups – was channelled through the Tanzanian port.

By all accounts, his role within the MPLA had always been problematic. He constantly griped that because the top structure of the political movement was composed mainly of *Mestiços*, his party was 'too white'. Things came to a head in 1973 when he was involved in an assassination attempt on his boss, Agostinho Neto. The Soviets got a whiff of it and warned the MPLA chief, but the sad thing is that once Neto took over the country, he had become weary of all the stringent socialist constraints through which that people had laboured over several decades. Communist or not, like Mozambique's Samora Machel, he would have liked closer ties with the West.

Machel subsequently died in a still-unexplained plane crash, while Neto succumbed while undergoing relatively minor surgery in a Moscow clinic under circumstances which have never been properly explained. Clearly, the Soviets (and Putin today) have always done things their own way.

Meantime, Chipenda used his position as head of *Chipa Esquadrao* to good effect and eventually the word got about that he was also working for South African Military Intelligence. This was a man who wore a diversity of hats.

Shortly after Operation Savannah ended, he sent his merry band of *Chipa* veterans – almost *en bloc* – southwards across the border with South West Africa. In a pre-arranged agreement to which his troops agreed, he handed them over to the South African Army.

The unit was then moulded into what was later to become known as 32 Battalion by Colonel Jan Breytenbach (which I cover in detail in Chapter 30).

It is interesting that there were also some former Rhodesians in Nova Lisboa who were 'on call' should things get out of hand, as one of the volunteers phrased it. These fellow African expatriates had left the old country to make new lives for themselves and their families in what the majority regarded as a 'Promised Land'.

It looked good when they first arrived. They were given as much farmland as they could use and embraced by all as precursors of still more families to arrive from the 'White South'. As one of them explained, they had been made to feel totally comfortable and accepted by the locals in their new environment, but then Angola had been welcoming new settlers for five centuries.

Quite a few of the 'Rhodies' had built lovely homes in the hills surrounding the city. There was even talk of starting an English school as well as a 'Club Rhodesiana'. Just then, all these good intentions were moved onto the back burner because contact with MPLA units (as well as the occasional UNITA guerrilla group) was becoming more regular and also much more intense.

Whenever a fire-fight did take place, those involved would return to the city with their wounded and the occasional irregular KIA and the news would ripple through the community. To a chorus of wailing and many tears, most of the European locals would start telling each other that things were getting serious.

A day or two later, everything would be forgotten and things would return back to normal. Until the next time…

Though I stayed on at my hotel – my magazine paid, so the expense didn't come out of my pocket – everything centred on one of the houses in town that was being used as an operational headquarters. If we weren't out in the countryside, we'd wait for instructions or help with training. The 'Home Guard' as they called it, was mostly WAGs (wives and girl friends) of our associates who would do the washing, cleaning and nursing and have food waiting for their men when they returned, usually towards dusk.

This worried me, because it was obvious that these rather limited hostilities were largely limited to daylight hours with everybody back home for supper before the sun went down. But, I was told, it was the unit's set routine and adhered to almost like clockwork. In my opinion that did not seem too healthy and I said so. When I asked whether there were others out there manning defences and road blocks during the dark hours, my query raised eyebrows.

One of them collared me afterwards and asked why I wanted to know. I told him that my logic was simple: If the MPLA was aware of us settling down into some kind of regular pattern, they might not only try to attack the city after dark, but it wasn't impossible that they'd wait in ambush for our people to return to their positions in the morning.

The fellow scoffed. He actually said that I shouldn't worry my little mind with things that were totally inconsequential; it was all being dealt with.

But two days later, on an off-duty day when I remained back at base, several of the pickups rushed back into town from the front as we were having breakfast. One of the vehicles had been ambushed as it left town and was badly shot up. Those telling us what had happened brought back the body of one of our fighters on their truck.

Pandemonium followed. Within moments we had a dozen of our women wailing and just about everybody within walking distance coming to look at the body, which was not a pretty sight because he had been caught in an RPG blast. Obviously, this rigmarole was both odd and unnecessary because Nova Lisboa had seen its share of violence over the previous year and there had been an awful lot of people killed.

The following evening, at a morbid dinner with a few of our guys at my hotel, I suddenly had a little fellow – an *umfaan,* who could not have been more than five or six years old – come off the street to give me a note.

It was all quite informal but the message was clear. *'Go Home! If you do not you will die,'* it read

The kid belonged to one of the labourers in the immediate vicinity of the hotel and he was tracked down soon enough because a waiter recognised him. On being questioned, the youngster said that a black soldier had given him the piece of paper. He'd even walked with him to the door of the restaurant where I was discreetly pointed out; the boy was told to give the letter to 'that white man with the beard' and he was handed a few escudos for his effort.

Obviously, this was troubling. While most of my colleagues laughed it off, I took it seriously, to the extent of barricading my hotel room door with a chest of drawers before I went to bed.

When I got a second letter a few days later, telling me that I would not be warned again and that I would be killed if I remained in Nova Lisboa, I thought that possibly the time had come for me to head south. Some of the Rhodesian farmers had also decided to pull out and it was an opportunity that might not happen again all too soon.

So I upped sticks and headed out with them on the long road south, first through Silva Porto, then on to Cuangar and finally along the Kavango River to Rundu in Caprivi where more adventures awaited us.

Only years later did I learn that while all these shenanigans were happening in Angola's second city, a fairly large group of South African troops backed by armoured cars had been delayed from entering Nova Lisboa, in large part because of my presence there. What Pretoria did not want was its clandestine military presence in Angola being exposed, the same presence I was asked about in that Luanda bar a short while before. I was after all, regarded by the authorities back home as a something of a nonconformist journalist. As somebody commented, who knows what I might have done with the news…

Somehow, they had to get rid of me and 'death threats' seemed to offer a likely solution to sending me on my way.

In truth, that irregular band of fighters that held the city could just have easily have bundled me off into the bush and shot me. But then, as I was made aware in subsequent years, there is usually a measure of honour among men in uniform, whatever their political hues…

The bottom line that underscores all these events is that I must be one of the few contemporary journalists to have joined an army in order to get my story. No question, it made for a bit of excitement.

Meanwhile, some of our other colleagues who had not joined us in Luanda but who were wandering about Angola in search of stories were making headway. ITN's Mike Nicholson had already achieved something of a breakthrough by reporting to London that he had seen South African soldiers in South Angola. Others spoke of mercenaries attached to UNITA forces, but they had no proof. Mike had wandered into a forward South African position at Silva Porto, now Menongue, made his report and filed it, but this was subsequently denied by the South African High Commission in Trafalgar Square.

Not long afterwards, having been joined by Fred Bridgland – the Reuters man in Lusaka – he boarded the Lonrho company jet on what was to have been a routine tour of 'Unitaland', otherwise known as Savimbi country. One of their stops while heading for Benguela on the coast was at Rundu, a South African military town and strongpoint near the northernmost border of South West Africa.

Once the aircraft was stationary on the runway, the two journalists stayed on board and spotted rows of Eland armoured cars, stacks of ammunition ten metres high, artillery pieces and hundreds of khaki-clad South African soldiers.[3]

On the apron were two or three South African Air Force C-130 transport planes being loaded with this stuff and taking off and landing in relays. They did not need to be told that everything they saw there was going straight into Angola to support the war effort. Caprivi's Rundu had effectively become the staging-post for the South African invasion of Angola.

Only weeks later I was stuck in Lusaka in Zambia in a desperate bid to get back into Angola again, together with all the other inkslingers, listening to reports of South African, Russian, American, rebel Portuguese and mercenary goings-on next door.

Worse, I'd been covering the same ground as ITN only weeks before, and which resulted in a series of adventures which got me arrested on charges of espionage and briefly jailed in a Congolese detention centre.

Those episodes take up four chapters in my book *Barrel of a Gun*, published by Casemate in the United States in 2010.

---

3 The South African armoured cars were listed as Elands by the military: air portable, light armoured cars based on the French-built Panhard AML. It was used by South Africa for long-range reconnaissance.

12

Cuba's Revolutionary Role in Angola

Pretoria's decision to go into Angola in force – which was what Operation Savannah was all about – was very carefully considered. Washington played a role – for a while – principally because Castro had sent in his army to support Luanda's Marxist regime.

A year before Lisbon's official independence handover, there was already a considerable amount of evidence, subsequently verified, that both Cuba and the Soviet Union had been actively fomenting their own version of a Peoples' Revolution geared for the communists to take over Angola *in toto*. Some of that emerged years later when a batch of Cuban state documents related to Castro's role in the Angolan war was leaked.

One of these documents was a letter from Luanda written by the leader of a delegation entrusted to make direct contact with Agostinho Neto, future president of Angola, shortly before independence.

Datelined Luanda, 11th August 1975, it came from Raúl Diaz Arguelles, a Cuban leader of what was termed The Tenth Direction and addressed for the attention of the Minister of the [Cuban] Revolutionary Armed Forces. Clearly, the messenger was an emissary with powerful sway. The communication arrived at its destination in Havana some months before the South Africans launched their somewhat ambitious Operation Savannah in what was regarded by some as a desperate bid to pre-empt the kind of Cuban gains that Arguelles had envisioned.

Headed 'Report on the visit to Angola and on conversations sustained with Agostinho Neto, President of the MPLA, its Politburo and head of the Angolan army', Arguelles told his superior that after they arrived in Luanda and made contact with the MPLA, the party arranged for hotel accommodation for the group. But immediately Neto heard that the Cubans had arrived, he countermanded and arranged for some of the more senior dignitaries to stay at his home and others to be lodged at the house of a senior MPLA functionary.

Much else emerged in this document, including the offer of military training for Angolan cadres in Cuba itself, links to FRELIMO, the Mozambique liberation group, supplies of weapons and other materiéls with which to fight against enemies of the people as well as strong condemnation of the forces of imperialism and capitalism and the rest.

The paragraph marked (c) is of interest because it has a significant bearing on would take place in the months ahead:

> That we came to visit the actual situation in order to properly assess what our aid should consist of, taking into account the aggression on the part of the FNLA and of Mobutu to the MPLA and the development of possible future actions until independence in the month of November. That we knew that the reactionaries and the imperialists would try all possible methods to avoid the forces of the MPLA take power, since this would mean that having a

progressive government in Angola, and based on this situation we brought militant solidarity from the Commander-in-Chief, or party and government…

Towards the end of this missive there is a statement that declares that Cuba …must help [the Angolan people] directly or indirectly to solve this situation, which definitely entails having the people resist powerfully against the reactionaries and international imperialists.

While it sounds like a lot of communist hogwash, Castro's intent to get involved in Angola is clear.

In the months following, Havana went into overdrive to help Neto's MPLA consolidate its position as the dominant force in Luanda (as well as many other cities in the north) and along the coast to the south. That included Benguela and the ports of Lobito and Mocamedes (later Namibe).

I arrived with the rest of the international press corps not long afterwards and like most people in Luanda, very few locals – and certainly not anyone linked to the Capitalist Press – were privy to what was going on, literally under our noses.

The CIA knew of course, because one of the first things Langley did was pass this information on to their South African associates in Pretoria…

To understand the nature of some of these convoluted developments, one needs to look back a little, and here I am indebted to what my old friend, editor, freelance combatant and journalist Yves Debay wrote in one of his magazines.[1]

As he declared, by 1975 the West had been heavily reliant on the Middle East for its oil requirements for decades and with time, would become even more so.

But, as we saw after the Six Day War, the Suez Canal became acutely vulnerable to closure. Sink a single ship in the main navigation channel and almost all Europe's Middle Eastern oil would have had to be routed around the Cape.

That had been the case before and Moscow's strategic planners said it could happen again. More salient, were it to happen – with the Soviet Union practically controlling the sea route from their African naval and air bases (that not only involved Soviet Tupolev TU-95 Bear bombers and TU-16 Badgers, but their warships too) – this powerful military presence would indubitably present the West with an enormous long-term threat.

Debray states:

> Without question, the Soviets would have derived invaluable strategic and economic advantages from a take-over of South Africa…further to getting hold of Pretoria's fantastic gold reserves, they could also lay their hands on the mineral wealth of southern Africa as a whole.
>
> As a western political observer put it when commenting on Soviet expansion in Africa at the time: 'From Cape Town, the Soviets will, in the long run, gradually control the policy of Europe and preside over its destiny, like they're doing in Finland'.

By late 1974, sizeable quantities of military hardware had already been shipped to the MPLA, followed shortly afterwards by 250 Cuban technicians and advisors who arrived in May 1975, just as the country was in the final move towards full independence.

---

1 Yves Debay; Angola and South West Africa: A Forgotten War (1975–89), *Raids Magazine*, No 44, July 1995. Yves was killed by a sniper's bullet in Aleppo, Syria in 2013 while reporting on the civil war for his magazine.

But nobody outside the upper echelons of Agostinho Neto's party was aware of these developments or even that Cuban troops were being clandestinely flown into remote airstrips by Soviet planes.

The Border War was already something of a feature of life in an increasingly embattled South Africa, but for the previous decade it was adequately dealt with the by the army and air force. This new development involving an acknowledged communist state with clear African aspirations (Cuba had already been involved militarily in the Congo, Somalia, Eritrea, with Egyptian forces in the Yemen, Algeria and with the Polisario Front against Morocco in the Western Sahara) obviously illuminated its intentions.

By 1975, when Angola was assured of full independence that November, both Havana and Moscow knew that the first move to achieve the objective of eventually ending up in Cape Town had to be initiated from Luanda. With the Portuguese showing their heels, Neto was urged to act.

Neto's military wing FAPLA secured Luanda harbour before independence, so the first Cuban freighter, *Vietnam Heroica* could berth. That vessel would deliver the initial batch of Castro's people, the *barbudos* (bearded ones, all Cubans) who were to play an increasingly significant role in Angolan military affairs at a fairly senior level. Additionally, thousands of tons of Soviet arms and equipment were airlifted into Angola by aircraft flying regular shuttles between Guinea's Conakry and Brazzaville in the Congo.

Although supported by the CIA, the small South African effort as well as mercenaries in the field linked to the pro-western FNLA collapsed. Lightly equipped, badly trained and lacking discipline Holden Roberto's men were no match for the communists who were generously supplied with artillery, particularly 122mm D-30 and M-46 130mm pieces, Soviet weaponry that had already proved versatile against the Americans in Vietnam.

Also, it did not help that Roberto had originally received almost all his funds from Larry Devlin, the CIA station chief in the Congolese capital and, more to the point, just about everybody involved knew this was taking place…

It should be mentioned that Cuba's links to the MPLA – and to its revolutionary leader Agostinho Neto – had been consolidated very early on in the so-called 'Liberation Struggle'.

Almost since the guerrilla war against Portugal had started, that Caribbean island had hosted fairly large squads of prospective Angolan guerrillas in a variety of training courses that prepared them for war. Obviously, this would all take place under cover and much of it only emerged after the fall of the Berlin Wall, though clearly, there had been whispers within the expatriate Cuban community in Miami for some time.

It was also from Miami where mercenary pilots needed to fly fighter aircraft for the Congo's Mobuto had been recruited some years before, something I deal with in great detail in *Mercenaries*, an earlier book.[2]

Meanwhile, a good deal of Angolan subterfuge was being coordinated by Moscow, whose commissars divided training and support needs between participating countries like Tanzania, Ethiopia, Algeria, Libya, Guinea (Conakry) and several Soviet states that included Bulgaria, Czechoslovakia, Romania and others.

Gradually Cuba came to head the list, underscored by a memorandum from the *Centro de Informacion de la Defensa de las Fuerzas Armadas Revolucionarias* dated 22nd November 1972 (three years before the South Africans launched Operation Savannah).

---

2 Al J. Venter, *Mercenaries: Putting the World to Rights with Hired Guns*, Casemate Publishers, US and the UK, 2014, Chapter 4 (Cuban Mercenaries in the Central Intelligence Agency's Air War in the Congo), Chapter 4, pp54-70.

It was written by Major Manuel Piñeiro Lozada to Major Raúl Castro, Fidel's brother and headed: Shipment of Comrades to Angola and Mozambique.

The document speaks for itself and I quote:

> For some time now we have discussed the possibility of entering Angola and Mozambique with the objective of getting to know the revolutionarily movements in those countries. These movements have been a mystery even for those socialist countries that gives them considerable aid. This research would help us give more focussed aid to those movements.
>
> I don't consider it necessary to delineate the strategic nature of these countries. It takes only pointing out that a change in the course of events of the wars that are developing in both countries could signify a change in all the forces on the African continent.
>
> For the first time two independent countries in Africa from which the bigger war could be waged would have common borders with the region with the principle investment and strongest political military knot of Imperialism in Africa exist: South Africa, Rhodesia, Zaire and the Portuguese colonies.
>
> Our comrades in Angola's MPLA solicited us this May for the following:
> a) That we train 10 men in Cuba in guerrilla warfare, taking into account the positive experiences they have had with people trained in Cuba (they are heads of various guerrilla detachments).
> b) That we send a crew to fly a DC-3 from Zambia or the Congo [Brazzaville] to Angola for the purpose of transporting equipment [our] guerrillas. They explained that because of great distances to the Northern Front and the borders with Zambia and the Congo it is extremely difficult to maintain the supplies by land and it is from that front where they have contacts and are planning urban actions in the capital Luanda, which have military and political importance.
> c) They want to send a high level delegation to Cuba to discuss relations with our Party.
>
> We suggested that we thought it a good idea to send some of our comrades to the interior of Angola to learn about the terrain of battle and to shoot a film, to which they agreed, and they proposed postponing their solicitations until the return of our delegation.
>
> The delegation would be protected by 150 troops directed by one of the commanders trained in Cuba.

It is worth taking another look at one other event that had a bearing on Cuba's subsequent involvement in the former Portuguese colonial territory.

Late 1965, a few years after many African countries had been handed full independence to run their own affairs by Britain and France (and the Congo, by Belgium), Argentina-born Che Guevara spent a while in Central Africa for the purpose of studying the prospects of revolution, as it was described in a letter home.

By then Guevara was a member of Castro's Politburo and the so-called 'Liberation Wars' in Angola and Mozambique were in full flow. Somebody in Havana must have believed that prospects in what he termed in his writings *The Black Continent* were excellent for expanding the Marxist Credo among the uninitiated.

Guevara spent a lot of time in the eastern reaches of Mobuto's Congo, some of it with Laurent Kabila who was eventually to become president of this vast country, even though, were we to judge from his letters home, Guevara regarded Kabila as the ultimate nincompoop. The revolutionary also had dealings with groups of Angolans who were trying to help their co-conspirators oust Lisbon's influence from Africa.

None of it was easy, and we get an insight to some of the problems faced from a letter that Che Guevara wrote to Oscar Fernandez Padilla in the Cuban capital. The original document came from Havana's *Archivo del Comite Central* [Archive of the Central Committee].

Padilla's code-name was Rafael while Guevara went under the *nom de guerre* Tatu, which interestingly, is the word for three in Swahili.

The document, originally in Spanish, read:

> Rafael,
> I attach some letters for you from Flavio. Not all is well in terms of organization. Changa insists that he has no money, and that is the reason why he doesn't set up the camp in Kigoma [the Tanzanian port on Lake Tanganyika]. Now, Olivia has left with Kabila without leaving money. I gave him all my reserve money, 8,150 (surmised to be US dollars) which they should reimburse me (5,000) so we can always have money available. The 50,000 came to me like a ring to a finger, since I was out of money and now we have the politics of buying everything, even yucca.
>
> I am completely in agreement in preparing the clandestine base with these characteristics: if possible, buy or make a contract with a warehouse where the principal nutritional products can arrive without bringing much attention, have a … near the lake and relatively far from Kigoma with a natural loading dock…[illegible] find one or two boats that can go without being suspicious over there. The best thing would be to have two… on this side and cross twice (back and forth) in the night.
>
> But that depends on various factors. [illegible]…
> Tatu

The fact that Che Guevara signed himself as Number Three suggests that he already saw himself as third in line in the Cuban power hierarchy, directly behind Fidel Castro and his brother Raúl.

What is important here is that none of it would have happened – *or could have happened* – had there not been solid collusion with radical influences at the head of the Portuguese military hierarchy, not only in Lisbon but in Angola itself.

What happened was once the new revolutionary military leadership in Portugal decided that all Metropolitan troops would be withdrawn from Africa, the Portuguese military authorities in Luanda – led by Admiral Rosa Coutinho – declared that the best course of action would be to cooperate fully with Agostinho Neto's Marxist MPLA.

That was the unofficial version. What has since emerged is that Admiral Coutinho had not been dubbed Red – thus Rosa Coutinho – for nothing. He was a full blown, communist cadre of long standing and the fact that he had been appointed to the topmost position in Portugal's largest African colony, suggests that there were others who thought like he did to have shuffled through what was clearly a highly controversial appointment.

From the start of his tenure, Coutinho maintained close links with Neto and other senior members of his party. They visited regularly at each others' homes, exchanged gifts and as some wiseacre commented, covered one another's backs so that neither UNITA nor Holden Roberto's FNLA could make headway in the peace process. In fact, Coutinho all but ignored the other political contenders.

Luanda, by now, was under full control of the MPLA and it was the admiral's job – by his own volition – to see that it stayed that way.

Other documents that emerged from Havana's CIDFAR or *Centro de Informacion de la Defensa de las Fuerzos Armadas Revolucionarias* (and subsequently in Lisbon), make it clear that Admiral Coutinho was not only aware of Cuban political aspirations in Angola but actually helped make it happen.

To begin with, he knew about clandestine parties of Castro's people entering the country either directly or through Brazzaville and Pointe Noire and secret arms shipments that were being landed along the coast north of Luanda.

If there was any proof needed of Admiral Coutinho's collaboration with his erstwhile enemy, it is found in a final personal note he wrote under the letterhead of his sumptuous Governor-General's office in Luanda, dated 22 December, 1974.

The original, in Portuguese, reads as follows:

Republica Portugesa
State of Angola
Office of the Governor-General
LUANDA, 22 December 1974

Comrade Agostinho Neto
The UNITA and FNLA insist in replacing me for some reactionary guy who may play along with them. If this happens, the whole project we've guised to handle the power solely to the MPLA would crumble apart. Those puppet movements get their support from whites whose sole intention is to perpetuate the heinous Portuguese imperialism and colonialism – the one based on the Faith and Empire motto, that is to say, reeking of moist-smelling churches and of the popish, plutocratic exploitation.

Those Imperialist forces intend to counter our Prague secret agreements that comrade Cunhal signed on behalf of the PCP [Portuguese Communist Party] so that, under the aegis of the glorious PC [Communist Party], of the USSR we may extend communism from Tangiers to the Cape and from Lisbon to Washington.

Empower the MPLA in Angola is vital to topple that bastard Mobutu, and imperialist lackey, and secure Zaire as a platform.

After the last secret meeting with the PCP comrades, we advise you to immediately start to execute the second phase of the plan. Wasn't it Fanon who said that the inferiority complex can only be overcome by killing the coloniser?

Comrade Agostinho Neto, give your MPLA militants secret instructions to terrorize the whites by every means, either by killing, looting or arson, in order to provoke their flight from Angola. Be cruel especially with children, women and elderly in order to discourage the bravest. Only terror will drive those bloodsucking white dogs out of this land to which they are so attached.

Both the FNLA and UNITA won't be able to count with the white peoples support, their finances and military expertise. Uproot them in such a way so that, with the white mens' fall (sic) the entire capitalist structure will collapse and a new socialist society may be installed, or at least the former won't be easily rebuilt.

Revolutionary salute, the Victory is certain
Signed António Rosa Coutinho, Vice-Admiral

It is interesting, that throughout, the informal *da* (you) in Portuguese is used in the familiar, amicable way and not in the deferential *de* that would customarily be used in exchanges of this

The first indication that Cuba had military intentions in Angola came with Operation Savannah, when the South Africans moved into Angola. They came up against a sizeable Cuban force, backed by modern Soviet weapons and armour, including tanks. (Author's collection)

Fidel Castro had been a long time planning to get involved in all the former Portuguese territories and in this regard he became the ultimate Soviet surrogate.

Emblem of Cuba's *Las Fuerzas Armadas Revolucionarias (FAR)* – Revolutionary Armed Forces of Cuba.

Cartoonists had been having a field day, ever since the start of the 'Liberation Wars': East against West.

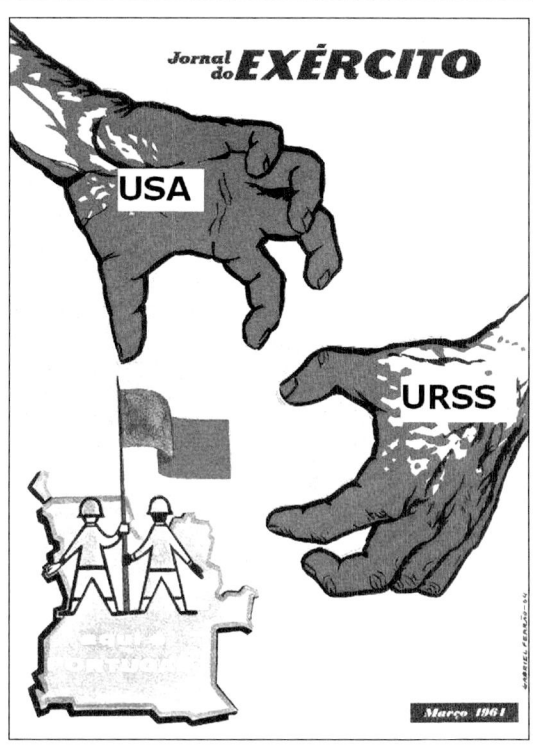

Cuba's military was able to give a good account of itself in Angola as its members had already been involved in several African wars. Castro was to send 16,000 men to Ethiopia's Ogaden to fight a proxy war on behalf of Moscow.

In the early 1960s Che Guevara made several clandestine probes into the region, including visits to both Congos as well as Tanzania.

Cuban troops march as part of guard of honour at the Mausoleum of José Martí, Castro's historic revolutionary mentor.

On arrival in Angola, Cuban soldiers were warmly welcomed by Neto's MPLA and lower ranks mixed easily with the populace.

Once active in Angola, Cuban propagandists used every opportunity to emphasise close links between Castro and the Angolan hierarchy.

Across the board, Cuban officers and NCOs tended to keep themselves apart from the Angolan populace. They mucked in when they needed to but were sometimes criticised for being unnecessarily aloof.

Castro maintained close links with African leaders opposed to Portuguese rule. Amilcar Cabral, head of Portuguese Guinea's PAIGC revolutionary movement, was among his favourites. (Author's collection)

nature. Simply put, that indicates strong, sociable links between the two men that obviously went way back.

Though the 'Red Admiral' might not have been aware of it at the time, his actions – as well as those of his communist and socialist compadres back home – ended up costing hundreds of thousands of Angolan lives in the 30-something years of dislocation and civil war that followed the departure of his own people in 1974/75.

Additionally, millions of people were forced to flee their homes or were displaced by revolutionary violence, one of the reasons why today's slum communities in Luanda are among the largest on the continent.

The noted Australian military correspondent Robert Moss, who made his name in Britain writing for the *Daily Telegraph* and as editor of *Foreign Report* and the *Economist's* 'Confidential Weekly' had his own take on the Cubans, some of which follows.

One of the historic battles of recent Angolan history was called the Battle of Quifangondo, which took place on 10 November, 1975, a day before Angola became an independent state.

A couple of years later, Robert Moss offered us a graphic account of what happened in his report titled Battle of Death Road, published in *The Sunday Telegraph* on 6 February, 1977.

We were already aware by then that the Marxist MPLA, by various means including violence, had successful gained control of the Angolan capital, while the two rival liberation movements, the National Liberation Front of Angola (FNLA) and the National Union for the Total Independence of Angola (UNITA), fought for a foothold themselves before independence could be declared.[3]

A fairly large FNLA force had gathered to the immediate north of Luanda, made up of 1,000 fighters together with 120 mostly white Portuguese Angolan soldiers under the command of a former Portuguese colonel – formerly PIDE/DGS – Santos e Castro.

There were also two Zairian Army battalions led by the 7th Battalion commander Colonel Mamina Lama and several dozen South African troops under the command of Brigadier Ben Roos, the man who was to head South Africa's Special Forces units. Prior to that, the FNLA – attacking from north-eastern Angola – had defeated the MPLA at Porto Quipiri before marching to Quifangondo which, about two hours march from Luanda, was almost within sight of the city.

There is a good deal of confusion about what actually took place in that final period and in which specific time-frame, except that Holden Roberto ignored good advice from the South Africans that a frontal assault would not work: there were simply not enough resources to make that final push, considering that Cuba had mustered a sizeable force to protect Luanda. But he decided to go ahead anyway and one disaster followed another, to the extent that after Quifangondo, the FNLA were relegated to the back burner and were never again to become part of the overall struggle.

Robert Moss is exceptionally detailed in his reports when he tells us that the FNLA column had advanced to the area of the Bengo River and was supposed to strike across the bridge at first light on that momentous final day. But somehow the orders got garbled, officers overslept, and the attack did not start until just before eight.

It was the direction of the attack rather than its timing that doomed it, Moss says. Facing Holden Roberto's men, on the other side of the Bengo River was a large force of MPLA soldiers commanded by Cubans, right down to section level.

They were very well-armed, he tells us. I quote: 'They had jeep-mounted rocket-launchers, heavy mortars, the huge 40-barrelled Stalin organs that terrified black troops, together with plenty of machine-guns and anti-tank guns.' They had dug themselves in on hilltops at Quifangondo with

---

[3] The Battle of Quifangondo – Wikipedia.

their guns commanding the only road to Luanda from the north, now bordered by swamp because of the rainy season.

When the Portuguese commanders suggested that the main offensive down the exposed road should be supported by flanking movements on foot through the swamp, the black FNLA officers refused to send their men out, complaining that the swamp was full of crocodiles and 'man-eating snakes.'

The South African and American advisors with FNLA were alarmed by the planned offensive, and it was suggested that Roberto should attempt a broad encircling movement from the east. But Roberto, burning with impatience to plant his flag in the capital before Independence Day, insisted on taking the direct route, down what has since become known as Death Road.

What is notable is that at the request of the FNLA leader, the SADF provided that attacking force with three outdated Second World War 140mm howitzers (which was as advanced as they had at the time). These had been set up on high ground at Morro do Cal which overlooked the combat area, but as it turned out afterwards, lacked the range to have any impact on the outcome.[4]

An air strike by SAAF Canberra bombers initiated the onslaught and shortly afterwards, a pair of 130mm cannon bought by Mobutu Sese Seko from North Korea were brought to bear.

From Luanda's side, the battle was well planned. The Cubans and FAPLA units waited until the entire attacking force was boxed into a predetermined killing zone between the coast and a lagoon before bombarding them. Most of the FNLA's armoured cars together with Jeeps carrying CIA-supplied recoilless rifles were destroyed in the first hour. It was estimated that the Cubans sent in about 2,000 rockets which totally demoralised the attackers, who then fled.

Colonel Santos e Castro's Portuguese Angolan commando force was also in disarray, due to the loss of most of their armoured cars and the death of some of their crews in the previous day's battle. His forces had consolidated a short distance north-east of their earlier occupied position on a ridge line; leaving the South African artillery together with a small SADF force there to protect the approaches from Cuban/FAPLA encroaches.

Shortly afterwards, Brigadier Roos threatened to withdraw his guns from northern Angola if they were not protected by a line of troops forward of their emplacements. Roberto was apparently furious because his Portuguese Angolan allies had left the South African guns vulnerable to attack and possible capture.

Sensing more problems, Roos shortly afterwards pulled all his men back to Ambriz from where they were taken onboard the South African warships, SAS *President Steyn* and SAS *President Kruger*, Type 12 former Royal Navy frigates, with the replenishment ship SAS *Tafelberg* providing logistical support.

The *President Steyn* used inflatable boats and its Westland Wasp helicopter to extricate 26 South Africans successfully from the beach and the guns, having been towed to Zaire, were picked up shortly afterwards and landed at Walvis Bay, South West Africa's major port.

That effectively ended Operation Savannah.

There was no question that the CIA orchestrated much of what happened at Quifangondo as well as subsequently, for no other reason than that Washington (and specifically the CIA) had a vested interest in the outcome of this war.

In his reports, Moss suggested a rather uncharacteristic lack of attention to detail on the part of the Americans, which might be determined either way. Perhaps Washington had no wish to

---

4   Edward George: *The Cuban Intervention in Angola, 1965–1991*, Cass Military Studies, Frank Cass, London 2005.

see Luanda taken by a force comprising a bunch of fresh-faced South African youngsters parading down the Marginal in their armoured cars.

Brigadier Roos afterwards complained of another reason for failure and unquestionably, being on the spot, he was in a better position to judge than anybody else.

Moss takes up the story:

> In the days before the attack on Luanda, the CIA had organised an emergency airlift of weapons for the FNLA. Mortars and light infantry weapons were flown into Zaire in big C-141 transports and ferried on to Ambriz by Zairean air force planes and the FNLAs own Fokker Friendships, expropriated from the old civilian airline.
>
> These weapons included ten new 120mm mortars and some 106mm recoilless guns. But according to the South African brigadier, the weapons arrived without handling instructions or sighting equipment. There was no time to prepare the FNLA or Santos e Castro's people as to handling procedures.
>
> This account is disputed by American sources. Washington subsequently claimed that there was no failure on the side of the suppliers and that there must have been a mix-up on the ground' [Either way, it was dereliction of duty on the part of whoever was responsible to overseeing the venture].
>
> This, in turn, might well have been related to the political climate in Washington. Because of the legal requirements that had been imposed on the CIA to report its operations to Congress, the officers assigned to liaise with Holden Roberto were pulled in and out of Angola like yo-yos.
>
> Although the Americans were the principal armourers for the FNLA (who had also benefited from many other sources including China, which had earlier provided several hundred instructors to train FNLA troops at Kinkuzu in Zaire) they failed to provide continuous or effective tactical advice and logistical supervision on the ground.
>
> American instructors for the 120mm mortars and the 106mm recoilless guns turned up in the end – after the battle for Luanda had been lost. Even when they did arrive, they came without range tables for the guns.

An issue rarely touched on with regard to post-independent Angolan developments was the level of preparedness achieved by the Cuban military, a vital aspect considering the eventual outcome of the war.

Though repeatedly thrashed by the South Africans, the Cubans were streets ahead of the majority of African armies who were certainly no match either in training and the kind of advanced equipment that Castro's people received from Moscow. By comparison, the entire FNLA military wing was, as somebody phrased it, 'a cake walk' and it showed in the manner in which Holden Roberto's forces were defeated, virtually within hours of the first shots having been fired along the 'Road of Death'.

That the FNLA was supported by some South African artillery – three heavy guns – and a few dozen men was of no consequence. The Angolan Army had the backing of several thousand Cubans together with hundreds of rocket launchers, and a lot else besides. There was simply no stopping them, had there even been time to properly prepare.

I spoke to Ben Roos about that cataclysmic battle at Quifangondo several times (because we shared Vleesbaai on the South Cape coast as a holiday venue). I'd actually spent six months there writing one of my books, and while he was reticent to offer anything about what had obviously been a 'balls up' (his words) he did say afterwards that the South Africans had been badly shafted by the Americans.

Thoroughly introspective by nature, he added (in Afrikaans) *'ons het daar 'n baie groot les geleer'* (we learned a very big lesson there).

I doubt whether he ever again accepted anything at face value, especially where it involved the security of the nation. His view was that his people should make like the Israelis (who he knew very well because over many years he had a lot to do with the Jewish State) and 'learn to depend only on yourself.'

There was one other aspect that emerged at the time and that was the incredibly close ties between the Soviets and their Cuban allies. The piece that follows was sent to me by a friend who has since passed on, so I am not certain of the source.

But it does tell you just about everything with regard to Castro's role in Angola's wars:

> The origin of the norms that made up the military culture of the Cuban Armed Forces can be traced to Cuba's vast Soviet training and indoctrination programmes which sought to instill Soviet 'combat conditions' inside the armed forces of Soviet allies and satellite states. With Cuba as a close ally since 1959, many Cuban officers were sent to Soviet military academies where they were exposed to the same instructional material as Soviet students.
>
> Referring to the *Fuerzas Armadas Revolucionarias* (FAR), a Soviet publication noted that hundreds of qualified cadres had been prepared in higher military training institutions of the Soviet Union.
>
> Another publication stated: 'In 1961 one of the oldest training establishments in the USSR, the MV Frunze Military Academy and other military academies began to train highly qualified Cuban officers.' The Frunze establishment is the rough equivalent of the US Army's Command and General Staff College at Fort Leavenworth, Kansas or the British Army's Staff College, Camberley. Officers in their late twenties up to 32 years at the rank of captain or major enter if they pass competitive entry examinations.
>
> The Red Army also helped set up and staff military academies inside Cuba such as the Camilo Cienfuegos Artillery Officers School which taught the standard Soviet military curriculum. Moreover, large numbers of Soviet military personnel worked to mentor, train and indoctrinate Cuban military personnel into Soviet military culture, both inside Cuba and abroad when Cuban officers were deployed on operations.
>
> Furthermore, Cuban troops used Soviet training manuals to guide their use of Soviet-produced armaments.

Significant here is that Cuba's involvement in Angola follows participation in a string of Third World conflicts, often at the behest of Moscow.

Castro answered numerous 'calls' of this nature, the most important – apart from Angola – was its involvement in Vietnam where it was directly linked to operating prisoner of war camps that held American servicemen. There is also evidence of Cubans having been involved in torturing prisoners and, of its own volition, conducting medical experiments in torture techniques.

Details of these activities were made public by former US Marine Lieutenant Colonel Elmer Davis, director C-130 Product Line, Kellstrom Defense in Florida (a Merex Company). Davis tells us that 17 American airmen were taken to Cuba for these medical experiments and that none survived. Castro also gave the go-ahead for the formation of an engineering battalion called the 'Girón Brigade,' responsible for maintaining Route Nine, a major enemy supply line into South Vietnam.

> Their facilities included a POW camp and field hospital very near the DMZ, just inside North Vietnam. Meanwhile Cuban interrogators worked in Hanoi at a prison known as the

'Zoo'. We know of these operations and some of what happened to our servicemen after some managed to survive and be repatriated in the winter of 1973, during Operation Homecoming.

Davis goes on:

> Following his release Major Jack Bomar, a 'Zoo' survivor, described the brutal beating of Captain Earl G. Cobeil, an F-105F electronics warfare officer, by Cuban Major Fernando Vecino Alegret, known by the POWs as 'Fidel'.

Regarding Captain Cobeil, Bomar related, 'he was completely catatonic. … His body was ripped and torn everywhere…Hell cuffs appeared almost to have severed his wrists…Slivers of bamboo were imbedded in his bloodied shins, he was bleeding from everywhere, terribly swollen, a dirty yellowish black and purple [countenance] from head to toe.'

> Because of his grotesque physical condition Captain Cobeil was not repatriated but instead, was listed as 'died in captivity,' with his remains returned in 1974.[5]
>
> Incredibly, Fidel's torture of Major James Kasler is well known because he somehow managed to survive the Cuban's torture.
>
> Much less is known about our 17 captured airmen taken to Cuba for 'experimentation in torture techniques.' They were held in Havana's Los Maristas, a secret Cuban prison run by Castro's G-2 Intelligence service. A few were held in the Mazorra (Psychiatric) Hospital and served as human guinea pigs used to develop improved methods of extracting information through 'torture and drugs to induce [American] prisoners to cooperate.

We now know that Havana *did* end up exporting many of its intelligence 'skills' to Africa while Castro's troops were active there. His G-2 intelligence service had a large office near the waterfront in Luanda and going by British-based Paul Trewhela's book *Inside Quatro* (there are 10 Cuban entries in his Index, including two of seven pages) a number are linked to the ANC's Quatro base.[6]

Additionally, there is a 30-page chapter titled 'The ANC Prison Camps' as well as a detailed analysis of the 1984 ANC mutiny in Angola, brutally put down and with the lives of many dissidents lost.

If you wish to understand some of the machinations behind today's political hierarchy in South Africa – and specifically the way President Jacob Zuma is motivated, Paul Trewhela's *Inside Quatro* provides quite a few answers…

---

5 *Miami Herald*, August, 22 1999, and Benge, Michael D. 'The Cuban Torture Program', as well as testimony before the House International Relations Committee, Chaired by the Honorable Benjamin A. Gilman, November 4, 1999.
6 Paul Trewhela: *Inside Quatro: Uncovering the Exile History of the ANC and SWAPO*: Jacana Media, Johannesburg, 2009.

13

Angola's New Political Dispensation and South Africa's Border War

> Just about everything that took place in Sector 10 – that northern area of the Border War which was most active militarily in what had become one of Africa's most expansive insurgencies – would have originated in the former Portuguese 'province' of Angola. The guerrillas had to move through Angola to get to present-day Namibia to fight. They were supplied and supported by the Angolans, their weapons came from and through there and, most salient, when everything went 'toes up', they could quietly slink back into Angola.

At the same time, it was never quite that simple. Many insurgent groups that infiltrated the operational areas in Ovamboland and further east – into Kavango and Caprivi – did not survive the vigorous counter-measures employed by the South African Army, as always, backed by several squadrons of helicopter gunships.

In this regard, the South Africans were different to some Western counter-insurgent forces in the way they countered what was blandly referred to as 'terrorism': the enemy was always ruthlessly pursued wherever and whenever he showed his face, almost always by sending forces into the African bush to seek out this adversary. When found, they killed them.

South Africa's tactics were consistently proactive and in most cases, somewhat different to how the Portuguese conducted their land campaigns. Whereas Lisbon's Special Forces were outstanding, the ordinary foot-soldier was generally reluctant to head out into the unknown for days at a stretch. They would venture forth regularly on routine patrols, as instructed, but would usually expect to be back at base before nightfall, which has never been the way to fight an insurgent war.

The insurgents were aware of this of course, which meant that they tended to dominate the dark. More of that later…

One of the fallacies generally put out about the guerrillas linked to the People's Liberation Army of Namibia (PLAN – SWAPO's military wing) was that their enemy was an inferior bunch and lacked the kind of guts and resolve that might have been expected of an insurgent force that fought long and hard for many years. The troops would like to tell their friends back home that SWAPO was afraid to mix it in the field. Others called them cowards and said they were badly trained and lacked motivation.

Simply put, that is just not true. No other colonial-era insurgent group in modern times fought for so long and quite as forcefully as did SWAPO's military wing. Group after group of guerrillas were pushed forward to do combat and the fact that many were killed or captured was hardly a reflection on SWAPO's will to conquer. Truth is, they were up against enormous odds and an extremely well-trained military force that, like the Israelis, believed they were battling for their own and their families' survival.

Many anecdotes emerged during the course of the war of guerrillas giving the security forces the run-round, sometimes for a week or more at a stretch. They would lay their mines, initiate ambushes and then disappear back across the border to fight another day. It was the oldest challenge in the book, and Mao was the most prominent contemporary exponent, followed soon afterwards by North Vietnam's Giap.

SWAPO's combatants did what they did at a tremendous disadvantage because PLAN never had air cover. In fact the only fighter aircraft or helicopters that came anywhere near the South African border – and then circumspectly, even though they had air superiority – was the Angolan Air Force.

The most effective of all counter-insurgency units active in both Sector 10 and in neighbouring Kaokoveld to the west (and later in the war, in cross-border raids which took them into Angola) was Koevoet which was operated and run by the police, both South African and South West African. The word Koevoet means crowbar in Afrikaans, signifying, as its founder, Brigadier Hans Dreyer once told me, the need to vigorously dislodge the insurgency from the local population. It was also sometimes abbreviated to Operation K, or SWAPOL-COIN, both of which are self-explanatory.

I went out several times with Koevoet combat units and many of the photos that I took and which are used here deal specifically with this crack counter-insurgency unit.

Though a para-military organisation and not directly linked to the SADF, Koevoet elements – usually on the charge – liaised readily with the security forces. When an insurgent track became 'hot', the unit commander would call in gunships to finish the job.

While the unit's initial directive was to conduct internal counter-insurgency reconnaissance, Koevoet soon became one of the most effective combat forces deployed against SWAPO during the war. Consisting of some 250 white and almost 1,000 black operators, it achieved an outstanding combat record, killing or capturing more than 3,000 guerrillas and fighting an estimated 1,600 engagements.

Tiny by comparison with other fighting groups, Koevoet was what would be termed in modern military parlance, a Pseudo Unit, composed almost entirely of former SWAPO guerrilla insurgents who had been 'turned' after they had been captured. Similar ploys were used by the British in Kenya against the Mau Mau and before that, in the Malayan Emergency of the 1950s and 1960s against 'Communist Terrorists', or colloquially, CTs.

The unit had several additional strengths, including remarkable tracking skills. Their staying power in the field was phenomenal: kills were sometimes made days after the first track had been picked up in the dry, arid country adjoining Angola. Not that this was unusual in time of war, but their adversaries were young and fit and running, literally for their lives. Yet Koevoet regulars stayed after them, most times moving at the double and also on foot.

Finally, there was the ability of their officers, both commissioned and non-commissioned ranks, to 'talk' approaching Alouette helicopters onto the fray moments before a full-blown contact became imminent. This was helicopter warfare at its most expedient and the tactics employed are likely to be studied by protagonists of this form of counter-insurgency warfare for a long time to come. Certainly it has an application in many of the brushfire African wars with which the international community is saddled at present, specifically by the French in combating AQIM in West Africa's Sahel.[1]

---

1 France has been engaged in a series of insurgent campaigns against groups of dissidents in several of its

A thoroughly integrated black and white unit, there were few of the usual military trappings that one customarily finds among combat units in the field.

During time spent with them both in Ovamboland and, for a while in the adjoining Kaokoveld region – where conditions on the ground were even more unforgiving – I was regarded as little more than one of the team. Scribblers embedded with military units enjoy certain perks, but not this time. My food was the same as that of the others and so was my seat in the Casspir armoured personnel carrier. My bed roll was also my responsibility.

Mutual trust between helicopter pilots and 'K' operators was deeply imbued and this became especially evident during follow-up operations. The pilots would proceed exactly as the 'K' commander requested – in contrast to dealing with conscript soldiers – who operated under similar conditions in the African bush but hardly ever achieved the same results. In later instances the pilots would sometimes take charge from the air and direct the movement of men on the ground to best effect.

As several SAAF chopper pilots would concede afterwards, a Koevoet contact was almost always a different situation to those called in by regular army units. Pilots like Arthur Walker, Neall Ellis, Heinz Katzke and others would often land in hazardous terrain, pick up the 'K' commander and his black team leader and go airborne to make an assessment, perhaps directing flushing fire at a position to unsettle an insurgent group waiting in ambush. Then they would land in an area that had not yet been properly clearly and drop them if another contact appeared imminent.

In the words of South African Air Force gunship pilot the late Arthur Walker, a double winner of the *Honoris Crux* in Gold, 'Koevoet section leaders would never rush blindly into a contact.' 'Nor', he told me, 'would he let things drag on so that the enemy had time to regroup or reorganize…they'd usually stay right on their tails and when they believed the moment was right, they'd go for it!'

Getting into the final phase of a full-blown contact with well armed and increasingly well-trained SWAPO insurgents was something salutary to those who went out with any Koevoet unit. If you understood the basics of military interplay, it was certainly an exercise in skill that came from a lot of experience: an event combined with an intuitive cunning that sometimes fringed on the atavistic.

Distance and fuel considerations in the vast terrain of southern Africa's largest conflict – especially where helicopters were concerned – were obviously of paramount importance in a country where roads were few and almost all were mined.

Major Walker spoke about another quality that he and his fellow pilots admired and in this regard he referred to Frans Conradie who, with this unit, achieved the highest kill rate of the war. Often under the heaviest fire, Frans always had time for a laugh, said Walker. He was never known to 'lose his cool'.

'Of course that had a kind of magic effect on the men he led into battle – they'd follow him anywhere – black and white …' he added. But then Conradie used experience garnered as an accomplished forward air controller: he had done the course some years before.

One time a Koevoet team scored 11 kills as a result of the remarkable powers of observation of Arthur Walker. It was evening and the pilot was flying back to Ondangua from Eenhana base in the east of Ovamboland when he spotted some bicycles lying at the edge of a small clump of

---

former West African colonies, most recently in Mali. There it is grappling with irregular strikes made by an Islamic State affiliate that calls itself AQIM (Al Qaeda in the Islamic Maghreb). Chapter One titled 'France's Terror War Against al-Qaeda in West Africa' of a revamped and updated and enlarged edition of the author's *The Chopper Boys* covers this conflict, together with some outstanding combat photographs. The book was published by Helion in Britain in 2016

bushes. He was immediately suspicious: a single bike, or perhaps two in this bush country, but not several…

Along with his Number Two, Major Walker started circling the area in a bid to establish why the cycles were there and who owned them. Then the two gunships were hailed from a distance by a Koevoet team, call-sign 'Zulu Victor'. First reports indicated that they had had an uninspiring day in the area searching for fresh spoor between Oshigambo and Onkankolo.

'Zulu Victor' asked what he was up to because he had spotted him circling in the distance instead of heading back to base. The aviator told him about the bikes and the Koevoet team changed direction.

At that stage the bicycle owners were still not to be seen, but the 'K' team rapidly spread out and moved in. With about 75 metres to go 'Zulu Victor' suddenly came under attack. The fight was on.

Walker and his Number Two had to hold fire for most of the contact as the Koevoet team – according to their distinctive fashion – drove headlong into the enemy. The close-quarter battle continued as the two choppers covered a large open area around the bush. In the subsequent chaos, the gunship took out several insurgents that tried to bolt.

In the end, all 11 SWAPO saboteurs – dressed in civilian clothes – lay dead alongside their carbines, rifle grenades, an impressive array of TNT explosives as well as safety fuses and detonators. It later emerged that this group was one of the most successful enemy strike units the war had fielded so far.

Their leader, known by his combat name, was 'Jet Fighter'; his side-kick 'Nicky' and their team of Russian-trained engineers had successfully eluded the security forces for over a year. During that time they had destroyed a host of communications equipment, planted landmines and acquired a reputation for ruthlessness. Had it not been for Major Walker following an instinct, coupled with his usual enthusiasm for a punch-up, the SWAPO squad might have been active a while longer.

Frans Conradie, Koevoet's top 'scorer' got the kudos once he got back to base and back at base another party followed, which was the way it went in this guerrilla struggle that had already enmeshed huge tracts of the region. The intrepid Conradie was responsible for 98 kills in 1981 and more than 80 in 1982, which was the year before he died. By August 1983 – he was killed in a road accident in September that year – his tally had already topped 60.

Nor was getting to grips with SWAPO cadres in this expansive bush war an easy act to follow. By the time a rebel group was ready to move from Angola across the border into Namibia – sometimes 50 or 100 strong – they were a well-trained and equipped force. The majority had solid military expertise and most senior commanders had spent time in the Soviet Union, East Germany, Cuba or Libya learning specialist skills.

Technically, in handling Eastern Bloc hardware, some SWAPO combatants were every bit as versatile as the average South African conscript, the majority of whom had the advantage of a decent western education, experience and training.

As counter-insurgency commanders go in Africa's low-key insurgencies, Frans Conradie must rate somewhere near the top.

Leading his own combat group through the bush, he survived well over 150 contacts in a career that spanned a decade. He was never seriously wounded in action, though he once took an AK bullet between the ribs, the impact absorbed by one of the curved-steel AK magazines in his Soviet-style chest webbing. A personal choice, he preferred the Kalashnikov, maintaining that in difficult African conditions it was the best infantry weapon around. He would argue that if they ran short, there was ammo galore that he and his men could take from the enemy.

In following in his footsteps on several patrols, I found it interesting that each kill achieved was a physical head count. An enemy did not become a statistic until he – and in some instances, a 'she'

– lay prostrate on the ground, weapon and pack usually neatly arranged alongside other bodies and ready for photographs and classification. That was the way the police used to work in South Africa and Conradie was no exception.

It was a further contradiction that the man was a cop and that he died in a road accident. Having returned from a week-long sortie to the moderate-sized garrison town of Oshakati in Ovamboland, he was heading for home after having had more than a few pints with the boys when his vehicle overturned. Conradie was pinned in his seat and bled to death before they could get him to hospital.

Before dawn there were few people in Oshakati or Air Force Base Ondangua who weren't aware that Frans Conradie had gone on his final bush operation. The following day, an entire region – whites as well as blacks who had come to know and respect this man – mourned his death. His comrades flew home with his body draped in the South Africa flag, a special flight laid on by the South African Air Force. Frans Conradie was finally laid to rest with full military honours.

Though still a lowly lieutenant – he had worked his way to a commission through the ranks – there were generals present at his graveside that hot September afternoon. Later that evening those with whom he had shared action in remote regions of Africa for the previous three or four years, used the money that Frans had specially laid aside for just such an event.

He'd often joked about the $200 he had put away to buy the drinks 'so you boys can laugh when I die and not cry'. That comment, stated in his quaint, strident voice and usually accompanied by a characteristic half-grin, was in keeping with his mién. Affable, some would call it.

At the wake they talked about little else but Frans; Frans the fighter, Frans the unflappable when under fire; the practical joker; the lover; the military historian with an awesome library of reference works; the party-giver; the provider of good things to his mates; the punctilious – for he was a stickler for detail when in the field – the collector of military trivia (including a remarkably diverse collection of Cuban and Soviet belt buckles taken from those whom, he would joke, wouldn't be needing them again) and Frans the tactician. In this role he was a superlative operator, in planning and in the final execution.

There are dozens of anecdotes that illustrate his life, but one needs an appreciation of military logic – or possibly illogicality – to understand most of them. The fact that he had never lost one of his own in combat had been a source of great pride.

It was actually Frans Conradie's physical ability which impressed me the most. In many respects he was arguably one of the finest (and fittest) trackers in the operational area, often following a spoor for days, usually on the ground and ahead of his back-up vehicles.

His staying power too, was regarded as phenomenal. Sometimes he would start on the spoor in the dry, desert-like sand of Ovamboland at first light and follow it at a steady running gait, keeping it up until sunset: Either that or until he made contact with the enemy. He could easily cover 50 kilometres at a stretch in often-difficult terrain where the POM-Z was king.

He was also the only policeman to have called in a jet strike to wipe out an insurgent pocket that was showing stiff resistance. On that occasion, 15 more of the enemy died. He is reputed to have killed groups of ten on four or five occasions, usually going into the contact with his 20mm cannon – mounted atop his Casspir – blazing and music bellowing from the speaker alongside.

God knows what the enemy thought of the crazy white demon hunting them, which might be why he acquired the moniker among some SWAPO cadres of *bwana mkubwa*, Swahili for 'Big Boss'.

The turret gun also had a story to it. It had been scrounged (with the help of a few pals in the Air Force) from an old SAAF Vampire jet fighter: an original Hispano-Oerlikon. Conradie modified it slightly, cutting down the barrel so that it became easier to handle.

Yet, in so many ways – and in contrast to Koevoet – the average grunt doing his military service was no different to those tens of thousands of Portuguese troops who had spent years in Angola's so-called 'Liberation Wars'. Or, for that matter, several hundred thousand American soldiers who fought a difficult struggle against a far more resolute enemy in Vietnam.

The Americans would refer to their adversaries by a dozen different epithets, of which the word 'Gook' predominated. South African and Portuguese conscripts were no different and SWAPO's cadres – and those few FAPLA troops with whom they came into rare contact – were given similar names, not always disparaging. SWAPO militants were usually referred to as 'Swaps'.

At the same time – and it took a while, as the war progressed – you could not help but detect a grudging admiration that some of the South African soldiers had for those revolutionaries who came across the sometimes ill-marked frontier to wage war. It was Koevoet, 32 Battalion and the helicopter gunships that got the kills, but for the average 'troopie', he was fortunate if he spotted a live and active insurgent during his entire tour of duty up north.

After one of my visits to the 'Operational Area' (or more commonly, the 'Op Area') as we referred to the region adjoining Angola, I ended up writing a reflective piece for *Soldier of Fortune*, one of the American magazines for which I wrote. The intention was not to draw comparisons, but in the end, you could not but help doing so because all wars are, if not the same, then similar. Except for those currently being fought east of Suez…

The piece was billed 'Troopie Patrol Along Angola's Border' and as I said at the time, those were the 'old days': tough when they happened, but speckled with memories for those who were there.

The main player was a youngster who called himself Peter Dreyer, a serving soldier who I actually got to know because I spent several days in his camp. At the same time, he could have been a combatant in any man's army. Tough, lean and wiry, like a terrier, he could march for days at a stretch and often through the night as well if the trail was 'hot'.

His appearance belied his origins and said it all: torn khaki fatigues, bush hat tucked in on the sides to allow for, as he put it, 'better hearing', T-shirt with sleeves ripped off and looking as if it had been on his back for a month, buckle-down webbing and R4 automatic carbine in .223 calibre. A sparse seven-day growth of beard could not conceal Dreyer's youthful features.

The young South African had turned 19 on his last 11-day patrol along the Angolan border. A decade earlier, he would probably have been indistinguishable from the thousands of young Americans and Australians serving in 'Nam.

In the broader context he enjoyed the same kind of life as those boys; all had folks and a girl back home and after dark, bedded down in his narrow slit trench that had taken half an hour to dig in the dark when out in the bush on patrol, he would spend time reflecting upon what they might all have been doing just then.

Dreyer's thoughts were the stuff of a hundred wars before him and countless thousands of soldiers on patrol in wartime. But, in Vietnam – and in Iraq, Syria and Afghanistan today – the terrain and weather were very different. Namibia, he'd discovered long ago is a dry, mostly dusty land, especially in the north where the terrain gives way to almost desert conditions for much of the year.

Only, while war lasted, it was called South West Africa.

While with him in the bush, Dreyer tended to fight his own kind of war, usually with animated vigour. His mind was tuned to absolutes; there was no middle way. It was either for or against – and SWAPO was definitely against – especially in a conflict so close to home. As the crow flies, Ovamboland is about a thousand or so kilometres from the red brick municipal house in which Dreyer was born and bred in Mafeking (of Boer War fame).

With the Border War in full swing, the SADF quickly adapted to new tactics, including the establishment of a South West African military force. (Author's photo)

Units soon became thoroughly integrated and it worked well, with many of the African troops coming from the Ovambo region. (Author's photo)

Koevoet's Casspir IFV was soon regarded as an outstanding combat vehicle for Third World (and especially African) conditions. (Photo: sourced to Georgy Konstantinovich-Zhukov: Military History Emporium)

Oshakati became the headquarters of Sector 10, with its distinctive water tower doubling as an observation post. (Author's photo)

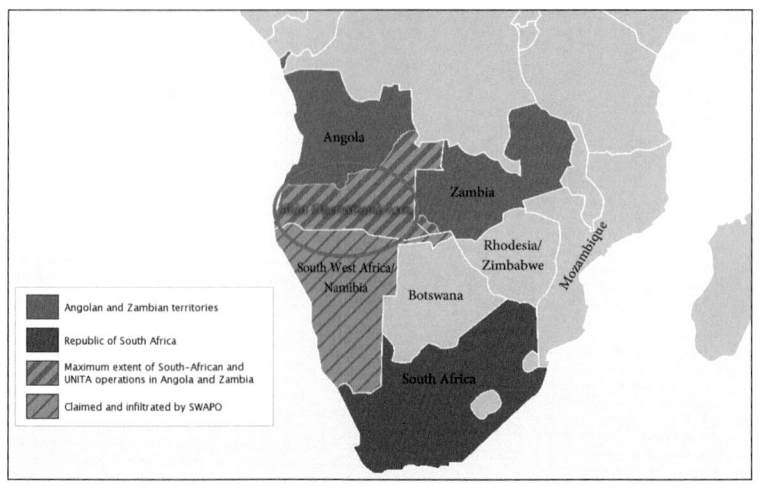

Peter Baxter's map showing the focus of military operations in the region adjoining south Angola.

Koevoet soon adopted the Casspir IFV as its 'vehicle of choice'. It made good sense since the machine was originally designed by Pretoria scientist Vernon Joynt with this kind of mobility in mind. Koevoet's kill rate throughout the Border War exceeded that of any army unit. (Author's photo)

Most Koevoet troops were tribal Ovambos – former insurgents who had been captured and turned to fight against their former comrades. (Author's photo)

Koevoet contact, following an ambush in a remote corner of Ovamboland. (Author's photo)

The author went out with Koevoet combat groups many times, both in Ovamboland and in the Kaokoveld, sometimes accompanying police Captain 'Sakkie' van Zyl, seen here on his haunches. A former security policeman, this man had one of the highest strike rates in the unit. (Author's photo)

South Africa's Casspir IVF was so successful during the course of the Border War that it was later adopted in many conflicts world-wide, including those in the Middle East, Central Asia, Sri Lanka and several other countries, including UN 'Peacekeeping' operations. This vehicle, still in use worldwide, has the advantage of having a shaped hull that affords it good protection against anti-tank mines. (Author's photo)

After-action rituals with some Koevoet units included securing dead insurgents killed in a contact to the fenders of one of the Casspirs. The bodies were then hauled back to base, ostensibly for identification or fingerprinting. We only discovered long afterwards that Koevoet combatants – all police officers – were paid a bounty for each member of the enemy force killed (Author's photo)

As a newcomer to the process, it took him a couple of days to get into the routine of spending more than 12 hours a day humping gear through some of the most inhospitable country on any continent and, as he was soon to discover, it was never easy going.

The sand in this region is soft. For much of the distance it became a punishing, uphill struggle, like trudging hard along a remote beach. It was interesting that throughout Ovamboland there are no stones, so if you ran out of ammo you didn't even have rocks to throw. It was only vaguely comforting that the enemy was faced with similar problems.

With darkness, one of the lasting recollections of this isolated bush region were the night sounds that echoed across the veld from beyond. Someone once described the all-embracing resonance as a kind of symphony of the African night and something to which most city folk never quite become accustomed.

So it was, in early April 1981, during that second two-hour watch after the songs and drums from the nearby Ovambo kraal had settled to a monotonous murmur that a bush baby suddenly screamed above his head. It sounded like a woman being raped. In less time than it takes to sound a general alert, the entire 30-man patrol was on their elbows, alert with their rifles pointing outwards.

What was astonishing was that the galago, a small nocturnal primate – bush babies or *nagapies* in the lingo – would fit comfortably in a pair of cupped hands and that it could create such mayhem. It happened, quite routinely as Dreyer was to find out for himself.

Few of the men slept easily that night. An hour earlier, most of the men had been roused by the sharp call of a jackal, barely 50 metres from where they lay in a calcite depression. It was an ominous, hollow cry and to the superstitious in the ranks might have spelled disaster.

The outer sector had reported back briefly by radio, but the young lieutenant, barely 15 months older than Dreyer, wasn't satisfied until he'd checked out the direction of the call himself. Called 'Horse' by his men, he returned 20 minutes later, not entirely convinced that the sound had not been human, even if he said nothing at the time.

Then most of the men fell into a fitful sleep, punctuated by Africa's discordant uneasiness. There were others out there in the dark watching, too, of that they had no doubt. More echoes followed, like the sharp screech as another animal of the night made a kill and woke some of the men after midnight. There was something relentless about it all, futile and helpless.

The guys would probably have been a lot more alert had they known that at first light they would encounter the tracks of a 50-strong insurgent force headed southwards out of Angola. Their tracks emerged a couple of clicks from where they had slept. The guerrillas could as easily have chosen the narrow tracks on that side of the Odilla watershed and then, at least, some of the men would have been able to justify a fruitless seven-day march without a blood spoor to follow.

The possibility of contact was real enough on all these patrols. But in reality, a fire-fight rarely materialized in its conventional, accepted form. More likely, the South Africans, like the enemy, might spot a couple of shadowy figures moving like fugitives along the sparse tree line. They might sound a challenge, shots would follow and then, possibly, a search.

If something did come of it, there would be another 12-hour chase, often at the double, with airborne troops in helicopters leapfrogging ahead in attempts to set up stopper groups. A kill might result, but more often than not, that simply did not happen.

Like Dreyer's group, the enemy was hungry. In Ovamboland that year they slaughtered 50,000 head of cattle because the rains had been unusually sparse. Locals had barely enough to keep themselves alive, let alone feed an insurgent force.

Yet few of the men in the patrol complained, if only because the majority were still young enough to adapt.

They tended to accept that the patrols were tough, but being out in the bush was a lot better than swatting flies off their food and faces back at base. In any event, these were the same kinds of hardships which had already been weathered by a generation of southern African fighting men before them, first by the Portuguese in adjoining Angola, Mozambique further to the east and later, Rhodesia.

To the majority, it was an African conflict, one of many. In the past, French, British, Portuguese, Spanish, Belgian, German, Italian and other colonial troops had fought their battles and had done so without fuss. Afterwards, they quietly buried their casualties in Africa's red soil and moved on.

Looking at the level of ongoing misery on that continent today, it might never have happened.

The average South African operational patrol could – according to demand or circumstances – last anywhere from a few hours to several weeks.

On average, between seven and 11 days was the norm, though long-range penetration groups sometimes went out for months at a stretch and often hundreds of kilometres behind enemy lines. Those were the Special Forces boys – the Recces – as well as the now-infamous 32 Battalion, but we scribes were hardly ever allowed to spend operational time with them. Everything they did, we were told when we asked, was 'classified'.

In a region as arid as Ovamboland, the men tried to haul along as much water as possible on their patrols and for good reason. It was not always feasible to organise re-supply, though in a real emergency when the men started to seriously dehydrate and occasionally even pass blood in their urine, the order would come through to 'chopper' in water bladders. These rubber balloons each contained about 100 litres, enough to keep a 20-man patrol going for a day or more.

Because there were no flowing streams in these great arid wastes during dry seasons – especially once you were operating away from the great Kunene River – most available water pits were usually covered by a green bacterial slime. Or sometimes they were poisoned either by our own forces, clandestinely, or theirs.

The majority of troops appeared to cope, though water purifying tablets helped. One week-long sortie with a mounted patrol in 1978 left me in the hospital for days after I was obliged to drink foul water to stay alive. You need to understand real thirst under desert-like conditions to appreciate that kind of quandary.

On average, the troops each tried to pack six one-litre water bottles, but weight was invariably a problem there. They were issued with a 'rat-pack' a day, which contained a reasonable supply of provisions, but made for still more weight. After the second or third time out, the troops were less likely to take along many of the cans that came with the victuals and anyway, to a hungry man in the bush, a packet of 'dog biscuits' more often than not makes for an adequate meal.

With weapons, ammunition, spare batteries, mortar bombs, claymores, anti-personnel mines, additional food, water and a dozen ammo clips each, the average South African troopie counted himself lucky if he set out from base with less than 40 kilos on his back. Packing this weight, he was expected to average 20 or 30 kilometres a day, much of it through the soft sand, which can be hell to anyone experiencing it for the first time. The radio 'tech' marched much heavier; he usually settled for another 10 kilos, including his rifle.

The 'heavyweight' prize patrol went to the machine-gunners. On a seven-day sortie when I went along, Number One Bren was loaded down with additional magazines as well as three belts of 7.62mm ammo and his load topped 50 kilograms. The bearer did not complain, though his muscles stood out like cords. Rather him than me…

No patrol in those distant days worked along any set pattern in the bush. The objective was to search for the enemy and, if possible, destroy. While some foreign observers – notably the Israelis – were critical of this kind of military procedure, routine patrols in the expansive African bush served good purpose. With the South Africans, they prevented ground saturation of much of that frontier region by guerrilla cadres. Vacate an area, even for a short time and it would be exploited soon enough by the other side. That was lesson also taught to the Americans in Vietnam.

The Rhodesians experienced some of it in December 1972, when Operation Hurricane was initiated by guerrillas.

Much of the activity in the bush centred on tracks, seeking, finding and following them, something that eventually became a much-cherished skill in South African army ranks. A number of the more experienced scouts – many of them city-bred white folk – could, from a short series of spoors, tell you about a man's pace, his weight and possibly his height. It was possible to 'read' whether the subject was alert, his mood – depressed or elated – and certainly whether he was carrying heavy or light (heels dig deeper into the sand if the former).

An interesting comment made by one of the experts attached to South West Africa's Special Operations Unit was that city boys often developed better as trackers than farmers' sons. Some were even sharper than locally born Africans, though even the enemy had to concede that the primitive little yellow-skinned Bushman had no peer in this field, especially in arid regions.

Put a Bushman on the spoor and all things being equal, contact would invariably result, given the right pace and enough daylight. That was one of the reasons why SWAPO, on sight, would kill any Bushman its units encountered in the Operational Area.

It was a tragic sidelight of this war because entire communities of these usually-placid little folk would sometimes be wiped out.

Some interesting observations were made how the Portuguese fought their wars in Africa and though it took time, the South Africans (and the Rhodesians before them) adapted quickly to African conditions. After all, they would argue, they were born there, '*so we're African*!'

In the majority of cases, so were their fathers and grandparents. The Venter clan – my family – goes back 14 generations, when the first three Venter brothers landed at the Cape a few years after Jan van Riebeeck in 1652.

Not so the average Portuguese combatant. Most of their hearts and minds were firmly embedded in Europe. It got worse with time, when young Portuguese soldiers would be critical when told by their officers that they were 'fighting for Portugal, your homeland.'

In the minds of most of them – the majority of Angolan troops excepted – Africa was just about as alien as Mongolia and in the latter stages of the war, they would not be afraid to say so. Worse, these attitudes tended to affect the way the Portuguese fought their wars, for the simple reason that their souls were not in it. Much of it devolved around mind-set and commitment.

Towards the end of Portugal's conflicts, quite a few South African soldiers, mainly Special Force operators, spent time with Lisbon's units and they were outspokenly critical. While they got on well with their European contemporaries – *Comandos Africanos* and *Fuzileiros* especially – they regarded the average conscript with disdain, often undisguised. Offered the choice, they certainly would not go on ops with a regular Portuguese Army unit.

The issue was adequately encapsulated by Colonel Reid-Daly, founder-commander of Rhodesia's Selous Scouts. He was several times detached to serve with the Portuguese Army in Mozambique and remained critical of the Portuguese war effort in the neighbouring state as long as hostilities lasted, and while that was Mozambique (and we are dealing with Angola here) many of Reid-Daly's observations are insightful. During all the operations in which the Rhodesians took part in the Tete Panhandle, he recalled, the Portuguese were found to be completely base-bound. They fought much as the Americans had fought in Vietnam, he declared.

The upper command was quite happy to let the insurgents control the bush while government forces held on to the towns, communications links and strong points. Reid-Daly said that in Tete, patrols lasting from four to six weeks should have been normal and supplied by air. That idea, when he first propounded it, was regarded as preposterous by the upper command. At that time, the Portuguese would not consider anything beyond three days, spending each night in camp if at all possible.

Reid-Daly:

> One of their worst faults on the march was that the column was noisy and straggling. They talked loudly instead of maintaining silence, which even FRELIMO knew was one of the first principles of counter-insurgency warfare.

After dark, he soon discovered, when an ambush had been set up, Portuguese soldiers would cough and fidget.

> It was as if they were warning the enemy to keep clear, so that they would not be compelled to fight. Clearly, that was an impossible situation.

On the other hand, some of the *Flechas,* parachute and black commando regiments were excellent operators in the bush. Most were superior to FRELIMO, and many of the kills in Mozambique were attributable to their people and to the air force.

While most operational plans were carefully prepared by the brigade staff, Reid-Daly found that they seldom allowed the battalion commander scope for flexibility or personal initiative. It all had to be done according 'to the book'. There was even a marked reluctance to change plans in spite of fresh information coming in and other developments as the operation progressed.

A sorry example of this was the failure to capitalize on the discovery, towards the end of 1967 by one of the helicopters during an operation in the mountains near Cahora Bassa, of a large insurgent camp about 500 metres across. It was only a day later that an infantry attack was launched: the Portuguese officer responsible wasn't prepared to change either the original plan or the sequence of events he and his colleagues had mapped out earlier.

Reid-Daly was with them when this happened. He insisted that they scrape together another body of men and try a vertical envelopment. That would have been possible because there were eight Alouette gunships available. By the time the operation only got off the ground the insurgents had disappeared into the bush.

Reid-Daly believed that the Portuguese soldiers with whom he came into contact on these operations were very badly equipped, considering the nature of the war. Apart from the standard G-3 rifle (7.62mm NATO calibre) they had no illumination flares, no claymores and none of the elementary means of protection issued for this kind of combat as a matter of course in most armies of the world.

Also, the average grunt from Europe simply had no idea of how to use smoke grenades to call up helicopters, or how to use small mirrors to attract the attention of aircraft – all little things that most bush fighters take for granted in remote or isolated regions.

Whereas the South Africans and Rhodesians maintained excellent liaison between pilots and ground forces – it was obviously in their interests to do so – that did not always happen in the Portuguese territories and no one really did much to improve the situation. There were many exceptions of course, with some elements working in close liaison with one another, but it was certainly not commonplace. Outside the mess, they just were not talking to each other.

It was the same kind of superficial superiority that I'd observed at close quarters in Angola's Sector D: the 'Blues' regarding themselves as superior to the 'Browns'.

14

Civil War: The Start

> Although the **MPLA** may have been somewhat more genuine in its leftist convictions than either the **FNLA** or **UNITA**, there was little to distinguish any of the three groups from each other ideologically. When the press made any distinction amongst them it was usually to refer to **MPLA** as 'Marxist', but this was ill-defined, if defined at all, and simply took on a media life of its own. Each of the groups spoke of socialism and employed Marxist rhetoric when the occasion called for it, and genuflected to other gods when it did not. In the 1960s, each of them was perfectly willing to accept support from any country willing to give it without excessive strings attached.
> William Blum, from *Killing Hope: U.S. Military and CIA Interventions since the Second World War*[1]

There are many interpretations (including my own) of how Angola's post-independence civil war developed. It lasted 27 years, from 1975 until 2002, though there had been quite a lot of sporadic fighting before then. In an effort to remain impartial, I am quoting the certainty of the Wikipedia version. Stripped as it is of ideology and any kind of 'hidden agenda', it makes for a refreshing presentation. I quote:

> The Angolan Civil War (in Portuguese *Guerra civil angolana*) began in 1975 and was essentially a power struggle between two former liberation movements, the MPLA and the National Union for the Total Independence of Angola (UNITA), Holden Roberto's FNLA having been all but side-lined early on.
>
> Additionally, the Front for the Liberation of the Enclave of Cabinda, to the immediate north of the Congo River (FLEC) and which was composed of an association of separatist militant groups, fought for the independence of that oil-rich piece of real estate from the Luanda government. The various phases of war can be divided roughly into three periods of major fighting – from 1975 to 1991, 1992 to 1994, and from 1998 to 2002 – broken up by fragile periods of peace.
>
> By the time the Luanda government [assisted by a powerful South African mercenary force, short on numbers but, almost to a man, skilled Special Force operators] finally achieved victory in 2002, more than 500,000 people had died and over a million souls internally displaced. It is axiomatic that the war devastated Angola's infrastructure, and severely damaged the nation's public administration, economic enterprises, and religious institutions. In some sections, society is still suffering from its effects.

---

1 Bill Blum: From his chapter in *Killing Hope: U.S. Military and CIA Interventions since World War II,* titled 'Angola, 1975 to 1980s: The Great Powers Poker Game'.

The Angolan Civil War was notable due to the combination of Angola's violent internal dynamics and massive foreign intervention. The war became a Cold War struggle, as both the Soviet Union and the United States, along with their respective allies, provided significant military assistance to parties in the conflict.

That was not the start of it. Only months after Lisbon decided in April 1974 that it was pulling its forces out of Africa, the various factions started jockeying for power and it soon became brutal.

The MPLA had already formed FAPLA, its military wing (which replaced EPLA and had the same intent) on August 1 and went into the immediate offensive to counter UNITA gains. Once these adversaries had converged on Luanda, they systematically set about trying to eliminate each other by a succession of assassinations and surprise night-time raids that sometimes left many dead.

There was more fighting in the countryside, as we have already seen with South African involvement in Operation Savannah, which attempted to counter Cuban military involvement.

The activities of Daniel Chipenda's *Chipa Esquadrao* became another factor in this chaotic juggling for some kind of strong-arm pre-eminence, which ended – and then only briefly – in January 1975 when the three major groups signed the controversial Alvor Agreement.

Essentially, Alvor – its terms were being abused even before the ink was dry – involved a 'sharing of power' in what was considered to be a coalition government with nationwide elections promised for the following November. That quickly fell apart as the various nationalist factions, totally distrustful of each other and unwilling to share power, attempted to take control of the country by force.

What we do know and what was confirmed by various sources, including Yves Debay (who devoted a lot of space to these events in his publication *Raids*), sizeable quantities of military hardware was shipped from China (probably shipped to Dar es Salaam in Tanzania and routed through Zambia to the MPLA late in 1974). That was followed by 250 Cuban technicians and military advisors six months later.[2]

The Americans had also been active. William Blum tells us that since 1969, the FNLA leader Holden Roberto had been on a $10,000-a-year retainer from the CIA, which in those days, as somebody commented, was a 'hellova lot of money for one man to booze his way through'. Washington must have been aware by then that Roberto was a chronic alcoholic and why they ever backed him still puzzles most of us 'Africa observers'.

In January 1975, the CIA was authorised to pass $300,000 to Roberto and the FNLA for what were termed 'various political action activities, restricted to non-military objectives. The last qualification was absurd – this was war, though things soon changed.'

Two months later, in March 1975, the FNLA – certainly the most quarrelsome of the factions – attacked MPLA headquarters and later gunned down 51 MPLA recruits, in retaliation for several similar attacks launched by Agostinho Neto's gunmen months before. These incidents all served to spark what was to become a full-scale civil war, with UNITA aligning itself with the FNLA against the MPLA. The scheduled elections would never take place which was something Lisbon's 'Red Admiral' Rosa Coutinho ensured: they were never intended to.

The Australian writer Robert Moss reported in the *Daily Telegraph* that while the Marxists in Luanda hailed Agostinho Neto as Angola's first black president, the supporters of the two anti-Soviet movements, UNITA and the FNLA, danced in the streets of Nova Lisboa (renamed Huambo) and Ambriz. The MPLA was quickly able to boast the diplomatic recognition of the

---

2 Yves Debay, *Raids* magazine No 44, 1995: ISSN 0963-1852.

Soviet bloc, the Marxist African states and capitalist Brazil. Meanwhile UNITA and FNLA proclaimed their own State, the 'Peoples' Democratic Republic,' and claimed that they controlled 11 of Angola's 16 provinces.[3]

William Blum:

> Also in March, the first large shipment of arms arrived from the Soviet Union for the MPLA. The [US] House investigating committee subsequently stated that 'later events have suggested that this infusion of US aid [the $300,000], unprecedented and massive in the underdeveloped colony, may have panicked the Soviets into arming their MPLA clients.'
>
> The Soviets may have been as much influenced by the fact that China had sent a huge arms package to the FNLA the previous September and had dispatched over a hundred military advisors to neighbouring Zaire to train Roberto's soldiers only a month after the coup in Portugal.
>
> The CIA made its first major weapons shipment to the FNLA in July 1975. Thus, like the Russians and the Chinese, the United States was giving aid to one side of the Angolan civil war on a level far greater than it had ever provided during the struggle against Portuguese colonialism. Meantime, American personnel did considerable flying between Zaire and Angola carrying out reconnaissance and supply missions, and the CIA spent over a million dollars on an ambitious mercenary program, which we will deal with in the next chapter.

In his series of article for London's *Telegraph* Group,[4] Robert Moss set the scene for what has since gone down in the annals of recent Angolan history as 'The Battle for Death Road'.

As he explains, Holden Roberto's FNLA army was pushing south in a desperate attempt to seize Luanda before Independence Day. They had been driven out of the capital in July, when the MPLA launched a surprise attack, in which Portuguese pilots – flying civilian airplanes of the Portuguese-Angolan airline, TAAG – had flown reconnaissance missions with their Fokker F-27s. But by early November, the Marxists' position in Luanda was no longer secure.

> Fighting around Dondo to the south, where the hydro-electric plant that supplied the capital's electricity was located, resulted in blackouts. Luanda's water supply was also cut off for days. Further, the anti-Soviet forces had managed to isolate the capital from its food supplies; the richest farming lands in the Central Highlands around Nova Lisboa were securely in UNITA [and FNLA] hands.

Indeed, there seemed to be a chance that the defenders of Luanda could be starved into submission.

In a series of exchanges with Serguei Kolomnin, press secretary of the Union of Russian Veterans of Angola, Marangoni, one of those involved with anti-MPLA elements, details events on the FNLA and South African side of that momentous morning.

He confirmed that on the eve of the 'Battle of Death Road', it was Cuba's revolutionary forces that launched a large scale intervention on behalf of the MPLA and airlifted the first group of Castro's Special Forces to Luanda. They were urgently needed to man the six Grad 122mm multiple rocket launchers supplied to Neto's forces by the Soviet Union.

---

3   Robert Moss, 'Battle for Death Road', *Sunday Telegraph*, London 13 February, 1977.
4   Robert Moss: *Ibid*.

Not the most formidable weapon in the Soviet armoury, Marangoni tends to be dismissive of the BM-21 weapons system. He always maintained that unlike the 81mm mortar, which he dreaded, the Grad was a relative lightweight. But it did frighten the hell out of the soldiers at the receiving end because of the enormous blast effect, black soldiers especially, he commented.

> My experience in Africa was that the weapon was more of a stun gun and did not result in many casualties…but since it was usually the attacker who won battles [in Africa] and those who were being attacked almost always retreated, these missiles intimidated the enemy because they made so much noise. In this case, it was the MPLA and their Grads who were doing the damage, so the FNLA – largely untested in any real battle – made a run for it when things seemed to get rough.

With Angola, he declared, it was invariably the non-Africans who did the real fighting – the volunteers, mercenaries, advisors, internationalists and the rest who decided the outcome of most clashes. 'These were the troops of conquest while the others were tasked with the basic occupation of conquered land and that also happened significantly.'

The night of 10 November was a significant event for both sides, with Angola's independence due to be declared the following day. Until then, Holden Roberto had lingered well behind the lines at his base well north of Luanda where he had maintained a measure of command over previous months. When he did eventually arrive in the vicinity of Quifangondo the next morning, he discovered his forces in disarray, many of them retreating in fragmented groups towards the north-east.

Pedro Marangoni, the Brazilian freelance fighter who had thrown in his lot with Roberto's crowd had some interesting comments to make several years later about what took place at Quifangondo. It was obviously a turning point in the war and resulted in the FNLA losing its pre-eminent position among the competing forces in Angola. That mantle was subsequently passed on to UNITA.

In his letters to the Russian Serguei Kolomnin, he made the valid observation that the force that gathered along the Bengo River was hugely uncoordinated. Also, he said, 'an interesting fact is that Luanda's MPLA never really considered us as being mercenaries, they only used that as a propaganda tool because [after mercenaries had been taken prisoner in northern Angola] my captured Portuguese colleagues weren't tried with the British and American and had a more humane treatment.' Three of them were captured at Quifangondo with several others taken at the Battle of Caxito some months before.

It was also interesting that he said that when he withdrew under heavy shelling from the Cubans to the high ground at Morro da Cal at about six in the evening before independence, the landscape was totally deserted. 'The only vehicles there were the headquarters Jeep and our Panhard VTT.'

The next evening, November 11, after the great battle, along with Colonel Santos e Castro, only 26 men stood at the front in the Morro da Cal, all special commandos. The FNLA simply ran wild without command and followed the Zaireans into retreat.'

The first to abandon the fighting lines apparently were almost all the FNLA officers and NCOs.

Among those who did not emerge from this early campaign that involved a peculiar group of Portuguese, British and American mercenaries was George Bacon, always a controversial figure, both at home and abroad. Certainly Bacon was what the media like to call a 'Spook', though he would never admit it, even to his few friends.

Jack Murphy, an eight-year United States Army Special Operations veteran who served as a sniper and team leader in 3rd Ranger Battalion and as a senior weapons sergeant in a military free-fall team in 5th Special Forces Group, says that when he first did research on George Washington Bacon III – MACV-SOG Operator, 'CIA para-military officer, mercenary and eccentric' – there was very little information about him until he started to make inquiries.

Eventually, he relates, 'some interesting people began to get in touch with me. George Washington Bacon was the real deal. Spending most of his life in the shadows, I found references to George by name or by his call-sign in over a half dozen books. But without the help of several sources who wish to remain anonymous this background about George and his life would not have been possible.'

Murphy takes up the story, George Bacon's final foray in Angola

Crammed into the back of a door-less grey Land Rover, the mercenaries accelerated, sliding across the muddy road as it twisted through the Angolan jungle.

As a veteran of MACV-SOG reconnaissance missions into Cambodia and having worked as a CIA Para-Military Officer in Laos, George would have known that something was wrong. Fellow mercenary, Gary Acker, had voiced his uncertainty as they raced to link up with another FNLA patrol.

George clutched a 9mm Uzi while Acker manned a German MG42 machine gun. The Portuguese driver was about to lose control of the vehicle until Douglas 'Canada' Newby ordered him to slow the hell down. 'Canada bought most of us another minute of life,' wrote Acker afterwards.

George would have understood the precarious situation they were in. FAPLA, the Angolan army – on its own pathetic militarily, but now bolstered by Cuban professionals – was once again on the offensive and he had just finished prepping a bridge with TNT explosives for demolition in order to delay the enemy advance.

FNLA recruiting drives in England and the United States had signed up a number of adventurers to fight in Angola. Some were qualified for the work having had military experience in the US Marines, British Parachute Regiment, or the SAS. George Washington Bacon was in a category all his own, recalled British safe-cracker and mercenary David Tompkins.

He goes on: 'Another recruit was George Bacon, a political science major and holder of the CIA's second-highest award, the Intelligence Star. He was considerably overqualified for the work; he should have been a CIA station chief in Kinshasa, not a grunt in Angola.'

But there was more to George Bacon. Much more…

Rounding a bend in the road, with the vehicle barely under control, the Land Rover ran right into the back end of a stake-bed truck, the Land Rover's hood actually going under the bed of the truck before they came to a halt. Acker spotted a Soviet BRDM armoured vehicle and suddenly realised they had just crashed into the rear end of a Cuban/FAPLA convoy.

'In seconds, the Land Rover was being turned into a sieve by enemy gunfire,' said one report afterwards. Bacon and several others were killed.

George Bacon took the long route to Africa, as he put it, 'to take up the fight against communism once more.'

He flew to Angola in 1975 and attempted to join the FNLA but was turned down. The other anti-communist movement, UNITA, also rejected him, perhaps because they suspected him of being a CIA informant.

In late 1975 an American freelance, David Bufkin, was recruiting mercenaries to join FNLA to help fight the communists in Angola, while a second recruiter worked England. It was, as Murphy suggests, 'a shit show from the very beginning, FNLA representatives promising the world, good pay, good kit, and top notch soldiers.' None of it was true.

Former Marine, Gary Acker linked up with Bufkin when he responded to one of his newspaper ads. Bufkin meanwhile also began publishing a paper called *Mercenary Forces Group* and this may have been how George happened across the FNLA recruiters, looking for an 'in' after failing to join up on his first try.

On February 6th, 1976, Bufkin, Acker, Gearhart, and George Bacon flew from Kennedy Airport in New York to Charles de Gaulle airport in France before getting a connecting flight to Kinsasha, Zaire. After paying the mandatory bribe at the airport, the would-be mercenaries stayed for three days at the city's plush Intercontinental Hotel where George received a phone call from the American embassy ordering him to 'come in' and fly home immediately. Was George truly off the reservation and freelancing in Angola or was he a part of a covert CIA mission?

McAleese and an FNLA Officer arrived and briefed the newcomers on their second night at the hotel. It says a good deal that though a brilliant combatant who has served with distinction in many wars, Peter McAleese is perhaps the only man to have been kicked out of the Special Air Service three times. If memory serves, he was booted from the British SAS twice and the Rhodesian SAS once, mostly for drunken brawls at the bar. Regardless, this British veteran with an excellent service record was an experienced soldier and, by all accounts, a strong leader.

The former SAS man cut to the chase, FNLA was losing the war against the communist FAPLA. He also told them about the lunatic Costas 'Callan' Georgiou who was on the run from both the enemy and now the FNLA as well. McAleese issued 'shoot on sight' orders with regard to the Cypriot.

Callan, as it transpired, was a clinical psychopath who had joined the FNLA and was soon taken to executing his own men in a misguided bid to terrorize his troops into obeying his orders. The last straw was a massacre at the small town of Maquela in north Angola in which Callan and his inner circle lined up and gunned down more than a dozen British FNLA recruits, the majority of whom had signed up for 'non-combat' roles.

The youngest was 16 years old, a few had military experience while most had none at all. One was a street sweeper by trade.

Of course their recruiter in England had filled their heads with lies about how they would be truck drivers and have other support positions. In Angola, Callan expected them to take up arms against the Cubans. This led to the recruits revolting against him and inevitably to the killings. It was a straight up murder and now Callan was a hunted man. He continued to fight the Angolan Army and its Cuban backers and was later captured by communist forces.

While at the hotel in Kinshasa, Acker learned that Bufkin hoped that he (Acker) would be killed in combat because he was afraid the former US Marine might talk to the FBI when they got back the US. Searching his hotel room, they found that Bufkin had a go-bag packed with an Uzi, three spare magazines as well as a Walther P-38.

As the mercenaries began to talk amongst themselves, the gravity of Bufkin's deception suddenly became apparent. He owed them all money and had been lying about the situation in Angola from the start. He had told them that the FNLA had 250 mercenaries including a commando element. The reality of the situation they were all stuck with was a handful of professionals trying to herd a bunch of poorly or untrained trained civilians in combat and into a losing war. Something had to be done.

Acker, Gearhart, and George Bacon strong-armed Bufkin back to his hotel room and confronted him. While Acker wanted to ice him right then and there, cooler heads prevailed and the trial of David Bufkin was held by the mercenaries on the spot. It was decided that rather than return to the US as he planned, Bufkin would be press-ganged into service as a front-line trooper, just like the rest of them. Peter McAleese found out about the verdict later and upheld it.

Between them, Fidel Castro and the future Angolan leader Agostinho Neto – ably assisted by Portugal's communist military chief in the country, Admiral Rosa Coutinho – carefully orchestrated the takeover of the country's government.

Dr Jonas Savimbi, the UNITA leader and his cohorts were effectively sidelined.

All manner of improvised weaponry emerged, including this makeshift 'armoured vehicle' that the author encountered when heading home from Nova Lisboa. (Author's photo)

Headline of the day:

Arms purchases

Minister P.W. Botha and Adm. Biermann were updated on the matter of supplying the FNLA and UNITA by Lt.-Gen. Armstrong on 17 July 1975, as soon as they returned to Pretoria. Lt.-Gen. van den Bergh did not hesitate. Within two days after the meeting at Klippan, he was overseas, possibly Paris. On 17 July 1975 a telegram was received in which he confirmed that he obtained weapons "subject to packing, immediately available – a boat was standing by to ship the consignment". In the telegram he mentioned that "I am not planning to finalise the order of the goods before I have been able to talk to Holden." He did, indeed, shortly afterwards, conduct an interview with Holden Roberto, but a meeting with Savimbi was cancelled. Apparently, the weapons mentioned in the above mentioned telegram (or a part thereof), were purchased, because the list somewhat matched the first consignment of weapons shipped to Matadi in August, and transported to Kinshasa for further distribution.

It is difficult to establish exactly how the weapons purchased by South Africa were distributed from Kinshasa.

Brought to you by:

http://www.warinangola.com

Naturally Pretoria got involved, distributing weapons among its putative allies, mostly with the help of the CIA through conduits provided by Congolese leader Mobuto. This is one of the documents that emerged at the time.

On the fringes of this 'catastrophe about to happen' tens of thousands of juveniles of every possibly political persuasion were taught to fight. (Courtesy of Roland de Vries)

Apart from Neto's MPLA, Savimbi's UNITA was able to rally its forces in a bid to prevent a military rout. In doing this, the Swiss-educated guerrilla was remarkably successful. (Author's collection)

The entire country was apprehensive. In parts of Cabinda, locals took to the bush because they believed they might be massacred during the elections.

Overnight, bands of brigands – allied to one faction or another – started to make their presence felt. Throughout, the MPLA maintained control of most urban areas.

The Chinese also played a subversive role, making contact with some FNLA commanders in the north of the country, usually by flying into remote airstrips.

Collateral damage was a factor that had to be reckoned with. This South African Airways Boeing 747 took several hits (circled) while approaching Luanda International Airport. (Photo from an anonymous source at the airline)

Basil Davidson, a radical British commentator, was at the forefront of providing Agostinho Neto good support in several London newspapers. While the MPLA was still fighting the Portuguese he met several times with the Angolan rebel leader in the Angolan bush. (Author's collection)

Getting some basic kit issued, Acker commandeered Bufkin's Uzi but later gave it to Bacon when he picked up an MG-42 in Angola.

Loaded into a Panhard scout car and a Land Rover, this rather sorry lot of putative mercs headed out for Angola, but the brand-new armoured car soon broke down, so they cross-loaded everyone into the Land Rover. At the frontier checkpoint, George used his language skills to negotiate their passage in French with the border guards.

George and Acker conducted some scouting patrols, seeking out egress routs back to Zaire and doing a basic area reconnaissance. They also trained 10-20 man groups of Angolan FNLA troops in marksmanship and weapons-handling.

On February 14, the mercenaries got word that the Cubans were on the move. 'Unsourced' aerial photography showed that Cuban convoys had been advancing during the night. Acker went out with a British mercenary named Dave (not Dave Tompkins who had already left Angola after being wounded by one of his own landmines) to establish a blocking position while Bacon loaded up several men and explosives into one of the unit vehicles. His mission was to blow up two concrete bridges to further delay the enemy advance.

The plan was for Acker and Dave to bring heavy fire on the enemy convoy as a harassing action to slow them. By first light, George would have the bridge prepped for demolition and once Acker's element broke contact, they would race the Land Rover across the bridge. At that point George would blow the bridge, in theory, again delaying the Cuban advance.

'It's important to remember that these were symbolic actions,' Acker wrote much later for *Soldier of Fortune* magazine. 'We were surrounded and outnumbered thousands to one. Within days Tomboco fell, Damba was abandoned without a shot being fired and then Maquela do Zombo was taken by the Cuban-led Angolan force.

> Stalin Organs [Katyusha Rockets] and MG-42s weren't the only things we shared with the Germans on the Eastern Front: We were dead meat. Cubans were closing in and they were exerting every effort to catch us in Sao Salvador.

Acker took up a position in his blocking position and waited all night alongside the road but the enemy never showed. Meanwhile, back at George Baker's position at the bridge, one of the black Angolans had accidentally shot himself. After giving the black mercenary medical treatment, the American set to work on rigging the bridge with TNT. He dug deep into the earth around the concrete pylons to ensure that the bridge would be properly destroyed.

When dawn came, Acker and Dave returned and formed back up with Baker's element. The bridge was ready to blow, but the former SOG commando wanted radio confirmation from a higher authority that they were to initiate the demolition plan. Thus far, they had seen no sign of the Cubans. Failing to establish comms with Sao Salvador, 'Canada' Newby told them to link up with a second patrol in Cuimba.

George Baker clambered over the ammunition and explosives stacked on their Land Rover so that Acker could orient himself facing towards the rear with his German-made MG-42 machine gun. Three mercenaries sat in the front including the driver, Fernando and 'Canada' Newby. Two more strap hangers stood on the running boards, hanging on tightly as they took off for Cuimba.

'I don't like this, George,' Acker said as they drove. George Bacon, in turn, shook his head but said nothing.

A veteran Special Forces commando, the American must have possibly have had a premonition of what was to come. Continuing down the road, their vehicle slowed as they spotted a young Angolan carrying an AK and wearing a chest rig full of magazines. Fernando asked him who he was and the kid replied that he was with FNLA. Taking the statement at face value, the driver continued down the road. Acker, and surely Bacon, were furious: they had just passed an enemy scout.

Moments later they turned around a bend in the road and literally ran into the Cuban convoy. Slamming on brakes, the Land Rover skidded to a halt.

An enemy rifleman standing next to a BRDM armoured personnel carrier opened fire first, a single shot blasting through the windshield. After a brief pause, the floodgates opened and the FNLA vehicle was raked with enemy fire.

'Aluminium panelling ripped and popped before my eyes and glass flew through the air like leaves in a tornado,' Acker wrote of the one-sided fire-fight.

He was hit multiple times in the fusillade of rifle fire. Bacon reacted immediately, throwing open the back door and pushing Acker out. The other mercenaries jumped from the side doors and were gunned down by the Cuban and FAPLA troops. Attempting to crawl to cover, Acker found himself surrounded by the enemy. Becoming entangled on something, he looked back to see what was holding him up.

Acker's shoelaces had somehow become snagged on Bacon, who was now leaned back against the Land Rover, his eyes motionless.

He had probably been hit in the initial barrage of gunfire, then hit a few more times once they got out of the truck. His shin bone was sticking through the upper portion of his boot. George Washington Bacon was killed on St Valentine's Day, 1976.

Surrounded and outgunned, the seriously injured Gary Acker played possum, a ruse that worked as the enemy came to loot his watch and other belongings. They laid George's body down next to him. Before long someone saw Acker breathing and finally took him prisoner.

'Canada' Newby was screaming at the FAPLA troops, begging them to kill him. He'd been shot through both legs and was in serious pain.

It was only as they were trucked away that Acker saw the entire convoy. In addition to the BRDM there were two T-54 tanks, a bulldozer, and dozens more trucks. The enemy convoy stretched back on the jungle, seemingly forever. They had run right into it.

'Canada' was provided medical treatment but did not survive the surgery. George's body was unloaded at Damba where the mercenaries' remains were filmed by a television crew and broadcast on Angolan TV for propaganda purposes.

George Bacon's friends learned of his death on reading the newspapers several days later. The reporters had misspelled his name, but they knew damn well who it was.

A friend and fellow SOG veteran received an anonymous phone call that day. Bacon's passport would be frozen for the next year and there would be no recovery operation. Days later, the entire FNLA force inside Angola was routed under the weight of the Cuban and FAPLA advance.

Peter McAleese conducted an aerial reconnaissance in a Cessna airplane, spotting 2,000 enemy soldiers and 75 vehicles closing on Sao Salvador. Back on the ground, he initiated 'Operation Breakout', the contingency plan to retreat back to Zaire. For the survivors, the war was over.

As for the captured foreign mercenaries being held by FAPLA, they were to face a kangaroo court for their crimes, both real and perceived. Gary Acker spent seven and a half years in an Angolan prison before he was finally released. He was lucky to escape with his life.

What became of George Bacon's remains are unknown.

Questions and uncertainly continue to surround the circumstances under which George Bacon came to Angola and whether he was not actually acting under the auspices of the Central Intelligence Agency. Although he received a call from the American embassy in Zaire while the group was still in Kinshasa to return home, it is certainly possible that he was working in a compartmentalized program where the left hand didn't talk to the right hand, simply because they didn't have a need to know.

Back in Washington DC, George's Morris Minor automobile sat unattended in a parking lot. The local police had been told to leave it where it was and it sat there for years, a close friend driving by to see it every so often, recalling many fond memories of George.

A Chief of Station who was serving in that part of Africa at the time denied that Bacon was working for Langley when it all went down. However, with the amount of smoke and mirrors that deliberately obscures the actions of any intelligence agency it is hard to be sure.

George Bacon was committed to fighting communism, whenever, wherever it showed itself. It is easy to think that if America had not been fighting the communists in South East Asia that he would have gone over there and started a war himself. He certainly did not need any prompting from the CIA to go to Angola and take the fight to the Cubans.

He was a secret soldier fighting a shadow war. From Vietnam, to Cambodia, to Laos, and finally Angola, George Washington Bacon was a man who lived his life exactly the way that he chose.

From what records we do have from his time with the CIA is this: he went operational with the CIA's Para-Military service in 1971. There is no record of when his service ended.

The trial in Luanda, the Angolan capital, was held in June and July, 1976, and the verdicts handed down were sentences that ranged from 16 to 30 years for nine of those involved and four of the prisoners executed by firing squad.

They were Costas Georgiou (aka 'Colonel Tony Callan') 25, originally from Cyprus though a British citizen who had served briefly in the army, Andrew McKenzie, 25 and Derek Barker 35, both also British and a 34-year-old American national Daniel (Danny) Gearhart. McKenzie, who had been wounded in action and was wheelchair bound, insisted on standing when he faced the firing squad.

Deals were eventually made with both Washington and London to get their imprisoned nationals released. The convicted British were expelled from Angola in 1982 and the two remaining Americans followed a couple of years later.

15

The Trial

> By definition, mercenaries have always been a dying breed.
> British journalist Ian Bruce in *Comment*, London, February 19, 2002

Some astonishing revelations emerged from the People's Revolutionary Tribunal that tried the 14 mercenaries captured in north Angola early 1976.

A series of question centred on where the money had come from that was used to fund the mercenary operation. Taken together with salaries and advances, flights, hotels and the rest it amounted to more than $4 million in the first few months, with promises of much more to come. In the process, quite a lot of money was lost because several recruits took their initial payments and scarpered, never to be seen again.

In Luanda, while the trial progressed, there was a strong consensus that Washington was behind it all and in retrospect, with John Martin's revelations below, and at least one CIA agent involved – George Bacon – they were probably right. Unquestionably there was also European input, some of it Belgian and linked to the Katangese copper mines.

John Martin, a journalist with the London *Observer*, dealt with some of the more devious aspects of mercenary involvement when he disclosed that the entire operation had been financed by the United States Embassy in London and that the contact man was Major James E Leonard, assistant military attaché. This was given to him by a 'burly, red-faced East-Ender' who called himself John Best.

Best declared that the cash came from four sources: through couriers direct from Zaire; a Leeds professional man, a so-called 'Doctor' MacDonald Belford; bank transfers from Belgium (which made sense because the Congo/Zaire had been a Belgian colony) and from the Zairean Embassy in London.

The courtroom in Luanda was given numerous specifics about the weapons issued to the various mercenary groups. These included Belgian FN rifles, almost all new and still in their factory grease, British sten guns that dated from the Second World War, Chinese automatic rifles, an anti-aircraft gun of unspecified origin, two and three-inch mortars as well as 106mm recoilless rifles flown in from Kinshasa, said to be of American origin. There were also various types of machine-guns, Chinese stick grenades, outdated American bazookas and German pistols. Another of the men disclosed they also had Land Rovers which had come from Petrangol, the Angolan oil company.

At the end of it, the small mercenary force was routed. Those who got away were just plain lucky. Others were not.

Among the former was Robin Wright, a sprightly young American journalist who had spent time with the mercenary contingent and afterwards travelled to Luanda to cover the trial. I'd met Robin a few times during her Southern African peregrinations, once in Salisbury, the Rhodesian capital, with a mutual journalist pal Chris Munnion who, almost until the week he died was working for London's *Daily Telegraph*, as he had been doing for most of the previous quarter century.

Chris, pint sized, always smiling – even in adversity – was a legend in Africa and with the *Daily Mail's* Peter Younghusband and John Monks of the *Daily Express*, the trio were almost always leading the pack. Chris, small as he was, could drink most of us under the table and was a regular at Salisbury's Quill Club.

It was also Munnion who penned the rather acerbic comment about war correspondents, though some of the old hacks who had seen a thing or two looked down their noses at what he said. But he did make good sense.

I quote: 'Why the title "war correspondent" should carry so much glamour, I really do not know. War has been the most dispiriting, soul-destroying experience I have ever had, especially in Africa. Ordinary people in a war behave very differently. It does de-humanise all concerned and carries no glamour whatsoever.'

Chris also shared with us some of the exploits of Robin Wright while she was on assignment in Angola, how she entered that country shortly before the debacle – she flew in on a small plane with Holden Roberto – and then, after a series of disastrous battles and with only moments to spare, escaped on the last boat to leave harbour. That had taken place just as the first Cuban tanks were coming into town.

A remarkable and enterprising news-gatherer, Robin was not afraid to put her life on the line to get the story. Thereafter she was awarded a Fellowship by the Alicia Patterson Foundation to study the dismantling of Portugal's African Empire.

Robin Wright had originally gone to Angola to report on five British mercenaries, 'regular blokes', she called them, lured from day jobs in London as factory workers and bricklayers with a promise of tax-free dollars as 'Soldiers of Fortune' in Africa. They commanded a pro-democracy militia in a small town, but had very little ammunition with which to defend themselves and those around them.

Early in 1976 this American correspondent found the mercenaries in the town of Santo Antonio de Zaire on the Angola-Zaire border where the Congo pours into the Atlantic Ocean. Angolan forces backed by Cuban troops stormed the place with armour and machine guns and shortly after, civilians and soldiers ran for their lives.

Robin Wright's first-hand report of the attack appeared in the *Christian Science Monitor* of February 9, 1976 under the title 'Angola's Dogs of War':

> [This reporter] was present during the surprise assault on this coastal city which is the northernmost point before the Zaire border.
>
> The attack began at 8.45am on February 6th with the sound of Soviet tanks and the crash of mortars falling on the hospital and airfield on the outskirts of town. At first many people thought the sounds were thunder from the gale-force wind of the rainy season that was drenching the steamy little town located six degrees below the equator.
>
> There had been no warning of the attack…
>
> Within seconds of the first shelling the entire town was in chaos. People and troops fled down the streets towards the river, the only exit on the peninsula.
>
> At the port where half a dozen fishing boats were docked, women and children were fighting and pulling each other out to get a place.
>
> …This reporter and one mercenary headed for the single, small motorised boat that had just been repaired the night before. Approaching the vessel – smaller than a tiny tug-boat – we saw it, too, was swarming with people clawing for space.

Of the 350 people in Santo Antonio de Zaire that day, only 22 made it out alive, including Robin and two mercenaries. The attackers slaughtered the rest.

She returned to Angola when the captured mercenaries – including the dreaded Callan – went on trial, and the revolutionary government tried to call her as a witness. She refused to testify on the grounds that she was a journalist and not a participant in the fighting. Accusing Robin of spying for the CIA, the Angolans put her in prison which she describes as 'a memorable week'.

In 1977 she won the Overseas Press Club award for the best reporting in any medium requiring exceptional courage and initiative.

Her Angolan exploits read almost like an adventure story and I give it to you in full.[1]

> If I hadn't lived through it, I'm sure I'd never believe it. Few dramas have ended in such tragedy. Few comedies have contained such pathetic slapstick. And no cast of characters were such perfect parodies of their stereotypes.
>
> The action of this adventure stretched over four days, the period I spent with five British mercenaries in the oil-rich northern Angolan city of San Antonio do Zaire. I had flown in to report on how these hardcore 'dogs of war' were changing the tide of the bitter civil conflict, helping the National Liberation Front (FNLA) hold the small strip of towns in the north from incursion by the Russian- and Cuban-backed Popular Liberation Movement (MPLA).
>
> But the story I found in that steamy little ghost town just six degrees below the equator hardly fitted my expectations. The five mercenaries were so busy administering the area they barely had time for the war.
>
> The first afternoon I found them all seriously gathered around the elegant dining room table in the former Portuguese governor's mansion, rifles and grenade launchers strewn on velvet chairs, their dirty bush fatigues clashing with the plush gold and white striped fabric. Hunched over a map of the town, they were intently planning strategy – but not the type expected.
>
> 'Douglas, you check on the bakery and distribute the bread,' the commander said in his thick Scottish burr. 'Stewart, you make the rounds of the hospital and clinic. And Mike, get the women organized in fishing brigades. We need more food.'
>
> 'The boys' had been in San Antonio, the northernmost town before the Zaire border, for three weeks and had yet to see any action. Other than the 7 am roll call and assignment of duties, the mercenaries rarely saw their 350 African troops. The rest of the day was spent searching for food for the few hundred residents who had not left for safer terrain in Zaire, trying to scrounge vehicles not sabotaged by fleeing Portuguese, and checking on the sick at the tiny hospital.
>
> Not a single shot had been fired since their arrival, not even in training sessions, because of the shortage of ammunition. 'At best we have 20 minutes of fire power,' the commander lamented. 'We can't waste it on the Africans. It'd take years of training to make them into effective troops. So we just drill them in the morning and dispatch them; they think they're defending the city, but it's all a grand charade.'
>
> Only once had a weapon been fired: when the fish weren't biting one of the boys tossed a couple of grenades into the water. 'That gets them jumping,' he chuckled.
>
> But for this type of work they were perhaps better qualified than waging war against the powerful MPLA. Most of the mercenaries were unemployed bricklayers, assembly line

---

1 Robin Wright, with acknowledgment to the *Christian Science Monitor* and the Alicia Patterson Foundation.

workers or repairmen. A few were petty crime offenders; some were school dropouts and most were marital misfits. Few had any army training and then only as non-commissioned officers.

The men I spent four days with were typical of the mercenaries fighting with the FNLA: There was Mick, the intense 39-year-old former private eye who claimed he fought with the French Foreign Legion. But as with most of his boasts, it was highly suspect.

Then there was Stewart, the mid-30s Scottish labourer whose crew-cut and tattoos – including the names of his brothers across his knuckles – made him a caricature of a mercenary. He had been involved in several petty robberies and thus was the most enthusiastic about fulfilling the full six-month contract in Angola.

Brummie also fitted the stereotype with his shaved head, thick neck and hefty frame. A jovial con artist, he had convinced four of his friends to go into Angola with him in the same way he had talked them into working under him as bricklayers in England.

Then there was Douglas, the ever-laughing big bear of a man, with more tattoos and another shaved head, revealing several scars from marital rows. 'My wife threw a mean ashtray,' he would explain. And finally young John, a rather melancholy ex-marine from Plymouth; he joined up mainly to spite his unfaithful wife and was also bored with his assembly-line job.

The whimsical way all five of them had 'tripped' into the war – with less than two days between the offer and their arrival in Angola – was as bizarre as their experience in the North.

They had been called together on a Friday night, January 23, at a Sussex pub where a friend told them attractive tales of a lush climate, friendly people, wealthy sponsors and lots of bounty – plus 300 tax-free dollars a week. The next morning – without passports, inoculations or equipment – they and 14 others flew to Brussels, then to Zaire to join the FNLA.

A 'special agent' got them through Heathrow Airport in London without papers and the Belgians 'just looked the other way,' they claimed.

In each case, the objective in joining was clearly money. 'Why not, we have to make bread some way,' Brummie rationalized. Two weeks into their jobs and some did not even know the name of the liberation movement they were fighting for.

'Tell me again, what's this FLA stand for?' Douglas used to ask regularly, not even getting the acronym right. And it was common to hear them referring to Roberto Holden instead of Holden Roberto, the FNLA president. After a brief stop in San Salvador, the northern headquarters, they were dispatched to San Antonio, where disillusionment set in quickly.

'We got here and found absolutely no organization. We had to start from scratch,' Mike explained. 'You'd never guess they had been fighting for several years. And there was corruption everywhere. The FNLA regional commissar is a boozer who hoards everything to sell across the border for liquor and cigs. He's hopelessly drunk by mid-morning and since we've been here, he hasn't done a bloody thing for the locals – except milk them.'

They were also lacking in basic equipment. The best arms were Russian AK-47s captured from the MPLA – but there was so little ammunition that few were used. Most troops used vintage American sten guns and carbines that were useless against the sophisticated artillery of the MPLA.

'We were told we'd get the latest in everything. But this stuff is useless,' Brummie scowled. 'And when we complained, Roberto ignored us. The only people who came around were the Americans.'

'The Americans?' I quizzed.

Sure, the four CIA blokes who flew down here to check the score. Usually brought survival kits, food, stuff like that. But once they brought us 40 carbines. Trouble is, they sent 10,000 rounds of the wrong kind of ammunition.'

The most notorious mercenary of them all in the civil war period was a brutal Greek Cypriot psychopath named Costas Georgiou – alias Colonel Callan – who had served briefly in the British Army before being dishonourably discharged. In Angola he executed 14 of his own recruits for 'disobeying orders'. (Author's collection)

Some of the mercenaries the author encountered when he joined *Chipa Esquadrao* in Nova Lisboa. (Author's photo)

THE TRIAL

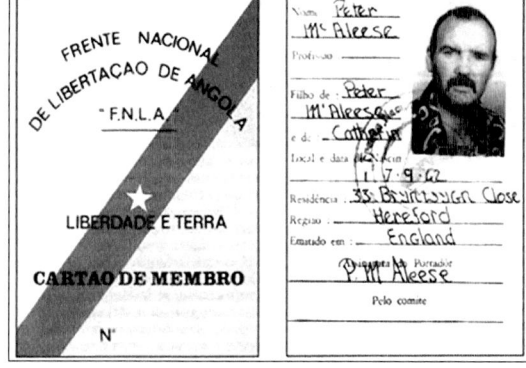

At the time mercenaries from all over the world were being recruited by the Rhodesian Army. My contact in Nova Lisboa confided that they hoped to do the same in Angola. (Author's photo)

Former British and Rhodesian SAS operator Peter McAleese ended up being recruited by the FNLA. He quickly distanced himself from Callan. This was his Angolan ID card.

Portuguese merc leads FNLA troops: "When our party of 18 guys got there, we found that there was 40 or 50 Portuguese there and they had the very best of what there was ... They were all armed with pretty good things." — Chris Dempster

Some of the mercenaries that joined the FNLA were a rum bunch with little or no military experience.

The author, seen here in Nova Lisboa (Huambo today) with his issued FN rifle while serving briefly as a mercenary with Daniel Chipenda's *Chipa Esquadrao*, was lucky to get out of Luanda unscathed. South Africa had invaded Angola's south (Operation Savannah) and since the media in the capital were a fairly close-knit group – and included many Cuban and Soviet 'journalists', suspicion fell heavily on him that he was a South African spy. He eventually left Nova Lisboa shortly before 'Kaas' van der Waals and his Task Force arrived in the city (Chapter 16).

Angolan newspaper cutting published after his arrest. It showed 'Colonel' Callan issuing orders at the front.

One of the mercenary officers in the mercenary unit in which the author served. (Author's photo)

American journalist and author Robin Wright.

American former Special Forces operator and CIA agent George Bacon who was KIA in the final stages of the FNLA withdrawal. He is seen here with one of his contacts in South East Asia.

FACING THE FIRING SQUAD

British mercenaries in Angola war trial

By JOHN HILL

COLONEL CALLAN
COSTAS GEORGIOU

THESE are the 10 British mercenaries soon to go on trial in Angola ... and face the threat of death by firing squad.

It is the price they could pay for their ill-fated part in the Angolan War.

And as they wait for their trial—due to begin on June 8— the anguish of their families grows.

For since they were arrested three months ago, the new Angolan leaders have refused to let the men send messages home.

The Foreign Office in London said: "We have been trying to get details from the Angolan authorities. But, so far, they have not responded."

Fainted

But, last night, one mother was giving thanks because, at long last, she knew that her 20-year-old son, John Nammock, was at least alive.

Mrs Noreen Nammock, of Hazelwood Crescent, West London, said: "Through a mix-up over the spelling of his name, I had been unable to discover whether he was really still alive.

"Now, because of details about his date of birth and past from Angola, I know that he is there.

"I nearly fainted when I heard the news. For months I have been ringing every telephone number I can think of where there might be some clue about him.

"He is the elder of my two sons and comes from an army family.

"John is the adventurous kind, whose ideal

of life is to be parachuting out of planes.

"I have been taking tranquillisers to help me sleep at night.

"Now I feel 100 times better—even though I am so worried about what will happen to him."

Caution

The list of Britons to be tried — announced by Angola's Justice Minister Dr Diogenes Boavida — is still being treated with caution by another mercenary's mother, Mrs Catherine Lawlor,

of Broom Hill Road, Farnborough Hants, said of her son also called John:

"I am 99 per cent sure that he is being held by them but I dare not positively believe it yet.

Fear

"Then there is the fear of what happens next.

"John is a strong character. — you do not go through Royal Marine training without becoming self-sufficient.

"But I would dearly love to be able to go to Angola for the trial."

● HE is foremost among the accused mercenaries, who knew him as "Colonel" Callan.

Georgiou, aged 25, is said to have ordered the deaths of 14 of his men for refusing to fight.

He is also alleged to be responsible for the massacre of 100 African villagers. He was born in Cyprus, but his parents live in London.

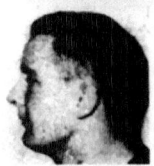

Kevin Marchant
● HE once served in the Royal Artillery. His wife, from whom he is separated, has said: "He never cared about the money— only the fighting. Marchant, aged 25, comes from Borehamwood, Herts.

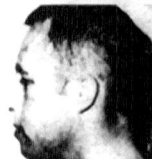

Michael Wileman
● HIS mother, who has six children, lives in Peckham, London. Wileman, aged 19, was still in council care when he signed up with the mercenaries.

John Barker
● He was captured while trying to flee Angola by swimming across the River Zaire. Barker, aged 30, is believed to have lived in Farnborough Hants.

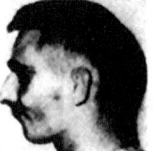

Colin Evans
● HE is a father of four, but separated from his wife. Evans, aged 28, is a former regular Army soldier. His father lives in Dewsbury, Yorks.

Cecil Fortuin
● HE was born in Capetown, but brought up in the Midlands. Fortuin, aged 32, was left for dead after being injured in Angola during an enemy advance.

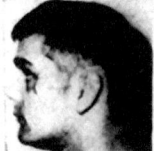

Malcolm McIntyre
● His real name is Malcolm Wright. He is aged 27, a father of two, separated from his wife and was unemployed before joining the mercenaries.

John Nammock
● HE is an ex-Parachute Regiment soldier who lived in West London. Nammock, aged 20, comes from a family with a long Army connection.

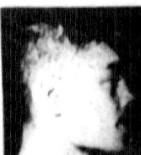

Andrew McKenzie
● HE is another ex-Parachute Regiment man and a friend of mercenary Michael Wileman. McKenzie, aged 26, left the paras after six years.

John Lawlor
● HE is a former Marine from Farnborough, Hants. Lawlor, aged 23, once did a term of duty in Ulster. Was reported killed in Angola.

The headline says it all – the end of 'Colonel Calan'.

The San Antonio unit did have one 106mm cannon, but it too was quickly rendered useless in one of the many tragi-comic episodes of the four days.

On the morning of February 5, we heard that Quinzau, some 100 kilometres south, had been taken by the MPLA, so the boys organized the troops for their first and only mission. Everyone set out rather dramatically in a caravan to the cheering of the few locals who were left. But just a few miles down the road the 20-ton truck that carried the 106 and most of the Africans overturned on a narrow bridge.

People were stepping on each others' backs, shoulders and heads to get out before the truck sank, as empty ammunition boxes floated down the river and frogs jumped in and out of the 106. From that point on, the mission was a hopeless farce.

When the 'advance team' got to the Quinzau area, Douglas ordered his men to disperse in the bush, which they promptly did – in reverse. Douglas looked around to find that his 70 men had all fled, so he followed suit. 'I couldn't fight alone,' he said, still stunned and indignant.

Brummie, deployed east of the town, had also to give up the defence line when he found his men had put all their ammunition in backwards on their bandoliers and in their magazines. 'It would have taken hours to put it all right,' he groaned. 'Stupid Afs, I can't imagine how they've held out this long.'

'It didn't take long for us to realize we joined a loser,' Stewart added. 'Not two percent of these men would stay if the city is attacked. The only reason they're here now is because we feed them. When you come down to it, the five of us are all this place had to defend it.'

'During my visit, it seems nothing went right for the mercenaries. Even an attempt to raise the morale through the first payment of the African troops in eight years backfired. After each soldier was given 500 escudos and each commander 1000 escudos, there was a small war among those who felt cheated and demanded more. The troops probably saw more action that day than in the entire eight years they had been fighting.

As it turned out, the timing of payment was another of the many pathetic episodes, for it was the very next day that the MPLA advanced on the city and wiped out the FNLA.

There were several indications of the approaching column, but again the boys did not take them seriously. On February 6, the town's water and electricity went off, despite the fact the plants were in order. Later that morning, people started walking quietly from the city, parcels balanced on their heads and children in tow. There was no indication where or why they were leaving, but apparently they knew.

Most mysterious, however, was the tree pruning done the night before the invasion. All around the governor's mansion the trees had been cut to below window level, a major operation since the structure had only a single story. At first we didn't understand. Sabotage? The answer was simple: MPLA infiltrators had cut the trees to pinpoint the headquarters to the advancing column.

There were other eerie elements on the morning of the invasion. The day had started slowly because of a fierce rainstorm. None of the boys was enthusiastic about the morning rounds. Part of the problem was the death the previous night of a 17-year-old girl who haemorrhaged after a miscarriage. The mercenaries had all taken turns stopping at the small hospital on the outskirts of town to check on her. There were no doctors or midwives in town, and the few pharmaceuticals at the hospital were unmarked, thus useless. The mercenaries had a small bottle of penicillin and at each shift the boys would give her a spoonful mixed in milk.

But it didn't help and she finally bled to death, her soldier-husband at her side in the pitiful and dirty little maternity ward full of other women and their howling babies. Her husband had walked down to give us the news and ask for a sheet to bury her in; there were no coffins or morticians in town. There weren't even sheets at the hospital.

He was still sitting at the dining room table sobbing, sheet-coffin tucked under his arm, when the storm appeared to get worse. Thunder cracked non-stop, scaring many of the soldiers. 'It's the MPLA, it's the MPLA,' someone hollered, setting off a panic.

At first we did not believe it. There had been absolutely no warning, no firing from the FNLA troops, no communication from San Salvador, nor any advance notice from troops deployed further south. But after we heard the rapid burst of machine gun fire, there was no choice but to move – and fast.

As could be expected, no one was prepared. Brummie, Mike, Stewart and Douglas set out to estimate the troop's strength – their own and the enemy's – but it was no use. Chaos had broken out. Mothers ran screaming down the city's main boulevard, dragging terrified children along behind. Troops dropped weapons and headed for the Congo River, the only way out of the peninsula town to safety in Zaire.

One of the African commanders stopped only long enough to report that the hospital was the first building hit by the incoming tanks. It had been destroyed and there was no hope for survivors, he screamed through the deafening gunfire. Then he too headed for the river.

There was no alternative but for us to also make a break for the water, to board the single small tugboat that could take us to safety. Within a period of 20 minutes we all met at the dock, a major accomplishment since the MPLA had quickly moved into town.

People on both sides of me were shot down by machine gun fire. And right behind Brummie and Mike – the last two to make their way to the pier – was an ominous T-54 Russian tank.

In one of the few strokes of luck, the tugboat had been repaired just the day before and was ready to take a handful of us out. But even our exit was not without mishap. Shortly after John and I boarded, the tug capsized from the churning waves of the storm and the weight of the many Africans who were vying for space. It was uprighted with just minutes to spare. The MPLA was by then on the beach and firing into the water.

The motion had jerked the ropes off the pier and only Stewart and Douglas were able to board. As we took off with chaotic speed, we saw Brummie and Mike still standing on the pier. 'Dive in,' we yelled. 'Swim. Swim out.' But nothing could be heard through the barrage of fire and the screams from the shore.

There was that last minute long-eye contact before we faded into the fog of the rainstorm that offered protection from the three tanks and troops that loomed on the beach. But there was nothing we could do.

Several days later, from the safety of Zaire, we learned that Mike had been killed and Brummie taken prisoner of war.

It is difficult to write about these men as 'dogs of war.' Unemployed and naive, they got caught up in a messy and hopeless situation. They often showed compassion for the local Africans and never walked out, which would have been the easier and smarter thing to do. They never even had a chance to fight.

It is impossible to condone what they did. But it is also hard to condemn.

16

Task Force Foxbat – The South African Army Moves into Central Angola

Though I was unaware of his role at the time, Lieutenant-Colonel WS 'Kaas' van der Waals[1] **played a significant role in getting me ousted from Nova Lisboa. As deputy head of Task Force Foxbat under Lieutenant-Colonel Eddie Webb, his forward elements had reached the outskirts of Nova Lisboa and were waiting for me to go so they could move in. As a journalist, I was a security threat and Pretoria could not risk my reporting on this ongoing subterfuge.**[2]

As Brigadier-General van der Waals recalls today, his overall commander, Major General Constand Viljoen, then Director General Operations of the SADF's General Staff, called him into his office at Defence Headquarters in Pretoria and suggested that he make his way to 1 Military Area, the northern border area adjacent to Angola, then under the command of Brigadier Dawid Schoeman.

He takes up events that followed.

Having made contact, Brigadier Schoeman informed me that I would have to join him as soon as possible at his headquarters in Caprivi. It was from there that Dr Jonas Savimvi's UNITA would receive the bulk of our support. He emphasised that I would be directly responsible to him and him alone. On the face of it, that sounded a bit ominous.

What I was aware of was that strictly speaking, the brigadier was not a military man. As a Citizen Force officer he had worked his way up through the ranks and done a very good job of it, considering that he was a politically well-connected, prosperous maize farmer from the western Transvaal.

A lieutenant-colonel when hostilities in South Angola started, and because of his expertise in agriculture and the SA Army's emphasis on agricultural 'upliftment' of the population in the Border insurgency, he was appointed commander of 1 Military Area as a brigadier. Thus it happened that this non-professional officer suddenly found himself in charge of Operation Savannah, South Africa's biggest wartime operation since the Second World War.

---

1   WS 'Kaas' van der Waals, is also the author of *Portugal's War in Angola 1961–1974*, published first by Ashanti in South Africa in 1993 and later by Protea Books, Pretoria 2011. The book has since been published in Portuguese to national acclaim.
2   See the full report in Chapter 11.

1 Military Area with its Headquarters in Rundu was divided into three sub-areas: Ovambo, Kavango and the Eastern Caprivi, each under command of a commandant or in contemporary terms, a lieutenant-colonel.

His orders issued personally to me by the brigadier at Pretoria's Waterkloof Air Force Base on 19 September 1975 were comprehensive:

- I was to stop the MPLA's advance from Lobito to Nova Lisboa
- Defend Nova Lisboa as Angola's second city and the 'Centre of Gravity' of the Central Angolan Highlands at all cost until the 11th of November 1975 when the Angolan nation would finally become independent
- Train two brigades of UNITA, one offensive and the other defensive, before 11 November 1975; and in the process, provide Savimbi and his general staff with advice

Obviously, the task ahead was a major meat and potatoes job. It was certainly the most difficult and comprehensive challenge I'd faced so far in a fairly lengthy military career that started as a paratrooper, or in South African military lingo, a Parabat.

My first meeting at Army Headquarters was with the SA Army's Director of Operations, Brigadier Jannie Geldenhuys, and my predecessor as Vice Consul in Luanda.

What I quickly discovered was that the first stage of what Brigadier Schoeman had in the mind – stopping the MPLA's advance from Lobito to Nova Lisboa in Angola's Central Highlands – was already very much in the hands of the enemy. There were regular armed clashes with the political and military opposition taking place, invariably with Cuban and Soviet support. In short, Luanda's forces were making good headway. That was the bad news.

If Lieutenant-Colonels Breytenbach and Linford, who headed Combat Groups Alpha and Bravo, were having a relatively easy time moving up the coast towards the west, mine was a much tougher job, and for several reasons.

Except for the operational presence in Central and Eastern Angola, there was already a substantial training task ahead that required a fully fledged South African Army training team. UNITA would provide the recruits and basic weapons and we would offer leadership, instructors and infantry support weapons. The way I read it, an operation to stop the MPLA advance from Lobito – which included a strong motorised force as well as armoured vehicles – had to be launched without any delay.

My obvious requirement for this operation was at least six Eland-90 armoured cars, which meant two pairs with 90mm guns mounted for each of the two approach routes to Nova Lisboa, together with a small reserve.

But, I was soon told, our involvement was so sensitive (secret, would be more appropriate) that any involvement by our armoured cars was out of the question.

It was suggested that instead, I should use 88mm anti-tank rocket launchers, a weapon that had its origins in the Second World War.

Ironically I was also told – almost in almost as many words – that due to political sensitivity I should not endanger the lives of my personnel. That was like telling an army commander about to go into battle to suffer no casualties… Absurd! But then that was the way Brigadier Schoeman conducted his business.

As a compromise I requested ENTAC anti-tank missiles and this was grudgingly accepted.[3]

---

3 ENTAC was a French-built wire-guided anti-tank missile which was bought in considerable numbers by the South African Army and used for the duration of the Border War, quite successfully as it transpired.

The next step was to submit detailed logistic requirements so that everything could be flown to Rundu in two C130 aircraft and, without delay, from there on to Silva Porto in southern Angola.

I decided on four ENTAC launching vehicles with 20 missiles each, two platoons of 81mm mortars and two platoons of medium Browning machine guns with adequate supplies of ammunition. My requirements were immediately prepared and ready to be loaded onto the aircraft the next day.

Personnel requirements followed and these were critical. I could select my own staff and promptly opted for ex-colleagues from 1 Parachute Battalion, Majors Nick Visser and Louis Holtzhausen for East and Central Angola respectively. The training team commander was chosen by the Chief of the Army, Gen Malan, personally: Eddie Webb, also an ex paratrooper.

On 23 September 1975 I departed for Rundu in two heavily laden South African Air Force C-130 aircraft accompanied by Brigadier Wally Black, General Viljoen's assistant as Director Operations of the SADF. Two signallers accompanied the force, WO2 Spider Hattingh and Staff Sergeant Maree.

In Rundu we were welcomed by the brigadier who promptly arranged for the aircraft to be offloaded. When I protested, saying that I had limited time to comply with my orders and that I needed the armament and supplies urgently, he replied in typical South African jargon that he knew our black customers [UNITA] and that you don't give them everything at the same time. Ironically some of the armament was still in Rundu when I returned after independence.

We finally left for Silva Porto in one aircraft with radio equipment when Dr Savimbi pleaded with me to bring the armament and ammunition urgently.

Our signallers installed our long-range radios at UNITA headquarters [the old Roads Department complex in Silva Porto] and we set up shop in a luxurious house close to the Savimbi residence. Leaving my signallers, I flew back to Rundu to await my training team.

Back at headquarters, I again met my ex-colleague and friend Jan Breytenbach who was then with a small team training FNLA [mainly ex MPLA Chipenda members] in Mpupa, an ex-Portuguese military base on the Cuito River. He didn't mention it at the time, but he was about to set out from the coast with Delville Linford [Combat Groups Alpha and Bravo].

I had three priorities, all urgent: getting training procedures started; launching an operation to halt the MPLA advance and taking stock of the general UNITA and MPLA situation, which required a detailed operational appreciation. Our training team arrived on 27 September after Savimbi and I had inspected the old prison facilities in Capolo on 26 September.

Capolo, a small town roughly 60 kilometres south of Silva Porto, was ideal from a security point of view; its facilities were good and it also had a disused 700-metre landing strip which could be useful. Based there was a small force of 25 officers, warrant officers and NCOs under command of Major Nick Visser (as Lieutenant Colonel Eddie Webb had not yet arrived). We were given two weeks to have the first group battle-ready.

Recruits, initially an African force of about 700, varied in age from young boys to old men, many suffering from malnutrition and TB and hardly the kind of tough, determined and malleable fighters that would be required for the task. There were also language problems: very few UNITA personnel understood English and quite a number not even basic Portuguese.

Training nevertheless progressed satisfactorily and by the 15th October we had put four companies through their paces – two offensive and two defensive – as well as two mortar platoons: 81mm and 60mm. Additionally, we had a 106mm recoilless gun crew.

We had also trained 60 bright young UNITA soldiers as a leader group and a further 60 as instructors. They would continue with training after our departure.

Of all the cities under UNITA's control Nova Lisboa was the most critical, with N'Zau Puna its political head. Apart from Silva Porto there were also military headquarters in Quibala in the north, Cangumbe under Chivale in the East and Serpa Pinto in the south-east. In the distant south-west Vakulukuta Kashaka commanded several dispersed UNITA units in the Cunene district.

Savimbi's military strength was estimated to be about 10,000 armed, 20,000 mostly unarmed or under training and a further 10,000 ready for training.

Armament was diverse and included six Panhard armoured cars, three with 90mm mounted guns and three sporting 60mm mortars, either donated by Mobutu or left behind by the Portuguese Army when they departed for Europe. Additionally, there were four 120mm mortars, a dozen 81mm mortars, some 106mm recoilless guns, a pair of 75mm guns, a reasonable number of 7,62mm light machine guns as well as a variety of 7,62mm rifles, the majority the same F1s issued to the author when he joined *Chipa Esquadrao* in Nova Lisboa.

Ammunition was in short supply and UNITA's main logistic base in Silva Porto was in disorder by the time I arrived. There was virtually no fuel; for day-to-day use fuel was stored in the back yard of Savimbi's house in the town. Obviously, I would require a logistics expert to assist me: Major Peter van Nierop soon filled that gap.

As an ally, the FNLA had a rather limited and often disruptive presence in Silva Porto. Regarding Chipenda in Serpa Pinto I shared Savimbi's sentiments. The man was devious, he suggested, worried that it was not impossible that he might opportunistically revert to the MPLA. We both accepted that if he did 'change his spots', the consequences could pose a serious threat to what he termed 'UNITA's soft underbelly'.

Then there was the CIA. I had often seen a young white fellow in Savimbi's presence and was assured by the UNITA leader that I should not be concerned and I would meet this 'individual' later. He was, as he phrased it, a 'friend'.

Another sidelight was a Bellair Viscount aircraft that often landed at Silva Porto, especially from late October onwards when ferrying limited military supplies from Kinshasa. There was also an executive jet that belonged to British entrepreneur Tiny Rowlands, who headed the Lonrho mining conglomerate. It operated from Lusaka and was used to fly Savimbi to various international destinations. The crew refused to overnight at Silva Porto but often refuelled there, adding to our logistics problems.

It was on one of these flights that British journalists Mike Nicholsen and Fred Bridgland spotted South African troops and armour making preparations to go into Angola, after which they broke the story internationally.

The ongoing MPLA threat had escalated over in the past few months, so I need to summarise the situation as on the 6th October 1975:

> First, the MPLA and their military wing FAPLA – the so-called Popular Military Forces – posed a serious threat to the UNITA area of influence (controlled by Savimbi), coming as it did from the north and west.
>
> From the East to the Atlantic Ocean FAPLA occupied Cazombo, Teixeira de Sousa, Henrique de Carvalho, Alto Chicapa, Luquembo, Nova Gaia, Malanje, Salazar, Dondo and Luanda.
>
> From Luanda southwards, FAPLA occupied Porto Amboim, Gabela, Novo Redondo, Vila Nova do Seles, Lobito, Benguela, Norton de Matos (Balombo today), Babaera, Sa da Bandeira, Rocades, Pereira de Eca and Evale. The strength of the Angolan Army was not known, but we were aware it had armoured vehicles and strong Cuban support. Clearly, this

THE SOUTH AFRICAN ARMY MOVES INTO CENTRAL ANGOLA

was unsettling, though at the time I was not to know that Colonels Linford and Breytenbach would soon capture many of those towns.

Cut off from the sea, a land-bound UNITA could not expect any proper means of receiving supplies from the west and this was especially serious with regard to fuel. Supplies had to come in by air, which posed an additional drain on the resources of the South African Air Force.

FAPLA threatened Nova Lisboa on two fronts, along a southern route from Benguela (where an Angolan Army force of roughly 350 men occupied Babaera late September, 1975). A further force of 350 men and three armoured vehicles was positioned at Mariano Machado. This force was being monitored and checked by two battalions of UNITA which forced FAPLA to use the northern route from Lobito via Norton de Matos where the two elements could combine forces. On this route a FAPLA company and an armoured car – supported by a reserve company and three armoured cars – occupied Sousa Lara on 29 September 1975. That left only a small force of 150 UNITA soldiers at Monte Belo; the only opposition between FAPLA and Nova Lisboa.

My immediate priority after our arrival at Silva Porto was to halt FAPLA's advance on Nova Lisboa as soon as possible and as far to the west as I could manage it. This would prevent the MPLA military forces in the region from gaining a foothold in the fertile Central Highlands.

I had already appointed Major Louis Holtzhausen as force leader and arranged for the Panhard armoured cars in his command to be repaired by our technical experts. The ENTAC missile launchers and their crews with 20 missiles had arrived and were ready for deployment by the end of September.

I'd also requested crews for a troop of Panhard armoured cars from South Africa and these arrived days later. Some long wheel base 4x4s specially designed for the rough conditions likely to be encountered followed: dubbed Sabres, they came with .50 Browning machine-guns mounted at the rear.

Eight days after our arrival we were ready for action but were then delayed by Savimbi's absence. We wanted him to be present to prevent friction between our troops and several other UNITA units designated to participate in the operation. Another reason was linked to diplomatic and political considerations: until independence on 11th November, Angola was still nominally Portuguese.

Savimbi returned on 2 October and decided to personally accompany the combat team which left for Nova Lisboa on 3 October.

Moving at night via Alto Hama, the combat group reached Luimbale where they were joined by a battalion of UNITA infantry under Major Lumumba, in Savimbi's eyes, his ablest commander in Central Angola.

None of us had proper maps or charts of Angola, so we were obliged to use tourist maps, which told us almost nothing about the terrain ahead. Major Holtzhausen consequently secreted his armoured column in the bush and went forward with Savimbi to reconnoitre.

About 10 kilometres south of Norton de Matos they met up with forward UNITA foot patrols and were told that there was a FAPLA force in the village. It also emerged that a UNITA detachment, in an earlier contact with FAPLA, had spotted a Soviet T34 tank.

By first light on 5 October the column set off, led by Holtzhausen in his Sabre. Between Massano de Amorim and Norton de Matos the column moved through a mountain range with the two Panhards in the lead, followed by a mobile UNITA contingent, but stopped short of the target town.

Major Holtzhausen and his 19 South Africans then returned to Silva Porto the same day, having left Major Lumumba and three Panhards (now manned by UNITA crews) in defensive positions to the east of Norton de Matos.

An interesting development took place about then. It comes from military author Paul Els who, on going through the files of the late Rowley Medlin found this vignette which he titled 'The Battle of Norton de Matos'.

The skirmish took place on the same day that the column, led by Holtzhausen, almost reached that strategic little crossroads town and just as the South Africans were preparing to match wits with FAPLA. They were about three kilometres from the outskirts of Norton de Matos.

Faced with FAPLA armoured cars and tanks, Holtzhausen and his UNITA group was in the process of advancing towards the Balombo River Valley. The South African had been briefly halted to deal with a small group of enemy soldiers and then managed to continue on. He had reached a bridge over one of the branches of the Balombo River when he was stopped. Ground cover, he recalls was scarce, while the terrain looked dangerous with lots of dead ground.

Then, from across the way, two signal flares were fired into the air by the enemy and moments later a heavy barrage of artillery fire was brought down on this medium-sized penetrating force.

An enemy tank, previously hidden, moved into a hull-down position and with its first shot, hit Holtzhausen's command vehicle while he was in the process of reconnoitring the set-up. His personal aide and signaller, Sergeant Maree was flung out of the vehicle and was badly wounded. The major was close enough to the explosion to have his glasses blown off his face.

Always enterprising, Holtzhausen ran to the vehicle and grabbed his portable radio before taking cover at the side of the road.

Moments later two of his missile-launch vehicles moved forward and took up positions on either side of Holtzhausen's disabled Sabre. Independently, they started firing on the enemy positions which were now clearly visible. The commander then ordered his Panhard to open fire and with its first salvo, knocked out two of FAPLA's armoured vehicles. The column had been led into a perfect ambush.

Throughout, Holtzhausen recalled afterwards, enemy firepower was both heavy and accurate. It was clear they had carefully prepared the ambush position, even pre-registering targets.

While this was going on, a light aircraft started dropping hand grenades on the combined South African/UNITA force. That was when Holtzhausen realised that just about all intelligence provided by the UNITA headquarters was inaccurate. He had been told nothing about this heavily defensive position at the bridge; he should have because a UNITA patrol had pushed forward to check out the area.

Even worse, the first shots from FAPLA had hardly sounded before Major Lumumba and his entire force of 500 UNITA troops made an abrupt about-turn and abandoned the 19 white SADF soldiers at the approaches of the bridge: they were left to fight on alone. Savimbi's troops totally ignored the basics they had been taught by their South African instructors and ran for their lives.

Meanwhile, Holtzhausen and his tiny group were pinned down alongside an exposed stretch of road. Heavy fire was heading in at them from a variety of Soviet weapons that included multiple-rocket 122mm Katyushas, D-44s (85-mm divisional guns) as well as a variety of other artillery pieces.

As he recalled afterwards, there were more RPG-7s headed in his direction than he had ever experienced before, many of these rockets self-destructing over their heads. The distinctive booms from Soviet T-34s, which had heavy 76.2 mm (three-inch) guns mounted, added to the drama.

This was the first time that this South African group had encountered such a volume of missile, tank, machine gun and mortars, coming at their exposed line and in concert.

His own missile launchers, still waiting, were manned by WO2 Lotheringen, WO2 Sid Brown, Staff Sergeant Patterson and their loaders. A short distance ahead stood the remaining Panhard, with Corporals Scheepers and van Rensburg.

Informed by Jacobs that he could see about 200 enemy soldiers making a flanking movement to cut off their retreat – and presumed to be Cubans because of their uniforms – their commander utilised his reserves of two .50 Browning machine guns mounted on vehicles and the two 106mm recoilless cannons.

After the first burst of the two cannons and accurate machine gun fire, the Cuban contingent pulled back and did not attempt another cut-off action.

It is worth mentioning that 40 years later, when the now-retired Brigadier-General van der Waals addressed a group of Angolan Army veterans at a function in Luanda to which he had been invited, he was able to chat to his erstwhile enemy General Lara. Now also retired, Lara told him that they had no idea that it was the South African Army that was involved at Norton de Matos. 'I thought they were a bunch of Portuguese mercenaries,' he declared, admitting too that they had 'given a pretty good account of themselves'.[4]

I had already informed headquarters in Rundu that we were involved with what appeared to be a fairly well trained enemy. Also, that they were supported by Cubans and equipped with armoured vehicles including tanks. My advice was that we either got in properly or be pulled out. Half measures, I told my brigadier, would not suffice.

Meantime Commandant Eddie Webb had also joined us as commander of the training team. A week into October – in the absence of Brigadier Schoeman on sick leave and in response to my urgent request – we were visited by his second-in-command, Colonel Des Harmse, an experienced and well balanced professional officer.

We outlined the situation and said it was essential that we needed more armoured cars. We requested a minimum of six Elands, two each for the two western FAPLA advance routes, and two for a possible northern route. In the event of a threat on one of the routes the two armoured components could be merged to provide a solid defensive punch.

These cars could unofficially be 'sold' to UNITA, the idea being that their crews man them because no South African forces could be seen – by the media, especially – as having been deployed in combat.

It was obvious that in its state of unpreparedness, UNITA was simply not able to counter anything that FAPLA – with Cuban and Soviet support – had to offer. In fact, Savimbi had attended our discussions with Harmse and acknowledged this. He knew too, that it was essential to achieve at least one or two convincing early victories, not only to boost troop morale but also to give him the status of a significant player when, later that month, a fact finding mission from the Organisation of African Unity would visit Angola. Colonel Harmse returned firmly convinced that Savimbi urgently needed a great deal more assistance than he had received till then. General Viljoen, who visited Silva Porto the next day, agreed.

But there was a problem because the prospect of deploying South African armour – on account of the security mantle over the entire military operation – was initially not considered. And since Pretoria demanded that South African casualties be avoided, this meant that armoured cars were to be made available urgently.

---

4 Something else that emerged at that Luanda get-together was that many of the troops in the ranks of FAPLA at the time were not Angolan at all. They were Katangese soldiers who had supported the brilliant Congolese politician Moise Tshombe, who, at the behest of the man who became his arch-rival – Mobuto Sese Seko, was murdered in Algeria.

During Operation Savannah the twin prongs of Combat Groups Alpha and Bravo were led by Lt Cols Delville Linford and Jan Breytenbach (centre). Robbie, who formerly fought with the Portuguese is on the colonel's right.

South African Defence Minister (and later President) PW Botha went into Angola in spite of the fighting. He is seen here at the small town of Cela with Delville Linford to his right and Lt Col Eddie Webb on his left. (SADF photo)

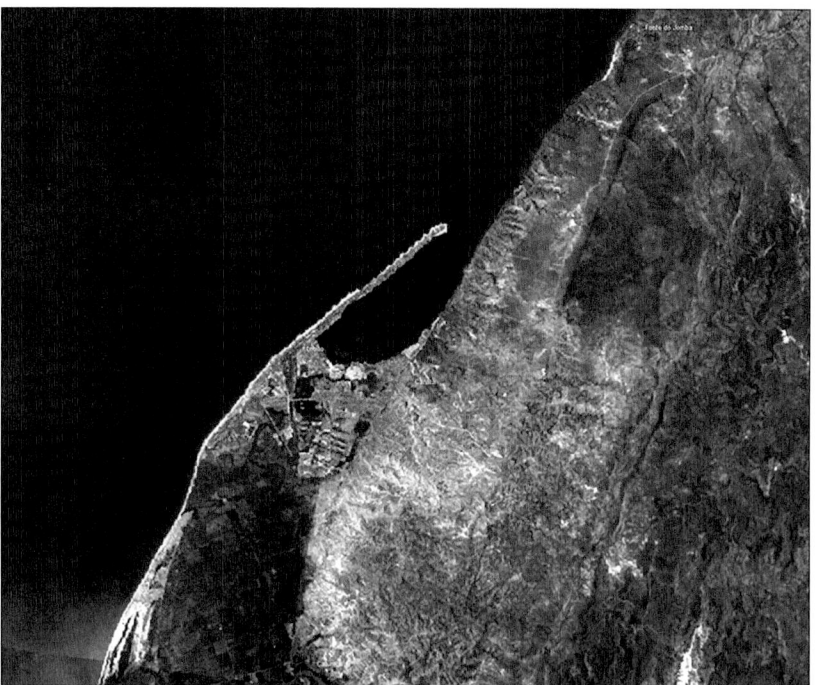

Satellite view of Lobito harbour which was quickly taken by South African forces.

Fighting groups inside Angola got some support from the navy: South African frigates had Wasp helicopters onboard that did some of the liaison work, especially in the north. (Author's photo)

The author left Angola late 1975 and then tried to enter the country again through the Congo. He was arrested (seen here) and held by that country's secret service on charges of espionage, all detailed in his book *Barrel of a Gun*.

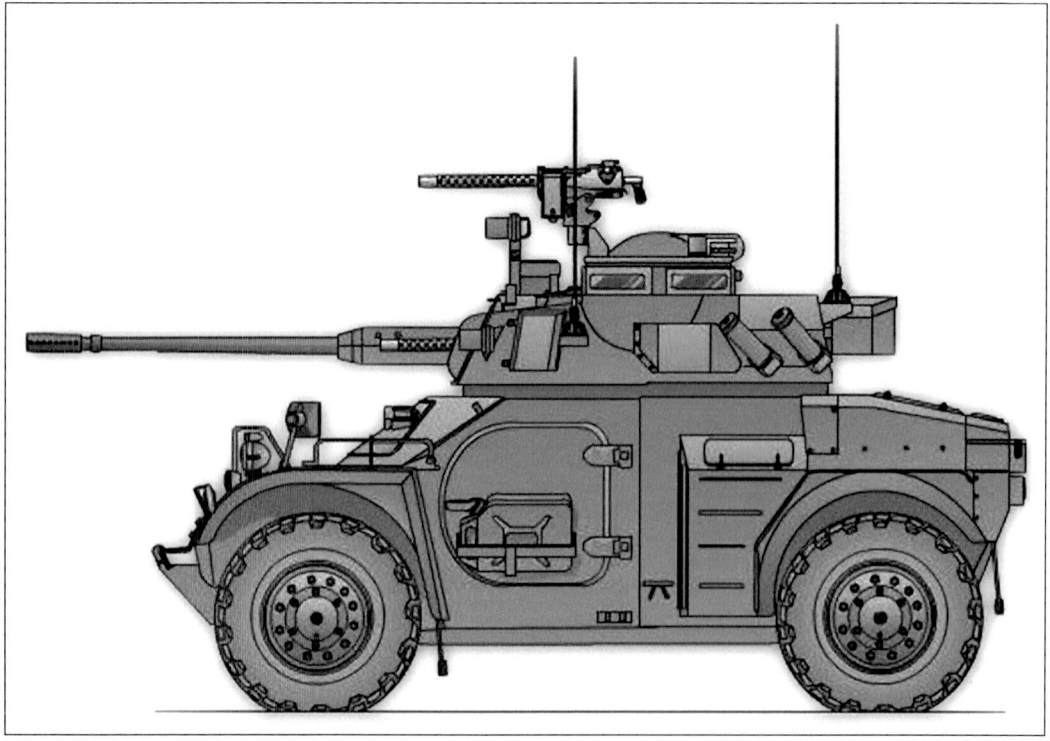

The Eland armoured car, this one with a 20mm cannon mounted was at the van of most South African attacks during Savannah. They were inadequate against some of the heavy stuff fielded by the Cubans.

After Op Savannah, the Border War started in earnest. (Author's photo)

On the 14th October 1975 South Africa's State Security Council took the plunge and approved the employment of Elands, a significant and more offensive expansion of South African involvement. The same day, Colonels Linford and Breytenbach's combat groups started their advance from Rundu.

While waiting for information about our reinforcements I could complete my aforementioned operational appreciation.

During a short visit to Rundu, I'd heard that a battle group [Zulu] was being prepared to clear south and south-western Angola up to Lobito. This would enable our people in Silva Porto – given the appropriate reinforcements – an opportunity to launch a 'blitzkrieg' northwards towards the Cuanza River. There was little or no FAPLA on this route during early October and Task Force Zulu and our newly-trained UNITA battalions could clear up behind us.

General Viljoen – as opposed to other senior officers at the SA Army HQ – regularly visited Silva Porto and kept me in the picture. This senior officer kept his fingers very much on the pulse.

With Holtzhausen deployed north-west of Nova Lisboa we gradually obtained a better intelligence picture. The threat against Nova Lisboa still existed and there was talk of a strong FAPLA force moving north from Mocamedes along the Sa da Bandeira-Nova Lisboa axis to link up with our elements on the road between Benguela and Nova Lisboa.

The intent, clearly, was a combined onslaught on the UNITA capital. This was circumvented by Task Force Zulu's successes later that month: both Colonels Linford and Breytenbach were clearly doing very well.

By the 17th October the first three UNITA companies having been trained at Capolo were ready for deployment. Two of them were sent to Major Holtzhausen to stabilise the Nova Lisboa front and one to Mussende where FAPLA was applying pressure in a southerly direction.

On that day we also received our armoured cars, two at a time by C-130 aircraft. I believed we would only receive the six (as requested) and was enormously pleased when Lieutenant du Raan – who arrived with the first cars and my friend Captain Neville Parkins, commander of the aircraft – told me that these were only the advance team of a 22-car squadron. They would come without support [infantry] troop and administrative echelon vehicles.

In a five-day period we took delivery of all 22 armoured cars, a squadron commanded by Captain GF Schoeman. The armour was fine, but it was a logistical nightmare – no fuel, no ammunition, no rations, no administrative echelon vehicles, nor troop carriers to transport the UNITA companies that were required to operate with the machines.

The cars were initially hidden at an abandoned Portuguese cavalry school next to the airport from where they were moved at night to Capolo to maintain an element of surprise. Through N'Zau Puna's intervention, we managed to obtain five heavy trucks to serve as echelon vehicles. Seven buses were commandeered by UNITA in Silva Porto to haul UNITA soldiers into battle, another first for this extended campaign.

While Foxbat was in the process of being formed and joint training of the armoured cars and UNITA's offensive companies took place at Capolo, a UNITA combat element was doing fairly well on its own on the western routes to Nova Lisboa, as well as near Mussende and in the Quibala area.

Webb and I could now do some proper operational planning based on the overall appreciation which I'd completed. We planned to act offensively on the Lobito route and to capture Sousa Lara. From there, I felt, we could also attack Quibala. We put forward my 'blitzkrieg' idea, to attack Quibala from Nova Lisboa in order to defend that city in some depth.

Headquarters in Rundu scotched the idea and ordered us to concentrate on the direct defence of Nova Lisboa.

Many of the youngsters in South Africa's black 32 Battalion and fighting a tough war in Angola were still their teens. They operated mainly behind enemy lines (which was why the exposed parts of their bodies were blackened), took enormous risks and came out of it at the end 'covered in glory'. The author took this photo while on ops with the unit.

Top: In Ovamboland, which the insurgents were constantly trying to infiltrate, patrols were constantly on the look-out for the enemy. **Right:** There was no shortage of anti-South African propaganda when the South African Army crossed the border into Angola. **Bottom Left:** Another SWA unit was the white-officered mainly Ovambo battalion. (Author's photos)

PROPAGANDA POSTER AT BORDER

O EXÉRCITO RACISTA DA ÁFRICA DO SUL É O INSTRUMENTO DA OPRESSÃO E REPRESSÃO NAMÍBIA E DA ÁFRICA DO SUL.

These posters properly mounted, were put up by FAPLA forces. They say that down south the racists are the instruments of oppression and repression.

Top Left: Anti-aircraft elements accompanied all cross-border raids. **Top Right:** The mobile G-6 - with a 155mm cannon mounted - came into the war towards the end. **Below:** SAAF Wasp helicopters played an important role in some maritime strikes. **Below Left:** Soviet SAM-8 (NATO: Gecko) ground-to-air missile launcher captured during Op Protea. **Below Right:** Body bags hauled back from the front. (Author's Photos except that of the missile from Pierre Victor)

Top left: Koevoet ops in Ovamboland. **Top right:** Eland armoured cars in Caprivi early in the war. **Top middle:** Wounded soldier airlifted back to safety. **Above right:** Ratel IFVs in Angola. (photo Cornie van Schoor). Bottom: SA Navy President Class frigate with SAS *Tafelberg* en route to Angolan waters (Photo Douw Steyn)

Top: A bunch of 32 combatants on ops in Angola take stock. **Right:** Temporary air force base (HAG) during cross-border strike. **Below:** Motor cycles eventually became a fairly successful mobile unit. **Below Right:** So too with the mounted force, commanded here by Lieutenant Johan Louw. (Author's photos)

Top: 32 Battalion patrol in the Angolan bush. (Author's Photo) **Bottom:** A pair of Impala ground-support aircraft about to land at Ondangua military airport. (Courtesy of the late Herman Potgieter)

Top: Lookout from one of the metal towers at Eenhana Base in Ovamboland. (Author's photo).
Below: Another of Herman's Potgieter fine studies – close-up of an Impala jet.

Top left: This photo shocked the nation when it first appeared in the South African news magazine *Scope*. For many, it ignored the realities of war, that lives are invariably lost in combat (Author's photo). **Top Right:** Searching for spoors immediately south of the Angolan frontier. **Middle Right:** SWA(Spes) patrol unit with dog. **Bottom Right:** Big and bulky South African Air Force Aerospatiale SA321 Super Frelon helicopters were rarely deployed to the Angolan border areas: they were unsuited to 'hot and high' conditions. **Bottom**: 101Battalion on ops in arid Kaokoveld country. Observe the mule carrying mortar bombs. (Author's photos)

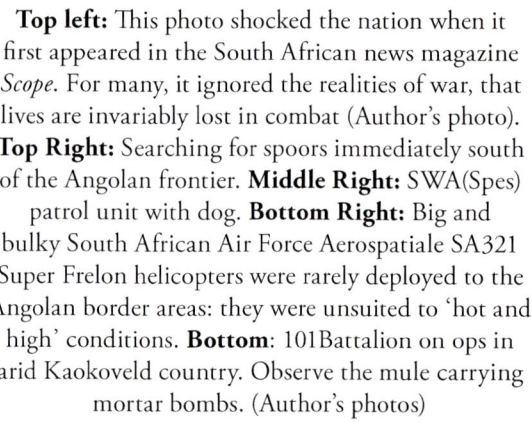

Top: Xangango –Vila Roçadas in colonial times - was a strategic south Angolan military town that lay on the Kunene River and became a regular target of the South African army, air force and Special Forces during the course of the war. The bridge was 'dropped' fairly early on. The author, who took both photos on this page, went on operations in the area several times.
Right: Early morning 32 Battalion strike deep inside enemy territory, an operation commanded by Lt Col Deon Ferreira.

Top: A South African Army 'Olifant' main battle tank (rear) during the Lomba River offensive in Angola. (Photo Roland de Vries). **Top Left:** A youthful Lt Ariel Hugo and crew with their 61 Mech callsign in Angola. **Right top:** The vaunted SA Army 155mm G-5 did enormous damage to Angolan deployments in the latter stages of fighting in south Angola. **Right:** Troops 'hand-starting' a Dakota with a rope when all else failed. **Below:** A pair of SAAF C-130 'workhorses'. (Photo Dean Wingrin)

Top: Executive Outcomes made much use of the rocket capability of the Soviet Mi-24 helicopter gunship, both in Angola and Sierra Leone. The author took this photo while Neall Ellis was flying his Hind out of Freetown. **Right:** Angola's rebel leader Dr Jonas Savimbi. **Bottom Right:** Soviet-supplied Mi-24 Hind helicopter gunships formed the mainstay of aerial strikes against the rebels. **Bottom Left:** UNITA played a significant offensive role in all these battles: most of the rebel weapons came from the Americans and South Africans.

Top Left: Executive Outcomes planning session with Angolan Army Special Forces commanders at the Cabo Ledo training base south of Luanda. **Top right:** Loading the full complement of Soviet air-to-ground rockets onboard the under-winglet pods of a Mi-24 gunship **Middle:** Static BMP-2 defences at the Saurimo air base in north-east Angola. (Author's photos) **Below:** Pierre Victor's sketch of a Soviet SAM-6, the missile that brought down several SAAF planes in Angola.

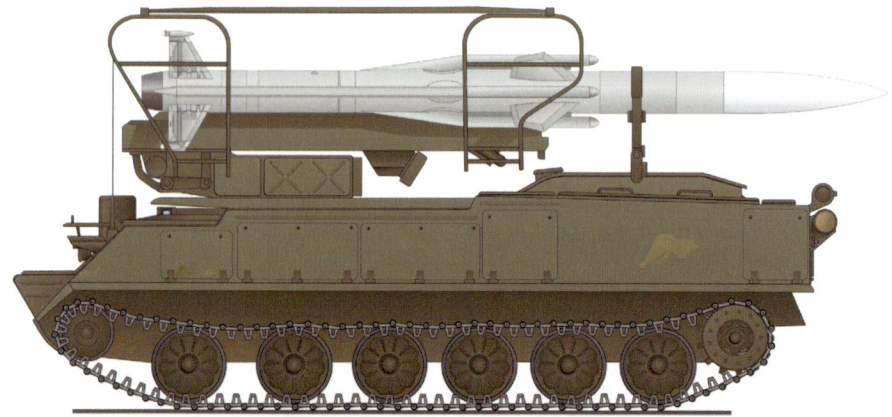

Right: The Soviet Union's Mi-17 (Hip) is unquestionably the most versatile 'workhorse' in any Third World conflict. 'Bokkie' earned Neall Ilis and partners a million dollars in Sierra Leone during the course of the civil war. (Author's photo) **Below Left:** Before Executive Outcomes personnel arrived in Angola, Soviet aviators were doing much of the flying. **Centre:** Dozens of Soviet air-to-air missiles were left lying around Angolan airfields when EO arrived. **Right (top):** EO 'stick' about to be dropped from a Hip. **(Right Bottom)** Dave Atkinson, who flew for Mugabe in the Congo. **Bottom:** Hennie Blaauw at an Angolan Army passing-out parade.

Top: Cuban troops - medals and all - atop a Soviet APC in Angola during the course of the war.
Below: A motley but extremely capable band of EO mercenary warriors at their operational base on the verge of Saurimo Airport, eastern Angola. (Hennie Blaauw)

Top: Times have moved on and these days it is Russian pilots at the controls of many of the larger aircraft in the Angolan Air Force. **Middle:** Government forces with Soviet hardware. **Below:** A selection of Angolan Air Force fighters and helicopters, together with a display of some of the MANPADS now found in some of the more unsettled regions in Africa, Libya included.

Top: Pierre Victor's fine drawing of an Angolan Air Force MiG-23. **Left:** Angola's diamond capital from the air. (Author's photo) **Above Right:** a clutch of RPG-7 rockets taken during an attack. **Below:** One of the best infantry fighting vehicles produced by the Soviets and subsequently deployed in many African wars, was the amphibious BMP-2. The photo was taken by the author, accompanied by Cobus Claassens during the attack on a rebel base adjacent to Sierra Leone's diamond fields in the east.

We had actually planned to seize and maintain the initiative by applying an offensive mindset which would put FAPLA on the defensive and prevent them from concentrating their forces on the various routes. But orders were orders and we could not go ahead.

Almost as if the Angolan command had read our minds, they took the initiative and only days later went on to launch a major offensive on the Central Front.

As part of this offensive, FAPLA's Lobito Force – with many Cuban troops in support – had already reoccupied Norton de Matos. Another FAPLA force, backed by nine armoured cars was already in the Santa Comba area, we were told by UNITA informers.

There was consequently a distinct threat that the two FAPLA elements could join forces at Alto Hama, just 65 kilometres north of Nova Lisboa, from where a combined attack on the city could be launched. Savimbi was on a tour of Europe and N'Zau Puna, in his absence, pleaded with me to let Foxbat loose.

Webb was in Rundu and three days later I placed Foxbat on standby to move. Meantime, I sent Holtzhausen and Holm to verify reports and assess the threat.

It was good that they did, because Foxbat was no longer the rag-tag and bobtail force of earlier. It now consisted of three companies of offensively trained and mobile UNITA soldiers. In addition there were five troops of 22 armoured cars; two 106mm recoilless guns mounted on Sabres; four UNITA-manned 81mm mortars; three ENTAC teams and to cap it, four 12.7mm heavy machine guns.

Also, as part of our Foxbat contingent – but not accompanying the combat group – were a further ten 106mm recoilless guns, four Panhard-90s and a Panhard-60 armoured car, all manned by UNITA.

Additionally we had a twin-engine Beechcraft Baron B55 light aircraft which UNITA had found abandoned at Nova Lisboa airport. We had the plane flown to Rundu for servicing and the fitting of a .30 Browning machine gun. Major Piet Uys, an experienced SAAF pilot, was detached to Rundu to fly the bird and that gave us a valuable aerial reconnaissance capability which, until then, had eluded our forces.

On the 25th October while Foxbat was moving to Silva Porto and Webb was on his way back from Rundu, our aircraft, which we'd dubbed 'Dinky Toy', started collecting information about enemy movements. It concentrated on all the access routes to Nova Lisboa. Operating along the route Alto Hama, Norton de Matos and Lobito, the plane overflew FAPLA forward lines and continued on until it was over the Atlantic Ocean. Thereafter the crew covered the Nova Lisboa, Alto Hama, Quibala road, giving us good information about enemy troop dispositions.

At this stage, I also had to deal with an untimely and rather silly dispute between UNITA and its 'official allies', Holden Roberto's disreputable FNLA. An entire battalion of FNLA troops at Santa Comba had fled southwards after clashing with a small Angolan government force.

Shortly afterwards they were intercepted and disarmed by N'Zau Puna, the UNITA commander. That night the FNLA and UNITA ended up battling each other in Nova Lisboa: just another 'sideshow' as the war progressed.

To prevent similar clashes in Silva Porto we used Foxbat's armoured cars to patrol the streets. The night of 25/26 October Foxbat moved undetected from Silva Porto to a laager area close to Alto Hama.

Various factors inhibited Commandant Webb and Foxbat – unlike Linford's and Breytenbach's Task Force Zulu – to move fast and with purpose in their bids to score successive victories; which the two officers did with characteristic aplomb.

One of the main reasons that caused Webb to pause was the fact that his forces would have to operate along three different approach routes to Nova Lisboa. There were also worries about the loss of South African lives.

To my – and later, also to Rundu's great frustration – this led to a series of pin-prick operations with massive expenditure of ammunition, especially along the western route. After that, Foxbat fell back to overnight consolidating areas (laagers) near Alto Hama and Teixeira da Silva, which complicated Webb's logistics still further, especially with regard to fuel problems. Also, because of minimal movement, he was unable to consolidate his operational successes.

The situation which had evolved was as follows:

On arrival in Alto Hama, Eddie Webb learned that Luimbale town had been taken the previous day by a FAPLA force of 250 men, two tanks and three armoured cars. He then tasked three troops of armoured cars and a UNITA infantry detachment to attack this force on the 26th October, causing 10 casualties and destroying the armoured vehicles while capturing ammunition and weapons.

The town was left to UNITA infantry to mop up while the rest of the force fell back on its laager area at Alto Hama, which resulted in them not following through on earlier successes.

A combat team consisting of one troop of armoured cars and a company of UNITA was separately deployed on the Santa Comba route to cover Foxbat's northern flank. This force again returned to the laager area a day later.

Massano de Amorim – unknown to us – had been vacated by the Angolan Army, was then attacked and our 4.2 inch mortars brought into play. The town was left in the care of two UNITA companies as a holding force, with Foxbat again falling back to its laager area.

At a meeting with the second-in-command of 1 Military Area in Teixeira da Silva on the 29th October, Webb was ordered to concentrate on the defence of the Lobito route. He was told to deploy a combat team on the Santa Comba route, as well as a further combat team along the Benguela route where a recent UNITA reverse had led to a FAPLA threat to the power station between Babaera and Mariano Machado.

A combat team under Major Holtzhausen on 29 October occupied defensive positions along the Queve River about 25 kilometres south of Santa Comba and clashed with a lightly-armed FAPLA force. On clearing the battle zone after the clash, the uniformed body of a Cuban colonel was discovered.

Thereafter, FAPLA reinforcements were spotted along the Santa Comba route by 'Dinky Toy' and Louis Holtzhausen's force was strengthened by another UNITA company.

A further combat team with three troops of armoured cars under Captain Schoeman advanced on the Benguela route that same day, and went on to take Babaera on the 31st October. With the UNITA morale along this route reinforced and Task Force Foxbat's progress neutralising the threat in that region, Schoeman's fighters also returned to Alto Hama.

Having been informed by 'Dinky Toy' that FAPLA had again occupied Norton de Matos along the Lobito route; Webb immediately dispatched a combat team to that area. They clashed with Angolan government and Cuban forces on 29 October and retook the town. Three UNITA companies were left behind as a holding force and the combat team returned to Teixeira da Silva. It was during this operation that 'Dinky Toy' crashed and its four-member crew all killed.

During the first few days of November, Webb consolidated arrangements logistically to again move in force along the Lobito route, having received intelligence that a strong FAPLA force was present at Monte Belo.

At this stage I planned on moving Foxbat – at speed – to an area north of Lobito in order to cut off FAPLA elements fleeing before Task Force Zulu's advance. This required joint planning and coordination as I feared Zulu and Foxbat might clash. Rundu again vetoed my request with no reasons given.

Our course of action was obvious and on the 2nd November Colonel Webb was once more ordered to advance along the Lobito route. The instruction was specific: he was not to overnight more than once in the same laager area.

A combat team led by Major Louis Holtzhausen and consisting of two companies of UNITA, three troops of armoured cars under Captain Schoeman, 106mm recoilless guns, Browning machine guns, 81mm and 107mm mortars reached Norton de Matos on 3 November. Having progressed, they ran into a well-prepared FAPLA defensive position at Caluita, a town about 16 kilometres to the west. After a long and heavy battle where the armoured cars played a critically decisive role, all opposition by Luanda's forces was overcome.

Advancing westward after the battle, there was some light opposition at Monte Belo but that too was destroyed. For two days Monte Belo served as the combat team's consolidation and recuperation area.

The advance was continued for three more days, our force reaching Sousa Lara without finding any significant opposition. In the process, they captured a large quantity of weapons – all Soviet – as well as good supplies of food.

Warned by the local population that the Cubans and FAPLA had laid a large number of landmines, the advance towards Lobito – without an engineering element to deal with the problem – was tentative.

On the 6th November – less than a week before Angola would officially become an independent state – our people took up a series of ambush positions on the main Lobito-Novo Redondo road to the immediate east of Lobito. That served as an effective cut-off force for Task Force Zulu where 40-plus FAPLA vehicles were destroyed over the next two days.

Unfortunately Captain Schoeman, the armoured car squadron commander, detonated a POM-Z anti-personnel mine and lost his left leg under the knee. He was evacuated to Norton de Matos from where he was flown to Rundu and thereafter to Pretoria where he died two weeks later.

Task Force Foxbat reached Lobito on the 7th November and was visited by Webb and Holtzhausen on 8 November.

It was decided that Foxbat would move back to concentrate on the defence of Nova Lisboa and make an advance to Quibala, while also protecting Zulu's right flank as it headed northwards along the coast. It should be recalled that officially, the South African contingent was supposed to be out of Angola by the 11th November 1975.

One day before the cut-off date, on the 10th November, Foxbat moved to Santa Comba with its excellent airstrip, a move that I had advocated from the beginning but had been vetoed by Brigadier Schoeman.

On 31 October 1975 General Viljoen and a member of the Bureau for State Security visited Silva Porto and discussed the military and political situation as it then stood.

They stressed that all South Africa's military activity would be limited to the 11th November 1975. Already, Phase Three of our involvement, the capture of Angola's Atlantic harbours was in progress and Luso, a major rail centre on the line to the Congo was taken on the 10th December 10 by Task Force X-Ray.

Headed by Captain Fred Rindel, his force – which included an armoured squadron, supporting infantry units, some artillery, engineers and UNITA irregulars – followed the Benguela railway line from Silva Porto (Kuito today) eastwards to Luso, which they overran. Their main objective was to seize the airport at Luso.

That achieved, it went on to serve as a supply point until the South Africans finally departed Angola early January 1976.

At the meeting with General Viljoen, I was tasked to draw up withdrawal plans for both Foxbat, the training team and, of course, myself. These plans had already featured in my aforementioned operational appreciation and would generally entail us being flown out by South African Air Force C-130 aircraft, with the Foxbat armoured car squadron moving independently southwards overland.

After General Viljoen's departure, a very downhearted Savimbi discussed the military situation with me. He emphasised that without our support the military gains made over the previous five weeks would be lost, probably within weeks.

UNITA were now a fairly competent fighting force, he declared, but he did not have the resources to counter the kind of Soviet armaments then flooding into Angola. Added to that, he reckoned, the Cubans were all regular soldiers from established Cuban units. Neither of us – nor the Americans – was yet aware that there were already about 10,000 of Fidel Castro's soldiers fighting alongside Luanda's government-led FAPLA.

I sympathised with him but emphasised that I had to follow orders. He then requested me to arrange for him to speak to Prime Minister John Vorster, in order to convince him that we should stay until at least early December when the Organisation of African Union (African Union today) would discuss the Angolan situation. Should his request be refused he would speak to President Kaunda in order for him to convince Mr Vorster that we should stay.

I promptly submitted this request to Rundu, after which General Viljoen again visited Silva Porto on 5 November to consider some of the more immediate options.

It was during this visit that he told me that I had been transferred to command 3 Sub-Area [Ovambo] of 1 Military Area and that I would have to return to the RSA to make arrangements for my transfer.

Savimbi visited South Africa for a meeting with Mr Vorster on the 10th November 1975 and as a consequence the South African military pull-out was postponed.

Shortly afterwards I was again visited by the local CIA representative to determine whether we would in fact be leaving Angola by 11 November. When I confirmed, he asked whether he could leave with us.

To which I replied 'You are welcome – be my guest'!

17

Fred Bridgland – Uncovering the Cover-Up

About the time all these events were taking place, the media went to great lengths to try and discover what was going on in Angola. Luanda was having none of it after I had gone in through Luanda and then tried again to come in from the south. Others converged on Lusaka, the Zambian capital and a few, like *The Scotsman's* Fred Bridgland and British television journalist Mike Nicholson used other means to discover what was going on.

First, a word about Fred Bridgland, author and award-winning journalist. In the early 1990s, while running the affairs of Ashanti Publishing in Johannesburg, I commissioned this award-winning British journalist to write a book about the still-ongoing war in Angola. The result was *The War for Africa*, which, if fractionally ambitious, set the scene for one of the finest books to emerge on that conflict. It is a brilliant work and it has surprised me and many of our colleagues that it was never republished.[1]

As one reviewer who calls himself 'Kiwi' commented in an amazon.com review, 'What the author does very well in this text is take you into the fighting on the ground and in the air in southern Angola in 1987–1988.'

He also states that the attentive reader will gain a great understanding not just of the organization, methods, and ethos of the various sides engaged in this epic Cold War struggle for Southern Africa, but of the Clausewitzian nature of war itself. How the actions of a few on the ground reverberate in policy choices and negotiations at the strategic level and how sometimes the frustrating limitations at the tactical level are required at the strategic in order to achieve the political goals of the state.

Aptly said, but now let's have Fred Bridgland's take on what eventually took place and resulted in his writing *The Battle for Africa*. I quote in full from his Introduction:

I stumbled upon the first and only Cuban-South African War unwittingly. It was a secret but highly momentous conflict which was to drag me, as a writer, along with it through all its 13 long years.

At the beginning of November 1975 Angola was falling through space towards an independence nightmare scheduled for the eleventh day of the month. It was already clear that self-determination

---

1 Fred Bridgland; *War for Africa: 12 Months that Transformed a Continent*, Ashanti Publishers, 1990. New British edition under discussion with Helion, 2016.

would be born in blood, not brotherhood. There would be madness and little sanity, despair, not hope; more cynicism than good humour; and no construction, only destruction.

For years three black Angolan liberation movements had fought each other more assiduously than they had waged war against their Portuguese rulers. When independence came, it was because the Portuguese right wing dictatorship in Lisbon collapsed and was replaced by a Marxist regime which embarked upon a major decolonisation programme. At the time the Portuguese Army was easily winning the war in Angola, although it was losing the conflict in its other major African territory, Mozambique [and of course, Portuguese Guinea].

The precarious situations in Portugal and its colonies were ripe for exploitation by the ruthless Soviet leader Leonid Brezhnev. The 'Brezhnev Doctrine', which asserted that Moscow-style socialist states had obligations to intervene in similar states if the continuance of socialism was threatened, had already resulted in the stamping out of Czechoslovak freedom by Russian tanks in 1968. The supine response of the Western democracies to the crushing of the Czechoslovaks encouraged Brezhnev to expand his social-imperial ambitions far beyond the Moscow's immediate back door into the swamps and pitfalls of the Third World, full of budding Brezhnevian clones and opportunists.

By the time the Portuguese flag was lowered in Angola, Brezhnev's 'forward policy' abroad for the realisation of Marxist-Leninist 'Scientific Socialism' was on a confident forward roll. Nearer home, Poland, Hungary and East Germany, as well as Czechoslovakia, had been cowed into submission by drab but hard-hearted stooges. Marxist-Leninist governments had recently been established much further afield in Vietnam, Cambodia and Laos and, along with Cuba and other long-established members of the socialist empire, it seemed that nothing could stop them lasting forever.

The Soviet invasion of Afghanistan had yet to come; along with the fierce resistance it inflamed which would begin to make Soviet power look less invincible. The internal contradictions of Marxist-Leninist dictatorship and oligarchism had not yet become sufficiently visible for one of history's greatest lies to be completely exposed.

It would be years before someone like the Czechoslovak author Milan Kundera felt sufficiently free to point out the differences between the plausible lie of socialist realism, floating boldly on the surface, and other sunken, less immediately intelligible truths about Marxist miseries.

'Anyone who thinks that the Communist regimes of Central Europe are exclusively the work of criminals is overlooking a basic truth', wrote Kundera.[2]

He went on:

> The criminal regimes were made not by criminals but by enthusiasts convinced they had discovered the only road to paradise. They defended that road so valiantly that they were forced to execute many people. Later it became clear that there was no paradise, that the enthusiasts were therefore murderers.

Brezhnev found in the Third World a willing audience for Soviet scientific socialism of naïve enthusiasts and devious strongmen: the latter gave their people non-liberty and poverty in the names of liberty and prosperity, and most of the people did not yet have sufficient experience, education or guile to see through the historic swindle.

---

2   Milan Kundera: *The Unbearable Lightness of Being*; Faber and Faber, London, 1984.

The weasel words 'of proletarian internationalism' were embraced as though they provided a short cut to the sublime, much as a brightly-lit Las Vegas gaming machine promises everlasting riches.

That the glossy, shallow slogans did not deliver the loudly-advertised rewards was not then widely perceived by poor people guiled into believing there existed a simple path towards acquiring the good things the world had to offer. Brezhnev was aided in his forward policy by the irresolution and torpidity of the Western democracies, 'flustered and panicked by the unflagging march of scientific socialist truth.'

After its humiliation in Vietnam, a deeply divided United States had little to give. It was too busy salving its own wounds. The Western European democracies – debilitated by oil crises and economic problems, student as well as trade union unrest, sapping debates about the value of NATO's deterrent weapons and guilt about their colonial pasts – had even less to offer.

The mid-1970's tussle between the Angolan parties, erupting into civil war, provided ideologically and, through satellites and local surrogates, numerous confrontations. In this test the Soviet Union acted with strength, commitment and purpose on behalf of its client, the Marxist MPLA.

The West's support for its protégés, the tribalistic FNLA and the formerly Maoist UNITA – which had experienced a miraculous Damascene conversion to the virtues of Western-style democracy when it realised aid from Peking would never match Moscow's to the MPLA – was weak, vacillating and faint-hearted. The West, whose cards were admittedly difficult to play at that time, compounded its own problems by behaving as though it had been dealt a dud poker hand; such initiatives as it did take were pusillanimous and unimaginative, while the Soviet Union always responded with decisive forcefulness. Also, the Soviet oligarchy, unfettered by any voters to whom it was answerable, acted openly and proudly in Angola while the West, subject to testy electorates, skulked and acted clandestinely.

Between November 1974 and February 1976 Moscow sent an estimated $US 400 million worth of weaponry to Angola and backed the landing there, in support of the MPLA, of a Cuban military expeditionary force which by mid-1976 was some 11,000-strong.

The US response was to send its clients $US 32 million worth of arms, the maximum which the Central Intelligence Agency was permitted to supply covertly, under American law. In another contribution to the war effort the West, with Britain's then Labour government playing a particularly important role, plumbed deeply distasteful depths. The US, Britain and Holland permitted the FNLA to recruit mercenaries in their countries with crisp new hundred-dollar bills.

The quality of the soldiers of fortune was dismally low. They were not the tough, professional adventurers who had made the title 'white mercenary' something genuinely to be feared and respected in the Belgian Congo of the 1960s. They were the new young unemployed of the mid-1970s and for the most part were the most socially ill-equipped of their generation. Poorly educated and from the most impoverished homes, they were real intellectual innocents in an African country which had lost its own innocence. Many had very little combat experience. Some had no military training at all, and two were London road sweepers recruited with the lure of $US300 a week and sent straight from their jobs to Angola.

The raw and unversed mercenaries were unable to stem the Soviet-Cuban tide. Many died. Several [as we saw in Chapters 14 and 15] were captured by the Cubans and four of them, three Britons and an American, were executed by an MPLA firing squad.

However, the West did have up its sleeve one truly substantial trick, its most secret weapon of all which went undetected for months and which almost reversed the course of events in Angola.

From September 1975 I was assigned by Reuter to cover the war in Angola. I was then working for the international news agency as its Central Africa correspondent based in Lusaka, Zambia,

Once the Angolan guerrillas had gained ground in Eastern Angola, Zambia's President Kenneth Kaunda gave them good support by allowing both the MPLA and UNITA to establish bases in his country.

The Freedom Monument in Lusaka depicts the traditional 'breaking of chains' which symbolised black domination by whites. (Author's photo)

British entrepreneur Tiny Rowlands, a close friend of Kaunda, allowed journalists Fred Bridgland and Mike Nicholson use of his private plane to surreptitiously enter Angola and observe the goings-on.

South African Air Force C-130 aircraft played a seminal supporting role during Op Savannah. (Photo: Dean Wingrin)

Savimbi's ties with Zambia did not last long after he started to sabotage Angola's rail links to the coast at Benguela: a strategic communications link for both Mobuto's Congo and the former British colony.

and given the task of reporting the UNITA end of the conflict from the guerrilla movement's bases in central and southern Angola. I usually travelled into Angola aboard the Hawker Siddeley 125 executive jet which had been put at the disposal of UNITA's leader, the energetic and highly educated Jonas Savimbi, by the British commercial conglomerate Lonrho.

On one of my journeys into Angola, on 1 November 1975, I was surprised by what I saw as I stepped from the Lonrho-UNITA jet at Silva Porto (since renamed Quito), which was then Savimbi's military headquarters. Two trucks crossed the airport tarmac towing spruce armoured cars decked in camouflage and with a crowing cockerel, UNITA's symbol, crudely painted in red on their sides.

The trucks halted. I ambled across to one of the armoured cars, in which sat a slight teenage white man with a thin, scraggy beard. I greeted him in Portuguese. When that brought no response, I asked him in English what language he spoke. 'English', he replied – except that the gravelly accent was a product of Southern Africa, not some genteel English country. I asked him where he came from and he replied grudgingly and gutturally: 'I am from Inger-land.'

I sauntered to the second armoured car where another young white sat in the driving compartment. He showed as little animation as the previous youth, but when I asked him where he came from he said: 'I am a mercenary.' Good, but from which country? 'I cannot say.' However, the accent, obviously developed at his mother's knee south of the Orange and Limpopo Rivers, spoke for him.

How long had he been in Angola? 'Two or three weeks', he declared. Had he fought before as a mercenary? Yes, he replied, 'in several places.' In the cabs of the trucks sat three other whites.

A polite 'Good morning' drew from one of them a heavily Afrikaans-accented reply. Before I could ask more questions a fawn Range Rover raced up and out stepped Skip, who passed himself off to reporters as an American journalist but whom, fresh from the failure of Vietnam, was now the CIA's resident liaison man with Savimbi.

Skip guided a series of American military experts into UNITA's bosom and supervised the arrival of arms deliveries by strange airlines registered in tiny Caribbean states. Some of Skip's military 'advisors' were straight out of the American nightmare – for example, an unsmiling tough in his late twenties who wore a black Texan cowboy hat, high-heeled boots and studded jeans and walked with a mean swagger while his tight, sour, gum chewing face sent a message: 'Look at me, admire me, but don't speak to me.'

(Other CIA specialists wore huge silver or wooden crosses flapping on their chests and told inquisitive reporters they were there to check on the fates of their Christian 'flocks').

With Skip that day on the dash across the Silva Porto tarmac, was a very tall, flaxen-haired white man in khaki shorts and blue shirt whom I had never seen before. The newcomer issued crisp orders in Portuguese to a couple of the black UNITA soldiers. Then, switching to English, he courteously ushered me to the Range Rover and I was driven to the palace of the former local Portuguese governor. Here, visiting journalists were housed in some luxury while, all around, Angola was descending into a Dark Age. The tall man's accent was South African, and I realised then that the Angolan story had become more complex than any of us journalists had dared to recognise.

Passing through Silva Porto again on 7 November 1975, I saw the flaxen-haired man once more. This time he was with a mixed group of black and white soldiers gathered around what looked like a French Panhard armoured car aboard a road transporter. I was driven away into town, and when I was brought back again later to fly on elsewhere, the Panhard was on the ground and the transporter gone.

It was difficult to know how to treat my encounters with 'Inger-lishmen' in French armoured cars deep inside Angola. It was the stuff of which Evelyn Waugh-style novels on Africa are composed.

However, brief encounters with two or three armoured cars whose Inger-lish crews declined to confess they were South Africans were not sufficient evidence to back up a story for an international news agency like Reuter on what I believed to be the truth – that the South African Defence Force, the most powerful military organisation on the African continent, had secretly entered the Angolan War at the bidding of the Western democracies, who felt unable to commit their own forces, and certain black African countries, including Kenneth Kaunda's Zambia.

It took me another 14 years to discover that the tall white man was in fact Commandant Willem 'Kaas' van der Waals of the SADF, a liaison officer in charge of instructor training of Savimbi's troops and responsible to make sure that UNITA's central Angola stronghold did not fall to Marxist forces.[3]

It would need patience, persistence and a large slice of luck to pin down the facts sufficiently firmly to meet Reuter's exacting standards on highly controversial stories.

When I returned from Angola to Lusaka on 9 November, one of my fellow passengers aboard the Lonrho jet was British television journalist Mike Nicholson, who had just made his first trip into Angola. Mike had established a reputation reporting from the world's trouble spots. He had gained particular celebrity the previous year during Turkey's invasion of Cyprus by positioning his crew beneath a descending heavily-armed Turkish paratrooper and welcoming him, on television, to Cyprus before he went off to kill Greeks.

Nicholson is a genial soul. On the plane I told him of my encounters with mysterious South Africans claiming to be English. In Lusaka I went home while Mike, away from his London base, struck up a friendship over drinks into the small hours at his hotel with two British pilots of Savimbi's jet.

The pilots obviously liked him and when they flew back to Angola on 10 November, the eve of independence, they invited the two of us to stay aboard the plane for a mystery trip after they had delivered a few items to UNITA's political headquarters in Nova Lisboa, Angola's second largest city which had been renamed Huambo.

There was no jet fuel in Nova Lisboa, and since Savimbi had to be flown that day on an urgent pre-independence mission to a neighbouring country, they were heading elsewhere to refuel. The pilots said they would show us something which would greatly interest us as journalists. The conditions were that we agreed not to report either the flight or anything we saw, or ask too many questions.

Before we could set off into the unknown we had to persuade a *Newsweek* correspondent who had flown with us from Lusaka that it was essential for him to go into the centre of Nova Lisboa to get press accreditation before he could begin reporting the Angolan War. Helpfully, we told him where to go and who to see, and as soon as he had gone we were off too.

The plane flew due south and had covered some 700 km over the immense forests and bush of central and southern Angola before it began to descend. Now the tree cover was thinner. The trees were more stunted and their crowns no longer overlapped, exposing stretches of sandy soil.

One of the pilots beckoned me to the flight deck and pointed to a silver river winding through the dry forest. The radio crackled into life and the conversation revealed that we were crossing the Kavango River, which formed the international frontier between Angola and South African-ruled South West Africa.

A woman spoke from the ground to the pilots in the same clipped South African English as the young men in the armoured cars at Silva Porto. She was ground control at the airport at Rundu, on

---

3   Jean Ziegler: *Les Rebelles – Contre L'Ordre du Monde*: Editions du Seuil, March 1988, p259.

the south bank of the Kavango, where the Republic of South Africa maintained a forward military base for operations against black SWAPO guerrillas fighting for Namibia's independence.

We touched down on a runway lined by machine-gun emplacements behind sandbags. Mike and I crouched on the floor of the plane for we had been told to keep our heads down and stay away from the exit door until we were back in the air. The plane taxied towards an area surrounded by a wall of sandbags some seven metres high. It passed through a narrow entrance into a vast, protected and surfaced area, and there we came upon the pot of gold at the end of Jonas Savimbi's rainbow.

We peeped over the bottom edge of the plane's small oval window as the pilots talked on the tarmac to South African Army and Air Force officers while the plane was refuelled. In the light of the clues I had already picked up, we realised that we were in the centre of what could only be Pretoria's staging post for military incursion into Angola. There were lines of Panhard armoured cars of the kind I had seen hundreds of kilometres inside Angola; there were whites sitting in the gunnery and driving positions as though preparing to leave immediately. The Panhard's immediate destination was a parking area where they were beginning to be loaded aboard Hercules C-130 and Transall C-160 transport planes painted in black and green camouflage and with all registration and other identification marks obliterated. Next stop for the transport planes and the armoured cars *had* to be Angola.

Soon we were flying back to Nova Lisboa. Savimbi's plane had landed, obviously routinely, at one of South Africa's most sensitive military bases. We had been given a glimpse into the heart of South Africa's unknown war in Angola. It felt surreal. The Lonrho pilots, for some reason best known to themselves which we never asked about, had guided us directly to concrete evidence of South Africa's embroilment in the Angolan calamity.

In Nova Lisboa we joined with Mike's film crew and flew by Beechcraft plane to Benguela for an eve-of-independence visit to the coastal town and to the neighbouring port city of Lobito. As we landed at Benguela we saw some 30 or so young fair-haired white men, stripped to the waist in khaki shorts, slink out of sight into a hangar just to the side of the airport's small terminal. Then, as we entered the building, a Hercules C-130 came in to land. It was painted in exactly the same way as those we had seen a few hours earlier in Namibia.

Before we asked more or demanded to see more, UNITA soldiers hustled us into a mini-bus. But as we drove away we passed a Panhard armoured car guarding the narrow approach road to the airport. Its camouflage paint was the same as that which we had seen on other armoured cars earlier in the day and the same as that I had spotted on the Panhards at Silva Porto earlier in November. The Benguela armoured car was surrounded by young whites in shorts relaxing in the African sun.

Nicholson's immediate problem was how to obtain television evidence of the obvious South African presence without the South Africans knowing they were being filmed. They would be bound to confiscate the film if they discovered it; otherwise the secrecy of the action – known to its planners as Operation Savannah – would be blown.

After being shown around Lobito by UNITA, Nicholson's cameraman prepared for the return bus ride to Benguela. He sat next to the driver, his camera held casually on his shoulder and his eye turned away from the viewfinder. He had lined up the camera at an angle he thought would frame the Panhard, better known in South Africa as an Eland. As the bus passed the Panhard we all waved to the soldiers while the cameraman casually depressed the operating trigger.

We flew to Nova Lisboa (Lubango today) for Independence Day, 11 November 1975. The following evening Nicholson and I flew back to Lusaka aboard Savimbi's Lonrho jet to file our Angolan independence stories, more than 24 hours after our colleagues had filed their reports from MPLA territory in Luanda, the Angolan capital.

From Savimbi's area there were no telephone or telex connections to the outside world. We landed after dark at Lusaka, where the twice-weekly British Airways flight to London was preparing to leave.

Mike sprinted from the Hawker-Siddeley to the VC-10 airliner and tossed the bag containing his precious film through the open front door of the plane with instructions to the stewards to phone Independent Television News studios on arrival in the British capital. The door closed, but then as the plane began to taxi towards the runway, it re-opened slightly and the bag was tossed out again, obviously for security reasons.

As the plane moved away Mike shook his fist in impotent rage and shouted: 'I hope you crash, you bastards!'

It was a good break for me because it gave me more time to flesh out the narrative for Reuter of my investigation into the cloak-and-dagger South African invasion before Mike's film would reach London by another plane. I decided that before I telexed my story to Reuter, I needed to question Savimbi. I flew back into Angola with Mike on 13 November and caught up with the UNITA leader in Lobito where he was addressing a rally of 50,000 people.

Afterwards, at a press conference in an abandoned hotel, Mike and I put to him our conviction that South African troops were the secret of UNITA's spectacular advances northwards over the three previous weeks. We did not tell him we had gathered the main evidence in his own plane.

Savimbi's replies were ambiguous, and understandably so, because behind the story of the South African presence was a longer history of Savimbi pleading for open support from the Western democracies, only to be guided by them to Pretoria for help on condition he denied knowledge of everything.

'There are no South African troops committed by the South African government here', he said. 'I agree that we have some white troops – not soldiers, but technicians – working for us here, doing things that we don't know how to do. I need people to fight with armoured cars that we cannot operate ourselves. The MPLA had the Russians with them. We had to address ourselves to people who could match them.'

As other journalists picked up the thread of our questioning, they joined in. One asked Savimbi whether the white troops fighting with UNITA were mercenaries in the shape of the first contingent of 4,000 Cuban troops who had arrived by then to support the movement's cause. He said it was clear that the MPLA could not have achieved the kind of things the Cubans had accomplished for them. He went on: 'So, in my own mind, if I have to get support from anyone, I will do it without any heavy conscience. It does not raise questions of morality ... I am doing it to save the fate of my country.'

Savimbi was upset by the pointed questions on South Africa, and later, as we returned to Lobito Airport he grabbed the *Newsweek* man's arm and said passionately: 'You journalists from Western countries, you say you want to oppose Communism, but you are the ones who just help Communism by the way you act. Why? You are weakening your democracy and giving a chance to the East to come up. We could not accept that the Communists will come here, but we knew that the MPLA was building up a strong army.'

Savimbi:

> Back in November 1974 I went to see every embassy of the Western countries in Lusaka. I told them 'The danger is this one, the danger is this one, the danger is this one' ... Everybody said 'We understand you, we are with you' ... but they did not act until the MPLA got us.

The failure of the West to respond adequately to the Soviet-Cuban build-up in Angola was at the heart of Savimbi's internal conflict.

Faced with a choice between helpless submission to Moscow's and Havana's MPLA associate or surviving to fight another day, he had no choice other than to accept from the West its gift of a poisoned chalice – help from black Africa's sworn enemy, white-ruled South Africa.

In that Lobito hotel Savimbi swerved and dodged in order to avoid admitting openly that he had received the West's South African bequest. But he did tell a parable which summed up his dilemma: 'If you are a drowning man in a crocodile filled river and you've just gone under for the third time, you don't question who is pulling you to the bank of the river until you are safely on it.'

I wrote my story of the South African invasion of Angola during the UNITA flight back to Lusaka from Lobito on 14 November 1975. I filed the copy that day and it became front page news around the world – except in South Africa, where it was censored.

For days afterwards we reworked the story and it made the front page of the *Washington Post*: the report actually changed the course of the war. Swiss Marxist philosopher Jean Ziegler said the *Post* report 'impelled the most powerful country in black Africa to change sides in the Angola War and support the MPLA.'

He went on:

> 'On 22 November 1975 Fred Bridgland published an unambiguous report about the presence of South African troops on Angolan territory. Nigeria, the leading political power of black Africa and supplier of petrol to the United States, changed camp, rejected UNITA and gave an immediate grant of 20 million US dollars to the government of [MPLA leader] Agostinho Neto.[4]

John Stockwell, a young career intelligence agent and Vietnam veteran who had been appointed head of the CIA's Angola Task Force, recorded afterwards that my story undermined the South African effort in Angola and fatally weakened the CIA's covert support for Savimbi. 'The propaganda and political war was lost in that stroke,' Stockwell wrote:

> There was nothing the Lusaka station (of the CIA) could invent that would be as damaging to the other side as our alliance with the hated South Africans was to our cause.

---

4   John Stockwell: *In Search of Enemies: A CIA Story*, Andre Deutsch, London, p202.

18

32 Battalion – A Crack Strike Force

> It was a curious anomaly that members of Holden Roberto's almost-defunct **FNLA** went on to provide South Africa with one of its best fighting units. 32 Battalion (initially called Buffalo Battalion) and under the command of Colonel Jan Breytenbach who, not long before had established what was to become the Reconnaissance Commando (later Regiment) – became an efficient and fearsome combat force dubbed *Os Terriveis* (The Terrible Ones) by those who opposed them.

At best, the battalion never exceeded 800 troops. Most times it consisted of roughly 600 or 700 riflemen and NCOs, mostly Angolan nationals under white South African and a handful of foreign officers. With time, this crack unit attracted professionals from many other countries including the United States, Australia, Portugal, Canada as well as veterans who had fought in Rhodesia.

Essentially a light infantry battalion, it went on to record more successes against the enemy than any other army unit. In terms of decorations for bravery, it was second only to the Reconnaissance Regiment.

32 Battalion had peculiar beginnings which stretched way back to the Task Force Zulu invasion of Angola late 1975 – otherwise known as Operation Savannah. Among some of the irregular troops encountered by the South Africans after they launched their two-pronged attack northwards, was a disparate unit that called itself *Chipa Esquadrao*.

Headed by Daniel Chipenda, a tough, uncompromising former senior MPLA commander who had fallen out with the ruling Luanda Marxist political clique, he had moved his command to Angola's central regions with headquarters in Nova Lisboa (Huambo today). I deal briefly with this, as well as my own involvement with Chipenda's people in Chapter 11.

There is still more background in a book I co-authored with the late Colonel Delville Linford, titled *As the Crow Flies*.[1]

Initially called Bravo Group and headed by Jan Breytenbach and Sybie van der Spuy, Chipenda's dissidents, as we have already seen fled to South West Africa. The unit was renamed 32 Battalion and consisted of two infantry companies, a mortar platoon, an anti-tank section as well as a machine-gun platoon. Not long afterwards, it was expanded to seven infantry companies, a reconnaissance wing as well as a support company that fielded 81mm mortar, anti-armour and machine-gun sections.

---

1 Delville Linford, with Al Venter: *As the Crow Flies: My Bushman Experience with 31 Battalion*, Protea Books, Pretoria, 2015. It is notable that almost all those Bushmen, with their families in tow, also sought succour behind South African lines. 31 Battalion was created, whereafter the majority of these little people served with distinction against the Marxist regime in Luanda.

Because most of the people who came from Angola spoke Portuguese, the unit was ideally suited for deployment in cross border raids and in the process, acting as a buffer between the SADF's regular forces and its socialist enemies. It also played a significant role in assisting Dr Jonas Savimbi's UNITA.

Although deployed as a counter-insurgency force, it was eventually also used semi-conventionally, especially during the later phases of the war – particularly at the Battle of Cuito Cuanavale, parts of which, including the destruction of the bridge across the Cuito River, featured in Chapter 23.

One of the remarkable strengths of 32 Battalion was its leadership element. I covered the Border War for many years and was to experience this for myself on cross-border operations with the fellows, once to make a TV documentary.

In charge at that stage was Commandant Deon Ferreira, one of the most forceful counter-insurgency field commanders in the SADF. Apart from foot patrols, I accompanied several 32 elements in a series of dawn strikes into Angola that involved eight or more Puma helicopters. Overall, the unit put up an impressive display of firepower, even though many of the young troops involved came straight into the army from school. About half of the white soldiers were barely out of their teens.

Youthful, extremely fit – in large part because of all the footslogging – and, by some accounts, recklessly impetuous – these youngsters slotted in well with their African charges. Small wonder they managed to achieve the battle honours they did.

The photos I took at the time were used world-wide, many distributed abroad by agencies like Gamma Presse Images, Sipa and others. Some are to be seen on these pages.

Mike Perry, an American correspondent writing for the *Spec Ops Channel* in January 2014 had his own take on the battalion. I quote him below:

> I had followed 32 Battalion's exploits throughout the 1980s in *Soldier of Fortune* magazine when they embedded journalists to go on missions and conduct interviews with the fabled unit. I remembered reading about their effectiveness in the field against their primary enemy at the time, which was communist Southwest Africa People's Organization, or SWAPO, a guerrilla organisation that found itself time and again supremely outclassed by these remarkable men.
>
> No matter how hard they tried to best '32', the end result was always the same: Dead insurgents and their AK-47s placed in piles after an ambush by what would become [one of] the most highly decorated, and controversial units of apartheid South Africa's war on communism.
>
> 32 Battalion's origins actually began not as a recruitment of South African soldiers, but mercenaries from the Angolan Civil War. That war ended in 1975, after the communists (MPLA) seized power and the remnants of an opposing force known as the FNLA sought refuge in other nearby countries, with many heading into South Africa in hopes of finding support and continuing the struggle…
>
> …for many of 32's members there remained a great desire to renew their efforts in Angola. Still angry that they lost, they did not intend to let that country grow in strength and export its own brand of utopia southwards.

Perry's assessment of the South West African People's Organisation – SWAPO – is instructive. As he says, SWAPO's intent was to use its guerrilla forces to reshape Namibia in the image of Angola, using that country as a base of operations.

SWAPO cadres operated mostly small, compact units, using terror tactics to achieve their aims, much the same as ZANLA and ZIPRA did during the Rhodesian War. It was the battalion's task to hunt down these foreign-based insurgents and for that the unit used its seasoned trackers to follow spoor before choosing the time and place to attack.

32 trackers knew the African bush better than most, the majority having been raised in the wild and customarily, they led ambush teams to encampments where many of the guerrillas were killed as they slept.

One of the operational strengths of 32 Battalion – and something that it developed into something of a fine art – was the ability of its small teams to infiltrate SWAPO bases without being spotted. For this reason, it was standard procedure for white operators in the field to cover their exposed parts of skin, the face especially, with a cream appropriately named Black is Beautiful. With time, these compact 'sticks' would become an enormous asset in gathering intelligence, to the extent that 32 reconnaissance leaders – some of whom had previously served in the Rhodesian Army – became legends in their own right. 32 Battalion soon became proficient at tracking much larger groups of guerrillas, having first established the lay of the land and chosen the time, manner and place for these attacks to take place.

The unit was excellent on improvisation, especially while Commandant Deon Ferreira ran the show. They experimented with the concept of placing a patrol well ahead of the main body of SADF troops in the hopes of running into the enemy, which happened often enough. The ploy then would then be to supposedly flee in total disarray in the direction of the main force. SWAPO, always eager to score points, would follow into the jaws of a well-prepared ambush.

As one unknown observer noted, this eventually led to the formation of a Reconnaissance Wing with training taking place under the legendary Staff Sergeant 'Blue' Kelly who, together with Ron Gregory, arrived towards the end of 1977 at a base situated at Omauni. Sergeant Major Pep Van Zyl initially helped with the selection and Kelly later moved on to Special Forces where he apparently had a distinguished career.

The observer goes on:

> Training was based on that employed by South Africa's Reconnaissance Regiment, with the emphasis on small unit tactics. A typical recce team would consist of three to five men, all dressed in SWAPO kit and armed with Eastern Bloc squad weapons such as PKM and RPD machine guns. Effectively, this would give them an edge in fire-power to compensate for their lack of numbers.
>
> There was special emphasis on demolitions, tracking, advanced medical aid, bush craft, navigation, fire control and small boat handling, canoeing especially. Every one of them would be small arms experts and jump qualified.

One of those who excelled in this dark art was Willem Rätte who ended his career in the SADF with the equivalent rank of half-colonel. On a recce of a SWAPO base, he and his companions cold-bloodedly entered the place after dark, only to discover that it was being partially vacated and equipment being packed on to trucks for removal. The three men calmly helped dismantle several 14.5 mm guns and moved them away from the base. SWAPO expected an attack and wanted the weapons in place to ambush Puma troop-carrying helicopters of the South African Air Force that they knew were operating in the area [In fact, During Operation Meebos in August 1983, a Puma with Captain John Twaddle in command and with 14 others onboard – including 12 national servicemen – was lost to heavy 14.5mm fire when the helicopter flew over an enemy camp].

After slipping silently away he radioed headquarters and informed them of the situation and the next morning the SWAPO base was destroyed, thanks to his timely warning. He later commanded the intelligence section of 32 Battalion.

Rätte, a small, modest-mannered man with a serious mién was both unorthodox and eccentric and I met him several times, once while on ops in South Angola when he arrived back in camp with two of his black soldiers after an extremely demanding recce behind enemy lines. What was interesting to me was that though a commissioned officer, he first reported his findings to the senior officer in charge and then fetched food for himself and his two buddies before the three of them bedded down in the bush on the verge of the camp for the night.

Rätte, already a captain, could quite as easily have found himself a more comfortable berth in the officers' enclave, but then that was Willem.

Today I continue to hold him in the highest regard: a perfectionist who would let nothing and nobody interfere with a well-planned operation.

32 Battalion, involved in unconventional South African ground as well as air operations – often in concert with one another – came up against many of the extremely sophisticated munitions deployed in Angola by the Soviet Bloc to counter both South African and UNITA efforts in the war. The unit was at the receiving end of much of it.

Yet, unlike what subsequently took place in Afghanistan and Iraq, the Angolans and their allies enjoyed few successes, and for two reasons. The first was that SAAF helicopters always flew at tree-top height, or just above the terrain's natural covering foliage. As anybody who has operated under Third World conditions, especially in Africa, knows well, the bush tends to dampen sound and very rarely would the roar of their rotors be detected until it was too late.

Even if FAPLA did have a bit of warning about choppers coming through, by the time these machines came into view, the operator still needed time do what was needed: a SAM missile system – MANPADS especially – has to be pulled out of its case, activated and locked-on to a target. All that rigmarole made things difficult in trying to bring down a plane, and by then the helicopters would in any event be long gone.

Secondly, much of Angola, even in the south, is wooded, often densely so. In places the bush dominates everything.

It is one of the realities of that guerrilla struggle – with the SAAF ranged over an area the size of France or Germany – that not a single SAAF helicopter or jet was ever brought down by a SAM-7. A couple of single-engine spotter planes were lost to SAMs, and that was about all that decades of MANPAD deployment could account for in this African struggle by the time it was all over. Portugal fared much worse, particularly in Portuguese Guinea, because their pilots put themselves in harm's way by flying at altitude…

SWAPO tried hard to redress that balance but it never happened. Yet it should have, because in one attack on a SWAPO base in the extreme southern reaches of Angola, Neall Ellis – leading an attack squadron of four SAAF Alouette gunships – had three SAM-7s fired at him in about as many minutes.

This is the way Neall Ellis related events, which subsequently appeared in more detail – and with a selection of photos – in one of the few books to be published about helicopter warfare in Africa, titled *The Chopper Boys* and recently re-released by this publisher.[2]

---

2   Al J. Venter: *The Chopper Boys – Helicopter Warfare in* Africa (Revised and expanded edition): Helion, UK, 2016. Much more comprehensive is John P Cann's *Flight Plan Africa: Portuguese Airpower in Counterinsurgency*,

Operation Super was a combined air-ground strike in which 32 Battalion distinguished itself almost beyond compare. That battle is the subject of study by several military academies today, in large part because of the way things eventually played out and the role that planning and independent action counted towards its success.

Like most South African counter-insurgency efforts, almost nothing came 'out of the box'. Indeed, those involved were counted on to think for themselves, often under severe pressure. It was taken for granted that team leaders would improvise and adapt, sometimes in a moment or two as and when the situation demanded. This is a quality in which the South Africans seemed to excel.

More to the point, this kind of effort might well be repeated in some future effort in one or more of the ongoing insurgent conflicts against al-Qaeda in north and West Africa.

As Neall Ellis recalls, 'the camp was certainly the biggest enemy base I'd ever attacked, some hundreds strong and frankly, we were a bit thin on the ground and in the air. Total forces on our side were 45 men from 32 Battalion led by Captain Jan Hougaard, all good soldiers, granted, but just too few of them, even if their number did include an 81mm mortar group. Air assets were equally frugal. We had four Alouette IIIs as well as five Puma medium chopper transporters for troop deployment. Because of this, our plan had to be pretty basic.

> We were acutely aware that any delay in bringing our ground forces in, or lack of fuel at the mini-HAG (our Helicopter Administrative Group) could cause us to lose both momentum and initiative.
>
> We knew where the camp was and the lay of the terrain, so the basic idea was to initiate our strike at exactly 0800 hours. From our own intelligence sources, we were aware that SWAPO guerrilla units in the field customarily paraded about then every morning: that was when daily orders were handed out and anyway, it suited us. The sun would be high enough to lighten shadows and enable those of us over the target to spot anybody hiding in the sparse bush.

The forthcoming battle was to take place in an area that was both remote and desert-like. The area, Cambino, was listed on the maps of the region and lay about 20 kilometres from Iona, part of the Marienfluss Valley, or 'Fluss', as the aviators called it. Though not far distant from the great Kunene River in south Angola, this was an extremely desolate region where very few indigenes had chosen to make their homes. In fact, the nearest proper settlement was several hours drive away, across dirt tracks.

Nellis:

> 'At our pre-flight briefing, it was decided that with my wing man Angelo Maranta, we would search for the camp and, once identified, deploy the 32 sweep-line together with several stopper groups.
>
> Four air force Pumas were tasked to airlift these forces into position. A fifth would haul in the mortar group. Once the men had been deployed, the two remaining gunships would provide top cover to two small groups that by then would have taken up positions to the far north of the camp; their job was to monitor the dirt track leading back into Angola and wait for enemy reinforcements. A secondary task would be to prevent any of the enemy, once detected, escaping in that direction.

1961–1974, also published by Helion.

The author went on several ops with 32 Battalion, usually under the auspices of Lt Col Deon Ferreira. He discovered in these young combatants – who would sometimes penetrate many days' trudge behind enemy lines – some of the best-motivated fighters of the war. (Author's photo)

Daniel Chipenda (seen taking the salute at his base in Nova Lisboa) eventually persuaded his entire Portuguese-speaking unit to head south and throw in their lot with Pretoria. These men were eventually moulded into what was to become 32 Battalion. (Author's photo)

32 BATTALION – A CRACK STRIKE FORCE

Colonel Jan Breytenbach, who went on to create three South African Special Forces units.

32 Battalion Emblem.

Some of the men who controlled South Africa's military destiny, Generals Magnus Malan (left) and Constand Viljoen (centre) with President PW Botha (right). (SADF photo)

Puma helicopter uplifts wounded after the Kaokoland attack in which 300 SWAPO were killed in a combined 32 Battalion/SAAF operation, the highest tally of the war. The gunships were commanded by Neall Ellis who provided the photo.

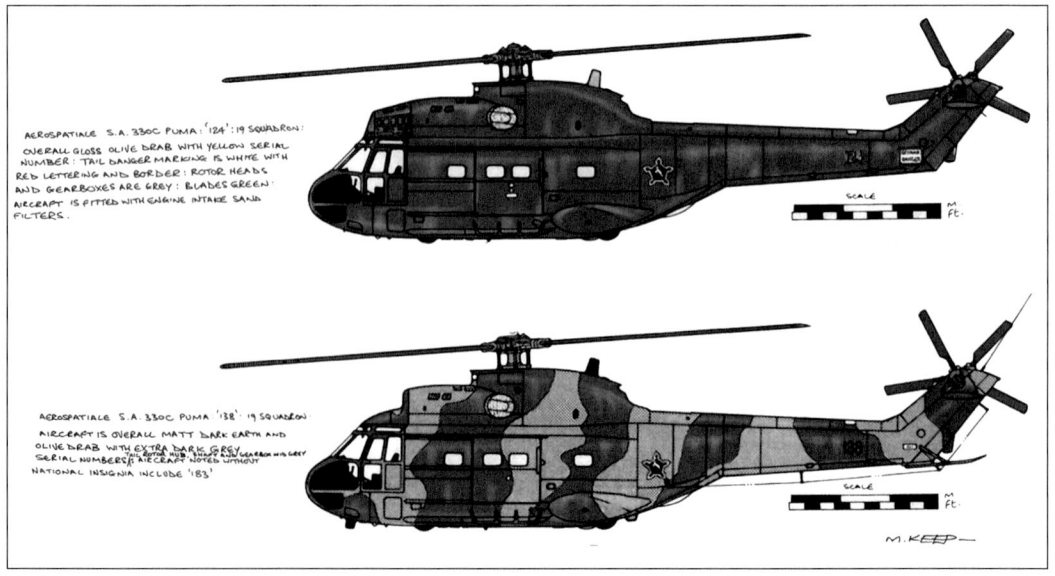

Two versions of SAAF Puma colour schemes during the war.

32 BATTALION – A CRACK STRIKE FORCE 279

The 32 Battalion flag.

One of the youngsters in customary 'Black is Beautiful' cammo paint during a 32 operation inside Angola. (Author's photo)

32 invariably came back with captured booty after their cross-border ops, this time radios taken in Operation Protea. (SADF photo)

While Operation Super – a combined 32 and SAAF helicopter effort – was enormously successful, the nature of hostilities quickly changed once Moscow started supplying the Cuban-led Angolan Army with tanks, including T54/55s.

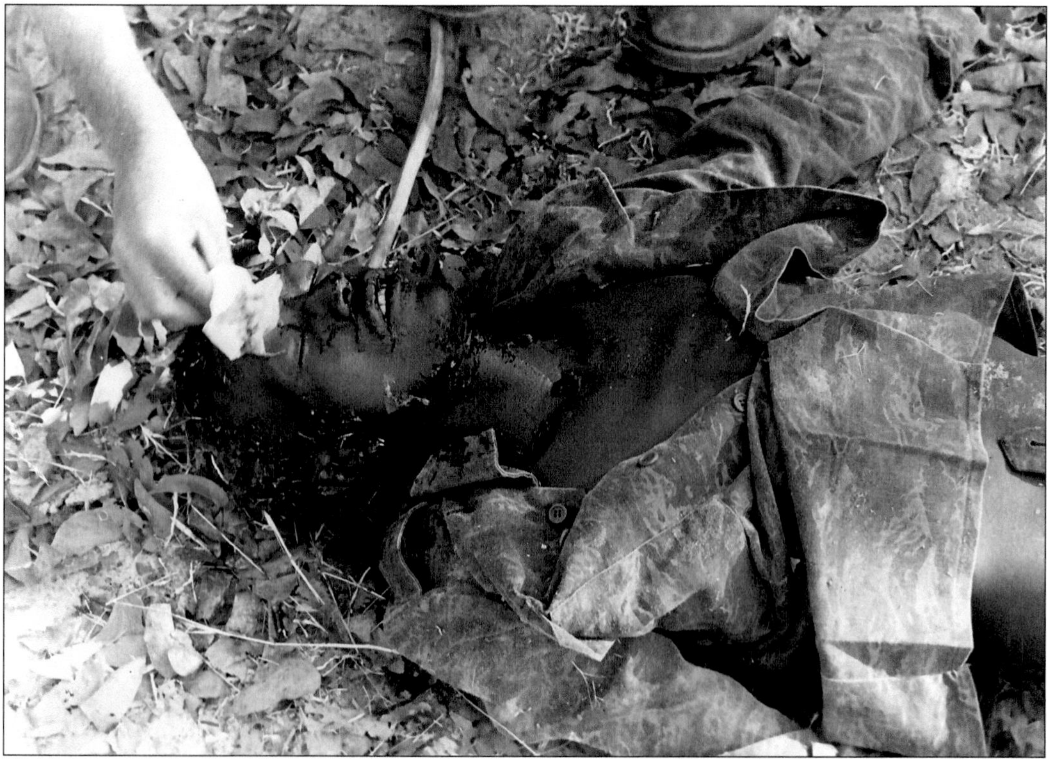

A 32 medic tends to one of the few SWAPO combatants who survived the attack. (Photo: Neall Ellis)

Our mini-HAG was to be established roughly 12 kilometres from target: that's where the gunships would refuel and rearm. If one of the Pumas couldn't get into an LZ in the contact area for a casualty evacuation, the wounded man would be flown back to our lines by one of the smaller choppers.

After a quick breakfast of dog biscuits and 'plastic' coffee' we went over the plan once more just to ensure that the intelligence picture hadn't changed overnight. I was also specific: everyone had to be perfectly clear about communications. The unit's 'Devil Dodger' wrapped up the procedure with a prayer and we went out to our aircraft. That was about 40 minutes before we were due to finally go in for the attack.

Once over the Kunene River, Ellis busied himself with navigation. From the start, he'd told his pilots, they needed to stay as low as possible: the other side was to have no warning of their approach. This was difficult as the Alouettes had no navigational aids and it was his job to track their course.

At the two minute mark I called for the climb and confirmed that the Pumas were in the holding area…everything was going well. As I lifted my machine over the ridge – which dominated the SWAPO camp – I could only hope that it would all work out.

The target area was in a large natural geological 'bowl', completely surrounded by a range of rocky, rugged mountains, like you get them in this corner of southern Angola. The Alouettes hugged the granite face in the hope that their approach would confuse the enemy and to use their camouflage to prevent visual detection.

By now I was worried about their anti-aircraft capability: the intelligence boffins had disclosed they'd been taken into the area by truck, so weight certainly hadn't been a problem. Also, we were aware they had something heavy like 14.5s. We'd had a lot of information brought in by the scouts, but very little about anything in that department.

Somebody had mentioned SAMs the night before, but I shrugged that off. Too remote an area, I said. I was wrong…

For that minute or so before the camp became visible, Neall Ellis and his pilots had been expecting to see a rebel emplacement stretched out on the ground below. There might be a tent or two, perhaps an improvised cooking place, he had reckoned earlier and said as much during the pre-flight briefing.

But once there, we could see absolutely nothing on the ground, not even vehicle tracks. Our four choppers were greeted by flat scrub, an endless rolling and featureless world of semi-desert that stretched all the way to the horizon.

Circling, I went into another orbit. Even if the camp was deserted, I argued to myself, we should *still* be able to pick up some kind of path patterns that come with constant use, even in this desolate terrain. More to the point, where the hell was the parade ground?

Obviously, that was out there somewhere, but all I could see was a large number of dew-soaked rocks, dark brown and featureless. I sent Angelo Maranta to the north of the area to search for any signs of the camp.

Just then, Coetzee called over the intercom. He'd spotted a few tents below. I turned and looked at the area he indicated but still couldn't see anything. The gunner remained adamant. He had tents visual, he insisted; he described them as kind of square and dark brown in colour. Then the scene unfolded; dark brown rocks suddenly became bivouacs and path patterns emerged like a spider web on the ground below. In places clothing had been hung out to dry and camp debris, carefully concealed, came into focus.

Jackpot!

As he recalled later, under just about every bush lay inert 'toy' soldiers, sometimes five or six to a cluster. One small shrub looked like a starfish. These guys had covered their torsos, but not their legs…he'd never seen so many enemy troops on the ground before.

> Suddenly I became aware that they were all over the place. The camp was built around an old derelict kraal and covered an area of roughly a thousand metres square. It was huge as these things go in the African bush. This was no small reconnaissance squad in search for opportunities…
>
> Just then, my main task then was to get our boys on the ground. I was aware that once SWAPO started to take the gap, it could become a flood. Also, we'd have to keep them guessing as to whether they had been spotted or not. I instructed Maranta to widen his orbit, to climb higher and to try and act as nonchalant as possible. That's when I decided to drop the sweep-line to the west of the camp as well as stopper groups along the river lines to the south and south-west in a kind of encirclement.

Earlier, Nellis had spotted a conical hill quite close by on which the mortar team could be deployed. It overlooked the camp and once on top, the soldiers would be able to observe the fall of their mortars and make their own adjustments. He radioed instructions to the Pumas: Captain Hougaard and his men – all 45 of them – must be landed as quickly as possible.

> We'd been over the target by now perhaps a minute or two. Still, the enemy hadn't made any effort to reveal their positions. But I could see that some of them had started a slow crawl towards the edge of the camp. Then I spotted the Pumas approaching below and it was that activity which alerted the enemy. They suddenly knew we were onto them, which was when I opened fire for the first time.

Experience had proved often enough in the past in such actions that after one person tried to escape – usually in blind panic – the rest of the bunch invariably followed. Also, said Nellis, when that happened, it was one huge problem to contain, especially when faced with a combat situation. Just then, he recalled, almost as if by command, all hell had broken loose as the rebels started to retaliate in force.

> I heard a thump of a bang towards the rear of the chopper as an RPG rocket exploded behind us. Meanwhile, Maranta shouted over the radio, 'SAM launch, Nellis! Six o'clock!'
>
> I looked down and all I could see was the thick, distinctive, whitish-grey smoke trail of a SAM-7 twirling up into the sky at a furious speed. Simultaneously I swung the Alouette sharply around in a bid to find the firing position. As I turned through that 180 degree arc, a second SAM was headed in our direction, which made it two in less than minute, only this one was headed for Maranta's Alouette.

I shouted into the mike: 'SAM launch: nine o'clock!' That one missed as well, and several more MANPADs were fired at the circling helicopters over the next few minutes, none of which found their mark.

Just then, our immediate attention was focused on the SAMs, or rather, their firing positions. Neutralise the operators, we knew, and that would take care of the problem, for the time being at any rate.

The missiles were easy enough to trace because their exhaust vapours rose lazily into the air behind them. I banked hard, got closer to the source and then spotted a couple of those responsible trying to take cover under some bushes that seemed totally inadequate for the purpose. Coetzee, my gunner, killed them both with a single burst.

By now both Maranta and I had become principal targets. Many more RPGs were being launched and quite a few self-destructed above our heads. Although fairly ineffective against aircraft unless the hit is direct, RPG-7s detonate with an extremely loud blast. Also, the explosions are accompanied by large puffs of black smoke, almost like something out of a Second World War movie.

There was flak everywhere and this caused a few distractions. While I was trying to direct a battle, another SAM-7 shot past my nose. Once that firing position had been identified, Coetzee killed its missile team as well. As I was to compliment him afterwards, he didn't waste much ammo. Meantime, the Pumas were coming in fast and I shifted my position to mark the spot with a smoke grenade and to offer top cover.

Their LZ was about two clicks from the camp and with the breakout of the enemy that we'd been expecting, I'd spotted some of them scurrying in that direction. Once disembarked, the troops from the four Pumas formed up quickly and started moving towards their objective.

Our next job was to drop off the mortar group and this was done without problem. After they'd been put down, the larger choppers returned to Marienfluss to uplift more stopper groups, together with additional fuel and ammunition.

At about that point the enemy must have realised that they'd been outflanked. Effectively, the efforts of the gunships had contained the group, which Ellis now reckoned was several hundreds and it was then that the insurgents started directing heavy fire in the direction of the men who had been airlifted in. Some of their mortars also came into play; they dropped several patterns onto 32 Battalion troops heading in on a sweep-line.

None of it was effective enough to stop the forward motion of the attack. Nonetheless, it was pretty disconcerting. Apart from all the other hot stuff coming their way, there were mortar bombs passing through the orbit of the gunships above. Maranta neutralized some of those emplacements soon afterwards.

Once the South Africans on the ground started moving through the outer perimeter of the enemy camp, they came under a concerted counter-attack fire and progress slowed. This was not a serious problem as the gunships had effectively limited the breakout. But by now, ground fighting had become intense.

At one stage Coetzee was killing isolated pockets of enemy that had taken up positions five or eight metres from our men. And since the lethal radius of a 20mm cannon shell is something like five metres, the troops on the ground had to keep their heads down when we sent in support fire. It was close.

After the battle, some of the soldiers had to be treated for light 20mm shrapnel wounds. Another time, two of the enemy had climbed a tree to get a better line of sight on the advancing troops and Coetzee picked them off as well.

About 20 minutes after the sweep-line had been dropped, the Pumas returned with the rest of the force which had been taken in as stopper groups. Maranta was detailed to give top cover to a Puma dropping call-sign Blackie.

While this helicopter was in the process of flaring, immediately prior to setting down, a group of about 30 of the enemy had managed to identify the landing zone. Maranta answered the challenge and got involved in a really stiff fire-fight, He neutralized the position, but it took some minutes and not before his own gunship had taken some none-too-serious battle damage from small arms fire.

Meantime, Ellis was giving top cover to the Puma dropping off another call-sign. That helicopter had just begun its short finals when the he picked up some of the enemy running along the same gully into which the Puma was going to land.

As he explained, the defile was rocky with steep sides and the rebel group could not climb out of it. They were trying to escape, to no avail. It was like a duck shoot. All that Coetzee had to do was fire above their heads and the ricocheting shrapnel did the rest.

Ellis continues:

> By the time the Puma had taken off again, a few more of the guerrillas had progressed to within 50 metres of the LZ and its commander was himself involved in a contact only seconds after touching down. His position exposed, we had a few anxious moments before we were able to take out the survivors. By this time Maranta and I were short on fuel; we were also out of ammunition.
>
> Bent and Schoeman positioned their gunships overhead to carry on with the task of controlling the sweep-line and providing close air support.

The 32 Battalion commander Captain Jan Hougaard had his first real casualty just as the first gunships were pulling out. A sergeant was badly wounded and Maranta put down to take him out, handling the evacuation under some really heavy 'incoming'. He had landed only metres behind the sweep-line.

After refuelling and rearming, the two gunships returned to the scene to relieve the others who now also needed avgas and re-gunning. Both gunships had positioned themselves to the north and east of the camp to act as airborne stopper groups.

Clearing-up operations took the South Africans into late afternoon.

The final body count was 187 SWAPO dead with a single capture. The insurgent taken into custody was the camp cook, who made it clear that he was not all that interested in making war.

South African casualties, in contrast, were a handful wounded, only one of which was serious, overall, an incredible tribute to the remarkable abilities of a relatively modest band of 32's combatants.

A particularly interesting insight here comes from former Brigadier-General Tony Savides, who – with his friend and colleague Major-General Roland de Vries – were both responsible as a pair of youthful majors in the SADF for compiling the initial mechanised infantry doctrine for the SA Army. It was from those sets of premises from which the 'Ratel concept of mobile warfare' evolved – which invariably applies to extremely difficult African conditions.

His view with regard to this form of mechanised warfare is that while the role, capabilities and exploits of 32 Battalion as a 'guerrilla', counter-insurgency or 'irregular' (and even 'motorised or foot infantry') force are well-known and documented, he has looked at the unit's role as 'mechanised infantry'. As he declared in several communications with the author, this interest stemmed from work he has been doing on the history of the Ratel Infantry Combat Vehicle (ICV)

Savides goes on and I quote: One needs to look beyond the 'standard' view of 32 Battalion and its capabilities and exploits, but rather at the apex of its potential, which suggests 'mechanised operations'. This can cover any phase or facet of the Border War – from the unit's use of mine-protected vehicles such as the Buffel or Casspir, right through to its activities in the Conventional Phase (1987/1988).

'For the purposes of my interest, this would include assaults onto defended objectives such as moving over long distances in vehicle column(s), the use of tactical formations while still mounted, or assault formations while mounted and then dismounting just before or directly onto the objective, manoeuvring under fire or delivering covering fire from the vehicles.'

It must be remembered, he goes on, that 'the so-called conventional phase of the Bush War (1987–1988) was far from what many other forces would term "conventional": we must think "Bush" here, not open plains.'

From several accounts it would appear that 32 Battalion – even before the introduction of the Ratel 90/ZT-3 Squadron – sometimes executed operations that, but for the fact that they were not in Ratels could be viewed as 'mechanised' – even if only from an infantry (as opposed to all-arms) perspective.

'This included being mounted in mine protected vehicles that afforded a degree of armoured protection, an ability (albeit limited) to fight from the vehicle on the move and the capacity to advance up to, onto or through the objective; coupled to being able – still on the move – to deliver covering or direct fire in support of the mounted or dismounted elements.

'The type or degree of opposition is relevant in that such "mounted" operations were, on the one hand, not advisable against well-prepared defensive positions while, on the other, an assault against mere infantry on the move or in the open would not qualify. In the former, the troops would de-bus well ahead of the objective, while in the latter, they would push on through regardless of odds.

'There were still occasions where lesser-prepared, yet still formidably-defended bases or positions were assaulted; in almost every case throughout the spectrum, there was always reasonable to heavy resistance.'

The first time that 32 Battalion elements deployed in a truly conventional mode was probably – equipped with Buffel MPVs – when they were part of the assault on Xangongo during Operation Protea in 1981. They tended to do this all the more once hostilities entered a more conventional phase.

'The versatility to move mounted over long distances in order to reach, avoid or circumvent opposition is an extremely important aspect linked to this kind of "mechanized" unconventional warfare; and in this 32 Battalion reacted with aplomb. They often provided lead elements, guides and even combat components in cross-border operations for the more heavily-constituted units such as 61 Mech or ad-hoc all-arms combat groups.'

Or as Major General Roland de Vries, that master craftsman of African mobile warfare added as a postscript, 61 Mechanised Battalion Group and 32 Battalion represented the 'African Way of Warfare': mixing conventional with unconventional styles. Similarly, paratrooper companies operating with 61 Mech became mechanised with their Buffels, adapting to the concepts of mechanised warfare.

Other SADF/SWA units, such as 101Bn and 31Bn also executed such 'mechanised' operations in their Casspir and Buffel MPVs, albeit mainly in the shallower cross-border zone; although they also penetrated deeper into Angola together with 61 Mech and others during such operations as Protea, Daisy and in the conventional phase.

Koevoet too, he added, was well-known for its highly-mobile assaults on insurgents and their temporary bases; but, with the exception of their combined operations with 61 and 63 Mechanised Battalions in April 1989, Koevoet was rarely involved in operations that could even remotely be classed as 'mechanised'.

However, that they used their armoured mine-protected vehicles (Casspir and Wolf) to great effect and often in a mounted assault with 'all guns blazing' cannot be doubted.

Operation Savannah, for all its short-term successes – did point towards an enormous deficiency in the mobility of the South African Army in any future military confrontation in southern Africa, which we all knew was coming. The order was given to design and build a variety of infantry fighting vehicles, of which the Ratel came out on top (as did the Casspir for the South African Police). Once these appeared in numbers along Angola's southern frontier they became a feature of the kind of mobile warfare which led to numerous successes, often against modern Soviet main battle tanks. The reasons were fundamental: Ratel crews were very well trained and were consequently a lot better motivated than the enemy. I became aware of these attributes fairly early on for the simple reason that my son was one of them. Also, these 'thin-skinned' IFVs were highly mobile and had a firing rate many times that of any enemy armour they came up against.

19

Airborne: Countering the Angolan Threat

> In their African wars the Portuguese had their *pára-quedistas*, the Rhodesians their Fire Force and the South African Army the Parachute Battalion, or more colloquially, the Parabats or 'Bats'

While the best-known action of South Africa's parachute forces was Cassinga – the unit's nickname 'Parabat' is a portmanteau derived from the words 'Parachute Battalion' – the unit performed numerous decisive operations in battle, the majority on Angolan soil. In the process, the 'Bats' produced a number of highly decorated soldiers. The account in this chapter by Brigadier-General McGill Alexander, himself a seasoned airborne warrior, provides an overview of South African airborne operations during the war.

The paratroopers of 1 Parachute Battalion were among the first to be deployed, and fought with distinction throughout the war as both conventional infantry and in their primary airborne role. Unfortunately they were, for the most part, penny-packeted as platoons or companies attached to other units. Many good opportunities to employ airborne troops were lost because commanders never understood how to use them or were not prepared to risk using them and because the paratroopers were, especially in the early years of the conflict, not fully prepared for an airborne role.

However, there were a number of parachute operations carried out in company and platoon size as early as 1974 and 1975, and later, once the insurgent war had escalated, larger airborne operations were launched and a viable capability developed.

Fire Force – South African Style

Towards the end of 1975 the South Africans had virtually exhausted their available full-time forces during Operation Savannah, the involvement by South Africa in the Angolan Civil War. A decision was made to call up units of the part-time Citizen Force (CF) in order to make up the shortfall.

In 1972, a CF parachute unit had been established to accommodate the many hundreds of conscripts who had been trained as paratroopers during their initial one year of full-time National Service. This unit, 2 Parachute Battalion, was tasked to call up one company for three months to participate in Operation Savannah.

This company was only deployed inside Angola for a few weeks early in 1976 before a political decision was made to withdraw all South African elements form that country. The paratrooper company thereafter deployed to the South African Air Force (SAAF) base at Ondangua in northern Namibia. By then SWAPO guerrillas had capitalized on the chaos in Angola and stepped up their campaign of infiltration and insurgency inside Namibia.

South African forces in Namibia were involved in skirmishes with SWAPO groups on an almost daily basis, and the paratroopers were employed as a 'reaction force', flying out in Puma helicopters to the scene of any contact with guerrillas, to take over the action from ground forces. This concept, instituted by Major-General Constand Viljoen, then the General Officer Commanding 101 Task Force, soon became a permanent feature of the war in embattled South West Africa.

Parachute companies from both 1 and 2 Parachute Battalions would rotate to always provide one company at Ondangua in this role.

In 1977 a second CF unit, 3 Parachute Battalion, was established to absorb the increasing numbers of paratroopers being produced by the National Service system, soon extended to two years initial service. This battalion immediately also commenced sending companies to the area adjoining the Angolan frontier.

Back in Rhodesia, where the insurgent war had seen a marked increase since early 1973, a similar requirement had developed. Known by the Rhodesians as 'Fire Force', it was based on a far more pre-active technique than the 'Reaction Force' of the South Africans.

The Rhodesians had the advantage of hilly terrain throughout much of the country (as opposed to almost table-top-flat northern South West Africa/southern Angola) and sent out observation posts (OPs) into areas known to be used as infiltration routes by guerrillas, or even infiltrated guerrilla groups, by means of 'pseudo' special forces. Their Fire Forces (they formed several) were highly mobile, and moved to a dirt airstrip anywhere near where OPs or their own pseudo groups were operating.

As soon as a guerrilla force had been pinpointed, the Fire Force would be called in to destroy it. Troops would be air-lifted in, using Alouette III 'G-Cars', while an Alouette 'K-Car' helicopter gunship (with a 20mm cannon mounted in the side-door) would provide fire support and serve as an airborne command post. The company commander directed the operation from the air while orbiting the battlefield in the K-Car.

Restricted to a limited number of the small Alouette helicopters, the Rhodesians found it difficult to transport sufficient numbers of troops to the contact area. They consequently resorted to using paratroopers, flying half their force out in helicopters and the other half in one or more C-47 Dakotas. Their level of activity became so high that at times some paratroopers were carrying out up to three combat jumps in one day on these small-scale operations. Their success rate reached phenomenal heights.

Impressed by their achievements, the South Africans attached some of their paratrooper officers to Rhodesian Fire Forces to learn the ropes. Fired with enthusiasm, they tried to implement the offensive Rhodesian ideas in Namibia, where, more often than not, they met with considerable resistance from the non-paratrooper military establishment who favoured the positional, reactive approach for the employment of the paratroopers.

As the Rhodesian Bush War escalated and built up to a climax, the SADF became directly involved. Among other forms of assistance, two Fire Force groups were deployed in the south of Rhodesia as part of Operation Bowler, manned by South African paratroopers who were dressed in Rhodesian camouflage fatigues.

With their own Pumas, Alouette gunships and Dakotas at their disposal – and employed by the Rhodesians in a highly mobile, pre-active manner – the South Africans achieved an excellent success rate, killing large numbers of guerrillas. With their own pathfinders joining the Rhodesians on their OPs, the South Africans experienced one of their most active periods.

They were simultaneously deployed on two fronts (Namibia and Rhodesia), manning three company-sized Fire Forces against three insurgent movements (SWAPO, ZANU and ZAPU).

In Rhodesia, companies from 1, 2 and 3 Parachute Battalions rotated for tours ranging from one month to six weeks, ensuring that a company always manned each of the two Fire Forces. This operation was maintained for six months, between September 1979 and February 1980, when the election finally took place and Rhodesia became Zimbabwe.

Back in Namibia, the Fire Force role continued to be the staple activity of the paratroopers on a more or less constant basis over a period of 13 years. The full-time paratroopers of 1 Parachute Battalion did tours of duty in this role of between three and four months at a time, while the part-time paratroopers of 2, 3 and later 4 Parachute Battalions did tours of just over two months' duration. The South African military authorities insisted on calling it a 'Reaction Force' and later a 'Mobile Reserve', but to the paratroopers it was always 'Fire Force'. Customarily, there was usually a company of paratroopers on standby on the edge of the tarmac airfield at Ondangua.

Over the years, 1 Parachute Battalion – so as to allow fairly sophisticated airborne operations to be conducted on a small scale – refined the technique for Fire Force. With the aid of night-vision equipment, they were eventually carrying out nocturnal strikes which were referred to as Lunar Operations.

Cassinga – The Classic Parachute Assault

By 1978 SWAPO had built up its forces in Angola to the extent that it was launching increasingly effective infiltrations into Namibia. Secure in the knowledge that Luanda's MPLA government – backed by then by a substantial Cuban military element – was giving them full support, SWAPO guerrillas were operating into Namibia with impunity.

South Africa's military chiefs, charged by their government with preventing these incursions, realised that drastic action would need to be taken for the initiative to be regained. Until then, the paratroopers had been operating across the border inside Angola with 32 Battalion, carrying out small-scale harassing activities and shallow reconnaissance missions. Generally, however, the South African forces were only active on the South West African side of the border on a purely reactive basis.

SWAPO had established its forward operational military headquarters, its major recruit-training base and a main logistics centre as well as a rest and recuperation (R&R) resort, all centred on the former mining settlement of Cassinga.

Located some 260 kilometres north of the Angolan/Namibian border, this base was identified by South African military intelligence boffins as housing more than 1,500 SWAPO guerrillas, a number of Cuban instructors as well as a considerable number of civilians: mostly refugees from Namibia who supported SWAPO. The South Africans, however, denied that there were large numbers of civilians present, and claimed that those who were there were victims of abduction, forcibly brought to Angola to be trained by SWAPO.

The headquarters at Cassinga was known to be responsible for planning and co-ordinating all guerrilla operations into what they and the rest of the world called Namibia. These operations were conducted from several forward operational bases, none more than 50 kilometres north of the border.

A plan was devised by the South Africans, largely at the instigation and under the guidance of artilleryman and paratrooper Lieutenant General Constand Viljoen, Chief of the South African Army, whereby an airborne force would attack Cassinga, while the forward operational bases would be attacked by a mechanised force. Prime Minister BJ Vorster was persuaded to authorise the raid.

Earlier that year a decision had already been made to establish a parachute brigade, also largely at the instigation of Viljoen. He was the one person who had recognised the strategic potential of a balanced airborne force when, as the Army's Director of Operations, he had ordered the first operational parachute drops in the Caprivi in 1974.

As an artilleryman, Viljoen viewed the airborne concept in far broader terms than merely an infantry capability on the tactical level such as the Fire Force. He had the vision to identify a need for organic direct and indirect fire-support, an engineering capability and proper logistic sustainment for independent airborne operations of a strategic nature. Hence the appointment, early in April 1978, of a parachute brigade commander in Bloemfontein to establish a brigade that would include the one full-time and two part-time parachute battalions.

It was envisaged that an airborne artillery regiment, engineer squadron, signal squadron and maintenance element would also form part of the new brigade's order of battle. This new brigade, yet to be formalised and named, was tasked with carrying out the assault on Cassinga.

It was to be a battalion-sized operation. For various reasons not one of the three units could provide a full battalion at that stage, so a composite battalion, formed from all three, launched the attack.

Neither were any of the three existing parachute battalion commanders appointed to command this temporary unit; instead, the honour went to Colonel Jan Breytenbach. He was certainly the most experienced officer of his rank in the SADF at the time, having fought in the Suez operation in 1956, in the first action of the war in Namibia in 1966, in the Nigerian Civil War in 1969, in Rhodesia and Mozambique in the early 1970s, and had commanded a battalion in the Angolan Civil War in 1975. He was also the first commander of South Africa's Special Forces (the Recces) and had formed the famous 32 Battalion of counter-guerrilla specialists. A veteran of previous helicopter assaults and operational parachute drops, Jan Breytenbach was the ideal man to command the paratroopers for this, the SADF's largest airborne operation.

Citizen Force paratroopers were called up to Bloemfontein, where the battalion was formed and given refresher training under heavy security for a week. On the evening of 3 May 1978 the battalion was flown to the air base at Grootfontein in northern South West Africa, 1,350 kilometres distant. There the paratroopers spent the night in an empty aircraft hangar.

More than 600 of these troops were poised for the attack to take place the next day. The brigade commander, meant to exercise control from an airborne command post, opted to rather jump in with the battalion. Under his command were the composite parachute battalion, a reserve of one company and another company to protect the helicopter administrative area (HAA) that would be set up close to the objective. For the actual parachute assault by the battalion, less than 380 paratroopers were to be dropped (barely half the strength of a complete parachute battalion). These were divided into four under-strength companies, a mortar platoon and an anti-tank platoon, together with the battalion headquarters. The fourth company formed the battalion reserve on the ground.

An almost full-strength company of 116 men formed the brigade's immediate airborne reserve, while half a company provided a protection element for the HAA to be established inside Angola, and half a company stood by as an additional reserve to be parachuted or trooped in by helicopter if necessary.

Nine transport aircraft were used. Four C-130B Hercules and two French-built C-160Z Transall aircraft dropped the paratroopers who formed the assault battalion. Two more C-160s carried the airborne reserve, the aircraft relieving one another so that one was always in the air on immediate call. A fifth C-160 stood by at Ondangua, loaded with additional ammunition, palletised and rigged for airdrop.

Pre-dawn on Thursday 4 May 1978, four Canberra bombers and four Buccaneer strike aircraft took off from Pretoria to fly directly to Cassinga. Shortly after 0600 hours the nine transport aircraft took off from Grootfontein. The C-160 carrying the reserve ammunition landed at Ondangua, where it stood by throughout the operation.

One of the two aircraft carrying the airborne reserve (rigged and ready to jump) went into a holding circuit above the border, while the other landed at Ondangua. They relieved one another throughout the day. The six aircraft carrying the force continued northwards across the frontier where they also went into a holding circuit.

Meantime, a dozen Puma and five Super Frelon helicopters loaded with half a company of paratroopers and drums of helicopter fuel, flew out to an isolated clearing in the bush, 22 kilometres east of Cassinga where they established a HAA. Also located inside the HAA were a medical aid post and the Mobile Air Operations Team (MAOT), whose commander would control all air movement in the vicinity of the objective. The helicopters refuelled and stood by to extract the paratroopers once the raid had been completed.

Already in the air at that time was a DC-4 Electronic Warfare aircraft, for monitoring and jamming enemy radio traffic and to provide early warning of any enemy interdiction or interception attempts. At 0730 hours, two Mirage III CZ fighters took off from Ondangua. A light Cessna 185 spotter aircraft arrived soon afterwards over Cassinga as the strike went in, orbiting above the objective to provide a radio relay and observation platform for the airborne troops once they were on the ground.

The attack on Cassinga commenced at 0802 hours while the majority of SWAPO troops in the base were on their morning muster parade. First the four British-supplied Canberra bombers swept in to drop anti-personnel bombs, followed in quick succession by four Buccaneers doing precision bombing of pre-selected targets. The two Mirages then strafed the recruits' camp and the enemy transport park. In was immediately clear to all the attackers involved that Cassinga was a significant military establishment.

Like the fast attack aircraft, the slower troop transporters approached from the north, but coming in at only 200 feet above ground level. Two minutes out from the DZs, they pitched up to their drop heights of between 600 and 800 feet and split apart for their individual final approaches. One aircraft dropped a two-platoon company east of Cassinga to form a stop line.

To the west of the objective, three aircraft dropped the actual assault force (two companies, each of only two platoons), the mortar platoon, battalion headquarters and four-man brigade headquarters.

Seconds later the remaining two aircraft crossed from east to west, dropping two rifle platoons to the north of Cassinga, with one rifle platoon and the anti-tank platoon to the south. The plan was designed to effectively seal off the objective before launching the ground assault from the west.

However, the drop was less than successful. Subjected to small arms fire during the run-in and with the target obscured by smoke and dust from the air strike, most of the aircraft dropped their paratroopers late.

For those who were to form stop lines this meant that many guerrillas and civilians escaped before they could close the 'box'. But for the assault companies it had almost disastrous consequences. Many of the paratroopers landed on the wrong side of the Culonga River, a relatively narrow but deep and swift-flowing stream.

Several paratroopers landed in the river, losing much of their equipment and almost drowning. A third of all the mortar tubes and bombs were lost in the river as well as half the medical supplies and much other equipment. A strong wind was blowing and most of one company was scattered across a rocky hillock. One of the northern stop line platoons was inadvertently dropped right on top of a tented recruit camp. They were fighting even before they hit the ground.

All the drops experienced some small arms fire during the parachute descents, which took place over bush and open forest, with many paratroopers being hooked up in tall trees. Two of the

South African Parachute Battalion shoulder emblem.

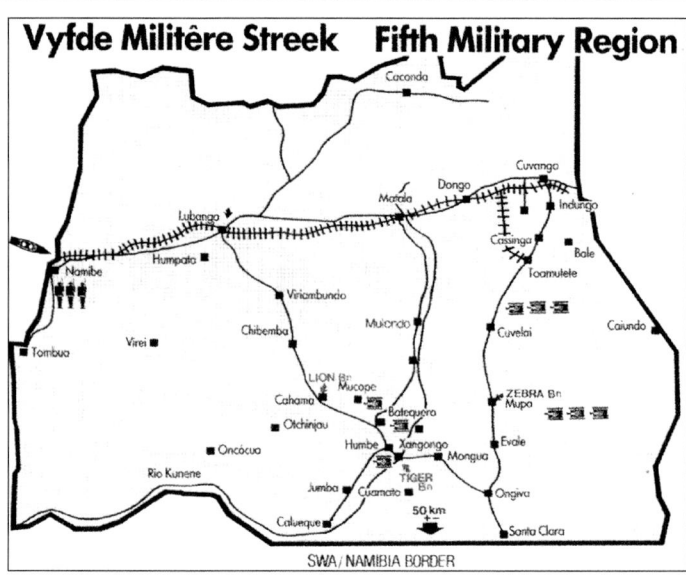
Operational map used for Op Askari.

Pumas taking the 'Bats' into combat in South Angola. (Author's photo)

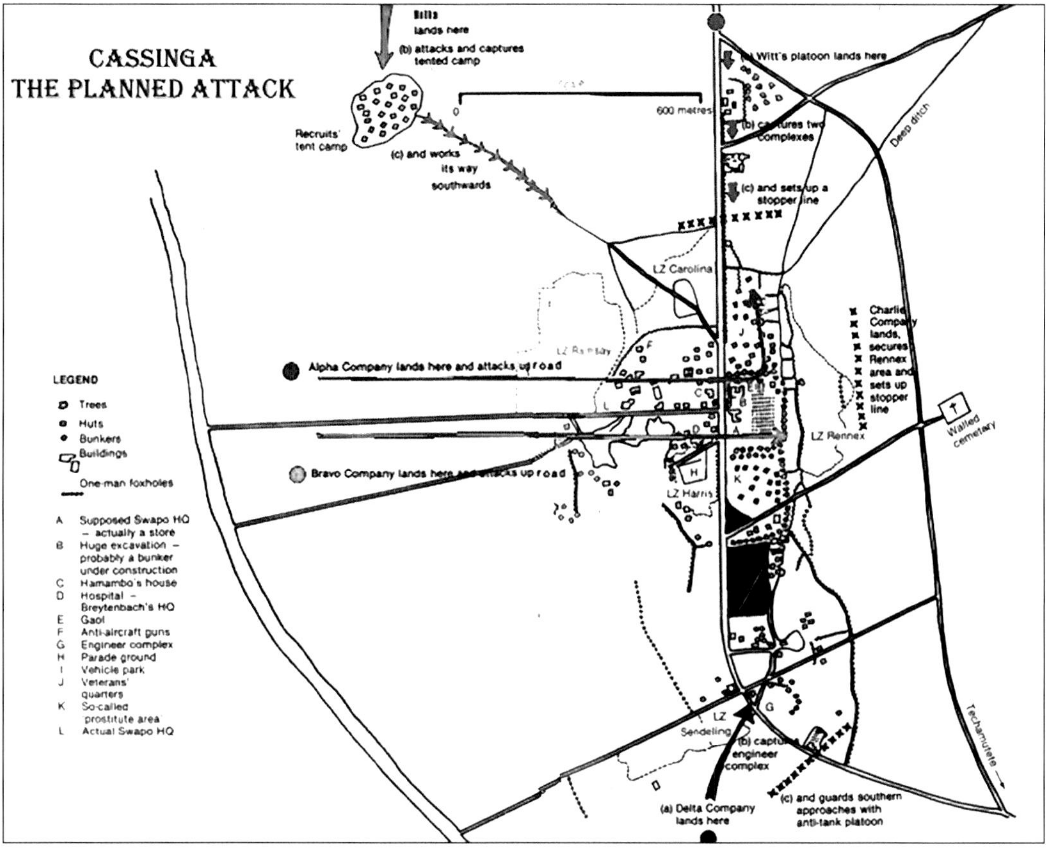

Map showing deployments during the Cassinga attack.

One of the SAAF Canberra bombers that struck at enemy emplacements at Cassinga. The aircraft had no identifying markings. (Photo: Pierre Victor)

One of the first photos to emerge from the onslaught following a Canberra bombing raid on Cassinga defences. (SADF photo)

Aviation specialist Dean Wingrin provided this shot of a C-130 doing a Parabat air drop.

Troops in line of battle at Cassinga. It was a tough slog for both sides.
(Photo: Kin Bentley from his Blog)

Some of the bunkers abandoned by the enemy in a subsequent Angolan battle. If there was time, they would invariably be booby-trapped. (Author's photo)

One of the South African Air Force Buccaneer bombers deployed in the Cassinga attack. (SAAF Photo)

During the course of many of these cross-border strikes, the South Africans would sometimes return with captured hardware. In this illustration, a conglomeration of artillery in the foreground and Soviet Gaz trucks behind.

A Puma helicopter drops a stopper group during an ongoing operation in South Angola. The choppers were at their most vulnerable during these phases where helicopters and men were exposed to ground fire and Alouette gunship cover usually sufficed. (Author's photo)

The Parachute Battalion never left any of their casualties behind: no matter what, they would bring them all out, even if covered in a poncho. This time it was Rifleman Edward James Backhouse from 3 Parachute Battalion who came home.

POM-Zs were regularly encountered by attacking forces: a simple but deadly weapon extensively used by both SWAPO and FAPLA in the war.

Soviet 'Black Widow' anti-personnel mine, such as the one that killed a young cadet officer during Operation Daisy.

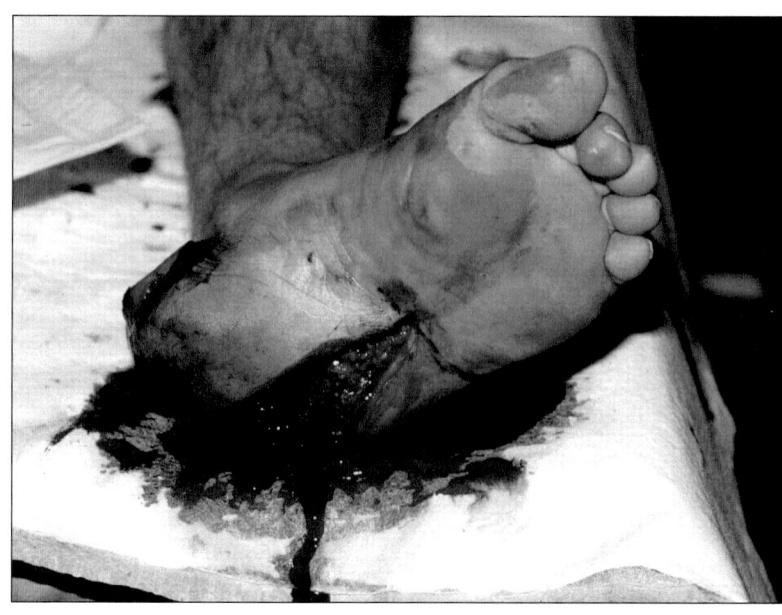

Anti-personnel landmines were a pervasive threat to attacking forces in Angola.

companies were involved in fire-fights with fleeing guerrillas in the bush as soon as they touched ground.

About six men were injured on landing, one suffering a nasty leg fracture and another severe concussion. One man, never accounted for, is believed to have drowned in the river. He could also have been shot in the air before landing in the river, his heavy equipment dragging him under the water.

Above the chaotic battlefield, Commandant 'Archie' Moore, Officer Commanding 1 Parachute Battalion, in the Cessna aircraft, was able to direct some of the paratroopers to a ford across the river. But that plane had to withdraw when it drew fire from an anti-aircraft gun.

It took Breytenbach over an hour to restore order, get his assault force across the river and form up for the attack. Not realising just how far south they were, he commenced the attack along the wrong axis, realised the mistake, changed the axis and ultimately attacked from south to north, but not before paratroopers from different companies had accidentally exchanged fire in the close, bushy terrain, fortunately without casualties.

Initially, resistance was light, but it soon stiffened. In the north, a platoon had been clearing some isolated buildings when a Forward Air Controller with the paratroopers mistakenly authorised an air strike on them. A fifth Buccaneer, armed with rockets, had been doing a combat air patrol above Cassinga. It now attacked the buildings, and two paratroopers were badly wounded by shrapnel before the strike was called off.

Many guerrillas and civilians had fled, but eventually the stop lines managed to get into position after the inaccurate drop and Cassinga was almost sealed off.

To the south, the anti-tank platoon, armed with RPG-7 rocket launchers, had moved down the road leading to the town of Techumatete, laid tank mines and occupied ambush positions. Just 16 kilometres away, Techumatete housed a Cuban armoured battalion, so it was to be expected that a counter-attack from that direction would be launched.

Meantime, the two assault companies had fought their way to the centre of Cassinga where they were held up by what could have been a twin barrelled ZU-23 and two ZPU-2 anti-aircraft guns deployed in a ground-defensive role in the vicinity of the SWAPO headquarters. It is possible that the ZU-23 was disabled by the air strike, as it seems it did not fire on the paratroopers. One of the companies tried to by-pass them, but was pinned down by fire from some of the remaining anti-aircraft guns. The other assault company was also pinned down, initially by sniper fire, and then also by anti-aircraft gunfire.

All efforts to silence the guns proved futile. The pinned-down paratroopers were too close to the guns to call in an air strike, and it was observed that each time the paratroopers killed the crews manning these guns, fresh crews would leap out of the nearby trenches to replace them. The paratroopers were deeply impressed by the bravery and determination of the SWAPO defenders.

As a consequence the assault was held up for two hours, all the while the South Africans trying to attack the guns from different directions. Eventually, one of the company commanders took a few men and worked his way towards the weapons by clearing trenches with grenades. Many civilians who had sought shelter there died in the vicious close-quarter fighting between the paratroopers and guerrillas who were determined to defend their weapons.

The guns were finally silenced with mortar support. Two paratroopers died in the battle in and around the trenches and several more were wounded, including the battalion commander. Others were wounded during house-clearing actions.

With the guns finally silenced, the paratroopers were able to take their objective and further resistance rapidly evaporated. After he had reorganised his force, Breytenbach's paratroopers searched the base, set fire to buildings and began destroying weapons, ammunition and stores while gathering documents.

The helicopters were then called in from the HAA to extract half of the battalion and the serious casualties to the HAA. With them came Lieutenant General Constand Viljoen, the paratrooper Chief of the South African Army, who was determined to see Cassinga for himself. But the helicopters had barely lifted off when one of the Buccaneers reported that an armoured column was approaching from Techumatete. The anticipated counter-attack was about to begin. The Buccaneer engaged the Cuban armour, which then detonated one of the mines laid by the strike force's anti-tank platoon.

With one tank disabled, the anti-tank platoon knocked out several armoured personnel carriers before they withdrew to join the remainder of the battalion on the emergency helicopter LZ. Two Buccaneer aircraft destroyed several more tanks and an anti-aircraft gun, while the Mirage fighters knocked out most of the APCs.

The helicopters extracted the last paratroopers as the remaining Angolan tanks arrived at the LZ. It was a 'hot extraction', conducted in considerable confusion and under fire, and the helicopters flew their loads of paratroopers directly back across the border. They then returned to the HAA to collect the remainder of the force, and by nightfall all but the one missing paratrooper were back at base.

The mechanised attacks on several other targets had all gone according to plan. It was estimated that close to 800 guerrillas and civilians were killed in the airborne attack, as well as about 150 Cubans and a number of MPLA soldiers. In effect, the main SWAPO operational headquarters in the region was destroyed, the guerrilla force's morale shattered and its international image dented.

The South Africans – according to SAAF reports – had knocked out three tanks, 17 Soviet APCs, seven trucks and three anti-aircraft guns.

In turn, the paratroopers lost three men killed in action, one missing believed killed, 12 wounded and six injured during the drop. Within three days all Citizen Force paratroopers had been demobilised and were back at their civilian jobs: they had been in uniform less than two weeks.

It was the largest airborne operation to be carried out by the South Africans, and was considered to have been singularly successful. Yet although the concept of the Cassinga operation was sound from a military airborne doctrinal view, many aspects of the operation had gone wrong.

The paratroopers undertook a detailed and critical self-analysis to correct failings in any future airborne operations.

The attack on Cassinga was extremely controversial, as SWAPO claimed the base had been only a refugee camp and that almost all of those killed had been innocent civilians, 'brutally slaughtered' – as was phrased in international media reports – by the aggressive paratroopers. The myth of innocents having been killed continues to this day, despite all the evidence to the contrary.

Controversy aside, the airborne assault on Cassinga was a classic example of an independent, strategic operation. It was independent because no ground forces were involved (the paratroopers were supported only by the Air Force).

The operation was strategic in terms of the objective that was attacked, namely, the main operational HQ of SWAPO. However, within six months, SWAPO was again conducting its insurgent war quite effectively. A guerrilla army is not reliant on fixed infrastructure for the prosecution of its campaign, and its organisation is sufficiently malleable to recover quickly from setbacks caused by conventional military attacks.

Nevertheless, the ability of the SADF to strike so deeply into this area caused SWAPO to re-assess their concentration of base facilities. In future they would disperse their layout and shift some bases to Zambia: This resulted in a decrease in guerrilla activities in Ovamboland and an increase in the Caprivi Strip.

Other Airborne Operations

Based on the lessons of Cassinga, the brigade – now named 44 Parachute Brigade – subsequently planned further independent actions under altered circumstances. Though not strategic, they were important for building the concept of independent airborne operations. One of these, Operation Safraan, was to have included a battalion-sized parachute drop onto an insurgent base in south-western Zambia in March 1979.

Three companies from 1 Parachute Battalion were poised in their aircraft – hooked up and seconds away from jumping – when the message came through: 'Stop drop! The air force has bombed the wrong target!' It later transpired that there had been a security leak, and the actual base was vacated the night before.

A more successful operation later that year was Operation Stoompot, when a company from 1 Parachute Battalion was dropped into the Njinji Forest in Zambia. There they spent several weeks searching for guerrillas. A number of insurgents were killed, bases uncovered (abandoned by the guerrillas as soon as they realised that paratroopers were hunting them) and weapons and documents seized. One paratrooper was killed in a skirmish.

There were many other airborne operations by the South African paratroops in which vertical envelopment as a form of manoeuvre took place. Most were of company size, but some involved a full battalion. These quite often involved a parachute drop, usually at night, but there were also helicopter assaults.

Overall, parachute operations tended to entail the deployment of stop lines so as to enable units like 32 Battalion to launch ground assaults at first light. However, there were also search and destroy operations carried out by parachute insertion in the shallow area across the Angolan border, and cordons thrown by dropping paratroopers around suspect areas on the other side of the border.

A company from 1 Parachute Battalion conducted a parachute sweep operation inside Rhodesia in 1979, working in conjunction with Rhodesian Forces. During Operation Daisy in 1981, 3 Parachute Battalion was dropped deep inside Angola at night to form a cut-off force during a major mechanised ground attack. Faulty intelligence unfortunately caused the operation to have very limited success.

Offensive helicopter operations were frequently undertaken during the early and mid-1980s. Three successful and significant helicopter assaults on insurgent bases were carried out in the arid, mountainous south-western corner of Angola, two by companies from 1 Parachute Battalion and one by elements of 32 Battalion.

In the dense bush of southern Angola across the border cut-line north of Ovamboland, companies of 1 and 2 Parachute Battalions launched numerous helicopter actions against guerrillas. These entailed attacks on identified bases as well as search and destroy operations.

The 1980s saw a conspicuous growth in the South African parachute forces, with 1 Parachute Battalion expanding to effective two-battalion strength and 44 Parachute Brigade gaining Citizen Force artillery, anti-aircraft, engineer and supporting units. A third Citizen Force battalion, 4 Parachute Battalion, was also established.

During that decade the Headquarters of 44 Parachute Brigade planned and conducted numerous airborne exercises, utilising the parachute battalion group concept. In the process a detailed doctrine on airborne operations was compiled, drawing heavily on past operational experience. Equipment and vehicles were designed, developed, tested and eventually brought into service with units of the brigade.

By 1990 the brigade had developed and exercised the capability to drop a battalion group of 600 paratroops with light artillery, logistic and command vehicles, as well as engineer and maintenance support and light anti-tank armoured cars, all in a single wave of 18 aircraft (a dozen C-130s and C-160s as well as six Dakota C-47s).

In South West Africa meanwhile, the insurgency war had taken on a far more conventional nature. Cuban forces in Angola had built up to significant levels and the MPLA forces were equipped with large quantities of Soviet heavy weaponry. SWAPO and South African National Congress (ANC) forces, trained in conventional operations and also equipped by the Soviets, were deployed alongside both MPLA and Cuban elements in the Angolan civil war. Pitted against them were the forces of UNITA, surreptitiously equipped by the USA and heavily supported by South Africa.

During 1985 and especially 1987/88, major clashes took place in south-east Angola when the MPLA and Cubans attempted to take the UNITA headquarters at Jamba. The battles around the Lomba River and Cuito Cuanavale saw the first employment of tanks by the South Africans in this war.

Over this period the paratroopers were employed mainly in smaller operations in the western and central parts of southern Angola, as well as in the ongoing Fire Force role inside Namibia. However, one light parachute artillery battery and the pathfinders were employed in the conventional battles in southeast Angola, though not in an airborne role.

The last parachute action to take place in Angola was Operation Pineapple, in which two companies from 1 Parachute Battalion participated. It took place in June 1988 and entailed the dropping of the companies roughly 200 kilometres inside Angola at night, followed by a 50 kilometres march to lay ambushes on the road between Cuvango and Cuvelai. Once again, faulty intelligence resulted in the expected convoys not passing, though several clashes with Angolan forces followed.

But by now, the Cold War was coming to an end. The Soviet Union was faced with disintegration and world communism was in a state of collapse. International events were overtaking the war in Angola, and continued Soviet support for the MPLA and the Cubans had begun to wither. Additionally, ongoing hostilities were draining the Cuban economy and morale.

By now, the South African ability to wage an extended conventional war was virtually exhausted and it was no secret that as a result of an ongoing UN-imposed arms embargo against Pretoria that had lasted decades, the Cubans and Angolans dominated the skies. Economic realities and the effects of years of international sanctions were forcing the South Africans to reconsider their involvement in this resource-sapping conflict.

International diplomatic negotiations led to an agreement being reached for the implementation of UN Security Council Resolution 435 for the granting of independence to Namibia. In terms of this agreement, there would be a phased withdrawal of Cuban forces from Angola and of South African forces from South West Africa, soon to be granted independence and renamed the Republic of Namibia.

The run-up to the implementation was characterised by a great deal of suspicion and posturing on both sides. Armed clashes continued to take place, initially in southern Angola, and later restricted to the continuing insurgency war between SWAPO and the SADF inside Namibia. It was at this time, towards the middle of 1988, that a composite and very powerful airborne unit was formed by the South Africans as part of 44 Parachute Brigade.

Known as 14 Parachute Battalion Group, it comprised full-time and part-time parachute elements drawn from existing parachute units, its members serving for a few months at a time on a rotational basis. It included four infantry companies, a support company, artillery battery, anti-aircraft, engineer and armoured anti-tank elements.

The unit, trained in amphibious operations, and using Walvis Bay in Namibia, rehearsed for a combined amphibious/parachute assault on the Angolan port of Namibe. Known as Operation Kwêvoël, it aimed at destroying the harbour and railhead used to supply the main artery for the Cuban and Angolan forces ranged along the Namibian/Angolan border. In theory, this would have prevented an attack on pre-independent South West Africa by the poised Cuban 50th Division by severing its logistic lines.

This operation was never implemented, and 14 Parachute Battalion Group was deployed instead in defence along the Angolan/South West African border until the mutual withdrawal of forces began. The paratroopers then returned home, with the exception of one company, which did duty as the resident Fire-Force at Ondangua. It remained there as the last combat element of the SADF to be withdrawn prior to Namibia's independence.

Yet before that happened, a battalion-sized tactical air-landed operation (TALO) was carried out during the final bout of fighting between SWAPO and the South Africans. In direct contravention of the cease-fire agreement for the implementation of Resolution 435, large numbers of heavily armed SWAPO guerrillas crossed the border from Angola into South West Africa on 1 April 1989.

The demobilisation and withdrawal of SADF units had reached an advanced stage, the few remaining units were confined to base and technically the UN Transitional Assistance Group (UNTAG) was now supposed to be in control of the operational area.

But UNTAG forces were not yet on the ground and that resulted in SWAPO bands clashing with police elements. As a consequence, vicious fighting erupted all along the border. The UN was forced to allow the South Africans to mobilise and go into action in a bid to bring the situation under control.

The need for reinforcements in the Kaokoland in the west, against the Cunene River border with Angola, resulted in 14 Parachute Battalion Group being flown from Pretoria to the airstrip at Ehomba. There, the paratroopers carried out a TALO and immediately commenced with Fire Force actions. A highly successful operation, it was the final action of the war for the paratroopers.

Nevertheless, the planned raid on Namibe was not the last independent strategic airborne contingency to be prepared by the parachute brigade. In October 1989, on the eve of the elections to be held in soon-to-be independent Namibia, the brigade was instructed to prepare for Operation Skydart. This was to be a parachute assault by two battalions and an artillery battery on the capital city of Windhoek in the event of SWAPO carrying out a *coup d'etat* before the elections had been held.

Though it never happened, the enterprise was planned in great detail and comprehensively rehearsed. That it was a viable undertaking illustrates the level of expertise that the brigade had achieved. It should be added that the envisaged force levels would have required virtually every transport aircraft in the SAAF and it would have been the largest airborne operation ever undertaken by South Africa.

After this, altered political circumstances, changes in personnel and a rapidly diminishing defence budget spelt an end to the concept of independent strategic airborne operations in South Africa.

The vision disappeared in the flurry of changes that took place in the decade of the 1990s.

20

Into Angola with Charlie Company

> **Manie Troskie is a paratrooper who saw a lot of action in Angola as the Border War developed. He once made the point that there was always some form of rehearsal or re-training prior to an operation, especially if it was 'cross-border'. With the attack at Cuamato, he said, there was simply no opportunity. So the men had to rely on what they had learned from previous engagements; referring to routines such as fire-and-movement and trench clearing drills. As it happened, they were all brilliantly executed, adding that while there were several more casualties on that second day, 'nobody else within our ranks was killed.'**

The author was with Theo Kluyts's squad when Charlie Company hit Cuamato. Kluyts later served as a member of the operational HQ of 1 Parachute Battalion.

The stench that reached up at us as we jumped from the choppers was unmistakable: a pungent odour of death that hung over the bush was a fetid premonition of what lay ahead. It was a remnant of the previous night's firefight, a battle that had claimed lives on both sides, two of them from Charlie Company.

There was no conscious acknowledgement of any of it among the troops in the helicopter as we approached the DZ. Rather, it permeated a vast, sandy terrain dotted by stunted mopani trees: a presence more foreboding than real. Being summer, the heat was intense even that early in the day and it hardly made things easier.

Small-arms fire crackled around the perimeter and there was no mistaking the heavier thuds of 12.7s and 14.5s, Soviet heavy machine-guns that have been used by one side or the other in hundreds of large and small wars on just about every continent over the past half century, many in Africa. The fact that the enemy had deployed these heavy weapons on the outskirts of Cuamato – and in such numbers – surprised us because SWAPO did not often use them. Nor could you miss the whack and whoosh of the occasional RPG-7.

We were lucky. The Puma that took us in dropped us on the periphery of the camp, well away from the main defences and we were spared the big stuff. Still, we'd been warned; there was enemy just about everywhere and by the time it was over, there were perhaps a score or more of them dead in our fairly modest quadrant.

We, in contrast, were still very much alive. The majority of the youngsters barely offered the bloody, blasted bodies a glance as we swiftly made our way through one trench-line and bunker hole after another: most littered with still more cadavers and the detritus of the war.

Except…except for one man. His image remains etched in my mind as if it had happened yesterday.

I found him sprawled face down, the back of his head blown into unrecognisable pulp. He must have been the base commander because apart from the blood, the rest of his uniform was spotless. Nor could you miss the fact that it had been neatly ironed before having been donned, probably a short time before the fight started. Lying prostrate outside an improvised command post that had radio aerials protruding out the back, the officer still clutched a pair of binoculars in his left hand. His other arm extended grotesquely out from under him, as if, even in death, he was still directing his men in battle. He couldn't have been more than 25 years old.

We did not bury the man, or any of the others who died that day. Instead, we left that for their *confreres*: they would arrive some time after the last South African Air Force helicopter had chattered back across no man's land into the sanctuary of South West Africa.

In the interim, Charlie Company, the unit to which I had been attached, – or 'embedded' – the terminology used today – had two of its own dead to contend with, both still in their teens and as far as we were concerned, two too many.

In many other respects, Cuamato was different from most other Border War operations and for once, the fat lady smiled.

On the day of the strike, there were more than a dozen of us cramped – with our packs and weapons – into the back of the Puma after take-off from the tiny hamlet of Cuamato three or four kilometres from the enemy camp. The chopper threaded its way through the early morning mist to a spot on the map that had been arbitrarily chosen the night before by the head of 32 Battalion, Commandant Deon Ferreira, his rank equivalent to that of a half-colonel in US Forces. With his counterpart from 1 Parachute Battalion – the Parabats – this bluff, burly, no-holds-barred veteran of dozens of campaigns said very little but did lots.

Heading out that morning, images of the previous night's engagement were fresh in our minds. To everybody onboard, the prospect of a contact was imminent…as some call it: 'dry-mouth real'.

Most of the troopies who crowded shoulder-to-shoulder aboard the chopper were still in their teens, their tautly-drawn faces reflecting no emotion. Peter McAleese and I were the oldest, by a long chalk. Formerly with Britain's Special Air Service, followed by a lengthy spell with the Rhodesian Light Infantry – McAleese had been detached from Jan Breytenbach's Pathfinder Company of the SADF's 44 Parachute Brigade and given charge of this squad. He was still tense after the previous evening's fire-fight.

No question, my presence was a bit more tenuous. As a scribe – I was the unknown factor: these youngsters had no idea how I would react under fire.

It mattered little to the young men going in that morning that the events ahead were the culmination of a succession of hot pursuit raids carried out in Angola over previous months. Envisaged targets included the western headquarters of SWAPO, the insurgent South-West African People's Organisation.

The operation involving Cuamato in mid-January 1981 was initially aimed at the larger southern city of Xangongo, further towards the west. An untidy, sprawling, typically-African conurbation, it lay on the northern shore of the Kunene River and featured often enough in the war in the past.

With time, Xangongo was to become a focal point of hostilities in that sector, though several spans of the great bridge along its southern approaches had already been destroyed in a South African Air Force strike. The word put out by Pretoria at the time was that it had been the work of the Recces, but that was all part of an elaborate charade played by both sides. Disinformation, the media called it.

The plan to hit Xangongo had been prepared at Defence Headquarters a month or so before and provided for a joint attack by both the paratroopers and Ferreira's 32 Battalion. Ancillary support would come from 31 Battalion, comprised of troops recruited within the Bushmen community of the Kalahari and originally founded several years before by another old friend, Lieutenant-Colonel Delville Linford.[1]

Outstanding trackers in primitive terrain, these little San people had been persecuted by the Angolans for years, to the extent that like vermin, they were often shot on sight whenever encountered by Angolan security forces.

Sensing an opportunity to counter the balance, Pretoria recruited a number of Bushmen to the SADF, and with solid skills taught by South African military instructors, 31 Battalion was moulded into an aggressive and competent fighting group.

The arrival of a squadron or two of Pumas and Alouette helicopter gunships in South Angola that muggy January afternoon in 1981 caused little surprise. Except for a few very old men and women, everybody else in Cuamato had fled, leaving strings of vehicle tracks across the dry terrain to testify to the recent departure of scores of military trucks. In retrospect, that alone should have alerted South African intelligence boffins that Cuamato was not the isolated settlement in the middle of nowhere, as it was perceived to be.

Undeterred, the comparatively modest force of South African Airborne wasted no time in securing a perimeter defence around the town. Trenches were dug, patrols sent out and radio communications established with Sector One Zero, the regional SA Army headquarters back at Oshakati.

By noon on the first day, all units were in place and only the flies worried us. By evening – though we were miles from any kind of permanent water – mosquitoes arrived and there were trillions of them.

Meanwhile, senior officers poured over a succession of maps and aerial photos spread out in the temporary command post, while sparse reports of SWAPO activity elsewhere was being monitored. Deon Ferreira called his officers together for a late afternoon Order Group. His force numbered perhaps 300 men, though at the end of the day it was the paratroopers that bore the brunt and took the most punishment.

There were problems, of course: in wartime there always are. For extensive operations involving choppers, Xangongo lies relatively distant from Ondangua, the main SAAF base in Ovamboland. That meant that a Helicopter Administrative Group – a HAG – needed to be established at a point roughly halfway to the target town of Xangongo which would allow for these machines to refuel.[2] Cuamato had been chosen for this purpose and the hamlet would also become the tactical headquarters for the coming fray.

It was supposed to be routine to start with, since intelligence sources had indicated no major Angolan Army presence in the area. There were elements of the paramilitary ODP (a variation of the civilian police) as well as TGFA (border guards) spread about, but they were hardly a threat. That was about it, the colonel was assured. There was certainly no mention of a major FAPLA base less than five kilometres from where we were pottering.

Yet, looking over photos I took immediately after the battle and included here, there is no question that a series of clearly discernable military strongpoints – as well as complex strings of trench lines – can be seen stretching off in all directions. Somebody in Pretoria must have been made answerable for that oversight because it cost lives.

---

1 Delville Linford (with Al J. Venter): *As the Crow Flies: My Bushman Experience with 31 Battalion*. Protea Books, Pretoria, 2015.
2 Actually, 'Helicopter Administrative Area', or HAA in English. HAG was the Afrikaans – *Helikopter Administratiewe Gebied* – though it was also referred to as a Hag by English-speakers.

More to the point, had the base remained undetected until the HAG was firmly in place and the Angolans resorted to using their heavy weapons and mortars to bombard the newcomers – as undoubtedly they would have done, because they had the resources – they could have caused havoc.

The first suggestion that something was amiss at Cuamato came late that first afternoon of January 15, the day we were all set down by the helicopters.

Several SAAF Puma and Alouette helicopters had earlier flown the 100 kilometres from the main embarkation point at Ombalantu to Cuamato, just 35 kilometres north of the Angolan border. The idea was that they would pave the way for Operation Vastrap 5, due to commence the day after. Puma mission chief was HAP Potgieter – another half-colonel – who piloted one of the machines.

The first pair of Alouette gunships flown in to provide top cover for ground forces once the fighting had started were piloted by Lieutenant Arthur Walker and Captain Mike McGee. Their mission chief was Captain Heinz Katzke, ferried in on board one of the troopers.

Things were quiet at first, but not long after the aviators had settled in and started to brew up, an advance Parabat reconnaissance group was greeted by salvos of rocket and machine-gun fire from positions out east. These were followed by the unmistakable thumps of 82mm mortars. Then it dawned: the South Africans had a battle on their hands.

What we did not yet know was that the route taken by the patrol led directly towards a major military base that, until then, nobody knew anything about. The installation was huge, and manned not by SWAPO irregulars, but by a large number of well-drilled and equipped Angolan soldiers. More important, this was all regular Angolan Army, not the ill-trained, badly-motivated bunch of local, souped-up conscript troops.

Mike Pearson, then a youthful Parabat lance-corporal, has vivid recall of events that afternoon. As he remembers, the sections under corporals Hennie Viljoen and Pepe Tommasi – accompanied by Lieutenant JC du Plessies and Sergeant 'Min Dae' Wessels – went out to check for any evidence of enemy activity in the area. He reported as follows:

> In was late afternoon by the time we came across a long, straight road heading north. We were standing among the bushes when, undetected, we suddenly saw a bunch of enemy soldiers cross the road about 500 metres ahead. Apart from the lieutenant and 'Min Dae', there was also Doug Winning and Rob Anderson, and our group wasted no time going forward until we intersected with their tracks.
>
> This was obviously a serious business, so we crept quietly forward for another 200 metres until we heard voices. Continuing, we had a group of five or six of them visual sitting on a termite mound. That was when we went down low.
>
> The lieutenant and I crawled under a fallen tree and had a clear view of those guys. We waited for the two corporals, Viljoen and Tommasi to join us, having already told them of the situation by radio. But then, unexpectedly, one of the gooks started walking straight towards us; he got to about ten or 12 metres from us and started to unzip his fly. The guy was taking a piss…
>
> The problem just then was that with Viljoen and Tommasi coming up behind, the man who had stopped to pee heard them approach. I already had a bead on him and as he turned to make a run for it, I nailed him. We managed to drop a couple more on the termite mound before the rest bolted.

Undeterred, our people crept forward until we came to the edge of the tree line. There we discovered that all the foliage and shrubs had been cleared for about 70 metres, and once the enemy at the base opened fire, we had no option but to take up defensive positions.

The firing was intense. It was so bad that after a couple of minutes every one of us prostrate on the ground was covered in foliage as everything was aimed in our direction – especially the 14.5s and 12.7s. Fortunately their barrels weren't adequately depressed and the rounds went high, lopping off twigs, branches and sometimes the tops of trees. This was what was falling on our heads.

Having called for reinforcements, it did not take long for the helicopters to bring in the troops, including Sergeant-Major Peter McAleese and a French guy whose name I can't remember. It was actually the sergeant major who, after jumping up, shouted that we couldn't lie there forever. That was when he asked us who was going to join him and make a dash for the trenches.

Well everyone did and we fired as we ran across a large open area. I recall emptying my magazine half way across and stopped to insert a fresh one thinking that the bastards were going to nail me. But they did not, and certainly not for want of trying.

Once we got abreast of the first line of trenches, the enemy seemed to take fright and they hopped like jack rabbits to get away from us. Sergeant 'Min Dae' Wessels made the mistake of leaning forward and looking into a trench before hurling his grenade: he was shot through the head, neck and chest.

Lieutenant du Plessies was a hellova lot luckier. He took a round in his pack, but it was deflected upwards and ricocheted under the skin on his back, clipping the back of his head. De Bruyn, the radio operator was shot at about the same time.

There was a lot of praise within the unit afterwards for the way that Danie Els provided covering fire with his LMG. Said one of his mates: the guy was relentless…he managed to keep a lot of enemy heads down. It was Steven MacDougal that sent the original signal back to the nearby HAG on his A-53 radio that he carried on his back: the message was terse: 'we are under attack'.

In clipped tones, he told headquarters that two members of his squad had been wounded and urgently requested casualty evacuation as well as back-up. Within the next half hour or so, another three platoons were hauled in by the Pumas.

MacDougal: 'The new arrivals weren't much help either because as the fire intensified, they, like us, could do nothing but duck.' Still more reinforcements were flown in, but the odds remained tough. To Ferreira, the situation had become untenable.

In his customary uncompromising manner, he told his commanders to get their act together and find out what the fuck was going on.

It was about then that 'Chunky' Truter, one of the paratroop youngsters was killed. He took a shard of steel in the brain after an enemy mortar landed in the middle of his squad. It was a lucky shot for the enemy but it did serious damage.

I was present after he had been carried into Cuamato village by his mates, Then, after a short spell of lapsing in and out of consciousness 'Chunky' breathed his last. I visited his mother in Cape Town a few months later to tell her that just before he died, he'd quietly called for her. She never got over his death.

As Charlie Company section leader Manie Troskie recalled afterwards, 'Chunky's' death had a hellova effect on all of us. 'If any of our group had reservations about killing, a kind of primitive hatred seemed to emerge from nowhere. Most of the guys were still in their teens, but overnight we'd become focused, our instincts brutish and certainly beyond the comprehension of most ordinary folk who have never seen this kind of action.'

But then, that's the way it is with all wars, which was why Charlie Company went in the next day and thought nothing about killing as many of the enemy as they encountered in an engagement that lasted several hours.

It was getting dark when the rest of us at Cuamato – only a short hike across the sands away – watched in awe as firepower poured out of the base and it did so in all directions. Had it all been concentrated where MacDougal and the rest of the group were cowering, they would almost certainly have been wiped out.

Casualty details were vague at first and came in snatches…'One of our boys dead…Casevac required…things are bad… really bad!' By then another man had been wounded, which was when somebody asked whether it had become too risky to send in the choppers to haul them out.

Tasked to handle the situation by his commander, Captain Heinz Katzke said that he was reluctant to use his gunships. Support was needed for the Parabats who were under fire, he agreed, but it had suddenly become too risky, and for three reasons: the flak was too heavy, the bush too sparse, and pretty damn soon it would be night. He suggested that they wait a bit and for those caught in the mêlée, to walk out in the dark.

That was what finally happened, with the seriously wounded and the dead ultimately hauled to safety by their mates on improvised sets of stretchers. Don recalls helping to carry his buddies out on litters made from tree branches hastily cut into lengths and threaded through the sleeves of their bush jackets, 'with a fireworks display of tracers around us.'

Only then was it established that along one stretch of the base perimeter, large numbers of enemy troops were entrenched in a parallel set of trenches, in places only 30 metres from where the paratroopers were trapped. Both sides had kept firing, though after things had kind of settled in, the two adversaries started hurling insults, the Angolans in Portuguese (which none of the South Africans understood) and the Parabats in Afrikaans, which to those listening on the other side could just as easily have been Mandarin.

To Rifleman George 'Org' Hennig – for a long time he owned the famous De Bos Restaurant in Pretoria – it was the worst kind of contact imaginable: 'The first we knew that there were enemy around was when the bush seemed to catch alight…we were under attack and it was fucking heavy,' recalls Hennig today.

As MacDougal said, it did not help that the entire region was pancake flat, the nearest row of hills several days' march distant and all the high points in enemy hands. These were defensive positions and every one of them had been carefully constructed by the enemy…it was from there that the guys took a pounding.

'Even more terrifying,' he remembers, 'was that we couldn't even pull back…to do so would have meant us crossing a couple of hundred metres of open terrain with almost no cover…we would have taken a horrible loss. So we lay flat on our backs and watched strings of tracers whistling past only centimetres over our position, though that did not stop most of the boys pulling out cigarettes and lighting up…' It stayed that way until dark.

After the sun had set and the rest of the squad was back in Cuamato with the wounded attended to, Ferreira pulled back all his non-essential troops and told his officers that they would wait until dawn before 'getting down to business'.

I would go in with the first wave, he said when he pulled me aside, adding that it would be the first time a South African journalist had been allowed to accompany his men into combat, never mind that everything pointed to a fully conventional battle ahead.

'You sure you still want to go in – two men already dead and there could be more tomorrow?'

The prospect was sobering, but I'd come that far, I replied.

Peter McAleese, who headed our section during the Cuamato attack, checks documents taken from one of the enemy. (Author's photo)

Cuamato water tower, used by the enemy to observe our arrival and after we had taken the town, by our forces. (Author's photo)

Angolan Army weapons – including some large-calibre guns – were scattered all over the camp. (Author's photo)

Though distant from our frontier, vehicles brought up supplies by road along *Oom Willie se Pad* – Uncle Willie's road – and then uplifted by Pumas. (Author's photo)

One of the men getting his wounds attended to after the first night's fire-fight. (Author's photo)

Cuamato village, with a small detachment of chopper gunships that were based there for ground support. (Author's photo)

Impala jet during one of the airstrikes.

Puma heading home, late afternoon. (Author's photo)

Puma helicopters 'parked' in Cuamato village waiting for orders. Meanwhile, the crew cooks up a brew. (Author's photo)

Darkness settled uneasily on both sides of the front. As the night wore on, we could hear the occasional blast as approaching Angolan Army vehicles detonated anti-tank landmines that both the Recces and 32 reconnaissance elements had been laying along the only approach road to the base. You cannot miss the distinctive hollow thump of an anti-tank mine being detonated.

Questioned about vehicles using the roads, the Bushman leader of his fighting group said that the way he gauged the situation, enemy trucks arrived full and left empty. That meant that a steady stream of men and supplies kept arriving at the base, obviously bolstering FAPLA defences. Also, the blackness was irregularly punctuated by mortar and small arms fire, but it was erratic and there was no damage.

The single biggest problem facing the officers that evening – they had since been joined by Major General Jannie Geldenhuys, who was in command of this northern war out of Sector One Zero – was who would actually lead the attack on the base the next day? That was when the name of one of the young officers attached to the Parachute Battalion was put forward.

Captain Johan Blaauw was in command of the Parabat contingent at Cuamato and unlike most of the officers, he was soft-spoken and unobtrusive: most of the time you did not know he was there, until he offered a comment. Then everybody listened, unusual for a junior officer. Interestingly, he was also articulate.

What mattered most in this young captain's mind was that his unit had already taken seven casualties – two dead and five wounded. He needed to even things up, he declared, looking his colonel straight in the eyes.

According to Blaauw's intelligence NCO, an even younger Theo Kluyts, the captain had been severely affected by the events that had taken place earlier. Respectfully, but inordinately direct, Captain Blaauw told Lieutenant Colonel Ferreira that there was no question that the job was his. While 32 Battalion might have been blooded more often than had Charlie Company, his men had a score to settle. He said that of all the officers at the order group, he was not only best suited for the task, but circumstances also made him – and the rest of his unit – the most motivated.

Moreover, he reminded the senior officers present, this would not be the first time either his men or he himself had seen action. They had proved themselves in a series of heavy actions in Operation Smokeshell a short while before.

Smokeshell was the code-name for the objective – the operation's name was Sceptic – though this unfortunate choice of name, often rendered Septic by the soldiers because of its shortcomings, caused it to be referred to as Smokeshell, which, as Brigadier-General Alexander pointed out, has a 'finer ring' to it.

There had been other battles before that, all successful. In fact, Sceptic was Charlie Company's first operational deployment, though Captain Blaauw had seen lots of action himself before that as a lieutenant, including two operational para drops inside Angola, one of them at Cassinga in 1978. He was awarded the *Honoris Crux* as a platoon commander during Op Savannah in 1975.

Consequently, Captain Blaauw declared, his hands firmly on the map table in front of him, he and his men knew exactly what had to be done.

Doubtful at first, the head of 32 Battalion looked around at the other faces gathered around. There was no dissent. Nor did General Geldenhuys object when apprised of the situation. That much decided, the order group turned to other matters.

It was decided that before Charlie Company was to go in, the base would be softened at first light by a napalm and conventional bomb strike involving SAAF Impala jets. That would be followed by a succession of heavy barrages from 32 Battalion's mortars.

There were at least four of these Aeromacchi light ground-attack/fighter jets already waiting at the Ondangua Air Force Base about 130 kilometres to the south when orders were radioed through. Often used far beyond their advertised capabilities as ground-support aircraft in this

Border War, the planes were only finally withdrawn from the front line over Angola in the late 1980s.

The appointment of Captain Blaauw as strike leader was fortuitous, and for several reasons. Youthful, imaginative and aggressive, he had already proved himself, invariably leading from the front. At the same time, Cuamato was unique in other respects, not least that the placing of the FAPLA military base close to the town was an intelligence blunder of significant proportions. The South Africans had no knowledge of enemy numbers, their weaponry, base layout, defensive doctrines and so forth. Essentially, the men would be going in 'blind'. The fact that the attacking force was to take only two or three more wounded in an assault that lasted a good part of the following day, was remarkable.

Second, there was no time for any kind of re-training or rehearsals, both normally essential in those conditions. Nobody needed to tell the captain that he could not just storm a base and hope. In the end, that was exactly what he did.

As the South Africans were to learn later, the layout of the enemy base was fairly complex. There were trenches, fox-holes galore and underground bunkers just about everywhere. Several of the officers declared that they had never come across an Angolan base so well prepared in enemy territory.

What amazed Theo Kluyts was that even though the Angolans (probably with Cuban help) had cleared an area around the base to a depth of about 200 metres (for an improved field of fire) the base itself was well camouflaged both from the air and on the ground. In some places fresh branches and dead bushes were pulled haphazardly into position to avoid any suggestion of a human presence, very much as had been the case in Vietnam.

'That made it quite difficult to determine where everything was', declared Kluyts. 'To me, it was obvious that they'd made the base pretty difficult for any kind of ground attack, which was why I actually asked one of the pilots afterwards to take me up so I could get a better understanding of the layout.

> I did a sketch of the area and gave a copy to the 32 Battalion intelligence officer, which, I believe, resulted in them later building a scale model at the training area of 1 Parachute Battalion in Bloemfontein.

Having bedded down for the night in the shadow of one of the solid brick Portuguese colonial structures in Cuamato, everybody was up before dawn. We nibbled at our rat packs but the minds of most of the men were elsewhere.

The call to move towards the staging area followed shortly afterwards and we were told that the first two Parabat 'sticks' would leave the ground in 10 minutes: it would take us only a couple of minutes to reach contact point.

Orders issued by ground staff immediately before take-off were brief: we would have roughly eight or 10 seconds to get onto the ground from a hover of anything between two and three metres. After that, the Pumas would pull away and head back to base to fetch the next bunch.

Word had come down from up top that I'd got my clearance: there was no problem with me accompanying the strike. But if I did not jump with my group, the officer warned, there would be no going back. Also, he had no objection to me 'carrying': especially since we'd be going into the kind of terrain where it was expected there would be enemy all over the place.

I was issued with a folding-stock AK and two magazines. I asked for a couple of grenades and got them.

It had become clear to everybody in Cuamato the previous night that the events of the day before had left its mark on the 'Bats' who crowded into the Puma around me. There were no smiles and none of the banter usually encountered under training. Immediately prior to boarding, automatic fire across the way picked up sharply and we had to accept the odds: this time we would be the attackers.

The real battle started as soon as the boots of the first of our detachment touched the ground.

Crouched in the bush, perhaps 30 or 40 metres from our hovering Puma were two of the enemy, both clad in FAPLA cammo. One was armed with an RPG-7 rocket launcher and the other cradled an RPD machine-gun in his arms. On reflection, they could probably have taken our chopper out in a flash, but curiously, in one of those quirky developments that characterise so many Third World confrontations and make no sense at all, fate decreed otherwise.

Instead of fighting, both men simply dropped their weapons and raised their hands. Having raced hard that first 100 metres to find cover, most of the men were already breathing hard, in part, because retaliatory fire had picked up along the line, which probably extended a good three or four hundred metres in all directions.

Peter McAleese was the first to reach the two Angolan soldiers and he wasted no time in cuffing them to ground, at the same time kicking their weapons away. He spent a short while going through their pockets and then, using the kind of universal sign language that everybody understood, ordered them onto their feet again. We took both men with us as we moved forward through sparse bush country and when we were halted once more, they were bound and sent back to base on the next chopper. 'Interrogation,' McAleese explained.

Asked afterwards why they had not fired as our choppers came in, one of the Angolan captives answered that it was pointless. 'We shoot and shoot, but still more of these machines come.' He suggested that his people were totally 'outgunned'

Time and sequence of events often have little relevance in battle and it was no different at Cuamato. Asked later how long the onslaught lasted, I had no idea. It could have been an hour, or possibly two, or perhaps only 20 minutes. Images, sensations, feelings: all were compressed into the immediate. That and the elation of still being intact and having weathered the first two mortar and RPG barrages, together with the relief of seeing some of your own people walk out of an all-encompassing layer of smoke, in a situation that appeared hopeless moments before.

That flank probably felt the same about us when the situation was reversed, for this kind of man-to-man contact is invariably unspoken, except when you're telling somebody to get down. We watched our flanks and our rear, not so much because the enemy might be lurking there, but rather to spot problems within our own lines.

You were aware too, that you were the subject of scrutiny, which was comforting: Peter McAleese kept his beady eyes on me throughout.

The routine was the same as the attack drove forward. We'd move ahead from one trench-line to another, all the time consolidating. Fire was sporadic, with enemy mortars more troubling, for the gunships as well because they had to be wary of entering the potential trajectory arc of fired mortars.

We would constantly encounter bunkers and all had to be cleared. At one of these locations, a couple of squadies moved in, but in coming out of direct sunlight, they could discern nothing in the dark recesses that were partially underground. Still, in one case, a troopie persisted and moved forward, until somebody at the far end opened fire and wounded him in the arm. He dropped to the ground and crawled out on his hands and knees. Two of his mates silenced the attacker with grenades.

At another bunker filled to the rooftop with firewood, Manie Troskie and one of his oppos moved in, but movement within its narrow confines was limited and it was all fairly cursory. Sensing a presence in the gloom beyond, both men crept silently back towards the entrance, turned once more before exiting and emptied their magazines into the gloom. Two dead enemy soldiers were later found slumped at the far end of the bunker. As Manie reflects today: 'it could just as easily have been us…'

Then we almost lost the captain. I'd been on Blaauw's tail in the latter stages of the attack while he and several of his men were clearing trenches and at one set of fortifications that led directly to a bunker, he almost came unstuck. He had already killed one FALPA soldier who had been waiting for him around a narrow bend in the trench line when he decided to throw a grenade into the adjacent bunker. If there was one enemy soldier in the area, the captain reasoned, there could be more.

'There was nothing planned,' Captain Blaauw recalled afterwards. 'The entrance to the bunker lay immediately ahead, so I grabbed a grenade, drew myself up out of the trench, pulled the pin and hurled it into the entrance.'

I was immediately behind the captain taking photos when the grenade exploded in the bunker and with it, ignited several drums of fuel that had been stored there, creating a massive back-blast that all but enveloped the officer. Though he did not actually catch fire, Blaauw was seriously burned, his hair and all his exposed skin seared. In fact, his entire face was scorched black.

The captain was quickly moved some distance behind our lines before he was airlifted out. Within hours he was in hospital in Oshakati.

Meantime, the rest of the unit took up positions adjacent to two Gaz ammunition trucks that were burning fiercely: the Soviet vehicles had probably been targeted in an earlier air strike. Though there was still some enemy action coming from more distant positions, the air around us was constantly being shattered by exploding rockets, mortars, grenades and small arms still left on the trucks abandoned by FAPLA troops. To my mind, we were a lot more at risk from those explosions than from the enemy, which was when McAleese decided to take the unit forward, a sensible move.

Once through a second line of trenches, the camp was all but ours. There were still small clusters of the enemy about, but when detected they ran and our guys would pick them off. We were aware too, that there were more of them still hiding underground, but all those bunkers and tunnels would be systematically cleared by late afternoon.

Speaking about the Cuamato attack years later, Alouette gunship pilot Arthur Walker recalls that that very first afternoon – prior to all this happening – things couldn't have been more settled.

'The Puma and Alouette guys were just parking off, the pilots sitting under the trees and making coffee. We were actually preparing to spend the evening there,' reckons Walker, who was to win his first Honoris Crux Gold decoration at Cuamato.

Awarded for acts of conspicuous bravery, HC decorations came in four classifications, bronze, silver, gold and diamond, the last being South Africa's highest decoration for bravery and roughly equivalent to the Victoria Cross or the Congressional Medal of Honour. It was never awarded. There were only six Honoris Crux Gold decorations handed out during the entire 23 year Border War and it says a lot that Arthur Walker got two.

What struck us as unusual at Cuamato, recalls Walker, was that apart from the operational commander Ferreira, an entire headquarters contingent arrived at the HAG, almost as if everybody wanted to get into the act. 'It included air force and army commanders, the majority gathered around to fine-tune the next day's operation towards Xangongo and nobody having the faintest idea that a huge enemy force was only a rifle shot away.'

As he remembers, this number included Air Force Lt-Col JB West (Military Air Operations Team – SAAF liaison officer) and the SAAF officer-in-charge of fighter backup, Brigadier Piet Bosman 'Bossie' Huyser. Jannie Geldenhuys came in from Oshakati soon afterwards.

Walker:

The contact call following the first shots exchanged near the as-yet-undetermined enemy base was soon followed by a report that two of our troops had been wounded. Not long afterwards, a helicopter extraction was asked for, which was when we were alerted.

So Captain Mike McGee and I went off in our gunships to try to secure a landing zone. The idea was that a Puma would follow and pull the casualties out. To our surprise, Mike and I came under some really heavy anti-aircraft fire, with even RPG-7s headed in our direction… stacks of them,' recalled Arthur.

The troops on the ground threw yellow smoke to mark their positions, which was when Mike and I went ahead with an attack in a bid to suppress the increased anti-aircraft fire. We were trying hard to allow for Puma access, but because it was now getting dark and the sky illuminated by tracer…which was pretty dramatic, especially for the guys watching on the ground, it did not take us long to realise that those guys were pretty well equipped.

We detected three emplaced 14.5mm ZPU twin-barrels, never mind who-knows-how-many 12.7s and, of course, the RPGs.

Against these, he explained, the gunships each had a single, laterally-mounted 20mm cannon and fired from a low and relatively slow orbit for accuracy.

We'd see the muzzle flashes when they were aiming at us and then the tracers. It all seemed to come at us in a kind of slow motion, just like in the movies. Then suddenly this stuff was whooshing past your head. Naturally we'd fire back, using their tracers to direct our aim at source…but it wasn't something that would have worked in the daytime.

My engineer and gunner was Sergeant Danie Brink and he kept firing until we ran out of ammunition, which wasn't long, because our gunships normally only carried 150 rounds.

I broke out of the orbit and called to Mike on the radio…told him I was going to re-arm… we certainly had not given up the battle yet, but that was when he suddenly radioed that he was coming under some really heavy shit and was going to crash.

Walker explained that the two gunships were flying about 500 feet above ground level while in orbit, and if you came under fire under those conditions, he said, it was best to get down low and fast.

But in his rapid descent, McGee must have become disoriented, which is why he thought he was headed into the dirt.

In the darkness I couldn't see him,' said Arthur, 'so I turned around in a bid to search for his machine and even put on my navigation lights. I told him to fly towards me, but that caused even more problems.

We did not expect to draw all that fire, but that's exactly what happened, though it did give Mike the brief opportunity to recover. After that I escorted him clear.

Heinz Katzke, who was in command of the gunships, made the point that the area was already well lit up with all that flak flying about. In addition, there were the lights of Cuamato, which were clearly visible in the south. 'It's worth noting,' he added, 'that the Alouettes were not equipped for night operations, though sometimes, needs must…'

Using evasive manoeuvring to interfere with the aim of the enemy gunners, including sharp turns and height changes, Walker and McGee finally broke free.

'Mike followed me back to the base, where we landed and shut down to re-arm, re-fuel and reassess the situation,' Walker elaborated, 'but we realised it was pointless. The position where our casualties were lying was just too close to the enemy, less than 200 metres.'

While all this had been going on, recalls Walker, 'we still had not assessed what exactly was down there… In fact, when we went up, we had no idea that this base even existed,' Walker told Mitchell. 'Obviously our intelligence was flawed.'

Later that night, the command element gathered in Cuamato and determined that the men would go in again at first light on what was then accepted as a significant enemy position. Ferreira warned that it would a tough exchange.

By then, too, the Pumas had returned to Ombalantu across the border, with Walker and McGee as passengers. They had left behind their gunships to be serviced for the second day's battle ahead.

Four Pumas headed back north to Cuamato before dawn the next day, bringing Walker and McGee with them. The flight was accompanied by four extra Alouettes flown by Katzke and Willem Ras (as the first pair) with Billy Port and 'Klip' Reynolds to supplement firepower.

Judging by performances past, the enemy might confidently have been expected to have taken the gap during the night. Isolated, totally cut off and with no effective air cover, the Angolans must have realised that come first light, they would come under heavy attack from a well-armed, well-trained and motivated 'First World' military force.

Standard operating procedure for FAPLA had usually been to 'shoot and scoot', which had happened often enough in the past. But not this time at Cuamato…

By then the South Africans had to accept that the Angolans had established a full-on defended area. On open ground, with sandy soil and light grass cover, the aviators discovered a huge military complex traversed by Soviet-style zigzag trenches: 'from where we were flying, it was all straight out of the manual and included numerous firing emplacements and positions for 82mm mortars,' recalled one of the pilots afterwards.

'When we went out again,' said Walker, 'it was an altogether different game. 'But even then we thought the enemy might have pulled out and we did not expect any real resistance. So when we moved off, we sent up four gunships, with two remaining behind to be serviced, the idea being to check out the situation from up close. Almost immediately a lot of heavy stuff came our way and even some SAM-7 ground-to-air missiles… about five were fired at us. None of the MANPADS hit, but they came close…'

Looking back, Walker reckoned that the lack of success with SAM-7 ground-to-air missiles was because of the extremely low level at which the South Africans normally flew, sometimes just clear of the tops of the terrain's tree cover. As he commented, the Angolan troops operating the heat-seeking Strelas did not have time to allow their missiles to engage before blasting off.

'They fired in haste before they could lock on…it needs a few seconds to zero in with the missile,' explained Arthur. In effect, they were dispatched ballistically and were thus no more accurate than the similarly unguided RPG-7s they were also using.

He reckoned that it could have been because of the K-Car gunship, as this Alouette configuration was termed. Hovering over the battle in a command and control capacity and fitted with heat shields to deflect exhaust gases upwards through the rotor, minimised their signatures and was an effective combination anti-missile combination in that primitive bush war.

> So there we were, over an Angolan strongpoint with all manner of crap being thrown at us. It was obviously dangerous, and to some of us, a pointless exercise. So in the end the ground commander ordered us to withdraw before there were more casualties.

Walker acknowledged it was time to call in the Impalas, though he was surprised that that had not happened earlier.

> Our tactic under those circumstances would normally be for the jets to use their rockets and bombs to create devastation on the ground. Only then would the choppers move in to clean up. So, some 20 minutes later, the fixed wings came in, guided by a forward air controller sitting in a twin-seat Bosbok spotter plane high above the battle.

On their first run in, however, the Impalas encountered some really heavy flak, recalls Katzke. The pilots decided that they would go in at 20,000 feet, dive vertically down, release their bombs and pull out at 15,000 feet. There was a French-speaking Impala pilot who, after a while said in English, with a heavy accent: 'Our weapons are ineffective for this target.'

That done, it was time for the planned full-on assault on the Angolan base and, as Walker conceded, there were to be no more half-measures once the Paratroopers had been taken in by the Pumas. By then, said Walker, the Impalas had already screamed in, two at a time. There must have been at least eight such pairs of jet strikes, he recalled, after which, the gunships followed. But there were still a few more surprises.

'What we found amazing after all this, was that the anti-aircraft guns that should have been destroyed in the bombing runs were still firing,' he ruminated. 'As one group of Angolan gunners were killed – literally taken out by gunships and the ground troops – the defenders would simply call forward more men and put new teams onto the guns. Once again, we still couldn't understand why these guys kept fighting as hard as they did.'

Visualising those dramatic events nearly decades later, Walker paused, and then added thoughtfully: 'They fought hard…credit to them because it was a hellova battle.'

Katzke agreed, 'It was a tough fight…once our boys took the initiative, they went into the trenches and cleaned up. Those FAPLA troops that survived so far were fleeing helter-skelter towards the north and the base was finally taken.'

Walker:

> Then we withdrew and all the guys went back to Cuamato. So did our ground forces. Later that afternoon, the choppers returned to Ombalantu and more assessment followed, more planning. But this time the South Africans would only be mopping up.

The citation for Arthur Walker's Honoris Crux Gold noted that he had 'displayed exceptional courage and bravery under fire by remaining on station and providing the close air support required by own ground forces'.

Describing the manner in which he went to help Mike McGee, the citation continued:

> His courageous act prevented the loss of an Alouette and its crew. Lieutenant Walker's actions were not only an outstanding display of professionalism, devotion to duty and courage, but also constituted exceptional deeds of bravery under enemy fire…

21

Caught in an Angolan Minefield

Of all the disasters anybody involved in Angola's travails was likely to encounter, a brush with a landmine – both anti-tank (AT) and anti-personnel (AP) – was the most consistent threat. I was blown up by an anti-tank mine on an Angolan sortie (and so was my son Johan, while serving with 61 Mech). A soldier who followed me into a bunker at a SWAPO base was killed by an AP. In this regard, the average Portuguese soldier suffered many casualties because unlike Pretoria, Lisbon never really got to grips with a problem that was both insidious and all-too-often deadly.

From the early 1960s, a range of landmines were hauled across the border into Angola from the Congo. And later, while some efforts were made to develop mine resistant or mine-protected vehicles, the average grunt from the *metrópole* serving in Africa was stuck for most of the war with the troop-carrying Unimog, an all-terrain vehicle developed by Mercedes Benz for military use.

Soldiers sat back-to-back behind the driver's cab when out on the roads, their rifles at the ready to counter ambushes.

The undersides of these vehicles that the Portuguese eventually assembled in their own country under licence offered absolutely no protection to the kind of blast that resulted from detonating an anti-tank (or anti-vehicle) landmine. As hostilities progressed, many of these improvised troop carriers were reinforced by replacing sand bags with steel plating.

It was different further south. One of the first dedicated tasks tackled by Ian Smith's government in Rhodesia was to design vehicles that would offer their soldiers some protection from bombs hidden in the ground. Until that happened, Rhodesian Army Bedford trucks also relied on sandbags to protect soldiers travelling on them.

But by then the Rhodesians were making serious efforts at countering large numbers of anti-vehicle mines that insurgents were laying on their country roads. These included Soviet TM-46s, Yugoslav TMA-3s (with their three distinctive fuel cells and nicknamed 'cheese mines'), Chinese metal-cased Type 72s and a catalogue of others. The insurgents even acquired from Libya some British anti-tank mines of Second World War vintage that had been lifted in the desert and recycled.

Considering Salisbury's limited financial and engineering resources, the 'Rhodies' proved astonishingly successful in developing several prototypes. Illustrations in this chapter display some of the hybrids that came off their production lines, though never in any volume because Salisbury simple did not have the money.

Successful in this range was the 'Pookie', variations of which were later tried by the South Africans. Travelling about the Honde Valley adjacent to the Mozambique border or along roads that fell within the area covered by Operation Hurricane, we would often encounter 'Pookies' poking about in the most unlikely places.

The 'Pookie' was not a personnel carrier and it protected only its driver. It was specifically designed to detect landmines, such as they were at the time. The South Africans took a long, hard look at this machine and used the concept, in part, to develop their own successful 'Husky'.

In contrast to anti-tank/anti-vehicle mines – much smaller and more compact buried bombs – anti-personnel mines were a different matter. Light, transportable and often laid on paths between villages or near water points, they caused horrific damage to soldiers and civilians alike.

Some of these were small enough to fit in the cup of man's hand; but it could blow a foot off if stood on. The Russions went a step further by developing the so-called 'Butterfly Mine' (or PFM-1), so named because it looked as if it had sprouted a pair of wings.

Essentially a plastic bag containing a liquid explosive, these devices were dropped in their thousands in and around towns and valleys in Afghanistan during the period of Soviet occupation in the 1980s. Its specific purpose was to maim and kill children and in that, the 'Green Parrot' (as it was dubbed by NATO) was inordinately successful.

Eventually, Angola became a kind of testing ground – a laboratory, almost – for many of these bombs, with just about every member of the Soviet Bloc offering expertise as well as South African scientists testing some quite remarkable devices that were extremely difficult to detect once buried and almost impossible to lift if uncovered.

Millions of APs were laid by all the participants in Angola's multifarious conflicts and, unlike anti-tank mines – where Luanda and Pretoria would sometimes (though not always) provide charts where they had been laid and which could sometimes be used in later years to lift them – the smaller devices were buried in the ground just about anywhere. It was the classic example of indiscriminate killing, and still is in some of the conflicts east of Suez.

Some landmines were laid defensively, to prevent infiltration of enemy forces. The Rhodesian Army laid anti-personnel mines on a massive scale along its border with Mozambique. Mapped, coordinated and listed along the 'Cordon Sanitaire', it was a reasonably effective interim measure at keeping insurgents out. But because the cordon was easily accessed by wild animals and heavy rains would sometimes cause the mines to shift, their role eventually became problematic. Those mines killed or wounded more elephants than insurgents.

Once the war in northern South West Africa got serious – after the first insurgent incursions in 1966 – SWAPO devoted an enormous amount of effort towards mining roads in an area that stretched for many hundreds of kilometres.

Landmines were ferried together with other war materiéls overland from both Congos and Zambia, usually on the backs of combatants or civilians who had been shanghaied into the role.

It was not long before the main east-west trunk road linking Caprivi with Ovamboland – at that stage not yet surfaced – was targeted. Known as *Oom Willie se Pad* (Uncle Willie's Road), army convoys using this route were forced to run a sometimes-hazardous gauntlet and casualties were commonplace. I travelled it often enough and recall being held up quite a few times while army sappers made the road ahead safe. There is a marvellous photograph that I took of an engineer physically detonating an anti-tank mine on that road. The metal casing had been identified by a mine detector and after clearing away some of the sand over it, he attached a rope to it, and pulled from a distance of about 30 metres. The blast was awesome.

In the countryside, rural people suffered serious damage from these bombs and in the early years of conflict there were more civilians killed by mines than army personnel. With time, SWAPO countered the threat factor to some extent by tipping off friendly locals that landmines had been laid, but these were haphazard efforts because their cadres were constantly on the move, if only to avoid pursuing army units.

Once Portugal had pulled out of Angola, conflict in the neighbouring territory escalated, but by then Pretoria had embarked on numerous anti-landmine projects of its own and a host of mine-protected vehicles emerged from South African factories. The research that followed these developments was outstanding, involving special steels and a variety of counter measures, to the extent that South Africa today remains one of the leading international developers of mine-resistant vehicles.

South African-manufactured anti-mine vehicles like the Mamba and its competitor, the Nyala RG-31, together with many other modifications, are to be seen in dozens of conflict zones the world over. They are deployed in several Middle East regions as well as further afield, including the Yemen, Iraq, Syria and Afghanistan and by both the Indian and Pakistani armies. Locally-built variants are in use by the American, British, Canadian and several European armed forces.

It is worth mentioning that after a follow-up contract for the Mamba was awarded to the South African company OMC, rather than to TFM – who then decided to manufacture an 'improved Mamba', without the restriction of having to use Unimog components – the RG-31 Nyala was the result. With several modifications it was introduced to the US Army and later became one of the most successful Mine Resistant Ambush Protected (MRAP) vehicles on the planet.

By then the British began to appreciate the potential of commercial opportunities in these rather convoluted enterprises and Henred Fruehauf, the original manufacturer of the all-purpose mine-protected Casspir infantry fighting vehicle was taken over by TFM in 1981. That company improved the design to develop the Mk 2. The sequence of buy-outs and take-overs of these manufacturing firms within South African industry is instructive; even before 9/11 the level of competition in a constantly growing market was fierce and involved Britain's Vickers Defence Systems and Alvis Vehicles as well as British Aerospace.

More recently, the company was taken over by Pretoria's Mechem, one of the pioneers in the industry.

It is notable that in South Africa early landmine research – with a view to escalating hostilities along the Angolan border – was based on experiments with the Unimog and the ubiquitous Land Rover. Soon a range of mine-resistant vehicles were developed which included the Hippo and the Hyena APS (based on a Bedford chassis) followed by the Buffel and the Casspir.

The chief criteria was good off-road mobility, armour protection against small arms fire and anti-personnel mines, together with ease and speed of repair by a light workshop crew in the field, which was essential after a vehicle had detonated an anti-tank mine: it was either that or the wreck had to be abandoned, which was so often the case with Portuguese forces. These requirements led to the distinctive V-shaped hull (for mine protection) and a wheeled chassis.

Going back to the early days of the Border War, the initial mobility requirement was for good on-road mobility – because that was where the mines were planted (hardly any were planted in the veld, except on known vehicle tracks). Early mine-protected vehicles (MPVs) were not very good on off-road sorties, but the Buffel, followed by the totally revolutionary Casspir, soon changed this.

The brainchild of Dr Vernon Joynt, one of the unsung heroes of South African weapons research and development, the Casspir resulted from his work at the South African Council for Scientific and Industrial Research. Joynt perfected its V-bottomed armoured monocoque hull – to which he attached a leaf-spring suspension – specifically to deflect the force of an explosion outwards and protect its occupants against blast.

It is important to note that the Casspir (CSIR + SAP) was intended for the South African Police and not for that country's military. The army already had the Buffel and had started a project to deliver a mine-protected combat vehicle (MPCV) when a 'short-cut' saw the Casspir being introduced after its successes with Koevoet.[1]

---

1   See Koevoet involvement in the Border War in Chapter 13.

Notable too, is that incorporated into the design of a Casspir was the ability – after it had been blasted by an anti-tank mine – to fly in a repair team, remove the entire damaged wheel unit and replace it with another (which was always taken along on sorties).

The entire procedure – lasting perhaps an hour or two – underscoring the extremely versatile nature of some development projects associated with the Border War and in particular the role of Dr Vernon Joynt, who was regularly consulted on such matters by American scientists. As the old-time South African adage suggests, *'n Boer maak 'n plan*. (A Boer makes a plan).[2]

A significant feature of his Casspir IFV is that its main armoured steel body is raised high above the ground, further minimising the effects of blast. Interestingly, the capabilities of the Casspir were the basis of the outline capabilities required by the United States Marines for their Mine Resistant Ambush Protected (MRAP) vehicle project which saw extensive operational use in Afghanistan.

While serving with Koevoet, the police counter insurgency unit that used Casspirs to operate along the Angolan border, was that its members achieved significantly more many kills than any comparable South African Army unit. Rarely more than 1,000 strong and only about a fifth white – the balance was made up of black Ovambos, many of them insurgents who had been 'turned'. Koevoet killed or captured more than 3,000 SWAPO guerrillas in roughly 1,600 engagements, the vast majority involving Casspirs.

The 10-ton, 6.9 metre Casspir (which operates with a crew of two plus 10 combatants) was (and still is) designed to protect its occupants against the vicious blast of *three* Soviet TM-57 landmines detonated simultaneously, or roughly equivalent to 21 kg of TNT under a single wheel, or a double blast (14 kg of TNT) below the hull. One of the specifics is that occupants of the vehicle under wartime conditions should be strapped in: there are revolving portholes in the armour-plated frame from which to shoot.

Ironically, many Casspir occupants – combatants – preferred not to use straps, to the extent of sitting on the vehicle's roof because of a better field of fire. Still, even to those not secured, the Casspir offered excellent protection, although many injuries and even some deaths resulted from mine blasts, which could have been avoided had the heavy-duty, fitted straps been used.

At the end of it – there are still more than a thousand early generation Casspirs in service (2,800 of the original marks were produced in South Africa) – the vehicles were bought in quantity by more than 20 countries including the US and Saudi Arabia. Many news clips shown on our TV screens today from a Congo (still in a state of civil war) show Casspirs deployed in the white livery of the United Nations.

A Denel news report dated April 2013 said that a new generation of the armoured IFV, the Casspir 2000 was in production.

From a survivor's perspective – somebody who was actually involved in an anti-tank mine blast – my presence on board a Ratel IFV that momentous day in November 1981 was fortuitous. It was immediately after the Op Daisy attack (or to some, 'Oopsie Daisy' because it turned out to be a lemon) – and became a rather personal matter of being left either clinically deaf or permanently dead…

---

2   Eastern Bloc combat vehicles, in contrast – BTR-152, BMP-2s, BRDMs etc – were almost always abandoned after hitting a mine and even today, these remnants of long forgotten battles – thousands of them – are found along just about every secondary road in the country. The same situation held for Mozambique during its 15-year civil war with Renamo. After hostilities ended, a friend who lived in Vilancoulos travelled to Maputo by road and he was astounded by the number of vehicles blown-up or abandoned along that 700 kilometre stretch: there was a wreck just about every few hundred metres, he recalled.

A fairly lengthy operation launched several months after Operation Protea had knocked a hole in FAPLA's defences – our 61 Mechanised Battalion column penetrated several hundred kilometres into Angola's interior from Ovamboland – and ended as something of an anti-climax. It was actually the deepest penetration of Angola's interior by a South African armoured fighting group since Operation Savannah.

What we were not aware of until years later, was that SWAPO had been tipped off that we were on our way. That was probably the work of Moscow's man in the South African Defence Force, Commodore Dieter Gerhard, a 21-year KGB veteran while serving with the South African Navy.

The strike was ambitious because it covered a huge area of about 35 square kilometres and included several People's Liberation Army of Namibia (PLAN) bases at Chitequeta and Bambi on the road to Cassinga. SWAPO'S regional headquarters in the region was also targeted, but in the short time available it was impossible to cover all points of the compass.

At the end, 70 insurgents were killed, although relatively few in the guerrilla camp itself – and we lost several of our own, including a young candidate officer SF Coetzee who had followed me into a bunker in the main base and was killed by an anti-personnel mine that had been secreted under a thin layer of dirt on one of the steps we both used to get into the underground structure.

Physically I was a bigger man, with my larger, size-13 pair of boots and how I missed that booby trap, we'll never know.

The real drama only started the morning following the main attack. Our column was comprised of scores of vehicles – Ratels, Buffel troop carriers, supply trucks, communications vehicles, fuel and water bowsers, recovery vehicles and quite a few others – all of which been drawn in a traditional overnight laager formation. At dawn we were ordered to move out.

Within moments of the first truck pulling forward, an anti-tank mine was detonated, blowing a section of its mine-protected front-end apart. A minute later another vehicle, our only water-bowser, went up. Then one more, a troop carrier. All this was happening within a radius of a couple of hundred metres.

By now, just as our driver started to pull away, I'd clambered onto the turret of the command Ratel that had been my home for almost a week. We had two clear tracks in the irregular grass and bush-covered field ahead and he took the one to the right. I leant forward and was about to shout that he should swing towards the other one, clearly less used. Then it happened.

Our right front wheel detonated a TM-57 mine and in the blast (or so I'm told, because I knew nothing about it) the front half of the infantry fighting vehicle was hurled a metre or more in the air. Shortly afterwards I found myself lying on the ground several metres away.

I'd heard or saw nothing, except that I was alive. So was everybody else onboard that remarkable machine, including Lt Ariël Hugo, the young officer in command of Call-Sign 22, the same number that was painted foot-high on our hull.

I was left with a broken arm which resulted in a visit to the medical tent where several others who had been injured were also waiting. The upshot was that some of us were airlifted back to Sector 10 headquarters at Oshakati by Puma.

What was interesting about this event was the aftermath, which lasted a good part of what was left of the day.

Altogether five or six vehicles in that temporary base were destroyed by land mines, which was when the order was given to halt all movement. The force commander surmised that the guerrillas – clever buggers that they were and extremely efficient with it all – had done the impossible by penetrating our defences in the night and laid their mines. They'd probably moved about within paces of where I was sleeping in a shallow slit trench.

Totally paranoid by now that there must be many more mines buried in and around the base, I was worried about the adjacent helipad, my lifeline to the world outside, especially when I was ordered to get onto the chopper. If our adversaries were that good, I reasoned, surely the helicopter pad – carved out of raw bush the previous day – would also have been targeted by the enemy. Also, we were all very much aware that so far it had been anti-tank mines detonated: where the hell were the anti-personnel mines that the enemy customarily laid in tandem?

Experience had shown that they had been trained to lay them in clusters: four or five APs around every anti-tank mine.

The Pumas started to arrive a short while later and I was taken out on the third or fourth flight because there were others more seriously hurt. It was a relief to get away, but about 20 minutes into the flight we were called back to pick up another man who had been wounded. By then I'd hoped, somebody, *anybody,* would have swept the helipad for mines. But they had not.

What I did eventually learn, was that within hours of us flying out, a long line of men was formed up and, step-by-step they checked the entire area for mines. It took several hours, but they found plenty more, including quite a few of the dreaded APs. Two or three of these anti-personnel devices were uncovered, as I suspected they might be, on the helipad, just metres from where our pilots were operating. It was that close…

What was notable about my Ratel going up was not the fact that I was only slightly injured by almost seven kilograms of TNT or RDX exploding immediately under my position on the turret, but that nobody else on board was hurt. The other crew members were only badly shaken and, as with me, their eardrums smashed. It says much that the designers of this remarkable vehicle were able to factor in one of the most effective anti-mine coefficients developed in the post-Second World War period.

We are also aware that during the course of the war several Ratel IFVs were destroyed by enemy ground fire, but I know of only one soldier in a Ratel who died from a mine contact, though quite a few troops were killed in subsequent engagements with Soviet armour and artillery.

Buffel troop carriers and Casspir IFVs, the other machines fitted with blast-deflecting under-carriages, also made regular contact with anti-tank mines. In the case of the latter it was usually double-laid TM-57s (and in one memorable instance involving Koevoet Captain 'Sakkie' van Zyl, a triple TM-57s laid one on top of the other) that cost lives. That blast blew the Casspir several metres into the air but apparently nobody was killed.

Like father, like son, it is perhaps ironic that little more than a year later, my son Johan de Wet Venter – then finishing his military call-up in the SADF – was blown up by a landmine not far from where I'd been inadvertently targeted. He'd passed the rigorous Airborne Selection Course at 1 Parachute Battalion, but then decided to switch to 61 Mechanised Battalion Group.

Within a year, his unit had done some heavy fighting against the Cubans and FAPLA in a series of armoured strikes fairly deep into Angola.

The first I knew of his having been wounded was a call from somebody at 1 Military Hospital in Pretoria. They'd tracked me to Cape Town and suggested that I fly up as soon as possible, which I did. Johan told me that first evening that I was able to visit, that his unit had come up against some really stiff resistance, but, as he commented, Ratels were all-purpose fighting machines and his mates took the initiative each time. Also, he intimated, 'we're bloody well trained, Dad!'

It was not enemy fire that eventually laid him low, but a mine, or possibly more than one. The blast killed his corporal who was standing right next to him and he ended up with his arms ripped out of their sockets. Troopie Venter was hauled back to civilization with a bunch of others, most on stretchers that slotted neatly on racks fixed to the fuselage of a C-130.

Johan did not complain. He was given a few weeks off after he had been released from hospital and went back to his unit to fight another day. As he said, 'it could have been a lot worse…'

He had just turned 20, and curiously he never speaks about the war. His daughters do not even know that he was wounded.

Back to Operation Daisy: the first ever cross-border strike into Angola where General Constand Viljoen allowed a civilian TV crew access to actual combat inside Angola.

Media cynics back home scoffed at the programme we delivered a few weeks later for broadcast on the SABC. A female journalist on the Johannesburg *Sunday Times* said it was rubbish and that it could all have been just as easily staged in the Northern Transvaal, but then she was so far past the ANC's sphincter muscle that some of the hacks would speculate about her ability to breathe. In the end, facts spoke for themselves. Like Israel, being a relatively small country, the government could not hide the sort of casualty figures then coming out of an Angola at war.

My cameraman and I, by then, had already been on the border for a couple of weeks, mostly around Sector 10, but also with brief excursions into the Kaokoveld and Skeleton Coast (to fish, not to fight). Word came through that a cross-border attack would take place and it was suggested that we go along to film what Brigadier 'Witkop' Badenhorst, OC Sector 10, thought 'might be something the folks back home would like to see'.

Initially we were to travel with a bunch of soldiers in a Buffel, arguably the most uncomfortable modern troop carrier in any man's army. That soon proved impossible because the column stretched over several kilometres and had we carried on there, our camera and sound equipment would soon have become clogged with dust, or rattled to pieces by the never ending hard-edged jarring of the vehicle to which we clung.

I almost had to go down on my hands and knees to beg for 'another arrangement' which, in itself, was demeaning and not regarded kindly by military planners who like to do things by the book – and from a 'blerrie civvie' to boot!

The following day, its original occupants having been evicted 'under protest', we were led to the only vehicle available: a Command Ratel – Call-Sign 22, which, even with its 20mm cannon in place, still had almost enough space inside to sling a hammock.

This fantastic vehicle and crew greeted us almost like family and in a sense it was like being moved from Cattle Class to First Class. I was also able to experience this remarkable Squad IFV's abilities for myself under combat conditions and compare the 18-ton six-wheeled machine with many others in which I've been to war in various corners of the globe.

Developed indigenously by Sandok-Austral, the Ratel is still today considered a leader in the range of several dozen IFVs developed over the past half century. It has been copied several times, including Belgium's SIBMAS and the WZ-523 from Communist China. In performance (crew 4+6) and a wide operational range of 1,000 kms, it overshadows America's M2/M3 Bradley in several departments, including range – the Bradley manages only about half that distance.

In the broader picture, questions have been asked many times over the years whether the Ratel was as remarkable a fighting vehicle its designers originally intended it to be. Also, was this South African hybrid superior to many of the armoured personnel carriers of the day?

The unqualified answer to both questions is yes, and for several reasons, the first being that it was specifically designed for the kind of primitive African conditions in which this IFV would often find itself, and in doing so, it performed admirably. Had the Portuguese Army had anything like it, there is no doubt that things might have ended very differently by the time those African wars ended in 1974.

In later stages of South African involvement in the Angolan conflict, Ratels often disputed terrain and matched firepower with Soviet-built T-54/55 main battle tanks. They performed remarkably well, first because this infantry fighting was far more agile and manoeuvrable than anything the Soviets threw against them and their crews were a lot better trained. Suggest to somebody today to send out a battalion of thin-skinned battle-wagons against armour and the prospect would not even rate consideration. In Angola, the South Africans had little option.

Operation Daisy – 61 Mechanised Battalion Command Group at Chitiqueta with Roland de Vries sitting in the middle with his left shoulder to the camera. This was the deepest SADF combined operations penetration after Operation Savannah. (Author's photo)

With Operation Protea, some of the fighting vehicles headed north past the Etosha Pan towards Ruacana to avoid signalling intentions. (Roland de Vries)

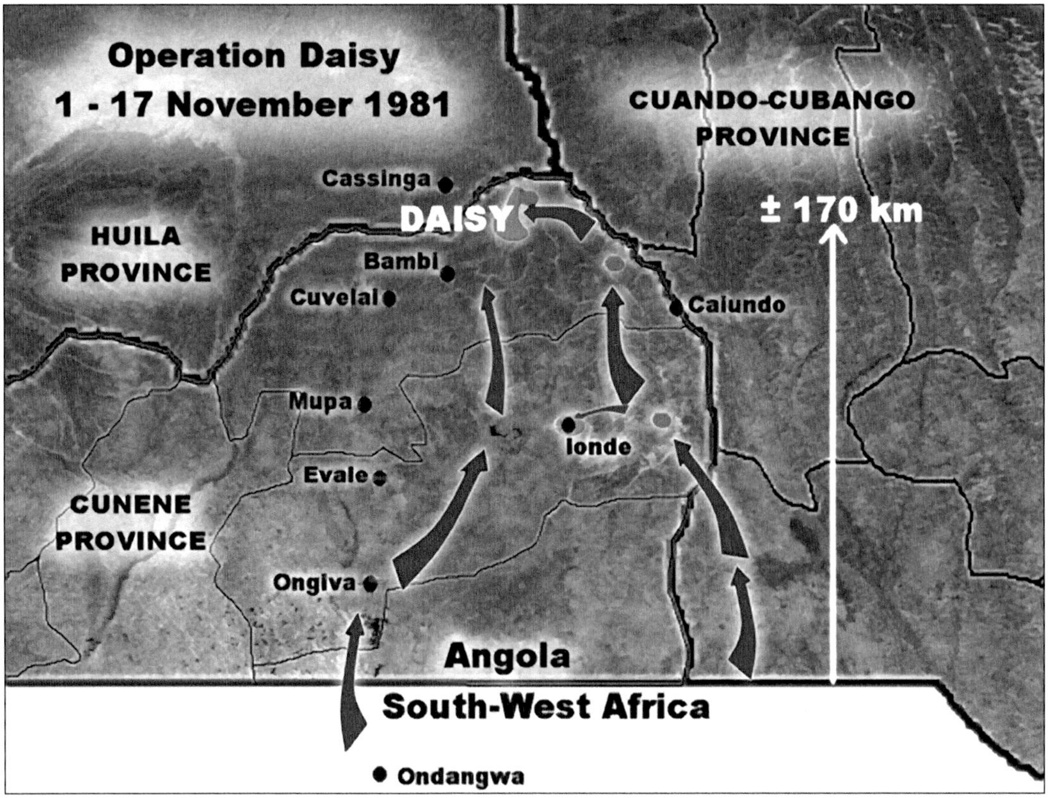

CAUGHT IN AN ANGOLAN MINEFIELD 329

Prior to every operation launched into Angola the men were gathered together for customary briefings and prayers.

Lieutenant Ariël Hugo who commanded Call Sign 22 on which the author moved into position and which took a big hit from a Soviet TM-57 anti-tank mine. (Photo: Ariël Hugo)

Troops moving forward on Buffel mine-protected troop carriers. Since Operation Daisy lasted almost three weeks this was a tough call for the men: although these mine-protected vehicle were relatively safe, they were hellishly uncomfortable.

The sharp end of a Ratel IFV attached to Charlie Squadron. (Photo courtesy of Roland de Vries)

As Major General de Vries says today, the young soldiers who took part in Op Daisy were eager for combat.

Enemy dead were moved back behind the lines to be finger-printed and if possible, identified. (Author's photo)

Because there was always the possibility of attack from the air, Op Daisy had several Triple-A units. (Author's photo)

CAUGHT IN AN ANGOLAN MINEFIELD 333

The right wheel of Ratel Call Sign 22 was destroyed by an anti-tank mine. The author suffered only a broken arm. (Photo: Ariël Hugo)

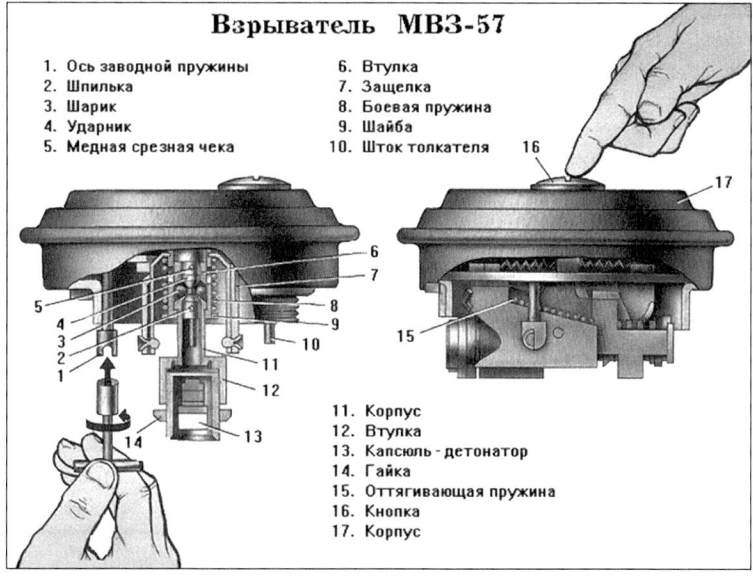

Cutaway of the Soviet TM-57 from a handbook in Russian captured along the way.

Lots of brand new Soviet military hardware was captured during these raids, usually handed over to UNITA for their use. (Photo courtesy of Roland de Vries)

Lieutenant Gert Minnaar was a member of the team headed by Ariël Hugo, who also provided the photo.

Obviously, the SADF had their *Olifant* (Elephant in Afrikaans) main battle tank, but in comparison to the almost 500 MBTs – T54/55s and later, T-72s – deployed operationally by the Angolan Army, they were comparatively few in number. Also, these over-heavy tracked juggernauts were difficult to move long distances across Angola's sandy terrain, parts of which were almost desert-like, the same problem incidentally that plagued FAPLA's armoured divisions.

The question most often asked in later years was how the Ratel IFV – under difficult Third World combat conditions – compared with enemy APCs during that period?

Overall, there was never any comparison. By definition an armoured personnel carrier transports men and equipment and rarely gets involved in a slugging match, unless of course it gets caught in one.

In contrast, Ratels deployed operationally in Angola went looking for trouble, and when they found it, those obstacles were destroyed, most times, anyway. Their basic design allowed them to be repaired in the field if the necessary equipment was handy, which it invariably was, together with the technicians needed to do the work. Like the Casspir, it took these professionals less than an hour to make our Ratel – Call-Sign 22 – operational again, and according to Lieutenant Ariël Hugo, they were sometimes able to hone that down to about 15 minutes if there had been no ancillary damage.

Would I today want to go to war in a Ratel in a country like Syria or Iraq, or Afghanistan especially? Probably not, for two reasons: in the first place, today's Middle East or Central Asian Islamic revolutionary is a very different fighting creature when compared to adversaries like FAPLA (or even FRELIMO). The majority of these African troops managed to do their jobs, even if inadequately trained, but they lacked the tenacity and the commitment of the kind of religious fanatic serving within the ranks of ISIS (Islamic State) today. Moreover, the Angolans never fielded a single suicide bomber…

Second, thin-skinned fighting vehicles were never intended to trade blows in open terrain with some of the fearsome firepower available to today's world of armoured combat.

Yet, looking back, there was one other factor that placed the Ratel ahead of the field of similar combat vehicles: like the Israelis, South African engineers designed their products with the thought in mind that it could be their sons that might be manning or using them. That factor alone created superior expertise, machining and workmanship which, throughout the 23-year Border War proved that what South Africa deployed in the ground war was almost always superior to what Moscow threw into the fray.

The South African Air Force might not have been able to match sophisticated 'Third Generation' military jets like the MiG-23 or Sukhoi in air combat with their 'front envelope' missile, but it was a different matter when it came to what was happening on the ground. Pretoria's battalions trounced FAPLA. While they had fewer men in the field, their equipment on the ground was streets ahead. Also, they were able to use resources at their disposal far more effectively.

One of the leading international figures in the development of several of these mine-protected vehicles (on the user side) is former Brigadier-General Tony Savides who served for many years as a permanent officer in the South African Army. His knowledge on the subject is regarded by his peers as encyclopaedic, and his comments on the development of the Ratel infantry fighting vehicle (IFV), or as he prefers, an infantry combat vehicle (ICV) – and its deployment in Angola – is invaluable.

I quote the Brigadier-General *in toto*:

The requirement for an ICV emanated directly from studies in the late 1960s and a move by the South African Army to 'Mobile warfare'. The user requirement was compiled in 1970 and finalised late 1972/early 1973.

While not specifically stated, the user requirement indicated a requirement for 'mechanised infantry' – hence the new battle handling that Major General Roland de Vries (then a major) and I were tasked to develop in 1975 and which was perfected by him and other combat commanders over the next decade or so.

Also of interest is that a 90mm variant was included in one of the first revisions of the user requirement – although it referred to a 'recoilless 90mm gun' (which only existed in the US so this was probably a 'lost in translation' aimed at a 90mm low recoil gun, as on the Eland armoured car).

In any event the 90mm variant was not pursued further. Fitting the Eland 90mm turret did indeed become an operational requirement eventually, but only from the Border War onwards and not Operation Savannah.

Several foreign contenders were evaluated between 1971 and 1973 together with a single local offering, the Springfield Büssing *Buffel* (no relation to the mine-protected vehicle of the same name).

Buffel was eventually selected as the basis for the new ICV – which was then named Ratel.

A British Saracen (the six-wheeled armoured vehicle built by Alvis and deployed for many years with the British Army) was used throughout the evaluations as a 'record vehicle' but was considered inadequate as an ICV.

The new, envisaged ICV was a completely fresh requirement, not a replacement for the Saracen (which, at that stage, was still used and intended to continue as the armoured personnel carriers of the South African Armoured Corps until disbanded in the early 1980s).

The first Ratel was the 'Ratel SS' (*sagtestaal* or mild steel) in 1973. Finally, in 1974, production of Ratel – as we know it today – got started. Thus, by the time Operation Savannah came around late 1975, the Ratel was well on its way. In fact, we evaluated the first Ratels off the production line that year.

Savannah therefore had little to do with Ratel – except to confirm the requirement for an ICV. Of course there were many other recommendations, including improved artillery, the need for mobile brigade headquarters and so on but time and money tended to play pre-eminent roles.

Also, the Ratel was never specifically developed for the so-called Border War but had as its primary function 'deployment with armour' (tanks). Operations with armoured cars and independent operations were thus secondary roles. Ratel's first deployment in its primary role was thus as part of 4 SAI (62 Mechanised Battalion Group) during Op Modular in Angola in 1987; so its (very successful) deployment from 1978 to 1986 was actually in its secondary roles. Altogether, some 1,600 Ratels were built.'

There were many variants – essentially relating to on-board equipment and use, rather than vehicle adaptation – and included the Ratel 90 FSV (Fire Support Vehicle, with a 90mm cannon), a Ratel 12.7 Command, Ratel 81mm Mortar, Ratel ZT-3 ATksMsl and the Ratel EAOS (Enhanced Artillery Observation System).

Some Ratels were used 'as is' as armoured ambulances while others were so deployed with the turret basket removed – this with much more interior space and ease of handling of stretchers.

A 'recovery package' was also developed and deployed – consisting of a clamp-on jib with a 'block and tackle' hoist at the rear and a front basket in which spare axles, sandbags and/or other equipment was carried as 'counter-balance'.

Current users of the Ratel infantry combat vehicle include: South Africa, Morocco, Jordan, Ghana and Rwanda.

> It should be mentioned, adds Brigadier General Savides, that the Hippo MPV was the forerunner of the Casspir and that the industry progressed from chassis-based to monocoque MPVs (except for the *Buffel, Kwêvoël* and one or two others which remained chassis-based). The first Mamba 4x2 vehicles – built by TFM Holdings – were based on locally-available 2-ton Toyota pick-up truck components (also a Vernon Joynt project). The Mamba 4x4s that followed came from Sandock Austral.
>
> Significantly MPV Holdings – which still builds armoured vehicles – had been involved in early developmental work and manufacture of the Casspir vehicle since 1977 and the dedicated manufacturing plant in Olifantsfontein, midway between Johannesburg and Pretoria was specifically built in 1979 to accommodate the production of this remarkable vehicle which remains in service world-wide.
>
> As he points out, the Mamba fitted the bill as a versatile cross-country 4x4, using excess Unimog components available in the SADF (among others, when Unimog soft-skinned ambulances were phased out by the Medics). While the Buffel retained the Unimog ladder-frame chassis, the Mamba was a monocoque and only had double-mine protection under its wheels and single-mine protection under the hull. He stresses that mine-protection standards quoted and used in those distant days differed substantially from NATO's STANAG 4569 Protection Requirement (Mines) that emerged later.
>
> What is certain is that neither the Casspir nor the Mamba in their original forms would have passed the applicable STANAG tests, which, in retrospect, were not so much about *limiting* the effects of blast, but rather about *permissible* injuries.

It is worth mentioning that Major General Roland de Vries's book *Mobile Warfare – a Perspective for Southern Africa*, was published in South Africa in 1987 while he was still a colonel. That work, seminal to subsequent developments at the time, outlined his thinking on the development of operational concepts and military doctrine for mobile conventional warfare within the Southern African context.

22

Special Forces: The Recces – Best of the Best

The South African Army's Reconnaissance Regiment – or the Recces, as they are colloquially known – distinguished themselves with great honour during that country's 23-year-long Border War. They paid a heavy price, of course: operators could expect to be deployed in operations against the enemy – primarily behind enemy lines – for an average of nine or ten months a year. Many of the operators did this for a decade or more, and then went on to join private military companies on active service in countries like Iraq or Afghanistan. Quite a few ended up in Executive Outcomes.

More striking are the statistics most commonly bandied about: By 1988 – as the war was drawing to a close – roughly 100,000 servicemen had applied for the pre-selection interview in attempts to qualify. In the end, roughly 480 aspirants successfully passed a series of extremely rigorous obstacles that could sometimes last weeks, often in the most exacting African jungle, bush or semi-desert terrain.

Of that tally, more than 80 were killed on operations. At the same time, about 55 per cent of Special Forces operatives were wounded in action.

Also interesting was the fact that the total strength of the Reconnaissance Regiment was never more than 250 Special Forces operators at any one time – and that for the duration of decades of hostilities.

A basic requirement for entry was the ability to speak two languages and be between the ages of 18 and 28 at the onset of training. Moreover, to become an operator one had to complete the following cycle successfully; that of pre-selection, then the tough selection course followed by an operational training cycle and finally, the first deployment, usually behind enemy lines.

The initial operational training cycle comprised (for most operators) of the following courses: basic parachute training; water orientation (small boats); survival; bush craft and tracking; 'know your enemy'; air orientation; demolition work as well as minor tactics. This complex set of disciplines would usually be followed by an operational deployment which many regarded as part of the process of achieving qualification. Only then was the badge awarded.

There were other quirks that individuals needed to overcome. For instance, packs that operators hauled along with them on external operations usually weighed in somewhere between 60 and 80 kilograms. For small-team operations or long-distance strikes it could be as much as 100 kg. The heaviest load ever carried by an operator was 130 kgs (286 pounds) – an event that took place deep inside Angola.

An anonymous source on the web went so far as to compare selection processes between various national Special Forces and came up with the following: True or false, he reckoned that 'of the 50 or so Special Forces-focused books I have read so far, the toughest described selection must be that of the Recces of South Africa.'

He went on: 'In his book *19 with a bullet*, Granger Korff recalls how after being selected – together with a handful of other paratroopers (whose own 'Hell Week' is (was) similar to that of the SEALs, without the cold water part) – he was made to run or march non-stop for eight weeks in the bush.' That was then, because rigours have been substantially modified.

Korff: 'One of the candidates was actually attacked by a lioness and his team fought her off barehanded. They would sleep with their backs to the trees, feet facing outwards, as any limb sticking out might be chowed by a marauding hyena, packs of which seemed to follow Recce trainees around in anticipation of a meal.

'The author recalls one of his teammates losing 12 kilograms over the course of the seven weeks that they managed to keep going. Since these same Recces were eventually to be dropped in small teams hundreds of kilometres inside enemy territory – with no hope of support or back-up – the selection process was designed accordingly.

As a comparison, last heard, the US Army's Delta Force's own 'endless timed march' had a duration of one week. The South African Reconnaissance Regiment selection course was eventually limited to five 'tough' days, with the accent in later years on psychological evaluation.

In a review of some of the achievements (and obstacles faced by fully-badged Special Forces operators) the following was tabulated:

1 At the beginning of 2014, just over 1,000 persons had qualified as South African Special Forces operators. Of those, around 200 are deceased.
2 Throughout its history, South Africa's Special Forces teams have been non-racial and some units even ended up having more black than white qualified operators.
3 The most highly decorated Special Forces operator to date is a black African operator from 5 Reconnaissance Regiment, who was awarded the *Honoris Crux* Gold in 1980. Only six HC Golds were ever issued.
4 Special Forces operators were allowed to wear beards while deployed on operations. Similarly, long hair – as displayed in some photographs – resulted from long periods on ops where hair cuts were impractical.
5 An unofficial form of achievement within the South African Special Forces is reached when an operator has completed a tough assignment behind enemy lines, traversing vast distances on foot with full kit. This usually ensured acceptance by the more senior operators.
6 During the Angolan war 95 percent of all Special Forces operations were carried out well within enemy territory – over distances of anything from ten to 2,000 kilometres beyond own deployments.
7 During reconnaissance of enemy targets and fixed positions, a Special Forces team was usually comprised of between two and four operators. Quite often they would conduct line-of-sight reconnaissance, sometimes from the verge of hostile positions and it was not unusual for the operators to penetrate inside those positions if required to do so. It was axiomatic that these installations were usually, as the saying goes, 'thick with the enemy'.
8 South African Special Forces have the highest statistical Killed in Action (KIA) ratio of any South African military unit since the Battle of Delville Wood in the First World War.
9 During the Angolan war, when deployed in cross-border operations among Soviet and Warsaw Pact forces, South African Special Forces operators came up against Russians, Ukrainians, East Germans and other Soviet personnel. Also present were Cubans, North Koreans, Vietnamese,

South African Navy Strike Craft – such as this one moored at Donkergat, operational headquarters of Douw Steyn's 4 Recce at Langebaan, near Saldanha Bay on the West Coast – played a seminal role in a succession of maritime raids on both Angola and Mozambique harbours. These remarkably versatile 'Minister Class' fighting ships were named after South African cabinet ministers and the strike craft flotilla was known as SAS Scorpion. Their

acquisition by the Pretoria Government followed a 1974 contract signed with Israeli Military Industries for the construction of three of their modified Reshef-class vessels at the Haifa facility of Israeli Shipyards. A further three were built by the Sandock-Austral shipyard in Durban, South Africa, with another three coming from the same facility several years later.
(Photo: Douw Steyn)

and various other Soviet-aligned military personnel. These included regular army, air force, navy and enemy Special Forces elements such as Soviet Spetsnaz Special Forces.[1]

10   During later stages of the Angolan war, the Soviet Union diverted much of its military supplies – initially intended for Afghanistan to Angola – including the most sophisticated Russian arms outside the Soviet Union itself. Angolan airspace at that stage was classified as the most hostile in the world, with the Soviet aircraft dominating Angolan skies for virtually the entire war. This meant that Special Forces operators never had the possibility of re-supply, support or evacuation on the majority of their operations. Once in, they were isolated until their return.

Historically, 1 Reconnaissance Commando was the first South African Special Forces unit, founded by General Fritz Loots, General Officer Commanding, South African Special Forces.

He appointed 12 qualified paratroopers (referred to over the years as 'The Dirty Dozen') as founder members. Included in this formation was Jan Breytenbach who was placed in command of what he sometimes referred to as his 'motley band of unconventional warriors.'

It was actually what took place in the Biafran War in the late 1960s that led to the formation of a Special Forces group in South Africa. This was eventually to become the famous Reconnaissance Regiment.

Colonel Breytenbach's role in that West African conflict – with Pretoria having given the nod (he was then a major) – was conducted under the auspices of the French Secret Service.

His group of operatives was limited to perhaps a dozen men, with a semi-permanent headquarters in Libreville, the capital of Gabon – of which there was rarely more than a handful who were operational inside Biafra at any one time. He tended to limit those inside the beleaguered Nigerian enclave to perhaps four or five individuals, one of whom was a radio operator and another who doubled as a medic, with solid experience of battlefield trauma.

Significantly, while he and his men were involved in many strikes against Nigerian Army units – the majority comprised of a series of long-range penetrations behind enemy lines – none of his men were killed or even seriously wounded.

There were a few wounds, including Breytenbach himself, who took a bullet in the gut. But here too, he was fortunate: 'It was a glancing shot in the stomach, in on the left and out under the skin on the right, without actually penetrating my body. A couple of Band Aids kept infection out… and yes, I suppose you could call it luck…' Interestingly, when Jan relayed this information to the author at his home in Sedgefield, he caught his wife Rosalind by surprise (he had never told her that he'd almost 'copped it' in Biafra).[2]

An interesting sidelight to Jan Breytenbach's Biafran exploits was that on his return to the Republic, South Africa's Military hierarchy accepted that the country needed to create a force that could handle the kind of unique and dangerous tasks for which the British Special Air Service was already renowned. Following a lengthy briefing to Military Intelligence in Pretoria, General Loots put the proposal to his senior commanders and the concept was given the go-ahead. Obviously, Breytenbach was to lead it.

He was quite effusive about it during my visit:

---

1   *Spetsnaz*: Soviet (and today Russian) Special Purpose Forces or Special Purpose Military Units), an umbrella term for special forces in Russian. Historically, the term referred to special military units controlled by the military intelligence service GRU (Spetsnaz GRU).
2   Al J. Venter; *Biafra's War: A Tribal Conflict in Nigeria that Left a Million Dead;* Helion, 2015.

A 4 Reconnaissance Regiment operator appropriately kitted out and ready to go into action from one of South Africa's French-built Daphne Class submarines. (Photo: Douw Steyn)

Danie van den Bergh took this photo of the strike craft that had earlier served as the *SAS Frans Erasmus*.

While Luanda harbour today is one of the most modern in Black Africa, largely because of Angola's massive oil industry, the adjacent areas though which the South African attackers approached their target was pretty run down, with several derelict vessels and underwater obstacles

A youthful Major Douw Steyn briefs his men on an upcoming raid on one of the Angolan ports.

Soviet aircraft carrier *Minsk* that visited Luanda about the time that the Recces sank three enemy ships in Angola's southern harbour of Namibe.

The port of Namibe today: it formed an important strategic adjunct to Moscow's ongoing hostilities in southern Angola during the Border War.

The South African submarine *Johanna van der Merwe* was often involved in maritime aspects of the war. It is permanently moored in Simonstown these days. (Photo: Dean Wingrin)

The Cuban freighter *Habana* sunk alongside its Namibe mooring by a Recce strike group. Two more ships were sent to the bottom on that raid, both Soviet. (Photo: Douw Steyn)

The South African naval tanker *SAS Tafelberg* took part – at a distance, with its onboard helicopters – in several raids in the south Atlantic and south Indian oceans. (SADF photo)

A Soviet Kashin Class guided-missile destroyer was rushed to Namibe from Luanda immediately after the South African attack.

The trouble was that I had some very different ideas from Loots…I wanted our main base to be at Oudtshoorn, and for several very good reasons.

To be able to do their job properly, Special Forces personnel need to fire their guns every single day; it is all part of training and readiness.

Additionally, Oudtshoorn was in the Eastern Cape, close to rows of mountains, a vast open Karoo terrain and some huge forests along the coast. For training, it was the ideal location. Also, we wouldn't be limited by space considerations. But the general had his own ideas – and it wasn't the only thing we differed on. He wanted what was to become known as the Recces to be based at the Bluff in Durban, on the verge of one of South Africa's largest cities which, frankly, was plain stupid.

I pointed out the shortcomings to him – including problems with weapons training – but my argument cut no ice, which underscored the fact that while General Fritz Loots headed an outstandingly elite and competent fighting force that in its day compared favourably with the SAS or America's Navy SEALS, he'd never actually experienced any real combat.

… Fact is, the man had made up his mind and that was that,' added the colonel, with undisguised disdain…

The six-month West African posting in Biafra was to have a significant influence, both on Breytenbach's career and on subsequent developments in the South African Army. On his return to Pretoria from Biafra, he was chosen in 1971 to found 1 Reconnaissance Commando. Even more significant is that while few soldiers anywhere have the privilege of forming a military combat unit of their own, Jan Breytenbach created three.

Britain's SAS emerged from David Stirling's efforts in the Western Desert during the Second World War; General Orde Wingate founded the Chindits; Portuguese veteran Alves Cardoso was responsible for Portugal's *Comandos Africanos* (as well as the *Flechas*), while the irrepressibly innovative Ron Reid-Daly created Rhodesia's Selous Scouts. As a young soldier, Ron also served with the British SAS in Malaya and was rewarded with an MBE for his efforts; some operator!

As for Breytenbach, apart from the so-called 'Recces', he was also tasked with taking in hand a large squad of recalcitrant Portuguese-speaking Angolan Army soldiers that had fallen out with the ruling Marxist clique in Luanda to form 32-Battalion, known colloquially as the 'Buffalo Battalion' (details of which can be found in Chapter 18).

That unit was literally 'forged in battle' during the South African invasion of Angola in 1975 and the creation of 44-Parachute Brigade followed. Another of Colonel Breytenbach's efforts was the formation of the South African Army's Guerrilla School, which he commanded until his retirement in 1987.

Although South Africa's 'Recces' are generally spoken of as a single Special Forces unit, there were actually several components, starting with the establishment of Jan Breytenbach's 'Dirty Dozen' in 1970. Training of 1 Reconnaissance Commando started in the Eastern Cape and was then formally moved to Durban in 1972. Meantime unit members underwent a series of specialized courses both in South Africa and in France. It was during this time that they were blooded on Angolan soil.

Two years later, in 1974, Special Forces Headquarters was established in Pretoria. In 1980 it moved to Swartkop Park in Pretoria, unofficially referred to as 'Speskop'. Also in 1974, 2 Reconnaissance Commando was created in Johannesburg. This was a Special Forces Citizen Force (Territorial Army).

By 1976, 5 Reconnaissance Commando was established in Durban and at Duku Duku, on the Natal's north coast. It was moved to Phalaborwa in the Eastern Transvaal in 1980. That year the Special Forces School came into being, part of 1 Reconnaissance Commando.

A major step was taken in 1978 with the establishment of 4 Reconnaissance Commando at Langebaan, formerly a whaling station on South Africa's west coast, north of Cape Town. Since 4 Recce was involved principally with water-based or maritime operations, it can justly be put on par with Britain's Special Boat Service.

Two years later (after the collapse of Rhodesia) saw the creation of 3 Reconnaissance Commando, comprised largely of former Selous Scouts. Similarly, 6 Reconnaissance Commando – consisting of former Rhodesian Special Air Service personnel, was established in Durban.

The integration of former Rhodesian Special Forces personnel into the SADF was not a success and within a year, the majority of these operators had moved on, some to join Britain's SAS where one member eventually went on to command one of the elite units. Those that remained were amalgamated with 1 and 5 Reconnaissance Commandos.

The final move came in 1981 when the Special Forces Reconnaissance Commandos were re-designated as Special Forces Reconnaissance Regiments, as follows:

Special Forces Headquarters (SFHQ) – Pretoria
1 Reconnaissance Regiment (1RR) – Durban
4 Reconnaissance Regiment (4RR) – Langebaan
5 Reconnaissance Regiment (5RR) – Phalaborwa

The number of operations conducted by the various Special Forces units over three decades run into the hundreds. Most of these remain secret and one of the problems facing anybody wishing to write about them invariably results in the scribe coming up against the usual 'blank wall'.

In preparing his own book *Iron Fist from the Sea* for publication, former Lieutenant Colonel Douw Steyn, founder member of 4 Reconnaissance Regiment, told me it did not take him long to discover that many of those involved in these clandestine operations simply refused to talk about what they did during the course of the war, even though he was one of their own.

As he records in Chapter 12 of his own book, while most, if not all, (of our) covert operations, especially maritime ones, were classified Top Secret and with a few notable exceptions, were never made public, there were always a considerable number of serving members, especially naval personnel and other supporting services, who were involved and well aware of Recce participation but sworn to secrecy. Thus very little was ever revealed. It is those components that make this book – co-authored by Arné Söderlund – such a unique and invaluable source.

One of the most fascinating – and ultimately historically important events of the Border War involved 4 Recce blowing the bridge at Cuito Cuanavale, an enormously strategic Angolan army and air force base in south-central Angola. By knocking out the bridge, it followed that several divisions of Soviet/Cuban/Angolan armour were stranded on the east bank of a fast flowing river and had no means to reach the safety of Cuito. All that hardware – many millions of dollars' worth of equipment, some of it high-tech – was abandoned within days and those involved in the battles fled, usually discarding their uniforms and rifles along the way.

Soviet and Cuban commanders directly involved in the battle had seen disaster approaching even before the bridge was destroyed and the majority were air-lifted out of the battle zone a day or two before the entire front collapsed in disarray. It was no secret that they left their 'compadres' and many of their fellow-officers in the lurch, the majority were ubsequently hunted down by UNITA and killed.

Codenamed 'Operation Coolidge', the battles that were waged in that region has become the subject of a great deal of controversy.

Essentially, the Battle of Cuito Cuanavale was a series of engagements between the Cuban-backed Angolan Army (FAPLA) and the SADF – as well as UNITA conventional and guerrillas forces – near the important town of Cuito Cuanavale during the latter part of the Angolan Civil War.

Wikipedia spells it out in simple terms, which centre on FAPLA forces initially being deployed to eliminate the UNITA position at Jamba and Mavinga, where the rebels had established their primary operating bases.

Following a number of failed attempts to take the settlements in 1986, eight FAPLA brigades mustered for a final offensive – *Operação Saludando Octubre* – in August 1987 'with extensive auxiliary support from one of Angola's closest military allies, the Soviet Union'.

They were joined by a number of Cuban armoured and motorised units, that had become more directly committed to the fighting for the first time during Havana's lengthy intervention. Soviet weapons deliveries to FAPLA were also accelerated, including over a hundred T-62 tanks and strike aircraft seconded from the Warsaw Pact's strategic reserve.

South Africa, which shared a common border with Angola through South-West Africa, was determined to prevent FAPLA from gaining control of Jamba and allowing insurgents of the Marxist South West African People's Organization (SWAPO) to operate in the region.

Saludando Octubre prompted the South African military to underpin the defence of Jamba and launch Operation Modular with the objective of stopping FAPLA's offensive. The Angolan government and its Soviet advisory personnel had failed to make contingency plans for South African intervention, and that despite advance warnings from *Umkhonto we Sizwe* of an imminent SADF counterattack.

The campaign which followed culminated in the largest battle involving armour on African soil since the Second World War and, according to some accounts, the second largest clash of African military forces in history. FAPLA was poorly disciplined yet well equipped, and Cuban air power proved to be a decisive advantage over the SADF. Nevertheless, the advancing FAPLA forces were frequently encircled and destroyed in running clashes with the much nimbler South African Ratel infantry fighting vehicles: effectively Soviet tanks battling South African 'thin-skinned' vehicles. The FAPLA offensive was halted with heavy casualties and abandoned shortly afterwards.

Notably, the SADF had a political imperative to avoid casualties wherever possible, and had orders to avoid the town unless it fell into their hands without a fight, so therefore made no attempt to follow up on its advantage and to capture the town.

By the mid-1980s, the Angolan armed forces had received a massive amount of modern Soviet equipment and had built up their forces in the south.

In 1985, with some 30,000 Cuban troops in support, numerous Soviet advisors deployed at all levels within the Angolan brigades, and a sophisticated Soviet air defence umbrella to deter the SAAF, they were ready to attack and defeat UNITA in its stronghold in the south-east of Angola.

The two-pronged offensive, drawn up by the senior Soviet advisor to Angola, with planning input from the Cuban and Soviet advisors on the ground, was named *Congreso II* and commenced in 1985. The main thrust, the assault on Mavinga, UNITA's main logistic base, was commenced from FAPLA's main logistic and staging base at Cuito Cuanavale, which caught UNITA unprepared, and was only stopped about 10 kilometres from Mavinga through South African intervention.

This offensive motivated the successful Reconnaissance Regiment attack on Namibe by South African Special Forces the following year, code named Operation Drosdy. As a result of the destruction of fuel supplies in the port, the advance on Mavinga from Cuito Cuanavale in 1986 was halted and eventually cancelled as UNITA then had the opportunity to attack Cuito Cuanavale and destroy further supplies.

In January 1986, as a result of the close call of 1985, the decision was taken to attach South African liaison teams to UNITA during their operation to disrupt the FAPLA build-up, named Operation Chuva. These teams were led by Colonel Bert Sachse and Commandant Les Rudman with Colonel Fred Oelschig in overall command and reporting to Chief of Staff Intelligence (CSI).

Deploying along possible access routes, these teams identified ways and means to disrupt the FAPLA advance and provided advice and practical training to UNITA forces deployed for the defence of Mavinga.

One of the plans was to deprive the advancing forces of logistic support and Cuito Cuanavale's strategic placement suggested a good opportunity. The small town with its airfield and military stores lay below the confluence of the Cuito and Cuanavale Rivers and on the east bank. Access to the east – and where the future tank battles took place – was over a single lane bridge with no other crossing points in the area.

The destruction of this bridge would achieve logistical disruption and limit the effect of any forces not yet deployed to the East, something dealt with in detail in the following chapter.

A short while later, mid-1986, the Reconnaissance Regiment launched its most ambitious cross border raid of the war, underscoring the enormously important role this Special Forces unit played in the struggle.

It was one of the most decisive South African military strikes since the end of the Second World War and the ramifications were felt all the way back to the Kremlin. It also resulted in, if not ending Soviet Navy involvement in the South Atlantic, then substantially limiting it.

Until then, to Washington's consternation, the Soviet Navy had been a major player in the region, with Luanda hosting a variety of key Eastern Bloc ships over the years, including major units such as the fixed wing aircraft carrier (with cruiser armament) the *Minsk*, the Soviet anti-submarine helicopter carrier *Moskva* as well as a full range of other large Russian warships like the *Talinn*, a guided-missile cruiser. All underscored Moscow's long-term interest in what was going on in Southern Africa at the time.

Aware that the port of Namibe in Angola's 'deep south' was being used to supply the Angolan Army and its Soviet and Cuban cohorts in a succession of thrusts eastwards in bids to cripple Jonas Savimbi's UNITA, Pretoria examined ways of halting the flow of both weapons and fuel from this strategic deep water harbour. The planners eventually settled on Operation Drosdy, the biggest single Special Forces operation ever launched by the South Africans.

There were 58 Recce operators in several teams involved, most from 4 Reconnaissance Regiment. The contingent included many specialist operators from 1 Reconnaissance Regiment at the Bluff.

South Africa's Navy played a critical role, with the French-built Daphne Class submarine *Johanna van der Merwe* captained by Commander Jan Rabie doing much of the legwork over several days in the approaches to the target – most times at periscope depth. Also involved were three strike craft and the supply ship SAS *Tafelberg* (Captain Chris Moon) with a pair of SAAF Pumas taken onboard for liaison and emergencies. Operations commander of the venture was a namesake, Lt Col JJ (Hannes) Venter.

The strike craft involved were SAS *Kobie Coetzee* (captained by Lieutenant Commander Gert Engelbrecht), SAS *Hendrik Mentz* (Lt Cdr Jonny Kamerman) and P1561, later renamed SAS *Jan Smuts* (Cdr Bryan Donkin). Naval Task Force Commander was Cdr 'Jock' Deacon, himself a strike craft veteran.

The raid was a remarkable success with no losses on the part of the South Africans. This was all the more surprising because the attack spanned several nights, Recce teams going in after dark and emerging intact well before sun-up. Using small craft, they remained undetected and managed to conduct their surveys unopposed, though there were a few narrow scrapes.

In the actual attack a lot of damage was affected ashore by blowing up three of four large fuel tanks as well as a host of electrical installations and the sinking of two Soviet ships *Kapitan Chirkov* (16,000 tons) and the 12,000-ton *Kapitan Vislobokov*, both loaded with ammunition and sunk at their moorings. Because the limpet mines used were fitted with anti-lifting devices, it took months to make things safe and the *Vislobokov* was so badly damaged it was eventually scrapped.

Also destroyed was a Cuban freighter, also with a cargo of explosives. This was the 6,000-ton *Habana* which capsized and sank after two mines tore her hull apart. She settled on the bottom, blocking off a quarter of Namibe's quay for three years until a salvage team from Havana could clear her cargo, mainly 152mm artillery shells. She was also eventually declared derelict, towed offshore and sunk.

Colonel Douw Steyn – then a major – was in charge of the shore component and he provides a remarkable insight to an operation, details of which have never been released before.

For a start, there were those in Moscow who felt that the South Africans had neither the ability or expertise to launch such a complicated military venture, to the extent that for a long time the Soviets believed the attack was initiated by a mobile land force. They took it very seriously though and sent a string of naval craft to Namibe, starting with the Kashin Class guided-missile destroyer *Stroymy* that arrived days later.

A couple of interesting asides emerged much later. Because the actual attack was put back one day because of technical problems (Steyn's reconnaissance teams had already been ashore the previous night) there was quite a bit of shipping movement. This was fortuitous because two of the three ships sunk were not yet at their berths: they were held up by a Greek and an Italian freighter that took an unusually long time to unload their cargoes. Only after they got underway were the *Habana* and the *Kapitan Chirkov* able to come alongside.

Additionally, the initial recce team had earlier reported the presence of a liquid petroleum gas tanker tied up at the harbour's iron ore quay. Curiously, it departed Namibe at 2200 hours, just as the strike force was heading in from deep water, both totally unaware of each others' presence. In fact, they must have passed each other in the dark and it would have been a very different story had contact been made.

The full story of Operation Drosdy can be found in Chapter 10 of *Iron Fist from the Sea*: (pages 332-357). Written by Douw Steyn and Arné Söderland and published in Britain by Helion, I would rate this work as the best single volume of military history to emerge from this period of Southern African hostilities.[3]

Additionally, it has details of an earlier 1981 Reconnaissance Regiment strike where Soviet ships in Luanda harbour were knocked out and Operation Kerslig – which took place in the vicinity of Luanda harbour – and caused heavy damage to the county's major oil refinery.

Captain 'Woody' Woodburne – who would later become chief of the navy – was appointed operations commander onboard the strike craft SAS *Oswald Pirow* (captained by Commander Arné Söderland). He was accompanied by strike craft SAS *Jim Fouche* (Cdr Fanie Uys). Douw Steyn, then a captain, commanded the raiding group while maritime liaison was provided by the hydrographic vessel SAS *Protea* (Captain Bob Pieters).

Though that operation was a success, with Angola being left with only two weeks' supply of petrol and the refinery taking six months to get on stream again, one of the operators was killed

---

3 Published by Helion in the United Kingdom, 2014.

in an explosion and two more seriously wounded. The rest of the attack force and their craft were able to withdraw into deep water before dawn.

It would be trite to say that the book reads like an adventure story: that it does which makes for a series of remarkable high-tech military operations. It is certainly comparable to anything published in recent years on Britain's Special Air Service. It says a lot that since the book was published in 2014, it has gone into several editions.

At the time of writing, there are plans – at the behest of Russian interests – to make a documentary on the South African attack. Meetings have been held in Moscow with those involved and the project is on schedule.

According to Colonel Steyn, the Russian veterans rate the attack as the single biggest defeat suffered by Moscow's forces since the end of the Second World War.

In a recent issue of *Scientia Militaria*, Dr Abel Esterhuyse, Associate Professor of Strategy at Stellenbosch University, reviewed the book and made the comment that the work is much more than a unit history.

He wrote:

> It traces the development of a unique seaborne capability by the South African Special Forces [providing] an outline of the creation of a specific military unit that housed these South African SEALS and offers a detailed outline of the history and unique operations this small group of men conducted between 1972 and 1990.
>
> The uniqueness of the unit is highlighted by the fact that, of the 480 soldiers who qualified as special force operators between 1978 and 1989, only 45 served in 4 Reconnaissance Regiment.

On a more personal note, while comparing 4 Reconnaissance Regiment to the American SEALS, the nature of work done by these South Africans are regarded by many as much more akin to Britain's Special Boat Service. Either way, 4 Recce was a most remarkable body of fighting men.

23

The Recces Blow the Bridge at Cuito Cuanavale

The damage to Luanda's war effort in the south of the country that would result from destroying the bridge at Cuito Cuanavale was not lost on Dr Jonas Savimbi. For a start, with the bridge gone – the only river crossing for several hundred kilometres and therefore immensely strategic – there would be no way back for the huge Angolan, Cuban and Soviet armoured force that had swept eastwards over the bridge in their efforts to wipe out the rebels. With grateful thanks to Douw Steyn and Arné Söderland for this material, linked to the Battle of Cuito Cuanavale from their book Iron Fist from the Sea: South Africa's Seaborne Raiders 1978–1988[1]

UNITA's Attempt on the Bridge

An attempt had been made to blow up a number of the poles supporting it in a clandestine attack. The operation was conducted by the UNITA Chief of Engineers, Captain Chicucuma with a team of 45 men, 39 of whom were bearers to carry all equipment to the departure point on the Cuanavale River.

At 2100 once the Zodiac inflatable boat had been assembled and launched, all equipment, including a dozen sandbags, each containing 3.5kg of explosive, was loaded and a team of six members made up of two rowers, two engineers and two commandos set out down the river. They reached the confluence ten minutes later, where they established that the flow was about two metres per second.

With no moon and in rainy weather, they moved swiftly down the meandering river but on approaching the bridge discovered that the flow varied from bank to bank and the boat was swept past. This forced them to land on the west bank and move carefully up-river to regain the bridge. The flow on the eastern bank was too strong and they thus commenced fixing the explosives to the piles on the western bank.

Unfortunately, while an engineer was attaching the cortex to the charges, the boat was swept away from under him and he fell into the water. The team quickly moved under the bridge and dragged the boat in with them as the sentry on the east bank came across to investigate the splash.

The sentry then started shooting into the water but was wounded by one of the commandos and fell into the river, continuing to shout for the other guards. The detonators were quickly set and the team emerged from under the bridge and withdrew amidst hectic firing into the river, to a RV point and safety.

---

1 Published by Helion in the United Kindgom, 2014.

Unfortunately, the attack, although resourceful, was unsuccessful. In May the same year, 4RR were tasked to carry out a reconnaissance on the bridge in order to obtain essential intelligence on its construction to enable a similar attempt at a later stage. This operation was given the name Coolidge.

Coolidge Preparations and the Recce

On being tasked to do the reconnaissance of a guarded bridge behind enemy lines, 4RR immediately realised that this was a new capability and planned a work-up and preparation phase to ascertain the required freshwater skills and identify the appropriate equipment for riverine work. This preparation phase consisted of two weeks of practical training and exercises in and around Donkergat, followed by a week on Angola's Kavango River.

The recce team would consist of two operators with a second pair fully trained as a reserve team. A six-man back-up team would provide direct operational support, while a four-man support team of signallers, a maintainer and a chef would accompany them for part of the deployment. As the target was behind enemy lines and in a staging area for a number of enemy brigades, the infiltration of the recce team required considerable planning and support from various own forces in the area.

The plan called for the team under the command of the Commander 4.1 Commando, Commandant Douw Steyn, to be inserted some 23 km upstream from the target and from there to paddle at night to a position a few km north of the bridge, where their kayaks would be destroyed and concealed before swimming to the bridge to conduct the recce. Once completed, the two operators would swim downstream to rendezvous with a recovery team. The operation was planned to take place over the period 22 – 24 July and a tactical HQ would be established roughly 30 kilometres east of the target.

The divers selected to conduct the recce were Staff Sergeant (SSgt) Anton Beukman and Sergeant (Sgt) 'Maddie' Adam. Prior to deployment, briefings were given to Colonel Oelschig and his teams, who, with UNITA, would provide the means of infiltration and withdrawal. They were also in a position to provide excellent intelligence on the target and enemy forces deployed in the area.

A meeting was also arranged with top UNITA officials in Mavinga on D-13 and their full support was achieved. The UNITA leader, General Jonas Savimbi, in an inscription to the Operation Commander, summed up their reasons for full support by stating 'Our region needs firm convictions for our people to remain free. The price is high. Let us meet the challenges of our lifetime.'

On 12 June, the teams and their equipment were flown to Rundu where they were finally briefed on the operation and the target. The next day, they conducted a helicopter familiarisation recce of the small town of Dirico and the Kavango River, where they would conduct their final preparations and rehearsal, deploying there on the 15th. Four days later on D-4 the teams were flown to Mavinga for further briefings and checks.

Finally, with all systems go, on the 22nd at D-1, the teams were deployed to a position 10km east of the Tactical HQ by helicopter and then by vehicle to the HQ, where Commandant Rudman and General Demosthenes, the UNITA Chief of Staff, did the final briefing. The following day the two groups departed by vehicle and later by foot to the launch and recovery positions.

By 2320 hours, with their inflatable kayak launched, the recce team commenced rowing towards the target and the operation was under way.

By 0030 they had, with great difficulty, disposed of the kayak and commenced their swim to a position some 800m upstream from the bridge, from where they could carry out an observation of all movements on or around the bridge. They swam underwater to the bridge, reaching it at 0130 and commenced a detailed inspection of the construction and the pillars with distances between them and depth below them being noted. By 0300 this had been completed.

They proceeded downstream under water for a further 800m before surfacing and swimming to a position 5.4km downstream, from where they were to establish contact with the recovery team by 0630.

Unable to make contact they continued on to the next position 17km from the bridge. At 0800 they came ashore and were able to establish comms. They were soon uplifted by Sgt 'Rassie' Erasmus in an inflatable but as the escorting platoon moved upriver, they drew selective fire. The team was eventually able to withdraw at 1500 that afternoon. During the actual recce, enemy attention was distracted by a covering mortar bombardment of the town by UNITA and the counter bombardment by FAPLA.

Although there were a few minor problems, the recce was a success and it was discovered that earlier intelligence on the bridge with respect to essential detail was incorrect, including the number of pillars and length of the actual span.

Cooperation and assistance received from the CSI Liaison Teams and UNITA had been superb and it transpired that Cmdt Rudman had personally conducted the reconnaissance of both the infiltration and recovery routes. Every team or sub-group involved had a senior UNITA Liaison Officer attached to it, with Gen Demosthenes remaining in the Tactical HQ for the operation.

Lessons and Techniques Learnt

Just as important as the intelligence gained was the new techniques and lessons learnt both in the preparation for and execution of the actual recce. During the preparations, it was discovered that the anchor used to hold a diver in position did not work in fast flowing water and this led to the use of large 'corkscrews' which could be positioned into the bank or shallows of the river and hold fast in a 6kt current. They did, however, prove to be rather unwieldy to carry and risky in a kayak.

It was also found during initial preparations that dry-suits were unsuitable in rivers, where obstructions, even reeds, could damage them. Thus, wet-suits were used for the actual operation. They did, however, also have some disadvantages, especially in the event of escape and evasion and thin rubber suits were selected, which would enable some clothing to be worn also.

Most important feedback resulted from the actual operation. The inflatable kayak, although easy to transport in the bush, proved to be unsuitable as it had no structural strength, was very difficult to row and, lacking a rudder, even more difficult to control in a current.

On a number of occasions it completed a 360 degree turn before becoming controlled again – not a pleasant experience when on a covert operation under the possible eyes of the enemy. Carrying capacity was also very limited and, as the diving equipment only just fitted in, would not be able to carry the explosives for an offensive mission. Just to really rule itself out of contention, it was extremely difficult to sink and conceal as cutting it open resulted in a noisy exit of air but not enough to ensure it would sink.

After being recovered, the divers reported that they had felt completely drained and that their skin had become extremely sensitive and sore, especially their hands, and they had not been able even to carry their equipment on recovery. This resulted from their swimming some 18km over a period of eight hours and it was apparent that energy supplements and some medical advice would be needed.

Another discovery was that, when coming ashore, their pistols were filled with silt and would be unlikely to function. On the positive side, the ARO rebreathers, although rather antiquated, functioned well and it was felt they would be suitable for a follow-up operation.

Coolidge – Preparations for the Operation

On 3 July, Operation Instruction 7/87 for Operation Coolidge B was issued by Special Forces Headquarters and final planning for the attack on the bridge commenced.

The initial consideration was to destroy the bridge before the Angolan offensive, Operation *Saludande Octubre* (Greetings October), commenced and thus delay it. It soon became obvious that to attack the bridge once the majority of attacking brigades had crossed the river and then deprive them of support would be more effective and allow them to be destroyed rather than merely delaying them behind their own lines.

The date for the execution of the operation was not given but it was specified that it should take place during the period of dark moon in August. The operation was to be conducted on behalf of UNITA and was not to be traceable back to South African forces. The OC of 4RR was appointed as Operation Commander and the participating teams were to be deployed not later than 22 August 1987.

Intelligence sources indicated that the enemy forces allocated for the Angolan offensive comprised eight FAPLA brigades (8, 13, 16, 21, 25, 47, 59 and 66) supported by the Cuban 50th Brigade (Bde). With the advance expected to commence on 17 August, an appreciation was carried out to ascertain the optimum date for the attack. D-day was thus to be 25/26 August, as it was estimated that, by then, 59 Bde, 21 Bde, 25 Bde and 16 Bde, along with elements of 47 Bde and possibly 66 Bde would be to the east of the river. Blow the bridge and they would all be stranded in no-man's-land...

It soon became apparent that this was not going to be an easy nut to crack. The latest intelligence was that the bridge itself was guarded by a company of FAPLA troops, deployed on the eastern side, where the guardhouse was located. Three T54/55 tanks were deployed about 300 metres from the bridgehead on the western side and a 14.5mm machine gun guarded each end of the bridge, which was illuminated with a lantern at night. Although they had two boats armed with 12.7mm machine guns, their serviceability was questionable and unlikely to be used at night.

With two guards on the bridge by day and five at night, it was apparent that the defences of this vital link had been considerably strengthened.

Planning and preparations began immediately with the operators building up their physical fitness and exercising swimming and diving techniques on the Berg River to get accustomed to operating in fresh water. The Italian-made, inflatable kayaks were replaced by standard Nautiraid folding kayaks which made a big difference.

The plan for the operation was based on the successful recce operation with respect to command and control as well as infiltration and recovery positions and procedures. There were a number of critical challenges, which needed to be answered, as they would dictate the size of the team. These included the number and sizes of the charges to destroy the structure as well as their placement.

An additional target was the wire stretched across the river just upstream of the bridge and which was used to guide and hold ferries when crossing. This would require a cutting charge. Another important consideration was the level of the river, which was dictated by the season and would be lower than during the recce. Although this was done, it appears that the drop in level was underestimated at the time.

Based on the results of a study into the above, it was decided that a team of twelve divers working in pairs would be required. Major 'Tuffy' Joubert was appointed as the Mission Commander with Major Fred Wilke as the Team Leader and SSgt Anton Beukman as his second in command.

The buddy-pairs making up the team were Team 1 – Major Wilke and Sgt Koos de Wet; Team 2 – SSgt Anton Beukman and Sgt Les Wessels; Team 3 – SSgt Gerrie Heydendrych and Cpl Pieter van Niekerk; Team 4 – Sgt Johan Oettle and Sgt Smiley van der Merwe; Team 5 – Sgt Henk Liebenberg and Sgt Adriano Manual; and Team 6 – Sgt Benji Burt and Sgt Phil Herbst.

The launching team, which included the reserve divers, Capt Johan Hechter and Sgt Pedrito as well as a reserve kayak and two rebreather systems, would fall under Captain Hechter but supported by Lieutenant Bezuidenhout, who would take over should the reserve team be deployed. The recovery team would be led by Major Julius Engelbrecht, assisted by Sgt Tablai and Cpl de Villiers and equipped with two F470 inflatables and two 30hp outboard motors.

Each diver would carry a satchel charge containing between 15 – 20 kg explosive and some high-density compressed foam on his back. The foam was to ensure neutral buoyancy as well as packing to hold the charge in place. All charges would have a 'sympathetic' switch which armed five minutes after activation (basically a salt pill that took that time to dissolve), while every second buddy-pair carried timer switches.

Every second charge also had a 30 minute 'bugger-off' device, which then armed the anti-lift device. With the charges fitted below the surface, any one detonation would send shockwaves to trigger all remaining charges almost simultaneously. The timers on the pillars would be set to detonate at 0700, 30 min after the charge on the ferry cable.

The first name of the major in the engineers who prepared the charges was Stoffel, but he was appropriately known as *Springstoffel* – *springstof* being the Afrikaans word for explosives!

To destroy the kayaks without wasting time, they would be cached on the bank and destroyed by two white phosphorous grenades (one forward and one aft) linked with detonating cord. A timer would ensure simultaneous detonation shortly before the main charges on the bridge detonated. Each member would carry a Browning HP 9mm pistol. With the exception of the team leader plus one other diver, who preferred the more modern Oxygers-57, the remaining divers chose to use the older ARO rebreathers, on which they had initially been trained.

A major consideration was the large number of crocodiles in the river and the danger they would pose to tired operators during a long swim. While consideration was given to carrying pungi sticks (a metal rod with a shotgun round at the end, which fires when pushed against the threat), it was concluded that they would merely overload the divers and also be an additional risk to each other.

Thus it would be a case of 'hope like hell it won't be you but keep your dive knife close to hand', and pray the crocs have settled in for the night.

Although the metal anchoring 'corkscrews' had functioned well, with all the equipment the divers had to carry, it became obvious that an alternate method was needed to keep the divers in place while fitting the charges. It was decided that a roll of thin rope about the length of the bridge would be used instead. This would be extended in line abreast on approaching the bridge with the buddy-pairs holding on to it and on reaching the target, the outer pairs would secure their ends to the bridge pillars.

As all the equipment would be infiltrated by helicopter, vehicle and finally by foot, every item had to be carefully packed to be light enough to carry but robust enough to withstand a long trip as, although the support staff would have emergency spares, they could not be expected to replace or repair items once behind enemy lines.

Deployment and Infiltration

On 15 August, the teams deployed to Fort Foot, the 1RR operational base in Rundu, for final preparations and exercise, spending four days rehearsing at Direco on a similar but long-destroyed bridge.

These very realistic rehearsals were of great value and enabled the team to find practical solutions for problems and to get to know the environment, although it was not a comforting sight to see the illuminated little red crocodile eyes lined up on the river banks and everyone made sure they kept their buddies on a short buddy line and knives close at hand whenever they dived.

A few operators on an inflatable boat always stayed close, ready to render assistance should a croc became a tad too nosey – a luxury not available during the operation! The debris under the bridge also helped prepare them for the obstacles they would encounter at Cuito Cuanavale. On completion, it was back to Fort Foot for final preparations and checking of equipment.

On the night of 22 August the teams were flown to Mavinga in a heavily-loaded Transall C-160, from where Puma helicopters took them to 5RR's Tactical HQ deep in the bush and close to the Lomba River to overnight.

The next day was D-2 and that night the launching and diving teams were ferried by Pumas to a UNITA Battalion base 46km north-east of the confluence of the Cuito and Cuanavale Rivers, where they were met by Cmdt Les Rudman and Col Gato, who would lead the UNITA escort.

On D-1, once the equipment was loaded into the vehicles and, (as they were now in a combat zone) all operators provided with AK 47s for the journey, they set off in a south-westerly direction and covered 26km, before arriving at a second UNITA base, from where they set off on foot just before last light, covering 10km before resting up 8km from the river.

On D-day they covered the last leg very cautiously and, with UNITA ensuring the area was clear of the enemy, arrived at the launching position 23km north of the bridge at 1700, where the divers happily handed their rifles back to UNITA and commenced assembling their kayaks 500 metres from the river.

Coolidge B – The Attack

On 25 August at 2030, all were ready and the six kayaks departed for the target, led by Anton Beukman, who had covered the route previously.

It was not easy navigating or rowing through the sometimes very narrow reed-lined waterways but they eventually arrived at a suitable place well clear of the town where they could cache the kayaks and prepare for the swim and dive to the target. The kayaks were tied together, anchored to the reeds and the timers for the grenades were set.

The team then swam carefully for approximately two hours to a spot some 1.5km from the bridge, under the impression it was where they had planned to deploy with the rope extended between pairs.

At this stage, Major Wilke discovered that his diving set had flooded but, as he could still carry out limited dives using his buoyancy compensator, decided to continue with the attack. The rope was extended with five teams linking up but the current and the need to remain under cover of the shadows on the western bank made it impossible to control the rope and it was eventually abandoned. Although unplanned, it was, in fact, a blessing, as barbed wire and other obstacles subsequently encountered would have snagged it and resulted in probable chaos.

It was well into the early hours of the morning when the bridge finally came into view and the team gathered to observe the target. As they were much later than planned, the cut-off time for the RV south of the bridge was extended to 0330 and the teams then set off independently in numerical order.

There was no wind and the water surface was smooth, which meant that anything breaking surface would be easy to spot. SSgt Beukman, in charge of Team 2, was carrying the cutting charge for the ferry cable strapped to his arm.

He armed it and, with his buddy Sgt Wessels, swam into the middle of the river and prepared to attach it to the cable, only to discover that it was about 1m above the surface. They had earlier heard the sound of a boat being rowed but could not confirm its presence in the darkness.

Cuito Cuanavale, though modest in size, was of enormous importance to the Soviets and the Angolans if they were to tackle Jonas Savimbi's forces at source. (Photo: 'Kaas' van der Waals)

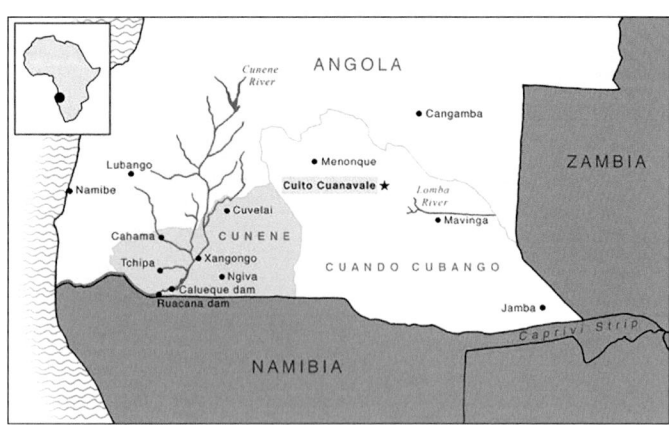

This map shows main areas of South Africa's military operations in south Angola (shaded area) with Cuito Cuanavale, centre and Mavinga (Right) UNITA's 'First City'.

Emblem of South Africa's Reconnaissance Regiment.

A small team of Recce operators 'blacked up' and ready to go into action. (Photo: Douw Steyn)

Iron Fist from the Sea, published by Helion in Britain, is rated by military cognoscenti as one of the most informative books to emerge from that period.

Angolan troops were powerless to halt the destruction of the bridge. (Uncertain source)

Recce training procedures in Saldanha Bay involving underwater navigation. (Photo: Douw Steyn)

Subterfuge was the name of the game. (Photo: Douw Steyn)

A more recent photo of a SA Navy Strike Craft of the kind used on several raids on both Angola and Mozambique port installations, as well as infiltrating strike groups in remote regions. (SADF files)

The bridge at Cuito Cuanvale today, newly built. (Photo: Roland de Vries)

They then heard firing and underwater explosions coming from the east bank and set off cautiously in that direction for their designated set of pillars with the current speeding them along.

Team 1 (Maj Wilke and Sgt de Wet), restricted due the rebreather problem, found themselves in an anti-swimmer obstacle of barbed wire on a cable but were eventually able to dive under it, finding that they were now on the wrong side of the river.

They thus decided to place their charges on the first set of pillars on the eastern side but, while approaching them, the strong current forced them against the river bank and obstacles forcing them to surface where they were immediately spotted. They were immediately fired on and dived towards deeper water but Maj Wilke, turning on to his back to see where the firing was coming from, was wounded in his right upper arm.

Swimming under the bridge, they finally surfaced 300m downstream, where they disposed of their charges.

Team 3 (SSgt Heydendrych and Cpl van Niekerk) were also off the western bank and approaching in the reeds when the firing commenced and could hear orders being shouted from the bridge. Both small arms and heavy machine-gun fire peppered the water below the bridge but they continued and some 50m away dived in about two metres of water.

They soon encountered a series of anti-swimmer obstacles and Cpl van Niekerk got caught on one but got free and was then hooked by a large fishing hook which luckily got entangled on his diving knife and he was able to free himself without injury.

With the water depth only 1m, they soon also drew fire and found themselves in another series of wire obstacles. After clearing them under constant fire and with the area illuminated by flares, they reached the cover of the bridge, but while preparing the charges found they could not sit up without drawing fire and were thus forced to move to deeper water, where they waited until the firing subsided. It was now after 0330, the cut-off time for regrouping, so they placed their charges on an underwater stump, initiated them and swam south downriver.

Team 5 (Sgt Liebenberg and Sgt Manual) were in deeper water and able to approach their target, the fourth set of pillars from the east bank, unhindered. It was about 0345 when they arrived on target and, being in deeper water, the continuing fire was ineffective. After placing and arming their mines, they continued south underwater until well clear of the bridge.

Team 4 (Sgt Oettle and Sgt van de Merwe), when about 100 metres from the bridge, moved towards the east bank to orientate themselves. From there, they heard a rowing boat on the river and, after a short while, firing broke out on the bridge and troops were observed crossing to that side. They thus dived and, in deeper water, approached their target, the third set of pillars from the left.

The first charge was placed and armed at 0412. Ineffective firing into the water did not distract them and as soon as the second charge was laid, they also continued south. Team 6 (Sgt Burt and Sgt Herbst), after observing the firing, dived and, when about 50 metres from the target, swam into a large underwater tree stump, which caused Sgt Herbst to lose his mine and mouth piece. A bit further on they encountered a number of obstacles and, on clearing them, drew fire and a hand grenade.

On reaching the pillars, Sgt Burt managed to just hold on and found it had already been mined. Losing his hold and pulled by his buddy, who had not been able to grab on to a pillar, they found a sandbank just downstream and weighing down his charge with a weight belt, armed it and they followed the other teams downstream.

Although Team 2 was one of the first to depart for the bridge, they had been delayed while locating the ferry cable and then by a wire net just under the surface. Their heads broke surface and soon drew fire aimed at their position. Finally reaching their target, the current forced them to place their charges independently.

While holding grimly onto one of the bridge supports and trying to get the mine in position, it became entangled with the antenna of his radio, breaking it off and thus depriving the team of its only means of communication with the other teams during the withdrawal. Their time on target was from 0400 to 0415 but they were able to place and arm both mines before swimming out from under the bridge.

Finally overcoming the strong current on the eastern side, they surfaced some 150 metres away and SSgt Beukman realised that he still had the armed cutting charge strapped to his arm and swiftly disposed of it in the reeds. Forced by fire from heavy machine guns, they dived and continued swimming south.

Exfiltrating from the Bridge

By this time, the other teams had regrouped at the second RV position, where an attempt was made to establish communications with Major Engelbrecht at the recovery position, but without success.

Although Team 2 had not joined them, Maj Wilke decided that as the cut-off time was long past, the group should continue south towards the recovery position in order to be clear of the target area by sunrise.

As Team 2 had been the first to depart and the remaining teams had all arrived, it was thought that the missing team may well have been ahead of them. They thus departed at 0410, keeping to the eastern side of the river to benefit from the cover provided by the high ground on that side. Most of the swimming was done on the surface partly due to Maj Wilke's wound but largely to conserve whatever diving capabilities the oxygen rebreather sets had left.

Team 2, realised that they could not catch up with the group and, just after daybreak, hearing the faint roar of explosions coming from the bridge, decided to exit the water and find a hide for the day, assuming that the enemy would have commenced searching downstream for those responsible. Finding a patch of reeds with some top cover, the cold, wet and hungry divers settled down for what proved to be a very long and eventually very hot day in their wetsuits.

They were none too soon as, early that morning, the enemy deployed MI-24 attack helicopters and foot patrols along the river. That afternoon at about 1500, the grass in the area was set alight but, with little wind, did not affect them.

As the main group steadily swam south, they tended to form a line with divers relieving each other in assisting the wounded Major, while Sgt Burt tried to keep them grouped.

Taking charge, he moved the group into the reeds at daybreak and they went ashore for a rest. Sgt de Wet and Sgt Oettle then treated and dressed the Major's wound, while another attempt was made to contact Maj Engelbrecht. Due to a tear in the watertight bag, the radio was wet and Maj Wilke then instructed that they should continue swimming towards the recovery position.

They were making good progress when a crocodile appeared and clamped its jaws on Maj Wilke's right swimming fin. He had seen the approach and had pulled his legs back just in time and was able to also kick the fin off. Sgt de Wet had also observed the approach and as the crocodile submerged, threw an M-26 grenade at it, while all the divers beat a hasty retreat to the river bank.

After the explosion, they recommenced their long swim but 20 minutes later came under enemy fire, which seemed to be aimed at the rear swimmers. The front swimmers had already rounded a bend in the river and were out of sight but those under fire immediately dived, three rejoining the group but, unknown to Maj Wilke, Sgts Heydendrych and Liebenberg took shelter in the reeds and decided to remain there until the enemy were clear.

The other three reported that they had been observed by someone cutting grass on the bank but the grenade may also have attracted enemy attention.

At about 1000, the remaining eight divers reached the recovery position and, after reporting that four of his divers were 'missing in action', Maj Wilke was carried out of the water and the bullet in his arm removed by the doctor, Lieutenant Shane Labuschagne of 7 Medical Battalion Group.

All the divers were provided with dry clothing and an AK-47 with two magazines, a reminder that they were still in a combat zone and not yet safe. At 2045, Sgts Heydendrych and Liebenberg arrived at the recovery position – much to the relief of all there. In view of the enemy presence and the need to get further treatment for Maj Wilke, it was decided to evacuate the divers and, escorted by one of the 5RR escorting teams with a UNITA platoon, they moved out on foot to the landing zone, leaving Maj Engelbrecht and his team with a 5RR team to wait a little longer for the missing team.

At last light that day (about 1915 on 26 August), Team 2 touched up their 'black is beautiful' camouflage cream and entered the river and cautiously started swimming on the surface with masks and mouthpieces slung around their necks below the surface. Enemy activity could still be heard and numerous fires could be seen along the banks.

At about 2140 SSgt Beukman was suddenly attacked by a crocodile, which came from behind, between his legs and clamped its jaws on his backside and thighs. Within seconds, he was at the bottom of the river and being shaken and rolled around like a rag doll. It eventually stopped and everything went quiet – all that the operator could hear was the gentle flow of the water past his ears as he was being pressed, face-down, against the sandy bottom.

Then his training and survival instincts kicked in and he managed to get his mouthpiece into his mouth and start breathing again. With the crocodile holding him down to drown, he reached for his diver's knife and started stabbing at the predator behind him.

The first three strikes were like stabbing into hardwood but the forth one plunged into what must have been its right eye and, and a few seconds later he realised he was free and no longer a menu item. Rising like a cork, he found Sgt Wessels frantically searching for him and they both swam to a sand-bank to assess the damage.

The wetsuit appeared to stem any serious bleeding and they decided to press on, knowing that the recovery team could not remain in a fixed position for long. At 2300, just as they came around a bend, they saw the red cyalume strung across the river and knew their ordeal was almost over.

The doctor soon patched up SSgt Beukman's wounds, which were not severe and the next morning, after exfiltrating by foot with SSgt Beukman on a stretcher, they were uplifted by a helicopter to Rundu, where the wounded operator joined Maj Wilke for further treatment and a number of rum and cokes!

The top secret signal from 5RR Tactical HQ advising SFHQ and 4RR that he was safe and in Rundu put a number of minds at rest – 'C. S/SGT BEUKMAN (CROCODILE DUNDEE) WITH PUNCTURED THIGHS AND BUTTOCKS, AND LUCKILY FAMILY JEWELS INTACT.'

The Aftermath

Although only six of the charges were successfully placed on the target, some 40m out of a length of 90metres was brought down. Initial repairs consisted of planks and ropes for personnel to cross.

With Soviet help, a temporary deck was erected, which allowed certain vehicles to cross but not any armoured vehicles for about a year, necessitating the use of ferries. With only two light casualties, the operation was thus regarded as a major success and achieved its aim, albeit for a limited period.

One operator summed it up quite subtly and accurately – 'the mission was simple: destroy a bridge in the middle of Angola, far behind enemy lines in a crocodile-infested river – simple, no problem!'

While 4RR conducted the actual attack, it could not have been mounted without the protection and support provided by 5RR and the UNITA forces while in the operational area and specifically behind enemy lines. All deployments were on time and in the correct position with the CSI Liaison Teams coordinating all planning with UNITA.

While the bridge had not been completely destroyed, the denial of its use for logistic support to the exposed brigades in the east soon took a toll, as they were now reliant on air supply or ferry.

It was not long before the enemy brigades started retreating due to the harassing and relentless attacks by the South African and UNITA forces. The effect of these attacks is highlighted in a telegram (No 91) from a senior Soviet Brigade Commander Advisor to the Advisor of the Military District Commander in Cuito Cuanavale on 11 November 1987, which stated 'The enemy hits each brigade separately and nothing is being undertaken to inflict a blow collectively. Thus all the brigades will be killed off one by one. There are few military personnel in the combat units. Commanding officers of all ranks are scared to start counteractions against the enemy.'

The source, Igor Zhdarkin, a Soviet translator operating at the front, recorded that 'the Angolan troops are almost completely demoralised; the brigades are on average at 45 percent strength. For every 10 to 15 shells launched by the enemy, the Angolans are able to send only one, if even that.'

There was thus no doubt that logistic support had been severely curtailed and all brigades were soon reduced to one third of their strength and became largely ineffectual. Thus Coolidge played an important role in ensuring the success of Operation Modular, the aim of which was to eject FAPLA forces threatening Mavinga and UNITA HQ in Jamba.

Intelligence prior to the deployment had indicated that there had been an increase in vigilance on the bridge with additional guards, although, during the operation, it became obvious that even this had been underestimated. Some attributed this to the FAPLA reaction after the nearly successful UNITA attack early in the year.

During the recce the previous June, however, this much-heightened state of vigilance had not been experienced. It is thus likely that the FAPLA and their Soviet advisors were well aware of their dependence on the bridge and with the opening of the offensive on 3 August, had made a special effort to ensure its protection, not just through numbers but through ensuring the constant vigilance of the force deployed.

On the other hand, it would appear that the underestimation of the water level under the bridge during the operation probably caught the divers by surprise, as it not only resulted in the water depths being much less than expected but also exposed a large number of underwater obstacles, all of which forced some of the teams to expose their positions. The fact that only one member was wounded during the withering fire and grenades exploding underwater while they were carrying and arming explosives, was nothing short of a miracle.

A few weeks after their return to Langebaan, the team was summonsed to Cape Town to receive the personal thanks of the State President and to give a first-hand account of their experiences.

Soon after returning from the Presidential meeting, SSgt Beukman was told to hand his diving knife in to stores. As no reason was given, and 'an order is an order', he did so with bad grace and was issued with a new one. Unknown to him, the knife was sent to Pretoria as requested by the Chief of the South African Defence Force, General Jannie Geldenhuys.

The General had arranged to have the head of a small crocodile mounted on a wooden base and, after appropriately placing the knife in the trophy, presented it personally to a very surprised Anton Beukman at a later function.

On completion of the report on the operation, the sheer courage and determination of all the operators under extremely hazardous conditions, and aware that they had been compromised, became obvious. All operators were thus justly rewarded with the award of the *Honoris Crux*, the most ever awarded for a single operation.

While not a seaborne operation, Coolidge B was probably the most hazardous operation ever undertaken by 4 Reconnaissance Regiment and will long serve as an example of the levels of professionalism, perseverance and courage displayed by its operators during conflict – later acknowledged even by its former foes.

Douw Steyn provided this remarkable aerial photo of Ongiva taken while war still waged in south Angola. This was the scene of many battles between South African forces and the Angolan Army which was significantly bolstered by Cubans troops and Soviet advisors. Note the ragged trench lines and mortar pits towards the bottom and centre right.

24

The Commanding Influence of the Ratel Infantry Fighting Vehicle on Mobile Warfare in Southern Africa

This is a thought-provoking account of how the author and a number of daring young commanders and soldiers tossed aside military textbooks in developing their own military doctrine for mobile warfare, South African style. It is clear that the Ratel infantry fighting vehicle wielded huge influence on the development and deployment of doctrine for mobile warfare during the 23-year long South African Border War.

The author answers a simple 'Yes' to the question raised whether the military doctrine of the South African Defence Force, devised during the Border War had served its purpose. He furthermore emphasises that significant lessons can be learned from the manner in which the SADF fought its military campaigns, a statement borne out by various authoritative publications recently circulated.

Major General Roland de Vries – a former commander of 61 Mechanised Battalion Group (1981–1982) and former deputy chief of the South African Army also recently published his book entitled *Eye of the Firestorm* in 2013, with a new edition from Helion in Britain in 2016.

General de Vries's report below, was originally published in *Scientia Militaria, South African Journal of Military Studies*, Vol 43, No. 2, 2015

Introduction

I was there, with other members of the project team on the historic day in 1975 when the first Ratel[1] prototypes rolled off the production line at Sandock-Austral in Boksburg. Roughly 40 years later – half the lifespan of the average man or woman – it is still in service of the South African Army as the trusted steed of the country's armed forces. This is no co-incidence.

What we conceived and developed was, and to my mind still is, the best vehicle for ultra-mobile African bush warfare ever to be made. Thanks to its swiftness, massive wheels, bush-breaking ability and variety of weapon systems, it reigned supreme on African soil through the 1980s. It

---

1 These six-wheeled armoured fighting vehicles were designed and manufactured in South Africa at a time when the country was being subjected to virtually total economic, political and military embargoes in the seventies and eighties. Ratels were employed in action in southern Angola for the first time in 1978.

was as tough and tenacious as the honey-badger, the *Ratel* in Afrikaans, after which it was so aptly named.

As a young mechanised soldier of the former South African Defence Force I soon realised that the Ratel six-wheeled armoured fighting vehicle would become the epitome of the long-standing cavalry dictum that strength lies in mobility. That swiftness is an elemental factor of warfare, making up for numbers on the battlefield by the quickness of marches and that an aptitude for warfare is an aptitude for movement.

Knowledge Starts with Practice

Many good books, such as the one on Ratel, soon to be published, offer comprehensive analysis of the SADF role in the war and the important part such unique military systems played in making the SADF one of the most formidable military forces of its time – for instance the Ratel and others such as the 155mm G-5 gun-howitzer, Casspir and Buffel Mine Protected Vehicles (MPV), Seeker Unmanned Aerial Vehicle (UAV), ZT-3 Anti-tank missile and others. These were all home-grown systems, which were soon battle proven and ideally suited for the conditions of the African battle space.

I am equally thrilled that I could write my own biography[2] portraying the role I played in that same war and about many other young officers who had made manoeuvre warfare a way of life – a band of daring young commanders and men who tossed aside irrelevant military text books and developed their own doctrine of Mobile Warfare, South African-style.

To have been able to contribute to the creation of the Ratel and the design of its training and its operational system through the seventies and eighties was a wow-experience to say the least! Likewise, was the privilege and honour to have commanded a first-line fighting unit extraordinaire such as 61 Mechanised Battalion Group (61 Mech) in 1981–82 and to have participated in the many conventional battles that were fought successfully from the early eighties until hostilities ended in 1989.[3]

There is a relevant question posed many a time about whether the military doctrine we had devised for mobile warfare (more or less 'on the hoof') had served its purpose and if it could be applied successfully in practice.

Fortunately, I find myself in a position to irrevocably pronounce my judgement. It is a big yes; simply explained by the way the SADF fought numerous manoeuvre battles while outnumbered and still won.[4]

My statement is borne out by various authoritative publications circulated recently proclaiming that significant lessons can be learned from the way the SADF fought its military campaigns.

An American veteran (Robert Goldich) of high standing recently wrote that by:

> Reading and studying South African accounts of the 23-year long Border War between South Africa and the Angolan liberation movement UNITA[5] on the one hand, and the Angolan

---

2 De Vries, Roland, Major General (Retired): *Eye of the Firestorm*. Naledi, PO Box 3136, Tyger Valley, Cape Town, 7536, 2013.
3 From Wikipedia, the free encyclopaedia (https://en.wikipedia.org/wiki/Roland_de_Vries).
4 Scholtz, Leopold: *The SADF in the Border War 1966–1989*. Cape Town: Tafelberg, 2013, page 247.
5 The National Union for the Total Independence of Angola (*União Nacional para a Independência Total de Angola*) was the second-largest political party in Angola, founded in 1966. UNITA fought with the Popular Movement for the Liberation of Angola (MPLA) in the Angolan War for Independence (1961–1975) and then against the MPLA in the ensuing civil war (1975–2002).

government and army (FAPLA),[6] supported by large Cuban forces on the other is almost hypnotically compelling.... The tactical and operational lessons from the Border War are mostly variations on usual military themes...solid and relevant training, doctrine, and attitudes; but that the most significant lessons of this conflict for the USA are far broader, and sobering, in nature....![7]

For this reason, I am enthralled to see books being published many years after the war by new authors such as David Mannall.[8] *Battle on the Lomba* is the compelling account by a young crew commander of the battle on the Lomba River in southeast Angola on 3 October 1987. On this day 61 Mechanised Battalion Group shattered a full Angolan armoured brigade, turning the tide of an overwhelming offensive. Mannall's vivid account of the battle proved to me that he had learned well...that what he had been taught during training could be applied in practice.

In saying so I cannot but otherwise recite the wise words immortalised by Mao Tse-tung in his military writings, namely that:

> Knowledge starts with practice, reaches the theoretical phase via practice and then has to return to practice. Practice, knowledge, more practice, more knowledge; the cyclical repetition of this pattern to infinity, and with each cycle the elevation of the content of practice and knowledge to a higher level.[9]

This the SADF had learned the hard way through superb training and successful campaigning!

It goes without saying that the South Africans had learned that fluid conditions are necessary for mobile warfare to flourish; that the answer to superior forces is greater mobility; that tactical victory is brought about by seizing fleeting opportunities following any ensuing confusion.

Were these wisps of wisdom captured in formal doctrine at the time? Not really. It was however captured adequately in several manuals and standing-operating-procedures in bits and pieces. The formulation of military doctrine for this new type of mobile warfare only happened many years after the border war ended. Clearly, what was important at the time of fighting was that the knowledge became internalised in the minds and spirit of those officers and men who had to stem the revolutionary as well as conventional onslaught.

---

6   The *Forças Armadas Populares de Libertação de Angola* was originally the armed wing of the People's Movement for the Liberation of Angola (MPLA – *Movimento Popular de Libertação de Angola*), but later became the country's official armed forces when the MPLA took control of the government in 1975. The MPLA was a political party that has ruled Angola since the country's independence from Portugal in 1975. The MPLA fought against the Portuguese army in the Angolan War of Independence of 1961–74 and defeated UNITA and the FNLA in the decolonization conflict of 1974–75 and the Angolan Civil War of 1975–2002.
7   Goldich, Robert. 'An Unknown War in the Far South of the World – South African Accounts of the Border War, 1966–1989'. (http://foreignpolicy.com/2015/03/12/annals-of-wars-we-dont-know-about-the-south-african-border-war-of-1966-1989/).
8   Mannall, David: *Battle on the Lomba, 1987*. Helion and Company Limited, 26 Willow Road, Solihull, England, 2014. This particular military campaign transpired during what the SADF referred to as Operation Modular.
9   De Vries, Roland, Colonel: *"Mobiele Oorlogvoering – 'n Perspektief vir Suider Afrika"* (Mobile Warfare – a Perspective for Southern Africa). F.J.N. Harman Uitgewers, Posbus 35226, Menlopark, Pretoria, 0102, 1987, page 173.

On Emerging Military Doctrine – Train as You Fight

It is important to realise that the Ratel was not originally designed for the bush war per se, but to fight alongside armour to protect the territorial integrity of South Africa against any conventional onslaught… to, when the time comes, 'entice a potential conventional enemy' into a grand killing area and then to destroy them by means of mobile aggressive action.'

Fortunately, this kind of war foreseen at some stage as part of South Africa's threat predictions never happened. Incidentally, there were adequate military doctrines available to cater for this type of military conduct, such as the doctrine called 'The Conventional Land Battle'. The latter was a derivative from American doctrine and somewhat outdated and would never have sufficed for the kind of bush war we were fighting up north in the 1970s and 1980s.

Fortunately, in the late seventies, the Ratel made its debut just in time to participate in the border war, especially when the clash of arms with our enemies from across the border became extremely serious. Ironically, these six-wheeled armoured fighting vehicles were destined to hold the line until December 1988 when peace came. These fighting stalwarts were required to fulfil the role of wheeled tanks in many of the high intensity battles fought inside southern Angola, even in fighting heavily outnumbered against enemy tanks such as the Russian T-55. It was only in November 1987 that a squadron of Olifant tanks was introduced during the final phase of Operation Modular to fight alongside the Ratels, to be followed by a second tank squadron in January 1988.[10]

The Ratel's primary role in fighting of this kind was to carry troops swiftly in and out of battle, and it was admirably suited for this purpose because it provided all the required mobility, firepower and armoured protection required for such combat conditions. High mobility combined with flexibility was the essence of this mobile war-fighting game.

The Ratel was not designed with full armour protection against all types of hostile fire – that would have made the hull too heavy and the vehicle too cumbersome. It provided adequate protection from 7.62mm armour-piercing rounds hitting it from the front, side and rear, and the slanted armour plating in the front could stop a 12.7mm armour-piercing round. But it was vulnerable to the formidable Russian 20mm and 23mm anti-aircraft rounds, which could slice through it from any side. What was really important, however, was that the Ratel could close with enemy formations under own heavy indirect fire support, whilst being protected against own and enemy shrapnel, due to adequate armour protection.

The infantry version's 20mm quick-firing gun and 7,62mm co-axially mounted Browning machine-gun provided the capability to lay down sustained fire; to suppress and neutralise or destroy hostile troops, even allowing the destruction of the enemy's light-armoured fighting vehicles during the close-in battle, and to produce high rates of fire to support own forces during fire-fights.

Sustained covering fire was also required to protect and support dismounted infantry and other friendly armoured fighting vehicles, to allow South African troops to move rapidly and more safely during battles – the ultimate aim in offensive operations is always to close with and destroy the enemy.

The Ratel's high mobility and long range – 1 000 km at high speed on roads and approximately 600 km across country – made it easier to achieve surprise. Initiative could be fostered and freedom of action could be maintained under the most difficult combat conditions.

---

10 De Vries, Roland, Major General (Retired): *Eye of the Firestorm*. Naledi, page 107 and 668.

All of this formed part and parcel of manoeuvre and fire-and-movement tactics under all weather conditions night and day. Decisive actions as well as sound command and control were enabled by the reliable tactical radio communications installed in the Ratel as a force-multiplying effect. The fighting whole was therefore greater than the sum of its parts.

All of this was possible because the basics had been provided through new doctrine designed at the Infantry School and at I South African Infantry Battalion (1 SAI) in the early seventies. This was initially based on the battle handling of the mechanised infantry section and mechanised infantry platoon and the aide memoires that went with it.[11]

The aforementioned doctrine would stand the test of time and was used successfully throughout the border war as a base-line for the design of the standing-operating-procedures (SOP) of units such as 61 Mech, forthcoming emerging doctrine on mobile warfare and subsequent training curricula. These doctrinal manuals gave commanders the freedom to experiment in the field and to initially concentrate more on application than on theory.

From these doctrines stemmed the many manuals referred to in a book soon to be published on the Ratel. Such as the 61 Mech SOP and the 'Rules for Bush Manoeuvring' that I had designed for 61 Mech, while serving as commander in 1981–82.

A provisional doctrine on the conduct of 'Pre-emptive Attacks' was also published by the Army College in 1980. There are many other examples to which one could refer, such as the unique battle formations and attacking methods employed by Commandant Jan Malan for the attack on FAPLA's 21st Brigade east of Cuito Cuanavale in January 1988. This was based on Malan's extensive experience as former training officer at 1 SAI and from the time serving as a young sub-unit commander in the field with 61 Mech.[12]

It was in the field and of practical necessity where certain tactical novelties (so well-known to our mechanised soldiers) such as the following, were created:

> Command initiative, point of main effort tactics, fire belt action, marching readiness, combat readiness and fire readiness.

What was lacking at the time was doctrine for mobile warfare at the operational level of war within the context of the African battle space. Fortunately, the commanders in the field where well-versed in the 'Joint Operational Planning Cycle' – an amazing planning concept we had learned from the Israeli Defence Force.

This catered adequately at the time for the planning and conduct of mobile operations at the tactical and operational levels of war. Such as the operational plan I had designed for the attack on FAPLA's 16th Brigade on 9 November 1987.[13] Incidentally, I used Field Marshall Erwin Rommel's plan for his surprise attack at Gazala in May-June 1942 as a base-line for planning. The planning concept relied heavily on what Rommel had explained in his 'Rules for Desert Warfare',[14] namely that:

> One should endeavour to concentrate one's own forces in space and time, while at the same time seeking to split the opposing forces and to destroy them at different times.[15]

---

11 Such as "*Die Gemeganiseerde Peloton in die Geveg*" (The Mechanised Infantry Platoon in Battle) and others, (of which much will be written in the book on Ratel).
12 Scholtz, Leopold: *The SADF in the Border War 1966–1989*. Cape Town: Tafelberg, 2013, page 323.
13 De Vries, Roland, Major General (Retired): *Eye of the Firestorm*. Naledi, page 654.
14 Liddell Hart, B.H: *The Rommel Papers*. Library of Congress, Catalog Card No 53-5656, 1953, Page 197.
15 De Vries, Roland, Colonel: *"Mobiele Oorlogvoering – 'n Perspektief vir Suider Afrika"* (Mobile Warfare – a

Lt Col (Commandant then) Roland de Vries briefs his section leaders on an upcoming attack during Operation Protea.

Briefing the troops at Ruacana before going into Op Protea. Unlike most armies, 'boots on the ground' were usually given a pretty good idea of what was likely to happen, as well as when and where. (Roland de Vries)

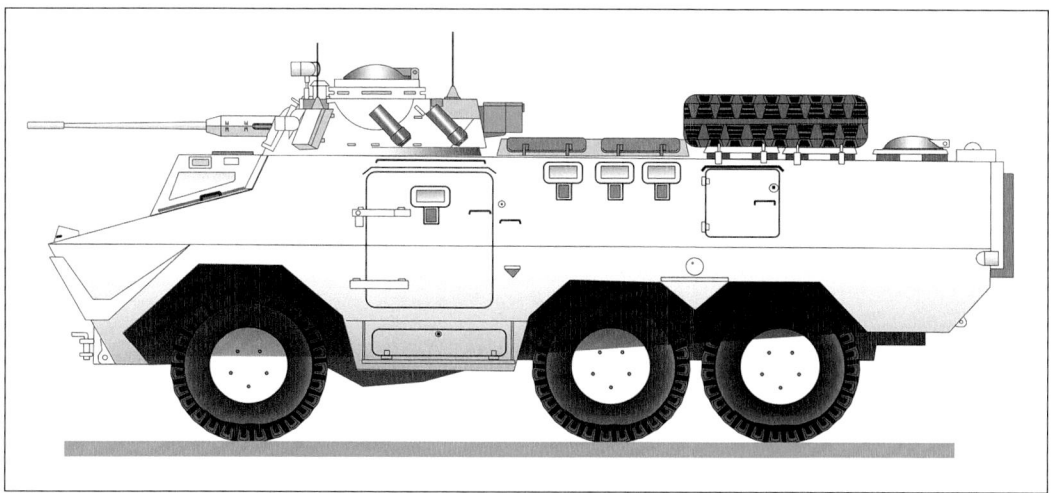

Detailed sketch of a Ratel infantry fighting vehicle: though 'soft skinned' these machines gave a lot better than they got against Soviet tanks. (Drawing by William Marshall)

The sad consequences of an enemy booby trap left behind in a house in Xangongo. Going into vacated enemy positions was always problematic. (Roland de Vries)

Camouflaged Ratel command vehicle, Operation Meebos, August 1982.

61 Mech Command Group, Operation Meebos. (Photo: Giel Reinecke)

A Puma together with a clutch of Alouette gunships in the Chitiqueta area during Operation Daisy. (Photo: Roland de Vries)

Op Sceptic.

Air support team, Operation Daisy. (Photo: Roland de Vries)

Enemy dead lying on an Angolan bridge after the attack. (Author's collection)

Ratel 90 – army recognition photo.

It was from experiences such as the above that I wrote my own book on mobile warfare[16] published in August 1987, just in time for the high intensity conventional battles then taking place in southeast Angola. All of the latter insights attest that military doctrine is a living subject.

Evolving operational concepts for mobile warfare practiced at units such as 61 Mech were based on manoeuvre and the optimum utilisation of terrain. This formed the core of the emerging military doctrine for mobile warfare, whilst the (general) principles of warfare provided the basis of how battles and campaigns were to be fought.

As such, doctrine ensured unity of opinion on the battlefield and the intention to secure or retain the initiative and exercising it aggressively to defeat the enemy at all times. This approach enabled units such as 61 Mech, 4 South African Infantry Battalion and 32 Battalion to incessantly develop opportunities, which enabled them to shift their main effort swiftly and to take advantage of enemy weaknesses many times during operations.

The military leaders and their soldiers who served at such units played an immense role in formulating, developing and refining the operational concepts and doctrine described above. This particularly referred to the conduct of joint operations, which involved more than one service, such as the army and air force, operating together.

This even applied to combined operations later on during Operations Modular, Hooper and Packer when 61 Mech, 4 South African Infantry Battalion and 32 Battalion fought closely intertwined with UNITA to achieve the common operational objectives that were set for them by their respective high commands.

In this unique way 61 Mech had become the combat experimentation centre for doctrinal development, not only for the South African Army but the South African Defence Force (SADF) as well. More so, it had become a finishing school, which produced outstanding combat leaders for close on four decades. What a sad loss this amazing potential was when on 18 November 2005 the unit was disbanded as an all-arms combat grouping by the newly formed South African National Defence Force (SANDF), which followed on the political changes in South Africa after 27 April 1994.

Did the doctrine for mobile warfare we developed at the Infantry School, at training units such as 1 SAI and operational units such as 61 Mech, 4 SAI and 32 Battalion work for us? It sure did for me!

Much More than Doctrine – Mobile Warfare had become a Way of Life

To the credit of the South African soldiers who operated their war machines under precarious conditions, mobile warfare had become a way of life. They had learned to make winning a habit and that practice makes perfect.

Embedded within the core of these operational concepts, the Ratel became their dream machine, the ultimate tool of their fighting trade.

It became the mainstay of all the conventional and semi-conventional operations fought in Angola, and was a force to be reckoned with. Operating by themselves or in combination with a variety of other lethally effective, locally manufactured weapon systems, the Ratels made it possible for the South Africans to influence the war and hold the line, even though usually outnumbered by huge margins; and this remained so until peace arrived at the end of December 1988.

Perspective for Southern Africa). F.J.N. Harman Uitgewers, Posbus 35226, Menlopark, Pretoria, 0102, 1987, page 52.
16 De Vries, Roland, Colonel: *"Mobiele Oorlogvoering – 'n Perspektief vir Suider Afrika"* (Mobile Warfare – a Perspective for Southern Africa). F.J.N. Harman Uitgewers, Posbus 35226, Menlopark, Pretoria, 0102, 1987.

It is therefore clear to see why the design of our equipment, the conditioning of our soldiers and dedicated training for mobile warfare were vital to us. In saying this it is important to understand that the South Africans were extremely well-versed in and adapted to mobile warfare and that the Ratel was well-suited for the job.

Our soldiers were imbued with a will to win, regardless of the odds. One of their secrets lay in the operational concepts and doctrine continuously developed, improved and applied; a unique theory which embodied mixed mobile, conventional and guerrilla warfare concepts. 61 Mechanised Battalion Group, 4 South African Infantry Battalion, 32 Battalion, 201 Battalion and 101 Battalion, which at times fought in combination with the formidable guerrilla units of UNITA, were foremost examples.

These South African units were commanded by young men who understood the bush-warfare game and excelled at it. I always thought of our small mobile brigade, out on a limb and fighting against overwhelming odds in south-east Angola in 1987 and 1988, as a modern equivalent of General Christiaan de Wet's commando of the Anglo-Boer War days, which was so beautifully described by Thomas Pakenham:

> De Wet's commando moved like a hunting cat on the veldt… It was not a majestic fighting machine, like a British column. It was a fighting animal, all muscle and bone; in one sense, the most professional combatant of the War.[17]

Warfare the African Way – Trials by Fire

The wide, densely covered, sometimes open, spaces of South West Africa-Namibia and Angola suited the exponents of insurgency, guerrilla and conventional-type mobile warfare: For the insurgent and the guerrilla fighter to evade and to strike at many places; for the exponent of mobile warfare to manoeuvre through the gaps, to concentrate superior forces at points of decision and to strike quickly when least expected.

In so much warfare in Africa as we experienced, it was not neat and clean, easily comprehended or linear, with peace and war at the opposite ends of the spectrum. At the blink of a commander's eye one could switch from conventional warfare mode to counterinsurgency and back again; or apply a combination of the two. Therefore, embedded in our operational concepts, within the African context, was the necessity to wrest the initiative from the enemy, which was achieved through high mobility operations and deep penetrations behind the enemy's static positions.

Many deep operations were launched from temporarily established helicopter bases. These fighting methods were well attuned to the African battle space, and many trials by fire resulted in doctrinal innovations founded on the lessons of the battlefield.

The South Africans purposely planned their operations to out-think and outsmart the foe, among other things by means of interesting out-of-the-box innovations which we called 'jackal operations'. This tactical approach basically amounted to the application of whatever type of battle craft and ingenuity would leave the enemy guessing or confused. It was a concept cleverly linked to what the renowned military author Sir Basil H. Liddell Hart referred to as 'the strategy of the indirect approach'.[18]

---

17 Pakenham, Thomas: *The Boer War*. Jonathan Ball Publishers, Johannesburg, 1981.
18 Liddell Hart, B.H: *Strategy*. Faber and Faber Ltd, London, 1967.

I defined it for my own satisfaction as follows: *'Attack with strength against weakness; hit the enemy in his centres of gravity; take the enemy from least expected directions; strike deep and ferociously; threaten his lines of communication, rear areas and command centres.'*

Another obvious winning factor was that the South Africans and UNITA made much better use of the neutral factors – space, dense vegetation and darkness – than FAPLA and the Cubans did. The dense bush and the night served as mediums for manoeuvring and were carefully utilised to offset a major deficiency in our mechanised land warfare capability, namely the lack of appropriate and adequate anti-aircraft weapon systems, including air fighter assets.

The shroud of the night was used for protection, controlled movement, dispersion and concentration of forces – to mask, to hide and to strike. Offensive mobile operations were the means by which to achieve this aim. It was also the main method of preserving one's own force and avoiding getting caught in any position where one was vulnerable to set-piece attack or destruction in detail by enemy fire. This was very important to the South Africans, as we were not prepared to sacrifice lives in futile exercises; blood was definitely not the price of victory.

Tactics that suited the requirements of the South Africans within this particular operational sphere were applied as far as possible. These practices had to be stretched at times, and at Cuito Cuanavale in 1987 to 1988, they were forfeited to some extent. Some of these characteristics were:[19]

- Ground was held only while it afforded a tactical advantage. When stationary for short durations, combat groupings leaguered in hides where all-round defence was possible. The artillery operated from well-camouflaged battery firing positions. Units such as 61 Mech and 32 Battalion were never stationary for very long and also operated from well-concealed hides. When stationary for short periods, troops dug shallow slit trenches for protection against possible enemy air attack and ground and artillery fire. Combat was offensive by nature.
- Manoeuvring was characterised by constant movement, controlled concentration and dispersion of forces – hiding, camouflaging and planning; then purposefully moving once again. It was a process of continuous operational assessment, intelligence gathering and quick decision taking; of being constantly aware of the situation. It was crucially important to know yourself, know your enemy and know where he was all the time. Excellent timing was another essential requirement.
- The battle sequence constantly applied was to see (or sense), decide and then act; but quickly, so as not to allow the foe the latitude and privilege of quality thinking, timely response and sensible engagement.

To encapsulate the aforementioned tactics: Some of the SADF's manoeuvre warfare concepts were rooted in values which were embedded in our subconscious minds and became second nature to us:

Make the battlefield fluid; strike deep; exploit your night-combat capability; use mobility and firepower to the fullest; keep on winning, notwithstanding the odds, because there is no alternative.

---

19 De Vries, Roland, Major General (Retired): *Eye of the Firestorm*. Naledi, page 204.

Lessons can be learned from our Fighting in Southern Africa

I believe that many valuable lessons could be learned from the South African Border War and those documented in the new book on the Ratel. Lessons which provide umpteen wisps of wisdom to be considered by those who are currently involved in the dilemma of fourth generation warfare[20] across the globe in places such as Africa and the Middle East.

One of the important lessons stemming from the South African experience is that one can emerge successfully from a protracted counter-revolutionary, vis-á-vis revolutionary, war, by employing similar tactics and strategies as your adversaries; by taking the war to the enemy; even by prolonging the agony and investing in fighting-over-time as we did in southern Africa.

As such, the South African Border War and the war in Angola in particular, could be widely used as a benchmark for the study of not only contemporary warfare, but future warfare as well. For instance, it was an armed struggle which typically evolved into a *transnational conflict* over time and which brought about all the imaginable political, diplomatic, military and social ramifications and complexities of war in Africa.

More so, this war included low as well as high intensity engagements across the full spectrum of warfare, playing out within a vast geographical expanse over an extended period of time – all elements and events resulting in valuable lessons from which to learn.

It is also significant to realise that southern Africa served as a leading laboratory for counterinsurgency warfare at the time. In recent years much has been written on insurgency and counterinsurgency from American and British perspectives, but as Dr. Michael Evans of the Australian Defence College, Canberra, observes: 'Only a quarter century ago, the Southern African region was one of the world's leading laboratories for the theory and practice of counterinsurgency.'[21] Evans upholds that much can be learned from this by scholars of strategic studies and by military practitioners.

John W. Turner, who wrote on insurgency wars in Africa, furthermore remarks that

> It is unfortunate that many lessons learned by the South Africans in the course of their counterinsurgency effort still remain relatively little-known.[22]

Turner proclaims that:

> the counterinsurgency war by the South African Defence Force (SADF) against the South West People's Organisation (SWAPO) in northern SWA (also called Namibia) in 1966–1989 is the only case of a clear-cut victory by security forces against a communist-backed insurgency with considerably foreign support based in supposedly invulnerable positions across the Angolan border.

And so one could carry on endlessly with the lessons to be learned from skirmishing in the far south, as Sun Tzu, 500BC so apply stated:

---

20 Also referred to as 'Asymmetrical Warfare' – Warfare in which opposing groups or nations have unequal military resources, and the weaker opponent uses unconventional weapons and tactics, as terrorism, to exploit the vulnerabilities of the enemy.
21 Evans, Michael, Dr: *South Africa and Contemporary Counterinsurgency: Roots, Practices, Prospects,* UCT Press, Sunclare Building, 21 Dreyer Street, Claremont, South Africa, 2010.
22 Turner, W. John: *Continent Ablaze – The Insurgency Wars in Africa 1960 to the Present.* Jonathan Ball Publishers (Pty) Ltd, Johannesburg. 1998, p. 34 – originally published 1998 by Arms and Armour Press, an imprint of the Cassell Group.

Well-preserved Eland Mk7, now the acknowledged 'Gate Guardian' at the Bloemfontein military school.

Know yourself and know your enemy, otherwise you will succumb in every battle.[23]

So be it!

Among others, what one would be able to ascertain from reading the forthcoming book on the magnificent Ratel is that the causes and effects and intended and unintended consequences of war and politics makes for fascinating study.

---

23 Hanzhang, Tao (translated by Yuan Shibing): *Sun Tzu's Art of War, The Modern Chinese Interpretation*. Sterling Publishing Co, Inc. New York/London, 2007, page 36.

25

Angola's Tank Battle on the Lomba:[1] David Mannall Tells Us How South African Armoured Vehicles Knocked Out Soviet Tanks

> …a series of bitter fights in South Angola – known as the Battle of the Lomba River – took place between the 9th September and 7th October 1987…**SADF** and **UNITA** forces prevented the Angolan Army – which had already suffered heavy losses – from crossing the river. The Soviets withdrew their advisors and left [what remained] of the Angolan Army without senior leadership. By the 29th September the South Africans had gained the advantage and launched Operation Modular, a significant armoured offensive. Four days later – on the southern bank of the Lomba River near Mavinga – they attacked and totally annihilated a **FAPLA** armoured battalion.
> From 'The Battle for Cuito Cuanavale': Wikipedia, the free encyclopaedia

That day, the 3rd October, would end like no other during our operational tour of Angola in 1987. What the Wiki website did not say was that following several hours of hard fighting – in which a couple dozen Angolan tanks were destroyed – the enemy fled. Government soldiers abandoned their armour, vehicles, BM-21 rocket launchers, artillery and, as they left the battlefield, many discarded their uniforms and dumped their AKs into the river. Some battle!

Known as 'Operation Modular', we were awake by three in the morning. Our weapons, vehicles and personnel were already made battle-ready for what we'd been told was likely to be a pretty significant contact with the Angolan Army. The last time we'd engaged that same brigade – a contact that lasted about an hour – their combat ability hadn't been regarded as much of a threat, either by the guys on the ground or our commanders towards the rear.

Sure they'd lobbed grenades and RPGs, and yes, there had been one fatality on our side – which happened because the infantry boys had been deployed alongside our vehicles, and we all knew that humans make for soft targets, but that was about it. What I wasn't aware of when we started

---

1 The author was instrumental in David Mannall's book *Battle on the Lomba* – one of the best to emerge from the war – originally seeing light of day. He introduced Mannall to the British publishers Helion. Major General Roland de Vries rates it an exceptionally graphic depiction of that enormous tank battle, the most expansive on the African continent since the end of the Second World War (even though it was largely six-wheeled Ratel infantry fighting vehicles ranged against Soviet T54/55 main battle tanks).

out early that morning was that by the end of that day, we'd have ended up killing or wounding a very substantial number of the enemy.

As before, as with every previous planned engagement – which was largely ranged against government forces – I liked to ensure that my boots, socks, underwear, tank-suit and the rest were all 'super' clean. It was very much a personal matter: as my mother always said – 'if you have an accident, it would be nice when you got to hospital for the nurses not to have to undress a dirty you.'

At the same time, I had absolutely no intention of pegging-off, even though every one of us accepted that there would be casualties. We'd been warned that it would be no ordinary skirmish: indeed, we were hurled into a grim and proper war and an awful lot of people were getting killed, even if there were something like 15 or 20 times more of their soldiers dying than our own. The stakes were high.

But I'm running ahead of myself. I should mention that in those far-off days, I was a pretty laid-back guy. That said, I took no chances when preparing for battle. As a section leader, others would rely on the decisions I made, which made me uncomfortably aware that were I to get it wrong, I'd have to live with the consequences, especially if one of our own guys were to get into trouble.

Our tactics were all pretty basic. My vehicle was part of a squadron of a dozen Ratel infantry fighting vehicles (IFVs) that included two command cars – my own and one other – and my call-sign was Three Two Alpha (32A). As a group, we were labelled Charlie Squadron and our emblem, proudly emblazoned on the frame of each vehicle, was a clenched black fist, clutching a bolt of lightning.

Roughly two hours before dawn, all dozen vehicle commanders checked communications and confirmed battle readiness. Then, abruptly, the order came down the radio-net: 'All vehicles start'. There was a surge of emotion as I realised we'd moved one more step closer to engagement.

I passed on the order to David our driver and he hit the starter. The powerful ten-litre turbo-charged engine of the Ratel IFV is housed in its own protective steel cocoon just three metres behind from where I was positioned – switch-kicked into action. Within moments the forest around me burst into a cacophony of deep rumbling roars as hydraulics systems started to tick over.

Then, the order: 'Charlie Squadron, move out'. I relayed the instruction to my crew: 'OK, guys, we're on our way…let's go'.

After two months in an extremely active combat zone, we'd all become a pretty well-oiled fighting unit, though I hadn't worked continually with the same people all year round, because some of the guys with whom we'd trained had been replaced. Others had become ill or moved on during our time in the operational area.

It was no secret that my driver, an extremely capable lad, had arrived on the scene, not exactly enthusiastic for what lay ahead. He wasted little time in demonstrating abhorrence for just about everything military. In fact, he despised the army and, as with quite a few of the conscripts, hated its impersonal, intrusive and multifarious authority. But as second-in-command of the little troop of four Ratels that made up our section, they took orders – as relayed down the line – from me.

Our gunner Herbert Zeelie – whom everybody knew as Herb – was an equally remarkable fellow. He had been one of the least *paraat* or disciplined members of the unit during our training phase. But with some additional coaching since he'd joined my crew, he'd already proved himself more than capable, responding promptly and unquestioningly to orders. That day, as I was to discover, he would demonstrate bravery and accuracy many times in the heat of the fray, which was a lot more than could be said for those across the line who opposed us.

As planned, Charlie Squadron was at the head of the battle group that was going into contact. The ghostly green shadows that appeared on our NVGs, or, more appropriately, night-vision goggles, initially offered only sketchy, speckled images of the world around us, at least until our eyes started to adjust to their use. Then I could clearly make out the protective steel casing of the IFV ahead, always by the single tiny penlight perched precariously on its rear. I could also distinguish trees and other potential hazards, though it took a while to adjust to what was still a very new dimension.

The first time we were issued with those sophisticated NVGs I was astonished at the amount of detail they displayed, sometimes in total darkness. Indeed, they magnified so much light that if someone dragged on a cigarette 20 paces away, it was as though they'd switched on a torch or even using a cigarette lighter. The luminosity that resulted would sometimes temporarily blind me, so I couldn't imagine going into battle wearing goggles because the muzzle-flash from a 90 mm cannon would spew flames two-metres deep on either side of the gun. Bang! And with a set of NVGs in place, you're blinded…

Nonetheless, cumbersome as they were, night-vision goggles were the best means of 'safely' navigating some of the heavily forested regions of south-eastern Angola after the moon had disappeared over the horizon before dawn. Headlights simply weren't an option: the enemy would in any event hear us coming and if we offered them an option of being able to spot our lights, they'd be able to range their shots.

As if in a choreographed ballet sequence, the squadron moved out in echelon, our advance marked by the distinctive high-pitch whine of the turbo-chargers spooling-up to assist in-line six-cylinder engines that pushed our 20-ton armoured beasts through the soft African soil.

By then I was in my usual position on board the IFV, standing on my crew commander seat, waist and upper body protruding out of the turret and going through the usual preparatory drills. This was also a time for communicating with other IFV commanders, each one of us directing and guiding our drivers – like the rest of our crews – hunkered down deep towards the front of these seven-meter-long vehicles. Our job was to alert the man at the wheel of any potential hazard as he slowly navigated a path across a difficult and primeval land.

David, after months on the job, was by now an expert at manoeuvring our Ratel through the bush and he responded readily to my directions. Most times he simply followed rows of deep ruts carved into the soft, desert-like sand by troops of vehicles immediately ahead. Herb, the 90 mm gunner, didn't have much to do, so he just sat back and waited, though under the circumstances, a snatched snooze was not a part of it.

There was no question in the minds of any of us that all this was for real. Skirmishes and contacts we'd encountered in the preceding months were symptomatic of an ongoing learning curve and we had come to accept the reality of these short, sharp fire-fights that gradually increased in intensity as the Angolan Army tried to secure a foothold on the southern banks of the Lomba River.

For a while FAPLA had been intent on reinforcing their in-theatre forces which, our commanders reckoned, already totalled something like 10,000 troops, never mind several hundred armoured vehicles like ours. There were also five or six squadrons of T-54/55 Soviet-built main battle tanks, in the argot, MBTs.

The build-up had been significant. We'd been made aware of increased political pressure from Fidel Castro and Cuba's Soviet sponsors in the preceding months in the enemy's bid to force inroads into the 'deep south', all of which led to increasingly aggressive counter-strikes on our part. What we were also told was that the Angolan Army was utterly committed to annihilating their prime objective: UNITA's rebel command under Jonas Savimbi in southern Angola.

His force was composed of elements of the 3rd Regular, 5th Regular, 13th Semi-Regular and 275th Special Forces Battalions, plus several thousand more guerrillas operating independently in the bush.

As the operation progressed, we'd been warned that we would eventually come up against a fully mechanised tank brigade that had earlier been dispatched to circle around the source of the Lomba and been spotted by reconnaissance elements sent in to spy the terrain. As before, enemy size and strength were both problematic, as was their deployment. Not long now, we'd been assured by some of the sceptics in our ranks, everything would be disclosed…

Being on the ground in these hostile badlands, we were not to know that two months previously FAPLA's 21st and 25th light infantry brigades – as well its 47th (armoured) and 59th (mechanised) and 16th brigades – had already moved out of Cuito Cuanavale in their bid to launch the biggest Angolan Army offensive of the 23-year war. Additionally, these ground forces had the advantage of solid air support, almost all of which came from their airbase at Menongue. Enemy air assets included Soviet Sukhoi and Mig-23 fighter-bombers, the majority deployed in ground-attack roles.

As fighters, we were centred on the 61 Mechanised Infantry Battalion Group, a unit of the South African Infantry Corps. While classed as mechanised infantry, it was a motley collection of infantry, armour and artillery, haphazardly interspersed as tactics and the terrain demanded.

Interestingly, the unit had originally been formed in 1978 as Battle Group Juliet in South West Africa as a force to prevent attacks on the region from SWAPO guerrillas in southern Angola and saw its first action in Operation Reindeer in early May 1978. Months later it was renamed '61 Mech' and became part of the regular order of battle.

Now, almost a decade later, we had reached the northern banks of the Lomba River near Mavinga and we were ready for them: there had been others before, but nothing with this volume of armoured clout.

Our immediate shortcoming was that the South African Air Force (SAAF) had no aircraft that could match squadrons of Soviet jets that had been deployed throughout the south, in large part because Pretoria had been stopped from acquiring any by a United Nations-imposed arms embargo. And anyway, the fighting that would take place was almost an hour's flying time from our own airfields in Ovamboland and Caprivi. We'd been told that if Cuito Cuanavale was lost by FAPLA, the next closest comparable outpost would be Menongue, roughly 300 kilometres from Mavinga and almost half the distance again from UNITA's headquarters at Jamba in the extreme south-east of this vast country.

By then, our own forces were approximately 500 kilometres inside Angola, and, to my surprise, it wasn't the kind of arid country we'd expected. South Angola, though desert-like in parts, had huge forested areas, some of which might even be described as jungle, with visibility sometimes down to less than 50 metres. The trouble was, this was hardly adequate for the kind of mechanised warfare in which we were to be involved. We'd been trained to accurately pick off targets at more than 2,000 metres, so somehow, we'd have to improvise. But so too, would FAPLA.

Conversely, some of the large trees that speckled the countryside were enormous and offered the singular advantage of excellent air-cover for our oversized vehicles from Angolan war planes. This was important in another respect: during this politically sensitive cold-war period, Pretoria actively denied that there was any kind of South African military presence in Angola. In fact, they told Washington, London as well as the United Nations, our infantry fighting units and the thousands of men who supported them, were simply not on Angolan soil…

As our squadron got closer to the Angolan battle lines across the way, the mood became tense and you could sense it from some of the utterances on our radio net. There was no more idle banter, no jokes and certainly nothing that was not essential. In the three hours after we'd pulled out of our temporary base at four in the morning, our minds had suddenly switched to operational mode.

Looking back on those distant days, and specifically that morning of 3 October as dawn finally broke over our moving convoy, I recall feeling curiously positive. I was totally prepared, my mind was calm and I was quite confident that the crew would do what was asked for them.

Fuck! We'd been training for this sort of thing long enough and were thoroughly familiar with our equipment, all of which had been primed for the impending action. Also, we'd already had a few contacts with advancing Angolan army units the month before, though none of those earlier sorties had been decisive. What we'd learned from our intelligence people was that an entire Angolan brigade had massed near the confluence of the Lomba and Cuzizi Rivers. There was a plan, they suggested that they might cross over to the northern banks, possibly because our earlier attacks had put their wind up.

From information available to us when we'd been given our battle orders the previous day, we'd been warned to expect a lot of resistance. As one of the senior officers expressed it: 'FAPLA's 47th Brigade has their backs to the Lomba River and that means that should they take a beating, they'll not be able to withdraw from the contact area which, as we've seen, is a frequent Angolan tactic…'

By then, battle-group leaders had made the decision that our unit – Charlie Squadron – would form the front line of the formation, while Alpha and Bravo anti-tank companies (our 90 mm contemporaries from the infantry unit) would form up on our flanks to prevent encirclement by enemy forces. Overall, the formation would resemble an oversized U-shape, with 20 mm infantry Ratels working in tandem with 81 mm mortar IFVs – as well as command vehicles – all active within a strategic pocket created by the 90 mm formations.

Just after sunrise we arrived to our staging point. There we disengaged from our support vehicles and fanned out into our pre-arranged formation, all the while relying increasingly on radio contact to ascertain our positions relevant to each other. We began moving forward, tentatively at first, anticipating contact at any moment, even though we'd been advised that the main body of the enemy force was still a couple of thousand metres ahead.

After about an hour, our progress was halted by a command from the captain. By then we were probably about a kilometre from the enemy but because of thick bush, they remained unseen. It was then agreed that our UNITA allies from one of their infantry platoons would move forward on foot, establish the rough positions of the waiting forces, engage briefly and then withdraw. Once enemy locations had been ascertained, our artillery batteries to the rear would start lobbing 155 mm shells over our heads and only then would Charlie Squadron take the lead and push ahead. In this instance, as we were only to discover afterwards, it was FALPA's entire 47th Mechanised Brigade.

As a point of reference: It remains my understanding that a brigade is at least three times the size of our battalion. More salient, these brigades bristled with some of the most modern equipment that the Kremlin could provide, along with some of the most high-ranking Soviet officers ever to conduct warfare outside USSR's borders, and, *our Ratel 90 was never intended for any kind of direct confrontation with armour.*

The brigade that waited for us that beautiful spring morning comprised at least two squadrons of a dozen T54/55 main battle tanks, fortunately not the newest in the Russian arsenal. They were backed by multiple squadrons of infantry fighting vehicles, very much like our own, like the BTR 60 with mounted multi-barrelled ZSU-23 heavy machine guns that could easily rip a Ratel apart with a single salvo, something that happened occasionally, with loss of life.

Looking back, it was perhaps just as well that we didn't know what lay ahead. We were certainly close enough to the line of fire to observe squads of scrawny, battle-hardened UNITA troops dressed in what seemed-to-be rags, with their AK-47s, RPGs and the very occasional Stinger anti-aircraft rocket suddenly materialising from the bushes around us and stalking forwards toward the enemy. Within 20 minutes the chatter of gunfire ahead had become intense: there was no turning back now.

Another ten minutes passed and still more UNITA combatants ambled past our positions after their brief fire-fights. Some were so nonchalant in their approach; they might have been on a morning stroll. Nervously, I gave these black-skinned warriors a grin and an optimistic 'thumbs-up'. We shared no common language, other than the international hand signal for 'everything's OK'.

But for us, things were definitely *not* OK. More chatter on our radios suggested that we were finally about to engage.

Then it came: 'Charlie Squadron, we're holding for the artillery bombardment' said the captain on our radio-net. And within moments came the crumps, and still more crumps with the occasional hollow 'thwump!'

None of could miss the almost ceaseless flashes of exploding munitions less than 200 metres ahead of us as dead-eye mortars and long-range artillery hurled a coordinated ripple of explosions onto nearby enemy positions. A minute or two passed and my headset crackled back to life: 'Charlie Squadron, let's move out'. The dreaded order came through in Afrikaans, first language of the SADF. As a crew commander, I was required to constantly monitor three radio channels. These were Squad-net (my little group of four Ratels), Troop-net (used by each of the Lieutenants that controlled the movements of their troops of 4 APC-90's), and of course, I was in constant communication through my helmet mike with Herb the 'deadly gunner' and David our driver.

'Okay boys this is it, let's move out. Herb, prepare to fire', I ordered and we began our slow forward movement, all the IFVs of Charlie Squadron in close formation, everyone else behind us. It was just after nine in the morning, five hours after we had first set out and for the following seven hours nothing happened behind our fighting group that didn't warrant consideration: my field-of-focus narrowed sharply towards everything immediately ahead and the rest of Charlie Squadron fighting alongside our machine. Our troop of four Ratels had become the fulcrum of our very universe.

Fellow combatants, or those of you who have experienced severe trauma like a vehicle accident, will know the meaning of everything suddenly going into distinct slow motion in those precious critical moments between life and death. Time becomes suspended, normal rules of reality are fuzzy and things you might normally accomplish during such intense duress afterwards seem impossible to have achieved under normal conditions.

So too, for me. After 18 months of preparation, the Battle of the Lomba River kicked off with the sun at arm's length over the horizon. Before I knew it, it was four in the afternoon. By then our Ratel – and those around us – had been in contact with dozens of Angolan tanks, but curiously, it didn't strike us that we were fighting against pretty impossible odds. Lieutenant Adrian Hind, our squad commander had been killed by enemy fire, his crew seriously injured and his Ratel destroyed, but on the opposite side of the battlefield, an entire Angolan armoured brigade – tanks, APCs and the rest – were annihilated.

It was actually much worse for the Angolan Army. By the time the battle had conclusively turned in our favour, their survivors – after losing most of their two dozen tanks – were beaten back into a rapid retreat, hundreds of their troops left behind dead and their wounded screaming for help. There were also more than a hundred FAPLA vehicles abandoned, their occupants relinquishing some of the Soviet Union's most prized and modern equipment. Among the items captured was a completely intact SAM-8 missile battery, an astounding intelligence coup because this weapons system had never before been seen by western intelligence services.

'Capture one of these SAM-8 launchers, the loader and its control vehicle and you've paid for the war', some 'big-cheese' general told us during a pre-war pep talk. Altogether there were three

SAM-8 batteries taken, although some of them a bit worse for wear, at least one ended up in the hands of American weapons specialists within weeks, a special flight having been dispatched to Pretoria by Washington to fetch it.

During the initial phase of the battle on the morning of 3 October, our entire formation moved forward with the IFVs of C-Squad spaced about 30 to 40 metres apart. My troop number 32 – was arrayed to my left, with 31 and 33 arrayed on the right.

First moments of actual engagement came just moments after a warning on the radio, 'all units…be advised…enemy snipers emplaced in the trees'. Moments after I'd acknowledged, the battle commenced.

It started with the staccato chatter of light machine-gun fire and, while trying to seek out the source, the bush directly ahead burst into life. I was faced with a ferocity of fire I'd never experienced before.

It took only moments to accept that enemy forces seem not to have dug themselves in as usual. Most of the opposing troops had taken cover behind some of the larger forest trees and we suddenly found ourselves right in the heart of the kill-zone. Our units were less than 200 metres from the nearest enemy concentrations and, within moments, all hell had broken loose. Months of drills and training abruptly kicked in. The rest of the day happened as if in a dream, surreal almost. We were simply going through the drills, my brain working at hyper-speed, identifying, evaluating, targeting, manoeuvring, and surviving.

Despite earlier 'ripples' of our own multiple rocket launchers and artillery fire, which had been used to soften the target area, we were faced with a well-established enemy front line no more than two or three hundred meters directly in front of us. All enemy positions were well camouflaged and lay concealed within a dense tree line. Behind that, enemy gunners were laying down a barrage of fire that ranged from concentrations of AK-47 and RPG-7 barrages to intermittent 100 mm tank and artillery salvos. I could see men moving around ahead of us, their muzzle flashes etched sharply against the dark forest backdrop and could clearly identify silhouettes of hard targets.

It was recommended that we enter combat 'hatch-down'. The problem with this approach was that to identify targets using periscopes or through the two-inch thick green glass surrounding the commander's hatch was just too inefficient for rapid target discovery. The upshot for me was that earlier I had established the best way to survive and that was with my head and half my body out of the hatch so that I could better see what was going on in the bush around us. I'd only just drop down when the crackling poc-poc-poc against the Ratel's mainframe told me that we were taking hits: the noise resembled a popcorn machine rattling on the body of the APC. That happened often enough because there were enemy emplacements – dozens of them – all around us and we could hardly miss the 'swoosh and blast' of the hundreds of rocket propelled grenades as they whizzed past, some exploding into the trees ahead and others self-destructing at 900 metres behind our positions.

War, as anybody has experienced real combat will tell you, is quite often punctuated by some furiously intense moments of lunacy contrasted by periods of downtime that can sometimes go on forever. In our case, explosives were being hurled in all directions as an incalculable amount of weaponry was fired at our positions which, at best, could only be regarded as improvised as we never had any real cover. Throughout the exchange, we faced a curtain of bombing, with the ground alongside my Ratel constantly kicked up by large-calibre explosions. Even the air we breathed was putrid and thick with cordite; for a while it seemed as if we'd been bracketed by a cacophony of blasts.

Retaining a good squadron formation, we gradually began making forward movement, always jockeying position, never staying in the same place for longer than was absolutely needed. Our job

South African armour – new adaptations of the versatile Olifant tanks – move into Angola.
(Courtesy of Roland de Vries)

An Angolan T54/55 knocked out near the Lomba River. (Photo: Hannes Nortmann)

A squadron of SAAF Mirage jets lined up on the runway near Pretoria. In large-scale cross border raids they would be on standby at Ondangua.

'Thin-skinned' Ratels into battle at the Lomba – it was an uneven match – infantry fighting vehicles ranged against Soviet T54/55 main battle tanks, but the superior manoeuvrability and much more rapid fire-power of the South Africans pulled it off. (Photo: sourced by David Mannall)

ANGOLA'S TANK BATTLE ON THE LOMBA 393

Enemy tank destroyed during the course of the battle.

Meanwhile, South African forces in their camps across the border operated out of secure bases such as this one.

Tank battle at the Lomba. (Sourced by David Mannall)

This photo taken from the turret of a Russian T54/55 by Camille Burger overlooks a crossing point at the Lomba.

South Africa's superior artillery, in particular its long-range G-5s and mobile G-6s knocked great holes in the enemy's defences, for which they had no answer. (Diagrams and Sourced by Pierre Victor)

South African soldiers take a look at one of the enemy tanks knocked out on the first day.

The Ratels became quite skilful at stripping the Soviet tanks of their mobility. (Photo: AR Taunton)

Captured portable ground to air missile systems – MANPADS – hauled back to base from Xangongo during Op Protea. (Photo: Roland de Vries)

Death Road, between Monongue and Cuito Cuanavale. (Photo: Camille Burger)

was to identify the next target, release perhaps a couple of 90 mm shells, and then move on. We never remained static in one spot for longer than 60 seconds.

During those first two hours we endured an intense amount of enemy fire from the tanks, and a lot more from small arms, RPGs, mortars and whatever else the enemy could bring to bear. I noticed that there were several Angolan Air Force MiGs buzzing overhead and reported this back up the chain of command, as if they didn't already know…

'Fuck boys, we got planes overhead!' was my unfrilled message to headquarters. But there was no time to be distracted by enemy aircraft because I had to remain focused on what was immediately ahead. In the hours that followed, I would continually snatch quick glances into the trees – for snipers – and into the sky, my Browning 7.62 mm turret-mounted machine gun always ready to pick off anything 'soft'.

This pattern was repeated hundreds of times as the battle progressed. 'Tank 250, eleven-o-clock'…fire when ready', I ordered. Herb quickly traversed his barrel onto target and *boom*… another shell on its way. Because the two forces were ranged in battle so very close together, our shells would most times strike targets dead ahead within a fraction of a second.

'Yes! Fucking good shooting, Herb!' I'd shout down the mike. Then I'd tell the gunner to lay another one there to make absolutely certain!'

BOOM! And the next round was also true. There was no time for congrats because we'd move swiftly towards another position in what had already become a hazardous game of hide and seek: us hiding and popping off shots and enemy tanks desperately swinging their turrets about while searching for something static to shoot at.

Then another target would appear, this time, perhaps, a personnel carrier. 'Gunner,' I called. 'Load HE (High Explosive)…target 300 metres…12-o'clock…*fire when ready*!'

The blast from our recoil was like a wallop in the nose, almost like getting slapped in the face by a heavy wet towel and something that we could never get used to.

'Target eliminated.' I called. Then after a moment or two: 'Next…' We would repeat the process over and over again, which is how it went for my well-drilled crew, one fluid fire-and-movement after the other, or as somebody else described it, like a well-calibrated machine.

What a phenomenal bunch of guys they were and we didn't regard it as peculiar that there wasn't anybody in my squad who was older than 21…

Looking back on these events, years later, it became clear that we probably needed a lot of luck to survive such a massive onslaught. But we were aware too that we could improve our odds by eliminating a target each time one came into view, which was often. An enemy tank or a BTR would appear, I'd indicate position and range, the gunner would zero in and that was it. Then we'd move to a new spot and wait for something else to happen.

It might have been dangerous but it was actually exciting as hell. We were playing games with our lives and until you've actually tasted that kind of risk, there are those who reckon you haven't lived. Fact is, you certainly can't explain that kind of experience to somebody who hasn't been there…

At some point during the early stages of battle, the APC to my left – 32 Charlie, or in the lingo 32C – lance corporal Bobby R screamed over the troop net that he was having problems with his gun man. His voice sounded desperate when he called: 'My gunner wont shoot, *my gunner won't shoot*'! he called, several octaves above his usual tone.

I immediately asked whether his gun had jammed. But no, Bobby said, when he came back online, the man had frozen, simple as that. Moments later he added something about the guy being paralysed with fear, and that too, was something that happened occasionally and in every war…

Bobby came back: 'I have one of their tanks targeting me at my 12 and the gunner is refusing to hit his fire-switch'.

'Okay Bobby, we've got you', I replied.

My instruction to David, my driver was immediate: 'Forward 11 o'clock 40 metres.' Then I told Herb to give me a HEAT round – High Explosive Anti-Tank – which he knew meant that we were going to go after the T54/55 that was threatening Bobby and his crew.

'*Now*!' I screamed into the mike.

Unlike our buddies who served in the South African main battle tank, the 'Olifant', we had no dedicated or auto-loader in the 90 mm Ratel. So between the gunner and the crew commander, we would load our rounds directly into the breach from the 29 bombs arrayed in place inside the turret.

Still more bomb-bays inside the vehicle held the remaining payload – and that meant another 42 bombs – but they were not accessible from inside the turret. The only way we could replenish turret stocks was to exit the APC and pass each bomb up into the turret where it would be stowed. But that was all pretty time-consuming because the rounds were large and the turret a somewhat constricted place.

It was a lot worse if we had to reload while under fire, which happened often enough because every one of the RFVs was a critical component in the uncertainty of what was going on all around us. We were trying to destroy enemy assets and they ours, and as with any battle, numbers mattered.

With 32 Charlie, it was impossible for the crew commander Bobby to try to help and possibly reach over the breach to hit the fire-switch. Had he been able to do so, he would have had his arm torn off by the breech which had a vicious recoil that reached back half-a-meter towards the innards of his machine

While my crew was shifting our position and loading 'tank-buster' rounds, I continued to maintain my chest-high position out of the turret. Meanwhile, I searched intently for the rogue tank that Bobby said was targeting his Ratel. Suddenly I spotted it in some thick bush, off towards our flank. I'd actually found it in seconds, but then wheren you're really up against it, time does seem to stand still.

Meantime, I was pouring a stream of fire from my mounted 7.62mm machine gun into the T54/55, desperately hoping to distract its crew and also to help Herb locate the target...which is why tracers are so valuable when people are throwing stuff around.

'Gunner,' I called. 'Watch for my tracer rounds…target 250…behind that tall tree, ten o'clock… fire when ready!' The target tank had already fired an HE round at Bobby's Ratel but it missed. Obvious another would follow pretty damn soon.

'Fire! Fire now!' I ordered and an enormous blast from our 90 mm followed. 'Bomb away and on target', Herb called, though he didn't need to.

'You fucking beauty, Herb!' I got back on the radio and called it in, 'Three Two, this is Three Two Alpha, we've eliminated the 32 Charlie threat. Now get that fucking gunner outta here.'

It wasn't long before 32 Charlie was withdrawn from the front line and we never saw the gunner in combat again. Bobby returned to the fray later in the day with a replacement gunner. What was really ironic was that Bobby's gunner – the Troopie who froze at a critical moment that might have cost the lives of everybody on board his Ratel – had been outstanding in all his training phases throughout the year.

I put it all down to an interesting lesson in life…

For the rest of the time, we continued pushing forward, sighting and eliminating targets and, as always, a lot of it was touch and go.

Since the start of Operation Modular, we had never been tested quite like this. In fact, there was no contact we experienced that had lasted anything as long. Nor were there ever such high-value targets. It seemed that each time we knocked out something significant – like one of their battle tanks – another seemed to pop up out of nowhere and replace it. Three hours into the battle and we were still coming under intense bombardment.

Still, while we were coming come up against a solid wall of enemy armour, Charlie Squadron was more than holding its own. But by then some of the crews – including my own – were beginning to run low on turret ammunition, which was when our commandant ordered a tactical withdrawal. We pulled back about a click, well out of sight of the enemy but close enough to our support units to replenish bombs, refuel and grab a bit of grub from a ration pack. There was almost no time to compare notes with my fellow crew commanders, though some of us were able to exchange a few words. Then, within the hour we were summoned by the big wigs, told how well we were doing and ordered back to the front line.

Meantime, the enemy had not been inactive. They'd reinforced their lines and the afternoon session immediately began with more contacts from T-54/55s and what was obviously a more organised defensive line. We got straight back into our routine drills, moving, firing, moving, improvising, and on the move again.

There is an expression in several languages that if you give an infinite number of monkeys an infinite number of typewriters, one or more of the works of William Shakespeare would eventually emerge. In our case, despite our superior training, an awesome number of projectiles were being thrown at us. Some of the larger calibres would have cleaved through a Ratel with enough kinetic energy to kill everybody. Indeed, that happened during the course of the war and obviously, casualties followed.

While the enemy was clearly badly trained or tended to lose focus whenever they came under concerted fire, their guys were at a distinct disadvantage in other respects when compared to us. Many of them were undernourished and, from what we'd experienced, the majority were inadequately trained. In some cases, some of the Angolan army troops were unwilling to fight for a cause they did not really understand.

In truth though, they were still a potent force and this ongoing battle was far too closely fought for them not have some success. The longer we fought, the greater chance the enemy would score hits.

So it happened that in the ongoing fog of exchanging fire that afternoon, a call came through the squad-net that one of the Ratels – it was identified as 33 – had taken a hit. Moments later somebody else reported that the strike was 'direct'. That was serious.

'Fuck! What's the situation? The crew?' I demanded.

Our captain came back sharply, his voice stressed. 'Confirm hit, vehicle immobilised…some of the crew sitting on the ground alongside.'

The incident was critical because there was enemy everywhere around us. But just then we had a few problems of our own, and the crippled Ratel was too distant for me to do anything about it. An infantry APC commander moved forward in an attempt to rescue the crew, confirming at the same time that the IFV had been blown apart. Literally, as if somebody had used a giant can opener to split it in half, which sometimes happens with 'thin-skinned' armour.

I never witnessed the incident which took place a couple hundred metres to our right, though shortly afterwards confirmation came through that we'd lost second lieutenant Adrian Hind. Also, his crew got mauled, one of his men losing an eye and some fingers, while a former school pal of mine, Graham, earned himself a bravery award for leaving his vehicle, sprinting across open ground to the stricken 33 and returning with a lifeless Adrian Hind who died shortly afterwards.

There was some chatter about how and why one of the enemy tanks had managed to target 33, but I prefer to believe that the tank got lucky. One needs to bear in mind that there were a lot of enemy tanks in the vicinity and any one of them could have popped up in the dense foliage and lobbed a shell. A direct hit from their 100 mm guns meant tickets for whoever took the strike.

We, on the other hand, in order to cripple or disable a main battle tank had to ensure not only a good shot but an outstanding one. It had to be delivered either directly onto its tracks, or even better, fired into the seam between its turret and hull. It didn't take any of us long to discover that a Ratel-90 could take four or five shots to kill a tank.

Fortunately, while we were deployed in Angola Herb, our gunner, never had that problem. We worked to a set pattern that if you missed with your first two shots you shifted your Ratel into another position. In turn, that forced the enemy gunner to have to 're-acquire' his target. But, if you remained static, it was pretty fundamental that we would then be offering our enemy too many chances to eventually get one of his shells onto target.

The right flank of Charlie Squadron took some time to recover from the loss of momentum caused by the loss of Troop 3's command unit, whereas on the left flank we continued to make good progress. We pushed hard against the forces arrayed against us but we'd suddenly acquired so many targets since the lunch break that we were again beginning to run low on bombs in the turret. I didn't need to be told that if this epic battle continued for much longer we'd need to pull back from the front line to replenish. However, any idea of leaving the other crews – my brothers-in-arms – to fight on without us, was to my mind, anathema.

I may have been fearful of what lay ahead at the start of the day but just then while we were immersed in battle there was no way I was leaving the rest of the gang without me by their side.

This state of affairs also presented something of a conundrum, because I was aware that the other crew commanders were also running short of ammo. But unless we were given the order to withdraw within the next five or ten minutes, 32 Alpha would be fending off T-55 tanks on its own…

So I chose my moment just after hitting the last hard-target in my field of fire, when I called back on the radio: 'Three Two, this is Three Two Alpha, I'm going to need to withdraw to replenish my turret.'

'Three Two Alpha affirm!' came the response from the troop commander who was obviously both stressed and focused on his own field-of-fire. I instructed David to begin a rapid withdrawal, keeping my head out of the turret to monitor his reverse: we didn't just then need to run into something large, like one of the big forest giants or worse, get stuck down to our axles in a bomb crater.

The reloading exercise, I knew, would require me to be out of the vehicle for several minutes: I'd work fast, but every shell that passed from outside would have to be secured inside by the gunner. That meant that we'd need to find somewhere relatively secure: we couldn't be left exposed and technically unarmed while completing the process. The immediate problem was that the further we retreated, the longer we'd be out of our fighting line and that meant leaving the guys to face the enemy without us. Every single one of our guns counted!

With bombs, shrapnel, bullets and the rest whizzing and pinging everywhere, we'd only reversed about 20 or 30 metres when, inexplicably, David slammed on his brakes. The Ratel slowed right down and I didn't like it. 'Keep going, keep going, Dave…*move*!' I shouted loud through the mike, telling him that the terrain was clear and that there were no obstacles in the way.

'OK, Corporal' he responded. He'd hardly begun to resume his pull backwards when a huge explosion suddenly rocked our Ratel. Something massive – we found out afterwards that it was a heavy-calibre mortar – had detonated just a few meters behind us. Shrapnel splintered onto the upper surface of the IFV as well as into the hub of the spare wheel locker that was usually positioned on top of the engine hatches and, in the course of events, seemed to absorb a lot of hits.

I didn't know it yet, but I was lucky, seriously so. Although I'd been monitoring our reverse manoeuvre with my head out the turret, I was shielded from the full impact of the blast by the thick steel hatch-cover which had been locked into its customary 90-degree upright position behind my head. Had David not momentarily slowed our reverse, that same mortar-round would've landed directly on the front of the vehicle, or possibly even on top of it, where I would have had no hatch-cover protection. It was that close!

We continued pulling back, but about 150 metres later I called down to the driver. 'Okay David,' I said into the mike, 'there is no real safe place to do this, but we've got to replenish. So stop now'. Realising that we had neither cover nor protection from the crazy maelstrom of battle taking place just a short distance away, I ripped off my helmet, jumped off the turret and almost cat-like, landed on the ground three-metres below where I'd been perched.

I couldn't miss a bunch of black streaks down the side of our vehicle: scorch marks from some of the shells that had glanced off our main frame. I wasted no time in opening the heavy steel door that covered external ammo stores, selected the appropriate ordnance, unlocked their bomb catches and passed the seven kilo bombs up to Herb in the turret. One shell at a time, we worked at hyper-speed, he locking the bombs away in their dedicated racks while David reached round from his cockpit to clear expended shell casings which cluttered the floor of the turret.

Good operational practice dictated that we hurled the casings out of the turret, but in the lunacy of the preceding hours, we'd not always had the time to do it because Herb's hatch always remained locked while the fighting went on. I would've been the only one able to do the job and that wasn't always possible given my multitude of tasks, target-spotting in particular.

As soon as we'd replenished the turret ammo, I told the other two that we should get back into line: there was no time to hang about in the rear. Also, with all that open ground around me, I was keen to return to the relative safety of my turret, obviously the safest option. While replenishing our ammo, several enemy shells exploded around us and the Ratel shuddered from some of the bombs that detonated nearby. Still, clearing the casings was a priority – if they were not removed, we risked having one or more trapped under the gun mechanism and that would have meant not being able to rotate our turret onto target.

Moments later we were back in line: the entire operation – it felt like an hour at the time – had taken something like six minutes...

By the time we'd returned to our original position in the formation we immediately began to take hits from a group of Angolan infantry who'd just exited a Soviet BTR-152 troop carrier which was a bit smaller than our Ratels and were usually fielded with 14.4 mm heavy machine gun mounted on the cab. Most of the enemy had taken cover behind a large tree which also shielded their vehicle.

I was about to order a first strike on their vehicle when I noticed a black dot travelling towards me, coming in almost in slow motion. In a moment the dot got larger but I already knew that I had an RPG-7 headed straight at us. There was no time to think. My legs buckled beneath me as I dropped into the turret. I looked upwards as the distinctive green grenade spun away missing my hatch-cover by inches. That was close!

No time to consider the implications, I called down to Herb on the mike: 'New target acquired!' I shouted. 'Load HE, large tree, 300 metres, follow my tracer-rounds...fire now!' He did, hitting the tree trunk squarely and obliterating half the cover the Angolan troops were using to shelter under.

'OK, good shot...tree gone! Let's take their vehicle...load HEAT...fire when ready!' And that he did, with only a handful of survivors fleeing back towards their own lines.

A moment later I felt a sharp pain in my back: I'd been hit. Scary at first because one doesn't know the extent of a wound I quickly realised that I was OK. I'd taken a piece of shrapnel and

Dion, the squadron medic, extracted it later that evening. That little piece of metal later become another memento of war.

Shortly after I got hit, call-sign Three Two started calling down the troop-net, 'I'm taking direct fire…tank…but I can't locate the target'. That was my troop leader: he had adopted the closed-hatch approach after he'd taken a shrapnel wound to his shoulder. But it did make for tricky target location and he was now dangerously exposed.

I responded immediately: 'Shit boys, we're not losing another vehicle today, let's go get this bastard'. The crew was with me all the way and followed instructions without question, even though we'd already survived a good six hours' madness. The number of close calls or near misses had been impossible to calculate and by then what the hell, we knew we were invincible.

'Three Two, this is Three Two Alpha…we're moving in on your position from your 3 o'clock. Now'.

Finding the enemy tank had suddenly become my only focus but as with most things, it becomes easier with practice. I reckon it was less than a minute before I spotted a barrel protruding from some heavy bush and, moments later, the muzzle-flash from a 100 mm cannon. By then I was almost behind that piece of enemy armour and had a full view of the rear of a Soviet T-54/55.

I told David to move us a little further down range to ensure that Herb had a decent sighting of the target. With a HEAT round locked and loaded, I told our gunner to hold everything

'Gunner new target acquired: 11 o'clock…200 metres. Follow my tracer…I'm aiming at his turret seam, and make this shot count, Herb, because we've got to slot him before he gets off another shot at Connor's Ratel. Fire when ready!'

The recoil from our shell resulted in the usual sensation of being punched in the face but when I checked a second or two later, I was able to report a bull's-eye. The tank had taken a mighty hit and then, to my surprise, its turret flipped right off the main body of the tank, all three or four tons of it. I'd heard of this happening, but never actually seen it for myself

'Three Two, this is Three Two Alpha,' I reported over the net. 'We got that fucker…'

A few weeks later we began to see some of the propaganda leaflets used against FAPLA. One of these showed a broken Russian main battle tank with its turret lying upside down alongside. I can only believe this wrecked T-54/55 to be the same unit we'd cleaved open that afternoon.

Months later I was told by one of our officers that I was to be nominated for a bravery award for this action and some other bits and pieces in combat, but like some of the other guys who were commended, we heard nothing further.

C'est la vie. I'm alive, and those for whom I was responsible had also survived. That means a lot when we'd eaten a few shovelfuls of shit together and emerged at the other end relatively intact.

Others hadn't been so fortunate.

Postscript: In the aftermath of the Lomba Battle, Igor Zhdarkin, a Soviet officers who was involved in that campaign published a book on his Angolan experiences in 2008. He pulled few punches, suggesting that his experiences in Africa were cathartic.

Titled *A Russian View of the Angolan War*, with the subtitle *We Did Not See It Even in Afghanistan: Memoirs of a Participant of the Angolan War (1986–1988)*, the book was originally published in Moscow by Humanities and Social Sciences ONLINE. It forms part of a collection of memoirs in the series *Oral History of Forgotten Wars* by the Africa Institute of the Russian Academy of Sciences in Moscow.

Zhdarkin's recollections opens with the retreat from the Lomba River crossing from where he and FAPLA's 21st Brigade began their long march to join the other Angolan army brigades, which, he says, 'were regrouping in the aftermath of the disastrous rout to prepare for the defence of their key base at Cuito Cuanavale.'

He goes on: 'The retreat was indeed a harrowing experience, as the title of the book reveals, since FAPLA troops were under continual bombardment by the SADF, along with the sniping, mining, and other harassment by the UNITA forces on the ground.' As the author relates, even Russians who had served in Afghanistan had never experienced such 'horrors' as the barrage of SADF artillery across the Lomba River.

> Under fire from the G-6 guns and Mirage and Buccaneer aircraft, FAPLA brigades panicked and deserted the field in flight, leaving behind their Soviet equipment in a graveyard of tanks, trucks, ammunition, and other materiel.

At one stage of the retreat (claims Zhdarkin), they were even bombed with 'chemical weapons containing poisonous gas,' against which, he maintains, they had no gas masks for protection (page 269). This is the usual nonsense offered up by legions of Soviets whenever they suffer defeats: had it been true – it would have been easy to verify – the use of a weapon of mass destruction would have made world news at the time. Instead, there was nothing...

Finally, and after nearly two months of retreating under fire, the author was able to join the Soviet advisors of the 59th and 16th Brigades awaiting the defence of Cuito Cuanavale then seriously threatened by the South Africans.

The most revealing commentaries are those concerning the author's opinion of the participants. On first impressions of Angola, he found Luanda 'more horrible' than other places he had visited. 'Just a pile of shit,' he described it, as he viewed 'the dirty airport and the ragged women and children on the floor' (a scene also observed by the book reviewer from where this report originally came) 'and the piles of rubbish covering the streets of Luanda.'

As for Angola's soldiers, it was Zhdarkin's view that they were 'unsuitable for war.' Not only were they 'afraid to take part in combat actions,' they were also unwilling to follow the 'reasonable advice' of their Soviet advisors. Consequently, it was necessary for the advisors to tell the Angolans that they were wrong and beat them up accordingly.

As the author explains, because many Soviet advisors were not familiar with the peculiarities of the black Angolan mentality, 'they often found it difficult to relate to them and obtain results.'

In contrast, says the reviewer, Zhdarkin 'does not say anything bad' about the South Africans. 'They fought well and competently because they were whites, because I myself am white and because South Africa related to us as whites to whites.' (page 369).

> He was also impressed by the 'ultimatum' delivered to Soviet soldiers inside the shells fired by the SADF artillery: 'Soviets leave Cuito Cuanavale. We don't want to touch you – our so-called white brothers. We want to cut up the Angolans'.

PART III

BACKBLAST: CIVIL WAR AND ENTER THE MERCENARIES

There's no honourable way to kill, no gentle way to destroy. There is nothing good in war ... except its ending.
  Purported to have been said by President Abraham Lincoln

In war the morale is to the physical as three is to one.
  Napoleon

If you can see the whites of their eyes going into a fire-fight, somebody's done something wrong...
  Unknown

Anybody who believes that the pen is mightier than the sword hasn't spent time in Somalia, or in Beirut in its bloody heyday. Or even Baghdad or Afghanistan's Helmand Province in more recent times.
  Al J. Venter

26

The African Adversaries

It was charisma, a certain dogged determination and more often than not, the utter ruthlessness of individual revolutionary leaders that made so many Black African liberation groups function efficiently, or relatively so.

Kwame Nkrumah was the most prominent of Africa's political firebrands to emerge after the Second World War. Preferring to be called *Osagyefo*, or 'Redeemer', he headed the party that took the British colony of Gold Coast into nationhood. He was to rename it the Republic of Ghana.

His counterparts in East Africa, *Mzee* Kenyatta of Kenya, Uganda's Milton Obote and Julius Nyerere of Tanganyika (with the amalgamation of Zanzibar it soon became Tanzania) were revolutionary figures who, for a while anyway, became the respected heads of their fledgling nations. Nyerere liked his people to refer to him as *Mwalimu*, the Swahili word for teacher.

Obote unfortunately – like Robert Mugabe and the tyrant Jean-Bédel Bokassa of the Central African 'Empire' – soon hoisted his own colours as a certifiable psychopath. While the Zimbabwean leader and Obote ended up murdering tens of thousands of their own people, Bokassa was a basket case of note who liked to cut the ears off naughty children.

In an absurd ceremony that would have done justice to the Court of Louis XIV at Versailles – and attended by many African Heads of State as well as the entire Bangui Diplomatic Corps – he crowned himself Emperor. Not one of the Western dignitaries present had a word to say about this ridiculous farce, probably because they believed they would be labelled racist.

That was the way it was with Africa in the 1970s, though the international community soon cottoned on to the fact that the man was mad and there were numerous allegations – together with evidence – of his being a cannibal. That did not stop him wasting the country's fortunes by building several 'triumphal' arches, as he declared, 'to commemorate my glory'.

The madcap Idi Amin Dada, a former heavyweight boxing champ while serving with the King's African Rifles in East Africa – a British colonial unit that garnered an illustrious record in the Second World War – followed with some loony antics of his own. A cruel man, Amin presented himself to the world as a rather absurd, buffoon-like figure. Like Mugabe, he did a very good job of discrediting African people in the eyes of the world.

During Amin's eight-year 'reign' he not only promoted himself to the rank of field marshal, but also volunteered himself as 'King of Scotland', so that the Scots, he would proclaim, 'could be free of British rule'… a theme which resulted in a brilliant film that went on to win an Oscar. Methinks Nicola Sturgeon might have showered him with platitudes.

Amin sometimes sent telegrams to the Queen of England, insulting and taunting her. Once he challenged the President of Tanzania to a boxing match but Nyerere very politely declined.

From 1977 until he was deposed, Amin demanded that his subjects refer to him as 'Your Excellency, President for Life, Field Marshal Al Haji Doctor Idi Amin Dada, VC, DSO, MC, Lord of all the Beasts of the Earth and Fishes of the Sea…' and so on…

While these contemptible people made headlines that were often hilarious, they were fortunately in the minority. Quite a few personable African leaders were to emerge and some, like South Africa's Nelson Mandela and Léopold Senghor of Senegal, went on to become much-admired international icons of moderation and progress.

Eduardo Mondlane of Mozambique might have enjoyed that same kind of status had he not been murdered by his lieutenants who, it was said on good authority in Dar es Salaam's diplomatic circles, included his successor, Samora Machel. That was never proved and Janet – Mondlane's American-born widow whom he met while studying in the United States – today lives in quiet retirement in Maputo.

Another leader assassinated by his own henchmen was Laurent-Désiré Kabila, said by those who knew him to have the intellect of a demented army corporal. The Cuban revolutionary Che Guevara met the man on one of his revolutionary 'fact-finding' missions to Africa and regarded him as a fool.

To be fair, Kabila was a lot sharper than he was given credit for. He was ruthless and crafty, because in the convoluted maelstrom of African politics, dim-wits simply do not rate. More to the point, the future Congolese leader was blessed with both the doggedness and atavistic guile to lead his bunch of crazies through the jungles of the Congo to eventually oust the equally manic Mobuto Sese Seko.

The same with Foday Sankoh, leader of Sierra Leone's Revolutionary United Front, an assorted group of rebels, many of them underage, who spent much of their free time cutting the hands and feet off women and children. I saw some of the results of their work at Freetown's Murraytown Amputee Camp while covering the war there in 2000 and I confess to never really having got over some of mutilations I saw there. These were hardly wounds of war, but horrific and mindless bestialities that some of those poor souls suffered at the hands of so-called 'Freedom Fighters'.

Considered a blunderer by his peers while serving in the Sierra Leone Army, Sankoh was as cunning and barbarous as any 19th Century anarchist. He must have been to have set Sierra Leone ablaze for almost a decade. It was British forces led by then-Brigadier David Richards – later to become Britain's Chief of the Defence Staff – that used good dollops of force to terminate that revolt.

Sadly, the majority of these African leaders were the products of colonial systems that believed in fair play and a fair measure of objectivity, essentially based on Europe's flawed but functional political dispensations. The problem was that societies from which people like Nkrumah, Nigeria's Abacha, Mugabe, Obote, Jacob Zuma, Mobutu and the rest emerged, very rarely practiced any sort of tolerance or objectivity in their own back yards.

Dostoevsky paraphrased it perfectly a century before when he wrote in *The House of the Dead* about excesses in his own society. His words were: 'Tyranny is a habit; it has its own organic life; it develops finally into a disease…blood and power intoxicate…'

In this regard, Angola was no different. Those who led the uprising were a diverse lot, some brilliant, others patently lacking in skills, but every one of them vehemently dedicated to ousting Portugal from their homeland.

For a long time, the revolutionary whip hand in Angola was jointly held by Holden Roberto's UPA (Patriotic Union of Angola) and the MPLA. UPA was eventually to transmogrify into GRAE, and finally into FNLA.

The MPLA, as we are aware, was headed by Dr Agostinho Neto, a charming young intellectual who nursed the movement through its most difficult years. Though a revolutionary through and through, he was certainly no despot.

Instead, Neto was a man clearly ahead of his time and there are many party stalwarts in Luanda today who maintain that he was murdered by the Soviets while being treated at a Moscow clinic, in part because he had begun to show a predilection for possibly drawing closer to the West.

Angola's first president seemed to have grown weary of Moscow's insistence on putting the party ahead of the individual. Shortly afterwards he was heard to say that after years of fighting and untold numbers of deaths, the guerrilla struggle was going nowhere. The Portuguese were of a similar mind and had already put out feelers for some kind of political settlement.

In spite of initial misgivings, it was the MPLA, with enough Moscow-led coercion and Third World subterfuge to do justice to any communist revolutionary group that eventually wormed its way into a position to take over the Angolan Government even before the Portuguese had left for home.

Curiously, as we saw in Chapter 12, the movement was assisted by the most senior Portuguese office holder in Angola, Admiral Rosa Coutinho. There is a lot of evidence out there today that show that Coutinho had been a communist for many years and though he played a prominent role in Angola's war, nobody was in any doubt where his true allegiances lay.

These were not the only players during that critical pre-independent phase. There were numerous splinter groups and off-shoots with such illustrious titles as CPA-CNE, FLEC, FLJKP and UNITA, the last, Dr Jonas Savimbi's UNITA, arguably the most successful African guerrilla group of the 20th Century, though his mind also went in the end.

But more of UNITA and its maverick leader later…

During the Portuguese epoch in Africa, all these freedom groups operated from neighbouring states and were headquartered either in Kinshasa, Congo-Brazza or in the Zambian capital, Lusaka. Groups opposed to the Portuguese presence in the oil-rich Cabinda enclave chose Brazzaville.

The UPA, or later, the Front for the Liberation of Angola – achieved prominence after the first bunch of barefoot crazies had crossed into Angola from the Congo and started murdering people. Curiously, there were some American intelligence operatives who believed that UPA might have been moulded into a rather promising guerrilla group.

Headed by Holden Roberto, the man who engineered the first full-scale attacks in March 1961, much of his support came from Western-orientated countries as well as pro-African movements in the United States, Britain, France and Belgium. Other countries that assisted financially and militarily were Tunisia, Ethiopia, Israel, the United Arab Republic, and, in the final stages, India.

Founded in 1954 as an illegal independence party within Angola, UPA was largely tribal-orientated. Its power rested with the half-million Bakongo people of northern Angola and while other tribes were involved, all senior positions were delegated by Roberto, who we now know, enjoyed the support of clandestine CIA-funded groups, including dissident Cubans based in Miami, Florida.

A number of these Cuban expatriates – many of them aviators – were later hired by the CIA to fly the Second World War aircraft in the Congolese Air Force against dissident rebel forces in the east of that country.[1]

Harvard T-6s already in the Congo were replaced by larger and more versatile T-28 Trojans, of which Washington delivered more than a dozen, as well as five long-range attack B-26 bombers, three Dakotas and two small twin-engine liaison planes. All were flown by mercenaries hired for the purpose, including Cape Town's Ares Klootwyk who had been trained in the SAAF, served in

---

1 Larry Devlin; *Chief of Station, Congo*, Public Affairs, a member of the Perseus Books Group, New York, 2007. The author crossed paths in Africa from time to time and remained in contact after he had retired from Langley.

the Royal Air Force where he flew jet fighters and then went on to man helicopters as well as fixed wing aircraft in both the Congo and Biafra.[2]

All this had taken place a few years before Holden Alvaro Roberto (alias Jose Gilmore, Roberto Holden, Ruy Ventura, Onofre *et al* – and also a brother-in-law of Mobutu) came on the scene. Born in 1923 near São Salvador, a town not far from the Congolese frontier, and while still an infant, Roberto's family moved into the former Belgian Congo where the future insurgent leader received most of his secondary education. The family then went back to Angola.

Prior to his revolutionary interests, Roberto returned to the Belgian Congo and worked in the Finance Department of the colonial administration in Leopoldville (now Kinshasa), Stanleyville (Kisangani) and Bukavu in the Congo's Eastern Province. During this time he retained close links with family interests in the Portuguese overseas province and consequently spoke fluent Portuguese, French, fairly good English, a little Flemish as well as his native Bakonga.

This 'Freedom Army' leader admitted to several journalists who interviewed him that most of his early support came from the American Committee on Africa and the Ford Foundation, largely as a result of the efforts of Eleanor Roosevelt and former United States Assistant Secretary of State for African Affairs, Mennen 'Soapy' Williams.

A curious individual, Williams led the pack in his anti-white African rhetoric. As part of the Kennedy Administration he is best remembered for declaring that 'what we [the United States] wants for the Africans is what they want for themselves.' This was reported in the press as 'Africa for the Africans,' contending that Williams wanted all people of European extraction expelled from the continent.

Naturally Williams was a strong protagonist of Holden Roberto, despite the FNLA leader crediting much of his success (as well as moral support from abroad) to Patrice Lumumba, the first Congolese black politician to make any impact internationally. 'My beloved Patrice', he always maintained, remained his 'guiding light' until Lumumba was murdered by the CIA because the Americans feared his close links with the Kremlin might get out of hand.

The largest 'black' educational institution in the former Soviet Union, Friendship University in Moscow, was renamed Patrice Lumumba University, a long-standing tribute to the man.

Notably, both Roberto and Lumumba were on first-name terms with Nkrumah, Roberto having worked in Accra for a while from 1958 onwards.

Above all, it was Washington that gave UPA/FNLA the impetus it needed to get its revolution into some kind of functioning mode. One Belgian diplomat I met in Kinshasa a few years after the first attacks took place maintained that were it not for CIA money, the movement would have floundered. It was his view that the United States fostered the UPA image as an effective counter to the more radical Congo-Brazza and Lusaka-based opposition.

It was obviously all Cold War stuff because from very early on, the MPLA enjoyed strong Soviet support: you got nowhere within the movement if you were not a loyal party *tovarishch*.

After more than seven years of fighting, Roberto's party took its first of many serious knocks in July 1968 when an Organisation of African Unity resolution withdrew recognition of his Angolan government-in-exile. OAU (African Union today) leaders declared in Addis Ababa that they would channel all future military and financial assistance to the MPLA, already in strong opposition to UPA/FNLA. The reason for the choice, the media was told, was that the MPLA appeared to be the more successful guerrilla grouping in Angola.

---

2   See Chapter 5 in *War Stories by Al Venter and Friends*, Protea Books, Pretoria, 2012 which details Klootwyk's three years spent flying against the rebels in the Congo.

Indirectly, Lisbon concurred that this was the logical choice. By the time I arrived in Luanda to cover the war for the first time in the late-1960s the Portuguese military authorities were candid that the MPLA threat was the most serious they had encountered since the start of the war. In fact, they made no bones about it: the MPLA and the Conakry-based PAIGC movement operating in Portuguese Guinea were the most effective guerrilla armies in sub-Saharan Africa, which became the most significant theme of my first briefing.

Of concern to Lisbon throughout, was that the MPLA got almost all its weapons from the Communist Bloc. The Mosin-Nagant bolt-action rifle was an early starter, followed by the Soviet SKS and obviously, AK-47 automatic rifles as well as PPsH-41 submachine guns.

It was interesting that a number of Portuguese units, including several Special Forces groups, actually preferred the AK; if not superior to their own G3, they believed the Kalashnikov was a lot more rugged. Koevoet, the South African police counter-insurgency unit was of the same mind. Many 32 Battalion operations involved clandestine cross-border raids into Angola; the unit liked to wear former Portuguese Army camouflage uniforms together with AKs to confuse locals into believing they were *camaradas*.

Angolan guerrilla movements also made extensive use of the Degtyarev light machine gun together with the DShK as well as heavier weapons like the SG-43 Goryunov. Support weapons included Soviet mortars, recoilless rifles, the RPG-2 and, when more readily available, the RPG-7.

As far as anti-aircraft weapons were concerned, the ZPU-4 was top of the list, supplemented towards the end of the war by Strela-2 ground-to-air guided missiles, more commonly called SAM-7. These sophisticated weapons were introduced into the Portuguese Guinea insurgency theatre of operations in 1973, and to Lisbon's consternation, ground-to-air missiles appeared among Mozambique guerrilla fighters a year later.

SAM-7s or Man Portable Air Defence Systems (MANPADs) were actually successful in shooting down several Portuguese Air Force Fiat G-91 support jet fighters in Portuguese Guinea as well as one or two Alouette helicopters. The consequences had a serious effect on morale among government forces because once the insurgents were able to prove they had the wherewithal to knock modern aircraft out of the sky, Portuguese Air Force bombing and strafing raids were immediately curtailed. Only after a variety of counter-measures were studied and implemented, including non-reflective paint on aircraft fuselages, were the jets again seen in action, and then only in the final stages of the war.

It should be mentioned in this context that shoulder-fired SAMs are relatively inexpensive and, at less than two metres in length, easy to use and move. Operated much like a rifle (as is the RPG-7) early versions of MANPADs were effective up to about 4,500 metres and for the guerrilla operating under primitive conditions, it was considered the ultimate offensive weapon.

Two Air Rhodesia Viscount civilian planes that had taken off from Kariba Airport towards the end of the Rhodesian conflict were shot down by SAM-7s; they were actually hit while still gaining altitude in the Zambezi Valley.

As with the missiles, most of the MPLA's arms, ammunition and equipment were – and still are – of Eastern European Bloc or Chinese origin.

It was the same with training. MPLA cadres were put through their paces by Soviet, Chinese, Cuban, Algerian and in a few instances, North Vietnamese guerrilla veterans. These military specialists from South-East Asia were put to good use in breaking the language barrier, especially since many rebel volunteers had originally come from Francophone Africa and since Vietnam was formerly a French colony, it made good sense.

Dr Agostinho Neto, in direct contrast to Holden Roberto, apart from being what his biographers called him: 'a quiet spoken intellectual and poet' was also a former Portuguese national who completed his tertiary studies in Lisbon.

For a while in the early days, Neto operated from an office in central Lusaka, though his movement's military wing – in large part because of CIA involvement in the region – had previously been based in Congo-Brazza. Increased French influence later forced him southwards.

Ultimately the Zambian government's militant stand against newly-independent Rhodesia was the deciding factor in Portuguese liberation groups gaining Kenneth Kaunda's support. The country's geographical position between three of the four erstwhile European-dominated Southern African states made the former British colony an excellent staging post.

Throughout the guerrilla struggle, Neto maintained a host of representatives in Europe – both East and West – as well as in Peking, Havana, Cairo, Lagos, Conakry and Algiers. In some of these countries they were given full diplomatic status.

His links with FRELIMO, the Mozambique insurgent group once headed by another American favourite, the late Eduardo Mondlane, were close. Following Mondlane's murder, Neto was said to have become more reclusive and even isolated from the party. He feared, correctly, that he might be next.

In contrast, Daniel Chipenda, who had once been a senior MPLA office bearer, was a competent but testy revolutionary and might even had become head of this radical movement had ambition not prompted him to move on.

Though he later fell foul of the elders of the founding party, he was initially the MPLA representative in Dar es Salaam. There, his job was to co-ordinate training and supply programmes with other liberation groups in Southern Africa.

It was an important posting because a large proportion of the military hardware used by the MPLA—as well as Mozambican and Rhodesian liberation groups—was channelled through Dar es Salaam harbour.

Chipenda must have used his position to good effect since it was said that he was working for both the CIA and South African Military Intelligence. This was why it came no surprise when he formed his own political and military grouping that he called the Chipa Squadron or, in the lingo, *Chipa Esquadrão*. It was this band of fairly seasoned fighters that went over to the South African Army almost *en bloc* after the Portuguese had pulled out.

The unit was eventually shaped into the SADF's crack 32 Battalion Special Forces group by Jan Breytenbach.[3]

Compared to earlier periods when there had always been what were termed 'trouble makers' among the indigenous black population – events that led to quite a few revolts – a new kind of political awareness began to emerge in the Portuguese territories early in the 20th Century.

Civil disobedience, though not widespread, caused Lisbon to pass the Portuguese Colonial Act in June 1933. While this recognised the supremacy of Portuguese over 'native people' and accepted that locals could pursue all studies including – if there was aptitude – being able to move on to

---

3 During the final phase of the Portuguese Army's withdrawal from Angola, the author travelled from Luanda to Nova Lisboa (since renamed Huambo) to join Daniel Chipenda's *Chipa Esquadrão* as a mercenary, largely in order to get the story he was after. The relationship did not last long. South African Army units had meanwhile invaded northwards from South West Africa (today's Namibia) and had made inroads almost as far north as Luanda. Obviously, his presence as a South African journalist impeded progress since the entire operation was supposed to be covert.

Tanzania's Julius Nyerere was at the forefront of driving white settler communities out of Southern Africa. Playing a convincing 'pacifist' card, he allowed the Soviet Union and China to use Dar es Salaam harbour to bring in billions of dollars worth of military equipment to wage a series of wars in Mozambique, Rhodesia, and South West Africa.

The anti-Lisbon 'liberation' leaders tried and failed to form a united front. Here Holden Roberto (left) meets some of those opposed to him in Kinshasa.

Meanwhile, the war in South West Africa escalated with landmines killing farmers south of the 'Red Line'. This vehicle belonged to a farmer in the Grootfontein area. (Photo: *Windhoek Advertiser*)

Moscow gave solid support to the rebels, making their aircraft available to shift war supplies. (Author's photo)

The author took this photo of a Russian 'trawler' on an intelligence-gathering mission off the South West African coast from a SAAF Shackleton.

THE AFRICAN ADVERSARIES 415

Cartoonists in Europe made the most of Portugal's unease…

Libya's Muammar Gaddafi provided facilities for thousands of 'liberation fighters' to be trained in his country.

Ghana's Kwame *Osagjefo* Nkrumah.

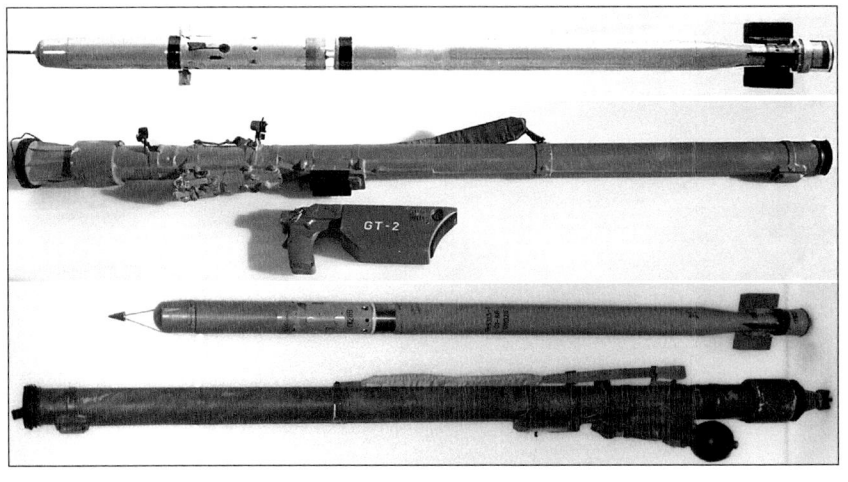

A selection of Soviet ground-to-air missiles fielded by the rebels.

Meanwhile, in Portugal itself, powerful support for the liberation groups came from an underground communist movement led by, among others, army major Otelo Saraiva de Carvalho (right), ironically, the author's escort officer while he covered the war in Portuguese Guinea.

Black Star Square, Accra, where Nkrumah of Ghana at first propagated the premise: 'Africa for the Africans'. (Author's photo)

university level, the reality was very different. Though some Africans from the 'Provinces' did manage to enter universities in the *metrópole* – they were hardly ever encouraged to do so.

After the Second World War – in which Portugal remained neutral (though the country did side with Britain in the First World War) – many more Portuguese settled in Angola than before. That flow became a flood in the 1950s, vigorously encouraged by the prime minister Dr António de Oliveira Salazar.

An interesting statistic here is that while the number of whites and people of mixed blood in a 1927 census showed a figure of almost 43,000, that tally had increased to several hundred thousand by the end of the colonial war in 1974. Almost all of them were to flee the country, the majority to Portugal and sizeable numbers to Brazil, the United States, South Africa, Canada and elsewhere.

The figure for whites and mulattos in Mozambique in 1928 in contrast, was 26,100. Again, this total multiplied several times by fairly strong South African inflows over the years which, in turn, fostered more Portuguese heading to the territory.

Still, the message about African self-rule was making the rounds and Angolan blacks were not insensitive to what was going on elsewhere on the continent. After the Second World War a group of young, reasonably well-educated black enthusiasts led by Viriato da Cruz and others formed the Movement of Young Intellectuals in Luanda in 1948 and went on to promote a largely ethnic Angolan culture. The body was taken over by aspiring nationalists who sent a letter to the United Nations calling for Angola to be given what they called 'Protectorate Status' under UN supervision. Many of these dissidents were arrested by PIDE, the Portuguese secret police; quite a few died in detention after being tortured.

Five years on and Angolan separatists founded PLUA, the Party of the United Struggle for Africans in Angola, the first of several organisations that advocated an absolute break from Portugal.

At that point, one of the moving forces in the Angolan political spectrum, Mário Pinto de Andrade, stepped up to the podium. Together with his brother Joaquim, the two men formed the Angolan Communist Party (PCA). In December 1956 they engineered a merger between the PLUA and PCA to form the Popular Movement for the Liberation of Angola (MPLA), which, after 13 years of guerrilla warfare, led to the country's independence.

Even here, there were tribal overtones. Most of the support for da Cruz, Mário Andrade, Ilidio Machado, and Lúcio Lara came from Luanda and the preponderant Mbundu people of northwest Angola. For centuries the Mbundus had been the most important tribal kingdom in a region which included much of north Angola as well as huge swathes of the Congo. From the earliest days of Empire, Lisbon assiduously cultivated good relations with these people as well as with the Bakongo, and in particular, their respective titular heads or chiefs.

With time, these relations soured. By the early 1950s the Portuguese could no longer count on the support of the Mbundu Royal Household.

A breakthrough for the political dissidents arrived in January 1961 when Angolan peasants in Malanje Province boycotted the cotton fields they were forced to harvest, quite often as hard labour and getting little reward in return for their labours. Incensed at being treated as second rate citizens and working under conditions that were slave-like in all but name, the workers burned their identification cards and attacked Portuguese traders in what was subsequently referred to as 'Maria's War'. It quickly turned ugly.

Portuguese military commanders in Angola responded by bombing several dozen villages with napalm and killing 7,000 Africans. Weeks later the dissenters upped the ante by storming a police station and Luanda's São Paulo prison. Seven policemen and 40 Africans were killed in February 1961, effectively signalling the start of limited hostilities against the colonial regime.

Conditions deteriorated further when the government held a state funeral for the deceased police officers. The funeral cortege that wended its way through the streets of Luanda saw the biggest turnout of the population the Angolan capital had ever experienced, with the emotionally-charged throng lining the route for kilometres. Incensed by the deaths of their compatriots, this multitude – almost all of them white – went on to massacre still more black people during rampages through Luanda's streets.

Black political militants then attacked a second prison later that month and the Portuguese once more retaliated with vigour.

John Marcum, the American historian and political scientist reported:[4]

> ...Portuguese vengeance was awesome. The police helped civilian vigilantes organise nightly slaughters in the [Luanda slums]. The whites hauled Africans from their flimsy one-room huts, shot them and left their bodies in the streets. A Methodist missionary... testified that he personally knew of the deaths of almost 300.
>
> Within weeks the government pushed the fledgling MPLA out of Luanda and into the Dembos region of the north where it established its '1st Military Region'.

UPA/FNLA leader Holden Roberto had meanwhile launched a series of his combined military incursions into Angola in March 1961, at the head of what was variously estimated to be between 4,000 and 5,000 militants, though several reports talk about a figure closer to 10,000.

His problem was that a tiny proportion of these irregulars had been militarily trained. While there were some automatic weapons, the majority were armed with ancient blunderbusses and machetes (pangas). Nonetheless, the mob was committed and such was their vehemence as they swept southwards, that the Portuguese authorities were taken completely by surprise.

The UPA went on to seize farms, government outposts and trading centres and murdered just about everybody the rabble encountered along the way.[5] At least a thousand whites and an unknown number of Africans were killed.

Commenting on the incursion, Roberto said that 'this time the slaves did not cower... they massacred everything.'

It took months for Lisbon's security forces in Angola to properly regroup and make an effective stand, all the while taking more casualties. But traditional Lusitanian doggedness persevered and finally government forces – backed by limited air power – started to have an effect. The Portuguese Army took control first of the hillside town of Nambuangongo where the local church was used as the rebel headquarters and then Pedra Verde, the UPA's last base in northern Angola, six months later.

In the first year of hostilities there were roughly 2,000 Portuguese and 50,000 Africans killed. Between 400,000 and 500,000 refugees fled to the Congo, or, as it was soon to become, Zaire. UPA militants used the opportunity to draw as many refugees into their movement as funds and facilities allowed and continued to launch attacks from the safety of the adjacent country.

---

4   John A Marcum: *The Angolan Revolution, Volume II: Exile Politics and Guerrilla Warfare (1962–1976):* MIT Press, Cambridge, Massachusetts, 1978.
5   Possibly the most explicit accounts of these attacks are to be found in one of the first books on the subject to appear in English. Written by Bernardo Teixeira and published in 1965, *Fabric of Terror: Three Days in Angola* comes with an introduction by American author Robert Ruark.

Violence throughout this period was uncoordinated and more often than not, mindless. It often included intra-factional brutality, like when a UPA patrol arrested almost two dozen MPLA militants (their supposed allies) and executed the lot. That happened during October 1961 in what subsequently became known as the Ferreira incident. While that was not the first time the UPA and MPLA had exchanged blows, the event did seal a growing enmity and sparked still more bloodshed.

Gradually the MPLA proved to be the more forceful of the two liberation groups, largely because Neto was receiving arms, equipment and training from the Kremlin. Also, his movement by then had quietly taken in scores of experienced fighters from other conflicts who had 'answered the call', including a number of Cuban militants. Meanwhile, the CIA recruited Holden Roberto, but he was both inept and ineffectual in command.

At Moscow's behest, Castro had been consistently following developments and Cuba entered the fray in force shortly afterwards. Neto had already met Che Guevara and soon got an infusion of cash from Havana as well as from East Germany.

In May 1966, Daniel Chipenda – then still a member of the MPLA – established the Eastern Front, significantly expanding the group's reach. But when that effort collapsed, Chipenda and Neto blamed each other for what has since been described as a 'tactical blunder that should never have happened'. However, it did and one of the results was that Luanda strengthened both its command structure and its forces in the east.

During the late 1960s the FNLA and MPLA ended up spending as much time at each other's throats as they did fighting the Portuguese. It got so bad that MPLA forces eventually assisted Lisbon's PIDE security agents in hunting down FNLA hideouts.

A brief word about Agostinho Neto the man

Born in September 1922 at Icolo e Bengo, south of Nova Lisboa in Angola's central provinces, he was educated to secondary level at a Luanda school. From 1944 to 1947 he worked in the Portuguese health services in the city and it was then that his zeal and initiative prompted the authorities to allow him to study medicine at Coimbra University in Portugal.

Not much is known about his politics at this stage, but one of his associates labelled him a 'visionary' because young Neto believed that eventually black people would rule his land. What is clear is that studies or not, Agostinho Neto became politically active and five years later, in 1952, was imprisoned for taking part in popular demonstrations against his hosts. Although freed shortly afterwards, he was imprisoned again from February 1955 to June 1957. Neto qualified as a doctor in 1958 and the same day he was awarded his diploma in Lisbon he married his Portuguese wife.

Dr Neto's MPLA was originally established in Luanda in 1956 as an underground movement advocating equal rights for all people irrespective of race, colour or creed. Prior to its exile to Congo-Brazza, The MPLA merged with a number of political groupings that had been declared illegal by the Portuguese authorities.

From early on, Neto was assisted by other radical members, including his close associate Mário Pinto de Andrade who lived outside Africa for most of his life. During the course of his studies at Lisbon, Frankfurt and Paris, Andrade joined both the Portuguese (underground) and French communist parties and spent time doing what his biographers term 'Political Training' in Moscow, Warsaw and Peking.

The date the MPLA commemorates above all others is February 4: it features in the name of Luanda's international airport. Then, in 1961 – almost six weeks before the first UPA attacks had taken place in northern Angola – MPLA guerrillas attacked the São Paulo prison.

Dr Neto always maintained that the large-scale UPA/GRAE attacks were premature. Had Roberto waited a few months, he reckoned, their joint efforts would have had a far more devastating effect on the Portuguese security forces. Luanda might even have fallen, he wrote afterwards and he was probably right, because following the first rebel attacks, Lisbon's defenders were forced the fall back almost to the city gates.

The MPLA also liked to claim responsibility for opening Angola's 'Second Front' in the east, along the Zambian border, an area of infiltration that the Portuguese military authorities in Luanda admitted in their briefings was already larger than Rhodesia by the late 1960s.

For a long time, most of the preliminary training that MPLA and UPA/GRAE/FNLA recruits underwent was completed in Zambia, Zaire, Congo-Brazza and Tanzania.

A number of insurgent training camps were pin-pointed early on in various African states bordering on Southern Africa and these included Dolisie and Pointe Noire in Congo-Brazza; Kinkuzu, which was a large UPA/FNLA camp some miles south of Kinshasa in Zaire; Tanzania's Kongwa, Bagamoyo and Nachingwea towns as well as Sikongo in the Barotse Province of Zambia.

Many of the brighter young MPLA trainees were sent for advanced guerrilla instruction at military institutions. The huge guerrilla training base at Tclemen, Algeria, regarded by many as the ultimate in revolutionary training orientation in Africa, was rated by the West as a terrorist-style African 'West Point' and quite a few recruits loyal to Neto spent time there.

Portuguese military leaders maintained throughout that a major factor in favour of their own forces in the Angolan struggle was that UPA and MPLA – while opposed to Portuguese domination – went to war with one another as soon as they did. Of the two, MPLA guerrillas were by far the most resilient. They were better trained, tough, wily and totally ruthless.

General Bettencourt Rodrigues – the man who had originally arranged for me to cover these wars – once commented that 'many MPLA cadres have been well trained… they know what they want and they know how to get it.' He knew what he was talking about.[6]

I stayed in touch with him over the years and it was clear to anybody who knew the man that he was an outstanding field commander. It was also Bettencourt Rodrigues who pulled Lisbon's troops up by their bootstraps when he was finally posted to senior command in Angola.

The UPA/FNLA, in contrast, while a reasonably effective guerrilla force to start with, was soon weakened by a lack of discipline that seemed to dog its efforts all the way up the ladder to headquarters in Kinshasa. Holden Roberto ruled largely by decree and preferred the good life in the Congolese capital, especially since it was being subsidised by Langley. He ended up a chronic alcoholic and to the surprise of us all, was one of the few of the old guard who actually died in their own beds of heart disease in 2007.

There were other notable differences between the two guerrilla factions. Whereas MPLA guerrillas would *ask* villagers for food and normally pay for what they took, UPA fighters would demand it as their right and make no recompense. For Neto's guerrillas, it was one of the simple revolutionary principles picked up in Mao's China

More salient, MPLA cadres rarely touched the women of their hosts, something apparently drummed into them while they were in training. UPA men had no qualms about demanding solace from the wives of local tribesmen. In one area, an officer told me, a UPA officer had shot a tribal chief because he had objected to his men taking three young virgins of the village for their pleasure.

---

6 It was General Bethencourt Rodrigues that originally got me into covering Portugal's African wars, details of which are in the Acknowledgments section of *Portugal's Guerrilla Wars in Africa*.

'That would never have been tolerated in any area controlled by the MPLA', he said. The philosophy behind its strategy was basic and involved a simple maxim: 'Help us now and once in power, you will not be forgotten.' This was where the Chinese and Cuban influences immediately became apparent, Sector D's Brigadier Martins Soares maintained in one of his briefings.

MPLA units, he stated, were implementing the Chinese communist dogma: before it was possible to win a guerrilla struggle it was necessary to win the confidence of the civilian population. 'They must move as freely among the civilians as the fishes in the sea', the Chinese revolutionary leader wrote, an aphorism that became engrained in many subsequent revolutionary struggles on several continents. The MPLA enshrined it.

Perhaps the best illustration of MPLA efficacy and where they made headway, the brigadier said, was that when their young men returned to an area after being trained abroad, they spent time organising the villagers to tidy their living quarters and make more equable sanitary arrangements. It was healthier for the entire community, they would explain. They would then encourage young men of the villages to help their women grow more crops, something unheard of in stratified tribal circles where it had always been females responsible for tending to the needs of the family.

Applying simple administrative principles was usually enough to impress any village chief who had lived in the jungle most of his life. In any event, to these simple African folk, enthusiastic young MPLA guerrillas were more reliable than either the usually obnoxious Portuguese government functionaries with whom all had had fleeting contact, or their grab-all UPA adversaries.

It has to be mentioned that shortly after the first UPA incursions into Angola's north, Lisbon did initiate several moderating measures in a bid to bring the mass of the population back into the fold. Cautious at first, these edicts soon took on legs of their own.

The *assimilado* programme was begun, whereby certain colonial subjects (of colour) could be 'assimilated' into Portuguese society. These gestures also opened the way for qualified black combatants to achieve commissioned rank within the armed forces. A growing body of black civil administrators in government service – of whom more were required each year to manage the affairs of this vast country as the war progressed – was also wooed with promises of high office. Similar programmes were concurrently instituted in Mozambique and Portuguese Guinea.

But it was too little and far too late. There were already dozens of formerly French and British African states, now independent, and represented in the United Nations and whose voices could be clearly heard on short wave radio bands in Africa's darkest forests.

All demanded universal equality for the black man and if that was not forthcoming, force of arms should be used to achieve it, was the gist of it.

Also, former Portuguese dissidents were returning home as guerrillas, each one of them spreading the word: with a bit more effort, they told the populace, Angola, Mozambique and Portuguese Guinea would soon be theirs.

Nor had events that had taken place at roughly the same time in the United States under President John F Kennedy been lost on Lisbon. Portuguese Premier Marcelo Caetano – the man who succeeded Salazar – and his ministers tried to institute vaguely similar moderating policies in the overseas territories, but few were followed through by an entrenched colonial hierarchy whose members regarded any kind of concession to black people weakness.

For all this, the new, relatively enlightened political structure was hardly a one way street towards egalitarianism. It might be recalled that US President Lyndon Johnson had never been a consistent advocate of racial equality and his explanation of why he backed the Civil Rights Act of 1957 lays out some of his thinking, especially since these sentiments would be uttered quite vociferously by the ruling establishment in Lisbon shortly afterwards.

To quote Johnson verbatim:

> These Negroes, they're getting pretty uppity these days and that's a problem for us since they've got something now they never had before, the political pull to back up their uppityness.
>
> Now we've got to do something about this, we've got to give them a little something, just enough to quiet them down, but not enough to make a difference.

In this regard, much has also changed in the United States of America in the interim…

Two African leaders played critical roles in supporting so-called 'Liberation wars' wars in Africa's south. The first was President Kenneth Kaunda (**top**) who allowed Zambia to become a conduit for weapons and the transfer of guerrillas, initially against the Portuguese, then against the Rhodesians and finally to counter the South African military presence in northern South West Africa. Kaunda (**on the right**) is flanked by President Nyerere with President Machel on the **left**. The **bottom photo** shows Mozambique's President Samora Machel addressing a crowd shortly after he arrived in Maputo for the first time. (Photo Curto Grosso)

27

Consequences That Followed Lisbon Abandoning its African Possessions

In theory, Angola's former adversaries, having stopped fighting, should have been able to work things out for the future, something solid and lasting. The country desperately needed a fresh start with reasonably well-educated and pliant people in charge who would consider every possible option. It was a God-given opportunity with the so-called colonial yoke relegated to history. But then most of those in charge were Marxists and a real or imagined 'god' did not feature in either their hopes or their visions. Yet, 'tomorrow' did beckon and so, indeed it should have. But the Cold War intervened…

It was exactly the same with Mozambique and in Portuguese Guinea, that tiny enclave way up the west coast of Africa which was already calling itself Guiné-Bissau. The problem in all three former Portuguese territories was that domestic politics lurched radically Left.

Aware of this impasse, several Western countries – the United States, Britain, France, Germany, Italy, Canada, all four Scandinavian countries, together with quite a few others offered aid and training programmes. But because almost all this largesse came not in greenbacks but from a succession of aid programmes – Luanda, the newly renamed Maputo and Bissau – preferred to tread the tried and trusted Marxist path, again at Moscow's behest.

Consequently, in both Angola and former Portuguese Guinea there was no real peace, in large part because several different factions were each struggling to reach dominance and wanted not only larger chunks of the national pie but also to settle personal scores. It was vicious.

Mozambique's case was different to started with because FRELIMO held pole position and RENAMO was something that took several years to happen.

In Angola, Agostinho Neto's MPLA – backed by a very substantial Cuban military force – launched a campaign of attrition against both the FNLA and UNITA. A grotesque civil war was initiated even before the last Portuguese soldier had left Luanda harbour for home.

In Guiné-Bissau, the revolutionary PAIGC killed every former government soldier it could seek out, including their women and children as well as other family member of those who had worn the distinctive Portuguese Army camouflage uniform. It soon became so mindlessly brutal, some of the survivors told me years later while I was filming in that country, that many of the fire-fights between former black Portuguese soldiers and those linked to the new government were far more intense than anything they had experienced before. Ongoing battles around the town of Tite in the interior – Joao Bacar's old stomping ground – were dubbed 'Killing Fields'.

Similarly in Angola where conditions quickly deteriorated into civil war: there too bloodletting was commonplace.

Castro's influence had already become pervasive and, as we have seen, by independence thousands of Cuban troops had infiltrated the country clandestinely, air-lifted across the Atlantic in Soviet military transports. Planeloads of weapons and ammunition into that part of Africa from Eastern Europe followed.

In terms of both scope and intensity, the battles that resulted in Angola were not as intense as those that had taken place in Portuguese Guinea (and certainly nothing like the carnage currently on the go in present-day Syria and Iraq). Several different and identifiable factions did end up battling each other for supremacy, and with foreign help, it did not take the MPLA long to prevail.

Apart from the early days of terror, initiated by UPA from the Congo, nobody was cutting off the heads of victims. Instead, they preferred pouring gasoline over their victims and setting alight their bodies, something I was to witness myself. The procedure was repeated not long afterwards in the same kind of simmering discontent that sometimes produced full-blown revolts in a South Africa under the rule of an apartheid-driven government. Those involved called it 'necklacing', widely practiced in the townships.

Looking back, one observed a grim and unforgiving transition. While serving briefly with the dissident *Chipa Esquadrao*, then based in Huambo when that city was still called Nova Lisboa – and under FNLA control – we'd regularly come upon the consequences of what, at worst, could be called African versions of these dreaded 'Kangaroo Courts'.

Left wing activists living there and who were believed to be linked, even ambiguously to Luanda's MPLA were arrested, questioned, judged and horrifically tortured, sometimes in minutes. That achieved, these poor victims were burned alive, usually on the outskirts of Angola's second city. We would find their bodies, gruesome and misshapen some mornings while out on patrol, which was one of the reasons why I went to great lengths to secure the door of my hotel room before I turned in each night.

Hostilities continued almost unabated throughout Angola into the next millennium and only came to an end after the mercenary group Executive Outcomes had forced UNITA to the negotiating table. Dr Jonas Savimbi was himself lured into an ambush and assassinated by persons unknown in February 2002.

There is good evidence that he knew his attackers and there are those who maintain that some old South African friends might have been involved. Others mention Israeli Interests, while Fred Bridgland, in a brief discussion with the author, suggests it was an Angolan Army unit that killed him in the end. We will never know for sure. Certainly, knowing the man and aware of his customary traits, it is pretty certain he would never have met with a bunch of strangers in bush country without the usual precautions.

In a word, he trusted somebody and was betrayed.

The civil war that had already started by the time that Angola's independence decree had been signed on the 11th November 1975 plunged the country into a cycle of violence far worse than the country had experienced while under Lisbon's rule.

There are many reasons for this having taken place. Writing for *Revista Militar*, former United States naval aviator Captain John (Jack) P. Cann wrote in his article titled 'Securing the Borders of Angola 1961–1974' (published in December 2009) that radical policies were behind a lot of it. I quote:

> By 1956 the young Marxists of the Angolan Communist Party contributed to the formation of the *Movimento Popular de Libertação de Angola*. The MPLA developed roots among Luanda's urban and largely radical intellectuals, among its slum dwellers, and to a lesser

extent, eastward from the capital among the Mbundu, Angola's second largest ethno-linguistic group, and the Chokwe people.

These urban roots were composed largely of *mestiços* or mixed-race peoples, who controlled the party. The movement had little in common with the rural peasants of the east and south of Angola and made almost no effort to gain their true devotion. In December 1956 the initial MPLA manifesto was openly published in a direct frontal assault on the [Portuguese] government.

Predictably the national police, known simply by its acronym PIDE (*Policia Internacional de Defesa do Estado*), reacted adversely, and a number of the MPLA leaders were forced to flee into exile.

From 1957 onward PIDE action was so successful 'that the nationalists were not able to maintain more than the most rudimentary organization inside the colonies and could not communicate with those cells that did exist'. The parties were forced to conduct their affairs from neighbouring states and were deeply influenced by their foreign connections.

As the PIDE systematically wrecked the MPLA organization, primarily in Luanda, it became progressively weaker and isolated from its leadership that was now abroad and, as it had no strong constituency or bases elsewhere among the rural population, withered within Angola.

The MPLA in exile established itself initially in Léopoldville and aligned itself not only with other independent African nations and their socialist philosophy, but also with the communist bloc, including the Italian and French communist parties.

But then, as we are all aware, no insurgency can survive without some degree of popular support. Insurgents must have backing to offset the advantages the government has by its control of the levers of power, especially the military forces and the police. Most insurgencies cannot afford to confront the government directly; to do so is too costly and risks destruction of the insurgent force.

Instead, insurgents seek to erode the strength and will of the government by the use of guerrilla warfare and terrorism until it either collapses or capitulates on conditions favourable to the insurgents.

Guerrilla warfare and terrorism must, however, increase the base of popular support to sustain the momentum of an insurgency. The academic Bard O'Neill identified six methods that insurgents use to gain popular support. These are: (1 charismatic attraction, (2 esoteric appeals, (3 exoteric appeals, (4 terrorism, (5 provocation of government counterterrorism and (6 demonstration of potency.[1]

Before the civil war in 1975–76, approximately 400,000 whites lived in Angola. Nearly 350,000 of these people left the country during the war and their departure portended serious consequences for the MPLA. The people of mixed blood, *mestiços* or mulattos – which numbered perhaps 2.2 million – were the most important political, economic and social group. They [initially] held the reins of power in the MPLA.[2]

A question often asked is when the first group of insurgents entered Angola from the Congo could they not be stopped? More salient, was Luanda not aware of this very substantial flow of belligerents from its own intelligence sources in neighbouring countries? Indeed, Lisbon knew it

---

1 Bard E. O'Neill, ed., *Insurgency in the Modern World* (Boulder, Colorado: Westview Press, 1980, citing George B. Jordan, *Objectives and Methods of Communist Guerrilla Warfare*.
2 Richard Harwood, 'Guerrillas Demonstrate High Morale', *Washington Post*, July 22, 1981.

was coming, but it was a question of *when*. Had this taken place in Europe, it would have been easy to muster defences along the country's borders. But this was Africa.

Rene Pélissier, the noted French historian, made the point in a personal communication to this author that Angola's frontiers were, if anything, porous. He cites an example used in a book titled *Angola* that he wrote in collaboration with Douglas L Wheeler and which deals with Angola's northern Congo district, immediately adjacent to the country of the same name:

> [In 1960, shortly before the first attacks took place] the Congo district for its 37,000 square miles had 14 *conceilhos* (basic urban or semi-urban administrative units) or *circunscrições* (basic rural administrative divisions) and 37 border posts, for an average of 725 square miles per administrative division. This presence would hardly be effective in controlling a frontier, as the posts would be dozens of miles apart. Large numbers of people could and did cross undetected.

After the MPLA had taken over the Luanda Government, conditions did not improve. In fact, they deteriorated. The independence struggle was over and most cadres tended to sit back and wait for things to happen, which is the story of so much of modern Africa.

Obviously the Soviets and the Cubans played a formative role and helped counter threats from the [South African] south, but the everyday affairs of the country were allowed to lapse, and for several reasons which are dealt with in a lengthy 1984 summation [before Savimbi's death] written by US Marine Corps Major Robert Burke which encapsulates many of the problems faced by the MPLA in its early years.

Titled *UNITA – A Case Study in Modern Insurgency,* it follows the collapse of Portuguese power in the country and suggests that the Marxist government had serious difficulties in executing an effective counterinsurgency programme. It is also important to note that when this was published, Dr Jonas Savimbi's UNITA was still extremely active as a political and military force throughout most of the country.

> One of the major difficulties was the uninspired leadership of the [post-independent] MPLA', declared Burke. 'As president of the MPLA, José Edwardo dos Santos was then (and still is after almost 40 years) head of government, president of the party, and commander-in-chief of the armed forces.
>
> Yet he, like Agostinho Neto before him, is a colourless individual. He is shy, taciturn, and reluctant to make public appearances; [At the time] he lived in Futunga Belas, the presidential compound just south of Luanda. Once this site was a famous resort for the rich in the colonial era; now tanks are dug in around the main road that runs past the compound and Cuban guards' barracks next door.[3]
>
> Although the MPLA bureaucracy is more sophisticated and complex than UNITA's, dos Santos has none of the personal leadership qualities that Savimbi of UNITA demonstrates. Perhaps fear of the rebel leader's charisma provides some of the rationale for the MPLA's official stance toward UNITA.
>
> The MPLA regards UNITA as a group of 'bandits' that would disappear without aid from South Africa. Savimbi is viewed as 'the main enemy of the Angolan people and little more

---

3 'Angola: Wind of Change', *Africa Confidential*, 24 (September 21, 1983).

than an extension of the South African military machine to be dealt with by force rather than [by] political compromise.'[4]

Savimbi is the most wanted 'outlaw' in Angola. There are rumours that the government is not unanimous on this issue, but none of these has been confirmed.[5] This suggests that some elements within the MPLA might be willing to negotiate with Savimbi and establish a coalition government.

The competency of the MPLA government is questionable. Official visitors and diplomatic representatives have indicated that apart from the president and a few ministers, other members of the government are disinterested in running the country. Few members of the government in key positions take part in negotiations on crucial issues.

As indicated in a recent edition of *Africa Confidential*, 'The party members are vastly outnumbered by the non-committed and the main nucleus of power surrounding the presidency is outnumbered by the dissidents within the party secretariat and people's assembly.'[6]

Factionalism has been a serious problem for the MPLA. In 1977, two members of the government, Nito Alves and Jose Van Dunem, distressed over the poor state of the Angolan economy, staged an abortive coup that resulted in a massive purge and reorganization of the government. The commissars and directing committees in eight provinces were removed. In October 1983, dos Santos narrowly escaped an assassination attempt.

The MPLA has always had a mixture of ideologues and pragmatists who disagree violently over the direction Angola should take. The ideologues want a Soviet style economy while the pragmatists want more private enterprise and exchange with the West. In response to the internal rivalries that beset the MPLA, dos Santos has played a more active role in the selection of candidates for office.[7]

Nevertheless, the divisiveness within the MPLA has seriously impaired its efforts to counter UNITA. The MPLA government is similar to the oligarchic Salazar-Caetano regime in Portugal that kept the country isolated from the outside world. Censorship is widespread. The few foreign visitors allowed to enter the country are afraid to talk to anyone but official representatives. All interviews must be arranged by the Department of Information and Propaganda.

It took Jay Ross, a *Washington Post* correspondent, 23 days to obtain just one interview. The secrecy surrounding the MPLA probably has hampered its ability to gain more international recognition from the West, especially the United States.[8]

Although the MPLA has attempted to mobilize the population by socializing the economy along Soviet lines, it has made some concessions to realism. Nearly all Portuguese enterprises that were abandoned during the civil war have been nationalized. Other enterprises deemed essential, such as banking and finance, have also been nationalized. State farms and agricultural cooperatives have been established.

Yet the MPLA has recognized and protected, and guaranteed private activities and property, even of foreigners, provided they supported the nation's economy.

---

4 David B. Ottaway, 'Angola Unwilling to Make Peace with Guerrillas,' *Washington Post*, December 29, 1978.
5 Edward Girardet, 'Angola – Yet to Come to Grips with Independence', *Christian Science Monitor*, June 16, 1983.
6 'Angola: The throttling process', *Africa Confidential* 23 (December 1, 1982).
7 Irving Kaplan, ed., *Angola: A Country Study* (Washington, DC: The American University, 1979).
8 Jay Ross, 'Inaccessibility to West Fosters Misunderstandings of Key Nation', *Washington Post*, September 20, 1981.

Corporations such as Gulf, Texaco, Boeing and Mobil have not been nationalized because the MPLA derives much of its revenue from these companies and because the MPLA does not have the technicians to run them if they were nationalized.[9]

In this final section of the book, I deal with all these matters in some detail: battles fought by the new-found Angolan Army which called itself FAPLA (*Forças Armadas Populares de Libertação de Angola*), as well as the role of a fairly large group of South African mercenaries hired by the most inappropriately-named Executive Outcomes.

These so-called 'Freelance Fighters' had taken on the war on behalf of Luanda's Marxist government – for a healthy fee of tens of millions of dollars – and almost overnight found themselves immersed in a society well-versed in the military ethos, culture and traditions of the period. They would undoubtedly have understood much of the subterfuge that went with it and the fact that in order to achieve anything at all, goodwill was never enough. It invariably necessitated an exchange of cash or valuables.

I saw some of this myself when I accompanied former SADF Colonel Duncan Rykaart to the home of his Angolan commanding general on the outskirts of Luanda. Following our own vehicle was a pickup truck with a brand new electricity generator on the back. Because of constant power cuts in the capital, the South Africans decided this gift would reflect good intensions on their part and they were right, to the tune, in those days, of about $35,000, or double what such a machine would cost today.

It was notable too, that the luxury 4x4 standing in the general's courtyard also came from the South Africans.

That was only a part of it. The next phase involved the guerrilla war against UNITA, which by then was extensive, as we have seen from the manner in which the Cafunfo diamonds diggings were reclaimed from the rebels in the opening three chapters of this work.

In truth, the South African mercenaries who arrived in Angola in 1993 slotted into their new role as adjuncts to the Angolan military fairly easily because both they and the Angolan officers with whom they mixed had shared quite a few battles in the past, almost always as adversaries.

Most of the old hands in the Angolan army and air force had seen action against Pretoria's old guard, some quite a lot of it. So the mercenary commanders, and those heading the Angolan Armed Forces – now renamed FAA or *Forças Armadas Angolanas* (which succeeded FAPLA) – had quite a lot in common.

The single difference was that while the South Africans were mostly former Special Forces operatives who had distinguished themselves under fire in the Border War and knew their business, FAA's antics were a farce. The Angolan military had been fighting UNITA ever since the country gained its independence and for almost as long hostilities lasted (until the South Africans arrived) Savimbi's people ran rings around them.

Worse, by the time Executive Outcomes came onto the scene to launch counter operations against rebel UNITA units in the Angolan oil fields in the north (something dealt with in Chapter 30) this versatile rebel force controlled about 90 per cent of a country as big as a sizeable chunk of Europe.

It is also instructive that many of UNITA's crack fighting units had originally been trained by the South African Special Forces personnel, something that resulted in an initial cause for suspicion within the Angolan top command. Quite a number of dos Santos's defence staff questioned the motives of Executive Outcomes. Obviously, by the time the South Africans came up

---

9 Kaplan, *Ibid.*

against UNITA in this new mercenary phase, they knew exactly what to expect of their adversaries and once they started taking casualties, the dissenters within the Angolan High Command were silenced.

Commented former South African Army Colonel Duncan Rykaart, a shrewd and competent Reconnaissance Regiment senior officer hired by Executive Outcomes: 'UNITA troops, by and large, were good. In fact, they were *damn* good because they were always good listeners when we instructed them. In turn, *we* knew exactly what we were up against!'

Duncan Rykaart was to die in an air accident a few years after EO pulled out of Angola. The circumstances of the crash were never properly explained, though we do know that it was a former Soviet aircraft on its way to Somalia from Uganda's Entebbe Airport.

It should be stressed that not all South African military professionals approached by Executive Outcomes were prepared to involve themselves in a mercenary war against Jonas Savimbi.

Former South African Air Force Colonel Neall Ellis – he went on to Sierra Leone as a 'freelance' gunship pilot shortly afterwards to turn the war against the rebels around – refused to do so.[10] Offered a lucrative job by Eeben Barlow, CEO of Executive Outcomes to fly helicopters against UNITA, Ellis's response was that that was simply not on because 'I have to live with my own conscience.' Jonas Savimbi, he explained, had been a trusted ally and also a very good friend of South Africa in the past: 'so to try to destroy him now would be a betrayal of all that.' He declared.

Quite a few more South African former military professionals echoed those sentiments, eschewing the opportunity of making good money at a time when things were pretty tight economically back home.

While these dramas were being played out, a cataclysm of almost similar dimensions was being enacted in Angola, only this one involved hundreds of thousands of mostly white Portuguese nationals fleeing for their lives.

They left the country in great haste, some not even bothering to pack their possessions and arrange to have them shipped to Europe: they had the prescience to accept that with the civil war developing, very little would be leaving the country in an orderly manner anyway.

They were right, because when I visited Luanda shortly before the handover, there were tens of thousands of crates stacked on the wharves waiting to be shipped out on ships that never arrived. By the time things became normal again, all had been ransacked because Angola's new government could not be bothered to guard the possessions of what was now regarded as a former enemy.

For all of Lisbon's promises of establishing an 'air bridge', that never happened. Commercial flights to Europe continued and supplementary flights were scheduled and some were actually laid on. The war had crippled Portugal financially and there was never enough in the coffers to rescue hundreds of thousands of potential hostages to a newly-established communist government in Africa.

As a consequence, enormous numbers of Portuguese nationals fled towards the south where a huge 'rescue' organisation was established by the Pretoria Government. With the ongoing Border War ravaging those southern regions, it was not an easy task and many of those fleeing the drama being played out further towards the north were killed in the crossfire.

An interesting observation here is the manner in which the FNLA was being referred to by the opposition. According to whoever it was in London who wrote the article, if you were not an

---

10 Al J. Venter: *Gunship Ace: The Wars of Neall Ellis, Helicopter Pilot and Mercenary*; Casemate US and UK as well as Protea Books South Africa, 2011.

Giving the salute during the mechanised parade on 4 May 1988 to commence Operation Reindeer. (SADF files)

Even after the armistice had been signed, guerrillas continued to operate in the bush: one war was followed by another...

CONSEQUENCES OF LISBON ABANDONING ITS AFRICAN POSSESSIONS

One of the bridges near Luanda blown up in the civil war. (Author's collection)

The detritus of conflict was still around, like this Portuguese army truck destroyed by a landmine. (Author's photo)

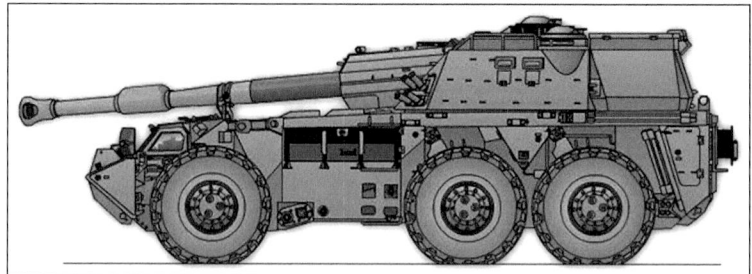

South Africa's armoury was enhanced by many new weapons systems which were developed after Operation Savannah, including this mobile 155mm howitzer labelled G6.

South African 140mm guns in action during a cross-border raid. (Author's collection)

Millions of people fled to the cities to seek protection from the war. Decades after hostilities they are still there, with Luanda's *Musseques* today holding millions of refugees. (Neil Walton took this photo in 2010)

Major General Bettencourt Rodrigues (on the right): the man who turned around Portugal's fortunes in the Angolan war.

A once-flourishing rail service abandoned in the face of hostilities.

This little boy – obviously Portuguese – arrived at a South African base with his black minder, a teacher in a small town and met with Roland de Vries who took the photo. They chatted a while and then left…

Memorial to those Portuguese who were killed while fighting for the South African Army. There are quite a few decorated heroes among them.

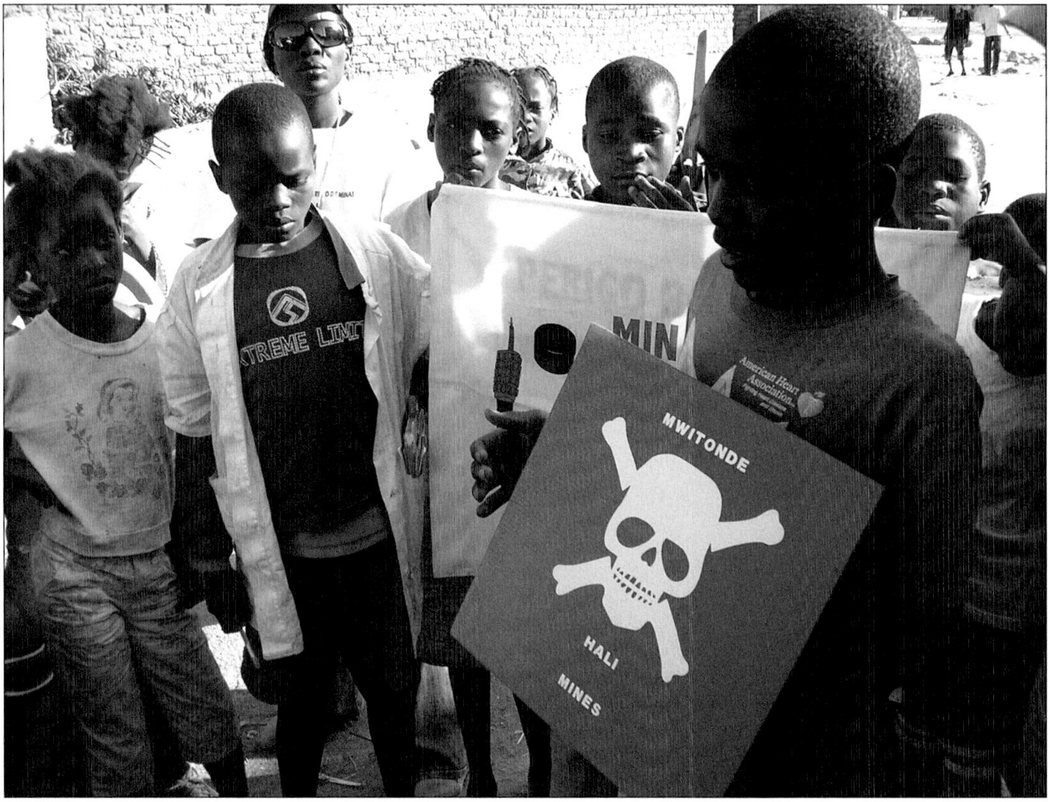

CONSEQUENCES OF LISBON ABANDONING ITS AFRICAN POSSESSIONS

One of the legacies of this conflict is landmines – millions of them – still being lifted by international aid groups.

Monument glorifying those who were involved in Luanda's wars.

MPLA supporter – an avowedly Marxist political organisation – it was axiomatic that you had to be a fascist.

Such were the perceptions of so many of the scribes who worked in Fleet Street during the 1960s and 1970s.

It was not long after the Angolan refugees crossed the South West African border that I experienced the makings of a human tragedy that unfolded during this cathartic period. I was in Sector 10 at the time – in Ovamboland – and had gone north into Angola with a raiding group. We ended up in one of the southern towns, not far from Xangongo. The story that emerged was fairly widely published at the time. I called it 'Collateral Damage', which I thought appropriate because it was about a little girl.

I remember it like it happened last week: as I wrote in my introduction, she was a waif, just a slip of a girl perhaps six or seven years old. Her hair was dirty and matted and streaked with mud, though it had probably once been dark.

The first time I saw her, the sun had bleached it. We found her when the patrol moved into a village near the hamlet of Mumbe in southern Angola, a region that had seen much violence over the past quarter century.

It was her features that appealed, a face that probably hadn't been washed in a month but that couldn't hide a smile that charmed. And her eyes, clear and blue that missed nothing. She had a rakish quality about her that was all mischief.

Her name was Lizbet, the old man told me, gesturing towards his charge. She clung to his bony protuberance that passed for a hand: a thumb with no fingers. 'The war,' he explained.

'Papa' she called the tall, rather frail old black man with an unusually dense head of pure white hair. In the African context it was magnificent but you couldn't ignore the humanizing touch of the comic.

When she spoke, he would stop what he was doing and listen carefully. It was obvious that he adored her. His proprietary looks and a gesture or two that only they understood said it all.

'*Sim* Lisbet', he would answer and they would spend a minute or two deliberating in Portuguese, or what passed for the language in the African bush. Someone in our group asked who she was. Nobody knew. It was unusual finding a white child in the heart of Africa a thousand miles from nowhere. Almost every one of us gathered on the banks of the great Kunene River that afternoon believed that we understood it all. We were wrong. Nothing had prepared us for this.

Here was a very dignified, very old black man, obviously much concerned about the security of someone who was clearly his responsibility. She, in turn, was totally misplaced. Lizbet was caught in the vortex of an African civil war. There was simply no ignoring her plight.

Some of the soldiers would have liked to pretend that she wasn't there; they found the intimacy between the two embarrassing.

We fed them both and they ate ravenously. She grabbed at the food before he did and he just smiled.

It was the summer of 1981 when it happened; the same summer that Charles and Diane were married. The battle for Beirut had just gone into overdrive.

In Angola, the Cold War had suddenly become hot. Cubans, Russians, East Germans (as well as the occasional Vietnamese) were being flown in like never before. Washington, meanwhile, had come out in support for the opposition, the curiously named Union for the Total Liberation of Angola. The Portuguese acronym is UNITA. It stuck.

UNITA was led by a mercurial, powerfully built graduate of Laussane University by the name of Jonas Savimbi, who would espouse Maoism to anyone who would listen. As far as Washington was concerned, that didn't matter. As they say in those parts: 'if your enemy is my enemy, then we are friends'.

It was the Americans that gave UNITA their first ground-to air missiles. There were other openers as well.

I had visited Savimbi's headquarters at Jamba a couple of times. There would always be talk of the handful of toffee-nosed Langley professionals there who tended to keep to themselves.

'They are Americans. They can turn the war around,' some UNITA cadres whispered when we asked. Usually the spooks were kept well hidden from the media. So were the Stingers and some of the other surprises that they brought with them.

The South Africans – when there were whites that still ruled Pretoria – were very active in Angola. The war, largely a guerrilla effort, was a low-key affair. As routinely as the seasons, the South African Army would feint or push into the hinterland a couple of hundred miles and then pull back.

The Angolans, in turn, would almost always retreat, leaving a lot of mines in their wake. Once the threat had passed, they would return to their old positions, lift those bombs that hadn't been triggered and settle down till next time. But that phase of the 23-year war is long gone. While Savimbi was still around, he was then more brigand than guerrilla, and the fighting went on, more intense than before.

I spent a while with one of the units that penetrated into the Angolan interior from what was then known as South West Africa, Namibia today. Eventually we found ourselves on the outskirts of Cassinga. But for the war, this remote settlement at the edge of what the Portuguese used to call *Terras do fim mundo* – Land at the end of the world – might have been one of Africa's biggest iron-ore projects. It was – and I suppose, still is – a region of great potential.

As one of the accredited correspondents, I had been cleared to accompany the long-range armored reconnaissance and strike force and our route took us through Mumbe.

The omens had been bad from the start. We took our first casualties within hours of setting out from Oshikango, a small town on the border. One of the infantry fighting vehicles just ahead of us – in a column a couple of miles long – hit a mine. The driver was incinerated; two others were horribly burnt. All were teenagers.

Five days later I, too, was flown out, another landmine casualty among many. With me it was only a broken arm caused by 20 yards of involuntary flight. I had been standing on the turret of one of the armored vehicles when it drove over a Soviet TM-57. That was after we had found the girl.

As with most towns in South Angola, the war had crippled Mumbe. There wasn't a building left intact. Most of the population had fled into the bush. Those pathetic souls that hung about when the South Africans arrived were either too old or too sick to go anywhere. Anyway, what new evil that hadn't already been tried by either Unita or Luanda could the racists foist on them? That was when one of the men spotted the girl.

We quickly discovered that the pair was inseparable. Like others in Mumbe, they had come to the makeshift army command post set up on the banks of the river to scavenge for food.

Lizbet's initial reaction to our presence was mixed. To begin with, she was guardedly friendly and then only because we offered succour. Our white skins didn't phase her; there were plenty of East Europeans serving with government forces and, no doubt, they had been curious about her as well. What she couldn't understand was that so few of us spoke Portuguese. Everything changed when someone pulled a coke out of an icebox. Judging from her reaction, it wasn't a first. She knew that there was nectar in the bottle and it didn't touch sides.

She asked for another and got it. After that we could do no wrong.

The presence of a little girl in the wilds of South Angola – a region that seemed to take its cue from the sixth ring of hell and where people were killed on a whim – presented us with some serious problems.

The first time we visited Mumbe, we weren't around long enough to appreciate the implications of her presence in the ongoing war. When we returned a couple of weeks later on our way back again (I rejoined the column by chopper after they had put a cast on my arm) matters took a turn. She was still there. And though the two of them had managed fine for years, we were worried about her. Who knew when any of us would be back? Would any of us come back? Such was the nature of this insurgent war that political and military scenarios changed constantly.

Chet Crocker, then Under Secretary of State for Africa, had tried numerous times to push through a cease-fire. Each time his efforts were thwarted. Angola – with some of the largest oil reserves on the continent – was a Soviet client state. As with the war in Afghanistan – then also in full swing – Moscow had as much interest in the outcome of this struggle as Washington. And since it was Gulf Oil that had originally developed Angola's oil fields, there were machinations on both sides.

Matters came to a head on our last evening in Mumbe. The sun had barely disappeared over the scattering of mopani trees to the west when the two arrived at the perimeter of the base. We had secured for the day and the order had gone out to the guards to shoot anyone who approached the camp. There are no 'Friendlies' in Angola's dark. It was fortunate that the man who spotted them disobeyed orders.

He did tell them both, in as many words, to fuck off. But when the old man persisted, one of the young conscripts was drawn to the commotion. It was he who told his corporal. Finally, the odd couple were escorted through barriers and brought before the only senior officer left with the column. All the others had been airlifted back to headquarters.

Having settled them around the campfire with more food, the old man was asked about his problem. It was 'a very serious matter' he had told the sentry when challenged.

'I am an old man,' he told the officer through a bilingual Angolan who translated.

'We can see that,' replied the Major diffidently.

'Soon I will be dead.'

'That's the way of all men.'

'Then, if I die, what will happen to her?' the old man asked, shoving his claw in Lizbet's face.

None of us had thought of that. It was only when he started to explain how it had all came about that we accepted its gravity. Lizbet had been with him since she was an infant. He was all she had: much more than a surrogate father considering the circumstances.

The old man's story was fascinating. When Lisbon unceremoniously dumped her African colonies in 1975, a brutal civil war broke out almost immediately. For a time there were Cubans and South African forces involved. Mozambique, the other Portuguese colony on the Indian Ocean coast was spared much of the pain, except that in the African tradition, anyone who was even *thought* to offer resistance was killed.

In Angola, those Portuguese civilians – many of them farmers, teachers, shopkeepers and administrators whose forefathers had been in the country for five centuries – were caught in the crossfire. Some tried to make a run for it. The nearest friendly border for many of them was hundreds of miles to the south. Most got through, some didn't. Among those who didn't were Lizbet's folks. She was the only one of seven in a vehicle to survive the blast of an RPG-7 rocket on the main road south out of Nova Lisboa: Huambo, as we know it today, had experienced some of the worst fighting of war.

The old man pulled her from the wreck early the next day after he had heard her cries as he was walking past. She was covered in the blood of the dead and he had taken care of her since then.

'How do you know her name?' the officer asked.

'Someone who had worked for the family in town told me; it's either that or another, except that the other child was killed with the others.'

'So it might not even be her real name?'

'Does it really matter?' the black man asked in a whisper.

What to do now? The old man's fears were valid, all the more so since hostilities in the area through which we were passing had flared up again. They could be caught in a fire-fight. It had happened before.

'Take her back with us,' one of the younger officers suggested.

'On whose authority?' the Major asked. He had already decided that he wanted none of it. Clearly, it was too much of a hassle. Anyway, it had a bit of racial tangle to it and could hardly be good for promotion. For my part, I couldn't get involved: I was there under sufferance as it was.

Throughout, Lizbet never uttered a word. It was obvious from our utterances that she was very much the subject of the debate. She remained seated in the dust at the feet of the old man, totally unfazed by all the fuss.

When it was over, her minder got up slowly, took her hand in his and walked out into the night. They had been offered a place to sleep, but he, proud man, thought the better of it. He had probably decided early on that they were not among friends.

It was only when we got back to base in Ondangua in South West Africa that I considered doing something.

I had come to know Brigadier *Witkop* Badenhorst, General Officer Commanding, Sector 10 (and in overall control of the war) pretty well over the years. A tough, no-nonsense field-commander, he had lugged it some of the distance into Angola with us. I was sure that had he been in Mumbe that night, he would have taken her back to base with him.

But first, I had to call my wife. Luke had been born a couple of years before, so why not a 'sister' for the family?

Madelon listened patiently as the story unfolded. I was speaking on one of those primitive farm phones that are still in use in much of rural Africa. I probably had half the country listening. When I finished it was she who asked whether I wanted to bring her home.

'Not so sure I can manage that. But what do you think?'

'Go for it!'

In reality, it was not that easy. Lizbet was the casualty of an ongoing war. Somewhere, somehow, she had family, no matter how distant; they were probably all in Portugal. We would need to communicate with them, in all probability through the Red Cross. Also, there were international conventions controlling such things. The Government – we were all aware – had control over who came into the country and from where.

There would, I was sure, probably be a thousand forms to complete. We, as a family would be vetted to establish our suitability as foster parents. First, I knew, I had to do my thing with *Witkop*.

'You must be crazy if you think I'm sending troops in there now that we've just come back,' he said when I tackled him in his office the next day. 'Do you know how many casualties we took?' We all knew that several of his soldiers had been killed, mostly by mines and booby-traps. There had been quite a few wounded.

'Anyway, you haven't even asked your wife.'

'I have', I told him. His face clouded. This hack really *was* serious.

It was not to be. Not just then, anyway. Washington had protested volubly about the South African armored incursion into the heart of Angola. Several towns in the path of the column had been occupied and quite a few of those who opposed had been killed. Pretoria was severely censured at the UN.

After a few days I couldn't wait any longer. I had to head back to Johannesburg because they were waiting for my story. And, though my initial enthusiasm had been tempered, I never lost hope that something would happen. It did. Badenhorst, never a ditherer, wasn't idle for long.

About a month later, in the middle of the night, I got a call from someone who had just returned from the 'Operational Area'. True to his word, the Brigadier had launched an operation. Several dozen paratroopers – Parabats, in the argot – were dropped on the outskirts of Mumbe from a South African Air Force C-130 very early one morning.

They encountered little resistance. Anyway, they put the word out, they were looking for the girl, not trouble. But she and the old man were gone. Nobody had any idea where to. Nor were those troops equipped to venture too far to search for them.

It must have been five or six months later before someone managed to establish a fix on the pair. Word had gone out that the South Africans were looking for the couple, but in an Africa where the basic infrastructure of society had long ago been obliterated, it travelled slowly. Even today very few phones in Angola work.

Eventually, I was to learn later, Lizbet and the old man had been spotted near Xangongo, formerly a regional capital. Like Mumbe, Xangongo lies on the river. In an area that is parched for half the year, they probably liked to stay close to it.

Once contact had been made, others took over. The Catholic Church, minimally active in a Marxist Angola since 'independence', was aware that her chances with an unknown family would certainly be better than on the banks of the Kunene and it passed the message through intermediaries that it would help. A local priest arranged for them to be taken south. But, he warned, it had to be done clandestinely. As it happened, it was weeks before they could move, A Cuban battalion had moved into the area and they were circumspect about any sort of unauthorized movement.

Defence Headquarters in Pretoria stayed in contact. Were we still sure we wanted her, they asked?

Sure we did. I suggested that they fly me to Ondangua to wait for her. Pretoria said that I should stay put. They implied that though things were happening, it wasn't as easy as that. They would wait for a 'window' in hostilities to bring her through. And even then it would be dodgy. By the time she had been taken as far as Ongiva, the largest town in south Angola, Madelon had started moving a few things about in the house. The little one would need some space of her own.

The last call we had was from someone at Military Headquarters in Ondangua. Never heard his name, just the message. Lizbet had left Ongiva early that morning on the final leg of the journey. She never made it.

Everyone in the vehicle in which they were travelling was killed in a double-boosted landmine explosion just that side of the border.

They heard the blast at the nearest army base and that was more than twenty miles away. One of their patrols was ordered out by *Witkop* to scour the wreckage.

I was never able to establish whether the old man died with her.

In is worth mentioning that the little girl who so very briefly had come into our lives was not the only abandoned white child encountered during the course of Angola's numerous conflicts. Roland de Vries, the 61 Mech commander also had an experience that he recorded in his book *Eye of the Firestorm*. I quote:

Battle Group 10 commenced settling down [on the outskirts of the south Angolan town of Humbe] for the night as the late afternoon started fading into dusk. The all-round defensive and mutually supporting posture had been set up. Local protection patrols were already deployed, and early warning and security arrangements were in place. Sentries had been posted and the first radio watch of the night was manning the sets. Other activities were up and running without any fuss or bother – it was all SOP.

Then, almost from nowhere, a distinguished-looking Angolan – bespectacled and smartly dressed – came riding sedately over to us on a dilapidated old moped motorised bicycle with a small tattered European boy perched on the front. There was no anxiety or uneasiness about him, and nobody challenged him as he chugged over to the command group through the ranks of war machines, almost as if it were a daily occurrence for him to encounter a battle group bristling with weapons of death and destruction.

We invited him to have a chat and he was happy to do so. He explained that he was the local schoolteacher at that same Humbe at which we had been hurling 140 mm shells only a few hours earlier. He felt no apprehension about the presence of the South African military and was quite willing to talk about the local situation.

Humbe's inhabitants and the police had fled that morning, he said, just before the air strike on Xangongo. And no, there had been no element of FAPLA deployed there for some time.

I was intrigued by the small boy, who was clearly of Portuguese origin; he explained that he was the stepfather of the boy whom he had found wandering around somewhere, a victim of the civil war that had been raging in Angola since the mid-1970s.

Our conversation over, our gracious black visitor and his adopted white son putted away into the setting sun towards the town. Before he left I took a photo of them with their moped, obviously victims of dreadful circumstances – but survivors nonetheless. It was a cheering thought.

I still have that the photograph and sometimes wonder what became of them. One day, perhaps, I'll be able to visit Humbe again and ask after them…

28

The Soldier of Fortune Syndrome

> If soldiering was for the money, [Britain's] Special Air Service (SAS) and the Special Boat Service (SBS) would have disintegrated in recent years. Such has been the explosion in private military companies that they employ an estimated 30,000 in Iraq alone – and no government can match their fat salaries. A young SAS trooper earns about $3,500 a month: on the 'circuit', as soldiers call the private world, he could get $16,000. Why would he not?
> *The Economist*, London: October 22, 2005

A fundamental mistake made by the majority of critics of Private Military Companies – and one which never escapes the attention of those involved with Executive Outcomes – was the 'pigeon-holing' of those who are or were prepared to do this filthy work. Many news reports categorise them as criminals.

The Press has been blatant in its condemnation of the work these people – almost all with enormous battlefield experience – perform. They use a variety of epithets, which if not snide are unflattering. Others call them retards, murderers, contract killers or worse.

Naturally the average so-called 'civilised' hack would not know a merc if he or she shared a drink with one of them in Downtown New York or Sloane Square. Nor would they acknowledge that lives had been saved – are being saved – by small groups of professional soldiers who are prepared to go in where few armies are prepared to tread: Angola, the Congo, Sudan, Nigeria, Sierra Leone, El Salvador, Yemen, Colombia, Libya and the rest. Most journalists haven't the courage to go to any of these places on assignment, never mind put their lives on the line for a just cause.

The perception, in the civilized world generally, is that mercenaries are semi-literate psychos with no scruples. And while Executive Outcomes always conceded the 'experience' bit, it was only because the majority of these veterans had been doing that sort of thing all along. Obviously, the majority were pretty good at it because warfare – which today involves a multitude of esoteric skills – was a chosen career.

The truth is that some so-called 'Dogs of War' could probably slot comfortably into all the categories mentioned, good and bad. Granted too, there is the occasional psychopath and over the years, I've met a few. But then most military establishments have their loose cannons.

Looking at a broader picture, it's axiomatic that the concept of killing people is repugnant to civilized people anywhere. While EO might have done an excellent job in destroying the rebel infrastructure in Sierra Leone, and before that, in forcing Savimbi to the negotiating table in Angola, the subject has always been unsettling.

There are those who feel that mercenaries indulge in violence for its own sake. Yet anybody who has seen these people at work from up close is aware that that conjecture is absurd. At the same time, one has to accept that the ideal does become blurred by perceptions spawned by recent history, like so-called Colonel Callan's mindlessly brutal role in Angola and what went on in the

Congo before Colonel Mike Hoare brought some order to a situation that had been totally out of hand. Obviously, there is sometimes an image factor that needs to be dealt with and it is not flattering.

What went on in the Congo in the early days is perhaps at the core of it, compounded more recently by the machinations of some American freelance operators who have since been charged with killing dissidents in Afghanistan.

Mercenaries everywhere were done another disservice by the large group of South Africans who, at the behest of Mark Thatcher, son of a former British Prime Minister and his sidekick Simon Mann, attempted to bring down the government of Equatorial Guinea in 2004. Almost all of those involved in that debacle were arrested and one or two subsequently died in prison.

In the earlier phase of the Congo, reports were reinforced by 'blood-on-the-hands ' photos of smiling mercenaries who held aloft decapitated heads of black men. This gory display of trophies was disgusting and it did not help that some of those pictures appeared in the news magazines of the time, in Europe in particular.

Fast forward to the 21st Century and just about everything has changed. Today's professional soldier-for-hire – in the main – is a pretty ordinary fellow. The majority probably would not be out of place in your local police force. About the only thing that sets them apart from the rest is that he is a veteran with a good run of combat to show for it. He has done his thing and more important, survived.

These are people not only familiar with the multi-disciplined precepts of most regular armed forces, but most are strong-minded individuals who are able to handle themselves with certain deftness, especially under fire. Few would jump into a ditch to escape if they were shot at while on patrol: instead, they would retaliate. Indeed, many have half a lifetime of professional military service and, to be blunt, are enormously proud of it.

Neall Ellis on his own, *twice* turned the war around in Sierra Leone and is a case in point, though admittedly he is not your typical hired gun, if only because most air force pilots are a good 20 or 30 years younger by the time they return their flying helmets to the ready room for the last time. Still, there are few combat pilots who have had as much experience as Nellis.

Into his sixties, he is still heading into battle, invariably at the controls of a gunship, most commonly a former Soviet Mi-24 Hind.

In Executive Outcomes' new phase in Angola in the 1990s, first deployments took place north of Luanda and around the diamond fields of Lunda Sul in the east. Soyo too, required pacifying once more (See details of the original battle in upcoming Chapter 30).

In Angola's distant east, the company chose as its headquarters the airport at the diamond city of Saurimo, not far from the Zairean frontier, today, the Democratic Republic of the Congo.

While this contract was renewed a year later, and then extended again for a further three months, it was officially ended early in 1996. By then EO had several hundred men in the field, the majority either chasing down UNITA rebels or training the Angolan Army. Concurrently, South African mercenary pilots were active throughout, whether providing close air support for their own people or assisting the regular army. There is no argument: Angola would never have managed without them.

Several developments contributed towards Dr Jonas Savimbi finally signing an accord with the Luanda government in November 1994. The first, in February 1994, was the recapture by FAA – with a strong EO presence in support – of N'dalatando in Cuanza Norte. Until then, this little junction town – which lies about halfway between Luanda and Malanje – had been pivotal to the guerrilla penetration of the oil-rich northwest.

Four months later EO was engaged – in conjunction with FAA's 16th Brigade – in a nine or ten week operation to retake the Cafunfo diamond fields. It was a blow from which UNITA never recovered, dealt with in this book in the first three chapters.

The alluvial diggings encompass miles of Angola's northern forest regions along the Cuanza River, and at that stage this valuable resource was supplying the rebels with about two-thirds of their diamonds. If Savimbi was of half a mind to continue with his war, he could not do without those diggings.

Finally, when Huambo – Angola's second largest city – fell to the government after battles that left thousands dead in September of that year, the UNITA leader sued for peace.

There was another issue constantly being raised by the media whenever contact was made with the mercenary force. That centred on whether any mercenary in the pay of a foreign government could actually be loyal. In other words, could any mercenary actually be trusted?

In Freetown, where journalists and these freebooters shared the same nightspots, the spectre of divided allegiances would be raised more often than was necessary and, once or twice, led to blows. As some of the hacks were to discover, a tavern is not exactly the place to ask a tanked-up war dog whether he is likely to defect to those whom he's fighting against and to whom he's probably lost a few of his friends.

Lafras Luitingh phrased it tidily when he said that while both Freetown and Luanda might have been pleased with what EO had achieved on the battlefield, 'that didn't mean we were always above suspicion'. He explained: 'black leaders who hired us would invariably judge us by their own standards. Of course, in their minds, that would sometimes make us complicit. After all, we are marketable commodities and obviously suspect.'

Luitingh accepted that some of the governments for whom his people (and other groups of mercenaries) fought had a right to be wary. Soldiers of Fortune are invariably 'bought', as it is usually phrased, by the higher bidder. It happened within the ambit of the major powers as well, he pointed out, only there 'turncoats are called spies'.

Because of this, he suggested, there was sometimes a real fear among African leaders that if a better offer did come along, these hired guns might switch sides. 'Our problem,' he stressed, 'is that we do what we do not for any cause, or ideal, but for money.'

But, he declared, there are limits. Financial motivation is always fundamental and obviously something that any African leader could understand. But it was also true that he and his EO colleagues would encounter suspicion about what some of them termed 'Real Agendas'. He accepted, too, that these misgivings stemmed from recent events. As he pointed out, 'History has left the world with a legacy of betrayals.'

This extremely perspicacious former Recce operator illustrated his argument by citing the Angolan experience. EO, he explained, had won several key battles in a country that had seen decades of war. Soyo was a part of it. But it had not gone unnoticed that in achieving its objective, Executive Outcomes had lost several of its best men. Yet, he declared, there were still senior Angolan officers who questioned, if not the company's allegiance, then that of several former SADF officers who were directing EO's efforts at winning the war.

> For instance, they would pose questions about our motives for coming across. After all, they argued, the two sides had been blood enemies for a generation. In their minds – and it was all part of the African psycho – the switch simply did not make sense and as a consequence, the suspicion bogey continued to follow us.

At the time that we discussed it, Luitingh had not been prepared to go over this option in such depth, though he had alluded to it once or twice. But it became a serious matter once we started to get into it and there were a few moments when his voice urged a conspiratorial urgency.

> As contract people – PMCs, mercenaries, War Dogs, whatever – our motives are *always* going to be suspect, if only because we fight for money: not ideals or politics or personal aspirations but hard cash. So, the argument went: what the one side offers the other can feasibly top.

But that was not the way the company worked, Luitingh insisted. EO, throughout its brief career maintained stringent codes of conduct and they were inviolable.

He used himself – well dressed, clean shaven, reasonably well read and informed about matters military – as an example of today's corporate Soldier of Fortune. As one of the top men in the organization, everybody who had anything to do with Luitingh had to concede that he was hardly what one would have expected of a 'merc'.

Lafras Luitingh joined the army after leaving school and for more than a decade – following his selection for South Africa's elite Reconnaissance Regiment – he did nothing but fight. His operations would sometimes take him on deep penetration insertions into Angola or Mozambique, often on foot. Other times they'd be put ashore in kayaks, launched from navy submarines or make clandestine high altitude HALO entries from air force C-130 aircraft.[1]

A tall, powerfully built man with a perennial smile, Luitingh had long ago learned to become uncompromisingly aggressive when he had need to. EO was formed after he had left the SADF with the rank equivalent to Lieutenant Colonel.

To his – and everybody else's surprise – he found it relatively easy to combine the art of survival of a fighting man with the battles sometimes encountered in the rarefied atmosphere of Yuppiedom. Clearly, this tough and fit combatant was a quick learner and, as a consequence of developing a good business brain in the process, a very wealthy man today.

Very early on, Executive Outcomes established its own brand of definitive criteria when fighting a war. Being in the business of conflict, everything that the company represented stood or fell by the core values it advocated.

Executive Outcomes offered Sierra Leone a feasible military solution for the kind of insurgency the nation faced, in much the way it had approached similar issues in Angola before. Basics were coupled to good old-fashioned military dog work together with a solid gumption to implement such programs to good effect.

Financial considerations, said Luitingh, were obviously the basis on which everything turned, or as he declared, 'just about all we do starts and ends with money. Consequently, it is a given to accept that we're not into welfare. In fact, we charge what we think the market will bear. And to get to that figure, we do our homework.'

There was a time, he suggested, when the people of Freetown really did think the company might switch sides, which was possibly to be expected because just about everything in Sierra Leone was based on a handshake.

Also, he added, 'the Russians had been running the Sierra Leone Air Wing before we arrived and they had screwed the government so often that there were some who queried whether the

---

[1] High Altitude Low Opening: delivery of military personnel or equipment from a transport aircraft at a high altitude by free-fall parachute insertion. Heights can be anything from 15,000 to 35,000 feet.

Conflicts in Africa seem to have attracted mercenaries almost since the end of the Second World War. It all started in the Congo, immediately after Belgium granted this enormous colony straddling much of central Africa an ill-timed independence. Among those who answered the call was Siegfried Müller, rarely seen without his Iron Cross, awarded while serving in Germany's SS. (Author's collection)

Bob Denard – who did a lot of freelance work for French Intelligence – fought in several African campaigns. He invaded the Comores Archipelago several times and for a dozen years, stayed on to become the uncrowned 'King of the Island'.

Rhodesia's war brought more mercenaries to Africa, attracted by the gung-ho nature of hostilities and the fact that South Africa got involved from time to time, as it did here – with its helicopters – deep inside Mozambique. (Photo: Richard Stannard)

Among the most famous mercenaries was Neall Ellis: on his own – as the only helicopter gunship pilot in Sierra Leone – he turned the rebel war on its head by driving the insurgents who threatened the government from Freetown's gates. Twice ! (Author's photo)

Another South African who flew Soviet MiG-17s in Biafra was former SAAF and RAF pilot Ares Klootwyk. Before that, he flew fighters in the Congo for three years. (Photo: Ares Klootwyk, from the author's book *Biafra's War*)

South Africans wouldn't do the same. And when you're faced with that kind of dilemma, a very real danger materializes if someone in command believes you might betray him.

'They start to see shadows where there are none.' It was the story of so much of Africa, he believed.

In Angola, Luitingh and his colleagues quickly countered that perception by getting into some of the most aggressive battles against UNITA that its military leaders had yet observed, with their own people taking still more fatalities. After that, things changed, especially once the group clocked up a succession of strikes that began to seriously hurt the rebel movement. That included killing some of Savimbi's most experienced field commanders, including several generals who were closest to him.

Luitingh: 'As soon as we could show that the other side was being damaged, things began to ease up. Also, you don't easily disregard casualties among people who are fighting for you.' It took a while, he added, but by doing what was expected, these 'Demon Boers' – as they had been described in Angolan newspapers and radio broadcasts in the past – were able to show the Angolans that they had themselves a bunch of fighters that were both professional and reliable.

Similar problems were sometimes encountered in Sierra Leone. Luitingh took the initiative during his first meeting with Chairman Valentine Strasser at State House in Freetown by arguing – with some aplomb, one of his sidekicks commented – that to betray the government would irrevocably destroy the credibility that the company had worked hard and long to foster.

This applied not only to Sierra Leone, he told the youthful Head of State who was then still only 25 years old, but to governments on three continents to whom EO was then talking.[2] It was a point well made and even the usually verbose Strasser couldn't argue.

'I told him we couldn't operate in this business without trust. We might be a band of brigands, I said, but we were an honourable band of brigands.' The Sierra Leone leader seemed to enjoy the quip.

Still more important, Luitingh explained, the company offered its services only to recognized governments. It was not interested in factions, or political parties trying to unseat rulers, no matter what kind of money was being put on the table. A year before, he disclosed, a dissident Nigerian group had approached EO with an offer of a 100 million dollars to train a guerrilla army to overthrow the tyrant Abacha.

> You can do a hellova lot with that kind of money, but we refused. In fact, we had no option: once you get into that sort of thing, you're going to have the international community on your neck.

Such actions might also be classed as international terrorism, he believed.

> Then you're into something that involves big governments, Washington, London, the United Nations, war crimes commissions at The Hague, Interpol. And then what?
> In the end we convinced Chairman Strasser that it was just not on... I know he believed us because he never again questioned our motives.

While Executive Outcomes lasted, it was active in almost a dozen African states. Apart from Angola and Sierra Leone, it accepted contracts in the two Congos, Uganda, the Sudan,

---

2 Prior to Executive Outcomes closing shop, they were in serious discussions with the Mexican Government about dealing with the Chiapas rebellion in the south of the country.

Mozambique and elsewhere. For a while, towards the end, it guarded South African farmers from cattle rustlers, though that option eventually became too expensive for its client base.

Prior to going into any country – and while still negotiating the contract – EO would state very clearly and in writing what they were able to offer and exactly what it was that the company intended to achieve. Having agreed on something of a template and with the price settled, other needs would be explored. These would include the extent of the threat, exactly who would fund what together with a timeline, sundry expenses and so on.

Discussions always involved the company's British associates and Michael Grunberg's experience was a reliable adjunct from the start. At a very early stage, these would detail finance, the apportionment of assets, what needed to be procured as well as liaison with local forces. The small print would contain specifics concerning equipment and weapons systems. Ancillary issues included support aircraft, logistics and exactly what EO would be expected to bring into the country.

Other aspects detailed security, internal movement, bases and airports to which the mercenary unit would have access. To get a permit each time a man entered a security area would have been impractical: consequently, the company demanded blanket clearances and though it took a while in Angola, they got them in the end.

There was also the matter of accommodation, which, in places like Freetown and Luanda, included serviced apartments with attendant domestic staff. All this would be tabulated and, after a bit of a haggle, both parties would sign. If the host country did not do so, EO would move on, as it did, several times.

Perhaps the strongest attribute shared by senior EO personnel was that, as a group, the men all had intimate knowledge and understanding of the continent on which they worked. Just about everybody in EO had grown up in Africa.

On arrival at Freetown, the men were to discover a remarkably empathetic environment. Freetown's kids weren't all that different from those in the 'Far South', as some Sierra Leone newspapers would refer to South Africa. Consequently, none of the men who went into Angola or Sierra Leone laboured under any of the misconceptions that might have encumbered Europeans and Americans who suddenly found themselves among disadvantaged folk.

It was that way in Somalia after the US Army arrived, something graphically depicted in Mark Bowden's *Black Hawk Down*. The book is a classic example of what takes place when you don't understand the people and the ambiance into which you're thrust. In such circumstances, mistakes lead to fatalities.

Also, the people around Freetown were indigent, as are the majority of black people in KwaZulu/Natal or the former Transkei. Almost from the time that Sierra Leone got its independence from Britain in 1961 the nation had been abused by a string of despots, as had South African blacks under apartheid, and more recently under President Jacob Zuma. Similarly, these West Coast people were little different from throngs of Angolans or ethnic Namibians among whom these former South African soldiers had worked and fought in the past.

And as Luitingh pointed out, Africa is the ultimate leveller. EO personnel did not have to be told what the region could – or could not – deliver. It was taken for granted that conditions were tough, if only because it was part of the day's demands.

Take one example after British Brigadier David Richards[3] arrived in Freetown with a relatively small force in a bid to bring order to a rebel uprising that was threatening to topple the government.

One of his officers, an army major who, totally against orders and accompanied by ten of his British soldiers, blundered into Magbeni, the Sierra Leone village controlled by a bunch of rebel lunatics with guns late in September 2000. Had this been an EO operation, nobody would have gone near the place until they had made an effort to find out who or what was there. This simple precaution is essential in any conflict environment in the Third World. American troops returned from Iraq and Afghanistan will echo that sentiment.

The consequences of the Magbeni catastrophe were serious. Apart from millions spent in getting a rescue effort off the ground, the operation that followed caused the death of a young SAS bombardier and the wounding of almost a dozen more British troops, two seriously. The British Army is not likely to make that kind of mistake again.

So too in dealing with the locals. From the President down, any kind of social interaction between EO and the people in the country in which they were operating had to be exemplary. If a man could not or would not relate comfortably with Africans – as all EO recruits were routinely warned on signing up – he had no place in the organization. And while there were examples of interracial strife elsewhere on the continent, and South Africans – as we are constantly reminded – are hardly paragons of racial virtue, EO would always stress that its people were required to be empathetic towards those with whom they had contact.

This was not a problem for the men who had been in elite units of the SADF. For them a man's race had never been an issue – even in the days when the severest racial strictures bedevilled life in South Africa. In any event, that country's Special Forces were always more than half-black. In fact, the elite, partly-Angolan 32 Battalion was 90 per cent African and the Ovambo 101 Battalion had only white officers and some white NCOs.

At the same time, while EO executives would quickly ingratiate themselves with a country's leadership, there was not all that much socializing between EO officers and the host country's military. That was in marked contrast to the cavorting that went on in Sierra Leone's bars once the newcomers discovered some of Freetown's wilder nightspots.

In the upper echelons of Angola's armed forces in contrast, 'gifts' would feature prominently. There was always something on the plane out of South Africa for prominent senior officers with whom the mercenaries had to do business.

Further down the ranks, life was informal, with the result that the people of both Luanda and Freetown soon embraced these newcomers. During the time I spent with Luitingh, the locals looked after us exceedingly well. Whenever the two of us drove around the city after dark – without an escort – we were almost never checked at roadblocks even though security controls in those days (as opposed to Nellis' term) were letter-of-the-law as far as the rest of the population was concerned.

---

3 Afterwards General, Sir David Richards, Chief of the General Staff and today after receiving his Peerage, Baron Richards of Herstmonceux.

29

Executive Outcomes – The Private Military Company that Altered the Balance of Power in Angola[1]

> Executive Outcomes gave us this stability. In a perfect world of course, we wouldn't need an organization like EO, but I'd be loath to say that they'd have to go just because they're mercenaries.
> **Canadian General Ian Douglas, Senior Negotiator for the United Nations**

The bedrock on which the reputation of Executive Outcomes was built came from the bitter two-month 'Battle for the Soyo', an oil installation by that name at the mouth of the Congo River in Angola's far north. The operation lasted just on two months, from early March to the end of April 1993 and was fought against the rebel movement UNITA.[2]

The actual battle lasted only a few days and involved only a few dozen operators, but was one of the hardest exchanges of fire yet seen in this West African territory.

In the process, three South Africans lost their lives, though everybody who stayed the distance was wounded at least once, some a dozen times over. Quite a few of the men suffered life-threatening wounds, a few seriously enough to be evacuated to hospitals abroad. In contrast, the rebel group lost several hundred men, including two of their top field commanders.

As a consequence of that tough, resilient action, the Luanda government liked what it saw. It was impressed by a group of men who, until a short time before had been a hated enemy and, as one observer stated, an equivalent gesture might have been an American Ranger Battalion fighting for Hanoi at the end of the Vietnam War.

Some of the hardliners in Angola's military, sceptical that South Africans – all mercenaries under contract – would risk their lives, were astonished at the outcome. Many had actually preached against Luanda taking on 'dubious' foreigners to fight their war. Further, these South Africans were dead serious: among their number were those who were prepared to put their lives at risk in order to achieve what they said they would. As a result, the Angolan Government hired a few hundred more of these veterans for an estimated $40 million a year and as a consequence Executive Outcomes was on the PMC map. The amount was one of several figures being touted at the time: one source mentioned something closer to $100 million, though from experience, that is doubtful.

---

1 Extracted from *War Dog: Fighting Other People's Wars* by Al Venter, Casemate Publishers, Philadelphia US and Newbury, England: Chapter 16.
2 *Uniao Nacional para a Independencia Total de Angola* (National Union for the Total Liberation of Angola).

The job, according to a deal signed by company representatives in Luanda, was to train 5,000 Angolan troops in both counter-insurgency and conventional military warfare and the contract was to last from September 1993 until January 1996. At the same time the Angolan Army was persuaded to buy a number of Russian T-54/55 main battle tanks as well 100 new BMP-2 infantry fighting vehicles from Moscow.

The air component – intended to support these operations – included MiG-23 and Sukhoi jet fighter/bombers, squadrons of Pilatus PC-7 and PC-9 ground support aircraft (with under-wing rocket pods) as well as Mi-24 Hind helicopter gunships and Hip multi-role transport choppers. All flew under the banner of the Angolan Air Force.

The arrival in Angola of EO, a small Pretoria security company with no previous record of any kind of military activity happened to coincide with the lifting of the international arms embargo on the Luanda government. Ultimately, in a series of military adventures that spanned almost the entire country, the company – after a series of lengthy engagements – was instrumental in forcing the Swiss-educated, Mao-espousing Dr Jonas Savimbi to the negotiating table.

But it was what took place at Soyo that set the scene for all this to take place. There, at one of Angola's principal oil facilities – perched precariously on the south shore of the estuary of the Congo River – the scene was set for a force of 40 men (and sometimes less than half that number) to fight a series of battles against a hugely preponderant UNITA guerrilla army numbering more than 1,000. What made the event significantly different from previous Angolan military exploits in its ongoing war against UNITA, was that the majority of EO's fighters had formerly served as members of elite South African Defence Force Special Forces units including the Reconnaissance Commandos, 32 Battalion, Koevoet as well as a handful from the Parachute Battalions.

Having been airlifted into Soyo by Mi-8 helicopters in what should have been a surprise attack, this tiny but 'highly effective work force' (as the company later phrased it) battled for the duration to hold on to the oil facility and the military base guarding it. They were eventually also to occupy the nearby ancillary port of Kwanza. The ordeal developed into a rugged test of endurance, sheer gut force, improvisation and tactics as the South Africans countered everything the rebels could throw at them.

There were days – and nights, especially – when UNITA would send its irregulars in relays – often hundreds strong – three, four sometimes five times in a row.

To the sound of whistles blown by their commanders, they would go in screaming *'Avante! Avante!'* and the fighting would go on for an hour or two. The rebels would withdraw and the next batch would follow a short while later.

Though the guerrillas attacked, probed, shelled, rocketed, mortared and regularly threw themselves at the defenders in numbers – and sometimes got to within metres of EO's defence perimeter – the tiny Executive Outcomes squad held on. As former Reconnaissance Commando Major Lafras Luitingh was to comment years later, 'we were able to contain it all OK, but believe me, only just…it could as easily have gone the other way…'

It did not help that many UNITA regulars battling along the South African perimeter were originally attached to Savimbi's own Special Forces, the brazenly bold *Groupos de Bate,* or that this experienced combat unit that had been fighting the Angolan Army for years had originally been trained by South African guerrilla warfare specialists.

Though FAA, the Angolan Army[3] offered some help (one of its tanks was brought ashore to bolster EO defences) many government troops thrown into the melee had no military – or any other – training. Indeed, only after it was over was it established that most of these youths had

---

3 *Forcas Armadas de Angola.*

been shanghaied off the streets of Luanda, put in uniform and had an AK thrust into their hands. Without further ado, they were then promptly shipped off to the front. At the first sign of a UNITA attack, many would slink off into the jungle, sometimes doffing their uniforms and weapons as they did so. They would only return to the base when odours wafting through the undergrowth told them that food was being prepared.

Though their officers shot them out of hand if they were caught – there were about 50 FAA soldiers executed that way, the majority by Colonel Pepe de Castro himself (who otherwise stayed well away from any actual fighting) – the South African defenders accepted very early on that an unwilling troop was invariably more of a hindrance than a help.

Then, once that minor war had ended and the South Africans pulled out – with the oil facility again in government hands – Executive Outcomes signed a formal agreement with the Angolans and over the next two years a lot more battles followed. This included the eventual recapture of Angola's diamond fields at Cafunfo (at the time one of the richest diamondiferous pipes in Africa and the subject of the first three chapters of this book) as well as the ousting of Savimbi and his command structure from many of the major centres in the border regions adjacent to Zaire.

Through it all, the reputation of this tough, resolute band of South Africans mercenaries hardly ever faltered, even though there were times when there was dissention within their ranks as to their actual purpose in the war.

In fact, the link was further cemented when, halfway through the Angolan campaign, EO's management was approached by an embattled Sierra Leone government to do something similar with its escalating insurrection rapidly spiralling out of control. After accepting a contract price of 'about $25 million', almost 200 men were sent to Freetown, again at very short notice. With that, company personnel – this time using their own weapons and helicopters – set about hammering Foday Sankoh's Revolutionary United Front into submission wherever they encountered them.

Not everybody was happy with the way all this came about. For many of those critical of the kind of tough, uncompromising military actions which Executive Outcomes propagated, wrote David Shearer in his substantive prognosis on the use of mercenaries, *Private Armies and Military Intervention*, the South African 'guns-for-hire' organization represented the unacceptable face of mercenary activity.[4]

Yet, added Shearer, while EO was condemned in liberal circles, the firm proved in the few years that it remained active that it could 'create a climate for peace and stability for foreign investment, focusing chiefly on military training and including a particular emphasis on Special Forces and clandestine warfare.' Shearer reckoned that it also saw 'a role for itself in peacekeeping (persuasion) services and was prepared to buy equipment appropriate to a client's needs.'

Not for nothing did EO describe itself in its promotional literature as a company with a 'solid history of success.'

Executive Outcomes began its business innocuously enough by handling private security back at its home base in Pretoria. Its founder Eeben Barlow originally qualified as a sapper in the SADF Engineers Corps where he trained in mines and advanced explosives warfare.

From there he was posted to 32 Battalion, one of the more aggressive South African units in the Angolan War that made something of a specialty of unconventional methods of warfare. White-officered, most of its members were disaffected Angolans who, having fought against the Marxist MPLA in a protracted civil war, ended up in exile in present-day Namibia (formerly the League of Nations mandate, South West Africa).

---

4 Linked in this venture to Ranger Oil of Canada.

After South Africa's 23 years of border conflicts came to an end in the late 1980s, Barlow did unspecified work in a covert South African Defence Force unit called the Civil Cooperation Bureau, or CCB. Only after he'd resigned from that clandestine force, did he and his partners establish Executive Outcomes, which operated as a normal security concern involved in private and corporate protection in a country where crime had become endemic following Nelson Mandela's election as President. Under Barlow's tenure, EO managed to recruit several weighty clients, among them the mining conglomerate Anglo American Corporation.

What happened next is regarded by some of those involved with EO in its earlier days more as a fortuitous turn of events than anything that might have been planned.

While with the CCB, Barlow, by now doing a lot of his work abroad, became fairly well known to British Intelligence and himself, in turn, familiar with some of their operators. His role within the apartheid-era secret group was the opening of both local and foreign front companies to be used in the kind of furtive work in which the CCB was then embroiled. He was also charged with handling bank accounts for these firms, some of which had links to South African sanctions-busting operations.

With EO innocuously on the map in South Africa, Angola just then was having serious military problems of its own, with Savimbi's guerrilla force managing to extend its influence throughout the country: by then UNITA dominated all but the major urban centres but it had not yet penetrated secure security swathes around the main cities of Luanda and Lobito.

It was the guerrilla strike on Soyo that eventually changed all that by proving that even on its own rural turf, Savimbi's best troops could be effectively countered.

Not the biggest of Angola's oil exporting facilities, Soyo represented an asset that represented good value to a number of oil companies that were operating in Angola at the time. These included Italy's Fina, Elf of France and Texaco, one of the American oil giants, all of which – including Sonangol, Angola's nationalized oil firm – used Soyo as a logistics base for their offshore operations. There was also Ranger Oil West Africa (ROWAL) – a joint venture between Ranger and Heritage.

With the rebels holding the place, all oil shipments from there came to halt. As a consequence, Luanda was hurting financially.

One item which fell into the hands of the guerrillas was a prototype of a rotating buoy then being tried out by ROWAL. An extremely complex and expensive item worth 'several million dollars' its owners wanted it back. Thus, through a series of intermediaries, ROWAL's directors made a formal approach to UNITA's representatives in Paris and asked whether permission could be requested from Dr Savimbi to have the buoy returned.

The reply that came back almost immediately was a very determined no. The portly guerrilla leader was of no mind to help his enemy balance its books and he said as much. He had the buoy and he was keeping it, was the gist of his message

Enter Tony Buckingham, a former SAS operator-turned-oil-entrepreneur who had links to London's Heritage Oil and Gas.[5] According to Lafras Luitingh, Barlow's partner in EO, Buckingham – astute as they come in this kind of business – was (and still is) extremely well connected in Britain, Westminster included. The gist of it was that he had come up with a solution to defeat UNITA.

By then, Buckingham had already been in contact with the Angolans in Luanda, where he approached Joaquim David, head of Sonangol, to do something about getting the buoy back.

---

5 *Private Armies and Military Intervention* by David Shearer: Adelphi Paper #316: International Institute for Strategic Studies/OUP, London, 1998.

David replied that he could not authorize anything to do with the military and suggested that he talk personally with Angolan President Eduardo dos Santos, which Buckingham did. That this British operator was able to gain access to the notoriously reclusive dos Santos – and at such short notice – says a good deal both for his influence and tenacity, even though he had done a number of successful deals in the country in the past.

Together with a group of military advisors, the President listened to what Buckingham had to say. The argument that he presented cantered about the possibility of hurling back UNITA's forces at Soyo and recapturing the oil terminal. That done, he suggested, their joint aims would have been achieved: he would get back his buoy and Luanda would again dominate the high ground at Soyo. Buckingham was promptly given $1 million to prepare a feasibility study.

Once back in London, Buckingham contacted some of his former SAS pals and suggested that there was good money to be made if they were to help him launch an operation to effect retrieval of the buoy. It would be a short, snappy operation, he said, perhaps accomplished over a weekend. He also disclosed that the Angolan President had confided that the facility was relatively lightly guarded.

It did not take long for his old Hereford friends to give him a thumbs-down. The proposal was absurd, they told him. Having studied the implications of what the venture would entail and spoken to individuals who were familiar with the region, he was told that the project was not only unfeasible, the mission fringed on suicide. Elaborating, they explained that with the Atlantic Ocean fringing the area on one side and, right alongside it, the Congo, the second largest river in the world, even getting in there would be difficult, never mind extricating the force if something went wrong.

Coupled to that, there was triple canopy jungle just about everywhere else. Even moving about the area off-road was difficult: the grass was two metres tall and there were swamps everywhere.

So, his friends argued, should things go toes up, escape, while not impossible, would be, as Anglos like to say, dicey. EO was to discover to its chagrin later, that whoever had made that initial study was spot-on.

It was said, but not confirmed, that some British operators had been trying to get two of their own companies, Saladin and KMS (Keeny Meeny Services, the name stemming from an incident in Malaya) into Angola for the job and had been unsuccessful. Operating much on the same paramilitary basis as EO, their personnel were not familiar either with the terrain or the local people. The South Africans, in contrast, on both counts, were.

Significantly, Saladin/KMS already had good experience in such matters. It was their people who trained the army of the Sultan of Oman and others. Indeed, they had been 'involved' in Aden, Malaysia and other traditionally British areas in much the same way that EO became embroiled in Angola and Sierra Leone. They also guarded British embassies in South America during the Falklands War and, it is said, EO was modelled on them. Because these people use primarily (and, in some cases, only) former SAS and SBS operators, the companies are sometimes referred to in the industry as the 'SAS Reserve'.

Having established the parameters in Angola, Buckingham flew to South Africa to talk to another old contact from the past, Larny Keller, a SADF Colonel from the apartheid era and just then involved in developing night vision equipment with Eloptro, a Pretoria high-tech company. It was Keller that brought Eeben Barlow's EO into the picture.

By now Buckingham had linked up with another of his friends from his Special Forces days, former SAS Captain Simon Mann. This was the same Simon Mann who, in mid-2004 was to find himself incarcerated in Zimbabwe's Chikurubi Prison with 69 like-minded mercenaries after organizing a botched coup attempt in Equatorial Guinea.

Ostensibly, while being briefed on the nature of the job and what might be expected of them, both Barlow and Keller were told that the project was extremely sensitive, which was why no other corporate player had been contacted to do the work. One option that might have been considered would have been to use the American private military company MPRI. But while that Washington-based concern is composed largely of former US Special Forces personnel, MPRI focuses its efforts on training and not fighting.

Within days in mid-February 1993, Larny Keller's house in Centurion, a large conurbation south of Pretoria, became Executive Outcomes' new 'centre of operations'.

As Harry Carlse, one of the former Recce operators who was eventually to become a section leader at Soyo tells it, 'Eeben called me on the Wednesday and asked me to bring along some of my friends. I took four guys and a fifth joined us later.'

Five 'platoon commanders' were contracted to handle recruitment, training and planning. All of them accepted the job. The men were Buks Buys, a former Reconnaissance Regiment major; Harry Ferreira, one of Barlow's old oppos from 32 Battalion; Phil Smith, a former Rhodesian who had also served with Barlow in 32; Lafras Luitingh, another Recce major and finally, one more individual from Barlow's sapper past, Mauritz le Roux. The first four were each tasked with recruiting thirty of their more experienced military colleagues from the past, while le Roux had to bring in a dozen SADF engineers.

At this point, the team was warned that what lay ahead, would not be easy. There would be a good bit of fighting ahead, they were told. In fact, Barlow suggested, there would be 'a lot of action and that it would be heavy going.' What they were not told was where all this would be taking place, except that the country involved 'spoke Portuguese'. Since there were ongoing civil wars in all three of Lisbon's former African territories – Angola, Mozambique as well as Guiné-Bissau (formerly Portuguese Guinea), it might have been any one of them.

Le Roux was further tasked to find a good supply of explosives, preferably C4, since all that was being offered by Luanda was some out-of-date TNT. He was cautioned that there would be 'some blowing of bridges' and possibly, mines to be laid. Training, too, would fall within le Roux's brief.[6]

Barlow stressed that since he was already getting strong pressure to move things along from Buckingham and friends. 'Whoever you guys hire will have to be ready to go within two weeks,' he told them. Once on location, there would be a short period of training and familiarization with Soviet-bloc weapons, standard issue throughout the Angolan forces.

The initial contract was for 30 days, he explained, and should EO be able to hold the target for that period, there would be a 30-percent bonus at the end of it. For that first month's work – the contract could be extended – everybody would get from a third to a half of their cash up-front, together with a full kit allowance that would be used to buy what was needed before they left South Africa. With that, the five-man leadership group set to work recruiting the roughly hundred men required for the job.

First results were not only encouraging, but enthusiastic. 'Yes', said just about everybody spoken to: they were all for it, they affirmed. 'When do we leave?' they all asked, after which interest waned. That came after the men had been told that there would be 'quite a bit of fighting'.

Altogether, about 80 men were interviewed for the job. While preference was given to former Special Forces personnel, only about three-quarters of the applicants passed first muster, among them, surprisingly, a few who had never been to war. One was an air force clerk who, like others

---

6 Lengthy personal interview with Mauritz le Roux when, with his friend and colleague Neall Ellis, they spent a week with the author at his home along the Columbia River in Astoria, Oregon.

The now-derelict lighthouse at Cabo Ledo – hundreds of years old – still stands, though the Angolan Army did its best to destroy it with artillery. (Photo courtesy of Jerry Buirski)

Executive Outcomes putting Angolan Special Forces through their paces. (Author's photo)

The Angolan Army training unit at the EO base at Rio Longa south of Luanda had its own water purifying unit, a legacy of what the instructors had used when they served in the SADF. (Author's photo)

One of the Hips used by EO out of the Saurimo diamond fields in the east with South African mercenary pilots. (Author's photo)

EO's enemy and erstwhile South African ally: UNITA's Jonas Savimbi.

Savimbi employed many private operators to bring his supplies in, much of it from the Congo. Most used vintage propeller-driven aircraft that could touch down on relatively short airstrips.

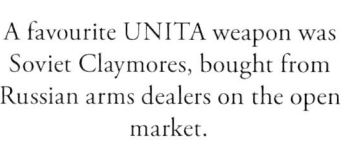
A favourite UNITA weapon was Soviet Claymores, bought from Russian arms dealers on the open market.

This Russian Mi-24 helicopter gunship was used with devastating effect against the rebels. (Author's photo, taken while with Neall Ellis in Sierra Leone)

An Angolan Air Force MiG-21 brought down by an American Stinger missile in Eastern Angola: Washington gave UNITA a number of them, with US Army personnel to train the rebels in their use.

in the group, had never seen any action. Also, 'while some of the men were in good shape, others were not anywhere near combat-ready,' said Harry Carlse.

Looking back a year or two later, Luitingh reckoned that because the job was so rushed – all of it at Luanda's strong insistence – there was not as much attention given to detail as there might otherwise have been. 'Which could be why some of the chancers got through,' he thought.[7]

'It worried some of the men that nobody was saying much to start with about where it was or what we had to do. We'd only be given the specifics once we arrived at our destination. What they did make clear from the start was that it would be no walkover', was Harry Carlse's view.[8]

There was no waiting around once formalities had been completed and papers signed. Each man was given the equivalent of a thousand or more dollars and taken to the local outdoor store to buy tropical gear.

Ground troops for the operation were offered 500 rands a day (at the time, about $150) for the lowest-ranking participant, which, at the time, was excellent money in South Africa. EO's leadership element was paid between 50 to a 100 percent more and though it might have been expected, nobody who signed took the money and ran. Many of these former soldiers had been like 'family' while still in the SADF: everybody knew everybody else and being a fairly closed society, that kind of illegality would have been difficult, anyway, explained Mauritz le Roux.

By South African standards, the emoluments offered were outstanding, and that at a time when you could do roughly the same with a single rand in South Africa as a dollar would buy you in America. Also, the economy was in a downturn and it was expected that EO would be inundated with applicants.

There were initially no ranks within EO, with the men being broadly graded according to positions held while still serving in the SADF. To start with, Barlow appointed team leaders, and the men were allowed to choose their own section leaders. All were warned that there would be no death benefits for members' families. Nor, he stated, was there to be any medical insurance.[9]

Unbeknown to Eeben Barlow and the others running the show, Tony Buckingham just then was fending off heavy pressure from Luanda to get the show on the road. In the simplest language he was told that he had taken their million dollars and they expected results, like, they said, 'within the following week!' In turn, Buckingham pressured Barlow to turn on the heat, to the extent that departure date to Angola for those who had signed was put forward to the next day, February 21st. That was barely a week after the recruitment program had started.

More serious, the biggest problem for everybody just then, was that instead of the more than a hundred men envisaged for the operation, all the five recruiters had been able to come up with was only 35.

True to his promise to Buckingham, Barlow dispatched Mauritz le Roux and four others to Windhoek. They flew to the Namibian capital on a commercial flight, from where, in a Cessna

---

7 The author travelled with Lafras Luitingh on the EO Boeing 727 to Freetown, Sierra Leone where many of the details of the initial operation were laid bare.
8 Personal interview Sandton, Johannesburg.
9 There is a considerable difference of opinion whether or not the earlier EO recruits were warned that there would be no death benefits for the members' families, or that there would be medical insurance, something that became standard with all EO personnel later. In fact, after Phil Smith was killed at Soyo, it took a long time and 'a little unconventional pressure' on the part of some of his buddies to get a settlement made to his wife Fiona. Smith – like Eeben Barlow – was a former 32 Battalion operator. The two had not only seen action together, but were also good friends and knew each others' families well. This blatant lack of family support by an organization making millions was regarded by many of those involved at Soyo as reprehensible.

404, they were taken to the old Cuban Air Force base at Cabo Ledo, more than an hour's drive south of Luanda.

Later dubbed 'Ghost Rider' – with the registration number of V5WAA painted on its tail – this aircraft would serve EO regularly for the next few months. But since travel to Angola required clearance from Windhoek's air traffic control, the pilot lodged a phony flight plan to the former military town of Rundu, in the north-west corner of the recently independent Namibia. Interestingly, the ruse worked for the duration.

Back in South Africa, Barlow was encountering more problems. Some of the original group had opted out and the team had to scratch hard for replacements. At the end of it, the total number of recruits still hovered around 40, all of whom were being sent to Angola in groups, some in small charter planes from Grand Central Airport in Johannesburg, others on regular South African Airways flights to Luanda.

As one of the men commented, 'there were sections coming up to Cabo Ledo whereas we'd been expecting platoons.' Still, by the end of the week, just about the entire crew had gathered at EO's new Angolan base.

As Harry Carlse explained, nothing took place quite so simply either. 'At Jan Smuts Airport – on the way to Windhoek – some of our guys who were travelling South African Airways were pulled over by airport security. We were a tough, rough-looking bunch and that immediately raised suspicions. They even queried if we were a military group.

'It did not help that we claimed to be a hikers. Nor that almost every one of us was wearing similar kit and that our tickets showed us heading for the same place. But we'd been briefed and the boys stuck to their story. In the end we got through,' Carlse explained.

EO established a temporary headquarters adjacent to the Cabo Ledo terminal's living quarters where, on the first morning the men were briefed, the spokesman explained that UNITA had attacked and captured Soyo the previous January, followed by the Angolan Army having been bundled out of the enclave with fairly heavy losses. All expatriate staff and local workers at the facility were evacuated.

'We were also told', said Carlse, 'that within the first day or two, the insurgents had been able to destroy many of the offices at the complex. So too, with any communication equipment they found. A week later they trashed Soyo itself, a town of about 4,000 people.' It puzzled EO management that much of the Soyo oil facility, the adjacent port as well as its ancillary offshore supply base that had been used to service offshore oil rigs were all left relatively intact.

Since the new headquarters at Cabo Ledo was adjacent to an existing Angolan Army military headquarters, with a detachment of FAA Commandos, the men took a good deal of interest in how their future compadres conducted themselves. What they found was not reassuring. The Angolan troops were a rum bunch. Most were ill-disciplined and lacked the most basic military skills. Many did not even know how to hold their weapons properly, never mind march. As for their shooting skills, said Carlse, 'I won't comment!'

Which prompted Buks Buys to suggest that since his own group of EO recruits and the Angolan troops in adjacent barracks were going to wage war together against a UNITA force of unknown strength, perhaps they should spend a bit of time coordinating their efforts. At the very least, he suggested, it was essential to put these black soldiers through their paces so they would have some idea of what to expect.

Simon Mann, having arrived only a short while before, scotched that idea. His argument was that since British and French soldiers were alike, their Angolans counterparts were likewise, since all armed services operated to roughly the same professional criteria, which of course was absurd.

He also told an EO gathering that he had received good assurances from Luanda that the FAA troops accompanying them into Soyo were 'totally up to scratch,' which got him some odd looks from the South Africans present. Also, he confided, he'd been told that the opposition they were likely to encounter at Soyo consisted of nine UNITA policemen armed with .38 Special revolvers.

Talking to a few of the men afterwards, one got the impression that it did not take Simon Mann – an Old Etonian – very long to be labelled by all as an arrogant and obnoxious prick. In spite of his previous so-called Special Air Service experience, he seemed hardly to have a grasp of what the operation entailed. Nor did things change once the fighting started, with the tiny EO attacking force ranged against huge numbers of the enemy.

What annoyed most was Mann's habit of constantly having to remind people of his role in an elite British unit. In dealing with this altogether South African force, he could be disdainful, even insulting of anyone or anything from that country. It perhaps tells you more that he took absolutely no part in the hostilities that followed, even though the manpower issue remained dominant from the start.

Which also makes you wonder how he ended up fitting in with the guys in a Harare prison a decade later, especially since some of the inmates in Chikurubi were also part of the Soyo mob?

With the entire group gathered at Cabo Ledo, a command structure was quickly established between the men. Roelf van Heerden (he of Koidu, Sierra Leone notoriety) helped with the planning, while Lafras Luitingh came into the picture because Barlow moved Buks Buys into the position of commanding colonel, though he too, by the time it was all over, never once set foot in Soyo.

Altogether four Executive Outcomes majors were appointed for the three sections planned. These were the Rhodesian War veteran Phil Smith, 32's Harry Ferreira, Lafras Luitingh and finally, Mauritz le Roux, the unit's engineering specialist.

Many of the younger Special Forces men found themselves with Luitingh, while Ferreira seemed to attract the more mature but still-active vets.

For his sins, Smith was stuck with what some of the more experienced operators termed 'the plebs': those with the least military know-how or combat experience. He had only three Special Forces veterans in his unit – an ex-Koevoet operator, a Recce as well as a former Foreign Legionnaire – while many of the others were physically out of shape and seemed more interested in the money.

Tactical planning for the operation was in the hands of Luitingh, Phil Smith and one of the section leaders.

While it was not Lafras Luitingh's job to liaise with Colonel Pepe de Castro, the Angolan commander who would be in overall control – the same man, incidentally, who was to lead EO's attack on the diamond fields at Cafunfo a while later – he appeared to slip into that capacity as things progressed. All agreed that it was a convenient arrangement, especially since Luitingh, as a former Recce major, had many years of combat experience.

For his part, partly because he could speak English, de Castro was to become a familiar figure among Angola's mercenaries. He was also designated by Luanda to be involved in all subsequent EO campaigns. Meanwhile, he tasked Lafras Luitingh with the job of ground commander of the operation.

The next day the group was issued with Angolan Army uniforms and identity cards. All showed them to be 'Advisors', though as one of the men asked at a briefing session, since almost none of them spoke any Portuguese, who should they say they were actually advising were they captured?

Weapons provided by the government included AKs, RPKs, PKMs RPDs as well as a handful of Dragunov sniping rifles. Training included sessions with former Soviet 60mm and 82mm mortars, as well as an update on section attacks, contact and grenade drills. There were also house-clearing exercises and some of the more arcane stratagems with which Special Forces like to amuse themselves. According to Carlse, the experienced men quite enjoyed it pretty much, but it was hard on those who were not prepared for anything really physical.

On March 3, with all preliminary work completed at the old Cuban base, the entire group, together with all their equipment, was flown north to the Angolan enclave of Cabinda, all of which lies on the north shore of the Congo River. En route, they passed over Soyo and the men crowded around the Antonov's port-holes to catch a glimpse of their ultimate destination and they were not disappointed. The plan was to spend the night at the Cabinda base and attack the following day.

Two large self-propelled barges operated by the Angolan Navy were to leave Cabo Ledo for the north at the same time, each with 500 FAA soldiers[10] onboard, together with the bulk of the heavy stuff, their ammunition and other hardware. There were also four T54/55 tanks, two to a vessel.

But on pulling out of Cabo Ledo, one of the barges had mechanical problems, which meant that everybody onboard that crippled craft had to climb over onto the second barge together with all their gear. In the process, the attacking force lost two of its tanks.

But that also meant that the expected time of arrival of the remaining barge was delayed. With its increased load, it could only manage a few knots and would arrive off Soyo a day late.

---

10 The Angolan Army (FAA) during the EO period was previously called FAPLA (*Forcas Armadas de Popular de Libertacao de Angola*), or the military wing of the ruling MPLA.

30

The Battle for Angola's Soyo – African History in the Making[1]

> Although the numbers involved were small – Executive Outcomes never had more than 500 men in Angola and were usually fewer, compared with Angolan armed forces of more than 100,000 men – [the mercenaries] were generally regarded as having played a critical part in securing victory for the government forces…
>
> British Government Green Paper *Private Military Companies: Options for Regulation*: Feb 12, 2000.

Taking the Soyo oil installation with such a small force was an inordinately tough call. It is almost certain that had the majority of EO operators been aware of what was waiting for them on the ground, the job would never even have rated consideration.

As we now know, they faced a long, hard battle to win back the oil facility and its surrounds as well as Kwando port. They were eventually also required to clear much of the surrounding areas that had been infiltrated by guerrillas. But first, they had to capture the main military base and that lay to the immediate south of two large oil storage tanks at Quefiquena.

The harbour was included in this configuration because, until then, it had served the needs of this vital enterprise as well as the even larger military base at *Campo Oito* – in Portuguese, Camp Eight – that was supposed to guard it.

As indicated by its name, *Campo Oito* lay eight kilometres south of Soyo, but what made it doubly difficult was that the entire complex was surrounded by some of the most magnificent primeval forest in Africa. In Vietnam War parlance, it would have been referred to as 'triple canopy spectacular', which, as the name suggests, made combat hazardous, often extremely so.

Under normal circumstances, trying to displace an estimated thousand well-entrenched enemy forces from positions that had been reinforced for more than a month should have required something like a brigade strength force, as well as armour and close air support. Indeed, Luanda promised it all, but in the end, very little materialized. An Angolan Air Force Hind did make the occasional cursory pass, mostly at heights in excess of 5,000 feet, but its efforts were useless: clearly, the pilot was afraid of coming under ground fire.

In his initial discussions with the Angolans, Eeben Barlow made several stipulations which he felt were critical to the success of the venture. The first was that the Luanda government pay for the operation in advance. Another was that while it lasted, EO would not be interfered with, either

---

[1] Extracted *in toto* from *War Dog: Fighting other People's Wars*, published by Casemate, the first of several editions, in 2006.

by the Angolan Army or the country's politicians. The same held for government commissars and political functionaries, features of the country's Marxist establishment. There was no argument from Luanda on any of the points raised by the South African.

Consequently, instead of attacking Soyo on March 4, Buks Buys sent in a three-man reconnaissance team to infiltrate the area the night before. Until then, the EO squad had to rely solely on intelligence provided by the Angolan Army, which, they soon realized, was sketchy. Most of it was obscure and invariably based on second-and third-hand sources. Usually they got it all wrong.

'FAA couldn't even give us the coordinates of the town', one of the men recalled. The men were thankful for the delay because apart from being able to reconnoitre the target area from up close, the supply barge with its support force and ammunition had still not pitched. The supplies onboard were to become a critical asset during of early stages of fighting. In fact, without them, the South Africans would almost certainly have been overrun.

Finally, a briefing for the entire group – together with an overview of both preparations in hand and what lay ahead – took place the next day at Cabinda's airfield with both Simon Mann and Tony Buckingham present. Also there was Colonel Pepe de Castro who was to follow the attack group to Soyo after initial landings had been made.

By now there had been several joint planning meetings involving EO command and FAA. It was agreed that the two tanks would provide immediate back-up, together with about a thousand Angolan troops, their ammunition and food. The South Africans would go in first – all 40 men in three Mi-17 helicopters – and would come in from the north, with the FAA element landing from the sea.

One issue raised at that final meeting by some of the men, was concern about the non-arrival of the on-site medical support team the recruiters said would be in place before they set out. The company had promised to establish a field hospital alongside the runway with Dr Francis Smit, the first medical doctor to be badged as a Special Force operator in the SADF, in attendance. But, as they were soon to discover, he was only to arrive weeks later, and then after much prompting by the men as casualties started coming in. Those fighting across the water were kept in ignorance of this fact, which was to have serious consequences later.

Undeterred, the force finally set out early on the morning of March 5, flying the entire leg across the Congo River barely a metre above the water. Buys would have liked to have the men on the ground before dawn, but none of the Angolans could fly at night. So first light it was.

Composed of three sections, which included two 12-man stopper groups deployed to east and west, the 14-strong Assault Group – that included Harry Ferreira, Lafras Luitingh, Phil Smith and Mauritz le Roux – went straight in with the Angolan chopper pilot putting his load down on the beach about a mile short of the oil storage tanks. The original plan was for him to land directly behind the tanks, but having reached the opposite shore and aware of a potential for trouble, the rather wild-eyed, trembling Angolan pilot would go no further.

This immediately presented the attackers with a raft of problems, not least that their packs were extremely heavy with extra ammunition, food and water. They'd never expected to have to hike anything like that distance through dense undergrowth, compounded by a swamp and puddles of mud sometimes half-a-metre deep.

The answer was for them to leave behind some of their heavier stuff which was not the best idea, but, as Lafras Luitingh admitted afterwards, there was no alternative. The first items ditched were their 60mm Patmore mortars and shells. The attackers were not to know it yet, but that was a bad mistake: waiting for them at Quefiquena was a UNITA force at least 300 strong.

EO's initial target, explained Harry Carlse, was UNITA's living quarters at the Quefiquena base. 'But being dropped so far away, it was a while before we could make contact with the original Recce team: it was their job to lead us in,' he explained. 'We'd also agreed beforehand that the stopper group, Team One, would provide early warning to the west of the LZ. Team Three took up a position to the east, while our group was responsible for the first assault.'

Instead of attracting fire immediately, the first of the EO teams moving forward took the UNITA guerrillas by surprise. They found a bunch of rebels congregating at the main gate of the target compound, obviously intrigued by unusual helicopter activity in their area. 'But when we sneaked up alongside one of the big storage tanks, they never even saw us. We opened fire and within twenty minutes we'd overrun their positions and forced them to vacate the compound and make a dash for it into the jungle' said Carlse. 'They left in such a hurry that their radios were still playing. There was money, clothes and weapons strewn about. Surprise was absolute and obviously, that pleased us.'

What also surprised the South Africans was that the defenders had secured their AKs with wire to the steel fence surrounding the complex. 'So when we hit them, they left their weapons behind as well.' It was obviously a measure to prevent troops from grabbing their guns and bolting, he explained. Still, fire from the base became intense and after a short consultation with the others, Mauritz le Roux decided to head back to the LZ and fetch the mortars.

Two men were designated to accompany him, but he had not been on the jungle track for minutes before they also disappeared. Only later did he discover that they had returned to the rest of the group; neither regarded the task a survival option.

'That was probably the loneliest walk of my entire life, as much as was possible in that difficult terrain, I moved at the double. Swamp waters prevented me from getting up any speed and naturally I was aware that I could have run into the enemy at any time. But I didn't, so I retrieved the tubes and a bunch of bombs and headed back, most times with the heavy foliage within touching distance on both sides…it was pretty hairy.'

Having got back to the others, the additional weapons came in handy for finally routing the remainder of Quefiquena's defenders.

At about this point, one of the stopper groups a few hundred metres down the road towards the west ambushed a green Renault, killing its driver. Inside they found the vehicle stuffed a metre high with piles of kwanza banknotes. Worth millions in the Angolan national currency, Executive Outcomes had hijacked the enemy battalion's pay for the month.

Similarly, a white Mitsubishi trying to flee the base was destroyed shortly afterwards and all its occupants killed.

After that, things did not go so well. With the element of surprise lost, UNITA opened fire on one of the other teams from about 300 metres but by retaliating fiercely, the rebels were driven back. It did not last: UNITA quickly regrouped and launched a vigorous counter-attack that halted any kind of forward momentum.

Carlse: 'Worse, the barge with all our reinforcements and armour had not arrived as it should have. It was six hours late and we had to fight hard to retain what we'd taken. When it eventually got there, the naval units came under concerted fire when UNITA forces – sitting on a patch of high ground that overlooked the region – laid down a hail of fire that included recoilless rifles, RPGs, mortars, light and heavy machineguns.' By now the South Africans were running short of ammunition.

Finally, at about noon, a 300-strong contingent of government troops arrived and none too soon. The 82mm mortars they ferried ashore provided immediate relief. With the South Africans taking charge, these African soldiers were spread around the outer defences, though it was immediately clear, with some of them wandering aimlessly and dangerously about, almost like schoolboys on a stroll, that they had absolutely no concept of what danger they faced.

More problems followed. Because of sustained fire, the barge captain, in bringing his vessel onto the beach, forgot to drop his retaining anchor. That meant that while the troops were able to clamber ashore, the vessel ended up broadside to the beach. Worse, it could not land its tanks.

One of these T-54s, a noisy, smoke-belching beast was eventually brought ashore on the fourth day, but because it attracted so much attention, – coupled to a hopelessly incompetent crew – the single piece of armour made marginal difference to the outcome of the battle, though it did eventually help EO to take the adjacent town. The other tank ended up buried in soft sea sand up to its turret and could not be dislodged. It is still there.

The additional FAA support, for all its shortcomings, did result in UNITA halting its retaliation for a couple of hours. A second attack followed when several hundred UNITA troops came forward in platoon-strength groups.

According to Carlse, it was an extremely determined effort, backed by mortars and rockets from further back. The defenders could immediately detect a new and single-minded discipline among the attackers coming at them: clearly, these fighters were Savimbi's Special Force *Groupos* and they knew exactly what was required of them.

Mauritz le Roux: 'They headed right at us, with the issue being made more difficult by a ring of three or four metre-deep oil retaining canals originally built as a precautionary measure to prevent spills from the nearby oil storage tanks. It was not long before they completely surrounded our position.

'When the rebels popped into these culverts, we could not see them, nor they us because they were at a much lower level than where we were. But they were actually only 15 or 20 metres below our lines and we could hear them talking among themselves.' That did not stop the infiltrators from hurling scores of grenades from down there and as le Roux recalled, it was then that some of the men started to get hurt.

'We retaliated, of course, but our numbers were small,' said Carlse, adding that the battle lasted about 90 minutes before UNITA pulled back again.

Then the unit's only medic 'Bossie' Bosman was hurt. In a bid to escape sustained mortar fire, he hurled himself headlong into one of the culverts. 'It wasn't an intentional option,' Carlse explained. 'Rather, he thought he would land on grass because the undergrowth was so incredibly dense.' As it happened, Bosman was fortunate to clamber out before the enemy grabbed him.

At about this point, said le Roux, some of the men realized that we had been short-changed by Buckingham. 'We were obviously in very serious trouble. There were very few of us facing huge numbers of the enemy and our so-called Angolan allies were all but useless.

It was about then that the men started to ask: Where were the nine policemen with revolvers that Simon Mann talked about at Cabo Ledo?

The most serious shortcoming of all was that there was no way that we could tell those people waiting in Cabinda what conditions on the ground around us were like. The radios with which the groups had been issued were short range and contact with headquarters across the water was impossible.

Consequently, there could be no back-up at short notice and obviously, no casualty evacuation should the worst happen. Also, we'd been told that there would be 'an open-heart surgery' clinic made available on one of the oil rigs, but we never saw anything like it. There wasn't even a doctor waiting on the other side for those wounded who were ferried out the next day.

Le Roux is outspoken about the way he and the other South Africans were 'exploited' by their British bosses with almost no regard for safety. As he commented bitterly, 'they would never have done that if the boys had been British…they wouldn't have been allowed to.'

Some really serious business started not long afterwards, with the guerrillas probing attackers' defences towards the south and east of Quefiquena. That affected some of the EO groups who had followed the initial group in, with some of them taking hits and having to make do with what was obviously an extremely precarious defence.

The section leaders felt that the biggest problem facing them at that point was the foliage that overwhelmed much of the complex. As le Roux recalls, the entire area was fringed by heavy jungle, so any kind of clear field of fire was out of the question. In places foliage actually overhung their positions, so that some of the men could barely see five metres into the undergrowth. UNITA ruthlessly exploited this advantage.

The Soyo campaign throughout, was a close-quarter operation, with the two sides sometimes only metres from each other. One of the defenders commented after it was all over: 'the rebels would infiltrate right up to our positions at night to attack. Or they would toss grenades at us. Then they'd call and taunt us, telling our blokes they were going to die.'

Another recalled that there were times when rebel fighters showed no fear: 'their perseverance amazed us all. Also, their combat tactics were excellent,' he declared.

Then Jeff Landsberg was wounded in the foot and his mates had to haul him to cover. With a small squad under Harry Carlse, this team had been trying to get at one of the enemy's artillery pieces – a D30 – but eventually that effort had to be abandoned because his men were not only visual to the enemy but also badly isolated from the main force. As Carlse reckons today, it would have been crazy to go on.

He takes up the story: 'with darkness that first night approaching fast, all three sections regrouped in an attempt to establish some sort of procedure. We knew that there would be a night attack because it was the way that UNITA operated. But at about this point, some of the EO guys said that they were worried about being sucked into something that none of them could handle. Obviously they were worried about casualties and they had a point. We'd been at it hard from the moment we'd arrived.

'Others declared that it had not been made clear to them when they took the job that there would be so much fighting. A few argued that rather, they'd envisioned training…this was a bunch of seriously rattled guys.

'As section leaders, we believed that our best option lay in setting up a defensive line alongside the compound that we'd captured earlier. By nine that night – almost within touching distance of the jungle – everybody had dug themselves a foxhole, most of which were spaced perhaps five or ten metres apart. Elsewhere there were large open areas that needed to be dominated and for which we knew, a large body of government troops had been deployed. By now they knew what was coming and did not need to be told to repel any attack.'

The main UNITA attempt came with midnight when the guerrilla movement launched its biggest attack yet: it lasted more than two hours. With all forces on call, the EO leaders were confident they could hold their positions. However, when their FAA allies did not react when ordered to open fire, it took the South Africans about a minute to realize that they were on their own: the Angolan troops had disappeared into the night. As some of the men reflected afterwards, they should have expected it, since so few government troops had been issued with more than a single magazine for their AKs.

As for their 'fucking illustrious officers,' as one of the EO men commented bitterly, almost all had hot-footed it towards the rear the moment the first shot sounded.

During this attack the South Africans took their third casualty with Harry Ferreira taking a bullet in his arm. A short while later Theuns Kruger was hit in the head by a piece of shrapnel

The Angolan countryside is littered with reminders of conflicts that took place decades ago. Nobody has ever bothered to remove this scrap, tens of thousands of tons of it. (Photo: Jerry Buirski)

Executive Outcomes air crew in Eastern Angola in front of their Hip: Pilot Carl Alberts (left), Angolan loadmaster and alongside him the mercenary regional commander Hennie Blaauw.

BATTLE FOR ANGOLA'S SOYO – AFRICAN HISTORY IN THE MAKING

An Angolan Army T54/55 tank that came to grief at Saurimo air base because the driver was drunk. (Author's photo)

EO training procedures covered the most basic disciplines, including how to handle the Soviet LMG: Jonny Maas shows how. (Author's photo)

Neill Ellis rates the Mi-24 Hind as among the most versatile helicopters available for Third World insurrections: its 12.7mm Gatling and winglet rocket pods make for formidable ground support roles. He helped to acquire this one for the Sierra Leone Air Wing. (Author's photo)

Soviet T54/55 main battle tank.

In order to capture Savimbi's alluvial diamond fields at Cafunfo, the Luanda Government bought 100 spanking new BMP-2s from Russia. Most were airlifted to the north-east. This one guarded the periphery of Saurimo Airport. (Author's photo)

from a grenade, though neither wound was serious.[2] But it was certainly indicative of how close the two forces were to each other because the grenade that wounded Kruger had been hurled from only metres away.

By now, all three section leaders were aware that if they did not react more forcefully, UNITA had enough manpower and seemingly unlimited supplies of hardware to eventually breach their lines. One of the more revealing comments about this attack, was that incoming fire was so fierce, that those of the men who did not have their kit bags in their foxholes with them, had them shot to ribbons where they'd placed them, just above their heads.

With daylight, work was immediately started in an effort to reorganise defences. Barely an eighth of the original FAA force was still around at sunrise, though they were joined by another group who slunk in guiltily when additional ammunition and water was handed out. It had originally been arranged before leaving Cabinda that a helicopter supply drop would be sent on the second day and this was certainly the most welcome sight of the operation so far. The defenders were not only able to pass on details back to base about the extremely serious situation in which they found themselves but also used the opportunity to ship out the wounded.

All the while EO was able to observe a white van moving backwards and forwards between UNITA's rear echelons and *Campo Oito*. It soon became clear that the vehicle was resupplying the guerrilla forward lines with ammunition and taking back the wounded. Le Roux reckons that they would have been able to do something about it, but the vehicle always remained just out of range. By now UNITA had also started lobbing heavy mortars at the South Africans – none too efficiently because most landed wide. For the rest of the time, they fired off artillery salvos of four or five shells at a time.

After dark, the previous night's drama was repeated, only this time defending FAA troops were a little more responsive. There was not a man among them who was not aware that if the South African position were to be overrun, they would be slaughtered.

Mutterings among some of the EO men was now becoming audible. More than half the force wanted out. This was not what they had come to Angola for, they insisted. Also, they argued, they were not all infantry trained and things were likely to get worse. As one of the more experienced fighters concluded, 'they resented having to work hard for that nice big pay check which, with all the percentage incentives now being offered, had become very fat indeed.' Cabinda had passed on a message of a massive bonus if the men were able to hold out.

At the same time, things were going badly for the government's troops. While the South Africans helped where they could, their Angolan counterparts were simply not able to withstand protracted fire. Some FAA soldiers became disorientated: others broke ranks and fled. Language, too, was a problem, even though four EO members could speak good enough Portuguese to make their presence felt.

But darkness brought more of the same. Though the EO officers had extended their lines forward about 300 metres – largely to avoid UNITA sappers getting into the retaining canal around the base – where they placed a large FAA squad in position. But by the time an attack came, again at midnight, the mercenaries were again on their own. All the Angolans had fled, even though more AK magazines had been passed around.

Sunday the 7th March, EO had planned in conjunction with the FAA commander to launch an early-morning retaliatory raid against the rebels, but none of the Angolan troops appeared. Instead, those who were left – about 100 of the original thousand – wandered into camp shortly before noon. As Mauritz le Roux says, the operation had become a monumental disaster.

---

2   EO forces in Angola and Sierra Leone never wore helmets, nor would they have done so even if available.

Nonetheless, the EO section leaders made good use of what black soldiers there were. Having spread the recalcitrants out in an extended line along the front and urged them to dig themselves in, everybody could do little more than wait for the next attack and that did not take long in coming.

To Harry Carlse, it was obvious that their lines could not hold indefinitely. The Angolan soldiers lacked both the tenacity and incentive to face seasoned guerrillas. So grabbing seven of his mates and calling the tank forward, they moved in among FAA ranks, with a man stationing himself every ten metres or so to fight alongside them. They quickly got these irregulars into something of a routine, encouraging them to coordinate magazine changes and to try to make something of an effective stand.

As he recalls today, the presence of this small group of South Africans right there among them worked wonders. 'Suddenly, with us shouting orders, showing them how and making a serious effort to retaliate with some verve and accuracy started to have an effect. We gave them the courage to do the same. And in the end, that's exactly what happened.

'When they looked again UNITA was on the run and our lines were able to move out even further.' The tank, meanwhile, was blasting merrily away at anything that moved and became a powerful rallying point in the fire-fight that followed.

With that, more of the EO men started to move up while others began to prepare food. Earlier Le Roux had cut some 44-gallon drums in half, cleaned them out and used them to boil water for cooking rice.

'We distributed great globs of rice while handing out ammunition. We also passed around still more AK magazines that were desperately needed by some of the African soldiers. Some still had only one with which they'd originally been issued and considering the circumstances, that was ridiculous,' le Roux commented.

What was also a little absurd, he added, 'was that once the rice was on the boil, more and more of these FAA troops would sheepishly emerge from the jungle.' At one stage there were so many stragglers arriving that le Roux thought a bus might have stopped close by and disgorged them all.

'We told them they could eat only if they stayed and fought and with that, we probably doubled our numbers.'

That evening, the third night the unit was out on its own on the edge of the jungle, Carlse remembers, presaged the first relatively quiet night of the campaign.

With the helicopter bringing in the casualties from across the water, shock immediately set in among those waiting in Cabinda. Buckingham was appalled, especially since some of the wounds were potentially life-threatening. And there was still no doctor!

It stayed that way until some of the men were flown to Windhoek four days later, by which time Landsberg's suppurating foot had started to rot in a climate that is a constant 99 percent humidity almost year round. Some of the South Africans made the point if some of the wounds were not treated promptly in that stifling climate, gangrene would be the result and without proper medical attention, the consequences, more than likely, would be terminal.

The story offered the Namibian hospital to which he and some of the others wounded were admitted was that he was part of a group of South Africans lifting mines in Angola. Looking back, Landsberg was indeed lucky to have kept his foot.

What soon became apparent to those watching a debacle that was growing more intense each day, was that this so-called control group in Cabinda had almost no conception of what was going on across the water. In fact, with no comms in place – apart from messages passed back and forth by the helicopter pilots – they simply had no way of knowing, except what they were told by the wounded.

This was another of Simon Mann's blunders since it was this man who originally vetoed buying more elaborate communication equipment that would have kept everybody in the picture.

For their part Keller and Buys were distraught at what the returnees were telling them. For a start, the numbers against which the tiny force was up against stunned them. Luanda had told them it would be a walkover, which actually underscored how little the average South African (and, for that matter, the Angolan top brass) knew about Savimbi's Special Forces.

Even Buckingham was perplexed enough to use his satellite phone to call his SAS contacts in the UK again to ask for a volunteers for a parachute drop. He offered good rewards for any takers. There were none.

Despite the brief measure of relief that the Mi-17 brought each time it went across, conditions within EO's ranks continued to deteriorate. By now about the half the team wanted out, especially since they had been almost continually under attack ever since they got there.

On the morning of the third day consequently, rather than have a mutiny on their hands, the section leaders – who had been forced to accept a more aggressive, independent role – made the decision: those who wanted out should go and that there should be no delay. They agreed that the dissenters had become more of an encumbrance than a help. Also, they sensed that a negative approach within the ranks was affecting the ability of the others to perform. In any event, contributing little, they were also using up valuable food, ammunition and water.

Luitingh asked his Angolan counterpart to request an airlift out for those who wanted to leave and the quitters were back in Cabo Ledo by nightfall. This immediately prompted Buckingham to offer an extra $3,000 bonus if the EO force could hold Soyo for 30 days. At the same time, EO was now reduced to less than 20 men on the ground and still facing a most determined enemy.

That said, the mercenary group still had a few advantages, one of which was in the air. EO had one very important asset: 'Ghost Rider', the same twin-engine Cessna that originally ferried the men from Windhoek to Cabo Ledo and that was now based in Cabinda, offered superlative support throughout the operation. Its job was to scout opposing forces' positions and where possible, provide ranging and other observations for the EO mortar teams.

It is worth mentioning that the plane was originally bought at a DEA auction in Miami after being seized for drug running in the Caribbean. Its role in the skies over Soyo just then was every bit as dangerous, in fact, even more so, since UNITA would use all the Triple-A it had, and in particular, its 14.5s to try to bring down the plane.

31

The Fighting Continues

> **For the mercenary is a simplistic fellow. Not for him the strutting parades of West Point, the medals on the steps of the White House or perhaps a place at Arlington. He simply says: 'Pay me my wage and I'll kill the bastards for you.' And if he dies, they will bury him quickly and quietly in the red soil of Africa and we will never know…**
> Frederick Forsyth: 'Send in the Mercenaries,' *Wall Street Journal*, May 15, 2000

The biggest battle of the campaign kicked off at first light on the morning of the fourth day. It was a series of touch-and-go sorties that at any time could have gone in any direct direction.

Throughout the night, Mauritz le Roux and other EO men on watch thought they heard an unusual amount of rustling in the grass around their position, but being exhausted from days of fighting, they put it down to wind. Only once the skirmish had been joined did they realize that UNITA had spent hours positioning its force for the coming onslaught.

It was extremely well organized, le Roux told me years afterwards. 'They moved quietly and competently into place. Not one of them allowed his position to be betrayed by the noise of metal upon metal. Nor did we hear a whisper among any of them…these guys had been solidly trained… they knew their stuff.'

Also during the night they could detect engine noises, possibly the white van moving about behind UNITA lines, but thought nothing more of it. It had been doing that from the start. One of Jonas Savimbi's officers captured some months later by an EO reconnaissance team admitted under questioning that more than 1,000 new men had brought forward earlier that evening, many of them *Groupos de Bate*, he declared proudly.

The EO officers were confident that whatever happened, they would be able to hold the 400 metres or so of frontline along which their forces were dispersed. They'd also distributed a huge amount of ammunition the previous evening, for just such an eventuality. There'd be no shortages when the attack came, they reckoned. Nor was there…

One of the mercenaries, JJ de Beer, had just been wakened for his watch when he stood up on the edge of his foxhole. In a passive, sleepy gesture he stretched his arms out above his head. With that, just about every enemy PKM, RPD, RPG, RPK and mortar within a half-mile range opened up. Without even thinking about it, he buckled his legs and plopped full-length into his hole. He remembers it being the first time at Soyo that they had come up against rifle grenades.

Though the war raged on the verge of a series of cassava fields for about three hours, it seemed to slacken a little every 30 minutes or so, which allowed both sides to take stock. UNITA used the break to haul back their wounded and dead, something at which they were quite adept. It was a Maoism that Savimbi had adopted from the very beginning of his guerrilla campaign: he'd argue that the enemy became demoralized if they had nothing to show for their efforts, particularly after long periods of slogging it out with the adversary.

EO too, had incurred losses. One of its men, Oosthuizen, had the sights of his RPG blow back into his face. The heavy steel rim on the weapon cut him severely. In fact, when you meet the man today, you can still see the extent of the wound. Blinded and in pain, Roelf van Heerden briefly got out of his foxhole to help him re-orientate himself and when he returned to his tiny piece of turf, he found that a rifle grenade had exploded right where he had been lying only moments before.

There were many extremely close encounters in the battle that served to remove just about every leaf in the trees and bushes above and around the defenders' trench lines. Louis Engelbrecht, a Koevoet veteran from the old South West Africa was using his PKM when he suddenly found that it would no longer fire on full auto. He'd cock his weapon and fire a single shot. Then he'd have to cock it again. That went on a while, until he discovered that an AK bullet had neatly lodged in the PKM's gas chamber. It had entered just below the supplementary barrel that operates the PKM's blowback system. An inch up, down or sideways, and he would have taken the bullet in his head. Lucky man…

At this point Harry Carlse remembers some of the mercenaries starting to act 'peculiar'. There were distinct signs of shell shock among several of the guys, he told me.

Their eyes would quiver from side to side and a few would act and talk irrationally, but not enough to get themselves killed. The ongoing attrition was affecting them, as it had some of the FAA troops. A few of the African soldiers had tried to bolt into the jungle before being cut down by automatic fire. Altogether 14 Angolan troops were killed in the attack, with more than 100 wounded, several dozen seriously.

For two or three hours or more, the battle went on. Then, gradually, to the astonishment of all, it slackened. According to Mauritz le Roux, something totally unexpected then took place. The defenders were both amazed and relieved to see UNITA commanders pull their men back and it did not take long for the entire area to be clear.

The guerrilla force, too, it seems, had had enough, though word later came through that their senior commander was killed by a mortar bomb which exploded right next to him.

It took a while longer for the dust to settle. Though elated to have survived that turmoil, the mercenary officers checked defences and pulled back those needing attention. Others were relieved from their posts when distress became obvious. But it all took time.

Meantime, more ammunition was handed out and preparations were started to cook the morning meal.

Throughout the Soyo campaign, which went on intermittently for another two months and afterwards as well – when EO marched towards the diamond fields – there were consistent reports coming through that indicated UNITA had hired a bunch of mercenaries, possibly also South Africans.

There was no question that Savimbi had used these freebooters in the past. Bob Denard had spent a brief time working with the rebels earlier in the war and at about the same time, Pretoria was abuzz with stories about agents recruiting seasoned soldiers for the other side in the South African capital city who clearly, once they went into action, would be exchanging fire with their old colleagues.

At Soyo, Angolan Army intelligence spoke about four white mercenaries having come across from the Congo during the first few days of the action. As a result, it was no surprise after the final battle that some of the EO officers were shown part of a scalp recovered from a soldier who had had half his head blown away. The blood-matted hair was blond while the bandana that the dead men wore was red.

EO sources subsequently claimed that more than 1,000 UNITA died in the battle for the Soyo oil complex. However, this did not make sense since Savimbi – at the height of his strength – never had more than 30,000 men in the field. In his most determined battles against FAPLA, Cuban and Russian brigades – with artillery, tank and aircraft action combined – they never exceeded more than 300 or 400 of their soldiers killed in any single conflagration, though there could often be a dozen such actions on as many successive days.

UNITA never did come back to Quefiquena in any kind of numbers, though attacks would take place there sporadically. Somehow their cast-iron doggedness had cracked.

In a contest of resolve, where luck probably played as big a role as experience and expertise, a small group of veterans from South Africa's Border War had won the day and the plaudits. What was also remarkable that up to this point, not one South African combatant had been killed.

About half the remaining South African force then took the initiative and decided to not unduly push their options: they asked to be sent home. To the majority, it was a sensible choice and Lafras Luitingh and the others did not argue. Those that wanted out were put on the first Mi-17 to touch down later that day, though they were told to leave their food, water and ammunition for those who stayed.

With the departure of that batch, Executive Outcomes strength at Soyo was down to 24 men, though the absconders were soon replaced by a fresh bunch of recruits. The newcomers were markedly better at playing at war than many of those previously recruited because EO's command structure could now be a lot more fastidious. They chose very carefully who would do their fighting for them and it showed in subsequent campaigns in Angola and Sierra Leone. For a start, all future recruits had to be able to prove that they were linked to one of the Special Forces units and have taken part in at least one major military campaign.

While the oil tanks at Quefiquena had lost their lustre for UNITA, the guerrilla force remained on the periphery of Soyo and its environs. Rather, with many of the main force having been sent back to bolster defences around the diamond fields, there were still groups of rebels sporadically attacking FAA convoys and strong-points. EO was constantly being called out to help.

One of the first of the areas that needed to be cleared, Luitingh and the others decided, was the town of Soyo itself. UNITA had spent good time and effort in a bid to ingratiate itself within the civilian population. Using the old TM 54/55 as well as a bulldozer that had been left behind by the oil contractors, about half the squad moved into town where they promptly annexed every civilian car.

One of the best of the lot was a white Toyota Corolla which immediately had all its doors ripped off, including the one over the trunk. With that, the company had made itself an improvised 'troop carrier' that could ferry 18 FAA troops to battle at a time, four or five of them in the trunk.

On the sixth day the entire EO force moved closer to town and occupied Cuanza Base, a small hotel-type facility that had previously been used by employees of the oil companies waiting for dispatch to their postings, vacation or home. It was an improvement on what they had before with a fully-equipped kitchen and, to the delight of some, their own gym and pool.

But the UNITA threat continued to manifest itself. Each day there were more attacks. Though minor compared to what the teams had gone through at Quefiquena, they were a reminder of why they were there. The main problem, the section leaders decided, was that the guerrillas were still infiltrating the area from the east and were still being supplied from the south.

With that in mind, a decision was taken to try to blow a large bridge to the south of *Campo Oito* which was still being used as a headquarters by Savimbi's people. It was decided that the attacking

A Soviet BMP-2 goes to war: this one in Sierra Leone, where it effectively helped rout the RUF rebels. (Photo: Cobus Claassens)

Peter 'Monster' Wilkins photographed these three Angolan Air Force MiG-23s at a Lubango air base years after the Border War had ended.

The twins, Louis and Nico du Preez, two former members of South Africa's elite Reconnaissance Regiment, with Cobus Claassens in the middle, all of whom fought for EO. (Author's collection)

A more recent photo of Angolan officers in training in Russia.

Mortar attack.

force would use two of the Zodiacs that EO had acquired by devious means to take the men in. Permission was sought from the local FAA commander who passed it on to Luanda.

Meanwhile, Phil Smith asked to do a reconnaissance of the area in one of the Pilatus PC-9s that were now able to use the 'liberated' Soyo airport and which, from time to time provided top cover in outlying areas where members of the company remained active. With its relatively low speed and under-wing rocket pods fitted to improvised hard points, these versatile Swiss trainers proved ideal for close air support throughout the campaigns that followed.

Having flown over the enemy camp, Phil Smith asked the pilot to do a turn over the first small town to the east of Soyo from where UNITA had consistently been lobbing 100mm shells at both Quefiquena and other positions held by either EO or FAA. They had barely circled the place the first time – from the air it looked minuscule, consisting of little more than some old colonial structures, surrounded by clusters of mud huts – when Smith spotted a white man running out of one of the buildings. He was surprised to see him carrying a MANPAD ground-to air missile in his arms. A moment later, he aimed it at the circling aircraft.

With the possibility of a missile attack imminent, the pilot hardly needed to be told what to do. He immediately thrust his stick forward and took the plane down low, but not before a couple of hundred rebels that had been hiding in the surrounding bush opened fire on the turboprop. As Smith told the others afterwards, they had RPGs self-destructing all around them and the sky was peppered with green tracers.[1]

Indeed, he admitted, they were lucky not to have been brought down. But then, not altogether unexpectedly, they took a hit somewhere mid-ships.

From what he could make out, the aircraft's fuel line had been punctured and the next moment, the engine cut. It was all that the pilot could do to look for somewhere to put down.

Fortunately the river was close-by and a stretch of open beach seemed the only logical alternative to crash-landing in a cassava patch. Radio comms with base meanwhile had one of the Hips heading towards them from Cabinda in a last-ditch effort to snatch the two men to safety. It was none too soon: following lift-off, the chopper pilot did a circle over the damaged aircraft and already there were figures emerging from the jungle and heading towards it.

The fact that the enemy was using white mercenaries from South Africa was an extremely disturbing revelation. EO could never come to terms with the fact that its men now faced some of their own people – former colleagues and, in some cases, close friends – every one of them recruited by UNITA. As they were to discover much later, some had even served together in the same units.

But it did not prevent one of the EO officers, JT Erasmus, a former Commandant in the Recces passing the word around that if any of the whites fighting them were captured, they were not to be killed. Rather, he ordered, they would be assimilated into their own ranks and discreetly returned to South Africa.

As Mauritz le Roux explained, 'we were there for the money, not vengeance. So that decision made good sense. After all, we were all South Africans doing a job as best as each of us saw fit.'

What did worry the Executive Outcomes command structure though, was that word had filtered through of clandestine offers being made by Savimbi: he would apparently pay anyone – UNITA or FAA – thousands of dollars for every EO combatant killed or captured. It was to be a repeat of the situation later in Sierra Leone with Foday Sankoh promising his gooks enormous rewards for bringing in mercenaries, dead or alive. Neall Ellis, Sierra Leone's only gunship pilot had a million dollars on his head…

---

1 Soviet tracers are green. The standard-issue RPG-7 rocket grenade self-destructs at 900 meters.

Apparently the Angolan guerrilla leader believed that if enough examples were made of those war dogs that fell into his hands, EO would have difficulty with its recruiting program.

More EO follow-ups took place in subsequent days, with the South Africans gradually gathering around them some of the more seasoned FAA soldiers that they had dealt with in the past.

Those Angolan soldiers that did show promise were coached in a variety of disciplines, including operational procedures, weapons handling and tactics. Basically they were shown what was expected of them under fire. Much attention was also given to marksmanship: troops were weaned off the customary Angolan bravado of firing from the hip. It pleased Lafras and his buddies to discover that there were some enthusiastic learners and quite a few of the brighter Angolans chose to stick close to the South Africans as long as their contracts lasted.

The first target to follow the battles at Quefiquena and Soyo was *Campo Oito,* which a column headed by EO's men captured on March 13th. It was a tough slog, with UNITA reluctant to vacate one of its strongest positions.

It was also there that the company took its first fatality. Buks Erasmus, a former 32 man and a mortar specialist – one of the best – was killed while some of his troops from Section One – with an FAA detachment in tow – were headed towards the UNITA headquarters. Struck full on by a HEAT Strim,[2] he was a brave men and under the circumstances, irreplaceable. For the next ten days, EO's people were almost completely surrounded by enemy regulars.

Meanwhile, news that UNITA had had been driven out of Soyo was beginning to make an impact abroad: Savimbi's men were not as all-powerful as his publicity agents liked to portray them. Numerous news reports that there had been mercenaries involved in the battles surrounding Soyo also got prominence.

What soon became clear was that while the events at Soyo were a departure for the Angolan Army who, for a while now had suffered a succession of defeats, the media was not being fooled by Luanda's claims that its own troops had been responsible. Too many of the original EO squad had returned home to regale friends with stories. The word was out: War Dogs had done it again!

The normally unforthcoming Eeben Barlow even did the unexpected by inviting a media team to Northern Angola to 'meet the boys' and explain what had taken place. That resulted in further coverage, with several of the world's biggest weeklies giving EO credit for driving out an insurgent army and helping to once more 'turn on the oil faucets'. The Americans seemed especially pleased.

By now, a new group of recruits had arrived in Soyo and with some of the old timers who decided to stay and collect a second check, one of the first tasks they were given was to smack a small town where UNITA were reported to control in some depth. The group set out early in the day in two trucks containing a bunch of EO volunteers together with a squad of FAA troops.

Reaching an area where an ambush might be waiting for them, some of the troops dismounted, with EO sending a number of its own men ahead to cover all eventualities. They had not gone far when UNITA troops, concealed in dense bush at the side of the road, opened fire. The men were caught completely off guard: According to Mauritz le Roux, Harry Carlse was shocked enough to drop his AK.

The first man hit was a relatively new arrival by the name of Cornell Taljaard, a former 4 Reconnaissance veteran. He took a hit in the leg and went down. Phil Smith immediately ran forward to give support, but was shot in the neck from up close and killed. With that, the rest of the column pulled back, leaving two of their own behind. Though reports about what happened to

---

2   Anti-tank Strim HEAT missile: The LRAC-F1 89 mm anti-tank rocket launcher (model F1) is a French reusable rocket launcher, some of which were obviously sold to UNITA, probably through third parties.

Taljaard are sketchy, it is known that he was tortured before being beaten to death by the women of a village in which the UNITA force was billeted.

For EO it was a heavy loss. Two of the best company men had been KIA and suddenly things again started to look grim. Up to that point, the tally was three dead.

The perpetual uncertainty of what lay ahead worried most of the men, coupled to a manifest lack of support from the Angolan command that sometimes fringed either on indifference or negligence. Though Soyo was theirs, these new developments taken together obviously had a detrimental effect on morale. In a sense it was dereliction on the part of the FAA commanders. Still worse, there was nobody present who could – or would – do anything about it.

Also, it was not lost on any of the mercenaries that initially they had been tasked for a single 18-hour strike, which Luanda had said was all it would take to recapture Soyo. At first the timeframe had been extended to three days, then ten and finally to two months. There did not seem to be an end to it.

At that point, about half the EO force, including many of the newcomers, decided that they'd had enough of this crap and asked to be repatriated.

After days of continuous fighting, including reinforcements having been brought in to supplement the main force, EO's presence finally did prevail. But it took another month for that to happen.

At the crux of it all, looking back, whatever UNITA handed out, they got back with interest, or to paraphrase Eric Linklater in an earlier conflict: the South Africans fought with dashing assurance. Unquestionably, much of it was due to the efforts of the original group that had stayed on longer than they had needed to, and again, it was money that motivated most of them. Together with the newcomers, they had used experience gained earlier to push the main UNITA force out of the oil areas.

Once EO pulled back and its members had gone home, the company left the Angolan Army in place to take care of things. At least that was the general consensus. Within weeks, the rebels were back and had retaken Soyo.

What was immediately apparent to everybody in Luanda was that the experiment of employing mercenaries had worked. Not only that, it had been an unmitigated success and an extremely difficult task accomplished. FAA had tried often enough in the past in its battles against UNITA and achieved almost nothing.

Moreover, it was the first real demonstration not only of EO dedication in achieving results against extremely heavy odds, but also of the unit's demonstrable combat abilities. More important, the effort showed some sceptics in Luanda – and there were quite a few to start with – that the South Africans were not only serious about what they did but had demonstrable military skills to make it all work.

As the insurgency continued, Luanda finally had to make a decision. Were they to hire a larger, more effective mercenary force or, as they had been doing all along, with questionable results, go it alone? The issue was decided for them by still more guerrilla successes. Not only was Savimbi by then in control of an enormous percentage of Angola's rural regions, all that really eluded his grasp were the country's larger cities.

Finally, in August 1993, Eeben Barlow signed a multi-million dollar contract to train 5,000 troops from FAA's 16th Regiment. Executive Outcomes would also bring in 30 experienced pilots with solid Border War combat experience.

More significant was the proviso that, with immediate effect, EO would start to advise Angolan Army commanders on front-line operations against Savimbi's forces, with the result that some EO officers eventually ended up directing the course of several major battles against the rebel force. In the end, the tide would swing completely the government's way.

Part of EO's deal with the government was to help it acquire some of the more sophisticated items of weaponry, which included thermobarics or, more commonly, fuel air explosives.[3] These are the same enhanced-blast weapons that were used to good effect by the Russians to dislocate the terrorist threat in Chechnya, especially around Grozny, the capital.

It is interesting that several sources have since indicated to this author that the Luanda Government employed enhanced blast/fuel-air bombs in some of their battles against Savimbi, in particular in dislodging the guerrilla leader and his entourage from his main fortress in the hills around Bailundo in the Central Highlands. In all probability, this was achieved with the remnants of an EO presence.

Certainly, once Executive Outcomes had gone into Sierra Leone to fight the RUF rebels, I was told by several serving officers that the company had intended using thermobaric weapons against rebel strong-points in the mountains near the Liberian border. I was actually present in Freetown when the possibility of using fuel-air bombs against the rebels was discussed. Before that plan could be implemented however, EO's contract in Sierra Leone was arbitrarily cancelled.

Since then, Colonel Bert Sachse, who for a long time was in command of EO in Sierra Leone, told me that all that really prevented his people using this weapon was the reluctance of some senior Sierra Leone commanders to wipe out Foday Sankoh's entire staff. In truth, apart from the fact that many of them had relatives among the rebels, quite a few were themselves on the RUF payroll.

In Angola, it is significant that video footage of thermobaric explosives being used against UNITA does exist, though the source of these controversial bombs has never been traced, at least not conclusively.

Obviously they must have come from South Africa but even today nobody is saying how, why or when.

At the end of it all, the role of the two former British Army veterans who created Africa's first Private Military Company must give us something of an insight to the way that things are likely to be handled in the future.

Both Tony Buckingham and Simon Mann were well-acquainted with both Angola and its government. They had worked with these people in the past. Had that not been the case, EO would not have got a foot in the door. Since Luanda welcomed people with whom they had done business and showed goodwill, the original link engendered confidence.

It did not happen overnight. The South Africans had to travel to Luanda – and elsewhere – to do the necessary. Indeed, they went in many times to thrash out the small print and much of this side of things involved General Luis Faceira of the Angolan Army.

It did not take long to become clear to everybody involved in the venture that EO's future role in Angola would hinge on a successful Soyo operation, if only because Luanda wanted to be certain that the 'Boers' (as the South Africans were sometimes disparagingly referred to) could actually do the job.

General Faceira's approach, which changed with time and became much more favourable, indicated to Barlow and his friends that the company's actions at Soyo had impressed the Angolan High Command. 'Immensely', he told Lafras Luitingh.

---

3 Special Report: 'The New Gods of War: Enhanced Blast Weapons' (Thermobarics/Fuel-Air-Explosives): Analysis, by Christopher D Kondaki, Global Information System (GIS). *Defense and Foreign Affairs Daily,* Washington DC, January 18, 2002. In this document Angola is listed as one of the countries in possession of thermobaric weapons. So, too, is Zimbabwe.

Not only had these foreign fighters acquitted themselves well under the most dangerous of conditions, they were prepared to risk their lives to make it work. The implications of a relatively small squad of 28 former South African Special Forces personnel, able to evict a much larger UNITA mobile force from a vital oil facility was not lost on anybody in Luanda's higher echelons.

Those 28 individuals were all that were left after a large part of the group had opted out once things became hot. Of this number, only about 15 had formerly been front-line fighters, though there were many times when the rear-echelon had to do some shooting, if only to avoid being overrun.

As Barlow's associate, Michael Grunberg told me when I made contact with his office in the Channel Islands, 'one must bear in mind that at that stage, the Angolans really knew very little of the internal machinations of EO – or, for that matter how they went about their business. Instead, it was a case of them keeping their fingers crossed.'

More important still, he pointed out, nothing like this had ever happened in Angola before and Luanda wanted more of the same. Especially since Savimbi's people were then still in control of some of the country's most lucrative diamond fields.

32

How Executive Outcomes Ran it's Campaigns in Angola

The Cold War is over, but with demand for military muscle stronger than ever around the world, hired guns are going corporate.
'Soldiers for Sale' by Adam Zagorin *Time* Magazine: May 26, 1997

Executive Outcomes' Soyo adventure was eventually to become synonymous with what a well-discipline bunch of 'War Dogs' could achieve in a regional 'Third World' conflict. To other PMCs active in distant lands, it offered what Kipling said of the Boer War: it was, he declared, 'no end of a lesson'.

While 'The Battle for Soyo' ranks right up there with Executive Outcomes having pushed Sierra Leone's RUF rebels from the precincts of Freetown, not much has appeared in print about either of these events, even though a lot of lives – the majority of them enemy – were lost in the process. What has been published about this extended African campaign has either been fragmentary or inaccurate, or in one notable instance, plagiarized.

In contrast, Mauritz le Roux's very personal impressions in previous chapters are remarkable. Not only was he there, in the thick of it, he was also one of the original movers behind the founding of Executive Outcomes.

An organizer with indomitable spirit, he has since gone on to found and nurture the Safenet Group, one of the most successful personally-owned Private Military Companies in the world, with its main offices operating out of Dubai. In keeping with his no-nonsense, low-key approach – and unlike most American companies of a similar ilk – he neither seeks publicity nor does he get it.

In recent years Safenet has been operational in many countries, including Iraq, Afghanistan, Egypt, Chad, South Africa, Sudan, Sierra Leone, the DRC, Liberia as well as a host of other trouble spots.

Mauritz le Roux obviously used his experiences with EO to good advantage because one of the comments made about his company came not long ago from the Regional Security Manager/US Military Liaison when he declared, in print, that Safenet 'had gone above and beyond in supporting the client throughout Iraq.' It had been an honour working with them and supporting their missions, he added.

As Mauritz said when he, Neall Ellis and I spent time together at the mouth of the Columbia River in the Pacific Northwest in the spring of 2005, 'Just about anybody can talk…I like to get on with the job.'

With that kind of approach, and a face that remains inconspicuous, Le Roux had protection teams working the 'Baghdad Beat' for quite a few years and during that phase, lost none of his men to hostilities. At the same time, he and his team battled their way out of several scraps with

Sunni fundamentalists. That included an attack in Falluja in the spring of 2005 when his group, travelling in convoy with no military escort, was hit by a 60-strong rebel group.

In the contact that followed, his attackers were routed. Le Roux's only casualty was his American client who, despite pleadings for him to travel in one of the protected vehicles, the man preferred to ride up front and exposed, alongside one of the machine-gunners.

'A great guy,' he said, adding that it was a catastrophe to lose him. 'But sadly, he wouldn't accept my advice. He was determined to be a part of it and we saw what happened. You need to be discreet rather than macho in the Sunni Triangle and my friend, great pal that he was, paid a terrible price.' Le Roux flew back to Texas with his client's body and attended the funeral. It says something that the American concern remains a client.

As might be expected, there are quite a few notables who were involved with him in the Soyo operation that now work for him in Baghdad, including Harry Carlse. Neall Ellis also briefly joined him.

All this underscores one of Mauritz le Roux's many strengths: he prefers people working for him who have fired a few shots in anger during the course of their professional careers. When things really matter, such as in a fire-fight, usually unexpected, he likes staff members who are able to extricate both themselves and those they are paid to protect from dangerous situations.

Compare that with the exploits of Blackwater USA, one of the most illustrious PMCs of the lot. Prior to us going to press with *War Dog: Fighting Other People's War*s late in 2005, Blackwater had lost almost 30 of its employees in contacts, ambushes and the like. The majority of those fatalities occurred in Iraq and elements with the now defunct company were indicted by the Federal Government on war crimes.

What Executive Outcomes did prove during the course of its activities in Angola was that a solid command structure, coupled to the correct choice of combatant, discipline that fringes on the exemplary and a level of dedication you do not often find among the ranks, it is possible for a commercial concern to achieve good results under austere conditions.

In a report I did for Britain's Jane's Information Group, I illustrated another reality: unconventional conflicts sometimes demand unconventional solutions. With decades of bush war combat behind them, this South African PMC managed to open doors that had been shut ever since Africa was vacated by the Colonial Powers in the 1960s and 1970s.[1]

Some considered Soyo as arguably the toughest single campaign fought by any group of mercenaries since Colonel Mike Hoare's final days in the Congo in the 1960s. The fraught economic situation was made even more horrific by an outbreak of Marburg, a deadly hemorrhagic fever related to Ebola.

Subsequent EO participation in Sierra Leone might have come close, but the level of competence among the rebels facing this mercenary group in the jungles beyond Freetown and in the approaches to the Kono diamond fields were no match to what Savimbi threw into the fray.

Considering the fact that there were a dozen or more battles fought in the roughly two months that Soyo lasted and the exceptionally low casualty rate among company personnel, what took place at this isolated oil installation in the jungle was both a tribute to their tenacity and a remarkable level of professionalism displayed under fire.

---

1 'Mercenaries Fuel Next Round in Angolan Civil War': Al J. Venter, Jane's *International Defence Review;* March 1996.

EO certainly vindicated any doubts that the company's adversaries might have had as to their efficacy outside the ambit of a conventional military force. And make no mistake; EO had critics aplenty, in Angola itself as well as in Britain, the United States and South Africa.

As Lafras Luitingh told me on the plane that took us to Sierra Leone not very long afterwards, what happened at Soyo was often emulated but never surpassed. In terms of sheer numbers and the paucity of equipment available, he said, a tiny group of South Africans managed to keep a far superior UNITA force at bay. The company played a significant role in preventing a major guerrilla force from neutralizing one of Angola's most valuable assets.

That Savimbi's people took Soyo again after the South Africans had pulled out was of no consequence. EO, Luitingh declared, had done what it had set itself to do and that was what mattered.

Ousting UNITA from Soyo a second time became a formality because this time round the attackers had support from both armour and helicopter gunships.

Once launched, the initial Soyo operation was the start of a most demanding regimen for the mercenary force in Angola. Within months of their return to this West African state, EO was very much in the thick of it. Their activities took them to the north and to regions that adjoined the Central Highlands in the interior. Only then did they tackle the east, though from the start, the company had an advanced operational base at Saurimo, the country's prominent but pathetically run-down diamond centre.

Looking at the broader scenario, some of Executive Outcomes' successes are said by insiders to stem from what Duncan Rykaart – a senior member of the company's original command group – termed EO's 'Four Interlocking Principles'.

This codification – informal but strictly adhered to throughout the expanded campaigns that followed in both Angola and Sierra Leone – was much discussed during my two visits to EO positions in Angola in 1995. They were also to become the basis of many of the core values established by management. As such, declared Rykaart, himself a former Special Forces operator,[2] they were sacrosanct. EO members ignored them at their peril.

Briefly, these fundamentals included air support for all ground operations, reliance on the individual in the field for good level of personal initiative and basic common sense and finally, logistics. Since most of EO's men had served long and hard in their own country's guerrilla struggles during the Border War, they were not unduly taxed by these demands.

It was notable that much of what ultimately took place under EO was dictated as much by the need to run an efficient business as to prevent loss of life in combat. The issue is perhaps best encapsulated by the credo, crude but emphatic, that was printed on some of the T-shirts issued to the men at Angola's Rio Lomba Special Forces training camp (more than an hour's drive south of Cabo Ledo).

Emblazoned across the back, in bold Day-Glo letters four inches high, were the words *Fit In or Fuck Off*.

The first of the four EO basics, that there was to be no ground operation without close air support, was routinely observed in Angola where there was never a shortage of government Hips and Hinds. These Russian rotor wings were used extensively in every punch-up into which the company was thrust. Angolan Air Force pilots flew some, but most were piloted by South Africans working for EO, though as the war progressed, the company itself increasingly played a more dominant role in air operations.

---

2 Duncan Rykaart was previously OC of 52 Commando of 5RR, and thereafter acting OC of 5RR after the death of Corrie Meerholz.

Executive Outcomes instructors with some of their Angolan charges. (Author's photo)

Soviet tank captured during the Border War. Though new T54/55s were acquired by Angola, many of these older versions remain in service.

Top: South African mercenary pilot Juba Joubert indicates where his Mi-17 took a MANPAD hit after taking off from Saurimo. Above: Point of impact, just below the main exhaust.

Colonel Hennie Blaauw with the Saurimo garrison commander at the EO base alongside the airport. (Author's photo)

Executive Outcomes Mi-17s always flew with sidegunners eager for a scrap if challenged. (Author's photo)

In Sierra Leone, by contrast, things were different. Because that tiny West African state had no combat pilots of its own, EO at first made use of the Government's solitary Mi-24 gunship (the Hips only arrived afterwards). A big obstacle that needed tackling after their arrival in Freetown was that the South African company was obligated to employ those Russian pilots already there since they were contracted directly to the state.

In order to establish a more effective system – which included more versatility, Executive Outcomes commanders had to find a way of bringing this asset under their control, not so easily achieved.

The Russians balked – as was expected they would – because it put a rather abrupt end to their monthly pay checks. They argued that they were doing a competent job, when in fact they were not. Their idea of top cover was, as at Soyo a short while before, hovering somewhere above 5,000 feet. South African gunship pilots, in contrast, thought 50 feet might sometimes be too high.

The issue was resolved, according to Barlow's financial mentor Michael Grunberg, by EO using the clout it had accumulated from organizing the supply of pilots, parts and ordnance to protect Freetown. Thus, the company took the helm and the Russians were ditched, but not before they sabotaged the Hind's electronics. In this spooky world of point and counterpoint, one of the Russian pilots was later found murdered, though another source maintains that the death had more to do with diamonds and the Russian *mafiya* than mercenary activity.

Notably, it helped EO's cause that there had also been a fairly serious language barrier between the components. With former Soviets flying these machines, EO's ground forces could not communicate properly with the men who were supposed to be providing air support. As they explained to Valentine Strasser, the Sierra Leone leader, 'when people are shooting at you, you do not need to waste time with translators.' Strasser was usually too spaced out on the hard stuff to comprehend very much of what was going on around him, but that message came through loud and clear.

EO eventually brought its own Mi-17s into play. Two Hips bought from the UN in Angola (and still in that organization's white livery) were flown halfway across Africa, though that did not prevent them from being 'arrested' in Nigeria while in transit because their pilots were South African.

The second EO canon centred on initiative and good common sense – values for which the majority of Third World forces are not especially renowned. EO's command and control approach encouraged resolute, often independent action to achieve these aims. As Hennie Blaauw, another of EO's combat commanders in Angola and formerly a colonel in command of one of the Recce units pointed out: 'That sort of thing doesn't feature in the handbooks.'

The third element comes back to discipline, enforced with a very strong arm. Anyone who stepped out of line – which excluded getting drunk as many times a week as you liked as long as you were not smashed on duty – was put on the first plane home. Every unit, no matter how remote, had its rules, which were rigidly applied, even if it meant ousting someone from a pivotal position. In the overall picture, it was 'liquor-inspired fisticuffs' that was usually the main culprit.

Two of EO's best and most valued combatants were peremptorily kicked out of the organization after they had tacked the British manager of Ibis Air – the airline founded by Buckingham and friends and used to bring in supplies – in a bar in Freetown. In a vicious attack that was described by one of those present as reflecting 'a pit bull mentality', they broke the poor man's jaw and some ribs. He was rushed home on an emergency flight.

Later, in both the Angolan and Sierra Leonian diamond fields, several of the men were fired for illicit dealings in precious stones. There might have been more, but diamonds are easily hidden and anyway, it was a difficult charge to prove.

The last was logistics. The key to EO's philosophy regarding conflict in Africa was, quite simply, that nothing happened unless it was made to happen. The South Africans had been dealing with

African governments for a while by now and, almost without exception, government support throughout had been found wanting.

Said Lafras Luitingh, in charge of EO's operations: 'all governments with whom we've been associated make promises…they make lots of them… always do, especially when the bottle is being passed around. But we've found, sometimes to our disadvantage, that these promises were rarely kept. By morning they were forgotten.

'Consequently, if we were to deploy a force on the ground in some remote region, we'd have to keep it supplied ourselves, which is why two Boeing 727s were bought in the United States at $500,000 each for Ibis Air.'

The aircraft were almost new but had been mothballed by the company that sold them because they exceeded America's newly-instituted noise limitation laws.

If anything were needed by the men in the field – from a toothbrush or a *sjambok* (quirt) to a toilet roll – it had to come on the weekly (and eventually fortnightly) Boeing flight that was allowed unimpeded access to Lungi [and the military sector of Luanda's international airport]. It was all part of the deal that EO was not subjected to any immigration or customs controls.[3]

As hostilities developed in Angola, the same system was adopted and relief flights became twice-weekly events after they commenced in 1994.

Michael Grunberg actually remembers being on the tarmac at a military field outside Luanda when the first of these passenger jets was delivered: it was still in its American Airlines livery. He also recalls that after regular flights between South Africa and Angola – and further north – had been introduced, EO pilots instituted a sophisticated logistics structure into the Sierra Leone operations envelope. It was passed on, together with the requisite international component to the West African air controllers at Robertsfield.[4]

Basically, in all theatres of military activity in which EO was active, the organization worked on the principle of the host nation providing the main component of military 'muscle' in order to get the job done. With the odd exception, this included arms, ammunition and land support vehicles together with the basic military infrastructure that any army should be able to come up with. Men in arms from the host nation were part of the equation. At the end of it, the company took with them everything else that might be needed to keeps its force in the field.

Its main menu included the kind of direction the men needed for the task at hand, their personal equipment, food as well as helicopters for close air support.

The movement of EO troops, replacements and casualties were also the responsibility of the company. Apart from the Boeings, two other aircraft came from Britain, former Hawker Siddeley Andover CC Mk2 twin turbo-prop transports that had previously been operated by the Royal Air Force's 32 Squadron, otherwise known as the Queen's Flight.

Depending on criticality, these were used to evacuate casualties either to London or South Africa, with one stationed at Luanda and the other at Lungi. Both had full aircrews on the company payroll and were maintained on the basis of 24-hour standby. It was a notable advance from the Cabinda debacle where the first doctor only arrived weeks into the campaign.

The Andovers ended up playing a crucial role in the war, even though they were not tasked that often. For a start, the troops had the reassurance that if things did come unstuck, they would be

---

3 That still did not prevent me from getting an AK shoved in my face and arrested for taking photos after I touched down with an EO contingent at Saurimo Airport. It took Blaauw and Rykaart half a day to extricate me from a situation that at one stage got ugly. In a prior confrontation between EO and the 'Ninjas', there was a 20-minute exchange of fire before the issue was settled.
4 Though relocated to Conakry in Guinea because of the civil war in Liberia, Robertsfield retained its original name for ease of recognition by the international aviation community.

airlifted to the best hospitals abroad, almost always with a company doctor in attendance. They could be airborne and on their way within an hour of a contact in the jungle, the Hips handling the first transit.

Consequently, lives were saved by flying some chronic malaria cases to the tropical fever hospital run by Canadians in the Ivoirean capital. More than once a Boeing was diverted to Abidjan if a doctor believed a case was life threatening.

As Grunberg observed, you had to give the company its due: when it came to health issues. 'Cost was never an issue.'

There were several more EO planes, including two King Airs, but these mostly worked Angola and the rest of Africa. One crashed in Uganda in bad weather, killing a senior EO director.

Also on company books was a Westwind jet located at Lungi and used by EO personnel for airborne surveillance work.

Things developed quickly following the two 30-day deployments in the Soyo area early in 1993. While producing nothing spectacular, the EO presence achieved its aims.

As a consequence, once the new contract was signed by the Angolan president, the Angolan Army immediately thrust numerous responsibilities at the organization. Almost overnight, a lot more men had to be recruited, almost all of them South African. The EO directorate was aware that they needed to be much more discriminating with regard to the calibre of their recruits than before. Again, it was a *sine qua non* for the newcomers to have had good combat experience, preferably with a Special Forces or an elite infantry unit and over a period of several years.

A significant aspect here is that Luitingh, Barlow and their cronies were interested not only in individual operators, but also support personnel with whom these people had been linked during their period of military service. They reckoned it was axiomatic that shared hardship bred trust.

Race was never a criterion. Despite apartheid, elite SADF units that had fought the Border War and in Angola were totally non-racial. In fact, they had just as many black troops as whites in their ranks, and, in some cases, in command positions over white soldiers.

The majority knew and understood the strengths and foibles of their officers and NCOs: after all, they had taken a lot of flak in each others' company in operations that spanned more than a decade. What mattered a great deal to EO's bosses was that during that period, these people had not only fought together but had sometimes saved each other's lives.

An interesting sidelight here is a former Recce who went to work for the company after the Border War had ended, and who had actually piggy-backed one of his wounded black soldiers for half a day in a bid to get him safely away from enemy patrols, successfully as it transpired.

Luitingh's viewed his company's black troops with immense respect. He regarded their welfare as his personal responsibility and would tolerate no officiousness towards '*my manne*' (Afrikaans for 'my guys'). He'd actually served with quite a few in his Recce days and was on first name terms with many of them.

There was no question that the company would be that much poorer without these black troops, he would say. They were strong, likable and everyone in the team had seen a good bit of action in his day, which made them invaluable when things got rough. He also liked to emphasize that there were few soldiers anywhere who were able to display such remarkable versatility with squad weapons as the African troops under his command.

In this regard, one of the men quipped, it was ironic that EO was now handling the same guns while working for the Angolan government that FAPLA and FAA had used against the South Africans when they were opposed to Luanda's Marxist regime.

33

Mercenary Air War in Angola

An air force of mercenaries has turned the tide of battle against insurgent rebels in Angola and West Africa.
'Gunships for Hire', *Flight International*: London, 21 August, 1996

The Angolan capital that became Executive Outcomes' new base of operations is one of Africa's most unforgiving conurbations. Luanda's poverty is of apocalyptic proportions.

Perhaps for this reason, the city was once described by Jon Jeter of the *Washington Post's* Foreign Service as a city 'awash in oil and mired in poverty'. This tragic economic situation was made even more horrific in recent years by outbreaks of Marburg, a deadly hemorrhagic fever related to Ebola. One of our colleagues, having visited the place, once said that the place was like a backstreet Mumbai open sewer, only worse, were that possible…

Approach Luanda International Airport from the air during the rainy season and you're greeted by an awful mish-mash of muddy pools, wrecked cars and three-metre high piles of garbage. And pullulating crowds that for all this, includes many faces that greet the visitor with a smile. At its heart, sadly, this is a place of nebulous neglect.

Getting up close does not help much either. The city is a hive of tens of thousands of nondescript, mud-coloured shacks and shanties, many of them roofless. This conglomeration stretches from one unbroken horizon to the other, a monochrome copy of Lagos *without* its Victoria Lagoon.

In an enlightened moment, British scribe Sam Kiley talked about some African cities having become 'grand Guignol horrors'. That's Luanda!

We arrived on one of the company's Boeings a little after dawn. Parts of the city were cloaked in a cold, clammy mist that sometimes creeps across the bay from the sea, especially in the cooler months. Frenzied movement on the ground below looked like something out of an old newsreel film: everybody scurrying about, buildings, tin shacks, slum tenements and roads pushed out sporadically like amoebic pseudopodia and most times ending in a congeries of bush or jungle or at a stream on the outskirts. To those who lived there, pain must have been a solvent: an Angolan version of Rio's *Favelas*.

In the middle of this apparition appeared Luanda's Aeroporto de 4 Febereiro, the country's only international air terminal. A bright neon sign on the roof announced in bold letters: *Bem Vindo*: Welcome.

Even while taxiing, it became apparent why the UN regarded Luanda as its most important staging post in Africa. By six in the morning, the roar of scores of aircraft – mostly ex-Soviet Tupolevs and some high-slung Ilyushins-76s – could be heard through the sealed bulkheads of our 727. There were also a few of the more familiar Antonov-12s, looking deceptively like American C-130s. Not for nothing did the crew refer to them as 'Hercskis'.

This same routine was repeated unwaveringly seven days a week, Christmas and Good Fridays included. Angola's starving millions were waiting for their bowls of gruel.

Because of the war in the interior – as it then was – many of the country's population centres in the interior were either cut off from the outside world or under siege. The way Jon Jeter described it, 'just about everyone was half a step away from starvation.' He painted a succession of vignettes that were both uncompromising and grim.

Writing from Kuito in the Central Highlands – it was a busy place when the Portuguese were still in control and trains ran between Benguela at the coast and the Congo's Copperbelt – Jeter set the scene:

> The cargo planes that keep this city alive land every few hours, trembling to a halt amid cracked concrete and yawning potholes. With the roads already close to impassable, relief workers worry that the approaching rainy season will shut the airport as well, hobbling their efforts to deliver food to thousands of peasants who pour into Kuito each month, chased from the countryside by an unyielding civil war.

And that in a country the size of Texas…

Coming into refuel, you couldn't miss the carnage. Like a giant knacker's yard, yesterday's war matériel lay about everywhere. On the verge of the airport were great heaps of rusting radar towers, scanners and reflector dishes. There were scrapped generators and pylons, all of it once Soviet, reminding everybody that in its day, Luanda was as important strategically to Moscow in the South Atlantic as was Castro's Cuba in the Caribbean. The airport was a junkyard and in this, it shared something with Mogadishu airport.

Some of the revetments that had previously sheltered Sukhois, MiG-21 and MiG-23 fighters had collapsed. Others had been washed away by tropical downpours that in 15 minutes can turn parts of Luanda into a swamp. Similarly with the military barracks at the southern end of the runway: it too was in ruins. So were airport repair sheds, their technicians having long ago returned to Mother Russia and the new order that awaited them there. In-between more wrecked Soviet jets and helicopters littered the periphery. It was a panoply of senseless waste, more so than at any other airport I'd seen.

Yet, in the middle of it all, there was a clear-cut division between civilian and military and the best part of the terminal was reserved for the Angolan Air Force, referred locally to as *Força Aérea Nacional de Angola*. When Executive Outcomes was still around in the 1990s, South African mercenaries who belonged there appeared to come and go at will.

Driving into town was something else. There were soldiers everywhere. We had been warned before leaving South Africa to be polite. If we weren't, they told us, EO couldn't help. Or rather, they would not.

A month before, an Angolan Army Colonel had an AK magazine emptied into his chest; he'd refused to show his ID card at an airport checkpoint. All of it was neatly encapsulated not very long before by one of John Edlin's acerbic comments, another Old Africa Hand then working for Associated Press: 'while Angola is a land of extremes, Luanda is populated by psychos.'

We had barely left the airport when a glistening pair of aircraft wings straddled the roadside. The fuselage of what was obviously a passenger jet lay half-a-mile on, occupied by squatters. The pilot – drunk, of course – had put the plane down short of the runway. Several passengers were killed, but he survived long enough for a military squad to smell his breath, frog-march him behind a building and execute him.

Though the accident had taken place several years before, nobody had bothered to move the wreck. There was no need to, an official explained. If they did, he argued, they might be depriving *povos*[1] of their homes. It was rumoured that two of the three engines were found to be repairable and both were sold for 100 crates of beer to a Lebanese businessman who, in turn, passed them on to an airline in the Middle East for real money.

Angola's civil wars – five or six of them, nobody's counting – have been hard. They've also been tough enough for the majority of the population to ignore the fact that for five centuries, the country was ruled from Europe with a benign kind of efficiency that rarely masked its brutality. Like it or not, much of the suffering that followed independence in 1975 was Lisbon's fault.

While Britain and France prepared its African subjects for the inevitability of *Uhuru,* Lisbon would have none of it. The capitals of the three African colonies, Angola, Mozambique and Portuguese Guinea, today Guiné-Bissau, were as much a part of 'Greater Portugal' as any city back home, they would argue. With solemnity, these Lusitanian apologists would declare that after five centuries on the 'Dark Continent', it was Divine Will that they were still there, which, on reflection was arrant dribble. It is notable, though, that Lisbon stayed on in Africa twice as long as the British held on to its American colonies.

And make no mistake; the majority of these Europeans really believed that God was on their side, which is why they fought so hard for 13 years – from 1961 onwards – to keep a grip on it. In the end, proportionate to the populations of both countries, Portugal lost more men in its African wars than America in Vietnam.

One of the more bizarre consequences was that just as the Belgians had done in the Congo, Lisbon handed over to a nation totally unprepared for self-governance and then too, one of the largest and richest countries in Africa. There was only a small number of university graduates among the indigénes.

Decades after independence, the Portuguese imprint on these African states is ineffaceable. For one, the official language is Portuguese. So is much of the culture in the cities. There were a couple of excellent little *Fado* bars in Luanda when I was there with EO. So is the food: most meals (for those who can afford restaurants' fare) offer *caldo verde* for starters, usually with an excellent Dáo on the table.

Forgotten is the trauma that resulted when the Portuguese were eventually bundled back to Europe in 1975, the majority absconding in great hurry only with what they could carry.

All that happened shortly before independence when Angola declared itself Marxist.

From Luanda we were taken by small plane to Cabo Ledo, EO's first major headquarters in the country once it had achieved a foothold.

As the aircraft banked over the coast, we spotted irregular groves of topsy-turvy baobabs. Beyond, almost like a sentinel on a promontory that jutted into the Atlantic, stood a lighthouse that Lisbon's engineers built more than two centuries ago.

There were not too many houses along this stretch of coast but the Iberian imprint among those that were there was unequivocal. When Portugal colonized Angola in the 16th Century, they brought with them their distinctive red clay roof tiles, still today as much a feature of the homes in Lobito and Luanda as in Coimbra and the Azores.

Cabo Ledo was originally taken over by former SADF Parachute Regiment Colonel Chris Grové. Not long afterwards the first FAA battalion of 800 men were being put through their paces by former South African Army veterans in preparation for the series of battles that eventually ended in the recapture of Cuito, Huambo, Uige and Soyo.

---

1 Peasants/people.

Meantime, little had changed at the old air force base. The runway was lengthened to accommodate larger Soviet jets and to receive some of the overflow when the main runway in Luanda was obscured by fog, but its terminal building was still an unpainted wooden shack about the size of your average storeroom.

As we stepped off the plane, we were met by Brigadier Nick van den Bergh, a powerfully built man with a full beard who had been a staff officer with 44 Parachute Brigade during the Border War. A pivotal figure in the company, he had been appointed by Eeben Barlow to handle EO's interests in this West African state.

Though he did the 90 minute road trip to Cabo Ledo often enough, Van den Bergh and his wife had made a home for themselves in Luanda: a simple triplex in a terraced block with few redeeming features. Situated in a noisy street with broken down cars outside, the place cost the firm three-quarters of a million dollars. It was a rip-off considering that the place was jerry-built and cluttered and he blamed the oil companies for almost systematically 'contaminating' the economy.

We stayed at the Van den Bergh home whenever we visited the capital and would lie awake each night listening to automatic fire reaching up from Luanda docks. The army had instructions to kill anybody who entered the area and obviously, pickings must have been good because there were casualties in abundance.

For all that, the South Africans shared the Cuban penchant for creating a reasonably comfortable environment for themselves at the base. About all that was missing was air conditioning.

To one side, spread over a couple of square kilometres, was a FAA airborne training base with enough BMP-2s scattered about to give the place the appearance of an armoured headquarters. From one of our verandas, we would watch them cluttering off on the day's exercises and clearly, nobody seemed to bother with maintenance; the machines belched fumes like old steam engines each time they were started.

By the time I got to Cabo Ledo, Executive Outcomes had about 20 men stationed at the base, half of them white, mostly communications, logistics and transport techs. There were also a few pilots like Namibian-born Werner Ludick of Lone Hill, whose job it was to ferry unit commanders about in the company King Air. His photos of the Pilatus Porters used by EO in combat and displayed in this book are still the best of the bunch.

The big event of the day was invariably the barbecue – or as the South Africans preferred calling it, *braai*. Bottles of Red Heart Rum would be hauled out and the guys would talk about home, the latest rugby scores and, of course, women.

In circumstances where you did not dare touch local sluts because a third of the population was infected with HIV, every night was party night.

On the third day, we went through to what was eventually to become EO's main training facility in Angola, a Special Forces base at the mouth of the Longa River, or as it is featured on the map, Rio Longa. The trip was an hour-and-a-half by road and we stayed the night: you do not travel around this country after dark, especially with roadblocks armed by troops who are almost always plastered.

We followed the coast for part of the way through the Quicama National Park, which had been almost totally eviscerated of wildlife. Important visitors would come to Angola a quarter of century ago and be awed by the range of animals; elephant herds that were sometimes hundreds strong, lion at every watering hole, buffalo, leopard and even the occasional rhino. By the 1990s, there were more people in Quicama than animals.

The elephants went first, for their ivory. Then most of the antelope were gunned down, sometimes with automatic fire, because Luanda was tardy with victuals for their troops. Finally the big cats were hunted for their skins, for which there was a big demand in Cuba. It seemed that every

More often than not, Angola presented an extremely difficult environment in which to fight an insurgency. Even infiltrating from seawards was invariably impractical because natural jungle overhung most river estuaries. If the enemy didn't get you, the crocs or pythons would (Photo: Jerry Buirski)

A batch of new RPG-7 warheads of the type supplied by Moscow to Angola. It was the second 'weapon of choice' of both the Angolan Army and UNITA, the first being the AK.

How the South Africans achieved results in their African wars: 'Flying Merc' column in Sierra Leone. It did not always matter that the attacking force had no armour – mobility and versatility invariably made the difference. (Photo: Cobus Claassens)

Russian training poster for the BMP-2. In Third World – and particularly in African conditions – this is an incredible weapon in the hands of trained fighters.

South African mercenaries gave strong support to ground units with these Pilatus PC7s: rockets had been fitted to under-wing hard points. (Photo: Werner Ludick)

Shortly before Cafunfo was taken, Blaauw's men captured massive supplies of arms and weapons at a jungle cache.

one of Fidel's pilots could not return to Havana without at least one photo of something he had killed.

EO's base on the river was one of the best on the continent. It fringed a great, tropical waterway and might have been an appropriate setting for a remake of one of Rider Haggard's great yarns: at one point near the estuary, the river was almost a kilometre wide. The camp itself was gathered like a safari boma around clusters of tall palms while lianas dangled everywhere: we could hear the monkeys cavorting as we arrived.

The 30-odd South Africans based there lived in tents, their metal beds raised several additional inches off the ground because of scorpions and snakes.

These reptiles were always a topic of discussion when newcomers arrived. The men took a devious delight in telling us about the numbers of mambas, puff adders, gaboon vipers and cobras that slithered in. Being so close to the river, pythons were also a problem and apparently, in that area they had become something of a threat to humans.

On my first evening, while visiting the unit's water purifying plant I was escorted down 'Python Alley'. It was too dark for photos, so we had to return the next day. When the time came, we made a wide detour to get there. 'Snakes,' my escort explained. I didn't argue.

The officer in charge at Rio Longa was Wynand du Toit, a legendary figure from South Africa's war days in Angola. Still in his thirties and like most of the others, with requisite beard, he'd devoted his life to conflict. Wynand's claim to fame was that as a member of an elite Reconnaissance Regiment, he had led a strike force into Cabinda in an attempt to sabotage Angolan oilfields.

Though things went well enough after being brought close inshore by one of South Africa's navy submarines, everything went sour soon afterwards because there was a squad of Cuban Special Forces waiting for them. During the course of the operation some of the South Africans were killed while Major du Toit was wounded and taken prisoner. He was to spend years in solitary in the worst of Angola's military prisons, though he actually thanks Cuban doctors for patching him up.

Curiously, not long before the Cabinda episode, he'd led a similar raid up that very same Longa River where he was then based. Once again a submarine had been tasked to take them a few kilometres offshore, from where they paddled the rest of the way in kayaks.

'It was a dark night and we entered the estuary, right under the noses of the guards…could have blown the bridge if we'd had the right stuff, but I decided after the first recce that the structure was too big for what we had. Couldn't carry too much in those little craft.' he explained.

For two nights, the combatants secreted themselves among thick reed beds that stretched out hundreds of metres from the river bank. Through it all, they never spotted a single serpent.

'If I'd have known how many there really were, I'd never have tackled the project,' he smiled.

In the aftermath of the South Africans attached to EO having settled in at Cabo Ledo, work began in September 1994 to prepare a battle plan to oust Savimbi and his forces from their strongholds in the north and north-east. Prime targets were the diamond fields, then under rebel control. While this was happening, EO instructors trained a battalion of FAA troops at several locations within a few hours' drive of the capital.

The envisioned combat force was divided into three elements: an offensive group (including air assault units with Mi-17 and Mi-24 helicopters); a mobile mechanized group that was equipped with FAA's new T-62 Russian tanks, as well as the Rio Longa training contingent.

In November, the Angolan Chief of Staff General Joao de Matos summoned EO's leadership to Luanda for a conference that cantered on the biggest prize of all, the recapture of Cafunfo. It was a particular difficult assignment, since all roads leading to the diamond diggings were in

UNITA hands and there were more than 10,000 guerrillas and their supporters on the banks of the Cuango River waiting for 'intruders'.

The Angolan Command was aware that Savimbi had ordered all bridges leading to the approaches to Cafunfo to be prepared for destruction, should government forces try to take the place. Thus, the attack would be two-pronged; one pincer headed out east from Luanda and the other from Saurimo, headed north-west.

Because of landmines, once conjoined at the junction town of Cacolo, the column would avoid all roads, itself a difficult decision because of the nature of the country that needed to be traversed. This part of the Angolan interior was still primeval, the kind that early explorers had always romanced about, a tough, unforgiving terrain. That it fringed the Congo to the immediate north, underscored its isolation.

Instead the strike force would 'bundu-bash' its way towards Cafunfo, roughshodding over whatever obstacles remained. Bridges would be built or temporarily laid with Russian TMM bridging equipment, brought along for the purpose. Those present at planning agreed that while the task was difficult, it could be done. This pleased de Matos, a bluff, chubby fellow who had already proved to the South Africans that he could be both ruthless and outspoken.

By the following January, another mechanized group was being prepared with BMP-2s at Cabo Ledo under EO Colonel Roelf van Heerden, formerly of the SADF's 82 Mechanized Brigade, and who was later to play a pivotal role in the Kono diamond fields in Sierra Leone.

Meanwhile, by mid-February, Grové, assisted by Colonels van den Bergh and Duncan Rykaart got their heads together with members of the Angolan General Staff. Heading the group as theatre commander of the operation was FAA General Marques and it was he who issued orders to prepare for an armoured thrust against UNITA at Cafunfo.

This was all pretty tough stuff. The plan included moving men and armour – almost a full division – from their two points of origin to the north-east corner of the country, a distance, as the crow flies from Luanda, of about 1,000 kilometres. In fact, with UNITA doing what it could to interdict any kind of movement, that included surrounding the air strip at Saurimo – with men armed with SAMs and rocket launchers – it ended up a good deal further.

To begin with, they had to move 22 new T62 tanks – in stages and on seven low-loaders – scores of kilometres to the crossroads town of Dondo, about half-way to Malanje. Beyond, they would proceed through the badlands under own power.

By now other EO men had assumed key positions. Col Hennie Blaauw formerly commander of 5 Reconnaissance Regiment was placed (together with his FAA counterpart Brigadier Sauchimo) in charge of Combat Group Alpha.

That order was reversed shortly afterwards when Blaauw was detached to take command of the Saurimo Sector, as well as Combat Group Bravo. His immediate boss was de Castro who, by then had taken most of the credit for what had happened at Soyo and been promoted to the rank of Brigadier-General. De Castro, good Party man that he was, took it upon himself to monitor all EO activities, a security measure that came from the top.

The force eventually included a motorized infantry battalion, which included 32 BMP-2s. Two at a time, these amphibious infantry fighting vehicles were flown out east in droop-winged Ilyushin 76s.

In the later stages, Saurimo became an indispensable cog in the envisaged program of attack. Though remote and with few facilities (or even a proper hotel) this dirty, dusty little outstation with no sewage system, few shops, banks that seemed to exist in name only and a road grid that ended in minefields on the edge of town seemed to attract diamond dealers from all over.

Like most other settlements within a 500-kilometre radius, hygiene hardly rated, which might be one of the reasons why two of the worst Ebola outbreaks in the past quarter century occurred just across the border in the Congo. Both were within half-a-day's drive of the place.

If you stayed a week at the decrepit old Hotel Lisboa or frequented the market – a huge, open-air fanfare of filth and cacophony where the entire community would gather during the day – you were likely to meet as many Israelis and Russians as French and South Africans. Each one of them was eager to crack the 'big one', though most of the larger stones moved surreptitiously because Angola has never been shy to tax transients.

Diamonds ruled just about everything that happened in Saurimo then as they still do today. In an environment about as enervating as it was dangerous, all talk seemed to centre on cut, colour, clarity and carat. Mention Saurimo back in Luanda and again you could end up discussing diamonds. You drew attention if you happened to mention that you were going there: Angola is a police state and the authorities like to keep tabs on what foreigners are doing in their country, especially where it concerns precious stones.

For all that, Saurimo was not the easiest of places to get to. Since UNITA dominated most of the countryside between the diggings and the coast, a charter was one of the few options left to reach the place and that could cost an arm.

Or you might cadge a lift from one of the Antonov pilots hauling in food for the US. The going rate at the time was about $100 for a single journey if you were lucky enough to find someone who was willing to take the chance. That also needed muscle because nobody without the necessary clearance was allowed to enter an Angolan *Aeroporto*: everything had to be arranged up front with more 'incentives' to the military running the show.

Even then there were risks. On our flights into Saurimo, EO's 727 would descend in a sharp, right-hand spiral from about 25,000 feet. We'd virtually swoop out of the sky and glide down onto the runway, often holding our breaths and seats to keep our breakfasts down. It could be unnerving, but as Werner Ludick explained, it was either that or missiles.

It was not only SAMs that concerned him. 'Friendly fire' from FAA troops manning anti-aircraft guns around the perimeter of the airport happened all too often to be ignored. Most times such incidents took place late in the day when cheap liquor or hash had taken effect.

For that reason Ludick repeated the process on leaving again. For ten minutes or so, he'd spiral upwards, making tight circles in the sky and would go on doing so until we were out of range of ground fire. Only then would he set course for home.

There were other problems that not everybody spoke about. Only months before I arrived, a Russian Antonov-12 was hit by one of UNITA's SAMs while preparing to land. Though the plane came down within sight of Saurimo and the Russian crew was able to walk away from the wreck, two of them were killed because they ended up wandering into a minefield. Both the town and its airport were completely surrounded by them. Even today, the war over, there are still mines all over the place.

Unlike EO's aircrews, Russian pilots rarely bother themselves with anti-missile precautions, was Ludick's view.

'Some of their pilots begin descent a hundred or so miles out and, let's face it, to some gook in the bush, that must present a pretty inviting target at 10,000 feet when you're handy with a MANPAD,' he commented.

34

The Mercenary Air War Continues

> EO's work force was largely made up of battle-hardened soldiers, most of whom had been at war for over 15 years, fighting for a way of life that they believed in deeply, however objectionable it may have seemed to the rest of the world.
>
> Elizabeth Rubin, *Harpers Magazine*, New York, February, 1997

There was always something happening in Angola's efforts to use its air superiority to good advantage while the war went on to keep pulses racing. Coping with Angolan pilots who were trying to fly the country's more advanced jet fighters was only one of them, which is why, even today, Eastern Bloc aviators always find work in these West African country.

During the war, there were many stories of so called 'near catastrophes', including several that did not have happy endings.

One of the more tragic incidents involved Arthur Walker as well as a young man, Danie Scheurkogel, known to everybody back at base in Saurimo as 'Skeeries', who shouldn't have been flying at all.

Scheurkogel was actually an EO non-combatant personnel officer based permanently at Saurimo and it was also his first operational flight. As the pilots recalled afterwards, he'd sit in on some of the after-flight debriefs and watch the proceedings through his thick 'coke bottle' glasses. Afterwards he'd ask to be allowed to fly with the guys.

'Just once,' he would plead. But there were always other priorities and anyway, the brass didn't want anybody taking unnecessary risks. On that fateful day, with Duncan Rykaart in Cabo Ledo, the pilot of the Pilatus PC-7 involved, Louwrens Bosch thought, what the hell, he'd give 'Skeeries' the experience of his life.

The outcome had disastrous consequences.It all happened not long after Savimbi's forces had been ousted from the Cafunfo diamond fields: driven out of the town and diggings in its environs, but not out of the region.

The usual pair of Mi-17s arrived there from Saurimo, did a dummy delivery to confuse Savimbi's artillery spotters across the river and proceeded to the real LZ. Just then a call came through on the radio from Louwrens Bosch who had been circling an area to the north of them all in a PC-7.

'I've been hit,' he snapped, adding that his plane was on fire. 'I'm going to have to put her down,' he shouted, adding that there were flames all around him in the cockpit.

Even more disconcerting to those listening was that Bosch had been operating alongside the river, well within the UNITA orbit of activity. With Arthur Walker and Carl Alberts in the one Hip and 'Juba' Joubert and JC Linde in the other, the situation was critical.

As Arthur Walker recalled afterwards, it was probably a SAM-14 that had caused the damage. He had flown with Bosch often enough in the past and knew that the Pilatus pilot would always joke about having eyes behind his head. In any event, stressed Walker, the man wasn't one to take unnecessary chances.

By Walker's reckoning, Bosch was one of the best pilots with whom he'd worked: 'Good man, brave, competent and resourceful and I don't only say that because he's gone: he really was one of the best. Whether at the controls of a Pilatus or a MiG-23, Louwrens would always reconnoitre a position beforehand and decide on what action to take. For him, it was that kind of war,' his old flying buddy commented.

A tragic sequence of events followed. Not only did Bosch crash-land his PC-7 in thick bush – which resulted in a wipe-out of his aircraft – but he and Scheurkogel were able to get out of the wreck and make their way to a nearby road, hopefully for a pick-up. All this time the pilot was able to stay in touch with the choppers heading his way: he used his little hand-held VHF Bendix King for comms.

Quietly, methodically, Louwrens Bosch guided the incoming Mi-17 towards him. The area, as he characteristically phrased it in Afrikaans, was '*vrot met die vyand*' (rotten with the enemy). He could hear them coming at them through the bush, he told Walker breathlessly, indicating too, that he'd been hurt in the crash landing.

A short while later Bosch radioed that he had the incoming Mi-17 visual. The enemy was also approaching fast, he warned. 'They're coming in hard…the bastards are really after us,' he told the pilots.

'The odds were impossible,' was Walker's contention several years afterwards. Undeterred, Louwrens Bosch set about trying to find somewhere for the approaching helicopter to put down in fairly heavy jungle country, but by then UNITA forces were closing in.

Looking back on what was to have been a rescue, it was Walker's view that things onboard their Mi-17 might have gone a lot smoother had their regular side-gunner been on board. But this was an emergency and the moment the order came they went up 'cold', with only themselves and their Angolan tech Tito Nunes to help. Ideally, they might have carried a search and rescue team, but there was no time to get anything like that together.

Walker: 'The last two clicks were what I suppose you'd call a hell-run. We were flying low and taking fire along the entire distance. They threw everything at us – even a couple of 12.7s. Of course, everybody and his uncle had his AK and they were shooting at us too. Meanwhile, we kept talking to Louwrens and by the time the two of them came into view, he was able to direct us almost right on top of his position.'

What happened next is not altogether clear. Because of the volume of fire, Alberts headed in at a steep rate of descent. As he flared, the ground was suddenly enveloped in billowing dust. The last thing they'd expected in a terrain covered in thick vegetation was a 'brown-out'. Also, communication with the Angolan tech Nunes didn't work all that well because he understood very little English.

The three men in the chopper felt it shudder as their wheels touched the ground: the crew thought they might have taken a hit. Moments later the Hip began to shake violently and then veered uncontrollably to starboard. Since they were on the ground anyway, Walker urged Nunes to hop out and lead the two men onboard.

'This was really one hellova situation for us, because by now we could see squads of UNITA troops racing down the road towards us,' Alberts recalled. The first group of enemy soldiers was coming at double pace over a small rise only two or three hundred metres from where we had put down and they would fire their guns intermittently as they rushed in.

Nunes hopped back aboard the Hip almost immediately. The men weren't there, he screamed, indicating with arms raised that they should get the fuck out of there. More volleys came whistling by and Alberts needed little encouragement.

He lifted his chopper off the deck but the shuddering became so severe the moment he pulled power that for a moment or two neither he nor Walker were sure they'd actually be able to control the machine. Somehow though, Alberts managed. Walker thought they'd lost their tail rotor, or at least part of it.

In those few moments in the hover before pulling away, the two pilots spotted a prone figure lying face down on the ground alongside the LZ. Both agreed afterwards that Bosch's blue flying jacket was unmistakable. From what little they could see from the cockpit, it seemed as if he'd taken a hit from the tail rotor.

In the investigation that followed back at base, it was concluded that because of the volume of dust whipped up in their descent, Bosch might have become disoriented and possibly walked into the rotor. Visibility on the ground was almost zero and the chopper wasn't completely stationary, so it was feasible. Of the other man, Scheurkogel, there was no trace.

It took about a minute before Walker and Alberts were able to get clear of that commotion and head away, but again, there was stuff coming at them from all over. At one stage they even clipped the tops of a row of trees in their desperation to escape.

Though the entire episode had lasted only a couple of minutes, Alberts had a tough time controlling the machine. In retrospect, it says a lot for his experience that they managed to get the crippled helicopter back to base at all. At one stage the vibrations got so severe that they thought the chopper might rip itself apart. Eventually he managed to put the Hip down on a road about five or six kilometres north of the town, but still behind enemy lines. By now 'Juba' Joubert and JC Linde were circling in their Hip.

Once down, the two South Africans did a quick damage assessment and decided that it was pointless to linger. The helicopter was in a bad way but not totally incapacitated. They would chance it, they told the other two, but suggested that they stay real close, 'just in case'.

As Walker recalls, the tail rotor had obviously hit something. The blades were twisted and one had all but been ripped off. In fact, looking at it afterwards, it was clear that the entire rotor was off kilter. In theory, they shouldn't even have been able to get airborne. But they did, which is also a tribute to Russian engineering ability. The machines they make are not pretty, but they work under the most arduous conditions, even when damaged.

On Roelf Van Heerden's instructions, two BMP-2 infantry fighting vehicles were dispatched to the site the next day and they had to fight hard to get to where the action had taken place. Having poked about a bit, they were forced to get out again and in the end, nothing was found. The Pilatus wreck, by now incinerated, was still where it had crashed, among the trees. There were scraps of flesh and some blood marks on the ground at the landing zone where a body seems to have been dragged to a vehicle, but of the two men, not a whiff.

Radio intercepts later spoke of a capture, but there never was any word of 'Skeeries'' fate.

There is no question that it was dominance of Angolan air space that finally turned this war around. That, and a vigorous ground campaign, spearheaded by a few hundred Executive Outcomes mercenaries.

The South African aviators were all SAAF veterans, many having cut their teeth on French-built Alouette IIIs or Mirages jet fighters or Buccaneers originally bought from Britain just before the anti-apartheid brouhaha started to bite.

Going into a fairly dislocated Angola where nothing is really as you expected it to be, including aircraft maintenance, things were very different from the days of South Africa's Border War. For a start, there were a lot more MANPADS around, including Stingers given to Savimbi's forces to counter the Soviet influence. Quite a few of the pilots including Neall Ellis (as we have already seen), Arthur Walker, Charlie Tate and 'Juba' Joubert either took hits from ground to air missiles or had narrow scrapes with them. In Joubert's case, he was hit at Cafunfo by a Strela SAM-7 missile and still managed to bring his damaged machine down.

Like almost all his colleagues, 'Juba' Joubert had seen years of action in chopper gunships in Angola's earlier wars. So, obviously, had Neall Ellis, who at some stage or another flew with them all. These aviators all did their share of combat in Sierra Leone afterwards.

Initially, the Angolan High Command seemed reluctant to allow the South African unrestricted access to the Angolan Air Force (FAPA's) fleet of MiG-23s, MiG-27 'Flogger' strike jets, and Su-25 'Frogfoot' close support planes.

So too with the PC-7s to start with. Equally abruptly, as plans neared fruition, many of the restrictions were lifted.

The Swiss-built PC-7 Pilatus turboprop trainers went on to give valuable service in close-quarter ground-support work in some of the more remote areas in which EO operated. Obviously slower than the jets, they gave the pilots the ability to do the kind of reconnaissance work that would have been impractical from larger aircraft. Also, during ground operations, one would sometimes be tasked as an improvised Telstar relay station between ground units and headquarters or air assets moving into the attack.

For combat, their under-wing hard points had originally been adapted for weapons systems by technicians in Luanda shortly after the aircraft arrived from Switzerland. This allowed them to field either two or four sets of 18-round 68mm SNEB rocket pods.

The Mi-17s fielded by the Angolans were also armed. They could handle an even heavier load and a variety of systems were experimented with on its four racks, including UPK-23-250 pods containing GSh-23L twin-barrel 23mm cannon. Also tried were GUV pods with the AGS-17 *Plamya* 30mm grenade launcher which went through a prototype stage.

Not everything worked. More successful on the Hips were two four-barrel 7.62mm 9-A-622 machine-guns. Because of technical problems, some of the crews of both the Mi-8s and the Mi-17s eventually settled for pintle-mounted 7.62mm PKMs firing from port and starboard and, once the clamshell rear doors had been removed, another from the rear. As for the pilots manning them, conversions were improvised. Former SAAF Mirage or Impala jet jocks would go solo after a few hours of orientation.

The South Africans were impressed with all these machines, the helicopters especially. Former SAAF Colonel Arthur Walker who had survived two decades of combat in Rhodesia, Namibia and Angola and who did several tours with EO (and was never once 'properly' wounded), found the Mi-17 rugged and reliable. Charlie Tate told me at Denel Aviation that on one of his first orientation trips with the Hip, he and Carl Alberts uplifted a four-ton container at the Rio Longa base. That was about a thousand more kilos than the manufacturer's permissible load.

The same applied to trooping. Hip specs allowed for about 20 fully equipped troops to be loaded. Never fazed by what the book said, the Angolans would raise that tally by half as much again. In one emergency near Cafunfo, a Hip was forced to aid another helicopter that had been forced down by ground fire and by the time it got into the hover again, there were 40 men onboard. All were hauled those last few hundred kilometres or so to EO's staging post at Saurimo, totally in the dark.

Without an air force of his own, Savimbi still managed to inflict serious damage. Airports were mortared wherever possible. His people proved their superiority in mortar barrages by using their NATO 81mm bombs (supplied through an intermediary dealer by France) to good effect. With a greater range than the East European 82mm issued to FAA, the rebels usually attacked from just beyond the range of what the Angolans had on offer.

Angolan Air Force Sukhoi SU-27 – NATO reporting name 'Flanker' – flown by South African mercenaries. (Photo: Pierre Victor collection)

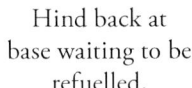

Hind back at base waiting to be refuelled.

An Angola Air Force Antonov AN-32 was one of the planes – with Russian pilots at the controls – used for air drops intended for the attacking mercenary force headed for Cafunfo. (Photo: Vano)

EO air crew at Saurimo base – all well-experienced in this kind of unconventional warfare while serving in the SAAF. At the back, from left: JC Linde, Sonny Janecke, Lourens Bosch (shot down and killed while flying a Pilatus PC-7 out of Cafunfo) and Arthur Walker. Crouched are Pete Minnaar and Carl Alberts.

A Sukhoi bomber that appeared to be permanently parked at Saurimo. (Author's photo)

Mi-24 helicopter gunship (NATO codename HIND) flown by South African merenaries in several African conficts, Angola's included.

A South African mercenary and one of the Angolan bombers. (Author's photo)

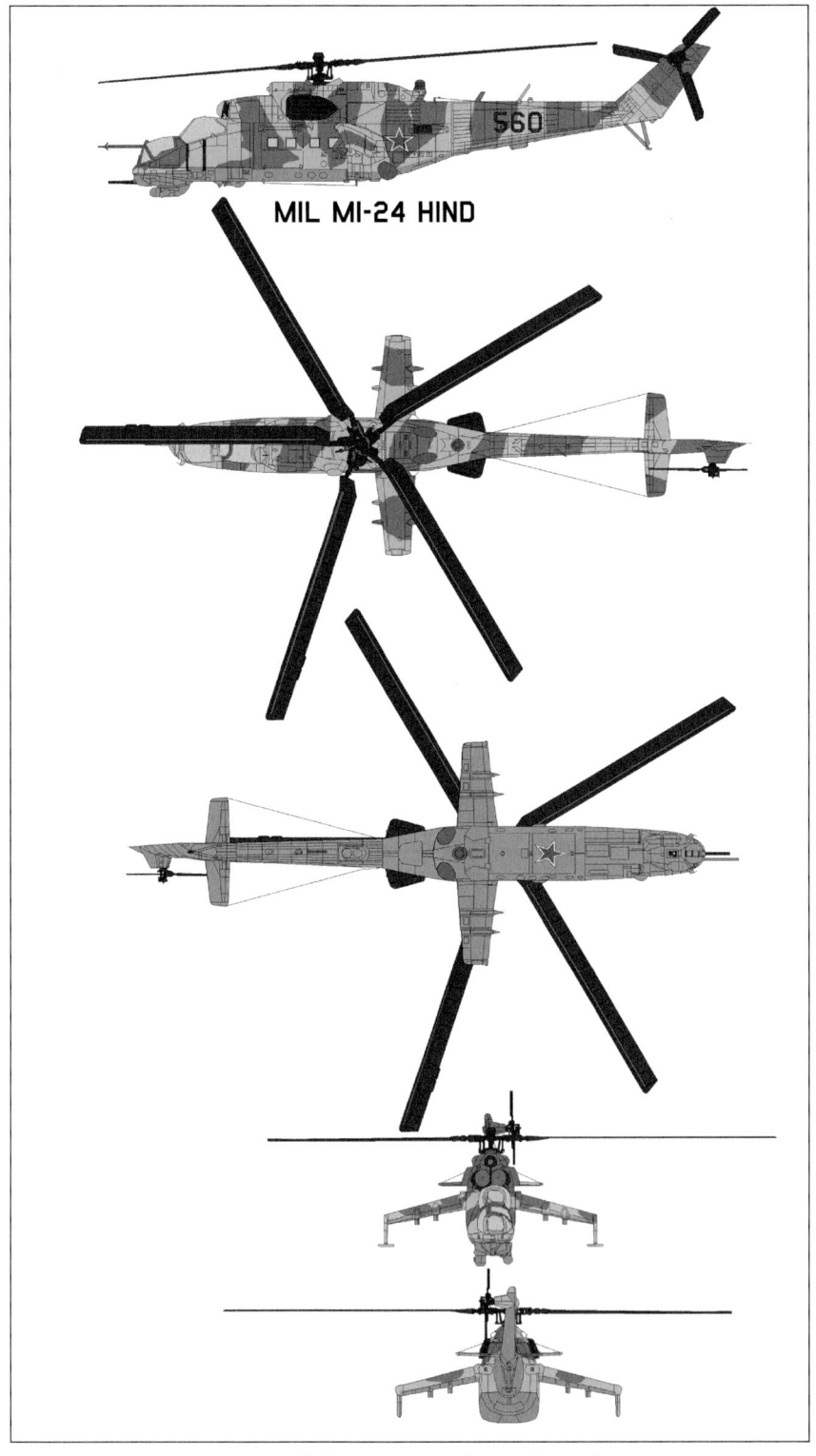

Diagrams of the Soviet Hind Mi-24 gunship.

The rebels also excelled in getting past enemy defences. Employing techniques taught by South African Special Forces instructors, they would use defectors' know-how and if needs must, would come straight through minefields in the way. Once, while EO worked out of Saurimo, a UNITA commando group – dressed in FAA uniforms – was able to penetrate airport security and destroy several aircraft on the ground. Two of the Hips then in EO employ were written off, one burnt to a frazzle after it took an RPG blast. The other, riddled by gunfire, was still standing, stripped of anything useable, in the base grounds when I was there.

In a remarkably well-orchestrated UNITA house clearing operation at the same time, EO lost 'Blackie' Swart. Badly wounded, the company airlifted him to Johannesburg but he was dead on arrival.

UNITA commandos who'd been responsible for this attack were members of one of Savimbi's crack Special Forces groups. Absurdly brazen, they would slide in just about anywhere and cause mayhem. As a consequence, according to Colonel Hennie Blaauw, his men had to be 'extra-alert'.

Once, after FAA's 45th Brigade had moved to Lucala, guerrillas penetrated a well defended perimeter and slit the throats of eight men as they lay in their sleeping bags. The perpetrators came and went like shadows, the bodies only being discovered in the morning.

Aircraft and armour were UNITA's two main targets. Earlier, prior to the 1992 cease-fire, the Angolan government had taken delivery of eight new Mi-24s: without spares the deal was worth about $40 million. The rebels destroyed most of them as soon as the talks were halted because they were shrewd enough to site their camps near important airfields.

Other aircraft knocked out on the ground included several C-130s, two or three AN-12s and at least one Ilyushin-76, blown away in a rocket attack. About a dozen more were accounted for by ground fire – 12.7mm and 14.5mm heavy machineguns as well as SAM-7s and SAM-14s, quite a few in the Huambo area. It could have been more because Luanda never credited UNITA with kills if there were no survivors.

Like the Nigerians in Biafra, Luanda would rarely acknowledge UNITA's prowess. Grudgingly, they would admit that the rebels were, as it was termed in the Angolan media 'bothersome', but to concede to any kind of successful strike or even that the air force might have lost aircraft as a result of their efforts was out. When a plane did go down, Luanda's spin masters would remonstrate with the international press and they did it exceedingly well, just as Mark Press in Geneva had done for Biafra a couple of decades before.

For instance, a King Air was brought down with a missile at the Cafunfo diamond centre late 1994. In the attack, shrapnel fragments killed and wounded several passengers and crew. For a while afterwards, Luanda claimed that something mechanical had been the cause.

EO's aircrews were linked to some remarkable tales of courage as the war progressed. Consider events that took place after the company had relocated part of its force to Saurimo.

At one stage Hennie Blaauw tasked a pair of Mi-17s – one flown by Charlie Tate and Sonny Janecke and the other by JC Linde and 'Juba' Joubert – to 'hot extract' an EO reconnaissance party that was about to be overrun by UNITA Special Forces.

Earlier, another team comprised of two whites, Renier and Steyn, a black tracker by the name of Handsome Ndlovu (a veteran of the Rhodesian War) and one of his pals, had been dropped by helicopter near the small but strategically situated hamlet of Cuango, well to the west of Saurimo. Almost immediately their radios went silent. After a search that lasted days involving every available helicopter as well as a pair of PC-7s, it was accepted that they had either been killed or captured.

EO maintained strict radio schedules because it was clear that there had to be good reason for the men not to call in. They never did and there was never a whisper about their fate. Only long afterwards did word come through that 'two white mercenaries' had been captured by the rebels and executed. There was no mention of the two Africans.

Unofficially, the word went out that they had been compromised by one of EO's radio operators at Saurimo who had been 'bent' by UNITA. It was said, but never confirmed that he died in an 'accident' shortly afterwards with no explanations given or asked for.

According to former Recce Colonel Duncan Rykaart, much of the early work of the mercenary force in the east entailed a program of destruction and disruption of enemy command and control centres. Small, long-range penetration groups would be dropped by helicopter and picked up after the job was done at designated LZs.

The object was to survey UNITA camps, supply dumps, strong points as well as headquarters and, ultimately, to prepare a route for an attack by land forces. Only occasionally did these small teams go onto the offensive.

An example of the remarkable ability to retaliate swiftly came when Saurimo received an urgent call from Simon Witherspoon, a former Recce and in his day, one of best operators in any man's army. It was sent on the second night of an operation in distant parts.

Having been inserted not far from Cafunfo, Witherspoon, Rich Nichol and their two trackers were running hard from a UNITA follow-up team through an unusually-dense stretch of jungle. Witherspoon recalled afterwards that the undergrowth was so thick that they could barely manage to cover 500 metres an hour. Worse, they were making little headway in a black night and the enemy was gaining, which was unusual because these were some of the fittest men in the unit.

It didn't take either Witherspoon or Nichol long to realise that their UNITA adversaries were closing the gap. And since the South Africans weren't familiar with the area, there was also the possibility of them being ambushed by enemy soldiers deployed further out. As he was to argue afterwards, they all had radios.

At that point several members of the chase team was about 300 metres to the rear, close enough for the South Africans to spot the reflections of their pursuers' torches off the wet foliage. He admitted that they had considered an ambush, but from the noise being made, they were hopelessly outnumbered. Whenever he stopped he could hear their scouts furiously chopping away at the undergrowth.

At that stage they were near the village of Sacassambia, about 35 kilometres north of where Renier and his group had disappeared in the earlier operation. EO's policy in these matters is clear: if they asked to be extricated, it was assumed that the situation was critical and such requests were serious: consequently, the unit reacted accordingly. In any event, all these men had been involved in combat for years and knew the ropes.

Considering all available options, a pair of Mi-17s left Saurimo at 0400 hours and arrived at the designated LZ just as first light was creeping over the tops of what was an extremely heavily foliaged region: it was typical triple-tier jungle. Also, there was a heavy mist that obscured visibility, which – according to the pilots – was scary because the region was undulating and there was also a mountain or two.

Since the crew hadn't brought night vision goggles, they were forced to rely on the fleeing party's strobe light. Finally, using their GPS sets, they were able to close in, break radio silence and establish comms.

With Linde at the controls and Tate's machine offering what support it could, the drama that followed was about as hairy as it gets. Though it soon became light, a heavy mist still clung to the slopes.

'It was really tough,' Joubert remembers. 'We would feel our way across the top of the forest and then suddenly a mountain would sort of appear out of the mist in front of us. At last Charlie spotted the strobe and he gave me bearings.'

As he tells it, the hillside sloped from left to right and the bush there was almost impenetrable. Meanwhile, the guys below had reached a small clearing but it wasn't big enough for his rotors to make a clear descent without causing some kind of damage.

The South Africans took the helicopter in anyway, with Joubert using his rotors to try to 'carve a passage' through the bush. It would have worked but for one tree that was sturdier than the rest and that caused damage to the blades.

'But we still weren't down on the ground. In trying to hover, I found that the machine had become seriously unstable. Meanwhile, Simon and the boys had emerged from the bush and shouted that we were still too high, so I beat the trees for a few more seconds and finally we were able to get them onboard.

'As I pulled power, the chopper began to vibrate and it was quite violent. The shaking continued as I gained altitude and I was forced to pull back on the throttle...but I knew too that we couldn't go on like that for long so I decided to put her down. If I didn't, I was sure that the old bird would break up,' he explained.

Joubert spotted a stretch of water ahead. To buy time from his UNITA pursuers – they must have been within RPG range by the time they lifted off – he decided to put his wheels down on the far side of a river. The moment they touched, he knew that he'd brought the helicopter down in water: they'd landed in a swamp.

'The tail boom immediately began to sink.' With Tate still circling nearby and having been given time to inspect the damage, the crew decided that they might just be able to make it back to base, several hundred kilometres away. Finally, the men set about extricating the machine from the mud and though it took time, they got it all clear in the end.

'We had to fly at reduced speed the rest of the way. Anything over 90 knots and the machine began to vibrate almost uncontrollably and then it would also yaw all over the place...obviously our light load helped.'

The same mistake wasn't made when another EO group was dropped with SAM missiles near Luremo, another diamond town on the Cuango River to the north of Cafunfo.

With its own airstrip, using chartered C-130s and DC-6 transports, UNITA regularly hauled in supplies, armaments and equipment, most of it out of Kinshasa.[1] The idea was for the EO squad to take up a position on the outskirts and try to bring down one of these aircraft. The problem was that though they were there for some time, the four-man attacking 'stick' was always in the right place at the wrong time.[2]

In the end the group had to be pulled out because just about all of them had contracted malaria.

Preparations for the attack on Cafunfo progressed steadily at Saurimo and each day also brought something new. EO's first casualty in the eastern sector of the war was one of them.

Early 1994, the town of Xinge – an important command post just north of the strategic crossroads of Cacolo – was increasingly being fingered in intelligence reports and what did not take long to become clear was that the place was rank with UNITA troop movements.

---

[1] For years, Savimbi relied on foreign companies to fly planes into some of the strips under his command in remote parts of the country. While most of these aircraft came from Zaire (Congo), others filed false flight plans and entered Angolan air space from Zambia, Namibia, South Africa, Zimbabwe, the Congo (Brazzaville), Morocco and several destinations, including one or two places in Europe. In the end, very few of these flights were apprehended by FAPA, the Angolan Air Force. The pilots involved were paid mainly from the proceeds of UNITA's illegal diamond diggings such as those around Cafunfo.
[2] 'Sticks' were usually four-man groups.

Under the command of Brigadier Bule, a competent though unconventional UNITA officer, this small town caused enough headaches for Hennie Blaauw to do something about it. Thus, – in concert with his FAA bosses – two mortar sections were landed by a pair of Hips about an hour's trudge to the west of Xinge. The intention was for them to spend the night in the area, set an ambush and hope for the best. At some stage they would mortar Bule's headquarters.

The plan was that they'd be extricated on request, probably the following day, Blaauw explained during one of the evening *braais*. The usual precautions were taken: LZs in several categories were marked on the maps, with a specified pick-up point together with one or two alternatives. Also listed were emergency locations where the choppers might go in if things got desperate.

This time round, the men had barely exited from the Hip in the dark before some kind of movement was observed by the men onboard. It was a short distance away and in the surrounding bush. Not being certain that it might be enemy, nothing was radioed to the choppers. In any event, with the men on the ground having been infiltrated, the choppers were already on their way back to their Saurimo base.

Throughout the night, there were reports coming in of unusual activity around Xinge. UNITA talked of the movement of helicopters, with radio reports claiming that they had fired on them, the usual inter-unit claptrap. In debrief afterwards, the aviators admitted that they had never actually been aware of having come under fire during the insertion. In fact, things might have taken a very different turn if they had. And while the situation on the ground was not yet serious, it didn't take long for things to turn nasty.

By morning, one of the teams had had its first contact with the enemy and Polly van Rooyen, formerly of 4 Recce almost had his leg blown off. Holding off a bunch of UNITA attackers, the South Africans went ahead anyway and mortared Xinge. Though it took a while to make comms with Telstar – the plane by then having taken up a monitoring position in the sky above them – they called for a helicopter to haul them out. They reported that van Rooyen – a big, robust man – was in excruciating pain and losing blood. Still, he never uttered a sound throughout the attack or during the subsequent extraction.

It was Carl Alberts that eventually brought his Mi-17 in and pulled both mortar teams out. As he recalled afterwards, it was done *in extremis*, almost within sight of Xinge, with 'Tattie' Tate's chopper in support.

Airlifted back to South Africa within hours, Van Rooyen's leg was saved and he stayed with EO in a non-combative capacity until the company folded.

We were to have a few rums and cokes in Pretoria when he told me his story.

Not long afterwards Hennie Blaauw was ordered to organize a fairly large force comprising mortar teams with protection elements to harry UNITA forces at Camaxilo. Not a big place and lying to the immediate south of the Congolese diamond town of Kahemba, it was an essential link in Savimbi's supply chain. Much of what he used for his war effort was routed through there.

Former Recce Carl Dietz was charged with getting the attack together, while the first helicopter involved in the operation was again crewed by 'Juba' Joubert and JC Linde and dropped its component. Charlie Tate and Sonny Janecke – with Dietz sitting in the jump seat – followed. Two of the fixed-wing PC-7s monitored the operation to provide top cover, if required.

A Pilatus had already gone ahead to scout the LZ and though he chose a position only about a kilometre from the town, the pilot said that it'd have to do because there wasn't anything else suitable for some distance. It was a one-off, thought the pilots, so what the hell. They would go in, drop the men and pick them up again immediately afterwards. The show was expected to last perhaps 30 minutes, max.

The job done, the helicopters went in again to bring out the men. There were no problems with Juba: he lifted out his team and headed southwards to wait for Tate and Janecke to do their thing.[3]

'Tattie' had barely touched down when the jungle exploded. Not only were they picking up fire from the direction of town, but from behind as well. Though the side gunners were supported by more PKMs on the ground, the Mi-17 was taking serious hits.

Within a minute, there were three men inside the chopper wounded, including one of the EO operators, Billie Erasmus. Dietz remembers seeing a solid stream of fuel running down the *inside* of the helicopter's windscreen and into the cockpit. They'd obviously taken a hit in one of the feed tanks, probably by an RPG.

In the babble of messages that followed – coupled to more shouts from the back about incoming, all of it muffled by the screams of the wounded – one of the engine oil pressure lights on the console flashed an emergency signal. With 'Natasha' screaming her customary warning that things were amiss, Charlie Tate had to make a decision: it was a question of fight or flee.

The first, he recalls, was never an option because it was obvious to everybody onboard the helicopter that they were outnumbered. He had serious doubts about the second.

Unaware of little but the immediate problems in his face, this former SAAF Alouette veteran took it for granted that none of the men would hang about outside. It was time to move so he pulled collective and got airborne. But only just, because the helicopter barely responded to its controls.

By the time Juba's Hip had joined forces, Tate's chopper was limping across the top of the jungle. Also, it was spewing volumes of fuel. Meanwhile, retaliation onboard had ceased because the men feared that a spark might ignite fuel vapours, which had enveloped everybody and everything. As it was, Juba recalls, the crippled machine billowed a huge white cloud of vaporizing fuel.

Barely three or four kilometres from where the ambush had taken place, Tate put his machine down. It was an LZ that had tree stumps protruding everywhere.

'What we had to do in double quick time was get everybody off, talk Juba down and hope to Christ that he'd then be able to get off the ground again with the additional load, which was huge and here we're talking about 40 men, together with the remainder of their equipment.' To his credit, Juba didn't even have to think about it: he landed his machine, loaded up and took off again, the entire operation having been completed in two, perhaps three minutes.

With Telstar in a low-level formation, they flew together until it got dark. Both aircraft arrived at Saurimo about an hour later.

The biggest tragedy of the event was that in the flurry and confusion of what was taking place when Tate was trying to get off the ground, four of the original group had been abandoned on the ground. Worse, though it was unintentional, the quartet of PKM gunners had – of their own volition – taken up defensive positions on the ground outside. They were actually protecting the helicopter from further attack and by all accounts, doing a pretty good job of keeping UNITA heads down.

As one of the men commented afterwards, paraphrasing the more familiar maxim 'they died so that the rest of our group could live.' It was a pithy reaction because for such a small unit, the loss was massive.

There was never anything forthcoming from UNITA about the fate of the four men that had been abandoned.

---

3 When the countryside or the jungle is too overgrown or too mountainous to land safely, a helicopter would hover over the men on the ground. Then they would either be winched up or climb up ropes lowered for the purpose. As the term implies, the positions from which they were snatched were indeed 'hot'. There were times when these soldiers came onboard with only a minute or two to spare.

Select Bibliography

Abshire, David & Michael Samuels: *Portuguese Africa – A Handbook*: Pall Mall Press, London, 1969
Afonso, Aniceto & Gomes, Carlos de Matos (co-ord.): *Guerra colonial,* Lisbon, 1998(?)
Afonso, Aniceto & Gomes, Carlos de Matos (co-ord.): *Os Anos daguerra colonial*, Matosinhos, 2010
Antunes, António Lobo: *Os Cus de Judas*, Lisbon, 1986
Antunes, José Freire (ed): *A Guerra de África*, 1961–1974, 2 Vols, Lisbon 1995
Attwood, William: *The Reds and the Blacks*, Harper & Row, New York, 1967
Beckett, Ian & John Pimlott (eds.): *Armed Forces and Modern Counter Insurgency,* Croom Helm, London, 1985
Birminghan, David: *A Short History of Modern Angola,* Hurst, 2015
Boon, Mike: *The African Way – The Power of Interactive Leadership.* Zebra Publishers, South Africa, 1997
Brandão, José: *Cronologia da Guerra Colonial*, Lisbon, 2008
Bridgland, Fred: *Jonas Savimbi: A Key to Africa*, Mainstream Publishing, London, 1986. A new and updated edition of this book is due out in 2017
Bridgland, Fred: *The War for Africa – Twelve Months That Transformed a Continent.* Ashanti Publishing Limited, Gibraltar, 1990. To be published in a new and updated edition by Casemate US and UK, 2017
Burgis, Tom, *The Looting Machine*: William Collins, London, 2015
Cabrita, Felícia: *Massacres em África,* Lisbon*,* 2008
Caetano, Marcello: *Depoimento*, Distribuidora Record, Rio de Janeiro, 1974
The Cambridge History of Africa Volume 8 c.1940 – c.1995: Desmond J. Clark (ed.), J.D. Fage (ed.), Roland Anthony Oliver (ed.), Richard Gray (ed.), John Flint (ed.) and G.N Sanderson (ed.); Cambridge University Press, Cambridge, 1986
Cann, John P: *Counterinsurgency in Africa: The Portuguese Way of War 1961–1974,* Hailer Publishing, St Petersburg FL, 2005, republished by Helion, Solihull, 2012
Cann, John P: *Brown Waters of Africa: Portuguese Riverine Warfare 1961–1974*, Helion, Solihull, 2013
Cann, John P, *Flight Plan Africa: Portuguese Airpower in Counterinsurgency, 1961–1974*, Helion, Solihull, 2015
Cann, John P, *The Fuzileiros – Portuguese Marines in Africa, 1961–1974*, Helion, Solihull, 2016
Silva Cardoso, António: *Angola: Anatomia de uma Tragédia*, Lisbon, Oficina de Livro, 2000
Carvalho, Nogueira e: *Era Tempo de Morrer em África,* Lisbon, 2004
Castilho, Rui de: *O capitão do fim,* Lisbon, 2002
Chilcote, Ronald: *Portuguese Africa*, Prentice-Hall, New Jersey, 1967
Chiwale, Samuel: *Cruzei-me com a História,* Lisbon, 2008
Cobanco, Jorge: *Onze Meses de Guerra em Angola,* s.l. 1970
Coelho, João Paulo Borges: *African Troops in the Portuguese Colonial Army, 1961–1974: Angola, Guinea-Bissau and Mozambique;* Eduardo Mondlane University, Maputo
Coelho, Joaquim*: O Despertar dos Combatentes,* Lisbon, 2005
Cornwall, Barbara; *The Bush Rebels*, Andre Deutsch, London 1973
Cunha, J. da Luz, et al, *África, a Vitória Traída*:Intervenção, Lisbon, 1977 [Background by pre-coup commanders in Angola, Mozambique and Portuguese Guinea]

Davidson, Basil: *In the Eye of the Storm*: Longmans, London, 1972
De Oliveira, Ricardo Soares: *Magnificent and Beggar Land: Angola Since the Civil War*, Hurst, London, 2015
De Vries, Roland, Major General (Retired): *Eye of the Firestorm,* Helion, Solihull, 2016 and also published by Naledi, Tiger Valley, Cape Town, May 2013
Diederiks, Andre, Colonel: *Journey Without Boundaries: The Operational Life and Experiences of a SA Special Forces Small Team Operator*, South Africa, 2007
Duffy, James: *Portuguese Africa*, Harvard University Press, Cambridge MA, 1959
Durand, Arn: *Zulu Zulu Foxtrot: To Hell and Back With Koevoet*, Zebra Press, 2012
Els, Paul: *Ongulumbashe – Where The Bushwar Began*, Group 7, Pretoria, 2003
Els, Paul: *We Conquer From Above: The History of 1 Parachute Battalion, 1961 – 1991*; Group 7, Pretoria 2011
Els, Paul: *We Fear Naught but God*; Group 7, Pretoria 2000
Estado-Maior do Exército. *Resenha Histórico-Militar das Campanhas de África, Vols. I–VI* [Historical Military Report of the African Campaigns, Vol. I–VI], Lisbon: Estado-Maior do Exército, 1989–2006
Felgas, Hélio: *Guerra em Angola*, Edição do Autor, Lisbon, 1968
Ferraz, Carlos Vale: *Nó ceg*, Amadore, 1983
Fraga, Luís Alves de: *A Força aéreana Guerra emÁfrica,* Lisbon*,* 2004
Garcia, Francisco Proença: *Análise global de uma Guerra,* Lisbon, 2003
Garcia, João Nogueira: *Quitexe-61,* Vila Nova do Ceira, 2003
Geldenhuys, Jannie: *At the Front: A General's Account of South Africa's Border War*, Jonathan Ball, 2009
George, Edward: *The Cuban Intervention in Angola, 1965–1991*, Routledge, London, 2005
Gibson, Richard: *African Liberation Movements,* Oxford University Press, London, 1972
Gleijeses, Piero: *Conflicting Missions: Havana, Washington, and Africa, 1959–1976*, University of North Carolina Press, Chapel Hill NC, 2002
Gouveia, Daniel Alves: *Arcanjos e Bons Demónios*, Lisbon, 1996
Greene, T.N. Colonel: *The Guerrilla and How to Fight Him,Selections from the Marine Corps Gazette*; Praeger, New York, 1967
Grundy, Kenneth: *Guerrilla Struggle in Africa,* Grossman Publishers, New York, 1971
Guerra, João Paulo: *Memória das Guerras Coloniais*, Porto, 1994
Guerra, João Paulo: *Descolonização Portuguesa*, Lisbon, 1996
Henricksen, Thomas*: Revolution and Counter-revolution,* Praeger, Westport CT 1983
Jorge, Paulo: *MPLA – Angola*, LSM, Canada, n.d.
Kitson, Frank: *Low Intensity Operations Subversion, Insurgency, Peacekeeping*. Faber and Faber Limited, London, 1971
Kitson, Frank: *Bunch of Five*, Faber and Faber, London, 1977
Lithgow, Nick: *LZ Hot: Flying South Africa's Border War*, Helion, Solihull, 2012
Lortie, Michelyne & Martin, Diane & Paquette, Claude: *Tout près de l'oubli,* Chesterville, Quebec, 2006
MacQueen, Norrie: *The Decolonisation of Portuguese Africa*, Longman, London, 1997
Mannall, David: *Battle on the Lomba 1987: The Day a South African Armoured Battalion Shattered Angola's Last Mechanized Offensive – a Crew Commander's Account*, Helion, Sollihull, 2014
Marcum, John A: *The Angolan Revolution Volume I: Anatomy of an Explosion (1950–1962)* and *Volume II: Exile Politics and Guerrilla Warfare (1962–1975),* MIT Press, Cambridge MA, 1969 and 1978
Martins, Manuel Alfredo de Morais: *Angola*, Lisbon, 2008
Mateus, Dalila Cabrita: *A Luta pela Independência*, Mem Martins, 1999
Mateus, Dalila Cabrita: *A PIDE/DGS na Guerra Colonial,* Lisbon, 2004

Mateus, Dalila Cabrita: *Memórias do Colonialismo e da Guerra*, Lisbon, 2006
McCuen, John, J: *The Art of Counter-Revolutionary War.* Faber and Faber Ltd., London, 1969
Mendes, Pedro Rosa: *Bay of Tigers: A Journey Through War-Torn Angola*, Granta 2004
Minter, William: *Portuguese Africa and the West*, Penguin, Harmondsworth, London, 1972
Minter, William: (ed.): *Operation Timber: Pages from the Savimbi Dossier*, African World Press Inc., Trenton NJ, 1988
Morris, Michael: *Armed Conflict in Southern Africa*, Citadel Press, Cape Town, 1974
Morris, Major, Michael, F. USMC (United States Marine Corps): *Flying Columns in Small Wars – An OMFTS Model.* A Thesis on the Angolan War of 1987 to 1988, United States Marine Corps, 2000
Morris, Paul: *Back to Angola: A Journey from War to Peace,* Zebra, 2014
Nguyen van Tien: *Notre Stratégie de la Guérilla,* Partisans, Paris, 1968
Nogueira, Inácio: *Cavaleiros do Maiombe*, Coimbra, 2004
Nortje, Piet: *32 Battalion: The Inside Story of South Africa's Elite Fighting Unit*, Zebra Press, Cape Town, 2004
Nortje, Piet: *Battle of Savate*, Zebra Press, 2015
Nunes, António Pires: *Angola 1966–74*, Lisbon, 2002
Nunes, António Pires: *Angola. 1961*, Lisbon, 2005
Paige, Jeffery M: *Agrarian Revolution*, Free Press, New York, 1978
Pacavira, Manuel Pedro: *O 4 de Fevereiro pelos Próprios*, Leiria, 2003
Pawson, Lara: *In the Name of the People: Angola's Forgotten Massacre*, IB Tauris, London, 2014
Pepetela: *Mayombe,* Lisbon, 1982
Pimenta, Fernando Tavares: *Angola no Percurso de Um Nacionalista*, Porto, 2006
Polack, Peter: *Last Hot Battle of the Cold War: South Africa vs. Cuba in the Angolan Civil War.* Casemate Publishers, Havertown PA, 2013
Porch, Douglas: *The Portuguese Armed Forces and the Revolution*; Croom Helm, London and Hoover Institution Press, Stanford CA, 1977
Paret, Peter, and John W. Shy: *Guerrillas in the 1960s*, Praeger, New York, 1962
Portuguese Ministry of Foreign Affairs; *Portuguese Africa – An Introduction*, Lisbon, 1973
Pélissier, René: *Les Guerres Grises: Resistance et Revoltes en Angola (1845–1941),* Editions Pélissier, Orgeval, 1977
Pélissier, René: *La Colonie du Minotaure, Nationalismes et révoltes en Angola (1926–1961)*, Editions Pélissier, Orgeval, 1978
Pélissier, René: *Angola – Guinées – Mozambique – Sahara – Timor, etc. Une bibliographic internationale critique (1990–2005)*, Editions Pélissier, Orgeval, 1979
Pélissier, René: *Explorar: Voyages en Angola et autres lieux incertains*, Editions Pélissier, France 1979
Pélissier, René: *Le Naufrage des Caravelles. Études sur la fin de l'empire portugais (1961–1975),* Editions Pélissier, Orgeval, 1979
Pélissier, René: *Africana. Bibliographies sur l'Afrique luso-hisanophone (1800–1980)*, Editions Pélissier, Orgeval, 1981
Ribeiro, Jorge: *Marcas da guerra*, Porto, 1999
Reid-Daly, Colonel Ronald Francis: *Staying Alive: A Southern African Survival Handbook*, Ashanti Publishing, Rivonia, 1990
Scholtz, Dr., Leopold: *The SADF in the Border War 1966–1989.* Tafelberg Publishers, Cape Town, 2013; UK edition Helion, Solihull, 2015
Shubin, Gennady and Tokarev, Andrei: *Bush War – The Road to Cuito Cuanavale.* Jacana Media (Pty) Ltd, South Africa, Sunnyside, 2011
Simões, Martinho: *Nas Três Frentes durante Três Meses*, Lisbon, 1966
Sitte, Fritz: *Flammenherd Angola*, Kremayr & Scheriau, Vienna, 1972
Spínola, General António de: *Portugal and the Future,* Lisbon, 1973
Stadler, Koos: *RECCE: Small Team Missions Behind Enemy Lines*, Casemate UK, 2016

Steenkamp, Willem and Al J. Venter (photos): *South Africa's Border War*. Ashanti Publishing, Gibraltar, 1989, new edition published by Helion in the United Kingdom in 2015

Steward Lloyd-Jones and Antonio Costa Pinto: *The Last Empire: Thirty Years of Portuguese Decolonization*, Intellect Books, Bristol/Portland, 2003

Steyn, Douw and Söderlund, Arnè: *Iron Fist from the Sea – South Africa's Seaborne Raiders: 1978–1988*. Helion, Solihull, 2014

Stockwell, John: *In Search of Enemies: A CIA Story*, W.W. Norton, New York, 1984

Sykes, John: *Portugal and Africa*, Hutchinson, London, 1971

Taber, Robert: *War of the Flea*, Paladin, London, 1970

Taylor Justin, *Whisper in the Reeds; The Terrible Ones, South Africa's 32 Battalion at War*, Helion, Solihull, 2013

Teixeira, Bernardo: *The Fabric of Terror*, Devin Adair, Old Greenwich, USA, 1965

Thompson, Sir Robert: *Defeating Communist Insurgency*, Chatto & Windus, London, 1966

Trinquier, Roger: *Modern Warfare – a French View of Counterinsurgency*, Praeger, New York, 1962

Turner, John, W: *Continent Ablaze – The Insurgency Wars in Africa 1960 to the Present*. Jonathan Ball Publishers (Pty) Ltd, Johannesburg, originally published 1998 by Arms and Armour Press, London, 1998

Van der Waals, Brigadier-General Willem: *Portugal's War in Angola 1961–1974*, Ashanti Publishing, 1993/Protea Books, Pretoria, 2011

Vaz, Camilo Rebocho: *Norte de Angola 1961*, Coimbra, 1993

Venter, Al J: *The Terror Fighters*, Purnell, Cape Town, 1969

Venter, Al J: *Africa at War*, Devin-Adair, Old Greenwich, 1974. Also published as *War in Africa* by Human and Rousseau in Cape Town

Venter, Al J: *The Zambezi Salient*, Timmins, Cape Town, 1974

Venter, Al J: *Challenge: South Africa in the African Revolutionary Context*, (ed.), Ashanti Publishing, 1988

Venter Al J: *War Stories by Al Venter and Friends*, Protea Books, 2011

Venter, Al J: *Gunship Ace: The Wars of Neall Ellis, Helicopter Pilot and Mercenary*, Casemate, Havertown PA, 2012

Venter, Al J: *African Stories by Al Venter and Friends*, Protea Books, 2013

Venter, Al J: *Portugal's Guerrilla Wars in Africa*, Helion 2013; also published In Lisbon under the title *Portugal e as Guerrilhas de A'frica*, Clube do Autor, 2015

Venter Al J: Venter; *Mercenaries: Putting the World to Rights with Hired Guns*; Casemate, Havertown PA, 2014

Venter, Al J: *The Chopper Boys: Helicopter Warfare in Africa:* Stackpole Books, Mechanicsburg PA/Greenhill Books, London, 1993: New edition from Helion and Company, Solihull 2016

Venter Al J: *Lebanon: Levantine Cavalry 1958-1990* (Forthcoming, 2017)

Venter Al J: *Somalia: Unending Turmoil Since 1975* (Forthcoming, 2017)

Venter Al J: *Conflict Stories by Al Venter and Friends* (Forthcoming, 2017)

Verdasca, José: *Memórias de um capitão*, Lisbon, 2004

Volker, Walter: *Army Signals In South Africa; The Story of the South African Corps of Signals and its Antecedent*; Veritas Books, Pretoria, 2010

Volker Walter: *9C – Nine Charlie! Army Siganallers in the Field. The Story of the Men and Women of the South African Corps of Signals, and Their Equipment*; Veritas Books, Pretoria, 2010

Wheeler, Douglas L and René Pélissier: *Angola*, Pall Mall Press, London, 1971. An updated and much-enlarged edition has been translated and published by Edições Tinta-da-China, Lisbon, under the title *História de Angola*

Zhdarkin, Igor: *We Did Not See It Even in Afghanistan – Memoirs of a Participant of the Angolan War (1986–1988), from A Russian View of the Angolan War*. Moscow: Memories Moscow, 2008. Translated into English by Tamara Reilly

Index

INDEX OF PEOPLE

Alberts, Pilot Carl 72, 470, 505-508, 510, 516

Bacon, George 223-225, 231-234, 241
Barlow, Eeben 429, 453-456, 461-463, 465, 482-485, 492, 494, 498
Beukman, Anton 355, 357, 359, 367
Blaauw, Captain Johan xvi, 47-48, 52-55, 58-67, 314-315, 317, 470, 491-493, 501, 503, 513, 516
Blaauw, Colonel Hennie 47, 58, 491, 513
Bosch, Louwrens 60, 63, 65, 505-507, 510
Breytenbach, Colonel Jan xvi, xxvi, 142, 148-149, 173-174, 185, 246-247, 249, 252, 256-257, 271, 277, 290, 299, 305, 342, 348, 412
Bridgland, Fred vii, xvii, xxxv-xxxvi, 126, 174, 187, 248, 261, 265, 270, 424
Buckingham, Tony 454-456, 461, 466, 468, 474-475, 484, 492

Cabral, Amilcar xx, xxii, xxxix, 135, 198
Caetano, Marcelo xx, 123, 168, 171, 421, 427
Cann, Captain John xvi, xx-xxi, xxvii, 95, 98, 100-101, 119, 133, 274, 424
Carlse, Harry 456, 461-463, 466-469, 474, 477, 482, 487
Castro, Brigadier Pepe de 60-62, 169, 172, 188-203, 222-223, 226, 260, 386, 419, 424, 453, 463, 466, 496, 503
Castro, Fidel 169, 172, 192, 194, 226, 260, 386
Chipenda, Daniel 179, 184-185, 221, 240, 247-248, 271, 276, 412, 419
Coutinho, Admiral Rosa xxxiii, 47, 136, 140, 171, 192-193, 221, 226, 409

Davidson, Basil xxxiii, 117, 230
de Matos, Norton 100, 248-251, 257-259, 502-503
de Vries, Major General Roland xvii, 227, 285-286, 328, 331, 334, 336-337, 363, 369, 374-375, 377, 384, 391, 397, 434, 440
Dreyer, Brigadier Hans 205, 209, 216, 382
du Toit, Wynand 50, 54, 502

Ellis, Neall ii, xvi, xl, 67, 73-75, 206, 274-275, 278, 280-281, 283-284, 429, 443, 447, 456, 460, 472, 481, 486-487, 507-508
Els, Paul 125, 159, 250

Ferreira, Deon xvi, 147, 272-273, 276, 305-306, 308-309, 314, 317, 319, 419, 456, 463, 466, 469

Geldenhuys, General Jannie 111-112, 246, 314, 317, 367
Georgiou, 'Callan' Costas 225, 233, 238
Grunberg, Michael 449, 485, 492-493
Guevara, Che xxvi, 123, 191-192, 196, 408, 419

Holtzhausen, Major Louis 247, 249-250, 256-259

Janecke, Sonny 510, 513, 516
Joubert, 'Juba' 67, 69, 72, 357, 490, 505, 507-508, 513-516
Joynt, Vernon 213, 323-324, 337

Katzke, Heinz 206, 307, 309, 318-320
Kaunda, President Kenneth 260, 264-265, 267, 412, 422
Kluyts, Theo 304, 314-315

Langley x, 143, 189, 233, 409, 420, 437
le Roux, Mauritz 456, 461, 463, 466-469, 473-474, 476-477, 481-482, 486-487
Linde, JC 505, 507, 510, 513-514, 516
Linford, Colonel Delville 142, 148-149, 173-174, 246-247, 249, 252, 256-257, 271, 306
Ludick, Werner 498, 501, 504
Luitingh, Lafras 444-445, 448-450, 452, 454, 456, 461, 463, 466, 475, 478, 484, 488, 493-494
Lumumba, Patrice 121, 249-250, 410

Machel, Samora 185, 408, 422
Mann, Simon 443, 455, 462-463, 466, 468, 475, 484
Mannall, David vii, xvi-xvii, 371, 384, 392, 394
Maranta, Angelo 75, 275, 281-284
McAleese, Peter 225, 232, 239, 305, 308, 310, 316-317
Moss, Robert 199-201, 221-222

Neto, Agostinho 110, 140, 169-170, 179-180, 185, 188-190, 192-193, 197, 221-222, 226, 228, 230, 270, 408-409, 412, 419-420, 423, 426
Nicholson, Mike 174, 187, 261, 265, 267
Nkrumah, Kwame 407-408, 410, 415-416
Nyerere, Julius xxv, 407, 413, 422

Pélissier, Rene xxxv, 86-87, 91-92, 98, 156, 426

Reid-Daly, Colonel Ron 218-219, 348
Roberto, Holden 141-142, 153, 169, 190, 192, 199, 201, 220-223, 235, 237, 257, 271, 408-410, 412-413, 418-420
Rodrigues, General Bettencourt xx, 420, 433

Rykaart, Colonel Duncan 48, 60, 62, 64, 68, 428-429, 488, 493, 503, 505, 514

Salazar, Dr Antonio de Oliveira xx, xxiii, xxxiv, 89, 105, 115, 248, 417, 421, 427
Sankoh, Foday 408, 453, 481, 484
Savides, Tony xvii, 285, 335, 337
Savimbi, Dr Jonas xxv, xxxi, xxxv-xxxvi, xl, 45-48, 52, 55, 59-60, 62-66, 92, 126, 141, 153, 158, 169-170, 180, 187, 226, 228, 246-251, 257, 260, 265-270, 272, 351, 354-355, 360, 386, 409, 424, 426-429, 436-437, 442-444, 448, 452-454, 459, 468, 472, 475-478, 481-485, 487-488, 502-503, 505, 507-508, 513, 515-516
Schoeman, Brigadier Dawid 245-246, 251, 256, 258-259, 284
Sese Seko, Mobuto 141, 251, 408
Smith, Prime Minister Ian xxxvi, 159, 321
Smith, Phil 456, 461, 463, 466, 481-482
Söderland, Arne xvi, 352, 354
Spinola, General Antonio de xx, xxxiii-xxxiv, xxxviii, 122-123
Stalin, Joseph ix, 199, 231
Steenkamp, Willem ii, 87, 141, 155, 267, 273-274, 319
Steyn, Colonel Douw xvi, 200, 340-341, 343-344, 346, 349, 352-355, 361-362, 368, 513

Stockwell, John 143, 169-170, 270

Tate, Charlie 507-508, 513, 516
Troskie, Manie 304, 308, 316

van der Waals, 'Kaas' xvi-xvii, 112, 141, 240, 245, 251, 267, 360
van Heerden, Roelf 60-61, 463, 477, 503, 507
Venter, Al ii-iv, xvii, xxxvii, xxxix-xl, 46, 60, 67, 86-87, 103, 149, 169, 177, 190, 218, 271, 274, 306, 326, 342, 351, 405, 410, 429, 451, 487
Viljoen, General Constand 141-142, 153, 245, 247, 251, 256, 259-260, 277, 288-290, 300, 307, 327

Walker, Arthur 70, 72, 75, 206-207, 307, 317-320, 320, 505-508, 510
Webb, Eddie 245, 247, 251-252, 256-259
Wilhelm, Kaiser xxxv, 88, 99
Williams, Glen 134, 141, 410
Wright, Robin 174, 234-236, 241

Younghusband, Peter 54, 174, 235

Zhdarkin, Igor 367, 403-404
Zuma, Jacob 203, 408, 449

INDEX OF PLACES

Accra xxxviii, 103, 410, 416
Afghanistan xix, xxxix, 55, 209, 262, 274, 322-324, 335, 338, 342, 403-405, 438, 443, 450, 486
Algeria xiii, xxxvii, 158, 190, 251, 420
Algiers xi, 176, 412
Angola i-iii, vii-xxiii, xxviii-xxix, xxxiv-xli, 45-52, 54-57, 59-60, 64, 68, 71-73, 75-76, 79, 83-91, 94-95, 98-101, 103-105, 110-112, 114-117, 122, 125-126, 128-129, 131, 133-138, 140-143, 146-151, 154-162, 164-166, 168-172, 174-179, 184-195, 197, 199-205, 207, 209, 212, 216-225, 231-240, 245-249, 251-254, 256, 259-272, 274-275, 279, 281, 286-290, 292, 297-298, 301-306, 314-315, 321-322, 325-327, 329, 335-336, 338, 340, 342, 344-345, 348-352, 355, 360, 363, 367-372, 379-380, 382, 384, 386-387, 391, 401, 404, 408-412, 417-421, 423-429, 436-445, 448-456, 460-465, 470, 473-474, 478, 482-489, 492-499, 502, 504-505, 507-509, 511
Asia xxxvi, 64, 76, 114, 215, 233, 241, 411
Atlantic Ocean xiii, xvi, xxi, xxxviii, 77, 85, 91, 103, 141, 146, 149, 155, 235, 248, 257, 259, 347, 351, 424, 455, 496-497

Beirut xl, 405, 436
Belgium xxxiv, 76, 79, 100, 175, 191, 234, 327, 409, 446
Benguela 77, 92, 100, 142, 149, 187, 189, 248-249, 256, 258-259, 265, 268, 496
Berlin 88, 100-101, 156, 190
Biafra ii, xxxix-xl, 342, 348, 410, 447, 513

Bissau ii, xi, xviii, xxii, xxxiii-xxxv, xxxviii, 124, 135, 423, 456, 497
Bloemfontein 290, 315, 383
Brazil 87, 90-91, 111-112, 123, 222, 417
Brazzaville x, 168-169, 190-191, 193, 409-410, 412, 419-420, 515
Britain xviii, xxxiii-xxxiv, xxxix, 43, 67, 75-77, 79, 86, 100, 103, 122, 173, 175, 191, 199, 205, 263, 305, 323, 348-349, 352-353, 361, 369, 408-409, 417, 423, 442, 449, 454, 487-488, 493, 497, 507

Cabinda xi, 50, 54, 104, 220, 228, 409, 464, 466, 468, 473-475, 481, 493, 502
Cabo Ledo 50, 54, 61, 169, 457, 462-464, 468, 475, 488, 497-498, 502-503, 505
Cacolo 55, 60-62, 503, 515
Cafunfo vii, 45-47, 52-55, 58-59, 61-62, 64-67, 69, 72, 428, 444, 453, 463, 472, 501-503, 505, 508-510, 513-515
Cambodia 224, 233, 262
Canada 86, 224, 231-232, 271, 417, 423, 453
Canberra xvii, 139, 200, 290-291, 293-294, 382
Cape Town xvii, xxxvii, xli, 80-81, 96, 102, 156, 176, 189-190, 193, 201, 218, 308, 326, 348-349, 367, 370, 373, 409
Caprivi 126-127, 150, 152, 159, 165, 186-187, 204, 245-246, 290, 300, 322, 387
Cassinga xvii, 151, 287, 289-291, 293-296, 299-301, 314, 325, 437

China xix, xxxiv-xxxv, 77-78, 158, 168, 201, 221-222, 327, 413, 420
Coimbra 110, 419, 497
Conakry xxxviii, 103, 190, 411-412, 493
Congo River 105, 220, 244, 451-452, 464, 466
Congo x, xvii, xxii, xl, 45, 53, 62, 65, 77, 80, 86, 88, 92, 100, 102-103, 105, 110, 112, 114, 121, 142-143, 159, 168-169, 190-191, 220, 234-235, 244, 254, 259, 263, 265, 321, 324, 408-410, 412, 417-420, 424-426, 442-443, 446-447, 451-452, 455, 459, 464, 466, 477, 487, 496-497, 503-504, 515
Cuamato xvii, 73, 101, 304-310, 312-320
Cuango 53, 503, 513, 515
Cuba vii, xxxv, 122, 140-141, 153-154, 158, 169, 171, 175-176, 188-191, 194-195, 199, 202-203, 207, 222, 262, 386, 419, 496, 498
Czechoslovakia 116, 190, 262

Dar es Salaam xxxiv, 158, 168, 176, 221, 408, 412-413
Dembos xxii, xxxvii, 104, 117, 418
Dondo 94, 222, 248, 503
Durban 143, 174, 341, 348-349

Egypt 76, 158, 486
England iv, 224-225, 237, 371, 407, 451
Ethiopia 76, 190, 195, 409
Europe xvi, xix, xxi, xxxv, 43, 55, 64, 76-78, 86-89, 98-99, 101, 105, 112, 114, 116, 122, 135, 141, 149, 168, 189, 218-219, 248, 257, 262, 408, 412, 415, 424, 426, 428-429, 443, 497, 515

Florida xxi, 202, 409
France xxii, xxxiii-xxxiv, xxxviii, 45, 55, 76, 79, 86, 100, 103, 118, 120, 122, 126, 144, 174-175, 191, 205, 225, 274, 348, 409, 423, 454, 497, 508
Freetown xxxiv, 67, 79, 408, 444-445, 447-450, 453, 461, 484, 486-487, 492

Geneva 175, 184, 513
Germany ix, xix, xxi, xxxiv, 76, 79, 98, 100-101, 122, 156-157, 207, 262, 274, 419, 423, 446
Ghana 103, 176, 337, 407, 415-416
Grootfontein 159, 290-291, 414
Guinea xi, xiii, xviii-xx, xxii, xxxiii-xxxvi, xxxviii, xl, 74, 76, 78, 86-87, 103-105, 115, 122, 124, 129, 135, 174, 190, 198, 203, 262, 274, 411, 416, 421, 423-424, 443, 455-456, 493, 497
Guiné-Bissau ii, xi, xviii, xxxv, 135, 423, 456, 497

Havana 140-141, 176, 188-193, 203, 270, 350, 352, 412, 419, 502
Holland 79, 156, 184, 263
Huambo 111, 221, 240, 267, 271, 412, 424, 438, 444, 497, 513
Humbe 99, 101, 441

India 76-77, 79-81, 159, 409
Indian Ocean ii, xxi, 85, 91, 105, 157, 171, 438
Iran ii, xxxvi, 76

Iraq xxxvi, 55, 76, 159, 209, 274, 323, 335, 338, 424, 442, 450, 486-487
Israel xxxvi, 140, 327, 409
Italy xxxiv, 76, 423, 454

Jamba xxxv, 126, 302, 350, 367, 387, 437
Johannesburg 102, 126, 168, 174-175, 183-184, 203, 261, 327, 337, 348, 380, 382, 440, 461-462, 513

Kaokoveld 205-206, 214, 327
Katanga 55, 76, 100, 112, 142
Katima Mulilo 126, 150, 159
Kavango 158, 186, 204, 246, 267-268, 355
Kenya xxxvi, 100, 205, 407
Kinshasa x, 119, 153, 224-225, 232, 234, 248, 409-410, 413, 420, 515
Korea 127, 158, 200
Kunene River 92, 99, 217, 275, 281, 305, 436

Lagos xxxiv, 103, 110, 412, 495
Langebaan 340, 349, 367
Laos 224, 233, 262
Lebanon xxii, xxxvii, xl, 159
Leopoldville xxii, 110, 119, 143, 410
Liberia xxxiii, 103, 110, 486, 493
Libya 190, 207, 321, 415, 442
Lisbon viii, xiii, xvi, xviii-xxii, xxiv, xxxiii-xl, 76-80, 82-84, 86-87, 89-92, 98-102, 104-105, 110-112, 114-115, 119, 122-126, 129, 134-135, 137, 141, 146, 149, 159, 174-176, 178, 180, 188, 191-193, 204, 218, 221, 262, 321, 411-413, 417-421, 423-425, 429, 438, 456, 497
Lobito 103, 108, 111, 142, 174, 189, 246, 248-249, 253, 256-259, 268-270, 454, 497
Lomba River 302, 359, 371, 384, 386-389, 391, 403-404
London xxxvi, xxxix, 45, 54, 76, 79, 97, 103, 111, 172, 174-176, 187, 200, 222, 230, 233-235, 237, 262-263, 267, 269-270, 380, 383, 387, 429, 442, 448, 454-455, 493, 495
Lourenco Marques xxi, 82, 146
Luanda vii, xviii, xxi-xxiv, xxvi-xxviii, xxxi, xxxv-xxxvi, xl-xli, 45-50, 54-55, 60-61, 77, 85, 89-93, 98, 100, 102-113, 116, 120, 136, 140-142, 150-151, 169, 174-177, 179-180, 183, 186-193, 199-201, 203, 220-223, 230, 233-234, 240, 246, 248, 251, 259-261, 268, 271, 289, 322, 344-345, 347-348, 351-352, 354, 404, 409, 411-412, 417-420, 423-426, 428-429, 431-432, 435, 437, 443-444, 449-456, 458, 461-463, 465-466, 472, 475, 481-485, 493-498, 502-504, 508, 513
Lubango xv, 149, 268, 479
Lusaka 158, 187, 248, 261, 263-264, 267-270, 409-410, 412

Malanje 53, 114, 248, 417, 443, 503
Malaya 173, 348, 455
Maputo xxi, 82, 102, 324, 408, 422-423
Mavinga 350-351, 355, 359-360, 367, 384, 387

Miami 190, 203, 409, 475
Middle East 141, 170, 189, 215, 323, 335, 382, 497
Mocamedes 149, 189, 256
Morocco 76, 190, 337, 515
Moscow xxxiii, xxxv, xl-xli, 64, 103, 116, 121, 135, 171, 174, 185, 189-190, 195, 201-202, 262-263, 270, 280, 325, 335, 345, 351-353, 403, 409-410, 414, 419, 423, 438, 452, 496, 499
Mozambique xi, xiv, xviii-xix, xxi-xxii, xxxiii, xxxv-xxxvi, xl, 73, 76, 79, 86-87, 90-91, 99-100, 102, 104-105, 115, 122, 124-125, 135, 147, 150, 159, 161, 185, 188, 191, 217-219, 262, 290, 321-322, 324, 340, 363, 408, 411-413, 417, 421-423, 438, 445-446, 449, 456, 497

Nambuangongo xxii, xxxvii, 117, 120, 418
Namibe 92, 189, 303, 345-347, 350-352
Namibia xiii-xiv, 81, 84-85, 87-88, 98, 101, 125-126, 142, 154-158, 171, 173, 204, 207, 209, 268, 272, 288-290, 302-303, 325, 380, 382, 412, 437, 453, 462, 508, 515
New York ii, 174, 225, 383, 409, 442, 505
Nigeria ii, xxxiv, xxxix, 70, 76, 79, 85, 103, 112, 270, 342, 408, 442, 492
Nova Lisboa 111, 177, 180, 183-186, 221-222, 227, 238-240, 245-249, 256-259, 267-268, 271, 276, 412, 419, 424, 438

Ondangua xxxi, 126-127, 206, 208, 287-291, 303, 306, 314, 392, 439-440
Ongiva 149, 368, 440
Oshakati 150, 208, 212, 306, 317, 325
Ovamboland 125, 157-159, 168, 170, 204, 206, 208-209, 214, 216-217, 300-301, 306, 322, 325, 387, 436

Paris xxxiii-xxxiv, xxxix, 92, 102, 112, 419, 454
Peking 263, 412, 419
Poland 116, 175, 262
Portugal ii, vii, xvi-xx, xxii-xxiii, xxxiii-xxxviii, xl-xli, 43, 76, 79, 82, 86-87, 89, 91-92, 98, 100-101, 104, 110-112, 114-116, 122-124, 136, 149-150, 161, 168, 171, 174, 176, 183, 190, 192, 218, 222, 226, 235, 245, 262, 271, 274, 322, 348, 371, 408, 415-417, 419-420, 427, 429, 433, 439, 497
Pretoria x, xiv, xvi-xviii, xxx, xl-xli, 49, 65-66, 87, 99, 103, 111-112, 125-127, 139-143, 148, 150-151, 155, 159, 166, 168, 170, 176, 184, 186, 188-189, 213, 227, 245-246, 251, 259, 268-269, 271, 276, 290, 302-303, 305-306, 309, 321-323, 326, 335, 337, 341-342, 348-349, 351, 367, 371, 373, 379, 387, 390, 392, 410, 428-429, 437, 440, 452-453, 455-456, 477, 516

Quefiquena 465-467, 469, 478, 481-482
Quibala 247, 256-257, 259
Quifangondo xxxv, 199-201, 223

Rhodesia xi, xxxvi, xxxix, 90, 102, 105, 111, 115, 125, 150, 159, 173, 184, 191, 217-218, 271, 288-290, 301, 321, 348-349, 411-413, 420, 446, 508

Rio Longa 50, 54, 458, 498, 502, 508
Rundu 126-128, 150, 186-187, 246-247, 251, 256-260, 267, 355, 358, 366, 462
Russia xix, 168, 472, 480, 496

Sa da Bandeira 149, 248, 256
Salisbury 102, 234-235, 321
Santos 65, 112, 132, 199-201, 223, 426-428, 455
São Paulo 77, 417, 419
Saurimo 46-47, 49, 51-52, 54-56, 60-61, 65-68, 72, 443, 458, 471-472, 488, 490-491, 493, 503-505, 508, 510, 513-516
Senegal xxxviii, 103, 408
Sierra Leone x, xiv, xxxiii, xl, 49, 56, 58, 60, 63-64, 67-68, 71-72, 75, 79, 85, 103, 408, 429, 442-443, 445, 447-450, 453, 455, 460-461, 463, 472-473, 478-479, 481, 484, 486-488, 492-493, 500, 503, 508
Silva Porto 186-187, 247-251, 256-257, 259-260, 266-268
Somalia xl, 159, 190, 405, 429, 449
Sousa Lara 249, 256, 259
South Africa ii, vii, ix-x, xii-xv, xvii, xxviii, xxxvi-xxxvii, xl-xli, 49, 54, 58, 61, 76, 87, 90, 99, 101, 103-104, 110, 115, 122, 125-126, 140-141, 147-149, 153-160, 168-172, 174, 176, 187, 189-191, 199, 203-204, 208, 215, 240, 245, 249, 256, 259-260, 268-273, 277, 287, 289-290, 302-303, 317, 323-324, 335, 337, 339, 341-343, 348-351, 354, 360, 369-370, 372, 379, 382, 395, 404, 408, 417, 424, 426, 429, 432, 445-446, 449-450, 454-456, 461-462, 478-479, 481, 484, 486, 488, 493, 496, 502, 507, 515-516
Soviet Union xix, 47, 103, 116, 154, 157-158, 168, 171, 173, 188-189, 202, 207, 221-222, 263, 302, 342, 350, 389, 410, 413
Soyo viii, 47, 52, 55, 60, 443-444, 451-452, 454-456, 461-466, 469, 475-478, 481-484, 486-488, 492, 494, 497, 503
Sudan xl, 442, 448, 486
Syria xix, 76, 140, 189, 209, 323, 335, 424

Tanganyika 100, 155, 192, 407
Tanzania 105, 158, 190, 196, 221, 407, 413, 420
Tete xxii, 104, 218
Turkey 76, 137, 267

Uganda xxxix, 407, 429, 448, 494
United States vii, ix, xvii, xix, xxi, xxvii, xxxvi, 45, 53, 55, 60-62, 65-67, 72, 74-77, 85-86, 90, 100, 102, 116, 122, 126-128, 134-137, 143, 148-150, 153-154, 168-171, 175, 183-184, 186-187, 190-192, 199, 202, 221-225, 231, 235, 237, 243-244, 249, 251, 256-258, 260, 263, 266-270, 275, 282, 304-309, 315-319, 323-327, 336, 339, 355, 379-381, 384-386, 388-390, 398-404, 420-422, 426, 429, 436-439, 441, 444, 448-451, 456, 460, 462, 466-469, 474, 481, 484, 486-488, 496, 502, 504, 506, 514

Victoria 103
Vietnam xix-xxi, xxxv-xxxvi, xxxviii, xl, 71, 114, 116, 126, 128, 140, 143, 170, 172-173, 190, 202, 205, 209, 218, 233, 262-263, 266, 270, 315, 411, 451, 465, 497

Washington xxv, xxxiii, xxxv, xli, 46, 129, 154, 174, 188, 193, 200-201, 221, 224, 232-234, 270, 351, 387, 390, 409-410, 425, 427, 436, 438-439, 448, 456, 460, 484, 495
West Point 45, 420, 476
Windhoek 87, 303, 414, 461-462, 474-475

Xangongo 99, 149, 285, 305-306, 317, 375, 397, 436, 440-441

Yemen 141, 190, 323, 442

Zaire x, 54-55, 115, 168, 191, 193, 200-201, 222, 225, 231-232, 234-237, 244, 418, 420, 453, 515
Zambezi ii, xxx, 97, 146, 155, 165, 411
Zambia xviii, 112, 126, 146, 150, 152, 155, 157, 159, 187, 191, 221, 263-265, 267, 300-301, 322, 420, 422, 515
Zimbabwe xv, 78, 146, 289, 455, 484, 515

INDEX OF MILITARY FORMATIONS & UNITS

1 Parachute Battalion 247, 287, 289, 299, 301-302, 304-305, 315, 326
1 Reconnaissance Commando 342, 348-349
3 Parachute Battalion 288, 297, 301
4 Reconnaissance Regiment xvi, 340, 343, 349, 351, 353, 368, 516
5 Reconnaissance Regiment 339, 349, 503
32 Battalion vii, 75, 185, 209, 217, 271-279, 283-286, 289-290, 301, 305, 314-315, 379-381, 411-412, 450, 452-453, 456, 461
44 Parachute Brigade 173, 301-302, 305, 498
61 Mechanised Battalion xvii, 285-286, 321, 370, 373, 376, 379, 381, 387, 440
101 Battalion 173, 380, 450

Angolan Armed Forces x, 47, 52, 60, 62, 64-65, 428, 443-444, 452-453, 462, 464, 466, 468-469, 473-474, 477-478, 481-483, 494, 497-498, 502-504, 508, 513, 516
Angolan Army 46-47, 50, 68, 154, 188, 201, 224-225, 248-249, 251, 258, 280, 306-307, 311, 314, 335, 348-351, 368, 384, 386-389, 400, 403, 424, 428, 443, 452, 457-458, 462-464, 466, 471, 477, 482-484, 494, 496, 499

British Army 153, 202, 238, 336, 450, 484

Combat Group Bravo 60, 64, 142, 148, 246-247, 252, 271, 388, 503

FAPLA xi, 47, 116, 136, 148-149, 154, 190, 200, 209, 221, 224-225, 232, 248-251, 256-260, 274, 298, 306, 314-317, 319-320, 325-326, 335, 350-351, 356-357, 367, 371, 373, 381, 384, 386-389, 403-404, 428, 441, 464, 478, 494

German Army xxi, 88, 101

Helicopter Administrative Group xi, 275, 306

Koevoet 65, 205-207, 209, 211, 213-215, 286, 323-324, 326, 411, 452, 463, 477

PIDE xiii, xxxiii, 110, 140, 150, 199, 417, 419, 425
PLAN xiii, xvi, xxi, 100, 122, 135, 141-142, 150, 158-159, 168, 170-171, 173, 193, 204-205, 219, 231-232, 274-275, 281, 289, 291, 300, 305, 324-325, 355, 357, 373, 388, 462, 464, 466, 484, 502-503, 516
Portuguese Armed Forces xi, xxxiii, 104, 138
Portuguese Army xi, xv, xxi, xxxv, xxxvii, xxxix, 88, 90, 99, 103, 105, 112, 117, 134-135, 141, 148, 157, 175, 183-184, 218, 248, 262, 327, 371, 411-412, 418, 423, 431

Reconnaissance Commando 168, 271, 342, 348-349, 452
Reconnaissance Regiment xiii, xvi, 47-48, 54, 58, 147, 271, 273, 338-339, 342-343, 349-353, 360, 368, 429, 445, 456, 479, 502-503
Revolutionary Armed Forces 140, 188, 194
Rhodesian Army xiv, 239, 273, 321-322
Rhodesian Light Infantry xiv, 173, 305
Royal Air Force xiii, 410, 493

South African Air Force xiv, xvii, 60, 73-74, 125-128, 134, 151, 200, 206, 208, 257, 274, 278, 280, 287, 293, 296, 300, 303, 306-307, 314, 317, 350-351, 387, 392, 409, 414, 447, 507-508, 510
South African Defence Force xiv-xv, xlii, 140-143, 145, 147, 150, 153, 160, 163, 168, 170, 172, 200, 205, 210, 245, 247, 250, 252, 267, 272-273, 277, 279, 285-286, 288, 290, 294, 300, 302-303, 305-306, 326, 328, 335, 337, 347, 349-350, 363, 369-371, 373, 379, 381-382, 384, 389, 404, 412, 428, 430, 444-445, 450, 453, 455-456, 458, 461, 466, 494, 497, 503
Selous Scouts 173, 218, 348-349
South African Army vii, x, xvii, xl, 47, 99, 111, 140-143, 145, 150, 155, 174-176, 184-185, 204, 218, 245-246, 251, 268, 286-287, 289, 300, 324, 335-336, 338, 348, 369, 379, 412, 429, 434, 437, 497
South African Military Intelligence xii, 185, 289, 412
South African Navy 106, 325, 340

INDEX 527

South African Police xiv, 125, 168, 286, 323, 411
Special Air Service xiv, 225, 305, 342, 349, 353, 442, 463
Special Forces vii, xiv, xxxv, xxxix, 47, 54, 58, 60, 66, 125, 148, 172, 199, 204, 217, 222, 224, 231, 241, 273, 277, 288, 290, 338-339, 342, 348-351, 353, 357, 387, 411-412, 428, 450, 452-453, 455-457, 463, 475, 478, 485, 488, 494, 498, 502, 513

Task Force Foxbat vii, 245, 258-259
Task Force Zulu 141-142, 151, 256-259, 271

US Army ix, 72, 202, 323, 339, 449, 460

ZANLA xv, 150, 273
ZIPRA xv, 150, 273

INDEX OF GENERAL & MISCELLANEOUS TERMS

African National Congress ix, xii, 154, 203, 302, 327
African Union ix, xiii, 260, 410
Angolan Civil War xvi, 153, 220-222, 272, 287, 290, 302, 350, 371, 487
Angolan Communist Party xiii, 417, 424
Angolan Government 46, 53, 154, 171, 257-258, 350, 370, 409-410, 451, 494, 513
Angolan War xxxvi, 46, 134, 175, 188, 267, 339, 342, 370-371, 387, 403, 433, 453

Bakongo 92, 409, 417
Boer Wars 209, 380, 486
Border War ii, vii, xvii, xxxvi-xxxvii, xxxix-xl, 62, 68, 71-72, 74, 87, 101, 150, 152, 154-155, 157-159, 166, 170, 172-173, 190, 204, 210, 213, 215, 246, 255, 272, 285, 304-305, 315, 317, 323-324, 335-336, 338, 345, 349, 369-373, 382, 428-429, 478-479, 483, 488-489, 494, 498, 507

Central Intelligence Agency x, 46, 121, 141-143, 169, 184, 189-190, 200-201, 220-222, 224-225, 227, 233-234, 236-237, 241, 248, 260, 266, 270, 409-410, 412, 419
Cold War xix, 64, 157, 171, 221, 261, 302, 410, 423, 436, 486
Commonwealth xx, 92, 172
Communist Bloc 143, 411, 425
Communist Party xiii-xiv, 136, 156, 193, 417, 424

First World War xxi, xxxiv, 43, 87, 92, 95-96, 98, 100-101, 155-156, 339, 417
FNLA xi, xv, xxxv, 114, 141-142, 169-170, 175, 177-179, 181, 183-184, 188, 190, 192-193, 199-201, 220-225, 229, 231-232, 236-237, 239, 241, 243-244, 247-248, 257, 263, 271-272, 371, 408, 410, 418-420, 423-424, 429
FRELIMO ix, xi, 150, 188, 219, 335, 412, 423

GRAE xi, 114-115, 408, 420

Honoris Crux xi, 206, 314, 317, 320, 339, 368

Luanda Government 45-46, 48-49, 136, 220, 426, 443, 451-452, 465, 472, 484

Mbundu 91, 417, 425
MPLA ix, xiii, xxix, xxxix, 47, 110, 114-115, 136, 140-142, 148, 153, 168-171, 174-175, 177-179, 181-186, 188-193, 197, 199, 220-223, 228-230, 236-237, 243-244, 246-249, 263-264, 268-272, 289, 300, 302, 370-371, 408-412, 417-421, 423-428, 436, 453, 464

NATO xiii, xxi, 72, 103, 122, 138, 184, 219, 263, 322, 337, 508-509, 511

Operation Coolidge 350, 355, 357, 359, 367-368
Operation Daisy v, xvii, 286, 298, 301, 324, 327-328, 330-332, 377
Operation Modular 112, 336, 350, 367, 371-372, 379, 384, 400
Operation Protea 279, 285, 325, 328, 374
Operation Savannah 142-143, 148, 150, 171, 173, 176, 184-185, 188, 190, 194, 200, 221, 240, 245, 252, 268, 271, 286-287, 325, 328, 336, 432
Organisation of African Unity ix, xiii, 251, 410

PAIGC xiii, xx, xxii, xxxix, 135, 198, 411, 423
Pretoria Government 159, 341, 429

Rhodesian War xii-xiii, xxii, xxxvi, xl, 168, 273, 463, 513

Second World War xi, xiii-xiv, xx, xxxiii-xxxiv, xxxvi-xxxviii, 77, 89, 120, 140, 156, 172, 200, 220, 234, 245-246, 283, 321, 326, 348, 350-351, 353, 384, 407, 409, 417, 446
South West African People's Organisation xiv, 154-155, 272
SWAPO ix, xiii-xv, xxxix, xli, 73-75, 126, 140, 142, 144, 150, 154-155, 157-159, 164, 169, 171-173, 203-209, 218, 268, 272-275, 278, 280-282, 284, 288-289, 291, 298-300, 302-307, 321-322, 324-325, 350, 382, 387

UNITA x, xv, xxv, xxxi, xxxv-xxxvi, xl, 45-46, 51-52, 55, 57, 59-67, 69-70, 72, 116, 126, 141-142, 154, 158, 169-170, 172, 175, 178, 185, 187, 192-193, 199, 220-224, 226, 228, 245-251, 256-260, 263-264, 266-270, 272, 274, 302, 334, 349-351, 354-357, 359-360, 366-367, 370-371, 379-381, 384, 386-389, 404, 409, 423-424, 426-429, 436-437, 443-444, 448, 451-455, 459-460, 462-463, 466-469, 473-478, 481-485, 488, 499, 503-506, 513-516
UPA xv, xxi-xxii, 114, 408-410, 418-421, 424

Vietnam War 140, 451, 465